T0380059

The Cambridge Handbook of Democratic Education

What kind of education is needed for democracy? How can schools respond to the challenges that current democracies face? This unprecedented Handbook offers a comprehensive overview of the most important ideas, issues, and thinkers within democratic education. Its 35 chapters are written by leading experts in the field in an accessible format. Its breadth of purpose and depth of analysis will appeal to both researchers and practitioners in education and politics. The Handbook not only addresses the historical roots and philosophical foundations of democratic education but also engages with contemporary political issues and key challenges to the project of democratic education.

JULIAN CULP is Associate Professor of Philosophy and Fellow of the Center for Critical Democracy Studies at the American University of Paris, France. His research focuses on ethics, philosophy of education, political philosophy, and democratic theory.

JOHANNES DRERUP is Professor of Philosophy of Education and Educational Theory at TU Dortmund University, Germany, and Guest Professor at Vrije Universiteit Amsterdam, the Netherlands. His research focuses on philosophy of education, democratic and moral education, and educational ethics.

DOUGLAS YACEK is a Research Fellow at TU Dortmund University, Germany. His research focuses on questions at the intersections of educational ethics, moral and democratic education, and the history of educational thought.

CAMBRIDGE HANDBOOKS IN EDUCATION

The Cambridge Handbook of Democratic Education

Edited by
Julian Culp
The American University of Paris
Johannes Drerup
TU Dortmund University
Douglas Yacek
TU Dortmund University

Shaftesbury Road, Cambridge CB2 8EA, United Kingdom

One Liberty Plaza, 20th Floor, New York, NY 10006, USA

477 Williamstown Road, Port Melbourne, VIC 3207, Australia

314–321, 3rd Floor, Plot 3, Splendor Forum, Jasola District Centre, New Delhi – 110025, India

103 Penang Road, #05-06/07, Visioncrest Commercial, Singapore 238467

Cambridge University Press is part of Cambridge University Press & Assessment, a department of the University of Cambridge.

We share the University's mission to contribute to society through the pursuit of education, learning and research at the highest international levels of excellence.

www.cambridge.org
Information on this title: www.cambridge.org/9781316512999

DOI: 10.1017/9781009071536

First published 2023

A catalogue record for this publication is available from the British Library.

Library of Congress Cataloging-in-Publication Data
Names: Culp, Julian, 1983- editor. | Drerup, Johannes, author. | Yacek, Douglas W., author.
Title: The Cambridge handbook of democratic education / edited by Julian Culp, Johannes Drerup, Douglas Yacek.
Description: Cambridge ; New York, NY : Cambridge University Press, 2023. | Includes bibliographical references.
Identifiers: LCCN 2022050938 (print) | LCCN 2022050939 (ebook) | ISBN 9781316512999 (hardback) | ISBN 9781009069885 (paperback) | ISBN 9781009071536 (epub)
Subjects: LCSH: Democracy and education. | Education–Aims and objectives.
Classification: LCC LC71 .C296 2023 (print) | LCC LC71 (ebook) | DDC 370.11/5–dc23/eng/20221209
LC record available at https://lccn.loc.gov/2022050938
LC ebook record available at https://lccn.loc.gov/2022050939

ISBN 978-1-316-51299-9 Hardback
ISBN 978-1-009-06988-5 Paperback

Contents

Contributors

Natalia Rogach Alexander is an Early Career Fellow in the Philosophy Department at Columbia University.

Brett Bertucio is Vice Principal at St. Monica Catholic School, Mercer Island, Washington.

Lauren Bialystok is Associate Professor at the Department of Social Justice Education, Ontario Institute for Studies in Education at the University of Toronto.

Gert Biesta is Professor of Public Education in the Centre for Public Education and Pedagogy, Maynooth University, Ireland, and Professor of Educational Theory and Pedagogy and Deputy Head of Institute for Education, Teaching & Leadership (IETL) at the University of Edinburgh.

Harry Brighouse is Mildred Fish-Harnack Professor of Philosophy of Education, Professor of Philosophy, Carol Dickson-Bascom Professor of the Humanities, and Affiliate Professor of Educational Policy Studies at the University of Wisconsin–Madison.

Drew Chambers is a PhD student in Philosophy and Education at Teachers College, Columbia University.

Julian Culp is Associate Professor of Philosophy and Fellow of the Center for Critical Democracy Studies at The American University of Paris.

Randall Curren is Professor of Philosophy and co-chair in the Department of Philosophy at the University of Rochester.

Richard Dagger is Emeritus Professor of Political Science and Philosophy, Politics, Economics and Law and E. Claiborne Robins Distinguished Chair in the Liberal Arts at the University of Richmond.

Johannes Drerup is Professor of Philosophy of Education and Educational Theory at TU Dortmund University and Guest Professor at the Free University of Amsterdam.

Yuval Dwek is a PhD Student at Teachers College, Columbia University.

Penny Enslin is Emeritus Professor in the School of Education at the University of Glasgow.

Franziska Felder is Professor of Inclusion and Diversity at the University of Zürich.

Ratna Ghosh is Distinguished James McGill Professor and William C. Macdonald Professor in the Department of Integrated Studies in Education at McGill University.

Johannes Giesinger is a fellow of the Center for Ethics at the University of Zürich.

Stefan Gosepath is Professor of Practical Philosophy at Freie Universität Berlin.

Michael Hand is Professor of Philosophy of Education in the School of Education and Director of Postgraduate Research in the University Graduate School at the University of Birmingham.

David T. Hansen is Professor and Director of the Philosophy and Education program at Teachers College, Columbia University.

Kai Horsthemke is Research Fellow in the Faculty of Philosophy and Systematic Pedagogy at the Catholic University of Eichstätt-Ingolstadt.

Sarah M. Iler is Assistant Director of Institutional Research in the University of North Carolina School of the Arts.

Mark E. Jonas is Professor of Education and Associate Professor of Philosophy (by courtesy) at Wheaton College.

Bruce A. Kimball is Professor Emeritus of Educational Studies at the Ohio State University.

Ben Kotzee is Reader in Philosophy of Education at the University of Birmingham and is Visiting Professor at Oslo Metropolitan University.

Anthony Simon Laden is Professor of Philosophy at University of Illinois Chicago and Associate Director of the Center for Ethics and Education.

Meira Levinson is Juliana W. and William Foss Thompson Professor of Education and Society at the Harvard Graduate School, co-director of the Graduate Fellowship Program at the Edmond & Lily Safra Center for Ethics, and Director of the Democratic Knowledge Project.

Jane Lo is Assistant Professor of Teacher Education at Michigan State University.

Colin M. Macleod is Professor of Law and Philosophy and the chair of the Department of Philosophy at the University of Victoria.

Bruce Maxwell is Associate Professor in the Faculty of Education at the University of Montreal.

Paula McAvoy is Associate Professor of Teacher Education and Learning Sciences and PhD coordinator for the Social Studies Program Area of Study at North Carolina State University.

Michael S. Merry is Professor in the Faculty of Social and Behavioral Sciences at the University of Amsterdam.

Avi I. Mintz is Associate Director of Curriculum at Newlane University.

Blain Neufeld is Professor of Philosophy at the University of Wisconsin–Milwaukee.

A. C. Nikolaidis is a PhD candidate in the Department of Educational Studies (Philosophy and History of Education) at the Ohio State University.

Martha C. Nussbaum is the Ernst Freund Distinguished Service Professor of Law and Ethics in the Law School and Philosophy Department at the University of

Chicago. She is an Associate in the Classics Department, the Divinity School, and the Political Science Department, a Member of the Committee on Southern Asian Studies, and a Board Member of the Human Rights Program.

Jürgen Oelkers is Emeritus Professor of Educational Science at the University of Zürich.

Roland Reichenbach is Professor of General Education Studies at the University of Zürich.

Ellis Reid is a PhD candidate at the Harvard Graduate School of Education.

Peter Roberts is Professor of Education at the University of Canterbury, New Zealand.

Anders Schinkel is Associate Professor of Philosophy of Education in the Faculty of Behavioural and Movement Sciences of Vrije Universiteit Amsterdam.

Krassimir Stojanov is Professor and Chair of the Faculty of Philosophy and Systematic Pedagogy at the Catholic University of Eichstätt-Ingolstadt.

Bryan R. Warnick is Professor of Philosophy of Education in the College of Education and Human Ecology at the Ohio State University.

Douglas Yacek is a Research Fellow in Philosophy of Education at TU Dortmund University.

Ilya Zrudlo is a PhD candidate in Educational Studies at the Department of Integrated Studies in Education at McGill University.

Acknowledgments

Compiling a Handbook of this breadth and scope is a daunting endeavor – one that is likely impossible, or at least thoroughly unenjoyable, without the help of colleagues, friends, and loved ones. Without the inspiration and moral support of these individuals, this Handbook would not be half of what it has become. We would like to express our special thanks to the following people, though the list that follows by no means covers all of the individuals that deserve our gratitude: Jens Beljan, Sigal Ben-Porath, Micha Brumlik, Carlo Burelli, Marcelo Caruso, Drew Chambers, Chiara Destri, Melanie Ehren, Matthew Farrelly, Jessica Feldman, Sarah Freedman, Kevin Gary, Michael Geiss, Dorothee Gronostay, Katariina Holma, Mark Jonas, Zoé Kergomard, Bruce Kimball, Phillip Knobloch, Marieke Krater, Nele Kuhlmann, Michelle Kuo, Anniina Leiviskä, Annabelle Lever, Ruprecht Mattig, Paul McCloud, Roland Merten, Doret de Ruyter, Stephen Sawyer, Harvey Siegel, Miranda Spieler, Hugh Starkey, Peter Vogel, Bryan Warnick, Rupert Wegerif, Lothar Wigger, Albert Wu, Anna Yacek, Douglas A. Yacek, Wendy Yacek, Roman Zinigrad, Tim Zumhof, and Danielle Zwarthoed.

We would also like to thank our research assistants, Tim Isenberg, Caroline Bossong, and Marieke Krater, for their diligence and care in preparing the manuscript for this volume.

Finally, we owe our gratitude to the Hirschhorn Museum for granting us permission to use Alma Thomas's "Earth Sermon - Beauty, Love and Peace" for the cover of this handbook.

Introduction

1

What Is Democratic Education and Why Should We Care?

Julian Culp, Johannes Drerup, and Douglas Yacek

Democratic education is central to the functioning and flourishing of modern multicultural democracies, and yet it is subject to increasing public controversy and political pressure. Waning public trust in government institutions (Miner, 2020; Stitzlein, 2020; Wilson, 2020; cf. MacDonald, 2019; Pew Research Center, 2022), sustained attacks on democratic values and customs from populist politicians and organizations (Brown, 2019; Müller, 2016, 2021; Runciman, 2019), political polarization and "sectarianism" (Finkel et al., 2020; Iyengar et al., 2019), and increasing trends toward privatization and chartering in the educational landscape (Abrams, 2016; Levin, 2001; Verger et al., 2016) have placed immense strain on the existing structures of public education and generally worked to undermine public confidence in democratic education. Practically speaking, this has meant that educators have been thrust into hazardous pedagogical terrain, in which students and parents are increasingly empowered to opt out of course content and evaluations on political grounds (Wilson, 2020), while teachers are expected to maintain scrupulous neutrality on politically and morally controversial issues, regardless of the intellectual merit of the opinions involved, or else face charges of indoctrination (Hand, 2008; Zimmermann & Robertson, 2017). This contentious educational atmosphere has made it increasingly difficult to foster coöperation, rational discussion and a sense of political community in students beyond partisan political divisions (Hess & McAvoy, 2015).

At the same time, several movements in educational and political theory have called some of the basic concepts, premises, and normative justifications of democratic education into question. According to the most critical of these perspectives, we should seriously reconsider the status of democratic education as an educational ideal and recognize its intrinsically hegemonic, bourgeois, or oppressive character. While in some cases these thoroughgoing critiques have led to important advancements in our understanding of democratic theory – for example, in our growing awareness of how power, racism, xenophobia, nationalism, and sexism have historically influenced political and educational theory-building – in other cases they have seemed to authorize anti-democratic or autocratic impulses under the auspices of academic scholarship.

In light of these developments, it seems to us to be of central importance to return to the basic concepts, theories, and values of democratic education, both as a social ideal and a political institution. Of course, "democratic education" has been defined in almost as many ways as its constitutive terms, "democracy" and "education," and we do not want to enter this particular debate in this introductory chapter (see, for instance, Brighouse, 1998; Brumlik, 2018; Callan, 1997; Gutmann, 1999; Kitcher, 2022; Merry, 2018; Reichenbach, 2022). Rather, we would like to make a brief case for democratic education as a core focus of educational theory and practice – that is, for *caring* about democratic education in a profound way.

In the first place, democratic education, in its broadest sense, expresses what we hope will result from our efforts to educate the next generation. Caring about democratic education means that, whatever curricular materials or pedagogical methods may be used in the process, we hope that our educational institutions are contributing to producing a happier and more flourishing society. At the individual level, this means that we hope students come out the other end of their education prepared to see themselves as worthy and able to participate in democratic decision-making, to uphold democratic ideals in their social and vocational lives, and to be prepared to protect the integrity and stability of democratic processes if they are threatened. Democratic education is, in other words, education *for* democracy (cf. Sant, 2019). It takes seriously the belief that human communities and individuals flourish most, or become the most just, when they commit to a basic principle of equality among all human beings and when they keep opportunities and social roles open to all those who strive to achieve them. To this end, education for democracy cultivates not only the will and ability to enact this basic principle in a comprehensive way, but also an active consciousness of historical injustices, so that the enduring effects of oppression, marginalization and demoralization can be counteracted and, ultimately, neutralized.

If caring about democratic education means enacting an education for democracy, then this implies something important about what democratic education looks like in practice. Democracy is not only a formal characteristic of political or educational institutions, but also an attitude toward our fellow human beings. Crucially, although this attitude may in some cases arise naturally in individuals, it is nonetheless in tension with other widespread and psychologically powerful human motivations and tendencies – for example, avarice, competitiveness, or the desire for power. Developing the ability to recognize our fundamental moral equality with other human beings, to make this recognition psychologically effective enough in our actions and decisions that it can overcome countervailing impulses, and to draw on this principle for strength when democratic ideals are challenged requires a rigorous and thoroughgoing educational program that creates democratically oriented habits, dispositions and virtues in students. In order to supply this comprehensive educational experience, democratic education will have to occur across the curriculum, in physical education, mathematics, and biology just as much as in social studies or civics. This insight prevents us from outsourcing the demands of citizen formation to one disciplinary location. It makes the concept of democratic education importantly different from terms like "civic education" or "political education," which focus more exclusively on the particular knowledge and skills necessary for effective participation in contemporary political processes.

Democratic education not only implies an education for democracy, but also that this education is *conducted* in a certain kind of way. Imagine a program designed to instill democratic habits and virtues that was taught in an authoritarian manner, allowing little to no room for students' own experiences and personalities and with harsh punishment schemes in place. Clearly, such an approach to "democratic education" would be a performative contradiction. However, the same goes for educational programs that too starkly individualize students, making education centrally a matter of individuals earning grades, accolades, credentials, and other forms of social recognition for their own personal advancement. John Dewey pointed out at the turn of the twentieth century that we seriously undermine the potential to cultivate and achieve democracy through our schools if we make education so individual an affair. The example he uses is the quintessential exam experience. What happens during exams? Students sit in individual desks, call up objective, impersonal knowledge to answer the standardized questions posed, remain quiet and still while they do so, and turn in their work at the end for an individual grade. If they decide – in the spirit of democracy – to communicate with each other and work together, perhaps even to help the weakest students improve their academic abilities, they are punished, sometimes with expulsion. Dewey urged us to ask ourselves, What could be more devastating for cultivating democratic sentiments and habits?

If we care about democracy and a truly democratic education, then this will not do. What counts as a characteristically democracy-promoting pedagogy, then? Dewey famously thought it was provided by the intrinsic "social control" of rich practical activities like cooking, sewing, woodwork, and gardening, and this is why these occupations made up the bulk of the school day at his laboratory school. In contrast, A. S. Neill thought it meant the almost complete forfeiture of curricular and educational decision-making power to students, particularly in an assembly-style structure composed of them and their teachers. Harold Rugg, a colleague of Dewey's and a fellow progressive, thought that "parliamentary discussion" of controversial social issues should form the core of the democratic educational experience. Freire thought, too, that only a thoroughly dialogical pedagogy would suffice, though it should be one in which students' home lives become the topic of instruction, particularly, the manifold ways in which oppression colors their experience. Countless further proposals have been made since these classic positions were staked out. Recently, programs that bring in important global issues and cosmopolitan perspectives have gained in popularity.

This is not the place to take a stand on this question, though it does seem to us that some combination of each of these elements would likely be necessary for providing a comprehensive democratic education. However, at a somewhat more general level, we can say that the two notions of democratic education – education *for* democracy and education *as* democracy (democratic pedagogy) – constitute two practical desiderata that limit and complement each other. For example, if we knew we could instill democratic qualities most efficiently by means of autonomy-denying methods, we would not want to do so because of our commitment to democratic pedagogy. On the other hand, if we allow democratic education to be too open-ended or student-centered in order to emulate the structures and procedures of democratic government in adulthood, then we fail to provide a compelling and effective education of sentiment and habit that furthers democratic flourishing (and personal flourishing, too). Indeed, not only would this prevent us from helping students develop democratic virtues; it inhibits us from counteracting anti-democratic influences in the larger culture – influences that shape students both outside and inside of schools every single day.

In light of this broad understanding of the importance and scope of democratic education, this handbook offers an expansive view of the formation of individuals for democratic life and includes theoretical traditions, topics, and thinkers that are not always immediately connected to this task when construed as civic, political, or citizenship education. More concretely, this volume provides readers with a comprehensive overview of the fundamental ideas, concepts, theories, aims and challenges of democratic education, both as a social ideal and as a contemporary institution. If educators are to provide students with a worthwhile and socially productive education within the current educational landscape, and if researchers are to understand the specific sociopolitical factors influencing the present educational moment, we believe that a broad engagement with the value and meaning of democratic education will be an indispensable resource to them. This volume will therefore not only introduce readers to the central contours of contemporary thinking about democratic education, but also function, we hope, as a clear signal of the practical and scholarly significance of democratic education. Given the current challenges to democratic education, we believe it to be an opportune time to send such a signal.

However, we believe that the reasons for compiling this *Cambridge Handbook of Democratic Education* go beyond the particularities of the present moment. Democratic education is a perennial concern of societies committed to the value of justice and the well-being of children. Debates about the meaning, purpose and aims of democratic education had already begun in Ancient Athens, in which the proper content of the *encyclios paideia* (general education) was vigorously disputed. On the one side, followers of Plato and Aristotle, though the two sages of Greek Antiquity expressed skepticism about democracy, defended the role of speculative and philosophically oriented studies for political formation, while followers of Isocrates and other sophists forcefully argued for public rhetoric and civic engagement as the prerequisite studies for democratic citizenship. This ancient debate has continued throughout Western history (Stasavage, 2020; Sen, 2005), with some educational thinkers taking the speculative, philosophical side and others the rhetorical side (Kimball, 1986). These issues became particularly poignant in the aftermath of the democratic revolutions in eighteenth-century Europe and America, in which it became apparent – to such figures as Thomas Jefferson and Horace Mann in the American context, for example – that access to a democracy-promoting education should be free and open to all citizens (though often excluding women, African-Americans and other groups). The discussion of what kinds of subjects and what kinds of pedagogy are appropriate for such an educational program are thus not only important in the present political situation. This discussion is a mainstay of open and free societies. The debates and deliberations over the content, methods, and aims of democratic education can be seen as so many indications of a healthy democratic community, so long as they are conducted in a humane and constructive manner.

In this way, this volume aims to be an enduring resource for those interested in advancing the discussion of democratic education well into the future. Not only does the volume encompass several chapters on the history of democratic education, including analyses of some of the major historical figures who have contributed to the discussion; it also engages with some of the central concepts, ideas, and ideals that have wielded influence over the programs and theories of democratic education in history. We hope to encourage readers to return to these issues and thinkers as a part of their study of democratic education, since they continue to provide fresh insight for the project of understanding and realizing democratic education.

There are four main themes that organize the handbook into four parts: (i) Historical Perspectives, (ii) Philosophical and Normative Foundations, (iii) Key Topics and Concepts, and (iv) Challenges. In *Historical Perspectives*, we include chapters on significant figures in the history of political and educational thought who have contributed significantly to our understanding of democratic education and whose ideas warrant perennial reconsideration. In *Philosophical and Normative Foundations*, we provide chapters connecting democratic education to important foundational ideas in ethics, moral philosophy, as well as social and political philosophy broadly construed. This part is essential to the handbook, for it shows that the discussion of democratic education is connected in myriad ways to some of the central issues in contemporary political and educational thought, such as the emerging field of educational ethics, moral education, political liberalism, and critical theory. The part dedicated to *Key Topics and Concepts* takes up some of the central issues in the research on democratic education today. This part provides the reader with a broad and systematic overview of some of the most pressing theoretical and practical questions in democratic education, including classroom debate and dialogue, controversial issues, global justice, punishment, patriotism, and free speech. The final part of the handbook addresses *Challenges* to the project of democratic education today. This part looks not only at intellectual movements that have contested the basic principles and aims of democratic education, but also movements in the public realm, such as the rise of populist political organizations, the changing media terrain and climate change.

With this thematic and conceptual orientation, we thus hope to have provided a distinctive and comprehensive treatment of democratic education, one that can serve as an enduring resource for researchers and practitioners who care about democratic education.

References

Abrams, S. E. (2016). *Education and the commercial mindset*. Cambridge, MA: Harvard University Press.

Brighouse, H. (1998). Civic education and liberal legitimacy. *Ethics*, 108(4), 719–45.

Brumlik, M. (2018). *Demokratie und Bildung*. Berlin: Neofelis.

Brown, W. (2019). *In the ruins of neoliberalism: The rise of antidemocratic politics in the West*. New York: Columbia University Press.

Callan, E. (1997). *Creating citizens: Political education and liberal democracy*. Oxford: Oxford University Press.

Finkel, E. J., Bail, C. A., Cikara, M., Ditto, P. H., Iyengar, S., Klar, S., . . . & Skitka, L. J. (2020). Political sectarianism in America. *Science*, 370(6516), 533–36.

Gutmann, A. (1999). *Democratic education*. Princeton, NJ: Princeton University Press.

Hand, M. (2008). What should we teach as controversial? A defense of the epistemic criterion. *Educational Theory*, 58(2), 213–28.

Hess, D., & McAvoy, P. (2015). *The political classroom: Evidence and ethics in democratic education*. London: Routledge.

Iyengar, S., Lelkes, Y., Levendusky, M., Malhotra, N., & Westwood, S. J. (2019). The origins and consequences of affective polarization in the United States. *Annual Review of Political Science*, 22, 129–46.

Kimball, B. A. (1986). *Orators & philosophers: A history of the idea of liberal education*. New York: Teachers College Press.

Kitcher, P. (2022). *The main enterprise of the world: Rethinking education*. New York: Oxford University Press.

Levin, H. (2001). *Privatizing education: Can the school marketplace deliver freedom of choice, efficiency, equity, and social cohesion?* Boulder, CO: Westview Press.

Macdonald, D. (2019). Trust in government and the American public's responsiveness to rising inequality. *Political Research Quarterly*, 73(4), 790–804.

Merry, M. (2018). Can schools teach citizenship? *Discourse: Studies in the Cultural Politics of Education*, 41(1), 124–38.

Miner, M. A. (2020). Unmet promises: Diminishing confidence in education among college-educated adults from 1973 to 2018. *Social Science Quarterly*, 101(6), 2312–31.

Müller, J.-W. (2016). *What is populism?* Philadelphia, PA: University of Pennsylvania Press.

Müller, J.-W. (2021). *Democracy rules*. London: Allen Lane.

Pew Research Center (2022). *Public trust in government: 1958–2022*. Available at: https://www.pewresearch.org/politics/2022/06/06/public-trust-in-government-1958-2022.

Reichenbach, R. (2022). “Une plante sauvage” – Über das Politische und die Politische Bildung. *Zeitschrift für Pädagogik*, 68(4), 445–61.

Runciman, D. (2019). *How democracy ends*. London: Profile Books.

Sant, E. (2019). Democratic education: A theoretical review (2006–2017). *Review of Educational Research*, 89(5), 655–96.

Sen, A. (2005). *The argumentative Indian*. London: Penguin Books.

Stasavage, D. (2020). *The cecline and rise of democracy: A global history from antiquity to today*. Princeton, NJ: Princeton University Press.

Stitzlein, S. M. (2020). The democratic potential of parental dissent: Keeping public schools public, legitimate, and educational. *Educational Theory*, 70(3), 355–72.

Verger, A., Fontdevila, C., & Zancajo, A. (2016). *The privatization of education: A political economy of global education reform*. New York: Teachers College Press.

Wilson, T. S. (2020). Contesting public education: Opting out, dissent, and activism. *Educational Theory*, 70(3), 247–54.

Zimmerman, J., & Robertson, E. (2017). *The case for contention: Teaching controversial issues in American schools*. Chicago, IL: University of Chicago Press.

Part One

Historical Perspectives

2

Plato on Democratic Education

Mark E. Jonas

2.1 Introduction

In this chapter, I turn to an unlikely source for democratic inspiration: Plato's *Republic*. I argue that, understood correctly, Plato's *Republic* provides insights into what a flourishing democracy looks like and how education can help produce such a democracy. At first glance, this claim will seem completely wrongheaded, as the *Republic* appears to advocate a form of totalitarianism founded on a rigid caste system that is entirely inconsistent with democracy.[1] Furthermore, it might be argued that the educational principles laid out in the *Republic* are also anti-democratic and are meant only for an elite group of future philosopher-kings. Plato's *Republic* seems to relegate nonphilosophical human beings to a narrow training in a craft and to submit them to a regimen of indoctrination intended to produce absolute obedience to the society's rulers, who themselves have unchecked power.[2]

While this interpretation of the *Republic* is certainly widespread, some interpreters have challenged this reading, suggesting instead that the *Republic* is not meant to be interpreted as a totalitarian political treatise.[3] Some of these commentators have argued that the political treatise at the core of the *Republic*

[1] The claim of totalitarianism is impossible to deny, if we take the *kallipolis*, the imaginary city that stands at the center of the *Republic*, to represent Plato's preferred political arrangement. As Taylor (1997) claims, "It is . . . uncontroversial that the ideal state of the *Republic* is a totalitarian state" (p. 32). However, if we deny the view that Plato meant the *kallipolis* to represent his preferred political doctrine – a view that there is ample reason to deny – then the *Republic* as a whole does not promote a totalitarian political theory. Commentators who have argued that the *Republic*, as a whole, may be more sympathetic to democracy than it is customarily assumed include Euben (1997), Jonas & Nakazawa (2021), Jonas, Nakazawa, & Braun (2012), Roochnik (2003), and Saxonhouse (1996).

[2] It is widely agreed that Plato does not explicitly address the education of the producers, but there is some disagreement as to whether that means they receive no education whatsoever beyond a bare education in their craft and an education in obedience. Guthrie (1975) and Reeve (1988), for example, argue that they get no education beyond this, but Barrow (2008), Bobonich (2002), Curren (2000), Dorter (2006), Kamtekar (2010), Vasiliou (2008), and Vlastos (1973), among others, argue that they must get at least some training in virtue. Others remain silent on the exact content of the producers' education, while acknowledging that there must be some education (Annas, 1981; Pappas, 2013). In a different vein, Mintz (2016) argues that Plato is inconsistent with respect to the producers' education as a way to intentionally encourage "readers to consider the conditions necessary for enabling all individuals in a society to flourish" (p. 13).

[3] Annas (1999); Clay (2000); Frank (2018); Jonas & Nakazawa (2021); Smith (2019); Waterfield (1993).

ought to be interpreted metaphorically – as representing the soul of a human being rather than a blueprint for civilization building. The foundational interpretive rationale for this reading is spelled out early in the *Republic*, when Socrates explicitly states that the point of identifying justice in the city is to help him and his interlocutors identify justice in the individual soul, which is the point of departure for the ensuing dialogue about the philosopher-kings and the society they are to rule (368e–369a). If we take Socrates' words at face value and keep those words in mind while reading the *Republic*, the totalitarian political doctrine largely recedes into the background and new vistas of interpretation open before us.

In what follows, I will attempt to reveal these interpretive vistas by making a case for an egalitarian reading of the *Republic*. While Plato does not provide an explicit defense of democracy, his criticism of corrupt democracies in Book VIII and his often-ignored advocacy of egalitarian communities in Books II, III, and IV offer contemporary educators insights into a mode of education that could strengthen contemporary democracies. Once this interpretation is in place, I will discuss the ways contemporary democratic educators might use Plato's ideas to support students in their development as democratic citizens.

2.2 Moderation, Happiness, and Egalitarianism in the *Republic*

To understand the relevance of the *Republic* for democratic education, we need first to briefly understand the relationship between virtue and happiness as expressed by Socrates in the *Republic*. In three separate moments within the *Republic*, Socrates offers us an image of contented and happy people. The way Socrates describes these individuals, and particularly how their happiness relates to the condition of their soul, contrasts starkly with the standard reading of Plato as a theorist of totalitarianism.

The first description of happy and contented individuals in the *Republic* is found in the first city he describes, the so-called city of pigs (371e–372e). The first city is made up of individuals who have distinct roles and responsibilities that are supposed to contribute to the happiness both of the individuals themselves and of the society as a whole. As Socrates maintains, these people have their basic needs met and live in peace, moderation, and good health; they share everything in common and there is no distinction between who is more or less valuable. The city is surprisingly egalitarian in that every person has an essential job to fulfill and no one's job is considered more important than anyone else's; nor are people wealthier than others nor command more respect or deference. From the most skilled craftspeople to the merchants and hirelings who support the craftspeople, everyone has a vocation that is central to the thriving of the community and that allows for everyone to participate fully in communal life.[4] This applies to men and women, the intelligent and nonintelligent, children

[4] It might be argued that the first city is not egalitarian because each person is expected to perform only those jobs for which they are naturally gifted. Socrates claims that there is a "diversity of natures" among people and some are suited for farming,

and adults. Socrates describes the resultant communal health of this egalitarian community in the following:

> First, then, let's see what sort of life our citizens will lead when they've been provided for in the way we have been describing. They'll produce bread, wine, clothes, and shoes, won't they? They'll build houses, work naked and barefoot in the summer, and wear adequate clothing and shoes in the winter. For food, they'll knead and cook the flour and meal they've made from wheat and barley. They'll put their honest cakes and loaves on reeds or clean leaves, and, reclining on beds strewn with yew and myrtle, they'll feast with their children, drink their wine, and, crowned with wreaths, hymn the gods. They'll enjoy sex with one another but bear no more children than their resources allow, lest they fall into either poverty or war . . . [T]hey'll obviously need salt, olives, cheese, boiled roots, and vegetables of the sort they cook in the country. We'll give them desserts, too, of course, consisting of figs, chickpeas, and beans, and they'll roast myrtle and acorns before the fire, drinking moderately. And so they'll live in peace and good health, and when they die at a ripe old age, they'll bequeath a similar life to their children. (372a–372d)[5]

Not only is this description of the first city attractive in its depiction of its peace, harmony, happiness, and communal flourishing, Socrates claims that it is "healthy" and "true," and he seems to consider it to be something worth striving for.[6] If the *Republic* were to end at this point, there would be no question as to Plato's (or at least Socrates') credentials as a committed egalitarian, if by these terms we mean simply that each person is able to live in a society that promotes their individual flourishing equally and equitably.[7] However, the *Republic* of

some are suited for cobblery, and some are not particularly gifted at anything and become merchants or hirelings. Whatever a person is most gifted at is what they will do to provide for the community. Many people in democratic countries would be concerned that the people not getting to choose what their job is means that the community is not egalitarian. Their thought is that a community is egalitarian only if it allows people to choose whatever job they want, whether they have any talent for it or not. However, in contemporary democracies, the reality is that countless people are not able to do whatever job they want, because there are other more talented people who get those jobs. Moreover, many people in contemporary democracies who are more talented than other people do not get the jobs they want, because other people have "better networks," or "know the right people," or simply have more undeserved social capital. In Plato's first city, this would never happen. The people who are actually the best at the jobs get the jobs. It is a genuine meritocracy. Although Plato does not spell out the mechanism that determines who is most naturally suited to which occupations, it is implied that every single person's skills and abilities are evaluated by the community so as to find those who genuinely are the most suited for every job. This means that every person, no matter what their social standing or "who they know," has the same opportunity to do any job, even if the reality is that only those with the most talent actually get the job. So, in a sense, the first city is far more egalitarian than modern democracies because it is the most pure form of meritocracy possible. But, importantly, it is a meritocracy that does not marginalize those with less "merit" but includes them in the flourishing communal life to the same degree as those with greater skills or talents for the vocations.

[5] All quotations from Plato are from *Plato: Complete Works*, edited by J. Cooper and D. Hutchinson (1997).

[6] Most commentators reject the viability of the first city: Annas (1981); Barney (2001); Blitz (2010); Cooper (2000); Crombie (1962); Devereux (1979); Howland (2004); McDavid (2019); McKeen (2004); Nettleship (1901); Pappas (2013); Reeve (1988). However, a few commentators have claimed that Plato genuinely believes the first city is a healthy and viable community (Jonas & Nakazawa, 2021; Morrison, 2007; Rowe, 2007a, 2007b).

[7] The first city and, as we shall see, the communities of auxiliaries and philosopher-kings found in Books III and IV are egalitarian insofar as each member of the community performs a vital function to the community and there are no members of the community that are given more political power than the others within that community to shape policy. Of course, that

course does not end here. Glaucon – one of the main interlocturs in the *Republic* – objects that Socrates' community is far too simple and insists that "if [the citizens] aren't to suffer hardship" they must have luxuries and conveniences "that people have nowadays." This riposte leads Socrates to abandon the first city and begin conceptualizing the famous *kallipolis*. Before he begins a new city, he makes it clear that the city Glaucon wants and the luxuries and conveniences upon which it must be built will make it an inferior and less desirable city. Socrates says:

> All right, I understand. It isn't merely the origin of a city that we're considering, it seems, but the origin of a luxurious city. And that may not be a bad idea, for by examining it, we might very well see how justice and injustice grow up in cities. Yet the true city, in my opinion, is the one we've described, the healthy one, as it were. But let's study a city with a fever, if that's what you want. There's nothing to stop us. The things I mentioned earlier and the way of life I described won't satisfy some people, it seems. (372e–373a)

As we will discuss in Section 2.3, the fact that Glaucon insists on having luxuries means that the peace, health, harmony, and equality of the above city will be replaced by a much less attractive community, especially to people who value harmony and equality.

The second instance in which Socrates depicts happy and contented people occurs in his description of the guardians of the *kallipolis*. Like the inhabitants of the first city, the guardians do not have any unnecessary luxuries, and they share everything in common and no one is left wanting (416d–e). Like the first city, while there are natural differences of intelligence or strength relative to each other, they all make important contributions to the group (455a–456a). He claims that by living in this manner the guardians "live a life more blessedly happy than that of the victors in the Olympian games" (465d) because they avoid the perils of those who want luxuries and conveniences. They avoid the false happiness of those who "build fine big houses, acquire furnishings to go along with them . . . and . . . possess what you were talking about just now, gold and silver and all the things that are [falsely] thought to belong to people who are blessedly happy." Although they occupy a caste of the radically inegalitarian society of the *kallipolis* – which is the necessary outgrowth of the feverish city Glaucon desires – the guardians live like the citizens of the first city in that they find happiness in a simple, moderate lifestyle that avoids the vice associated with the "endless acquisition of money" and the pursuit of luxury and convenience (373d).

The third time Socrates describes human happiness is at the end of the *Republic*, when he depicts the various forms of human beings that are characterized by different psychological constitutions. He claims the happiest human beings are

is not to say that each person is equal in terms or talent, intelligence, strength, etc. – something that is not possible among human beings who have natural differences from other human beings. There will always be differences of this kind. Nevertheless, while Plato does not call these communities democratic, it is clear that there is a kind of equality among citizens that makes the communities egalitarian in a way that exceeds what we would minimally expect for contemporary democratic communities.

the ones who pursue moderation and virtue and who avoid wealth and honor and the luxuries and pleasures they provide. The happiest human beings have "aristocratic" souls that are "rightly said to be good and just" (544e). Unfortunately, if people of this sort are not careful to follow moderation and virtue completely, they can be subtly persuaded by their appetites to begin pursuing things like wealth and honor that inevitably corrupt their souls. Socrates claims that it is "clear that there is a dangerous, wild, and lawless form of desire in everyone, even in those of us who seem to be entirely moderate or measured" (572b). That is, all human beings have appetites that continually urge them to forgo moderation and pursue luxury and licentiousness. If the "aristocratic" soul is not on guard, it can slowly be perverted to pursue luxury and vice. Socrates uses an analogy of "iron" and "bronze" parts of the soul, which represent the acquisitive desires, in contrast to the "gold" and "silver" parts of the soul, which represent moderation and virtue. In a careless person who is overly influenced by the wrong type of people, these two parts can battle each other: "Once civil war breaks out, both the iron and bronze types pull the constitution towards money-making and the acquisition of land, houses, gold, and silver, while both the gold and silver types – not being poor, but by nature rich or rich in their souls – lead the constitution towards virtue and the old order" (547b).

As the iron and bronze parts of the soul gain in strength, eventually the person gives themselves over to the desire for wealth, luxury, and vice. A few lines later Socrates describes their transformation: "Such people will desire money just as those in oligarchies do, passionately adoring gold and silver in secret. They will possess private treasuries and storehouses, where they can keep it hidden, and have houses to enclose them, like private nests, where they spend lavishly either on women or on anyone else they wish" (548a). Eventually, the person described above gives themselves completely over to their desires and becomes a tyrannical person who is "the most wretched" sort of human being (580c).

In summary, we see a consistent claim throughout the *Republic* that the best and happiest life for the individual is one of moderation and virtue and that the pursuit of excessive wealth and luxury leads away from happiness, not toward it. The same is true for the inhabitants of the first city in Book II, the guardians of the *kallipolis* in Books IV and V, and the souls of all human beings in Books VIII and IX. For Plato, happiness is found in a simple, moderate life in which people have their basic needs met and eschew wealth, luxury, and power. This latter point is essential, as Plato believes these things to have a corrosive effect both on the souls of people who acquire them and on the community in which they live. People who live in this moderate fashion are not ascetic and discontent but, on the contrary, are satisfied and happy, because they take true pleasure in virtue and community and do not crave the false pleasure of wealth and luxury.

2.3 Socrates' Critique of Immoderation and Elitism in the *Republic*

The result of the discussion in Section 2.2 is the following: Plato's vision of individual happiness requires that moderation and virtue be in place within the soul. However, this conception of happiness has a crucial further aspect. If we focus our attention on Socrates' three descriptions of human happiness in the *Republic*, it becomes clear that, for Plato, the happiest individuals live within a community that is defined by diversity of skill and vocation, mutual support, and social equality. Plato says this explicitly in his account of the egalitarian first city and implies it strongly in his description of the community of auxiliaries and philosopher-kings in the *kallipolis* (who are supposed to be the best intellectually and morally endowed individuals of the society). But the point also follows from his critique of immoderation and his asseverations that luxury and power corrupt the individual soul. If the highest good of a human life is moderation and virtue, and if societies undermine the pursuit of this good when they become competitive and stratified, then the individual needs an egalitarian community to support their growth toward human flourishing. It is this latter point that will concern me in this section.

Of course, there may likely be many who demur at my claim that Plato prefers an egalitarian community in which people live in harmony, where everyone values a happy life characterized by moderation and simplicity, and where everyone has equal standing with everyone else, even if there are natural distinctions between the community members' intellectual and physical strengths and weaknesses. People might claim that, in fact, the (in)famous tripartite structure of the *kallipolis* at the center of the *Republic* is radically inegalitarian with respect to lifestyles and privileges – where producers are relegated to lives of total obeisance, with the only "advantage" being that they get to pursue wealth and the luxuries that the city affords.

At first glance, this criticism seems justified. In the *kallipolis*, Socrates famously divides the city into the three classes of people – the producers, the auxiliaries, and the philosopher-kings, the latter of which have unchecked power. What commentators fail to acknowledge, however, is that the only reason Socrates creates these three classes is because Glaucon rejects the egalitarian first city as highlighted as not suitable to "people nowadays" who have grown accustomed to luxury and convenience. Glaucon insists that they should be allowed to pursue wealth and all the pleasures it affords. Socrates expresses some surprise and claims that apparently it is not a "true" and "healthy" city that Glaucon wants but a city with a "fever" and one that has "surrendered [itself] to the endless acquisition of money" (272e–273d). Despite Socrates' surprise, he is willing to create the city that Glaucon wants, which is confusing considering what we see in Socrates' universal condemnation of the pursuit of wealth and luxury (something he condemns not just in the *Republic* but throughout Plato's whole corpus). However, Glaucon clearly has not appreciated the central point of the first city – that individual and communal happiness depend on the avoidance of unnecessary wealth, luxuries, and conveniences. Hence, Socrates quickly realizes that if he is going to persuade Glaucon (and Adeimantus, another main interlocutor) that the just life is better than the unjust life, he will need to extend the metaphor of the city so that they can see justice more clearly. Socrates says this explicitly when, after hearing Glaucon's request to create a city with a fever, he claims that creating a city with a fever may "not be a bad idea, for by examining it, we might very well see how justice and injustice grow up in cities." This suggests that the city they will go on to create (the *kallipolis*) will contain injustice, which is exactly what we see.

When Socrates begins to create this city, he introduces a whole series of injustices that are necessary if the city is going to have wealth and luxury. He says that if the city is going to have "delicacies, perfumed oils, incense, prostitutes, and pastries . . . [and] paintings and embroidery . . . and gold [and] ivory . . . Then we must enlarge our city, for the healthy one is no longer adequate. We must increase it in size and fill it with a multitude of things that go beyond what is necessary for a city" (373a–b). He goes on to say that "we didn't need any of these things in our earlier city, but we'll need them in this one . . . And if we live like that, we'll have far greater need for doctors than we did before" (373c). So far, this city sounds like a far cry from the community he affirms in the first city, from the community he affirms in the community of guardians, and from the simple life he affirms at the end of the *Republic*, all of which eschew these kinds of unnecessary desires. But it gets worse. He argues that if the citizens want these things,

> Then we'll have to seize some of our neighbors' land if we're to have enough pasture and ploughland. And won't our neighbors want to seize part of ours as well, if they too have surrendered themselves to the endless acquisition of money and have overstepped the limit of their necessities? . . . Then our next step will be war, Glaucon, won't it . . . [which] comes from those same desires that are most of all responsible for the bad things that happen to cities and the individuals in them. (373d–e)

The unpleasant nature of these passages is entirely in keeping with what we saw in Section 2.2. The city that Glaucon insists they create is not a happy or virtuous city – certainly not throughout; it is instead a city that is morally depraved and full of immoderation, ill-health, and rapacity. This is what we should expect because it is the opposite of the communities that Socrates recommends in his praise of the first city, the guardians, and happy and just human beings. But what is typically ignored is that it also necessitates the introduction of a guardian class of people who will guarantee the continued ability for the city's citizens to indulge in their immoderation and license. Socrates says that "the city must be enlarged . . . by a whole army, which will do battle with the invaders and defense of the city's substantial wealth and all the other things we mentioned" (373e).[8] He claims that this class of guardians must not come from within the citizens themselves but must be selected and trained to do nothing else than manage the city to protect the citizens' ability to imbibe in their unhealthy and immoderate lifestyle. It is here that we see the introduction of

[8] Reeve (1988) claims that the guardians are "introduced to defend the polis, not simply against other hostile poleis, but also against unnecessary appetites, which are the root cause of such conflict" (p. 178). This interpretation that guardians protect against unnecessary desires is highly confusing, however; as we have just seen, the guardians' first responsibility is to go on to "seize some of [their] neighbors' land." The reason their neighbors' land needs to be seized is to allow citizens to satisfy unnecessary desires. The guardians need to defend their polis because their polis is full of tremendous wealth and luxuries generated by these desires.

hierarchy in the city. As we have seen, before the introduction of wealth and luxury, the citizens lived happily in an egalitarian community, where everyone contributed in ways that equally contributed to everyone else's happiness. The craftspeople and farmers made things, retailers sold things, and hirelings supported the craftspeople in their trades. No one had any more power or money than anybody else; every person was essential, and they lived "in peace and good health." Not so with Glaucon's city with a fever, where its citizens live not with peace, but war; and not with good health but an increased need for doctors. In Glaucon's city, hierarchy was the only way to allow the fever to continue; there would need to be people in power who could protect the wealth that the citizens enjoyed, which Socrates explicitly claims creates the need for a guardian class (373e–374b).

The problem is that, for these guardians to be clear-thinking enough to know how to protect the wealth, they must themselves not be tempted by it. If they were similarly addicted to a life of immoderation and luxury, they would not make wise decisions about how to protect the wealth that Glaucon insists on. Thus, Socrates provides an education and communal rules for them that protects them from the desires that characterize the immoderate citizens. He also insists that they must have unchecked power so that the citizens who are given to poor judgment and vice associated with wealth and luxury cannot threaten the wealth of the city. In this way, the egalitarian nature of the first city that Socrates praises is utterly lost thanks to Glaucon's insistence on luxury and convenience. There is now a class of people who have totalitarian power.

Fortunately, Socrates finds a way to reaffirm his commitment to the benefits of a simple, egalitarian society when he creates the egalitarianism found with the auxiliary community and the philosopher-king community. Even though the city itself becomes inegalitarian and addicted to money, he thereby continues to affirm his egalitarianism and moderation. Like the first city, both these groups have within their own group, natural differences in ability, strength, and intelligence, but they remain fundamentally egalitarian insofar as they share a common purpose and work together in their differences as a unified team. None of the auxiliaries rule over other auxiliaries, and none of the philosopher-kings rule over other philosopher-kings, just like no one in the first city ruled over their fellow citizens. Thus, while in the *kallipolis* egalitarianism and moderation has been lost, it remains alive and well in the guardians' communities. It is as if Socrates is saying:

> Glaucon, you can try to promote wealth and luxury as the ideal for human beings by insisting that the first city be ruined by it, but I am still going to promote my ideal of a healthy, simple community, by founding the guardian communities which have the same virtues and values of the first city. My ideal of what constitutes a "true" and "healthy" community still exists amongst the guardians' egalitarian communities in the unhealthy, totalitarian *kallipolis* which you have forced me to create.

Socrates sums up this view much later when he claims, "So isn't it clear by now that it is impossible for a city to honor wealth and at the same time for its citizens to acquire moderation, but one or the other is inevitably neglected?" (555c).

It has been customary to assume that Plato created the *kallipolis* to express his favored political ideal. From what we have seen, the opposite is the case. He created the *kallipolis* to show how injustice, greed, war, and the like grow up in cities and how, if they are allowed to grow up in cities, equality must forever vanish and totalitarianism must ensue.

To sum up, Plato is a committed egalitarian in the *Republic*, but because he is trying to help Glaucon see the dangers of wealth and luxury for individuals and for communities, he creates the *kallipolis* as a heuristic device to illuminate those dangers. Although this result undermines the all-too-common belief that Plato relishes political totalitarianism, there is still one more barrier in the way of reading Plato as a promoter of egalitarianism. In Book VIII, Plato's *Republic* contains a scathing critique of democracy as a part of his account of the decay of the individual soul when it turns to luxury and wealth. At first glance it is tempting to assume that there is no way Plato could be a committed egalitarian because he rejects democracy, calling it a corrupt political system. Since, at its most basic level, democracy promotes political equality among its citizens, it seems plausible that Socrates' rejection of democracy is an implicit rejection of egalitarianism and an affirmation of political hierarchy. What are we to make of this critique? And to add to the impression that Plato could not possibly be in favor of giving all citizens in a community the right to participate in their own governance, there is the fact that the Athenian citizens in Plato's time were allowed to participate in their own governance and as a result Plato's beloved teacher was condemned to death.

2.4 Socrates' Critique of Democracy in Book VIII of the *Republic*

As I have indicated in Section 2.3, it could be argued that my claim that Plato advocates egalitarian communities in the *Republic* cannot be true because of his criticism of democracy in Book VIII. At first glance, there seems to be merit to this criticism insofar as Socrates characterizes democracies as societies that are founded on citizens' freedom to pursue any desire they like. However, the kind of democracy he criticizes in Book VIII is radically libertine, where all people are free to follow every whim and fancy, and chafe at any restriction on their liberty whatsoever. He goes so far to say that "there is no requirement to rule ... or again to be ruled if you don't want to be" (557d), and that even criminals stroll around in public without any restrictions on their activities (558a). His criticism of democracy therefore seems to be directed at the radical liberty – really, anarchy – that comes from a completely laissez-faire approach to communal life. To my knowledge, there has never been, nor will there ever likely be, a democracy that matches his description. Thus, his criticism is not really of democracy per se (as the rule of the people and equality before the law), but of an extreme version of community-wide licentiousness that justifies itself by claiming to be "democratic." By the end of his critique it is clear that the problem he identifies with democracy is not really its theory of governance, but the effects that radical libertinism has on citizens – namely, that they develop an addiction to the unnecessary desires that characterize Glaucon's feverish city. He describes what happens to the soul of a person raised in a democracy founded on the principle of extreme libertinism:

> These desires draw him back into the same bad company and in secret intercourse breed a multitude of others ... won't they call reverence foolishness and moderation cowardice ... and won't they persuade the young man that measured and orderly expenditure is boorish and mean ... and give [other vices] fine names, calling insolence good breeding, anarchy freedom, extravagance magnificence, and shamelessness courage? Isn't it in some such way as this that someone who is young changes, after being brought up with necessary desires, to the liberation and release of useless and unnecessary pleasures? (560b–e)

Thus, we see that Plato's critique of democracy in Book VIII is *not* that it is egalitarian, but that it promotes the kind of unnecessary desires that are harmful to the mental and physical health of the individual and society, and – ironically – ultimately lead to anti-democratic and anti-egalitarian political circumstances. As we saw at the beginning of the chapter, egalitarianism is desirable when it helps people live in ways that promote individual and social health, but when, in the name of egalitarianism, a corrupt "democracy" promotes pleasures that undermine individual and social flourishing, then it is to be condemned – again, not because it is egalitarian, but because it damages individuals and society.

2.5 An Education for Healthy Egalitarianism in the *Republic*

Now that we have seen that Plato's criticism of democracy in Book VIII is not that he is opposed to egalitarianism, or even opposed to the rule of the people or equality before the law, but is only opposed to forms of democracy that encourage the kind of unfettered freedom that leads to the form of licentiousness found in democracies, we are now in a position to consider his beliefs about how people might be offered an education that promotes individual and social health. His beliefs on this are found in the education of the guardians of the *kallipolis*. These guardians are given an education that promotes moderation, courage, and egalitarianism within its members. Of course, because they are the guardians of a group of citizens that Glaucon insisted should be allowed to pursue wealth and luxury, they must necessarily have authoritarian control of those citizens, but that is not because Plato prefers authoritarian control. It is a necessary evil to protect the wealth and comfort that Glaucon insists his citizens should have. Plato thinks this wealth and the authoritarian control it makes necessary are an evil that should be avoided, but Glaucon will not hear of it. As we shall see, had Glaucon *not* insisted on the luxuries and conveniences, Socrates would still have recommended the same education to the guardians, except that they would not be guardians who go to war to steal other people's land or who rule unopposed over others; they would just be typical human beings who live in peace, harmony, and moderation, in the same way as the members of the first city did before they were introduced to the endless acquisition of wealth.

To see that the education of the guardians is one that could be available to all people, we need to return to the first city. To recall, everyone in the first city had an important role to play in the flourishing of the society. While some were more intelligent, stronger, or better craftspeople than others, they each had an essential role to play in the society and all were able to participate equally in the peace, harmony, and good health of the city. All of their physical needs were met and they enjoyed the arts, good conversation, simple delicacies, sex in moderation, and so on. They wanted for nothing and they did not consider themselves to be deprived of happiness. Let us suppose that after describing this society, Glaucon did *not* insist on giving these peaceful and content citizens wealth, luxuries, and conveniences, but instead asked Socrates how he (Socrates) would educate such people to be content with what they had. This would be a legitimate question, because as we saw in Section 2.2, Socrates claims that all people have appetitive desires in them (572b). Thus, each person has the capacity to be overcome by desires for wealth and luxuries. As such, there would need to be some sort of education in place that would help them not give into those desires, which would undermine the health of the individual and society.

What would have Socrates' answer been? His answer is made very clear when he describes the education of the guardians. While on the face of it, the education of the guardians seemed to be specifically meant for them to be rulers, its primary function was to teach them to be moderate and embody the rest of the virtues. Their early education was an education in virtue, and it was only their later education that was meant to provide them with knowledge of the "Forms" that they would need to rule others. In a healthy society, these people would not be guardians because there is nothing to guard and no need to steal land from other communities. The education of the guardians did more than teach them how to steal land. It taught them how to be moderate and just, living a life, as we saw above of egalitarianism and simplicity – the same life the citizens of the first city lived.

A standard objection to this point might go like this: Plato's depiction of the guardians is supposed to portray his elitist pessimism toward the educational potential of the masses. Plato thinks that most people simply do not have the cognitive and moral capacity for philosophical virtue. What makes you think that all human beings could be so educated?

Objections of this nature – which are quite common in the secondary literature – completely miss the educational meaning of the arguably most important scene in the *Republic:* The Allegory of the Cave. Plato is actually an optimist, or at least an egalitarian, with respect to the pursuit of virtue. He claims that the power to learn and be habituated into the virtues is found in everyone:

> And surely, once our city gets a good start, it will go on growing in a cycle. Good education and upbringing, when they are preserved, produce good

> natures, and useful natures, who are in turn well educated, grow up even better than their predecessors, both in their offspring and in other respects, just like other animals. (424a)

The important thing to notice here is Plato's claim that what "produce[s] good natures" is education and upbringing. In other places in the *Republic* he talks as if humans are born good or bad, but in fact over and over again in the *Republic* and across the dialogues, he lays far more stress on the role upbringing and education plays in creating the right kind of natures. He says, for instance, in Book VII that:

> If that's true, then here's what we must think about these matters: Education isn't what some people declare it to be, namely, putting knowledge into souls that lack it, like putting sight into blind eyes . . .
>
> But our present discussion, on the other hand, shows that the power to learn is present in everyone's soul and that the instrument with which each learns is like an eye that cannot be turned around from darkness to light without turning the whole body. This instrument cannot be turned around from that which is coming into being without turning the whole soul until it is able to study that which is and the brightest thing that is, namely, the one we call the good. Isn't that right? . . .
>
> Then education is the craft concerned with doing this very thing, this turning around, and with how the soul can most easily and effectively be made to do it. It isn't the craft of putting sight into the soul. Education takes for granted that sight is there but that it isn't turned the right way or looking where it ought to look, and it tries to redirect it appropriately . . .
>
> Now, it looks as though the other so-called virtues of the soul are akin to those of the body, for they really aren't there beforehand but are added later by habit and practice. However, the virtue of reason seems to belong above all to something more divine, which never loses its power but is either useful and beneficial or useless and harmful, depending on the way it is turned.

The fact that Socrates claims that the ability to learn is present in "everyone's" soul, but that those souls need to be redirected if they develop the capacity to "see" properly reinforces the view that individuals' natures are shaped by education. They develop a second nature, as it were, by how they are educated. It is the same with the virtues of the soul, which are "added later by habit and practice." This habituation creates natures that are virtuous. When this process is applied to all people the above "cycle" begins to happen – as their natures are developed, they pursue more education, and as they pursue more education, their natures are further improved. This leads to an increase in virtue and a decrease in the need for the endless acquisition of wealth that harms people and their communities.

The above does not mean that everyone receives the same education, however. In Socrates' egalitarian city, everyone is capable of developing the virtues through habituation, and everyone is capable of intellectual learning through having their sight redirected; however certain people have capacities for certain vocations that make their learning easier. Thus, according to Plato, people who have an innate predisposition that makes them good at farming will learn farming more quickly than someone who has an innate predisposition toward cobblery. Because each person has a soul that can be redirected, each person could *eventually* learn the other person's craft to a significant degree, but they will never learn as quickly as the one innately suited to it. It is the same with the habituated moral virtues. Plato believes that some people develop habits of virtue more quickly than others – he uses a variety of stories across the dialogues to explain the mythological origins of these differences – but he believes that all people are, ultimately, capable of virtue even if it takes some longer than others to develop them.

2.6 What Contemporary Democratic Educators Can Learn from the *Republic*

Having explored Plato's affirmation of egalitarian communities that are committed to moderation and virtue, we are now in a position to consider whether contemporary democratic educators have anything to learn from him. The answer to that question will depend largely on what each individual educator believes the point is of a democratic education. If educators believe that the point of democratic education is to make the given democracy stronger by encouraging a realistic moral egalitarianism as well as psychologically healthy individuals, then Plato has a great deal to offer. If, on the other hand, educators believe that the point of democratic education is to help students access all of the economic and material advantages the democracy has to offer, then Plato has little to offer.

I am writing this chapter to speak to the first group. The reader who believes that democracy should be equated with the maximization of wealth and capital need read no further. However, if an educator wants to think about the ways they might invite their students to help contribute to the flourishing of democracy by supporting the social and political equality of all citizens and by promoting values and virtues that increase the individual's ability to flourish, then here are some initial thoughts based on Plato's insights.

The first thing Plato teaches us is that we ought to help students question the dominant paradigm in many Western schools that the point of an education is to maximize their earning potential. Through discussions like the kind Socrates has with his interlocutors, we can help students think through the messages they are bombarded with over the internet, on television, through social media, and in the school ethos. These messages often aggressively communicate that a happy life is one characterized by wealth, luxury, and consumption in general. Using Socratic dialogues, teachers could help students discuss different visions of the good life and help them learn to distinguish propaganda from reality.

The second thing Plato teaches us is that there are certain vices that undermine the kind of democracy that seems most worth striving for: that is, a democracy in which individuals feel equal to one another in their ability to contribute to and enjoy the benefits of their social group. When students single-mindedly pursue wealth and the luxuries and conveniences it allows, they not only have potentially bought into a view of a happy life that is less happy than they think, but they also help set the conditions for radical material inequality. Teachers can help students realize that their attachment to goods and commodities often result in the diminishment of the quality of life of the underpaid employees of the companies who produce them. When students purchase the most up-to-date commodities they help make the owners and executives of those companies millions or billions of dollars, but often they do not increase the flourishing of the factory floor workers who perform the actual labor. Of course, there are some companies who treat their employees better than other companies, but the employees are rarely treated as equals in the company and rarely receive the kind of paid time off, flexibility of work schedule, and quality of job experiences that help lead to a flourishing life. While it may be true that some of these workers (if they are employed in democratic countries) have a right to vote and have the freedom to work or not work, they are also only minimally efficacious in lobbying to improve their own and others' working and living conditions. Voting choices afforded to the working class are often dictated by powerful lobbying groups who serve those already in power. Distributive schemes might be put into place to counteract some of these effects, but Plato's point is that the more we are wedded to luxury, the more we will *need* such schemes, and the more they will tend to create strife, disatisfaction, and – if things go really south – tyranny.

The third thing Plato teaches us is the importance of cultivating democratic virtues in our students. If democracy is going to flourish by remaining committed to a thoroughgoing egalitarianism, our students will need to cultivate virtues consistent with such a democracy. Virtues like generosity, justice, courage, moderation, civility, and honesty (to name a few) are the bedrock of a society committed to the flourishing of all people. We need our students to be generous and just enough to seek the good of others and not merely themselves; we need them to be courageous and moderate enough to resist the temptation to acquire material wealth and comforts that require the relegation of others to lives of drudgery; we need them to be civil and honest enough to interact with others in ways that dignify them without flattery or deceit.

2.7 Conclusion

In spite of the standard interpretation that the *Republic* is a dialogue that promotes totalitarianism, we have seen that it actually promotes egalitarianism. However, this does not mean that Plato thereby endorses all democratic communities. Plato unequivocally rejects democracies that promote unrestrained materialism, not because they fail to allow communal decision-making (which is the foundation of democracy) but because they lead members to live viciously. Educators can learn from the *Republic* insofar as it depicts the political and social dangers that arise in democracies that are founded on implicit and explicit messages that claim the happy life is one characterized by materialism and consumption. Plato reminds democratic educators that there are other forms of democracy that may be more desirable and teachers can go some way in promoting those forms of democracies in their students.

References

Annas, J. (1981). *An introduction to Plato's Republic*. Oxford: Oxford University Press.

Annas, J. (1999). *Platonic ethics, old and new*. Ithaca, NY: Cornell University Press.

Barney, R. (2001). Platonism, moral nostalgia, and the "city of pigs." *Proceedings of the Boston Area Colloquium in Ancient Philosophy*, 17, 207–27.

Barrow, R. (2008). *Plato*. London: Continuum.

Blitz, M. (2010). *Plato's political philosophy*. Baltimore, MD: The Johns Hopkins University Press.

Bobonich, C. (2002). *Plato's Utopia recast: His later ethics and politics*. Oxford: Clarendon Press.

Clay, D. (2000). *Platonic questions: Dialogues with the silent philosopher*. University Park, PA: The Pennsylvania State University Press.

Cooper, J. (2000). Two theories of justice. *Proceedings and Addresses of the APA*, 74, 5–27.

Crombie, I. (1962). *An examination of Plato's Doctrines: Vol. I*. London: Routledge.

Curren, R. (2000). *Aristotle on the necessity of public education*. Lanham, MD: Rowman & Littlefield.

Devereux, D. (1979). Socrates' first city in the Republic. *Apeiron*, 13, 36–40.

Dorter, K. (2006). *The transformation of Plato's Republic*. Lanham, MD: Lexington Books.

Euben, P. (1997). Democracy and political theory: A reading of Plato's *Gorgias*. In P. Euben, J. Wallch, & J. Ober, eds., *Athenian political thought and the reconstruction of American democracy*. Ithaca, NY: Cornell University Press, pp. 198–227.

Frank, J. (2018). *Poetic justice: Rereading Plato's Republic*. Chicago, IL: University of Chicago Press.

Guthrie W (1975). *A history of Greek philosophy: Vol. 4*. Cambridge: Cambridge University Press.

Howland, J. (2004). *The Republic: The odyssey of philosophy*. Philadelphia, PA: Paul Dry Books.

Jonas, M., & Nakazawa, Y. (2021). *A Platonic theory of moral education*. New York, NY: Routledge.

Jonas, M., Nakazawa, Y., & Braun, J. (2012). Appetite, reason, and education in Socrates' city of pigs. *Phronesis*, 57, 332–57.

Kamtekar, R. (2010). Ethics and politics in Socrates' defense of justice. In M. McPherran, ed., *Plato's Republic: A critical guide*. Cambridge: Cambridge University Press, pp. 65–82.

McDavid, B. (2019). Why the city of pigs and clocks are not just. *Journal of the History of Philosophy*, 57(4), 571–93.

McKeen, C. (2004). Swillsburg city limits: The "city of pigs": Republic 370c–372d. *Polis*, 21(1–2), 71–92.
Mintz, A. (2016). The education of the third class in the Republic: Plato and the *locus classicus* of formative justice. *Teachers College Record*, 118(10), 1–18.
Morrison, D. (2007). The place of the Republic in Plato's political thought. In G. R. F. Ferrari, ed., *The Cambridge companion to Plato's Republic*. Cambridge: Cambridge University Press, pp. 232–355.
Nettleship, R. (1901). *Lectures on the Republic of Plato*. New York, NY: St. Martin's Press.
Pappas, N. (2013). *The Routledge guidebook to Plato's Republic*. New York, NY: Routledge.
Plato (1997). *The complete works of Plato*. Ed. by J. Cooper & D. Hutchinson, Indianapolis, IN: Hackett Publishing.
Reeve, C. D. C. (1988). *Philosopher-kings: The argument of Plato's Republic*. Indianapolis, IN: Hackett.
Roochnik, D. (2003). *Beautiful city: The dialectical charter of Plato's Republic*. Ithaca, NY: Cornell University Press.
Rowe, C. J. (2007a). The place of the Republic in Plato's political thought. In G. R. F. Ferrari, ed., *The Cambridge companion to Plato's Republic*. Cambridge: Cambridge University Press, pp. 27–54.
Rowe, C. J. (2007b). *Plato and the art of philosophical writing*. Cambridge: Cambridge University Press.
Saxonhouse, A. (1996). *Athenian democracy: Modern mythmakers and ancient theorists*. South Bend, IN: University of Notre Dame Press.
Smith, N. (2019). *Summoning knowledge in Plato's Republic*. Oxford: Oxford University Press.
Taylor, C. (1997). Plato's totalitarianism. In R. Kraut, ed., *Plato's Republic: Critical essays*. Lanham, MD: Rowan and Littlefield, pp. 31–48.
Vasiliou, I. (2008). *Aiming at virtue in Plato*. Cambridge: Cambridge University Press.
Vlastos, G. (1973). *Platonic studies*. Princeton, NJ: Princeton University Press.
Waterfield, R. (1993). *Republic*. Oxford: Oxford University Press.

3

Aristotle on Education, Democracy, and Civic Friendship

Randall Curren

3.1 Introduction

There are a variety of interpretive, historical, and practical questions one might pose concerning the intersection of Aristotle's ideas about education and democracy, including: What civic purposes did Aristotle have in mind in framing his educational proposals? How did he envision those purposes being served by the education he proposed? Was he a proponent of democracy? Did he propose a form of democratic education? Would the adoption of his educational proposals be favorable to establishing, preserving, or strengthening a democratic society and system of government?

These are the questions this chapter will answer. Doing so will require a broad sketch of the respective roles of the *Nicomachean Ethics* (*NE*) and *Politics* in Aristotle's philosophy of human affairs (*ta anthropina philosophia*; *NE* X.9 1181b15), which he presents as a science of politics (*ton epistêmon en tais polisi; NE* I.2 1094b1). It is only within this framework that we can understand his views regarding the proper ends of constitutional systems and legislation, the status of democracy, and the civic purposes of education. The questions at stake will be primarily, but not exclusively, interpretive. There are various standards by which one could judge whether Aristotle proposes a form of democratic education, including his intentions, the compatibility of his educational proposals with contemporary democratic principles, and whether enacting them would be conducive to preserving or strengthening democracy. The question of conduciveness to preserving or strengthening democracy is largely empirical, and of no small importance.

There has been an immense outpouring of scholarship on Aristotle's *Politics* in recent years, much of it grappling with the status of democracy in Aristotle's thought but little of it engaging his educational ideas in any detail.[1] There have been several new English translations of the *Politics* (Lord, 1984; Jowett [in

[1] Scholarship on Aristotle's educational ideas has been overwhelmingly focused on character education and makes little or no reference to the *Politics*, but see Lord (1982), Reeve (1998b, 2012, pp. 250–77), Curren (2000), Nightingale (2001), Nagle

Barnes, 1984]; Robinson, 1995; Saunders, 1995; Kraut, 1997; Simpson, 1997; Reeve, 1998a; Keyt, 1999), many books and collections of articles on it (e.g., Patzig, 1990; Keyt & Miller, 1991; Miller, 1995; Curren, 2000; Kraut, 2002; Frank 2005; Kraut & Skultety, 2005; Roberts, 2009a; Garver, 2011; Deslauriers & Destrée, 2013; Pangle, 2013; Lockwood & Samaras, 2015; Riesbeck, 2016), and hundreds of journal articles. While the effect of this voluminous scholarship has been to promote a unified reading of Aristotle's philosophy of human affairs and clarify important aspects of his political philosophy, there are aspects of his stance toward democracy that are sharply contested.

These disputed matters notwithstanding, the answers defended in what follows are that Aristotle's educational proposals are intended to serve the singular civic purpose of facilitating a partnership of all citizens in living the best kind of life. Living the best kind of life inherently involves exercises of intellectual virtues, and being a partner with one's fellow citizens in living such a life inherently involves exercises of moral virtues and bonds of civic friendship. Aristotle's educational proposals are thus focused on cultivating moral and intellectual virtues and educating diverse children together, with a view to nurturing civic friendship. Regarding democracy, Aristotle classifies it as a corrupt form of constitution, but he defends forms of shared governance in the common interest – "mixed" and "middle" constitutions and an ideal form of aristocracy – that would qualify by today's standards as limited forms of democracy. Setting aside the narrowness of his conception of the best kind of life that education should facilitate, and his restrictions on who can qualify as a citizen and receive this education, the education he proposes is recognizably democratic. It is, within limits, egalitarian and intended to foster shared governance.[2] This is not to deny the disconcerting fact that Aristotle proposed limiting full citizenship to landowning males, thereby excluding women, slaves, farmers, and other manual and paid workers, but rather to hold that his thought nevertheless offers significant resources for understanding democracy and democratic education. Regarding its potential efficacy in advancing democracy, Aristotle's understanding of the role of common schools in promoting civic friendship and shared governance should qualify as an important contribution to the theory and practice of democratic education.

3.2 What Civic Purposes Did Aristotle Have in Mind in Framing His Educational Proposals?

Aristotle identifies the defining purpose of a polis (i.e., city-state or politically autonomous city and environs) as partnership (*koinonia*) in living the best kind of

(2006), Stalley (2009), and Destrée (2013). Joyal et al. (2009) place some key educational passages from the *Politics* in the context of Greek and Roman education.

[2] Citizen girls and women were excluded from governing and were consequently less than full citizens, but it is unclear whether Aristotle thought their education should be different from that of boys and men (*Pol.* I.3 1260b13–20, VII.16 1335b11–12; Reeve, 2012, p. 253).

life, so the fundamental civic purpose of education would be facilitating such partnership by nurturing the required personal attributes and social bonds. A subsidiary civic purpose of education would be to improve imperfect regimes or enable societies to make progress toward partnership in living the best kind of life.

The opening claim of Aristotle's *NE* is that political science is the master art concerned with the highest good or best kind of life for human beings (*NE* I.2 1094a18–28, 1095a14–19), and his *Politics* opens similarly with the axiom that a polis is properly a partnership of citizens in living the best kind of life. Every community "is established for the sake of some good," he says, and "the community that has the most authority of all and encompasses all the others aims highest, that is to say, at the good that has the most authority of all. This community is the one called a polis, the community that is political" (*Pol.* I.1 1252a4–6).[3] The *NE* is foundational to the *Politics* (see Adkins, 1991; Cooper, 2010; Frede, 2013; Ober, 2015), as it defines both the proper function of a self-governing society – facilitating a partnership of citizens in living well – and the virtues that must be cultivated in all citizens in order to fulfill that function. It closes with a rationale for the *Politics*, announcing the latter as providing the knowledge of legislation essential to cultivating virtue widely. These works are presented as together comprising *political science* (*hê politikê epistêmê*), and the *Rhetoric* (*Rh.*) can be seen as addressing the subsidiary art of persuasion (Garver, 1994; Rorty, 1996; Frank, 2005).[4] While the *Politics* itself can be read as displaying strategies of persuasion (e.g., for convincing leaders to engage in constitutional reforms), or as engaging its audience rhetorically (Pangle, 2013; Frank, 2015), Aristotle presents law and education as the primary instruments of statecraft, giving priority to education (*NE* X.9 1180b24–30; *Pol.* I.2 1253a30–35, V.9 1310a13–20) and following Greek precedent in framing law as itself an instructional enterprise (*NE* V.1 1129b19–26).

The civic purposes of education are identified in *Politics* VIII.1, where Aristotle says, "No one will doubt that the legislator should direct his attention above all to the education of youth" (1337a10–11). This is a remarkable thing for him to claim in a world in which only Sparta and Crete provided public education of any kind and theirs was limited to military training. The brevity of the supporting arguments that follow would also be remarkable, were they not summaries of arguments that run through both the *NE* and *Politics* (Curren, 2000).

Aristotle first explains that the better character produced by education yields a better *politeia*, meaning better citizenship, a better citizen-body, or a better regime (*politeuma* or members of the governing body) (1137a14–18).[5] He defines citizens as those who share in making political decisions and in holding offices, which in Athens would have included serving on juries, membership in the assembly, and eligibility for administrative roles filled by lottery (*Pol.* III.1

[3] Translations are those in Barnes (1984), except where noted.

[4] It is only recently that scholars have taken Aristotle at his word in presenting these works as comprising a *science* (Henry & Nielsen, 2015), but there is little dissent regarding the importance of reading the two works together.

[5] For a detailed account of the distinct meanings of *politeia*, see Mulhern (2015).

1275a22–3, 1275b17–21), so the education that makes a citizen-body better with respect to citizenship would necessarily make for a better governing body or regime. The translations of Lord (1984) and Simpson (1997) are thus on target in rendering *politeia* as "regime" in this context (1137a10–18). Another meaning of *politeia* is "arrangement of offices," so it is frequently translated as "constitution," as it is in this passage by Jowett (Barnes, 1984) and Reeve (1998a). This has Aristotle saying that better character makes for a better constitution, which is intelligible if one reads "constitution" as referring to the way a society is constituted with respect to governance, a constitution being in this sense a hylomorphic composite of form (i.e., arrangement of offices) and matter (the character of those who fill those offices or civic decision-making roles). I will use "constitution" in this hylomorphic sense in what follows (as in Curren, 2000).

Aristotle's second reason for legislative concern about education is that the practice of *aretê* (virtue, goodness, or excellence) requires prior education (*Pol.* 1337a19–21). This is presented without elaboration and followed immediately by the claim that because a polis has one end or purpose, "it is manifest that education should be one and the same for all, and that it should be public and not private" (1337a21–24). This is essentially a theorem of "political science" resting on the foundations laid down in the openings of the *NE* and *Politics*, and it concerns the fundamental civic purpose of education for Aristotle – equipping all citizens with the same virtues that are essential to them all living well together. It is best to begin there, and then circle back to the argument that education yields better constitutions or regimes.

In the *NE* and *Posterior Analytics*, Aristotle defines a science as pertaining to unchanging objects of knowledge (*NE* VI.3 1139b20–25) and having an axiomatic structure consisting of theorems derived from first principles by means of demonstrative deductions (*PoA.* 1.2.71b9–16, 1.13, 1.33.8830–34). The first principles define the nature and affirm the existence of the object of study. Ethics takes the best life for human beings as its object, but it pertains more broadly to the nature, function, and varieties of the human psyche, relying on psychology to identify the function that is said to determine the nature of the best life (*eudaimonia*, flourishing, or living well). It addresses the varieties of psyche or states of character that do and do not permit the fulfillment of that function in a flourishing life. Politics pertains similarly to the nature, function, and varieties of polises – the varieties of constitutions that do or do not fulfill a polis's natural function of enabling people to live as partners in the best kind of life for human beings (*Pol.* I.1 1252a4–6). The nature of a properly functioning constitution or political system is thus defined in a way that builds on the nature of a properly functioning psyche.

What, then, is the best form of life that a properly functioning political system should enable all of its citizens to share in? The axiom at the heart of the *NE* is (roughly) that the best life for a human being is one that is devoted to activity in conformity with the "best and most complete" virtue, by which Aristotle evidently means philosophical or "scientific" activity (*theôria*) manifesting theoretical wisdom (*sophia*) (*NE* I.7 1098a16–18; Kraut, 1989; Reeve, 2012). This presupposes the possession of moral virtues, given Aristotle's understanding of the foundational role of moral virtues in developing intellectual virtues (*Pol.* VII.151334b12–28; cf. Plato, *Laws* 631b–d). The habituation that shapes moral character forms an integrated cluster of behavioral, affective, perceptual, and doxastic dispositions. People who are well habituated and thus acquire the moral virtues grasp the moral facts (*to hoti*) that are the starting points of ethical and legislative science (*NE* I.7 1098b2–4), while others who lack this habituation do not. So, at least within the sphere of human affairs, one could no more contemplate what is knowable without possessing moral virtues than deliberate and choose well without them. There are many passages in the *Politics* that confirm Aristotle has in mind a life devoted to excellence in *theôria* when he identifies a polis's natural function as enabling people to live in partnership in the best kind of life for human beings (*Pol.* I.1 1252a4–7; cf. VII.2 1324a23–35, VII.8 1328a36–37; *NE* I.1 1094a1–18).

Given this natural, defining, or proper function of a polis, there will be true (just) and deviant (unjust) varieties of constitutions. As partnerships in living the best life, the former will aim at the common good (i.e., good of all citizens) and be consensual or governed through consent rather than force (*Pol.* III.3 1276a8–16, III.4 1277b8–30, III.6 1279a17–22, III.7 1279a25–39, III.9 1280b30–40, etc.). A political form of governance, transacted through discussion of what is good and bad, right and wrong (I.2 1253a7–18; Mayhew, 2013; Frank, 2015) would characteristically involve mutual advantage and consent to arrangements that promote it, and Aristotle repeatedly endorses governing through consent as a defining aspect of true, just, or legitimate forms of governance (I.13 1259b37–60a, III.10 1281a22–25, IV.9 1294b35–39, V.9 1310a15–17, VII.2 1324b23–31, etc.). Regarding mutual advantage or the common good, he holds that correct (i.e., true or just) constitutions *impartially* promote the good of all citizens (III.13 1283b36–42), explaining that the wish of political societies with correct constitutions is "to be composed of those who are equal and alike" (IV.11 1295b24–26; Kraut, 2002, pp. 385–91). It is also clear throughout the middle books of the *Politics* that Aristotle's understanding of justice makes *degrees* of justice relevant across the spectrum of less than ideal constitutions (Curren, 2000, pp. 70–79, 100–09; Kraut, 2002, pp. 173–74; Destrée, 2015).[6]

3.2.1 Nurturing Virtues and Civic Friendship

Living the best kind of life is a matter of engaging in activities that are at the same time both admirable (*kalon*) and personally satisfying. These are necessarily enactments of virtues, which Aristotle regards as interdependent, so education in both moral and intellectual virtues will be essential. Books VII and VIII of the *Politics* describe the best possible constitution or "polis of our dreams," and what we come to in the closing chapters of VII are public oversight of childbirth, childcare, and training of habits, and in Book VIII public schooling and theater.

[6] For other views on justice in Aristotle's works, see Miller (1995), Roberts (2009a), and Schütrumpf (2015).

All of this should build toward the development of the intellectual virtues that are foundational to living well, we are told.

Because the natural and proper end (*telos*) of a polis is partnership in such flourishing, a further task of education is to nurture the civic bonds or relationships that would constitute a partnership in living well. Aristotle conceives of this in terms of civic friendship (*politikê philia*), which he describes as "the greatest good of states and what best preserves them against revolutions" (*Pol.* II.4 1262b7–10; cf. *NE* VIII.1 1155a23–28, VIII.2 1155b31–34, VIII.4 1157a21–25, 1169b9–10; *Rh.* II.4 1380b36–1381a2). "Unanimity seems . . . to be civic friendship," he explains, "and such unanimity is found among good men; for they . . . wish for what is just and what is advantageous, and these are the objects of their common endeavor as well. Bad men . . . aim at getting more than their share of advantages, . . . [and soon] they are in a state of faction" (*NE* IX.6 1167b2–14).

Aristotle followed Plato in regarding factional conflict as a common defect of polises, but in Book II of the *Politics* he rejected the solution to this proposed in Plato's *Republic* – a scheme for common rearing of children in which parents would not know whose children were whose (Mayhew, 1997). Plato may have imagined that rivalries between families could be limited and greater civic unity achieved in this way. Aristotle's alternative proposal is to create common civic institutions that nurture friendships bridging all social groups, the most important of these being public day schools in which a city's diverse children are educated and "grow up together" at least a few hours a day (i.e., common schools) (*Pol.* V.9 1310a12–25). It is through such education that societies can be unified and made into a community, he contends (II.5 1263b37–38), while also referring to common meals and religious observances.

Aristotle's account of civic friendship is not fully explained, but what he seems to have in mind is, first, that common schools and other institutions should nurture virtues of goodwill, which when they are manifested and recognized reciprocally would constitute friendship (VIII.2 1155b33–35), and second, that they should nurture friendships of more intimate kinds that bridge different social groups and facilitate wider liking, trust, goodwill, and cooperation (Curren, 2000, pp. 131–39; Curren & Elenbaas, 2020).[7] A much-discussed passage in *Politics* III.9 has been read as implying that Aristotle thought spontaneously occurring "family connections, brotherhoods, common sacrifices, amusements which draw men together" are typically sufficient to make a society a "partnership. . . in well-being, for the sake of a perfect and self-sufficient life" (1280b32–1281a2). However, the schools Aristotle describes did not yet exist, the common meals he refers to (*Pol.* II.9 and 10) were created in Sparta as an egalitarian and unifying replacement for private dining clubs segregated by class, and his attention to publicly subsidizing the costs of participation in common meals and religious observances in *Politics* VII.10 suggests he saw a need for public intervention to prevent the segregation of citizens into groups that do not intermingle in friendly ways.

[7] For the classic debate on which this interpretation builds, see Annas (1990); Cooper (1990).

3.2.2 Improving Imperfect Regimes

The second dominating idea at the opening of *Politics* VIII, is that citizens should be molded "to suit the form of government" or constitution (1337a11–19). We learn in this passage only that better character yields a better regime, but in II.4 that, "A good citizen must have the knowledge and ability both to be ruled and to rule, and this is the virtue of a citizen to know the rule of free people from both sides" (1277b13–15). This is qualified as pertaining to *political* rule involving citizens, and it emerges that a *politeia*, in the sense of a system of citizenship or sharing in rule, is the form of constitution to which defective political systems should aspire. Aristotle says explicitly in *Politics* V.9 that, while education should suit the character of the constitution, whatever form it takes, the education that suits a constitution is not the kind of education preferred by the rulers of an unjust system (1310a12–25), but instead the kind of education that would preserve it.[8] Neither oligarchy nor democracy can survive "unless both rich and poor" share in ruling and being ruled (1309b37–40). So, the education that suits different constitutions will in each case turn out to be education in knowing how to rule and be ruled, and nowhere does Aristotle suggest that the common schooling that is the same for all would prepare children of different social classes for different roles in ruling and being ruled. The reforms associated with education that makes for a better constitution would move an oligarchic constitution that denies the poor a share in governing and unjustly favors the wealthy, or a democratic constitution that similarly dominates the rich and unjustly favors the poor, closer to the constitution that Aristotle regards as the best that is possible for most societies.

Aristotle calls this best constitution that most societies are capable of achieving a *politeia* (rendered in this use as "polity") or a constitution that is "mixed" in the sense of providing institutional roles for different social classes and "middle" in the sense of being limited to or moderated by a large middle class.[9] To preserve a defective political system one must reform it, aiming at the mean between oligarchy and democracy (*Pol.* V.9 1309b18–22) or a constitution that provides citizens, both rich and poor, with institutional platforms for protecting their interests and that favors a large middle class – a politically moderating mean between poverty and opulence. Political systems that exclude one or another class from governing would thus come to approximate a *politeia* or

[8] A matter that would require too much space to address here is Aristotle's stance on education in the spirit of defective constitutions and compliance with law. He regards such compliance as primarily owing to habit, or more accurately a state of character, and as important to the political stability essential to the common interest. Yet, he also surely recognized that a blind or undiscerning habit of obedience to law as such would be counterproductive to the extent that existing laws are bad and do not communicate moral truths about how members of societies can live well together. See Curren (2000, 2013).

[9] The established view (see Balot, 2015; Ober, 2015; Samaras, 2015) is that a "middle" constitution and *politeia* are ruled strictly by hoplite soldiers or the class of citizens who have enough wealth to equip themselves as heavily armed infantry (*Pol.* II.6 1265b27–29; III.7 1279a40–1279b4). I would argue that, while Aristotle may consider it ideal to favor moderate wealth (in the interest of virtue and living well) and limit citizenship to people of moderate wealth (and virtue), his guidance on improving imperfect regimes in the middle books envisions scenarios in which other classes retain shares in rule, and progress would occur by making a constitution more mixed and middle. The effect of making democracies and oligarchies more like polities or *politeia* (i.e., systems of citizenship or political rule) will be to make them more just as well as more stable.

system of political governance in which all citizens share in governing. The education that would moderate corrupt oligarchies and democracies, and thereby preserve them, would school rich and poor citizens together, making them more like one another, more capable of both ruling and being ruled, and more unified by civic friendship and trust.

Beyond this target for political reform that is realistic for most societies is the best possible polis described in *Politics* VII and VIII, a partnership in living the best life. The common schooling in such a society would be sufficient to make it an ideal form of *aristocracy* in which all citizens are truly virtuous and share in ruling and being ruled. As a system in which all citizens share in rule, it would be a *politeia*, and as a system in which there are provisions to ensure the wealth of citizens is moderate, it will be a "middle" constitution (Frank, 2005, pp. 138–80; Ober, 2015). As a classless society, as far as citizens are concerned, it would not be a "mixed" constitution providing distinct institutional roles for citizens of different classes (Curren, 2000, pp. 73–74, p. 105). Only in this best possible society will the virtue of a citizen and the virtue essential to living well fully coincide (III.4 1277a1–4; III.18 1288a37–38; Roberts, 2009b), but Aristotle does not expressly prescribe different education for citizens of less perfect societies. The proper aim of education seems in all cases to be the virtues essential to living well, but only in the best possible society is such virtue fully attainable.

3.3 How Would Aristotelian Education Advance These Civic Purposes?

A partnership of all citizens in ruling, being ruled, and living the best life would evidently require universal possession of the virtues that are manifested in living the best kind of life and a distribution of good judgment sufficient for collective practical wisdom (*phronêsis*) in sustaining a civic partnership in such a life. If the best kind of life necessarily involves exercises of theoretical wisdom (*sophia*) in philosophical or "scientific" activity (*theôria*), then Aristotle must have envisioned an education in theoretical and practical philosophy, the former of which he took to include mathematics, natural philosophy (i.e., sciences of nature), and theology (*Met.* VI.1 1026a18–19). So, would all citizens learn mathematics, natural and political science, and theology? Or did Aristotle think that most citizens would participate in the best kind of life through less demanding forms of intellectual activity? With regard to practical wisdom, it might be enough for many citizens to have adequate judgment concerning whom to trust, when listening to speeches in the assembly for instance, and for a few to have practical wisdom grounded in the ethical and legislative science that Aristotle provided in his lectures. *Phronêsis* brings together "particulars" of cases, discerned in perception, with "universals" or general truths about the human good and how human beings can live well together (*NE* VI.8 1142a13–15), and there can be no doubt that Aristotle regarded his own lectures in ethics and politics as an education in these universals.

Much of *Politics* VIII appears to have been lost, leaving us with little more than a discussion of education in musical performance as a paradigm of, or maybe a first step in elaborating, the "branches of learning and education which we must study merely with a view to leisure spent in intellectual activity" (1338a10–12). Music is not useful, so it is taught precisely "for intellectual enjoyment in leisure," Aristotle argues (1338a13–24), and while drawing *is* useful, it can nevertheless be taught in order to make children "judges (or contemplators [Nightingale, 2001], *theôrêtikon*) of the beauty of the human form" (1138b1–2). Nightingale (2001, pp. 168–71) argues that Aristotle focuses on music and drawing in this way because he thought that the closest most people could ever come to philosophical *theôria* is the contemplation of human affairs experienced by a spectator (*theôros*) at the publicly sponsored theater festivals of Athens. Destrée (2013) adopts a similar view, noting Aristotle's insistence that "there is clearly nothing which we are so much concerned to acquire and cultivate as the power of forming right judgment, and of taking delight in good dispositions and noble actions" (VIII.5 1340a16–19). Children are to *engage in* musical performance so they can learn to be good judges of it and "appreciate what is good and delight in it, thanks to the knowledge they acquired" (VIII.6 1340b37–38). Destrée agrees that Aristotle must have regarded such aesthetic *theôria* as an approximation of philosophical *theôria*, citing Kraut (2002, p. 200), who notes that "Aristotle is not referring to unaccompanied music, but to poetic or dramatic words that tell a story... that may embody a kind of truth" (p. 201). "Stories conveyed in song [may] express a form of wisdom" and stimulate "something like philosophical activity," Kraut writes (pp. 201–02), and one could add that in the context of public theater this would constitute a form of *collective* contemplation of the good and the just that may facilitate a partnership in living well. Kraut finds it "plausible" that Aristotle's curriculum also included mathematical studies, including astronomy, for children ages 14–17 (2002, pp. 199–200), while Reeve finds stronger grounds for thinking Aristotle envisioned higher learning beyond these studies.

Reeve is an outlier in holding, "That there must be public education in philosophy generally, and not just in ethics or political science, is *certain*, since philosophy is required for leisure and education in it is needed to make a city good (*Pol.* II.5 1263b37–40, 7 1267a10–12)" (Reeve, 2012, p. 255; italics added). The passage in *Politics* II.5 that Reeve cites invites the question of how a society governed by all its citizens could succeed without providing them all with an education in philosophy similar to what the philosopher kings and queens of the *Republic* receive, and Aristotle surely knew that the philosophical curriculum proposed for schools in Plato's *Laws* – the text of the *Laws* itself (VII 811b–812a; Bobonich, 2002) – included not just ethics and political philosophy but also theology (X 887c–907a). Is it really so implausible to think that Aristotle's ideal aristocracy – a system of shared governance by citizens who are fully virtuous, a condition requiring the possession of *phronêsis*, hence ethical knowledge (*epistêmê*) – would provide education in at least ethical and political philosophy, if not other forms of philosophy? Reeve notes Aristotle's reference in *Politics* VIII.2 to the existence of "liberal (*eleutherios*) arts quite proper for a freeman to acquire" to a suitable degree (1337b13–14); he infers quite reasonably that these arts would include all those requisite to being a "well-educated person" or *pepaideumenos*, a person who falls short of acquiring specialist or scientific knowledge but learns enough to be a good judge of diverse matters, just as the liberal study of music will fall short of producing virtuosity but enable the student to be a good judge of the performances of others:

> In every study and investigation ... there appear to be two kinds of competence. One can properly be called scientific knowledge of the subject, the other as it were a sort of educatedness. For it is the mark of an educated person to be able to reach a judgment based on a sound estimate of what is properly expounded and what isn't. For this is in fact what we take to be characteristic of a generally educated person. And we expect such a person to be able to judge in practically all subjects. (*PA*. 639a1–6; Reeve, 1998b, p. 58, trans.)

The extant manuscripts do not reveal when Aristotle may have thought that comprehensive "liberal" education of this kind should occur or how much of it should be compulsory, but the constitution he envisions would require at least a moderate level of collective possession of its benefits, and he is insistent on the fact that *all* (full) citizens will receive the same education. How would this come about other than through an attempt to provide all (full) citizens with a general education – an education in knowledge and judgment that enables them to engage in the most rewarding and admirable kinds of human endeavors and in collective self-governance?

3.3.1 Common Schooling and Civic Friendship

In addition to defending a common curriculum for all full citizens, Aristotle follows Plato's *Laws* in proposing public day schools in which children would all be educated together in the interest of civic friendship. These institutions must be egalitarian, in the sense of being open to all citizen members of the society and treating all those who participate as equals. They must also be part of a wider experience of justice and the relative equality that is essential to friendship and shared governance. Aristotle addresses this with particular force in *Politics* IV.11:

> Those who have too much of the goods of fortune, strength, wealth, friends, and the like are neither willing nor able to submit to authority. The evil begins at home; for when they are boys, by reason of the luxury in which they are brought up, they never learn, even at school, the habit of obedience. On the other hand, the very poor, who are in the opposite extreme, are too degraded. So that the one class cannot obey, and can only rule despotically; the other knows not how to command and must be ruled like slaves. Thus arises a city, not of freemen, but of masters and slaves, the one despising, the other envying; and nothing can be more fatal to friendship and good fellowship in cities than this. (1295b14–24)

Aristotle says more than once that participants in every community of any kind are friends "to the extent to which justice exists between them" (*NE* VIII.9 1159b25–31). The minimal condition for *philia* is mutual recognition of mutual goodwill (*Pol.* VIII.2 1155b33–35), so the implication of this is that people enact forms of mutual goodwill to the extent that they deal with each other in ways that are just. Such "friendships" or episodes of mutually recognized mutual goodwill could be as fleeting as a brief commercial transaction, but Aristotle regards good laws or norms of justice as providing a kind of habituation that promotes the formation of virtue. Justice and common institutions would thus establish a context in which dispositions of civic friendship could take root.

Aristotle's view of the origins of the wide civic friendliness that can unify a society is that it begins in a small number of substantial friendships that are civically important. His conception of how these initial "civic friendships" with "kinsmen, comrades, [and] partners" can lead to a generalized disposition of friendliness toward all fellow citizens is that it would involve forming some of these relationships in settings such as schools that bring different kinds of people together (*Eudemian Ethics* II.10 1242a6–9). In these settings, people with different group identities may become friends with one another, and those relationships would put a friendly face on kinds of people who might otherwise seem alien, untrustworthy, or threatening. This kind of transmission of friendliness was predictable from Aristotle's perspective, because we tend to like our friends' friends, "those who are like ourselves in character" and "those who desire the same things as we desire" (*Rh.* II.4 1381a15–20, b15, and b17–18). If these are psychological facts, then the more venues there are in which different kinds of people interact in ways favorable to friendship, the more the society will tend to be unified by civic friendliness and the less likely political polarization will be.

3.4 Was Aristotle a Proponent of Democracy?

Aristotle's typology of *politeia* classifies democracy as a corrupt (*parekbasis*) form of constitution that does not allow a polis to fulfill its natural (*phusin*) or just function. He considers it a system of lawless domination of the wealthy few by the numerous poor (*dêmos*), rather than a rule of law aiming at the common good and transacted through reasoned persuasion and consent (*Pol.* III.6–8). Lawless rule by many in their own interest is better than lawless self-interested rule by the wealthy few or by one tyrant, Aristotle acknowledged. Yet, his view of democracy is consistent with his view of the working poor as precluded by their labor from acquiring the virtue or judgment needed to participate in governance and with his identification of a polity, or "mixed" and "middle" constitution, as one in which those of moderate wealth – the hoplite class – govern.

The underlying principle of entitlement to share in governing seems to be that the possession of normal deliberative capacities and good judgment entitles a member of the society to be self-governing and is a pro tanto or prima facie basis for entitlement to a share in governing proportional to their good judgment or virtue. In the absence of a god-like king whose wisdom is incommensurably greater than the combined wisdom of everyone else in the society, this will require a form of shared political governance with some differentiation of institutional roles in governing by merit – a "mixed" constitution – but Aristotle treats the qualifications for citizenship as legitimately influenced by a variety of practical considerations (VI.4 1319b6–14, VI.6 1320b25–37). There will be no human right to citizenship, but all citizens will have a share in governing through a system that (in one way or another) seeks to fill offices that require individuals with especially good judgment on the basis of possession of such judgment (*Pol.* III.9 1280a9–b7; *NE* V.3 1131a24–28). Any such system will provide institutionalized roles through which the interests and judgments of people of ordinary capacities and judgment will be aggregated, and Aristotle offers some analogies to explain how this can yield a better judgment than that of a single person of greater wisdom (III.10–18). There are unresolved debates concerning the interpretation of these analogies and how little or much they illuminate the merits of democratic decision making (Waldron, 1992; Lane, 2013; Ober, 2013, 2015; Bobonich, 2015), but Frank (2015) offers a promising account of reasoned persuasion and acceptance of reasons as what mediates collective ruling and being ruled.

Setting aside the important questions of global justice and democracy that have reshaped political philosophy in recent years, Aristotle's preferred constitutions sound a lot like democracy (Frank, 2005, 2015; Balot, 2015; Ober, 2005, 2015). A "mixed" and "middle" constitution in which no one is above the law is arguably the very model of what democracy has meant since the nineteenth century. It is democratic in being a system of collective self-governance, and (interpreting "middle" generously) a system dominated by a large middle class is democratic because it is conducive to broad participation in living well, favors democratic solidarity or civic friendship, and is a bulwark against partisanship that undermines the very idea of impartial justice and a common good. The ideal aristocracy of *Politics* Books VII and VIII is also arguably a polity and, by modern standards, a democracy. To be sure, the artisans, traders, and farmers, who are necessary to this aristocracy of all citizens are not citizens. Yet, so far as citizens are concerned this "polis of our prayers" is a democracy of sharing in rule and being ruled and a model of egalitarian cooperation in living well, apart from the perfectionistic exclusivity of the (supposed) singular best kind of life to which it is devoted. So, in both his vision of the best possible constitution (a legitimate kingship being theoretically ideal but not possible) and in his target for the best constitution that is feasible for most societies, Aristotle is an advocate of a form of democracy (Ober, 2005, 2015).

3.5 Is Aristotelian Education Democratic?

Did Aristotle propose a form of democratic education? Would the adoption of his educational proposals be favorable to establishing, preserving, or strengthening a democratic society and system of government? There are reasons to affirm that Aristotle did indeed propose a form of democratic education, but any such reasons must appeal to an account of what defines democratic education, and there is no contemporary consensus regarding any such account. Democratic education might be defined substantively (e.g., as education in virtues of democratic citizenship), as inclusive and pluralistic (i.e., as *nondiscriminatory* in who receives it, *nonrepressive* in respecting a reasonable diversity of conceptions of the good, and possibly *common* in the sense of educating diverse students together), or as democratically governed (i.e., collectively by the society or by the stakeholders in individual schools, or through a sharing of educational authority by governments, parents, and professional educators) (Gutmann, 1987). Education might be democratic in one or more of these respects and not others, and these different ways in which it could be democratic may be mutually reinforcing in some circumstances but not others.

If what constitutes democratic education is parents being at liberty to educate their children as they please, then Aristotelian education is, of course, very far from democratic. The grounds on which it can be regarded as democratic are that it is, first of all, substantively a general education designed to promote individual flourishing, intellectual self-determination, and competent judgment in collective self-governance, especially in being able to judge who to trust. Second, it is a form of common education inclusive of all citizens that is intended to nurture bonds of civic friendship favorable to democratic cooperation and solidarity. Finally, it is publicly administered and provided, apparently without cost, to all citizen children. To the extent that its public administration is subject to processes of collective self-rule, it is democratic, and because the schools are day schools, parents retain a prominent role in their children's upbringing and education. So, although Aristotle did not conceive of the education he advocated as "democratic education," it is reasonable to see his proposals as formative contributions to democratic education as we know and contemplate it today.

Several aspects of Aristotle's educational proposals evoke concern: the singularity of his perfectionistic conception of the best life, the systematic state interventions that would be deployed to advance it, and the restriction of citizenship and public education to a leisured class that does not engage in manual labor. Can these be jettisoned or brought into alignment with principles of liberal democracy? Scholars disagree about the extent to which the unattractive aspects of Aristotle's politics can be separated from the attractive aspects, but the underlying ethic is arguably one of respect for human rational self-determination and valuing of human flourishing (Curren, 2000). From an ethical standpoint, the distance between Aristotelian and liberal-democratic ideals is smaller than it may seem, and there is merit in pursuing a neo-Aristotelian approach to liberal-democratic justice and education (Curren, 2013, 2023). In the spirit of Aristotle's scientific naturalism, there is much to be gained by examining the supposition underlying Aristotle's conception of the best life and liberalizing it (Curren, 2013, 2023), and much to be gained by examining his hypotheses about the effects of intergroup contact and using what we learn to strengthen democratic institutions and culture (Curren & Elenbaas, 2020).[10]

[10] I am grateful to Lawrence Philpot for his perceptive comments on an earlier draft.

References

Adkins, A. W. H. (1991). The connection between Aristotle's *Ethics* and *Politics*. In D. Keyt & F. Miller, eds., *A companion to Aristotle's Politics*. Oxford: Blackwell, pp. 75–93.

Annas, J. (1990). Comments on J. Cooper. In G. Patzig, ed., *Aristotles' "Politik."* Göttingen, Germany: Vandenhoeck & Ruprecht, pp. 242–48.

Balot, R. (2015). The "mixed regime" in Aristotle's *Politics*. In T. Lockwood & T. Samaras, eds., *Aristotle's Politics: A critical guide*. Cambridge: Cambridge University Press, pp. 103–22.

Barnes, J. (Ed.) (1984). *Complete works of Aristotle*. Princeton, NJ: Princeton University Press.

Bobonich, C. (2002). *Plato's utopia recast: His later ethics and politics*. Oxford: Oxford University Press.

Bobonich, C. (2015). Aristotle, decision making, and the many. In T. Lockwood & T. Samaras, eds., *Aristotle's Politics: A critical guide*. Cambridge: Cambridge University Press, pp. 142–62.

Cooper, J. M. (1990). Political animals and civic friendship. In G. Patzig, ed., *Aristoteles' "Politik"*. Göttingen: Vandenhoeck & Ruprecht, pp. 220–41; reprinted in Kraut, R., & Skultety, S. (Eds.) (2005). *Aristotle's Politics: Critical essays*. Lanham MD: Rowman and Littlefield, pp. 65–89.

Cooper, J. M. (2010). Political community and the highest good. In J. G. Lennox & R. Bolyon, eds., *Being, nature, and life in Aristotle: Essays in honor of Allan Gotthelf*. Cambridge: Cambridge University Press, pp. 212–64.

Curren, R. (2000). *Aristotle on the necessity of public education*. Lanham, MD: Rowman & Littlefield.

Curren, R. (2013). A neo-Aristotelian account of education, justice, and the human good. *Theory and Research in Education*. **11**(3), 231–49.

Curren, R. (2023). Enabling everyone to live well. In R. Curren, ed., *Handbook of philosophy of education*. New York and London: Routledge, pp. 42–56.

Curren, R., & Elenbaas, L. (2020). Civic friendship. *Insight Paper*. Birmingham: JCCV, University of Birmingham. Available at: https://www.jubileecentre.ac.uk/userfiles/jubileecentre/pdf/insight-series/RC_LE_CivicFriendship.pdf.

Deslauriers, M., & Destrée, P. (Eds.) (2013). *The Cambridge companion to Aristotle's Politics*. Cambridge: Cambridge University Press.

Destrée, P. (2013). Education, leisure, and politics. In M. Deslauriers & P. Destrée, eds., *The Cambridge companion to Aristotle's Politics*. Cambridge: Cambridge University Press, pp. 301–23.

Destrée, P. (2015). Aristotle on improving imperfect cities. In T. Lockwood & T. Samaras, eds., *Aristotle's Politics: A critical guide*. Cambridge: Cambridge University Press, pp. 204–23.

Frank, J. (2005). *A democracy of distinction: Aristotle and the work of politics*. Chicago, IL: University of Chicago Press.

Frank, J. (2015). On *logos* and politics in Aristotle. In T. Lockwood & T. Samaras, eds., *Aristotle's Politics: A critical guide*. Cambridge: Cambridge University Press, pp. 9–26.

Frede, D. (2013). The political character of Aristotle's ethics. In M. Deslauriers & P. Destrée, eds., *The Cambridge companion to Aristotle's Politics*. Cambridge: Cambridge University Press, pp. 14–37.

Garver, E. (1994). *Aristotle's Rhetoric: An art of character*. Chicago, IL: Chicago University Press.

Garver, E. (2011). *Aristotle's Politics: Living well and living together*. Chicago, IL: Chicago University Press.

Gutmann, A. (1987). *Democratic education*. Princeton, NJ: Princeton University Press.

Henry, D., & Nielsen, K. M. (Eds.) (2015). *Bridging the gap between Aristotle's science and ethics*. Cambridge: Cambridge University Press.

Joyal, M., McDougall, I., & Yardley, J. C. (2009). *Greek and Roman education: A sourcebook*. London: Routledge.

Keyt, D. (1999). *Aristotle Politics: Books V and VI*. Oxford: Clarendon Press.

Keyt, D., & Miller, F. D. Jr. (Eds.) (1991). *A companion to Aristotle's Politics*. Oxford: Blackwell.

Kraut, R. (1989). *Aristotle on the human good*. Princeton, NJ: Princeton University Press.

Kraut, R. (1997). *Aristotle Politics books VII and VIII*. Oxford: Clarendon Press.

Kraut, R. (2002). *Aristotle: Political philosophy*. Oxford: Oxford University Press.

Kraut, R., & Skultety, S. (Eds.) (2005). *Aristotle's Politics: Critical essays*. Lanham, MD: Rowman and Littlefield.

Lane, M. (2013). Claims to rule: The case of the multitude. In M. Deslauriers & P. Destrée, eds., *The Cambridge companion to Aristotle's Politics*. Cambridge: Cambridge University Press, pp. 247–74.

Lockwood, T., & Samaras, T. (Eds.) (2015). *Aristotle's Politics: A critical guide*. Cambridge: Cambridge University Press.

Lord, C. (1982). *Education and culture in the political thought of Aristotle*. Ithaca, NY: Cornell University Press.

Lord, C. (1984). *Aristotle: The politics*. Chicago IL: University of Chicago Press.

Mayhew, R. (1997). *Aristotle's criticism of Plato's Republic*. Lanham, MD: Rowman & Littlefield.

Mayhew, R. (2013). Rulers and ruled. In G. Anagnostopoulos, ed., *A companion to Aristotle*. Oxford: Wiley-Blackwell, pp. 526–39.

Miller, F. (1995). *Nature, justice, and rights in Aristotle's Politics*. New York, Oxford University Press.

Mulhern, J. J. (2015). *Politeia* in Greek literature, inscriptions, and in Aristotle's *Politics*: Reflections on translation and interpretation. In T. Lockwood & T. Samaras, eds., *Aristotle's Politics: A critical guide*. Cambridge: Cambridge University Press, pp. 84–102.

Nagle, D. B. (2006). *The household as the foundation of Aristotle's Politics*. Cambridge: Cambridge University Press.

Nightingale, A. W. (2001). Liberal education in Plato's *Republic* and Aristotle's *Politics*. In Y. L. Too, ed., *Education in Greek and Roman antiquity*. Leiden: Brill, pp. 133–73.

Ober, J. (2005). Aristotle's natural democracy. In R. Kraut & S. Skultety, eds., *Aristotle's Politics: Critical essays*. Lanham, MD: Rowman and Littlefield, pp. 223–43.

Ober, J. (2013). Democracy's wisdom: An Aristotelian middle way for collective judgment. *American Political Science Review*, **107**, 104–22.

Ober, J. (2015). Nature, history, and Aristotle's best possible regime. In T. Lockwood & T. Samaras, eds., *Aristotle's Politics: A critical guide*. Cambridge: Cambridge University Press, pp. 224–43.

Pangle, T. (2013). *Aristotle's teaching in the politics*. Chicago IL: University of Chicago Press.

Patzig, G., ed. (1990). *Aristoteles' Politik: Akten des XI. Symposium Aristotelicum*. Göttingen: Vandenhoeck and Ruprecht.

Reeve, C. D. C. (1998a). *Aristotle: Politics*. Indianapolis, IN: Hackett.

Reeve, C. D. C. (1998b). Aristotelian education. In A. Rorty, ed., *Philosopher on education*. London: Routledge, pp. 51–65.

Reeve, C. D. C. (2012). *Action, contemplation, and happiness: An essay on Aristotle*. Cambridge, MA: Harvard University Press.

Riesbeck, D. J. (2016). *Aristotle on political community*, Cambridge: Cambridge University Press.

Roberts, J. (2009a). *Aristotle and the politics*. London and New York: Routledge.

Roberts, J. (2009b). Excellences of the citizen and of the individual. In G. Anagnostopoulos, ed., *A companion to Aristotle*. Oxford: Wiley-Blackwell, pp. 555–65.

Robinson, R. (1995). *Aristotle Politics books III and IV*. Oxford: Clarendon Press.

Rorty, A., ed. (1996). *Essays on Aristotle's Rhetoric*. Berkeley, CA: University of California Press.

Samaras, T. (2015). Aristotle and the question of citizenship. In T. Lockwood & T. Samaras, eds., *Aristotle's Politics: A critical guide*, Cambridge: Cambridge University Press, pp. 123–41.

Saunders, T. J. (1995). *Aristotle Politics: Books I and II*. Oxford: Clarendon Press.

Schütrumpf, E. (2015). Little to do with justice: Aristotle on distributing political power. In T. Lockwood & T. Samaras, eds., *Aristotle's Politics: A critical guide*. Cambridge: Cambridge University Press, pp. 163–83.

Simpson, P. L. P. (1997). *The politics of Aristotle*. Chapel Hill, NC: University of North Carolina Press.

Stalley, R. (2009). Education and the state. In G. Anagnostopoulos, ed., *A companion to Aristotle*. Oxford: Wiley-Blackwell, pp. 566–76.

Waldron, J. (1992). The wisdom of the multitude: Some reflections on Book 3, chapter 11 of Aristotle's Politics. *Political Theory*, 20, 613–41; reprinted in Kraut, R., & Skultety, S. (Eds.) (2005). *Aristotle's Politics: Critical essays*. Lanham, MD: Rowman and Littlefield, pp. 145–65.

4

Rousseau on Democratic Education

Avi I. Mintz

4.1 Introduction

In 1794, amid much fanfare, officials in France had Jean-Jacques Rousseau's remains moved to Paris and placed among others deemed worthy of the highest regard in the recently completed Panthéon. Rousseau was honoured in 1794 for the same reasons that his work remains on the syllabi of political theory courses today: he articulated a vision of political community in which legitimate rule was to be based on the collective interests of all citizens. A deep egalitarianism runs through Rousseau's political thought – citizens are equally part of the sovereign body and the demands of that body's general will are imposed on all citizens equally. The leaders of the French Revolution celebrated Rousseau's influence and generations of political theorists continue to reckon with his ideas.

Rousseau's rank in the canon of Western educational philosophy is arguably even more elevated. Rousseau is a staple of introductory courses in educational theory. Of thinkers outside the last half century, the same could only be said of Plato and John Dewey. Rousseau today is best known as perhaps the most influential proponent of child- or student-centered education – and more narrowly, experiential or discovery learning – in which children learn through encounters with problems in their environment (rather than by reading about them or hearing a teacher discuss them). Rousseau presented these ideas in *Emile: Or on Education*, published in 1762.[1]

Rousseau also discussed education in other works, particularly in his *Considerations on the Government of Poland*. But Rousseau's ideas of education in those works highlight not the student-centered principles of *Emile* but rather a collectivist education in patriotism. Rather than allowing the children to discover principles and ideas on their own schedule, Rousseau calls for public schooling that explicitly cultivates patriots. In *Considerations of the Government of*

[1] Note on Rousseau's works: The translations of Rousseau's works cited in this chapter are *Emile* (*E*), by page number; *The Social Contract* (SC) by book, chapter, and paragraph number; *The First Discourse* (*FD*) by part and paragraph number; *Political Economy* (*PE*) by paragraph, *Considerations on the Government of Poland* (*GP*) by chapter and paragraph number; and *Plan for a Constitution for Corsica* (*CC*) by page number.

Poland and in some other works, Rousseau writes about the need to cultivate a strong attachment to both one's country and one's fellow citizens.

To modern ears, Rousseau's treatment of education in *Considerations* seems poorly suited to modern liberal democracies. Extreme nationalism seems to invite xenophobia and jingoism. Can the patriotic, nationalistic aim of education in *Considerations* be reconciled with the child-centered, individual education of *Emile*? Were either of these ideals (or both) theories of *democratic* education? In this chapter, I first discuss the individual ideal presented in *Emile* and I explain why educators and philosophers committed to democratic education embraced Rousseau's work. I then discuss the national aim of education that Rousseau articulated most prominently in *Considerations*. Finally, I discuss some of the scholarly attempts to interpret whether the ideals are contradictory. I argue that there has been an overlooked, unifying theme in his educational works grounded in his discussions of *amour-propre*. Rousseau believed that education – whether national or individual – must generate social cohesion, concord, and fellow-feeling; that is, education ought to provide a foundation for citizens to recognize each other's dignity and live harmoniously with one another.

4.2 Domestic Education, Education for Citizenship, and Democratic Education in *Emile*

Rousseau's *Emile* is an unconventional book on education in many ways. It is not merely a treatise on education; much of it is presented as a novel where the relationship of a boy, Emile, and his tutor, Jean-Jacques (and later his wife, Sophie), is a thought experiment designed to elucidate philosophical, psychological, and educational principles. But Rousseau also includes anecdotes from his own experiences in addition to those he imagines Emile encountering. A discussion of natural religion, "The Profession of Faith of the Savoyard Vicar," reads as though it is a completely separate essay (over 50 pages in Bloom's translation) that was inserted into *Emile*.[2] (Rousseau wrote that he included it "as an example of the way one can reason with one's pupil in order not to diverge from the method I have tried to establish" [*E* 313]).

To modern readers, *Emile's* scope seems remarkably wide. Today's books on education are typically divided into those for parents and those for educators. Among parenting books, there are some about infants, others about toddlers, and those that address further stages of development. Education books for teachers might focus on classroom management, pedagogy, curriculum, or communication strategies. *Emile* is comprehensive; it discusses child rearing and education with a tutor (though not in a classroom). Its five books are based on different stages of development. This first covers infancy (and Rousseau doles out advice on topics like nursing, swaddling, and bathing); the second covers toddlerdom through age 12, the third ages 12–15 (the age of "adolescence

[2] Jurgen Oelkers (2008) argues that the section on religion is key to interpreting the entire book.

without yet being that of puberty" [E 165]), the fourth ages 15–18, and the fifth early adulthood (including marriage and a discussion of girls' education).

That Rousseau divided childhood into stages is noteworthy. He insisted that children are not mini-adults and, therefore, the education suitable to them at different stages must be carefully thought out. Rousseau writes, for example, that, in education, the "wisest men concentrate on what it is important for men to know without considering what children are in the condition to learn" (E 34) and "childhood has its own way of seeing, thinking, and feeling which are proper to it" (E 90).

But, since this chapter is not a general survey of Rousseau's educational thought but rather a discussion of the connection of his educational thought to democratic theory, I must focus on what Rousseau says about education for democratic citizenship. Unfortunately, it is not clear that the education outlined in *Emile* is directed at citizenship, let alone democratic citizenship. Rousseau posits that educating the man and the citizen are two wholly opposed projects. "Civil man," Rousseau writes, "is only a fraction unity dependent on the denominator; his value is determined by his relation to the whole." On the other hand, "natural man" is "a numerical unity, the absolute whole which is relative only to itself or its kind" (E 39). Rousseau then gives examples of Romans and Spartans as exemplary citizens, men and women who were great patriots and took delight in their fellow citizens' accomplishments without jealousy. Rousseau argues that man and citizen are "necessarily opposed objects" which require "two contrary forms of instruction – the one, public and common; the other, individual and domestic" (E 40). Rousseau then dismisses the idea of public education because there is no longer a fatherland (or, he implies, there is no country worthy of a citizen's patriotic commitment).

Despite claiming that the individual and the citizen are distinct, Rousseau recognized that even the product of a domestic education will become a citizen, and he discusses what kind of citizen Emile will become. As readers discover at the end of Book V when Emile has traveled Europe to examine the variety of political regimes, Emile will take up residence in a country where he can live simply and peacefully. Thus, though Emile may, by necessity, become a citizen of some country, his education can hardly be understood as an education for robust participation in a democratic society.

A further challenge of discussing Rousseau's work in relation to democracy is that Rousseau would have been unlikely to view himself as a democratic theorist. The word democracy appears only at the end of *Emile*[3] and even there Rousseau merely notes that "we shall conclude that generally democratic government is suitable for small states, aristocratic government for medium-sized states, and monarchy government for large states" (E 466). In *The Social Contract* – published in the same year as *Emile* and reflecting ideas similar to the political analysis in *Emile* (E 459–67)[4] – Rousseau makes the same claim. But he goes on to

[3] On p. 465 of the 480 pages in Bloom's translation.

[4] Allan Bloom notes that *Emile's* analysis of politics has some notable omissions in comparison with *The Social Contract*. There is no discussion in *Emile* about the legislator and civil religion (*E*, p. 494, n. 61).

say there that a pure democracy is an unattainable ideal, even in a small state: "If there were a people of Gods, they would govern themselves democratically. So perfect a Government is not suited to men" (*SC* III.4.8). Nevertheless, one should not overlook the fact that democracy is the ideal. And Rousseau hardly endorses the large societies for which he says monarchy and aristocracy are suited.[5] Capital cities, in particular, are a frequent target for Rousseau as breeding grounds for vice. Indeed, one could read Rousseau; he deems them saying that life in large countries is so corrupt and debasing, they might as well be governed by a monarchy or aristocracy. Rousseau viewed tyranny as one of the greatest plagues of humanity (*E* 466) and envisioned societies in which people cared for each other, treated each other as equals.[6] He was a fierce advocate of popular sovereignty – calling for a radical increase in citizens' participation in public life. Indeed, Rousseau is credited as an early advocate of what is now called "participatory democracy," a form of governance in which citizens deliberate about the state's laws and some other important matters. (Advocates of representative democracy, on the other hand, call for the election of officials who deliberate about public policy while representing groups of citizens.) So, there is good reason to treat Rousseau as an advocate for democracy even if he might have seen himself as, more generally, a republican.

In addition to Rousseau's influence on democratic theory, there is another reason that it is valuable to consider Rousseau in the context of democratic education. Rousseau was highly influential among progressive educational philosophers and theorists who understood themselves to be developing an educational theory appropriate for democracy. At the beginning of the twentieth century, these progressives often invoked Rousseau. Indeed, when John Dewey and his daughter Evelyn surveyed progressive educational experiments in *Schools of To-Morrow* (1915), Rousseau's name arose often. The Deweys wrote there were a range of practices at the schools, but "most of these points of similarity are found in the views advocated by Rousseau" (Dewey & Dewey, 1915, p. 290).[7] These progressive educators thought that traditional schooling was appropriate for authoritarian regimes. Democracies, on the other hand, required citizens to take initiative rather than passively waiting for others' commands but democracy also required cooperation – citizens must be able to work with all citizens

[5] In *Considerations*, Rousseau (somewhat surprisingly to many readers), notes the danger or political revolution and outlines reforms while preserving the monarchy.

[6] When Emile is about to begin his life as a young adult in Book V, Jean-Jacques takes him away from Paris and says: "Adieu, then, Paris, celebrated city, city of noise, smoke, and mud, where the women no longer believe in honor and the men no longer believe in virtue. Adieu, Paris. We are seeking love, happiness, innocence. We shall never be far enough away from you" (*E* 355). In the *Plan for a Constitution for Corsica* (*CC*), Rousseau wrote, "If cities are harmful, capitals are even more so. A capital is a pit into which almost the entire nation goes to lose its morals, its laws, its courage, and its freedom . . . From the capital is exhaled a continuous plague which undermines and finally destroys the nation" (*CC* 132).

[7] Progressive educational theorists were explicitly reckoning with the role of education in democracy. It was no accident that Dewey titled his most important work on educational philosophy *Democracy and Education* (1916). In Chapter 9, Dewey explicitly wrote that nature as aim is "of recent influence" and that, "since no one has stated in the doctrine both its truth and falsity better than Rousseau, we shall turn to him" (1916, p. 112). I have argued elsewhere (Mintz, 2016) that Dewey uses Rousseau as a stand-in for his contemporary child-centered progressives whom he declined to identify explicitly. I discuss Rousseau's educational legacy among progressives more generally in Mintz (2012).

regardless of ethnic, class, religious, or other differences.[8] Rousseau, they believed, identified a way to cultivate the kind of initiative and independence suited for democratic citizens.

4.3 *Emile* and the Autonomous and Independent Citizen

Perhaps most striking to *Emile's* readers – both past and present – is Emile's freedom up to age 15. Emile has no classroom, no classmates, no traditional teacher, no set curriculum, no books, and hears no lectures. "Emile will never learn anything by heart" (*E* 112). He will not be forced to read – "Reading is the plague of childhood and almost the only occupation we know how to give it. At twelve Emile will hardly know what a book is" (*E* 116). Until the age of at least 12 or 15, he won't learn languages – "I number the study of languages among the useless parts of education" (*E* 109). Likewise, until that age it is "ridiculous" to study history. Rousseau notes that when a child studies geography, he may learn to list the names of cities and rivers but has no understanding of the subject: "There is not a single child of ten who can find his way from Paris to Saint-Denis," a nearby town (*E* 110).

Rousseau rejected these facets of schooling (which are as common in our own era as they were in his) because he made a set of assumptions about physiological development. He believed that children were not capable of grasping abstract ideas. When learning history, a child may be able to repeat facts but cannot grasp the complex context of those facts – a historical understanding of causes and effects (*E* 110). When studying foreign languages, a child is simply mapping synonyms onto his native tongue, Rousseau believed.

Rousseau was guided by an ideal about the value of children's freedom and independence. Books – "the instruments of their greatest misery" (*E* 116) – are not only filled with ideas young children cannot adequately grasp. They also do something more pernicious: they "teach us to use the reason of others ... to believe much and never to know anything" (*E* 125). Rousseau insists that submitting to the authority of others must be assiduously avoided (a topic I discuss in Section 4.4).

Rousseau sometimes called these educational principles the "inactive method" of education. He writes, "usually one gets very surely and quickly what one is not in a hurry to get" (*E* 117). Elsewhere he writes: "Dare I expose the greatest, the most important, the most useful rule of all education? It is not to

[8] The Deweys wrote, "Education that associates learning with doing will replace the passive education of imparting the learning of others. However well the latter is adapted to feudal societies, in which most individuals are expected to submit constantly and docilely to the authority of superiors, an education which proceeds on this basis is inconsistent with a democratic society where initiative and independence are the rule and where every citizen is supposed to take part in the conduct of affairs of common interest" (Dewey & Dewey, 1915, p. 163). They also wrote, "The conventional type of education which trains children to docility and obedience, to the careful performance of imposed tasks because they are imposed, regardless of where they lead, is suited to an autocratic society ... Children in school must be allowed freedom so that they will know what its use means when they become the controlling body, and they must be allowed to develop active qualities of initiative, independence, and resourcefulness, before the abuses and failures of democracy will disappear" (pp. 303–04).

gain time but to lose it" (*E* 93). He also calls this education up until the age of 12 a "purely negative education," and says, "It consists not at all in teaching virtue or truth but in securing the heart from vice and the mind from error" (*E* 93). From the earliest pages of *Emile*, Rousseau emphasizes this message: "What must be done is to prevent anything from being done" (*E* 41). Rousseau calls for governing without explicit instruction, which he argues is really "doing everything by doing nothing" (*E* 119).[9]

What the progressive educational philosophers, so deeply committed to devising a new democratic education, would have liked about these ideas is clear. Children are presented with ample opportunities to explore with the freedom and independence appropriate for someone who will be an adult citizen empowered to govern her own life and, with others, society in general. But Rousseau also articulated something else that proved appealing to those educators. Rather than force children to study something that was ill-suited to their development or their interests, one should wait for the child to desire to study it. That is, Rousseau understood the child's intrinsic motivation to be essential to learning. Forward-thinking educators of Rousseau's day proposed various ways to engage students in learning. They had dice and card games (just as we do now) to generate students' interest. Rousseau writes, "What a pity! A means surer than all these, and the one always forgotten, is the desire to learn. Give the child this desire; then let your desks and your dice go. Any method will be good for him" (*E* 117). Though Jean-Jacques does not teach Emile to read, Rousseau writes, "I am almost certain that Emile will know how to read and write perfectly before the age of ten, precisely because it makes very little difference to me that he knows how before fifteen" (*E* 117).

Learning takes place when children enjoy an activity or pursue something for the sake of some other goal (*E* 116).[10] When the child reaches 15 or so, the period of losing time ends. But Rousseau does not believe that one should then proceed to teach in a traditional way (*E* 172). In Book III, Rousseau outlines a pedagogical strategy to engage Emile in lessons that are now appropriate to his age.

Rather than lecturing the child (or assigning a book on the topic), educators must create an educational experience. Rousseau describes how Jean-Jacques would teach Emile geography and astronomy through a situation where understanding emerges from activity. Jean-Jacques takes Emile to the forest and pretends that they are lost. Emile is tired, hungry, and begins to cry. Jean-Jacques laments the predicament along with him but then notes the position of the sun in the sky. Emile, prompted by a few questions, deduces which direction is north from the shadows, then reasons that he needs to go south to emerge from the forest. Emile concludes, "Astronomy is good for something" (*E* 181).

[9] Lines such as this one appear frequently. For example: "The education of children is a vocation in which one must know how to lose time in order to gain it" (*E* 141); "Nature's instruction is late and slow; men's is almost always premature. In the former case the senses wake the imagination; in the latter the imagination wakes the senses; it gives them a precocious activity which cannot fail to enervate and weaken individuals first and in the long run the species itself" (*E* 215); "I shall repeat it endlessly: put off, if possible, a good lesson for fear of giving a bad one" (*E* 96); and "Keep yourself from giving it today if you can without danger put it off until tomorrow" (*E* 94). See also Rousseau's critique of parents who are overly eager to have their children learn to speak (*E* 93).

[10] Children must feel "the real and present advantage in either pleasure or utility" (*E* 116).

Because Rousseau calls for learning in immersive experiences where students discover facts on their own, he has been credited as the father of "experiential education" and "discovery learning."[11] Rousseau writes, "let him know something not because you told it to him but because he has understood it himself. Let him not learn science *but discover it*" (*E* 168; emphasis added).[12] The educator should not only avoid teaching a lesson directly, he should not even suggest what the child ought to learn (*E* 179). Rousseau wrote something of this process that would seem familiar to anyone acquainted with contemporary educational theory. Emile should learn to learn rather than acquire knowledge, and he should come to love learning. In studying geography, for example, "the goal is not that he know exactly the topography of the region, but that he grasp the means of learning about it" (*E* 171). Rousseau elaborates: "The issue is not to teach him the sciences but to give him the taste for loving them and the methods for learning them" (*E* 172).

Educators are keen to impart lessons to their charges but, Rousseau warns, "our didactic and pedantic craze is always to teach children what they would learn much better by themselves" (*E* 78). Rousseau recognized an important implication of this approach to pedagogy. Educators must not create an educational experience but then jump in as soon as the youth struggles or errs. One must wait until the youth recognizes them himself: if Emile "never made mistakes, he would not learn so well" (*E* 171).

Some of Rousseau's critics from the pedagogical right thought he called for a completely laissez-faire approach to education. Such an interpretation, however, neglects Rousseau's repeated calls for the tutor to create the conditions under which Emile will be prompted to investigate, just as getting lost in the forest is the occasion for the study of geography and astronomy. When Rousseau writes, for example, that the educator should not even suggest what Emile ought to learn because "it is up to him to desire it, to seek it, to find it" he advises next that "it is up to you to put it within his reach, skillfully to give birth to this desire and to furnish him with the means of satisfying it" (*E* 179).

Some of Rousseau's critics from the pedagogical left who consider the teacher's authority to be a threat to the student noticed that Rousseau was anything but laissez-faire and warned that Jean-Jacques' hidden agenda introduced a pernicious manipulation that undermined Rousseau's aim of educating an independent, free person.[13] Rousseau, however, saw no inconsistency in maintaining that Emile's tutor ought to be in complete control while Emile believed himself to be completely free. He confronted the matter head on:

> Let [your pupil] always believe he is the master, and let it always be you who are. There is no subjection so perfect as that which keeps the appearance of

[11] Concerning the importance of the use of the senses in children's learning, Rousseau was particularly influenced by Condillac. See Roosevelt (2021, pp. 101–07).

[12] Rousseau also writes, the governor "ought to give no precepts at all; he ought to make them be discovered" (*E* 52).

[13] A. S. Neill noted with disapproval Rousseau's authoritarianism (see Walter, 1996). Rosenow (1980) and Darling (1982, pp. 179–82) discuss the tutor's manipulation. For nuanced treatments of authority in Rousseau's *Emile*, see Iheoma (1997) and Michaud (2012).

> freedom. Thus the will itself is made captive ... Are not his labors, his games, his pleasures, his pains, all in your hands without his knowing it? Doubtless he ought to do only what he wants; but he ought to want only what you want him to do. He ought not to make a step without your having foreseen it; he ought not to open his mouth without your knowing what he is going to say. (p. 120; see also pp. 121, 124, 175)

The degree to which authority is valuable or detrimental in cultivating democratic citizens is a question of no small importance.[14] Must students exercise their autonomy in order to develop it? Rousseau, in *Emile,* answers with a qualified yes. Children and adolescents need to be free to discover and pursue their interests, but this discovery falls within a carefully delineated sphere for which the educator is fully responsible. Coercion and manipulation are threats only if they are detected. Emile "instructs himself so much the better because he sees nowhere the intention to instruct" (*E* 119). Rousseau warns that if one makes a child submit to commands "that is to want him to be credulous and a dupe when he is grown up" (*E* 178). Because the manipulation is hidden, Emile is "not accustomed to turning constantly to others ... [H]e judges, he foresees, he reasons in everything immediately related to him. He does not chatter, he acts" (*E* 119). Jean-Jacques even tells Emile as he transitions into adulthood that he was only apparently free, but now he is really free and must "learn to become [his] own master" (*E* 445).

Much like in Rousseau's political theory, where Rousseau believed he identified a way for citizens to be free under the constraints of the general will – famously writing that sometimes citizens may need to be "forced to be free" (*SC* I.7.8) – Rousseau's educational theory sought to reconcile the value of a child's freedom with the adult's knowledge and experience about how to best develop children's autonomy. Whether Rousseau's solution is persuasive (or even plausible) is a matter of debate. But autonomy and independence are not the only aim of Emile's education; indeed, they are only instrumentally valuable for Rousseau's broader educational project in *Emile,* and that broader project has important implications for democratic citizenship.

4.4 *Amour-Propre* and Citizenship

Rousseau argues that Emile should not only (believe himself to) be free from submitting to adults but that he should never become accustomed to commanding others. Children have needs that they cannot meet. According to Rousseau, how one attends to those needs makes all the difference. When a baby cries out for an object, Rousseau advises that one should take the baby to the object so he can grasp it himself, rather than fetch the object for him: "The first tears of children are prayers. If one is not careful, they soon become orders. Children begin by getting themselves assisted; they end by getting themselves served" (*E* 66).

[14] See Chapters 10, 12, and 35 in this volume.

Rousseau's emphasis on "wasting time" is rooted in a concern that one should avoid introducing notions of "domination and servitude," "empire and dominion" (*E* 48, 66). It is primarily in service of this idea that Rousseau constructs an educational philosophy where authority is hidden, where the child discovers ideas on his own, where the child pursues only what interests him.

Ideas of dominion are so dangerous because they "awaken and flatter" *amour-propre,* which could be translated as vanity, pride, or self-esteem. *Amour-propre* involves comparing oneself to others, in contrast to *amour de soi,* self-love:

> Self-love, which concerns only ourselves, is contented when our true needs are satisfied. But *amour-propre*, which makes comparisons, is never content and never could be, because this sentiment, preferring ourselves to others, also demands others to prefer us to themselves, which is impossible. This is how the gentle and affectionate passions are born of self-love, and how the hateful and irascible passions are born of *amour-propre.* Thus what makes man essentially good is to have few needs and to compare himself little to others; what makes him essentially wicked is to have many needs and to depend very much on opinion. (*E* 213–14; see also 243)

Emile's education has limited the way that he compares himself to others in that Jean-Jacques has painstakingly avoided putting Emile in situations where he obeys others (and thus feels inferior to them) or makes others obey him (which would arouse feelings of superiority).

Rousseau says that Emile's education is based on the need to delay comparisons to others as long as possible, and this need not begin until a child becomes a moral being around the age of 15 (and the subject of *Emile's* fourth book).[15] Rousseau's aforementioned comments about comparisons to others might lead to a reading of *Emile* that holds that *amour de soi* – self-love – is a virtue while *amour-propre* – vanity – is a vice. But the issue is actually more complex. *Amour-propre* is the root of prejudice and opinion (*E* 68), yet it is "useful" despite the fact that it is a "dangerous instrument" (*E* 244). Rousseau says, "we shall transform it [*amour-propre*] into a virtue" since "there is no man's heart in which this virtue does not have its root" (*E* 252).

Emile should thus be read not only as an educational philosophy of discovery learning or experiential education but, rather, an educational philosophy about turning *amour-propre* into a virtue. Such a reading would relegate the ideas which proved so influential to child-centered educational philosophers as but a means to that end. Comparison to others is inevitable, especially during adolescence. Furthermore, and importantly for the purposes of considering Rousseau's contributions to democratic educational thought, comparison to others is essential for citizenship. Recall Rousseau's question at the outset of *Emile:* "What will a man raised uniquely for himself become for others?" (*E* 41).

[15] Rousseau notes that Emile is 18 at the beginning of Book IV (*E* 243), but closes Book III by noting that Emile is in his 15th year and "*amour-propre,* the first and most natural of all the passions, is still hardly aroused in him" (*E* 208).

Emile has spent the first 15 years of life raised "for himself." Now that he can meaningfully engage in moral relations, *amour-propre* must come into play. But rather than looking at others and wanting to be ranked ahead of them, Emile will look at them as fellow humans who ought to be afforded the same respect as he would hope they afford him. Because Emile has not been raised to yearn for the admiration of others, and he has not spent his time jealous of others, the foundation has been laid, perhaps, for Emile to be that rare citizen who does not look down upon those of lower rank or defer to members of the upper class. Emile would view other citizens as his equals, recognizing no distinctions of class.[16]

In this discussion of education in *Emile*, I have argued that Rousseau's educational philosophy might be viewed as democratic in two senses. First, because of his emphasis on autonomy and independence in the child's self-motivated learning through experience, Rousseau's ideas suggest one way to cultivate democratic citizens, a vision that proved influential to child-centered progressive educators. Second, Rousseau also articulates a more complex vision of democratic education. Discovery learning and related educational ideas are means to a more important end: the cultivation of a citizen who recognizes the inherent dignity of all fellow human beings, one whose *amour-propre* is a virtue rather than a vice. Such a citizen will not tolerate antidemocratic class hierarchies.

My analysis here is not intended to be exhaustive. Indeed, Rousseau's argument in *Emile* is particularly interesting because of the robust role allotted to the emotions in Emile's education; compassion, for example, is particularly important in the development of Emile's *amour-propre* and thus compassion becomes a key political emotion.[17] Love is also important. The fifth book describes Sophie, her education, and her relationship with Emile. Sophie's education is, in many important ways, opposed to Emile's. For example, whereas others' opinions should not matter to Emile and he should not care about his appearance, appearances matter for Sophie (*E* 361, 364–65). Rousseau writes, "Opinion is the grave of virtue among men and its throne among women" (365).[18] Yet perhaps Rousseau's description of Sophie's education is evidence that Emile is not fully fit to participate in society. Sophie – with her knowledge of the ways of opinion and appearance – represents a bridge between Emile and society. His relationship with Sophie might therefore suggest that both of them have an incomplete education and, without one

[16] Rousseau's egalitarianism runs through his comments about how Emile's education will be designed. He writes, "Men are not naturally kings, or lords, or courtiers, or rich men" (*E* 222) and "man is the same in all stations . . . [T]o the man who thinks, all the civil distinctions disappear" (*E* 225). Rousseau suggests that political equality is necessary for people to care for fellow citizens (*E* 224). Thus, Emile would see all men as equal up to the age of 12 (*E* 160) and Emile's education about others (when he becomes a "moral being") begins with examining what he has in common with others (*E* 235). Emile's education will be arranged so that he "puts himself in no class but finds his bearings in all" (*E* 226).

[17] For a list of sources on the role of compassion in Rousseau's political and educational theory, see Mintz (2012, p. 264, n. 37).

[18] For an insightful critique that focuses on the precise nature of Rousseau's views on women and girls' education, see Weiss (1993). See Jonas (2016) on some of the ways that Rousseau's educational philosophy and philosophy of the family intersect.

another, meaningful political participation is impossible. (At least via Emile, since Rousseau does not envision granting women with the same rights and responsibilities as men.) Nevertheless, I must set that controversy aside to turn to the most important problem with interpreting Rousseau's educational theory. How can one reconcile Emile's education with Rousseau's views on public education?

4.5 *Considerations on the Government of Poland* and Patriotic Citizenship

In *The Social Contract,* Rousseau wrote that he would consider "men as they are, and the laws as they can be" (*SC* I.0.1). Perhaps fittingly, therefore, Rousseau said relatively little about education in that work, though he does discuss how civil religion can form citizens, making them "love [their] duties," more sociable, and tolerant (*SC* IV.8.31–34). Could one reconcile education through civil religion with the education of *Emile*? Perhaps Emile will reach such a conclusion about the value of civil religion on his own, becoming a patriot in whatever country he moves to after his marriage. Or perhaps civil religion is necessary for forming citizens who have not benefited from the type of education Emile experienced. More challenging to reconcile with *Emile,* however, is Rousseau's *Considerations on the Government of Poland* (*GP*).

Rousseau was asked to offer recommendations for Poland's constitution when the country was in the midst of political upheaval and was deteriorating in anarchy (*GP* 3.1). He completed his essay for Poland in 1772. He devoted a chapter to education, which he says is "the important subject" (*GP* 4.1) and calls not only for public schooling – the sort of institution into which Emile never sets foot – but a thoroughgoing attempt to foster a love of country. The schools are to be common to all, rich and poor alike, and free, or at least affordable, for the poor as well (*GP* 4.3). (The common education that Rousseau proposes is limited to boys, we may presume.)

When Emile eventually learned to read, he was given Defoe's *Robinson Crusoe,* a book that celebrates independence. In Poland, however, Rousseau advised that a child, "upon learning to read, he read about his country." Rousseau provided some details for his patriotic curriculum: "At ten he know all of its products, at twelve all of its provinces, roads, towns, that at fifteen he know its entire history, at sixteen all of its laws, that in all of Poland there not be a single great deed or illustrious person of which his memory and heart are not full, of which he could not then and there give an account" (*GP* 4.2).

Emile's curriculum contains no love of fatherland. While history and law are something Emile begins to learn at the age of 15, by 12 Emile would have no knowledge of the country's products or it provinces, roads, and towns. Indeed, as I mentioned in Section 4.3, Rousseau specifically criticized the teaching of geography in this way (*E* 110). Patriotism is the aim of national education in *Considerations* : "It is education that must give souls the national form, and so direct their tastes and opinions that they will be patriotic by inclination, passion, necessity" (*GP* 4.1).[19] Rousseau writes that a true republican loves his fatherland; "When he is alone, he is nothing" (*GP* 4.1). In contrast, Emile has spent much time alone and maintains a critical distance from his own country, traveling for two years to identify the best country to settle in.

Emile spent time doing whatever interested him. But in Poland children "should not be allowed to play by themselves as they please, but all together and in public" (*GP* 4.5). Emile viewed others as equals because, unlike Sophie, he was not raised to seek the approval of others. In contrast, Rousseau proposes that the children of Poland become accustomed, much like Sophie, "to living under the eyes of their fellow-citizens and to seeking public approbation." Children would play together in public in a way that "excites competition and emulation." Emile was shielded in his early life from ideas of subordination and dominance, but the children of Poland will be accustomed "early on to rule, to equality, to fraternity, to competitions" (*GP* 4.5). Rousseau proposes a mechanism for developing students' skills of shared governance in Poland – a "moot State." This student government, much like the official regime, would have a budget and meet to conduct business. Rousseau says that it is "the nursery of the Statesmen who will one day direct public affairs in the same capacity which they first exercise only in play" (*GP* 4.6). Emile's introduction to politics comes from study and travel alone, rather than practice.

There are some educational principles shared in *Emile* and *Considerations* – Rousseau says in *Considerations* that "I cannot repeat often enough that good education has to be negative" (*GP* 4.4). In *Considerations*, as in other political works, Rousseau treats *amour-propre* as a dangerous but potentially valuable passion.[20] Perhaps he envisions Polish schools adapting some of the educational principles of *Emile* in much the same way that child-centered progressives later would in schools. However, the emphasis on manufacturing patriotism in Poland has no equivalent in *Emile* and seems to undermine the autonomous judgment that Emile would develop.

Is there any way that these two works can be reconciled or are they an example of contradictions and paradoxes about which Rousseau often warns readers?

4.6 Autonomy, Patriotism, and *Homonoia*

Are these two ideals opposed? Perhaps, if they are, one might be inclined to argue that Rousseau simply changed his mind between the publication of *Emile* in 1762 and *Considerations* in 1772. This is not a promising explanation, however, because Rousseau had been consistently extolling patriotism prior to *Emile*. In his *First Discourse*, written in 1749 and published in 1750, Rousseau lamented the

[19] On patriotism as one of Rousseau's educational ideals, see Wain (2011, pp. 1–20).

[20] In his *Political Economy*, Rousseau writes of dangerous passions like greed and vanity but that, when citizens "feel themselves members of the fatherland," they "transform into a sublime virtue the dangerous disposition that gives rise to all of our vices" (*PE* , para. 36). In *Plan for a Constitution for Corsica*, Rousseau identifies vanity as an impediment to social cohesion (*CC* p. 154).

lack of patriots in society. He lamented the intellectuals around him who "smile disdainfully at such old-fashioned words as Fatherland and Religion" (*FD* 2.40), and the politicians who care about money rather than virtue. In his *Discourse on Political Economy*, published in 1755, Rousseau articulated ideals for state education that are consistent with those of *Considerations*, though in Poland the abstract is made concrete.[21] Finally, even while Rousseau was writing *Emile*, he wrote in *The Social Contract* that "when each Citizen is nothing and can do nothing except with all the others, and the force acquired by the whole is equal or superior to the sum of the natural forces of all the individuals, the legislation may be said to be at the highest pitch of perfection it can reach" (*SC* II.7.3).

If Rousseau's thinking did not change over time, perhaps he simply could not decide whether national or individual education ought to be the primary purpose of education. As Amos Hofman recently put it, "even after about a decade since the publication of *Emile*, Rousseau was still vacillating within the man/citizen dichotomy that characterized his philosophy of education all along" (Hofman, 2021, p. 89).

Hofman may be correct, but there are some other options that ought to be considered as well. Perhaps we might consider whether the differences between the two ideals are as stark as scholars typically assume. Denise Schaeffer (2013), for example, has argued that Rousseau remains committed to developing judgement in both contexts.

Grace Roosevelt (1990, especially chs. 5, 6) has, to my mind, offered the most compelling analysis of Rousseau's opposing educational ideals. Rousseau believed that different forms of government were appropriate to states of different sizes (and democracy was appropriate only for the smallest). Roosevelt argues that the education outlined in *Considerations* is appropriate for small, tightly knit states. Patriotism is necessary in a small country like Poland on the brink of anarchy because it will help unify its citizens as a free and independent state. In contrast, *Emile* proposes an education appropriate to a decadent, expansionist state – notably, *Emile* is set in France. The citizen, like Emile, in a large, aggressive monarchy ought to be raised to be a cosmopolitan humanitarian, "comfortable in the world at large and generally critical of his own government, but who nevertheless fulfills civic duties and social responsibilities with compassion and commitment" (1990, p. 172).[22]

Returning to the language I used to describe the two ideals, Rousseau highlighted the importance of patriotism for some regimes and the value of

[21] Rousseau wrote that education "is surely the most important business of the state" (*PE* para. 38) and thus should not "be abandoned to fathers' lights and prejudices" (*PE* para. 37). Rousseau essentially defined the good citizen as a patriot, and called for education to form the good citizen: "The fatherland cannot endure with freedom, nor freedom without virtue, nor virtue without citizens; you will have everything if you form citizens . . . Now to form citizens is not the business of a single day; and to have them be citizens when they are grown, they have to be taught when they are children" (*PE* para. 20; see also para. 29).

[22] Victor Gourevitch seems to endorse Roosevelt's analysis in his brief comments about man and citizen in his introduction to *Rousseau: The Social Contract and Other Later Political Writings* (Rousseau, 1997, pp. xxix–xxx). Gourevitch argues that national education is "concerned with happiness accessible to the greater number," while individual education is the best option available in some political contexts. (Gourevitch does not cite her work in the discussion, but Grace Roosevelt [1990] is listed in his "A brief guide to further reading" [p. xl].)

autonomy and independence in *Emile*. However, he believed that social cohesion is essential in any society. The patriot not only loves his Fatherland, he loves his fellow citizens. Rousseau's conception of patriotism is perhaps even more focused on citizens' relationships with one another than their relationship with the state. In both *Considerations* and *Emile,* Rousseau is concerned with how citizens view one another. Rousseau was a serious reader of the ancients and the concept that best describes the unifying educational aim across his works is *homonoia*. Philosophers like Plato and Aristotle understood *homonoia* to be central to any thriving community.[23] Translated literally, *homonoia* means like-mindedness, but might be better described as solidarity, concord, or harmony. It involves a sharing of both hearts and minds, a love for one's fellow's citizens as well as shared commitments. Basically, it is that which creates social cohesion in a political community. An education in patriotism, as Rousseau outlines in *Considerations* and calls for elsewhere, is one way of forming bonds between citizens. Humanitarian cosmopolitanism – the term Roosevelt uses to describe Emile's citizenship – is another. As I have described, Emile grows to see others as his equals who are worthy of respect and whose dignity is recognized regardless of their social status. In either case, education must turn *amour-propre* into a virtue. *Amour-propre* is thus the key to generating *homonoia* or a threat to it.

If Rousseau might seem foolhardy to modern readers for proposing two opposed ideals, one might reply that he was not the only one in his time grappling with the competing demands of citizenship and developing autonomy.[24] It was an era, after all, where Benjamin Rush (one of the signatories of America's Declaration of Independence) declared that, having freed America from tyranny, schools must help citizens prepare for their independence by converting "men into republican machines" (1786, p. 17). When Rousseau is read in the context of other Enlightenment thinkers like Rush, it becomes clear that it was no simple matter to identify the balance between cultivating commitments to shared governance and cultivating the capacity for autonomy required to participate meaningfully in collective rule

The tension is no less present in modern democracies. Should schools encourage patriotism? Or is patriotism suited to authoritarian regimes? One of the most contested issues in public schooling in democracies is the history curriculum. Should students encounter a version of history that celebrates a country's heroes and ideals? Or should they encounter the many ways that a country has failed in its treatment of populations within and outside of its borders? Since democratic patriotism is already a subject of a Chapter 23 in this volume, I will not explore it further here. But Rousseau's educational philosophy, both in *Emile* and elsewhere, points clearly to the pressing need for *homonoia* and social cohesion. In *Emile* and *Considerations* (and elsewhere) he discusses how *amour-propre* might be transformed into a virtue, proposing an education that is up to

[23] On Plato and Aristotle's praise of *homonoia* in Sparta, for example, see Mintz (2018).

[24] By the second half of the eighteenth century, intellectuals became intensely interested in citizenship education. Condorcet would write about education in France and Diderot about education in Russia, for example. See Gilead (2021, especially pp. 21–24).

the task of helping citizens recognize each other's dignity and live harmoniously. Rousseau may be fairly criticized for the inadequacy of some of his political and educational principles, but underlying his philosophy is a sincere hope that citizens can relate to each other better, wherever they may find themselves.

References

Darling, J. (1982). Education as horticulture: Some growth theorists and their critics. *Journal of Philosophy of Education*, 16(2), 173–85.

Dewey, J. (1916). *Democracy and education: An introduction to the philosophy of education*. New York: The Free Press.

Dewey, J., & Dewey, E. (1915). *Schools of to-morrow*. New York: E. P. Dutton.

Gilead, T. (2021). Introduction: Enlightenment and education. In T. Gilead, ed., *A history of western philosophy of education in the age of enlightenment*. London: Bloomsbury, pp. 1–43.

Hofman, A. (2021). Rousseau's philosophy of education. In T. Gilead, ed., *A history of western philosophy of education in the age of enlightenment*. London: Bloomsbury, pp. 69–96.

Iheoma, E. O. (1997). Rousseau's views on teaching. *Journal of Educational Thought*, 31, 69–81.

Jonas, M. E. (2016). Rousseau on sex-roles, education and happiness. *Studies in Philosophy and Education*, 35(2), 145–61.

Michaud, O. (2012). Thinking about the nature and role of authority in democratic education with Rousseau's *Emile*. *Educational Theory*, 62(3), 287–304.

Mintz, A. I. (2012). The happy and suffering student? Rousseau's *Emile* and the path not taken in progressive educational thought. *Educational Theory*, 62(3), 249–65.

Mintz, A. I. (2016). Dewey's ancestry, Dewey's legacy, and the aims of education in democracy and education. *European Journal of Pragmatism and American Philosophy*, 8(VIII–1). doi: doi.org/10.4000/ejpap.437.

Mintz, A. (2018). Sparta, Athens, and the surprising roots of common schooling. *Philosophy of Education*, 74, 105–16.

Oelkers, J. (2008). *Jean-Jacques Rousseau*. London: Bloomsbury.

Roosevelt, G. G. (1990). *Reading Rousseau in the nuclear age*. Philadelphia, PA: Temple University Press.

Roosevelt, G. G. (2021). Educational legacies of the French Enlightenment. In T. Gilead, ed., *A history of western philosophy of education in the age of enlightenment*. London: Bloomsbury, pp. 97–124.

Rosenow, E. (1980). Rousseau's "Emile," an anti-utopia. *British Journal of Educational Studies*, 28(3), 212–24.

Rousseau, J.-J. (1750/1997). The First Discourse on the arts and sciences. In *Rousseau: The Discourses and other early political writings*. Trans. by V. Gourevitch, Cambridge: Cambridge University Press, pp. 1–28.

Rousseau, J.-J. (1755/1997). Political economy. In *Rousseau: The Social Contract and other later political writings*. Trans. by. V. Gourevitch, Cambridge, Cambridge University Press, pp. 3–38.

Rousseau, J.-J. (1762/1979). *Emile: Or on education*. Trans. by A. Bloom, New York: Basic.

Rousseau, J.-J. (1762/1997). The Social Contract. In *Rousseau: The Social Contract and other later political writings*. Trans. by V. Gourevitch, Cambridge: Cambridge University Press, pp. 39–152.

Rousseau, J.-J. (1764/2005). *Plan for a constitution for Corsica*. In *The plan for perpetual peace, on the government of Poland, and other writings on history and politics*. Trans. by C. Kelly & J. Bush, Chicago, IL: Dartmouth College Press, pp. 123–55.

Rousseau, J.-J. (1772/1997). *Considerations on the government of Poland*. In *Rousseau: The Social Contract and other later political writings*. Trans. by V. Gourevitch, Cambridge: Cambridge University Press, pp. 177–260.

Rush, B. (1786). Thoughts upon the mode of education proper in a republic. In F. Rudolph, ed., *Essays on education in the early republic*. Harvard, MA: Harvard University Press, pp. 25–40.

Schaeffer, D. (2013). *Rousseau on education, freedom, and judgment*. University Park, PA: Penn State University Press.

Wain, K. (2011). *On Rousseau: An introduction to his radical thinking on education and politics. Vol. 3*. Rotterdam: Sense Publishers.

Walter, S. (1996). The "flawed parent": A reconsideration of Rousseau's *Emile* and its significance for radical education in the United States. *British Journal of Educational Studies*, 44(3), 260–74.

Weiss, P. A. (1993). *Gendered community: Rousseau, sex, and politics*. New York: New York University Press.

5

Dewey on Democratic Education

Natalia Rogach Alexander

5.1 The Democratic Character and Its Critics

Skepticism about democratic education is as old as Plato's *Republic*. Socrates charged Athenian democracy with miseducating its citizens: cultivating characters that are inconstant, superficial, easily swayed by appetite, obstinately unwilling to "admit any word of truth" (Plato, 1992, pp. 231–32). Democracies have certainly changed since Plato's time, but skepticism persists. In twentieth-century America, Walter Lippmann took inspiration from Plato in painting an unflattering portrait of democratic citizens. We're blinded by stereotype, prejudice, and propaganda. Since efforts to educate "omnicompetent" citizens will inevitably fail, those who put faith in democratic education are indulging in a "barren" fantasy (Lippmann, 1997, p. 79).

John Dewey once said that Plato's dialogues were his "favorite philosophic reading" (Dewey, 1930; LW 5: p. 154).[1] More "urbane" and "lucid" than the moderns (1925; LW 2: p. 140), the ancient Athenian taught Dewey to recognize the importance of education to philosophy. The social arrangements we inhabit shape who we become. Moreover, schooling is a powerful tool for molding and maintaining forms of social life:

> It would be impossible to find in any scheme of philosophic thought [other than Plato's] a more adequate recognition on one hand of the educational significance of social arrangements and, on the other, of the dependence of those arrangements upon the means used to educate the young. (1916; MW 9: p. 95)

While he admired Plato, Dewey couldn't have disagreed more with the *Republic's* apparent indictment of the democratic individual.[2] His life's work was devoted

[1] When citing John Dewey, I refer to the edition of his works published by the University of Southern Illinois Press. That edition is divided into Early, Middle, and Later Works. For instance (1930; LW 5: p. 154) refers to page 154 of Volume 5 of the Later Works.

[2] In this chapter, I focus on Dewey's reading of Plato. I set aside the question of whether Dewey was correct in reading Plato this way. Even if he was wrong, it helps us grasp his vision. Of course, Plato may not have been a simple-minded "Platonist" in the sense Dewey attributed to him. For a different reading of Plato, see Curren (1993a; 1993b; 1994).

to elaborating a competing vision of the democratic ethos and of the character it nurtures. He once remarked that to safeguard democracy, we ought to have "a sense of something fine and great for which to live" (1941; LW 14: p. 263). It isn't an exaggeration to say that his reflections on democracy and education were offered in that spirit. Not just a technical account of the minutiae of school curricula, but a rich and inspiring vision of who we might become if we're willing to make the effort. In this sense, *Democracy and Education* was itself a contribution to the American democratic ethos. The Deweyan "democratic individual" (1939; LW 14: p. 92) is neither the vacillating dilettante depicted in the *Republic*, nor the "omnicompetent" everyman whose existence Lippmann rightly doubted. In this paper, I offer a reconstruction of Dewey's alternative – and of its relevance to the present times.[3]

5.2 A Different Portrait

What kind of characters might develop in a flourishing democratic culture? What citizen virtues are needed to safeguard democracy against its ever-present enemies? These questions have to do with education *by* and *for* democracy. Dewey reflected on both. Still, it isn't easy to get a clear-cut portrait of the "democratic individual" (1939; LW 14: p. 92) from his vast 37 volume oeuvre. The best place to start is with his most famous book. Published in 1916, *Democracy and Education* is one of the most celebrated treatises on democratic education ever written. Packed with discussions of concrete classroom problems (should teachers emphasize discipline or interest? work or play?), it's commonly read as a handbook for "progressive" schooling. What isn't properly recognized is that *Democracy and Education* is part of the pragmatist's broad inquiry into human development and flourishing. Because that larger project has never been fully understood, Dewey's nuanced reflections on democratic education have often been reduced to a collection of clichés: the value of group-work, the importance of active participation, the urgency of connecting "bookish" studies to life. To be sure, Dewey's critique of the drudgery of early twentieth-century schooling was pioneering in its time. But the innovative classroom techniques he championed can't be understood in isolation from his overarching reflections on the centrality of growth to human flourishing and development.

Like Plato, Dewey wanted to connect reflections on schooling "to serious and thoughtful conceptions of life" (1916; MW 9: p. 339), to inquiry into human flourishing:

[3] Scholarship on Dewey's conception of democracy often focuses on epistemic justification and inquiry. See, for instance, Festenstein (2019, pp. 217–41), Misak (2013, p. 136). Bohman (2010, pp. 49–68) focuses on the "epistemic division of labor" in democracy. Rogers (2010, pp. 69–91) focuses on expertise. Rogers (2009) and Talisse (2011) debate the potential tension between Deweyan democracy and pluralism. In this chapter, my focus is different. My aim is to add to the existing literature specifically by probing the complex connection between democracy and *education* in Dewey's thought. Moreover, I take myself to be adding to the existing literature on Deweyan democratic education (see, for instance, Fesmire, 2015; Jackson, 2018; by offering a new reconstruction of Dewey's puzzling notion of growth, showing how it illuminates his portrait of the democratic individual and his conception of the relationship between education and democracy.

> [In Ancient Greece] the educational enterprise was taken seriously. *It was regarded as the systematic means by which the good life was to be arrived at and maintained*: the life full, excellent, rich, for the individual centre of that life, and the life good for the community of which the individual was a member. (1930; LW 5: p. 291, my emphasis)

Inspired by the ancient project, *Democracy and Education* was Dewey's modern answer to Plato's *Republic*.[4] Its most important notion is also its least well-understood. The proper goal of schooling, Dewey tells us, is lifelong "growth" (1916; MW 9: p. 56) – "the evolution of conscious life" (1916; MW 9: pp. 369–70). Schooling should shape "a character which ... is interested in the continuous readjustment ... essential to *growth*" (1916; MW 9: p. 370, my emphasis). The appeal to "growth" may sound superficially plausible, but not particularly illuminating. Dewey never explained exactly what he had in mind. No study to date has done full justice to this central concept. Getting a proper grasp of his position requires doing additional work, sifting through his vast *oeuvre* to reconstruct his understanding of human psychology. But the effort is worth the trouble.

William James' groundbreaking *Principles of Psychology* had a decisive influence on Dewey.[5] Its "biological conception of the *psyche* ... worked its way more and more into all my ideas and acted as a ferment to transform old beliefs" (1930; LW 5: p. 157). Another source was Darwin,[6] whose work "introduced a new intellectual temper" (1909; MW 4: p. 3). This frame of mind abandons "the superiority of the fixed and final" (1909; MW 4: p. 3) in favor of constant, incremental improvement. Not static perfection – continuous, gradual development became the goal of Dewey's forays into a number of areas: metaphilosophy, ethics, politics, aesthetics, and education. The pragmatist focused on identifying sources of confinement and suffering (the dullness of traditional schoolrooms among them) in order to improve how we live.

Inspired by James and Darwin, Dewey saw human beings as biological organisms whose activities are largely governed by (revisable) habits (1922; MW 14: p. 25).[7] *Democracy and Education* recognizes that habits can be useful: "Routine action, action which is automatic, may increase skill to do a particular thing" (1916; MW 9: p. 84; the point is echoed in 1922; MW 14: p. 121). Habits allow us to be good at repetitive, specialized tasks. Their importance shouldn't be

[4] It was also a response to Rousseau, who was one of Dewey's explicit interlocutors. Like Plato's *Republic* and Dewey's *Democracy and Education*, Rousseau's *Emile* offers a portrait of the democratic character, one whose "spirit of peace is an effect of his education which ... has diverted him from seeking his pleasures in domination and in another's unhappiness" (Rousseau, 1979, p. 251). On Rousseau's conception of human psychology and its influence on his political philosophy, see Neuhouser (2008).

[5] See James (1983). Dewey acknowledged James' influence in his autobiographical essay: "As far as I can discover one specifiable philosophic factor which entered into my thinking so as to give it a new direction and quality, it is this one" (1930; LW 5: p. 157).

[6] Darwin's significance for Dewey is captured in "The Influence of Darwinism on Philosophy" (1909; MW 4: pp. 3–14).

[7] *Human Nature and Conduct* (1922; MW 14) contains Dewey's account of how habits can be intelligently revised through the process of deliberation. It involves, among other things, taking an intelligent, sympathetic and imaginative survey of the habit's consequences.

underestimated. Like Aristotle, Dewey believed that virtues and vices are habits (1922; MW 14: p. 25). Though they're essential to our functioning, habits can limit our horizons. We can get stuck in routines. Overly rigid habits can prevent us from appreciating and interacting with the world in all its richness (1934; LW 10: p. 110). Blindly following unalterable habits can impoverish our lives. Worse still, defective habits can confine us and our fellow human beings. They can turn into prejudices that cause a vast amount of suffering. Dewey thought such defective habits underlie racism and sexism, "social diseases" that ought to be eradicated (1922; MW 13: pp. 242–43). These habits must be revised. Doing so will remove barriers to human flourishing. This is echoed in "Creative Democracy," which sees the democratic way of life as fundamentally committed to eradicating prejudice (1939; LW 14: pp. 224–30).

Growth can be "social as well as personal" (1916; MW 9: p. 85). It occurs when we revise our individual and collective habits in the interest of gradually removing barriers to human flourishing.[8] Why do we need growth? To solve the problems we face and to enhance our experience. As Dewey saw it, a perfect set of fixed habits is a utopian fantasy. The environment keeps changing (1922; MW 14: p. 38). New problems constantly emerge, making it impossible to achieve a permanent adaptation. As our habits evolve, so do the problems we face, necessitating further revisions. Sometimes, we start to appreciate previously overlooked forms of confinement and suffering. The challenge of remaking our habits in order to remove barriers to our individual and collective flourishing is one that continues as long as we live.

The Deweyan self embraces lifelong growth. Central to this process is the ability to engage in free, sympathetic, open-minded dialogue with others and to imagine the consequences of various habits in a responsible and compassionate way (1916; MW 9: p. 127 and 1922; MW 14: pp. 144, 169). This sort of dialogue helps us identify and solve problems. It also enriches our lives (1916; MW 9: pp. 8–9 and 1939; LW 14: p. 228). Deweyan growth isn't just a chore. It is itself an essential component of a flourishing life. As we revise our habits, we gain new ways of interacting with "the world of things and persons" (1925; LW 1: p. 188). We learn to appreciate hitherto overlooked aspects of experience. Letting go of confining prejudice, we come to see one another anew, as if for the first time (1934; LW 10: p. 59). All this enriches our lives.

Democracy and Education defines all genuine education as growth. It suggests that preparing students for lifelong growth in their community is the proper goal of schooling:

> The something for which a man must be good is capacity to live as a social member so that what he gets from living with others balances with what he contributes. What he gets and gives as a human being ... is not external possessions, but *a widening and deepening of conscious life* – a more intense, disciplined, and expanding realization of meanings. What he materially receives and gives is at most opportunities and means for *the evolution of*

[8] For a contemporary account of what this sort of growth might look like on the wider social level, see Kitcher (2017b; 2021a).

> *conscious life.* . . . Discipline, culture, social efficiency, personal refinement, improvement of character are but phases of *the growth of capacity nobly to share in such a balanced experience*. And education is not a mere means to such a life. *Education is such a life.* (1916; MW 9: pp. 369–70, my emphases)

The Deweyan democratic individual is a growing personality. Her capacities – intelligence, creativity, sympathy, autonomy – develop together with the democratic ethos she helps shape. She's willing "to break away from current and established classifications and interpretations of the world" (1925; LW 1: p. 170), prepared to revise individual and collective habits in an open-minded dialogue with other democratic citizens. Her mind is "individualized, initiating, adventuring, experimenting, dissolving" (1925; LW 1: p. 188). She treats other human beings with respect, as partners with whom she's engaged in a joint project and from whom she might learn (1939; LW 14: pp. 224–30). She's able to communicate and cooperate across social divides and to engage sympathetically with a wide range of human predicaments (1916; MW 9: p. 127). In considering the consequences of her actions and habits, she's responsible and sensitive to the needs of others (1916; MW 9: pp. 366–67). Shaping the conditions under which she lives enhances her autonomy. As she explores and seeks "the good life" in open-ended inquiry with fellow democratic citizens, she grows in her appreciation of the range of values and meanings of existence. A genuine "individual" involved in reshaping herself and the social world she inhabits by drawing on her "irreducible uniqueness" (1925; LW 1: p. 187), she's neither mediocre nor conformist. The democratic individual grows together with the form of social life she helps develop. Her growth-enabling skills allow her to contribute to the never-ending "evolution of conscious life" (1916; MW 9: pp. 369–70). She eschews fatalism in favor of making changes to "a world which is not all in, and never will be, a world which in some respect is incomplete and in the making, and which in these respects may be made this way or that according as men judge, prize, love and labor" (1919; MW 11: p. 50).

What does this have to do with democracy? As Dewey saw it, democracy isn't just a set of governmental institutions. It's a culture, an ethos, "a *personal* way of individual life . . . it signifies the possession and continual use of certain attitudes, forming personal character and determining desire and purpose in all the relations of life" (1939; LW 14: p. 226). Moreover, democracy is "creative" (1939; LW 14: p. 225, and 1927; LW 2: pp. 256–57, and 1937; LW 11: p. 182).[9] It "must be continually explored afresh" (1937; LW 11: p. 182). When, in 1941, he addressed young people disillusioned with democracy's failings, he told them it's "a moving thing . . . [I]ts possibilities are far from exhausted" (1941; LW 14: p. 263). He hoped he could imbue them with "a sense of unrealized possibilities opening new horizons which will inspire them to creative effort" (1941; LW 14: p. 263).

[9] On Dewey's thesis that democracy is creative, see Bernstein (2000, p. 226; 2010). For other reconstructions of Dewey's conception of democracy, see also Bernstein (2010), Pappas (2008), Rockefeller (1991), Rogers (2016), Ryan (1995), Seigfried (1999), Westbrook (1991).

Essential to Dewey's vision was his adamant insistence on "liberal democratic means" (1937; LW 11: p. 298) by which alone barriers to human flourishing should be gradually removed: "consultation ... conference ... persuasion ... discussion in the formation of public opinion" (1937; LW 11: p. 297), "the voluntary activities of individuals in opposition to coercion ... assent and consent in opposition to violence" (1937; LW 11: p. 298). Against the backdrop of the rise of totalitarianism, he emphasized the importance of liberty, autonomy and individuality:

> In re-thinking the issue in the light of the rise of totalitarian states, I am led to emphasize the idea that only the voluntary initiative and voluntary cooperation of individuals can produce social institutions that will protect the liberties necessary for achieving development of genuine individuality. / This change in emphasis ... attaches fundamental importance to the activities of individuals in determining the social conditions under which they live. (1939; LW 14: p. 92)

Dewey didn't seek one perfect, fixed way of being, to be imposed on citizens by philosopher-kings. He envisaged a society that provides its members with the conditions necessary for developing their "irreducible uniqueness" (1925; LW 1: p. 187) within the social matrix as they help determine the conditions under which they live, in consultation with others.[10]

Schooling should prepare democratic citizens to engage in free, open-ended inquiry into how they should live together – one that involves a wide range of perspectives in a conversation aimed at gradually enhancing human flourishing. Taking part in this enterprise is itself a lifelong educative project (1916; MW 9: pp. 369–70).

5.3 Reexamining Schooling

We now have a better understanding of Dewey's unorthodox position. Deweyan democratic schooling prepares human beings for lifelong growth in a developing community.[11] They're educated to take part in an evolving ethos – one that gradually removes barriers to human flourishing through free consultation, open-minded inquiry, voluntary cooperation, creative experimentation, and sympathetic mutual engagement. Although he sought ways to enhance human flourishing, Dewey was a liberal and a meliorist. He put democratic citizens – not philosopher-kings – in charge. We're responsible for seeking "the good life" together. Deweyan democracy evolves in a direction specified by its members, who have developed the skills they need to take charge of this process:

[10] Among other reasons, Dewey believed that "a progressive society counts individual variations as precious since it finds in them the means of its own growth" (1916; MW 9: p. 315).

[11] For instance, *Democracy and Education* argues that instruction should aim "to shape the experiences of the young so that instead of reproducing current habits, better habits shall be formed, and thus the future adult society be an improvement on their own" (1916; MW 9: p. 85).

autonomy, creativity, open-mindedness, readiness to overcome confining prejudice, initiative, intelligent criticism, flexibility, cooperation, sympathy, and respect for other human beings and for different points of view (among other virtues).

This means that democratic education should be expanded. "To teach children the constitution of the United States, the nature and working of various parts of government machinery" (1902; MW 2: p. 83) isn't enough. *Democracy and Education* criticizes early twentieth-century schooling for fostering apathy, estrangement, docility, and social divisions – instead of the skills needed for lifelong growth in a democratic community. The book advocates innovative teaching methods aimed at enhancing sympathy, communicative and cooperative skills (1916; MW 9: p. 127),[12] autonomy, creativity, initiative, flexibility, open-mindedness, and responsibility in considering the consequences of one's actions and habits (1916; MW 9: pp. 366–67). "Creative Democracy" emphasizes tolerance, trust, sympathy, the ability to respect different points of view, the habit of resolving conflicts through dialogue instead of force, readiness to overcome confining prejudice, the habit of respecting all human beings as engaged in a joint project of figuring out how we should live together (1939; LW 14: p. 228). These skills can be practiced in "miniature communities" (1916; MW 9: p. 370) that embody the democratic ethos. Character education doesn't consist in "merely adding on a special course for direct instruction in good behavior" (1934; LW 9: p. 192). The Deweyan school is "organized as a community in which pupils share," where they get "practice in the give and take of social life, practice in methods of cooperation" (1934; LW 9: p. 192). This sort of school isn't just a place of formal instruction. Like Jane Addams' Hull House settlement that inspired it, it's "a social center":[13]

> [T]here is mixing people up with each other; bringing them together under wholesome influences, and under conditions which will promote their getting acquainted with the best side of each other . . . It is not merely a place where ideas and beliefs may be exchanged, not merely in the arena of formal discussion . . . but in ways where ideas are incarnated in human form and clothed with the winning grace of personal life. (1902; MW 2: pp. 90–91)

In our time, Dewey challenges us to take a fresh look at our educative practices. Do they prepare democratic citizens for lifelong growth – or for a few "utilitarian ends narrowly conceived for the masses" (1916; MW 9: p. 200)? Do they encourage cooperation and sympathy – or narrow-minded, self-centered competitiveness? Are individuality, creativity, and autonomy stifled by dogmatic teaching methods? Are students developing the communicative skills needed to talk across social divides? What are schools doing to cultivate respect for other human beings and the ability to overcome confining prejudice? Are "bookish studies" (1916; MW 9: p. 159) connected with live issues of wide human

[12] Dewey's plea to cultivate skills that can help students communicate across social divides resonates with the concerns expressed in Anderson (2007).

[13] On the influence of Jane Addams on Dewey, see Seigfried (1999).

concern, with the problems facing our democracy? Are students being educated to explore and seek "the good life" together? Do schools provide all students with an education that prepares them for "a life worth living" (1920; MW 12: pp. 200–01),[14] regardless of their "race, sex, class or economic status" (1920; MW 12: p. 186)?[15]

Answering such questions is still "the task before us" (1939; LW 14). For democratic citizens aren't to be educated merely for being slotted into some predetermined pattern of life. They should be educated to take part in shaping it together. That's why the "humanistic" aspects of democratic education shouldn't be ignored:

> Democratic society is peculiarly dependent for its maintenance upon the use in forming a course of study of *criteria which are broadly human.* Democracy cannot flourish where the chief influences in selecting subject matter of instruction are *utilitarian ends narrowly conceived for the masses* … The notion that the "essentials" of education are the three R's mechanically treated, is based upon ignorance of the essentials needed for realization of democratic ideals. (1916; MW 9: p. 200, my emphases)

When, in Depression-era America, proponents of austerity argued against school "frills" like teaching "music and dramatics," Dewey countered that the "democratic social experiment" (1933; LW 9: p. 141) is a demanding project that requires increasing public access to education in the arts and humanities.[16] He would have been appalled by the current trend of sidelining these subjects, seeing it as deeply mistaken. A critic "… who is active in attacking our schools because of their 'frills' … disbelieves in the whole democratic endeavor" (1933; LW 9: p. 142). The arts (and other growth-enabling, creative studies) aren't just useless luxuries for the few. They enrich our lives. They cultivate our characters. They contribute to our ability to explore and seek "the good life" together. They help extend our sympathy for specific human predicaments. Sometimes, they help us overcome the prejudices that blind and separate us (1934; LW 10: p. 110). As I argue elsewhere, Dewey's *Art as Experience* offers us a nuanced, underappreciated account of the educative value of the arts and their role in enhancing the democratic ethos.[17] In an age when an overemphasis on science, technology, engineering, and mathematics (STEM) and technical training threatens to sideline subjects offering students a chance to explore "the good

[14] For a more recent exploration of this question, see Kitcher (2012; 2021b).

[15] In his concern about providing rich educative opportunities for all human beings, regardless of their "race, sex, class or economic status" (1920; MW 12: p. 186), Dewey may be seen as an ally of W. E. B. Du Bois. For Du Bois' critique of how racial injustice undermines education, see Du Bois (1997; 1999; 2001).

[16] Already in his earliest writings on education, Dewey reflected on the importance of the aesthetic (1897; EW 5: pp. 202–03). For the most complete account of Dewey's aesthetics, see *Art as Experience* (1934; LW 10).

[17] See Alexander, N. R. *Taking education seriously: Dewey and his Interlocutors* (n.d.). Dewey's vision of this resonates with recent defenses of the importance of the arts and humanities. See, for instance, Elgin (2009), Gooding-Williams (2021), Kitcher (2013; 2021b), Moody-Adams (2015; 2022), Nussbaum (2010). On pragmatist aesthetics, see also Shusterman (1992).

life" together, Dewey's vision of the "essentials needed" for democracy sounds as provocative as it did a hundred years ago.

5.4 An Antidote to Disenchantment

Why read Dewey today? Reconstructing his demanding vision of democratic education isn't just a scholarly indulgence. It reveals an important set of ideas that can help address some of our current troubles: confining prejudice, social division, estrangement, and disenchantment with democracy. Offered almost a hundred years ago, his diagnosis of democracy's troubles sounds eerily prescient. It could have been written today:

> The other especially urgent need is connected with the present unprecedented wave of nationalistic sentiment, of racial and national prejudice, of readiness to resort to force of arms. . . . We now know the enemy; it is out in the open. Unless the schools of the world can unite in effort to rebuild the spirit of common understanding, of mutual sympathy and goodwill among all peoples and races, to exorcise the demon of prejudice, isolation and hatred, they themselves are likely to be submerged by the general return to barbarism, the sure outcome of present tendencies if unchecked by the forces which education alone can evoke and fortify. (1934; LW 9: pp. 203–04)

We, too, are living through a "wave of nationalistic sentiment, of racial and national prejudice, of readiness to resort to force of arms." We, too, face the task of cultivating democratic individuals who will maintain and enhance our democratic ethos. As he watched the rise of totalitarianism in Nazi Germany, Dewey cautioned that "individuals who prize their own liberties and who prize the liberties of other individuals, individuals who are democratic in thought and action, are the sole final warrant for the existence and endurance of democratic institutions" (1939; LW14: p. 92). Properly educating democratic citizens is essential for safeguarding democracy.[18] "Without this basis, it [government] is worth nothing. A gust of prejudice, a blow of despotism, and it falls like a card house" (1888; EW 1: p. 240). We shouldn't act "as if our democracy were something that perpetuated itself automatically" (1939; LW 14: p. 225). Connected to the idea that democracy is a way of life is a provocative insight: it's up to us to make it work.[19]

[18] That's why Dewey believed philosophy of education isn't merely a peripheral subject; it's central to political philosophy: "For the habits formed decide in the long run . . . the kind of customs and institutions which come to prevail socially" (1941; LW 14: p. 323). For a more recent defense of the importance of education to political philosophy, see also Honneth (2015).

[19] Was Dewey too optimistic about democracy's prospects? He was certainly an optimist. But his faith in democracy was neither "Panglossian" nor "blind." Moved by Lippmann's criticisms, Dewey called them "perhaps the most effective indictment of democracy as currently conceived ever penned" (1922; MW 13: p. 337). The influence of prejudice, hatred, and propaganda on the democratic public troubled him deeply (1925; LW 2: p. 215). Still, he didn't see these problems as insoluble. The temper of classical American pragmatism is one of modest optimism premised on making an effort to improve

In our day, Dewey is important not just because of his insights into "progressive" schooling, but also because of his affirming vision of democratic life. It's a vital antidote to disenchantment. The great American pragmatist realized that skepticism can be a self-fulfilling prophecy. For close to a century, he resisted its seductive appeal, defending democracy against its ever-present detractors: radicals wanting to achieve social advances by undemocratic means,[20] philosophical skeptics,[21] disillusioned members of the public who had lost "confidence in the democratic way of life" (1941; LW 14: p. 263). When he spoke in 1941, Dewey could have been addressing all those taken aback by democracy's current troubles:

> It is also possible that, after suffering and agony, the change may be for a better society, making possible a freer and more secure life for all. *This better prospect can become an actuality only as our defense takes the form of creative activity to make the democratic way of life a deeper and wider reality than it has been* . . . We are still a young nation measured in years of existence. We are old in spirit if we cannot once more by the example of our own form of life point out the way in which the nations of the earth can walk in freedom and cooperative peace. (1941; LW 14: pp. 264–65, my emphasis)

It isn't just his faith in the possibility of improving our democratic culture that's important. It's Dewey vision of the promise of that culture. Against all those who view the democratic individual with scorn, he offered us a portrait of the democratic individual whose life is rich and flourishing. In our troubled times, it can still give us "a sense of something fine and great for which to live" (1941; LW 14: p. 263).[22]

Why care about democracy? One answer is that it's the "least bad" set of governmental institutions. Dewey saw it differently. Safeguarding and taking part in the democratic ethos enriches our lives. We join together in the demanding project of elaborating the meanings and values guiding our existence. We break through barriers by entering alien points of view. Finding

life. Our endeavors "carry the universe forward" (1925; LW 1: p. 214). Reforming democratic education can help us address some of our present troubles. Of course, success is never guaranteed – Dewey was clear-eyed enough to recognize this (1925; LW 1: pp. 313–14, 326). But to embrace skepticism and disenchantment is to abandon our responsibility for shaping and safeguarding democracy, creating a self-fulfilling prophecy. To be sure, we can never get to "perfect" education. Nor can we hope to create a "perfect" democratic culture or character. The best way to read Dewey is as a meliorist who suggested lines along which we can make gradual improvements. (In reading Dewey this way, I'm indebted to Kitcher 2017a). I offer a more in-depth probing of Dewey's optimism in Alexander, N. R. *Taking education seriously: Dewey and his Interlocutors* (n.d.).

[20] See, for instance, "Democracy is Radical," where Dewey argued against radicals who wanted to achieve their ends by undemocratic means (1937; LW 11: p. 298). Among other things, he wrote: "The idea that those who possess power never surrender it save when forced to do so by superior physical power, applies to *dictatorships that claim to operate in behalf of the oppressed masses while actually operating to wield power against the masses*" (1937; LW 11: p. 298, my emphasis).

[21] See Dewey's review of and response to Lippmann's work (1922; MW 13: p. 337). For an exploration of the Dewey–Lippmann debate, see Bohman (2010); Festenstein (2019); Rogers (2010). That literature addresses questions of expertise and epistemic justification. My focus here is different: democratic education.

[22] In this sense, Dewey's writings on democracy resonate with the vision offered in Whitman's *Democratic Vistas* (2010), which conceives of democracy as an educative culture that shapes a worthwhile life and a rich character. On the connection between Dewey and Whitman, see Rorty (1998).

unanticipated connections with others gives us a renewed sense of "community of experience" (1934; LW 10: p. 337). When we overcome the prejudices that confine us, we succeed in truly seeing other human beings and being seen (1934; LW 10: p. 59). Democracy isn't just the least bad set of institutions. It's an educative culture that helps us grow:

> This educational process is based upon faith in human good sense and human good will as it manifests itself in the long run when communication is progressively liberated from bondage to prejudice and ignorance. It constitutes a firm and continuous reminder that the process of living together, when it is emancipated from oppressions and suppressions, becomes . . . a constant growth of that kind of understanding of our relations to one another that expels fear, suspicion and distrust. (1950; LW 17: p. 86)

References

Works by Dewey

Dewey, J. (1888). *The ethics of democracy*. *EW* 1: 227–49.
Dewey, J. (1897). *The aesthetic element in education*. *EW* 5: 202–03.
Dewey, J. (1902). *The school as social centre*. *MW* 2: 80–93.
Dewey, J. (1909). *The influence of Darwinism on philosophy*. *MW* 4: 3–14.
Dewey, J. (1916). *Democracy and education*. *MW* 9.
Dewey, J. (1919). *Philosophy and democracy*. *MW* 11: 41–53.
Dewey, J. (1920). *Reconstruction in philosophy*. *MW* 12: 80–201.
Dewey, J. (1922). *Racial prejudice and friction*. *MW* 13: 242–54.
Dewey, J. (1922). *Review of public opinion by Walter Lippmann*. *MW* 13: 337–44.
Dewey, J. (1922). *Human nature and conduct*. *MW* 14.
Dewey, J. (1925). *Experience and nature*. *LW* 1.
Dewey, J. (1925). *The "Socratic Dialogues" of Plato*. *LW* 2: 124–40.
Dewey, J. (1925). *Practical democracy: Review of Lippmann's The Phantom Public*. *LW* 2: 213–20.
Dewey, J. (1927). *The public and its problems*. *LW* 2: 235–372.
Dewey, J. (1930). *From absolutism to experimentalism*. *LW* 5: 147–60.
Dewey, J. (1930). *Philosophy and education*. *LW* 5: 289–98.
Dewey, J. (1933). *Shall we abolish school "frills"?* *LW* 9: 141–46.
Dewey, J. (1934). *Character training for youth*. *LW* 9: 186–93.
Dewey, J. (1934). *The need for a philosophy of education*. *LW* 9: 194–204.
Dewey, J. (1934). *Art as experience*. *LW* 10.
Dewey, J. (1937). *The challenge of democracy to education*. *LW* 11: 181–90.
Dewey, J. (1937). *Democracy is radical*. *LW* 11: 296–99.
Dewey, J. (1939). *I believe*. *LW* 14: 91–97.
Dewey, J. (1939). *Creative democracy: The task before us*. *LW* 14: 224–30.
Dewey, J. (1941). *Address of welcome to the league for industrial democracy*. *LW* 14: 262–65.

Dewey, J. (1941). *Lessons from the war – in philosophy. LW* 14: 312–34.
Dewey, J. (1950). *John Dewey responds. LW* 17: 84–87.

Works by Other Authors

Alexander, N. R. (n.d). *Taking education seriously: Dewey and his interlocutors.* (Unpublished manuscript).

Anderson, E. (2007). Fair opportunity in education: A democratic equality perspective. *Ethics*, 117(4), 595–622.

Bernstein, R. (2000). Creative democracy – The task still before us. *American Journal of Theology and Philosophy*, 21(3), 215–28.

Bernstein, R. (2010). *The pragmatic turn*. Cambridge, MA: Polity.

Bohman, J. (2010). Participation through publics: Did Dewey answer Lippmann? *Contemporary Pragmatism*, 7(1), 49–68.

Curren, R. (1993a). Justice, instruction, and the good: The case for public education in Aristotle and Plato's laws, part I: Groundwork for an interpretation of politics VIII.1. *Studies in Philosophy and Education*, 11(4), 293–311.

Curren, R. (1993b). Justice, instruction, and the good: The case for public education in Aristotle and Plato's laws, part II: Why education is important enough to merit the legislator's attention. *Studies in Philosophy and Education*, 12(2–4), 103–26.

Curren, R. (1994). Justice, instruction, and the good: The case for public education in Aristotle and Plato's laws, part III: Why education should be public and the same for all. *Studies in Philosophy and Education*, 13(1), 1–31.

Du Bois, W. E. B. (1997). *The souls of black folk*. Ed. by D. W. Blight & R. Gooding-Williams, Boston/New York: Bedford/St. Martin's.

Du Bois, W. E. B. (1999). *Darkwater: Voices from within the veil*. Mineola, New York: Dover Publications.

Du Bois, W. E. B. (2001). *The education of black people: Ten critiques*. New York: Monthly Review Press.

Elgin, C. Z. (2009). Art and education. In H. Siegel, ed., *The Oxford handbook of philosophy of education*. Oxford/New York: Oxford University Press, p. 316.

Fesmire, S. (2015). *Dewey*. London and New York: Routledge.

Festenstein, M. (2019). Does Dewey have an "epistemic argument" for democracy? *Contemporary Pragmatism*, 16(2–3), 217–41.

Gooding-Williams, R. (2021). *Beauty as propaganda: On the political aesthetics of W.E.B. Du Bois*. Dewey lecture in Law and Philosophy. University of Chicago.

Honneth, A. (2015). Education and the democratic public sphere: A neglected chapter of political philosophy. In J. Jakobsen & O. Lysaker, eds., *Recognition and freedom: Axel Honneth's political thought*. Leiden: Brill, pp. 17–32.

James, W. (1983). *Principles of psychology*. Cambridge, MA: Harvard University Press.

Jackson, J. (2018). *Equality beyond debate: John Dewey's pragmatic idea of democracy*. New York: Cambridge University Press.

Kitcher, P. S. (2012). Education, democracy and capitalism. In P. Kitcher, ed., *Preludes to pragmatism: Toward a reconstruction of philosophy*. New York: Oxford University Press, pp. 344–62.

Kitcher, P. S. (2013). *Deaths in Venice*. New York: Columbia University Press.
Kitcher, P. S. (2017a). Dewey's conception of philosophy. In S. Fesmire, ed., *The Oxford handbook of Dewey*. New York: Oxford University Press, pp. 3–22.
Kitcher, P. S. (2017b). Social progress. *Social Philosophy and Policy*, 34(2), 46–65.
Kitcher, P. S. (2021a). *Moral progress*. New York: Oxford University Press.
Kitcher, P. S. (2021b). *The main enterprise of the world: Rethinking education*. New York: Oxford University Press.
Lippmann, W. (1997). *Public opinion*. New York: Free Press Paperbacks.
Misak, C. (2013). *The American pragmatists*. Oxford: Oxford University Press.
Moody-Adams, M. M. (2015). *Civic art of remembrance and the democratic imagination*. 56th Annual Bishop Hurst Lecture, American University.
Moody-Adams, M. M. (2022). Philosophy and the art of human flourishing. In J. Stuhr, ed., *Philosophy and human flourishing*. Oxford: Oxford University Press.
Neuhouser, F. (2008). *Rousseau's theodicy of self-love: Evil, rationality, and the drive for recognition*. New York: Oxford University Press.
Nussbaum, M. (2010). *Not for profit: Why democracy needs the humanities*. Princeton, NJ: Princeton University Press.
Pappas, G. F. (2008). *John Dewey's ethics: Democracy as experience*. Bloomington, IN: Indiana University Press.
Plato (1992). *Republic*. Trans. by G. M. A. Grube & C. D. C. Reeve, Indianapolis, IN: Hackett.
Rockefeller, S. (1991). *John Dewey: Religious faith and democratic humanism*. New York: Columbia University Press.
Rogers, M. (2009). Dewey, pluralism, and democracy: A response to Robert Talisse. *Transactions of the Charles S. Peirce Society*, 45(1), 75–79.
Rogers, M. (2010). Dewey and his vision of democracy. *Contemporary Pragmatism*, 7 (1), 69–91.
Rogers, M. (2016). Revisiting *The public and its problems*. In J. Dewey & M. Rogers, eds., *The public and its problems*. Athens, OH: Swallow Press, pp. 1–32.
Rorty, R. (1998). American national pride: Whitman and Dewey. In *Achieving our country*. Cambridge, MA: Harvard University Press.
Rousseau, J.-J. (1979). *Emile*. Trans. by A. Bloom. New York: Basic Books.
Ryan, A. (1995). *John Dewey and the high tide of American liberalism*. New York: W. W. Norton.
Seigfried, C. H. (1999). Socializing democracy: Jane Addams and John Dewey. *Philosophy of the Social Sciences*, 29(2), 207–30.
Shusterman, R. (1992). *Pragmatist aesthetics: Living beauty, rethinking art*. Cambridge, MA: Blackwell.
Talisse, R. B. (2011). A farewell to Deweyan democracy. *Political Studies*, 59, 509–26.
Westbrook, R. (1991). *John Dewey and American democracy*. Ithaca, NY: Cornell University Press.
Whitman, W. (2010). *Democratic vistas: The original edition in facsimile*. Ed. by E. Folsom, IA: University of Iowa Press.

6

Hannah Arendt on the Very Possibility of Democratic Education

Roland Reichenbach

6.1 Introduction

You have to agree with Kimberley Curtis when she claims that Hannah Arendt's political theory was "a kind of pedagogy about the wonder of the human condition of plurality" (Curtis, 1997, p. 34). Seemingly contrary to this description, however, it is indicated here that Arendt was not in the least of the opinion that you had to "educate" children in "publicness"! Because the public is not known for its leniency. Admittedly, public action represents a fresh start in each case, at times some kind of luck, yet always a risk, with which individuals prove that they are capable of practicing freedom. Arendt was more than skeptical of an education *toward* democracy as well as an education *as* democracy. Her exclusive understanding of the public realm and politics makes Arendt an irritating conversational partner for those who understand democratic education as, in the end, a variety of moral education. It could also be said that Arendt's thinking constitutes a provocation for all the pedagogues who would rather not distinguish between the social and the political dimension categorically (Reichenbach, 2021).

This apparent provocation is the focus of this chapter. In Section 6.2, Arendt is characterized as a pedagogue of the public realm and then, in Section 6.3, as an antipode to John Dewey. Section 6.4 illuminates Arendt's understanding of the political in its proximity to Jacques Rancière's thinking and, in Section 6.5, the question of whether this could be about a moral self-misunderstanding is raised. Concluding remarks assert the elementary political dimension of education – in line with, or yet despite, Arendt's insights and skepticism.

The pedagogical relevance of Arendt's thinking of the public realm is twofold. First, she is able to conceive an exquisite concept of the public realm that, from the perspective of political education, appears fundamentally more substantial and arguably more problematic than many of the blurred conceptions with which we are confronted in the relevant literature and which attest to the bareness of late modern political life. Second, Arendt as a pedagogue of the public realm is paradoxical and persuasive at the same time, in that it is especially easy to understand her belief that – and why – the practice of freedom, through which the public realm can always be born in the first place, is disruptive every time. The use of freedom, then, resembles a "plante sauvage," to use Alain Touraine's words (1997, p. 80), rather than an ornamental house plant. Therefore, from this perspective, it cannot be a serious task of late modern political education to arouse emotions of political self-efficacy, although this is – simultaneously, in an anachronistic manner and in a manner that has become not very convincing – proclaimed pertinently today in many places (Reichenbach, 2000b).

Following Arendt, it is possible to reconstruct where the boundaries of an education toward democracy have to lie so that democracy constitutes itself not only as an institution but also as a complete practice. Children and adolescents cannot be educated toward the public realm, but always, without doubt, toward the social realm; at most, those capabilities can be occasionally improved that, in general, enable human beings to engage and to withstand the rough winds of their counterparts. A "positive" pedagogics of the public realm would rather be understood as an affront against this idea of the public realm, inasmuch as the practice of freedom constitutes the democratic form of living. When it comes to pedagogical-political design wishes, therefore, Arendt's "pedagogics of the public realm" requires some form of abstinence – her "pedagogics" are completely in accordance with an *éducation négative*.

6.2 A Pedagogue of the Public Realm

For some time now, there has been a kind of Arendt boom, which – as with any boom– should be treated critically. The word "boom" not only refers to a strategic, marketing-bound exploitation of something that should essentially stay more humble; the delayed golden age of Arendtian thought may be connected to the fact that the concepts and opinions that have been shaped by her possess an unexpected actuality today. This applies most of all to her understanding of the public realm that Seyla Benhabib describes with good reason as "agonistic" (1995, p. 97ff.). This perspective whereby the public realm should be understood as a discursive, fleeting, and placeless fighting forum – a passionate fight for prestige and power – is of interest here.

Particularly noticeable is the stubborn refusal of Arendt – for some the most important political theoretician of the twentieth century – to adapt her understanding of politics and the public realm to so-called reality (or what passes as reality). This refusal is characterized by something almost ludicrous and, at the same time, by something worthy: to the proponents of realpolitik who do not give much credit to the *homo politicus* any more, she probably appears ludicrous; to those who still want to throw an anthropological and maybe existential philosophical glance at the possibility of the political life, she might seem worthy. Following Thomas Meyer (1994), it is possible to oppose Arendt and still appreciate her work greatly – she would rather "endure the desert and keep the consciousness of the oasis awake ... than to adapt the concepts to the circumstances in which there is, far and wide, no recognizable path left to the oasis" (p. 29). With Meyer, it can be claimed that a concept that would like to be more than a "melancholic memory of the oases during the walk through the endless deserts of history" (p. 29) would have to be more political, because an empirically unsubstantial concept would be "in itself unpolitical" (p. 36). Surely, you have to criticize Arendt in this course, but you also have to give credit to her initially, following Hauke Brunkhorst (1999) and against a common misunderstanding that Arendt's "perspective is never nostalgic. Her interest in past grandeur is completely focused on the current future (p. 9).

Now, the political realm in the spirit of the classical polis of which Arendt appears to be inspired is an expression of a *practice of freedom* of human kind (Arendt, 1994b). The political realm can be determined conceptually by its understanding as an attribute of value of politics with the criteria "communality," "public realm," and "freedom" at its center; "The political realm would then constitute good, successful policy – although not necessarily effective policy" (Vollrath, 1977, cited in Meyer, 1994, p. 23). In this sense, the political realm has to offer more than politics, namely the public life in which the actions of every individual set the conditions of everybody else's actions, and which is only able to be a "fleeting state of aggregation" in contrast to the "resilient consistency of mere politics" (p. 33). For Christian Meier, the classical perception of the political realm represented "a uniquely separate path in the history of humankind" (Meyer, 1994, p. 33). According to Thomas Meyer, Meier's reconstruction of the Greek political realm is more informative and more conclusive than Arendt's conception, because it would uncover "the internal relations of interdependence between the subjective and objective dimensions of the political realm" (Meyer, 1994, p. 33). Alternatively, the normative transformation of her public realm concept, which might not have been fully apparent to the author, represents its pedagogical appeal.

When Arendt is presented as a pedagogue of the public realm here, it has to be emphasized that the topic of education was not at center of her thinking. There is only one paper dedicated to the question of education. It was originally a a lecture that she gave in Bremen in 1958 with the title "Die Krise der Erziehung" ("The Crisis in Education") (Arendt, 1961, pp. 173–96). In this lecture, Arendt argues quite emotionally that there cannot be a "progressive education"; rather, education is a genuinely *conservative* activity in the sense that "by its very nature it cannot forgo either authority or tradition, and yet" – and here lies her modern problem – "must proceed in a world that is neither structured by authority nor held together by tradition" (p. 195). Nevertheless, "education belongs among the most elementary and necessary activities of human society, which never remains as it is but continuously renews itself through birth, through the arrival of new human beings" (p. 185). In education, the parents "assume responsibility for both, for the life and development of the child and for the continuance of the world. These two responsibilities do not by any means coincide; they may indeed come into conflict with each other" (p. 185f.). The child has to be protected from the world but ultimately also the world from the child (p. 186). According to

Arendt, the child has to be protected from the public realm, among other things, as perhaps the brightest and as a savage place in the world. "Everything that lives, not vegetative life alone," she continues, "emerges from darkness and, however strong its natural tendency to thrust itself into the light, it nevertheless needs the security of darkness to grow at all" (p. 186).

This illustrates that Arendt contemplated the (democratic) public realm as an unsuitable principle of education and development. Children are not "worldly" and "exactly the same destruction of the real living space occurs wherever the attempt is made to turn the children themselves into a kind of world" (p. 186). There "arises public life of a sort" among these children to be sure, but "quite apart from the fact that it is not a real one and that the whole attempt is a sort of fraud, the damaging fact remains that children – that is, human beings in process of becoming but not yet complete – are thereby forced to expose themselves to the light of a public existence" (p. 186f.).

6.3 An Opponent of "Progressive Education"

Regarding the question of education, Hannah Arendt has to be understood as the antagonist of John Dewey, as her merciless critique of "progressive education" (Arendt, 1961) makes abundantly clear. It is also not very convincing to read Dewey as a political philosopher, since he – as the social philosopher that he was – seems to lack any theory of political or democratic institutions, or a (critical) theory of power. It is therefore hardly surprising that Dewey has been received in German-speaking pedagogics quite readily, above all in form of the so-called democracy education (Beutel & Fauser, 2011; Beutel et al., 2022; Edelstein et al., 2009) in which the difference between the social and the political realm is of little concern. This certainly also has to do with the lack of an agonistic understanding of politics or democracy. In contrast to Arendt or Jacques Rancière (see Section 6.4), Dewey seems to be less critical – conceptually or terminologically – in regard to modern democratic society, as reflected in his concept of education, which is closely linked to the idea of community. "Much of our present education fails because it neglects the fundamental principle of the school as a form of community life," Dewey writes in *My Pedagogic Creed* (1981, p. III). In this context, democratic education is fully dedicated to the promotion of social intelligence within the framework of the school community by means of mutual problem-solving processes and the constitution of the "common good." Therefore, individuals are only able to learn how to understand "democratically" if they become part of a community in which common problems are solved mutually – discursively or through joint liberation, and through "a shared interest in the common good" (Carr, 1995, p. 52).

From the perspective of a pluralistic, migration society, which was not (yet) in Dewey's focus, the questions that arise, above all, are what is recognized and acknowledged as a problem and what is recognized as a "common" problem in present social, political, and legal circumstances?

In democracies, the education system distinguishes itself that it consists of democratically organized institutions according to Dewey ([1916] 1966). Schools as communities support the development of a democratic social life by themselves becoming "embryonic" societies that "promote social modes of behavior and intellectual dispositions which are inherent in democratic forms of living" (Carr, 1995, p. 52; Dewey, [1900] 1968). Apart from the fact that the metaphor of school as embryonic society is misleading (since a social *sub*system – such as the education system – is not able to represent society as a whole), the idea of "education *as* democracy" is already too unconvincing because education and school education always exhibit *more* and *other* qualities than "democratic" education, that is, they do not preexist solely in a "democratic" manner and they cannot be understood exclusively in a "democratic" manner.

For Dewey, democracy or, to be more precise, democratic education cannot be defended by providing it with a rational basis (Reichenbach, 2001). He appears to share not only mere skepticism toward such basic thinking with certain postmodern variants but almost the conviction that it can be foregone completely (Carr, 1995). He sympathizes with the critique of the abstract rationalism and universalism of enlightenment. However, his concern for a democratic form of living, which he sees compromised by social fragmentation, and his reformulation of the insight that individual freedom can only exist on the basis of social relations, which define the democratic form of living, stand testament to an attitude that cannot in all seriousness be given the ambiguous and already depleted label "postmodern." Dewey's focus on community makes it difficult to classify him in the first place, be it in the debate on postmodernism, the communitarian-liberal debate, or the overlapping of the two discourses.[1] According to Joas (1993), his idea that "democracy is to be understood as the highest increase in principles that form the basis of all communal life" (p. 50) had not been given a voice in Germany before 1945; this is why the classification of the community concept into antidemocratic thinking that became comprehensible after 1945 should not be overstated.[2]

The public realm – in the sense of Arendt, nothing else than (politically motivated) discursivity – bestows worldliness upon the public actors or the space between them. Arendt wants this worldliness to be seen orthogonally to all morals, quasi-morally indifferent, a fact that might offer some criticism as a self-misunderstanding by the author. The discourse arena, not bound spatially but only by human action, represents the condition for the end of individual solipsistic or worldless thoughtlessness wherein also the truth of the "banality of evil" (Arendt, [1963] 1986) can be found. Yet, discourses in which the thinking of individuals is expressed mostly end in perplexity. Arendt shows – and is this not pedagogically substantial? – how this (Socratic) perplexity represents the opposite of what could be called "practiced thoughtlessness" (Reichenbach, 2000a).

[1] Arguably, he has to be described as a "communitarian" liberal (Wellmer, 1993, p. 183).

[2] With "community," Dewey certainly uses a term that has – in contrast to Germany especially – an unambiguously positive connotation; yet, there is a much broader spectrum of meaning compared to the German term "Gemeinschaft" that can signify "community," (territorial) "municipality," or (utopian) "commune" (Joas, 1993).

Discourses irritate mere meaning – to initiate them, that is, to recreate the public realm in each case, corresponds to a practice of freedom.

6.4 The Political Realm

Talking and acting are operations that transcend the realm of the *only*-necessary and the *only*-useful. According to Hannah Arendt ([1958] 1998), *talking* was considered as a means to persuade and convince in classical Greek thinking (p. 26), and acting, basically nothing more than *speech* acts, included all interpersonal activities that aim at changing the existing world. Acting as the highest form of operation constitutes the human realm, that is, the political realm, while working (as the "lowest" form of an active life) encompasses all operations that are dependent on the nature of human needs and exhaust themselves in a cycle of production and consumption, but it produces no lasting world of things by itself. The operation situated one higher, producing, does not represent the place of human freedom in classical thinking – again, according to Arendt – although the lasting works created by humans stabilize human existence since it is thereby able to distance itself from nature's ephemerality.

To be political or to live in a polis means to settle relevant matters using convincing (or persuading) words – and not under duress or by force (p. 26f.); "in Greek self-understanding, to force people by violence, to command rather than persuade, were prepolitical ways to deal with people" (p. 26). Arendt continues that "under no circumstances could politics be only a means to protect society" (p. 31).

The term "public" can be described in two different ways. One is that something is rendered visible and audible to certain individuals prior to a community (p. 50) and the other is that the term signifies the *worldly* community (p. 52 ff.). These meanings are interconnected but not identical. The first meaning refers back to the fact that the public realm constitutes reality: "For us, appearances – something that is being seen and heard by others as well as by ourselves – constitutes reality" (p. 50). Being heard and being seen constitute reality, while each inner life has to "lead an uncertain, shadowy kind of existence unless" it would be "deprivatized and deindiviudalized" in order to appear publicly in a suitable form (p. 50). "The presence of others who see what we see and hear what we hear assures us of the reality of the world and ourselves" (p. 50). This is why "the intimacy of a fully developed private life," which is the result of the modern era or the decline of the public realm, "will always come to pass at the expense of the assurance of the reality of the world and men" (p. 50). Reality and therefore the human world is constructed in the public realm, whereas the subjective feeling removes the individual from the world and this subjective feeling makes it even impossible for the individual – depending on how intense their experiences are – to communicate reasonably. The insight that the private realm is, so to speak, "worldless" and that familial communities or communities that define themselves as families have an unpolitical and unworldly character is crucial in this context (p. 53). The attempt to make subjective experiences (of the private realm) a principle of the public realm has to fail every time. Accordingly, love serves as a clear example since it is unable to survive in the public realm: "Because of its inherent worldlessness, love can only become false and perverted when it is used for political purposes such as the change or salvation of the world" (p. 52).

According to Jacques Rancière (1998), the *le politique* (political realm) represents *la rencontre de deux processus hétérogènes* (the meeting or clash of two heterogeneous processes), namely governing or the government, which he calls "police," on the one hand and *égalité* (equality) on the other hand (p. 112). With the latter, a *jeu de pratiques* (game of practices) is intended that is led by the assumption that anybody is equal to anybody, having to verify or justify this equality without a problem (p. 112). Thus, the appropriate name for this practice which is understood as a process is emancipation. It could also be called "*la* politique" (p. 113). To govern, however, means to refuse equality as emancipation – the two processes are "incommensurable" as a consequence; in the end, governing not only refuses emancipation but even damages it (p. 113.).[3] With the political realm ("*le* politique"), therefore, a space or domain is constituted in which the government ("*la* police") and the practice of emancipation ("la politique") not supported by it clash. Accordingly, emancipation is the verification of equality by any being that speaks to any other being (p. 115) and equality represents the only political universal.[4] It exists and is only effective as a practice; it is not a virtue that can be submitted according to taste, it has to be *présupposé* (presupposed), *vérifié* (verified), and *démontré* (demonstrated) anew time and time again (p. 115).

It is without question that Rancière understands equality as an ideal of justice that has a regulative character, as all moral and political ideals do. The one who acknowledges it acts differently, or would like to act differently, or would like it if others would act differently. For this reason, equality (or inequality) is to be discussed to a lesser extent – not only according to Rancière – as a condition but, above all, as social practice. It can exist as an (albeit counterfactual) assumption effort only *between* human beings "that regard themselves as reasonable beings" (Rancière, [1987] 2009, p. 108). Now, when it comes to the state of equality (or inequality) in society, you are to

> choose if you attribute it to the real individuals or their fictional unity. You have to choose between a society of inequality with equal human beings and a society of equality with unequal human beings. Who has a taste for equality must not hesitate: individuals are the real beings and society is a fiction. Equality has value for the real beings but not for a fiction. (p. 155)

Following Rancière, one could say that equality represents a social practice and inequality a social fact. Equality is a *political* recognition effort which can be turned against the societal and social inequality that surrounds us.

[3] "Au lieu de dire que toute police dénie l'égalité, nous dirons que toute police fait tort à l'égalité" (Rancière, 1998, p. 113, emphasis in original).

[4] "Le seul universel politique est l'égalité" (Rancière, 1998, p. 116).

It is interesting to note that Arendt ([1958] 1998) does not use the term equality in her argumentation; she uses – as shown earlier in this section – the term freedom or equal liberty – "to be free meant to be free from the inequality present in rulership and to move in a sphere where neither rule nor being existed" (p. 33). Accordingly, this "sphere" is not to be understood spatially or locally, just as Ranciére's *terrain*, but as a social *practice*. This *speech* practice ideally differs from constraint or force (p. 25ff.); "in Greek self-understanding, to force people by violence, to command rather than persuade, were prepolitical ways to deal with people" (p. 26f.). Therefore, the polis democracy was informed by speaking – the original political *action* (speech acts). Since freedom can only be "practiced" in the political realm or even creates it, to rule was considered to be a "contradictio in adiecto" within the political realm (p. 27f.). In this regard, Arendt's reading of the political realm corresponds with Rancière's reading for the most part: rulership as "police" is incompatible with "*la* politique" as emancipatory practice of equality. For Rancière, however, "*le* politique" is created in a confrontation between the equal liberty thought (sensu Arendt) and rulership. It could also be said that Arendt refers only to "*la* politique" in her narrower understanding of the political realm, while she completely ignores "*le* politique." The fight for the political realm in the sense of "*le* politique" does not represent the political realm in the sense of "*la* politique" – in other words, the creation of enabling conditions of equal liberty practices is not the same as the equal liberty practice itself.

Arendt banishes "constraint and force from her notion of the political realm," writes Thomas Meyer and she identifies "its core, namely the communication of many, directly with power though – a kind of power that should become effective as a public force indeed, yet its rulership should not be reinforced and perpetuated" (1994, p. 26ff.). For Arendt ([1958] 1998) the discourse among beings of equal liberty characterizes the political realm, whereas all necessity is a prepolitical phenomenon (p. 31).

While such an understanding of the political realm appears to be highly exclusive, it would be wrong coincidentally to imagine the "free" life of the (comparatively) few (Athenian) citizens of the polis as a communication idyll. Arendt rather emphasizes the gap between the sheltered *oikos*, especially family life, on the one hand, and "the merciless exposure of the *polis*" on the other hand (p. 35). To surpass others and to distinguish oneself in front of them have their place in the public realm – the term *excellence* refers back to that (p. 48f.).[5] Occasionally, excellence contrastively implies or indicates its opposite; it then implies or indicates defamation and exposure. In return, a public action can also achieve excellence, as is never possible in the private realm. The intimate surroundings in the family are not capable of acknowledging excellence without blowing themselves up with this recognition effort (p. 48f.). Excellence requires a public space.

[5] Cf. Greek: *arete*; Latin: *virtus*. According to Meyer, "the Greek word arete with which Aristotle describes the spirit and form of the polis' life is translated as "prowess" by adepts. In doing so, it becomes clearer that the political virtue is less a certain volition than rather an everyday practical ability (1994, p. 61).

According to Arendt, this close relationship between public performance and excellence could not be destroyed completely during the modern turn, although the common social realm tries to anonymize excellence by understanding it as human progress and not any longer as the performance of individuals. "While we have become excellent in the laboring we perform in public, our capacity for action and speech has lost much of its former quality since the rise of the social realm banished these into the sphere of the intimate and the private" (Arendt [1958] 1998, p. 49).

6.5 And the Moral of the Story?

It is surely not unreasonable to criticize unreservedly the concept or the understanding of the political realm in the work of Hannah Arendt and also Jacques Rancière or other philosophical figures who are able to inspire the pedagogical or at least the pedagogical-philosophical discourse. Even if Arendt and Rancière cannot be accused of the nostalgic idealization of the Greek polis in a convincing manner, the exclusivity of the political realm, as it is presented here, is a conceptional problem. As much as the eye for the dimensions of the political realm can be focused and the latter can be protected from its equalization with the social realm as a result, an implicit moralization goes along with it, which is of no real interest pedagogically but is vulnerable from a political theory and democratic theory perspective, most of all because of the missing systematic thematization and classification of political institutions. To the appeal and problem of exclusivity, the undoubted positive connotation of the "true" political disposition of these two philosophers surely corresponds with the (philosophical) idealization of actual political practices, at least to a certain degree. In my opinion, this argument is less relevant with regard to Arendt – from a pedagogical perspective in any case – due to the fact that she regards the politicization of education as an evil anyway that leads to the understanding of "political activity ... as a form of education" (Arendt, 1961, p. 176). In this sense, it can, or has to be, concluded that the idea of an "education toward democracy" or an "education as democracy" represents a wrong track for Arendt. The realms of education and politics have to be divided strictly: "Education can play no role in politics, because in politics we always have to deal with those who are already educated. Whoever wants to educate adults really wants to act as their guardian and prevent them from political activity" (p. 177).

Arendt's thinking can be regarded – on the surface – as an antimodernistic political theory, as a nostalgic history of decay that laments the rise of the social realm at the expense of the decline of classical ideals of the polis, and as the loss of public space in the modern era (Benhabib, 1992, p. 90). What disturbs this surely idealized picture of the polis is that Arendt almost completely ignores the historical fact that the many (noncitizens) have, with their labor, enabled the political passion of the few (citizens) in the first place. Seyla Benhabib refers to the fact that the modern "rise of the social realm" has been accomplished at least by the emancipation of the groups that had been excluded from participating in public life in the classical polis – those who had to remain in the "shadowy interior of the household" to some extent. Benhabib is not alone in the conviction that Arendt underestimated or even ignored the moral of her polis ideal, but also that such a moral is implicitly present (Benhabib, 2006). Arendt defines public space as the only place in which freedom can realize itself – therefore, a space that should not be defined or occupied morally. She discards the Platonic ideal of a just state because such a moralization makes freedom in the political realm strictly impossible (Dossa, 1989, p. 19); for her, each "institutionalization" of public space – no matter what the premises – represents a destruction of the freedom practice and thereby of the political realm (Dossa, 1989, p. 79). The political realm is not at the service of what is necessary, not in the service of the solution of social, moral, or economic problems (Dossa, 1989, p. 85f.), but it is an *end in itself* – you may even claim *because* freedom is an end in itself for Arendt. Freedom (of the public self) is self-sufficient; this is why the political realm can be compared to theater, whereas theater is the altogether the most political art – entirely in the sense of Arendt. The close connection of theater and politics or of self-representation and the public realm has come under heavy – moral – criticism at least since Rousseau. Arendt's polis citizens are not moral beings in the classical sense, but they are also not unmoral beings according to Dossa (1989, p. 115). It appears that Arendtian thought wants to elude a "positive moral" at all costs as a result of Arendt's radical juxtaposition and separation of politics and morals (p. 108).

Arendt's close moral understanding appears not connected to her strict separation of the public realm from the private realm which can still be affirmed even if you try to emphasize the implicit morality of the public realm. Of course, if you regard the political realm as completely detached from what is necessary, the question regarding the moral becomes superfluous, as does the question of politics, as Gottsegen (1994) argues: "A politics free of matter of necessity . . . would be an unnecessary politics" (p. 234). Yet, inasmuch as political questions are not questions of truth according to Arendt but – completely Kantian – questions of opinion that you hold, public space is always also the space of self-representation *as* freedom (and, vice versa, of freedom as self-representation). The political realm or political action is – even if not the only – an important human endeavor that has a transcending and an individuating character at the same time.

Arendt adduces good reasons for not wanting to reshape the public realm and even to see it outside the moral realm to some extent; the public realm can only exist if it is not "domesticated" morally. The morality of the public realm does not consist in its specific and fleeting quality each time but rather and solely in the fact of its existence; in other words, it is crucial *that* there is a public space that individuals create by practicing their freedom as speech. It is only the existence of a public space that is able to secure – if at all – that the *others* are thought of, that the plurality of opinions, visions, and alleged truths *has to* be taken into account. And it is only public space that challenges individuals to take a stand and gives them the opportunity to change, although they do not intend to do so (Curtis, 1997). According to Benhabib (1995), "The cultivation of one's moral imagination flourishes in such a culture in which the self-centered perspective of the individual is constantly challenged by the multiplicity and diversity of perspectives that constitute public life" (p. 139). In this sense, a mediation takes place between moral thought (and its development) and the culture of the political realm. This connection may be overestimated where democratic politics is viewed solely through moral glasses, and it is probably overestimated where only the will to power is seen in politics. Arendt's political theory refers to the constantly *expressive* character of the political realm in life and thereby to its importance for the self, namely social reality, and thus to experience oneself (p. 139).

6.6 Concluding Remarks: Education as Conceiving the World

Hannah Arendt's "pedagogics of the public realm" is idiosyncratic; according to Arendt, the question of whether the public realm should be educated upon has to be denied. Her public realm is an arena of the discursive fight in which the individual actors try to distinguish themselves from the crowd and to make a little piece of history. Arendt emphasizes this "urge for self-representation," which is criticized wrongly in my opinion, probably because its modern forms are admittedly rather often superficial and frequently even vulgar. *Expression* constitutes the self and enables experiences of reality in a special sense, namely in the sense of *self*-experience. According to Arendt, the strict separation between the public and the private realm is the vital condition for a democratic form of life – a separation between light and darkness, however, that has been broken through and blurred under the psychological and mass media conditions of our culture long ago. Arendt's public realm serves the discourse and global change; it is progressive: "In politics this conservative attitude – which accepts the world as it is, striving only to preserve the status quo – can only lead to destruction ... unless human beings are determined to intervene, to alter, to create what is new" (Arendt, 1961, p. 192).

Arendt follows through on the dualism between the two classical realms of life in a consequent if not rigid manner and places education in the dark section clearly – in the section of inequality and asymmetry: "We must decisively divorce the realm of education from the others, most of all from the realm of public, political life, in order to apply to it alone a concept of authority and an attitude toward the past which are appropriate to it but have no general validity and must not claim a general validity in the world of grown-ups" (p. 195). Her vote for a clear demarcation between youths and adults appears strange today, as dating back to a time that was overcome long ago. Arendt, however, cannot be monopolized conservatively or progressively; on the contrary, her analytical separation between young and old can be turned, as a critical figure of thought, against a culture of general infantilization, against a society in which pedagogical and psychological forces assist with a noble motivation in condemning its members to the state of *lifelong post-adolescence*.

In other words, to read Arendt as a pedagogue of the public or the political realm (which coincide for Arendt) helps to think about the conditions of living together in which human beings not only try to live their own respective lives as long and problem-free as possible, but to live them with a certain passion for a common world – a passion, therefore, that, at least partially, frees it from absorbing self-thematizations and unfruitful self-psychologizations:

> Education is the point at which we decide whether we love the world enough to assume responsibility for it and by the same token save it from that ruin which, except for renewal, except for the coming of the new and young, would be inevitable. And education, too, is where we decide whether we love our children enough not to expel them from our world and leave them to their own devices, nor to strike from their hands their chance of undertaking something new, something unforeseen by us, but to prepare them in advance for the task of renewing a common world. (Arendt, 1961, p. 196)

Even if the following questions might appear emphatic or antiquated, they are still of central importance in my opinion: What kind of world – which "small scale model" – do the adults conceive, be it as parents, as teachers, or in another capacity, through their actions and inactions? Do they (still) conceive a world at all? What do they defend?[6] And do these pedagogical – or also unpedagogical – conceptions have any effect at all? If so, is it about the world as it is, as it should be, or both? And is it about, as Arendt argues, whether we love the world enough, on the one hand, and whether we love the children enough (p. 196) in order to be able to conceive of any world at all, on the other hand? Is possibly the *love for the world* the central political motive that governs or should govern pedagogical actions?

The "world" in question here does not represent nature, it is not the manufactured environment, it does not consist of institutions, and it is not a mere gathering of individuals; "world" rather describes an ephemeral space that can only come into being *between* human beings that express themselves in a thinking, speaking, and acting manner, and intervene, that is, they make themselves seen and heard (Arendt, 1998a). A pedagogics that disregards, ignores, or suppresses this space, a pedagogics that only "tames, trains, and instructs mechanically" but not "enlightens" (Kant, 1977, p. 707) could be called "worldless." Kant (1977) argues that the child should not become a "blind mimic" (p. 745). Today, pedagogics might appear "worldless" to itself if what and whether "mimicry" is still at play have become irrelevant in a purely "subjective" manner.

The world of human beings is problematic and incomplete, and education as introduction to this very world is too (Reichenbach, 2018). Education might even foster the discontent in civilization and in our own existence, at least temporarily, but then also point to it with an "in spite of all of that," with a "brave heart" (Kant, 1977, p. 747), without which political life – and that also means a

[6] Cf. Jacque Derrida's reference regarding the meaning of (French) *professer*, in the sense of displaying publicly what one defends (Derrida, 2001).

confident life – is hardly possible.[7] "Education," as Peter Roberts (2016) argues not without pathos, "is meant to create a state of discomfort, and to this extent may also make us unhappy, but is all the more important for that. Indeed, the fact that we can experience such discomfort is a source of hope and possibility" (p. 3).

However, the contemporary discourse in education science, education research, and above all education policy is not only characterized by the key objective of competency but *tyrannized* to a large extent.[8] What a mistake to see the goal of education first and foremost, or even exclusively, in the promotion of individual competency! As if individuals could act for themselves, confidently and autonomously so to speak, without depending on others in their behavior in an elementary manner. How could the realization of the necessity of the abilities of understanding and judging – in contrast to competency – be neglected in such a manner according to the apparently corrupted concept of (individual) autonomy? As if a meaningful existence could be possible in the vita activa without a corresponding and corrective vita contemplativa.

A lot of things change but some do not. Human beings want to understand the world and themselves and they depend on being understood by others. At first, this has not much to do with the production of individually desired and useful states. The meaning of understanding runs deeper: "Understanding begins at birth and ends with death" (Arendt, 1994a, p. 110). Understanding and knowledge are not identical, but they are closely related: "Understanding precedes knowledge and succeeds it. Prior understanding, which underlies all knowledge, and true understanding, which transcends it, have the following in common: *They give meaning to knowledge*" (p. 113, emphasis added). Understanding is symbolic representation (of the world) that would be as ethereal as speech, and senseless without the cultivation of inner pictures, that is, of imagination.

Indeed, it is not the task of pedagogues to conceive the world *as it is* (they are not at all able to do that – nobody is); but it should be regarded as their task to help the children and adolescents entrusted to their care to promote the understanding of the world and the diverging perspectives on it, that is, to increase the power of judgment (the competency to judge). In this process, knowledge, that is, the transfer of knowledge, plays a central role. Knowledge – as controversial as it may be – and the transfer of knowledge are connected intrinsically. "There is," according to Georg Steiner (2009), "no community, religion, discipline, or craft without masters and disciples, without teachers and students; knowledge is transfer. In progress, in innovation, as far-reaching they as well may be, the past is present" (p. 167). However, the creation and the transfer of knowledge are not only characterized by generational changes but also by generational conflicts (Hoffmann, 2002).

[7] Since "The gleeful heart alone is capable of experiencing delight in what is good" (Kant, 1977, p. 745).

[8] Richard Sennett (1986) suggests that the term "tyranny" was used synonymously with "sovereignty" in its oldest political meaning. Thereby, the notion of a (sovereign) ruler that "tyrannizes" society (through a principle) is implied (p. 424). Such a principle, however, does not have to proceed from "raw coercive power," it can just as well be based on "seduction." Also, this principle has not to come from one person, the tyrant, but can lie in an institution that becomes the "sole source of authority" or yet, following a common basic belief, "the only standard of reality" (p. 425).

The political dimension of education and teaching could – broadly speaking – be seen in revealing to children and adolescents a sense of the political realm. This is less a didactic or curricular affair than a question of style and interaction, of access to the world that can only ever show itself in specific objects that become thematic among human beings. The form of access has a political meaning if it supports the possibility of the – childhood or adolescent – practice of freedom.[9]

References

Arendt, H. (1961). *Between past and future. Six exercises in political thought.* New York: The Viking Press.

Arendt, H. (1963/1986). *Eichmann in Jerusalem – Ein Bericht über die Banalität des Bösen.* Munich: Piper.

Arendt, H. (1994a). Verstehen und Politik. In H. Arendt, ed., *Zwischen Vergangenheit und Zukunft. Übungen im politischen Denken I.* Munich: Piper, pp. 110–27 (original: *Between past and future*, 1968).

Arendt, H. (1994b). Freiheit und Politik. In H. Arendt, ed., *Zwischen Vergangenheit und Zukunft. Übungen im politischen Denken I.* Munich: Piper, pp. 201–26 (original: *Between past and future*, 1968).

Arendt, H. (1958/1998). *The human condition.* Chicago, IL: The University of Chicago Press.

Arendt, H. (1998a). *Vom Leben des Geistes. Das Denken – Das Wollen.* Munich: Piper (original: *The life of the mind*, 1971).

Benhabib, S. (1992). *Situating the self. Gender, community and postmodernism in contemporary ethics.* New York: Routledge.

Benhabib, S. (1995). *Selbst im Kontext. Kommunikative Ethik im Spannungsfeld von Feminismus, Kommunitarismus und Postmoderne.* Frankfurt a. M.: Suhrkamp (original: *Situating the self*, 1992).

Benhabib, S. (2006). *Hannah Arendt. Die melancholische Denkerin der Moderne.* Frankfurt a. M.: Suhrkamp (original: *The reluctant modernism of Hannah Arendt*, 1996).

Beutel, W., & Fauser, P. (Eds.) (2011). *Demokratiepädagogik: Lernen für die Zivilgesellschaft.* Frankfurt a. M.: Wochenschau Verlag.

Beutel, W., Gloe, M., Himmelmann, G., Lange, D., Reinhardt, V., & Seifert, S. (Eds.) (2022). *Handbuch Demokratiepädagogik.* Schwalbach: Wochenschau-Verlag.

Brunkhorst, H. (1999). *Hannah Arendt.* Munich: Beck.

Carr, W. (1995). Erziehung und Demokratie unter den Bedingungen der Postmoderne. In L. Koch, W. Marotzki & H. Peukert, eds., *Erziehung und Demokratie.* Weinheim: Deutscher Studien Verlag, pp. 35–56.

Curtis, K. F. (1997). Aesthetic foundations of democratic politics in the work of Hannah Arendt. In C. Calhoun & J. McGowan, eds., *Hannah Arendt and the meaning of politics.* Minneapolis, MN: University of Minnesota Press, pp. 27–52.

[9] I would like to thank Daniel Werner (University of Zurich) for his assistance with the translation of this text.

Derrida, J. (2001). *Die unbedingte Universität.* Frankfurt a. M.: Suhrkamp.

Dewey, J. (1900/1968). *The school and society.* Chicago, IL: University of Chicago Press.

Dewey, J. (1916/1966). *Democracy and education. An introduction to the philosophy of education.* New York: Free Press.

Dewey, J. (1981). *My pedagogic creed. The philosophy of John Dewey.* Chicago, IL: University of Chicago Press.

Dossa, S. (1989). *The public realm and the public self. The political theory of Hannah Arendt.* Waterloo: Wilfrid Laurier University Press.

Edelstein, W., Frank, S., & Sliwka, A. (2009). *Praxisbuch Demokratiepädagogik.* Weinheim: Beltz.

Gottsegen, M. G. (1994). *The political thought of Hannah Arendt.* Albany: State University of New York Press.

Hoffmann, N. (2002). Zum Zusammenhang von Generationswechsel und Innovation in der Wissenschaft – Ein fiktives Interview mit Ludwik Fleck. In A. Kinder, ed., *Generationswechsel in der Wissenschaft.* Bern: Lang, pp. 15–29.

Joas, H. (1993). Gemeinschaft und Demokratie in den USA. Die vergessene Vorgeschichte der Kommunitarismus-Diskussion. In M. Brumlik & H. Brunkhorst, eds., *Gemeinschaft und Gerechtigkeit.* Frankfurt a. M.: Fischer, pp. 49–62.

Kant, I. (1803/1977). *Schriften zur Anthropologie, Geschichtsphilosophie und Pädagogik 2.* Werkausgabe Band XII, Frankfurt a. M.: Suhrkamp.

Meyer, T. (1994). *Die Transformation des Politischen.* Frankfurt a. M.: Suhrkamp.

Rancière, J. (1987/2009). *Der unwissende Lehrmeister. Fünf Lektionen über die intellektuelle Emanzipation.* Wien: Passagen.

Rancière, J. (1998). *Aux bords du politique.* Paris: Gallimard/Folio.

Reichenbach, R. (2000a). "Es gibt Dinge, über die man sich einigen kann, und wichtige Dinge." Zur pädagogischen Bedeutung des Dissenses. *Zeitschrift für Pädagogik*, 46(6), 795–807.

Reichenbach, R. (2000b). Die Ironie der politischen Bildung – Ironie als Ziel politischer Bildung. In R. Reichenbach & F. Oser, eds., *Zwischen Pathos und Ernüchterung. Zur Lage der politischen Bildung in der Schweiz.* Freiburg: Universitätsverlag, pp. 118–30.

Reichenbach, R. (2001). *Demokratisches Selbst und dilettantisches Subjekt. Demokratische Bildung und Erziehung in der Spätmoderne.* Münster: Waxmann.

Reichenbach, R. (2018). *Ethik der Bildung und Erziehung.* Paderborn: Schöningh/UTB.

Reichenbach, R. (2021). Das Soziale, das Politische und die politische Bildung. In L. Gensluckner, M. Ralser, O. Thomas-Olalde & E. Yildiz. eds., *Die Wirklichkeit lesen. Political Literacy und politische Bildung in der Migrationsgesellschaft.* Bielefeld: transcript, pp. 115–35.

Roberts, P. (2016). *Happiness, hope, and despair. Rethinking the role of education.* New York: Lang.

Sennett, R. (1986). *Verfall und Ende des öffentlichen Lebens. Die Tyrannei der Intimität.* Frankfurt a. M.: Fischer (original: *The fall of public man*, 1974).

Steiner, G. (2009). *Der Meister und seine Schüler*. Munich: dtv.
Touraine, A. (1997). *Pourrons-nous vivre ensemble? Egaux et différents?* Paris: Fayard.
Wellmer, A. (1993). Bedingungen einer demokratischen Kultur. Zur Debatte zwischen Liberalen und Kommunitaristen. In M. Brumlik & H. Brunkhorst, eds., *Gemeinschaft und Gerechtigkeit*. Frankfurt a. M.: Fischer, pp. 173–96.

7

Paulo Freire on Democratic Education

Peter Roberts

7.1 Introduction

Paulo Freire is a pivotal figure in the development of democratic thought in education. His work has had a significant influence on other educationists engaged in struggles for more socially just forms of democratic life, and his ideas continue to be much discussed in today's world. Over recent years, Freirean theory has, for example, been considered in relation to neoliberalism (Espinoza, 2017; Tiainen et al., 2019), Indigenous resistance movements (Kee & Carr-Chellman, 2019), new discourses on "happiness education" (Guilherme & de Freitas, 2017), forms of openness and closure in education (Toh, 2018), the "post-truth" age (Farrell et al., 2017), and the global COVID-19 pandemic (Roberts, 2022). Freire has also been seen as offering something of ongoing importance in addressing perennial questions relevant to the development of a robust concept of education and defensible approach to moral education (Beckett, 2018; Veugelers, 2017). Some areas that have attracted debate in the past continue to do so today. An example is the nature of the teacher–student relationship in Freirean pedagogy (Barros, 2020; Chambers, 2019; Tan, 2018a; Wilcock, 2020). Freire has also been discussed in studies with a focus on aesthetics and literature (Bingham, 2016; Suissa, 2017; Todd, 2018; Vahl et al., 2021). From this necessarily limited sampling of current areas of interest, it seems clear that, whatever one thinks of Freire, his ideas will remain worthy of engagement in the years ahead.

This chapter maps some of the broad contours of Freire's position on democracy, as conveyed in both his written work and his educational practice. Freire addressed the theme of democracy in several different ways. He is perhaps best known for his attention to democratic *processes* in education, as elucidated, for example, by the contrast he draws between "banking" and "problem-posing" approaches to pedagogy. He also has much to say about democratic *dispositions*, referring to these as qualities or virtues that should be developed by all progressive teachers. There is, in addition, a clear view in his work of what a democratic *society* should look like. These different dimensions of a Freirean perspective on democratic education are closely connected with each other, and all will be considered in the present chapter. Freire's stance on democracy must be understood in relation to the specific contexts within which his pedagogy of the oppressed was forged. This does not mean his ideas cannot be taken up and applied by others in their own contexts. As Freire himself counseled, we must continually "reinvent" his work, remaining faithful to certain fundamental pedagogical principles while also adapting as appropriate to the particulars of our own time, place, and circumstances. Section 7.2 of the chapter shows how Freire's orientation toward democracy is related to his wider philosophy and his analysis of social change in Brazil. Section 7.3 focuses in a more detailed way on the educational elements of Freirean democracy. The final section provides brief reflections on contemporary challenges and possibilities in upholding Freire's democratic ideals.

7.2 Democracy and Humanization: Philosophy, Politics, and Practice

Freire's conception of democracy grows out of his ontology, epistemology, and ethic. Freire (1976) argues that, as human beings, we have a distinctive capacity to reflect critically on ourselves and the world and to intervene in reality to change it. From Hegel and Marx, Freire adopts a dialectical view of the world. He accepts the Hegelian principles of contradiction, negation, and change; like Marx, however, his interest is not just in the dialectical development of consciousness but in the concrete expression of oppositions and tensions through historically grounded social struggle. Building on Marx, Freire observes that as creative, curious, temporal beings, we can work with the products of nature, fashioning what we find into objects that will be both useful and beautiful. In the process, we also shape ourselves. We are conditioned but not determined by the systems and institutions that structure our society. Freire advances an ethic of humanization: becoming more fully human through engaging in praxis. Praxis – transformative reflection and action – affirms our ontological status as Subjects, integrated with, and not merely adapted to, the world (Freire, 1972a). Humanization is not an abstract process; nor is it something we undergo alone. We humanize ourselves through dialogue with others, in a world that is always dynamically in the making. Reality, as Freire understands it, is always in motion. This is true of both the objective sphere (including the world of nature and socially constructed material reality) and the subjective sphere (the inner realm of emotion, desire and thought). Both spheres are themselves undergoing constant change and they are also in continual interaction with each other. As we change the world through reflection and action, the new reality that results will, over time, demand further reflection. This process is continuous throughout the human lifespan. We are finite but necessarily unfinished beings, always with more work to do (Freire, 1998a).

Knowing, for Freire, is a similarly incomplete process. Freire parts company with Hegel, and with logical positivists, in stressing that we can never know in final or absolute terms. Given a reality constantly on the move, knowing is always provisional, and we must always be prepared to revisit what we hitherto may have taken for granted. We sometimes need to be a little less certain of our certainties (Freire, 1997a). Doubt can be debilitating but it can also prompt us to inquire, to ask questions, to probe further. Doubt does not mean we cannot act; we can, and must (in the normative sense of "must") be prepared to make decisions and take action, even where there are no clear or easy "solutions" to difficult social problems. Doubt does not have to be coupled with indecisiveness (Freire, 1998b). Nor does becoming less certain of one's certainties mean any interpretation of reality is as good as any other. Freire is not an epistemological relativist. His work suggests that some ways of understanding the world – and of living in it – are better than others (Roberts & Freeman-Moir, 2013). Freire identifies a number of intellectual virtues characteristic of those seeking to know. Knowers, he suggests, are curious and investigative. They ask questions and pose problems. They discuss ideas with others and seek to learn from them. They endeavor to uphold the highest standards of scholarly rigor in their field, developing both breadth and depth in understanding. They remain open to learning more. They develop the capacity to stand back sufficiently from an object of study in order to understand it more intimately. Knowing, for Freire, is not an individual act or state of mind but a social process, and seeking to know is not a temporary task but a lifelong commitment.

Freire's ontological, ethical, and epistemological ideas took shape as he worked, with others, in social and educational settings characterized by conditions that contrasted sharply with his ideals. He witnessed great poverty, ruthless exploitation, severe malnutrition, high rates of infant mortality, substandard housing, limited access to healthcare, and high rates of adult illiteracy (Freire, 1972a, 1972b, 1976). In rural areas, peasant farmers were subject to the dictates of wealthy landlords. In urban settings, workers endured long hours for very low wages, as corporate elites sought to maximize their competitive advantage. Such situations were utterly dehumanizing. Freire (1972a) was quick to point out that dehumanization, while a reality, was not inevitable. Dehumanization is a distortion of our ontological vocation. A major barrier in addressing oppressive conditions, Freire (1976) argued, was the sense of resignation among the poor: their situation, they surmised, could be explained by fate, or destiny, or God's will. Freire sought, through his educational endeavors, to provide opportunities for disrupting these deeply embedded patterns of thought. His efforts in this direction are described in some detail in his first book, *Education as the Practice of Freedom*.

Freire began composing *Education as the Practice of Freedom* while imprisoned in Brazil immediately following the military coup of 1964 and completed it while exiled in Chile (Schugurensky, 2011, p. 67). The book was not published in English, however, until after his best-known text, *Pedagogy of the Oppressed* (Freire, 1972a), had already enjoyed wide international circulation. In English translation, *Education as the Practice of Freedom* appeared, together with another concise early work, *Extension or Communication*, under two different titles: *Education for Critical Consciousness* (Freire, 1973) and *Education: The Practice of Freedom* (Freire, 1976). Freire's focus in *Education as the Practice of Freedom* was on Brazil's transition in the 1950s and 1960s from a "closed" society to one characterized by greater openness. This transition, he observed, was incomplete, with the process of opening that occurred in urban areas finding no equivalent in rural areas (Freire, 1976, pp. 8–9). With the military coup of 1964, there was a risk that the progress that had been made would be lost, with a "catastrophic return to closure" (p. 10). Freire argued that a more homogeneous openness was needed, but admitted that this would not come easily given the opposition mounted by reactionaries to transformative social change. Groups, on both the Right and the Left, tended to fall into what Freire called "sectarian" positions characterized by arrogance, antidialogue, and uncritical readings of reality. Sectarians, Freire maintains, cannot love, and therefore cannot create. They have a propensity to act without reflection. Freire favored what he referred to as a "radical" response to the challenges posed by Brazil's transition (cf. Aronowitz, 1993). A radical, for Freire, is someone who adopts a "critical, loving, humble, and communicative" posture (Freire, 1976, p. 10). Radical participants in the process of change will be strongly committed to their ideals but will not deny others the right to think and choose differently. Radicals understand the value of dialogue; they will argue for their position but will have no interest in crushing or conquering an opponent. They will recognize and resist the violence inherent in all relationships of exploitation and oppression. Those who exhibited these qualities were, in Brazil's case, very much in the minority. Separation, brutalization, and hatred prevailed, threatening to extinguish the hope that would enable Brazilians to see themselves as critical Subjects rather than colonized objects (pp. 8–12).

Freire identifies several key moments in the transitional period in Brazil, where moves toward democratization were repelled by those with an interest in maintaining the status quo. He argues that when those who have previously been "submerged" in reality call for greater involvement in Brazilian life, the "privileged elite," once they have grasped the threat posed by "the awakening of popular consciousness," begin to organize (pp. 13–14). Agitation for change is treated as a sign of ill-health, and aid in the form of institutionalized assistance is provided. "Assistencialism" is a cynical process of appeasement, treating the symptoms rather than the causes of social problems. Its goal is to render silent and passive those who might otherwise question. Those who, despite these measures, continue to call for greater participation are labeled "subversives" and every effort is made to restore order. From the elite's perspective, there is no alternative: "As the dominant social class, they must preserve at all costs the social 'order' in which they are dominant" (p. 14). To ensure this, they would need additional support from the government, and with the military coup of 1964, this was provided. This intensified the climate of irrationality, authoritarianism, and rigidity that had already been evident in some sections of Brazilian society, closing off the country to further democratic development. What was needed was the formation of a more open, dialogical, critical orientation to the world. This is the basis for Freire's understanding of critical consciousness, a mode of thinking and being that he regarded as characteristic of "authentically democratic regimes" (p. 18). Key features of this approach to reality include depth in the examination of problems, a willingness to reflect and revise, robust argumentation, and a receptiveness to taking what is best from both the old and the new. Critical consciousness is consistent with "highly permeable, interrogative, restless and dialogical forms of life" (pp. 18–19).

For Freire, democracy cannot be imposed but must be experienced (p. 36). Citizens need to learn, through "exercising" democracy, how to participate actively in the creation of their society. This would not be an easy transition for Brazil, mired as it was in its "closed, colonial, slavocratic, reflex, anti-democratic" past (p. 21). Under colonization, land was exploited, slave labor was employed, and entrenched patterns of "domination and dependence" emerged (p. 22). The Portuguese colonizers were motivated principally by commercial greed, and with large land holdings could form "self-sufficient economies" characterized by despotic rule, the issuing of decrees, and the denial of possibilities for dialogue (pp. 23–24). A culture of silence developed. Those who were exploited "housed" their oppressors within themselves. Brazil was kept in a state of relative isolation. Communicative relationships across provinces within the country, and with other nations, were restricted. The "gentlemen" of the privileged classes were granted access to municipal offices, but workers had few opportunities to participate in civic life. The establishment of an outpost for Portuguese royalty in Rio de Janeiro provided the impetus for some reform, including the establishment of schools and libraries, but prospects for gaining democratic experience remained limited to a minority. The balance of power was shifting from rural patriarchies to (re-)Europeanized urban elites, but the foundations for forming a genuine democratic state were not in place. Imposing a political structure requiring dialogue, solidarity, and responsibility on a feudal economic platform, with workers who were "defeated, crushed and silenced" would not work (p. 28). The abolition of slavery near the end of the nineteenth century disrupted the equilibrium that had been formed in maintaining a closed society, and with an enhanced emphasis on immigration and further industrialization, Brazil strengthened its economic base – accompanying this, in the first half of the twentieth century, with fresh advances in the arts and sciences. The country was finally beginning to "find itself" (p. 31), but there was still much work to do in building Brazil's democracy.

7.3 Democratic Education: A Freirean Perspective

Freire believed that education had an important role to play in enabling citizens to form a better understanding, through experience, of democratic life. In Brazil, however, education had, for the most part, been antidemocratic. It lacked rigor, eschewing theory and research in favor of verbosity and polemics. It was premised on the idea of a simple, one-way transfer of knowledge rather than a dynamic, dialogical exchange between teachers and students. There was a heavy reliance on rote learning, with few opportunities for reflection and discussion, and a profound disconnection between the curriculum and the realities of Brazilian life. Immersed in a predominantly verbal culture, Brazilians preferred "well-tuned" phrases and "easy" words over substantive investigation, analysis, and debate (Freire, 1976, p. 37). Some progress had been made in the preparation of technicians, professionals, and scientists via the country's universities. But the acquisition of specialist knowledge and technical skills, while important for Brazil's ongoing development, needed to be seen as part of a wider process of humanization. There was a lack of trust in the capacity of students to pose problems, ask questions, explore, and create. "Democracy and democratic education," Freire contends, "are founded on faith in men [and women], on the belief that they not only can but should discuss the problems of their country, of their continent, their world, their work, the problems of democracy itself" (p. 38). Educationists have nothing to fear in allowing students to critically analyze their social world in dialogue with others who are also seeking to know. Those involved in traditional Brazilian education had failed to take up this challenge, dictating ideas rather than allowing them to be exchanged, lecturing instead of listening, working *on* rather than *with* students. This approach to education was woefully inadequate in preparing citizens for democratization, for it "contradicted that very process and opposed the emergence of the people into Brazilian public life" (p. 38).

In *Education as the Practice of Freedom* Freire goes on to show how he developed and applied the principles of critical, dialogical, democratic education in his literacy work with adults. He details how the words that formed the heart of his literacy program were selected via discussion with participating communities, identifies some of the key themes that were addressed via pictorial representations of aspects of everyday Brazilian life, relays some of the observations made by learners, and outlines the methods employed to generate new words and extend reading and writing abilities. The program was successful in enabling adults to read and write in as little as 40 hours but its fuller development, into a postliteracy phase, was curtailed by the military coup of 1964. Freire was regarded as a subversive, placed under arrest, and then forced into exile. He continued to express a deep love for his country, but the tremendous impact he was to have with his work was, in the first instance, more keenly felt beyond Brazil. He lived for several years in Chile, and after a brief period as a visiting scholar at Harvard University, spent a decade in Geneva, Switzerland, in a position with the World Council of Churches. He was finally able to return to Brazil in 1980, having traveled widely as a speaker and consultant for educational initiatives in a number of other countries. By this stage in his professional life, he had already become one of the world's most widely known educational theorists, with *Pedagogy of the Oppressed* in particular attracting extensive international attention (Kirylo, 2020). His time at Harvard had resulted in another book – *Cultural Action for Freedom* (Freire, 1972b) – and this, together with *Pedagogy of the Oppressed* and *Education for Critical Consciousness* – cemented his reputation as a distinguished and distinctive contributor to educational theory and practice. After a comparatively "quiet" period in his publishing activities from the mid-1970s to the mid-1980s (with just two key works: Freire, 1978, 1985), Freire enjoyed a strong "second wind" as a writer. In the last decade of his life, he coauthored a number of dialogical books with other educators (Escobar et al., 1994; Freire & Faundez, 1989; Freire & Macedo, 1987; Freire & Shor, 1987;

Horton & Freire, 1990) while also completing several sole-authored volumes (Freire, 1994, 1996, 1997a, 1998a, 1998b, 1998c). Some of the books that appeared under his own name (e.g., Freire, 1993) also included material based on conversations with others. The posthumous publication of books such as *Pedagogy of Indignation* (Freire, 2004) and *Daring to Dream* (Freire, 2007) has provided further opportunities for scholars to engage his work in the twenty-first century.

Freire continued to revisit his early ideas on democracy in his later works. In *A Pedagogy for Liberation*, he admits that prior to the military coup in Brazil, he "gave to education some powers that were really beyond it" (Freire & Shor, 1987, p. 32). This was partly because "the moment then was very optimistic," with great hope among left groups that social change was possible and no shortage of willing volunteers in educational initiatives (p. 32). "After the coup," Freire says, "I was really born again with a new consciousness of politics, education and transformation" (p. 32). Freire notes that in his first book he does not "make reference to the political nature of education," revealing his "naiveté" at the time (p. 33). He learned from history, however, concluding that what was needed was "a political practice in society that would be a permanent process for freedom, which would include an education that liberates" (p. 33). Education, he goes on to argue, is not in itself or on its own the "lever of revolutionary transformation" (p. 33); rather, it must, in its liberating form, be seen as part of a broader process of social struggle. Education should neither be granted powers it does not have nor be dismissed as a waste of time. Critiquing traditional approaches to schooling can be important but this is not enough on its own; we also have to critique "the capitalist system that shaped these schools" (p. 35). Lessons are conveyed not just in the content of a school or university course but in the forms of pedagogy enacted in the classroom. In treating students as critical, knowing Subjects, and in demonstrating a passionate but well-justified commitment to ideas and ideals, teachers show what is possible and permitted in a democratic society. A teacher committed to liberating education gives "a testimony of respect for freedom, a testimony for democracy, the virtue of living with and respecting differences" (p. 34).

In the second chapter of *Pedagogy of the Oppressed* (Freire, 1972a) Freire draws his well-known distinction between banking education and problem-posing education. He argues that traditional education has suffered from a kind of narration sickness; it has been built on the idea of an all-knowing teacher issuing monologues to ignorant, passive students. Students are expected to memorize and repeat the content of the teacher's narration. Under this model of education, reality is presented as static, and knowledge is conceived as a gift to be bestowed by one person on to others. Freire makes a case for an alternative approach, anchored in democratic and progressive principles, built on the idea of posing problems, asking questions, and engaging in dialogue. In problem-posing education, a critical orientation toward the world is not only permitted but actively encouraged. Instead of a one-way transfer of knowledge, like a deposit in a bank, all participants in an educational setting learn from each other. Freire's advocacy of a more democratic approach to classroom life should not be seen as a denial of the importance of teaching. In later writings, partly in response to misreadings of his earlier work, he makes a point of noting that he is not just a facilitator but a teacher (Freire & Macedo, 1995). In arguing for problem-posing education over banking education, Freire does not claim that teachers and students are the same as each other. He shows that, while all participants have something worthwhile to bring to an educational dialogue, teachers and students have their own distinctive roles and responsibilities. Teachers can and should exercise authority – over academic content, in assessing work, and in the structuring of pedagogical discussion – but this is not the same as being authoritarian. The authoritarianism of banking education, Freire makes plain, is part of a wider oppressive system, and it is this, together with the active suppression of questioning and critique, to which he objects. The narration sickness of traditional education is, to put this another way, merely a symptom of a much bigger problem. Understanding Freire's position on banking education entails getting to grips with his views on the political nature of all pedagogical initiatives (Mayo, 1999).

Education, Freire never tired of insisting, can never be "neutral"; it always favors some ways of understanding reality, interacting with others, and living in the world over others (Freire, 1987, 1997b, 1998c). This idea may appear to be self-evident, but it was a marked departure from the dominant educational discourse in Brazil in the late 1960s and early 1970s, and Freire found himself having to argue this point again as neoliberal views took hold in the late 1980s and early 1990s. Both teachers and students are shaped by their circumstances, and education never takes place in a vacuum; priorities and trends will be influenced by what is perceived as important at a given time, by specific groups of people, for particular purposes. Past experience will always have some bearing on what participants bring to, and take from, an educational encounter. Education is "political" not just in the sense that it is subject to the laws and decisions made by politicians and policymakers; its political character is also revealed in the layout of teaching and learning spaces, the topics and reading matter selected for study, the assessment regimes implemented, and the pedagogical methods employed. Teachers who claim to be "neutral" are, in Freire's view, either being naive or disingenuous. Teaching in formal educational settings is a necessarily interventionist process (Roberts, 2000). But in acknowledging this, and accepting the responsibilities that come with educational intervention, teachers need not, and should not, set out to impose their views on others. To impose is to deny the democratic right to be different; it is to expect that one view will be accepted without a reasonable opportunity to ask questions, pose problems, and explore alternatives. To intervene in reality, in critical communion with others, is an expression of our ontological vocation of humanization; to impose is to impede the pursuit of this vocation. Imposition dehumanizes both those who are subject to it and those who are responsible for it.

For Freire, democracy is not just a form of government but a mode of being: a way of living in the world, with others, consistent with the ideal of humanization. As he puts it, "since the ontological orientation of men and women has evolved toward being more, democracy will be the form of struggle ... most appropriate to realize this orientation" (Freire, 1996, p. 146). Democracy, like humanization, is always an unfinished project; it is always in a state of becoming, posing new problems for us as we negotiate our way in the world. Every democratic moment places its own distinctive demands on us; there are no fixed "rules" for democratic life that apply equally well at all times, for all people, under all circumstances. To commit to democracy is to be willing to live with a restlessness that is never fully satisfied. This idea has important implications for education. Freire refuses to provide step-by-step guidelines for teachers seeking to employ democratic methods in classrooms. His primary focus is not on the "how to" of democratic education, but on the deeper principles underpinning democratic life. He is not interested in prescribing or proscribing curriculum content for democratic societies. He recognizes that laws and policies can enhance or impede opportunities for democratic expression and participation, but they are not enough on their own. Just as important are the democratic dispositions that underpin the decisions made and actions taken by those involved with the educational process. Freire speaks of these qualities as virtues to be developed by progressive teachers.

One of these key virtues, as signaled in Section 7.2, is openness. Openness means being open-minded, but this does not adequately capture what Freire means by the term. We can express an attitude of openness through our physical movements and via the subtle emotional signals we send in everyday interactions. As educationists, we should, from a Freirean perspective, be open to learning from the colleagues and students with whom we work. The investigation and exploration of alternative approaches to social, cultural, and economic life should be actively fostered, and we should always be open to the possibility of change (Peters & Roberts, 2011). Openness is necessary if we are to attend and respond, with equanimity, to others. Openness allows us to see what otherwise might be obscured by prejudice or ignorance. Openness requires humility. Facing the world with an attitude of humility does not mean denial of our own capacities as thinking, feeling, and willing individuals; it is more a matter of recognizing our own incompleteness as human beings. No one, Freire (1976) maintains, is ignorant of everything, just as no one knows everything. This may seem obvious, but we frequently forget it in our relations and interactions with others. Freire also stresses the importance of tolerance as a democratic virtue. It is not uncommon for tolerance to be conceived as merely "putting up" with others, but this is not the way Freire sees it. Tolerance does not consist in patronizing, tokenistic, or resentful gestures toward those with whom we disagree; nor does it imply the suppression of our own views. From a Freirean perspective, we have not only a right but a responsibility to offer what we can to debates over contentious matters (and it must be remembered that speaking is not the only way to contribute). The key to tolerance is recognizing that others have something worthwhile to offer too. Tolerance means not being fearful or defensive or reactionary in the face of difference but actively embracing the opportunity to talk with and learn from others who hold views at odds with our own (Nieto Ángel et al., 2020).

Learning to listen is another distinguishing attribute of democratic teachers, and this is closely linked with the other virtues already mentioned (Roberts,

2010). Humility and openness are necessary but not sufficient in developing the art of good listening. Similarly, if tolerance is to be demonstrated in the company of peers, and if an educational exchange is to be genuinely dialogical, it is essential that opportunities be granted for all voices to be heard. If we are to listen effectively, attentiveness to the Other is important (Rozas Gomez, 2007). We need, as far as possible, to reduce our focus on ourselves – without denying that we are active participants in the pedagogical process – while trying to remove any preconceptions about what our interlocutor might have to offer. It is not only the words uttered by the Other that should be of interest to us but also the gestures, expressions, and subtle movements that form part of an educational conversation. It is easy to become distracted – by noises in our surroundings, by the pressures of time, by our own thoughts – but we should seek to minimize the effects of these intrusions. For Freire, the imperative to listen applies in working with learners at all ages and in all educational settings, formal and informal. Listening plays an important role in generating the respect that is necessary for democratic education. As Freire puts it, "by listening to and so learning to talk with learners, democratic teachers teach the learners to listen to them as well" (Freire, 1998b, p. 65).

Freire also stresses the need for coherence and consistency in democratic education. He sought to exhibit these qualities in his own work, and he encourages others to do the same: "It is not what I say that says I am a democrat, that I am not racist or machista, but what I do. What I say must not be contradicted by what I do" (p. 67). This is not easy. Indeed, it is "truly difficult to make a democracy" (p. 67). Reflection on one's shortcomings in establishing this consistency can be painful, but such moments constitute forks in a road, where choices need to be made. We may fall back into reactionary ways, or we may lapse into cynicism. But we may also keep struggling, with ourselves as well as with the challenges posed by others, and recommit ourselves to our ideals. For Freire, there is always hope, even in the most despairing of situations (Chen, 2016; Roberts, 2016). Keeping hope alive relies on another virtue to which Freire regularly referred: commitment, even where there may be no easy or clear way to address a complex problem. Commitment does not mean blindly pushing forward, with our eyes fixed firmly on an unwavering goal. For democratic teachers, commitment must be subject to the demands of critical scrutiny, to questioning and debate. We must remain open to the idea that our goals may require some modification. We can exhibit the quality of restlessness that was so important to Freire while also demonstrating the patience that is necessary for thoughtful, considered commitment. Patience is a partner with other Freirean virtues, being necessary, for example, in learning to listen to others and in studying with rigor and discipline. Patience is needed in knowing that, if we are committed to the ideal of building a fairer, more democratic world, we cannot expect quick fix solutions; we must, instead, be prepared to settle in for the long haul.

In his work as an adult educator in Brazil, Freire was clear that democracy must extend beyond the right to vote. Three decades on from his first book, the situation for tens of millions of Brazilians remained deeply problematic, with a third of the country suffering from "hunger and pain day in, day out"; in such circumstances, "the vote is insulted and degraded" (Freire, 1996, p. 146). For Freire, democracy can only exist where there is "an orientation toward humanization"; "class, gender, and race discrimination, to which may be added any disrespect or diminution of another human being, denies democracy by denying that orientation" (p. 147). Freire supports the idea of citizens in a democracy being able to express their views freely, including via the press and in the form of protests on the streets, but also truthfully and respectfully. Freedom, as Freire sees it, should not mean "anything goes." There are limits to freedom, some of which are imposed by coercion, others of which are necessary. Both authoritarianism and permissiveness impede democracy. Authoritarians seek to dominate, manipulate, and control, sometimes with force, sometimes by more subtle means. Those who lapse into a position of permissiveness refuse to take responsibility for setting necessary limits. These principles are carried over to Freire's educational theory. Dialogue, as we have seen, is a key element of Freirean education, but this is not mere idle chatter or a casual conversation. Freedom and tolerance are important in allowing ideas to be aired and tested, and originality and creativity should be encouraged, but dialogue in an educational context must have a strong sense of structure and direction; it must be purposeful and rigorous (Freire & Shor, 1987; Roberts, 2000; Tan, 2018b).

7.4 Contemporary Challenges and Possibilities

In *Education as the Practice of Freedom*, it will be recalled, Freire aligns critical consciousness with "authentically democratic regimes" and with "highly permeable, interrogative, restless and dialogical forms of life" (Freire, 1976, p. 18). Each of these constituent elements has arguably been threatened by recent social trends, at least in some parts of the world. We have seen, for example, the rise of new forms of political populism built on the cultivation of fear, distrust, divisiveness, and hatred. In such circumstances, there is a lack of openness, a disregard for rigor, an excessive degree of certainty, and a refusal to engage in dialogue. These threats are, however, not new. They have always been there for democracy, and this is why, from a Freirean perspective, democracy is always a work in progress: a form of social organization, an ethos underpinning human interaction, and a state of mind requiring constant reflection and renewal. "A good democracy," Freire suggests, "warns, clarifies, teaches, and educates" (Freire, 1996, p. 156). As Freire sees it, "[t]eaching democracy" is possible, but this is "not a job for those who become disenchanted overnight just because the clouds turn heavy and threatening" (p. 154). Democracy requires substantial, sustained commitment and we need to keep fighting for it (p. 155). Democracy also needs to be defended against those who, through their actions, demean it. Here Freire has in mind politicians who, having been democratically elected, become corrupt. Too often, Freire shows, the response to such examples of "failures" under democracy is to turn instead to authoritarianism. Brazil has a history of falling prey to this tendency. What corruption demands, however, is thorough investigation and, where cases are proven, public denouncement, along with further educational efforts to allow citizens to be better informed when casting their votes.

In the last years of his life, Freire expressed particular concern at another threat to democracy: neoliberalism. Neoliberals, he argued, are too certain of their certainties (Freire, 1994, 1997a). They have a smug belief that the battle between capitalism and socialism has already been decided, and that the free market now provides the only realistic way forward for all countries. Neoliberalism denies history and promotes a fatalistic view of the world (Freire, 1996, 1998a). Freire could see that under neoliberal global capitalism, existing social inequalities would be exacerbated. The construction of knowledge as a commodity – as nothing more than information to be exchanged between buyers and sellers in a market – is also profoundly at odds with Freire's epistemology. The emphasis on choice and competition as key planks of neoliberal educational reform contrasts sharply with the spirit of cooperation and collegiality fostered by Freire. The ethic of self-interested individualism underpinning neoliberal thought stands in direct opposition to Freire's ideal of humanization and his commitment to social justice (Tiainen et al., 2019). Freire's conception of democracy is built on a recognition that seeking what is best for others, and not just for ourselves, is ultimately for the good of all. We are not, in Freirean terms, "self-contained" individuals; we are, rather, *social* beings, occupying a world, and facing its myriad problems, in the company of others. We can pursue collective ends without undermining the integrity and distinctiveness of each person involved in doing so. Neoliberalism is premised on the idea of individuals seeking to satisfy wants, and in twenty-first-century capitalist societies multinational corporations play a powerful role in *creating* those wants. Freire's ethic of care, commitment, and love rubs against the tendency to focus just on what we want, and his notion of critical consciousness encourages us to ask searching questions of the culture of relentless consumption that underpins contemporary economic life.

Freire observed that it was not uncommon to link democracy with capitalism and socialism with authoritarian regimes, but he resisted this tendency. "While I am a radical and substantive democrat," he said, "I am [also] a socialist" (Freire, 1996, p. 114). It was on this basis that he joined the Brazilian Workers' Party and supported Luiz Inácio Lula da Silva ("Lula"), who would later become President of Brazil. (Lula served two four-year terms from the beginning of 2003 and returned, against the odds, to reclaim the Presidency in Brazil's 2022 general election.) Freire's commitment to democratic socialism also underpinned his work as Secretary of Education in the municipality of São Paulo (Freire, 1993; O'Cadiz et al., 1998; Weiner, 2003). Freire did not mince his words when discussing capitalism, describing it as "evil" (Freire, 1996, p. 188). In his later work, he placed his own "universal human ethic" – the ontological and historical vocation of humanization – directly against the ethics of the market (Freire, 1998a). He abhorred the practices of exploitation he had witnessed in capitalist societies and was deeply distressed by continuing hunger and poverty in Brazil. Writing in the last decade of the twentieth century, he reported that 33 million

Brazilians were "starving," with "many more below the poverty line" (Freire, 1996, p. 185). He was, at the same time, also aware of the abuse of power and denial of basic human rights in some communist countries. He did not unpack the terms "communism" and "socialism" in systematic detail, but his preference was for the latter and his sense of what a socialist society should look like was shaped by a range of different intellectual influences. His efforts to bring socialist and democratic ideals closer together echoed a similar struggle he had in earlier years to overcome what he saw as a false opposition between Christianity and Marxism. Freire interpreted the Christian gospels as a call to social action and his reading of Marx provided theoretical sustenance for his practical commitment to the liberation of the oppressed. For Freire, Christianity, socialism, and democracy were, or should have been, united by an underlying ethic of care for others, and he retained his faith in the capacity of human beings to build principled and strategic alliances with this fundamental point in mind.

One of the obstacles to realizing the dream of a socially just democracy, as Freire saw it, was the propensity among groups on the political Left to turn on each other, allowing their differences to become a weakness rather than a strength. Battle lines would be drawn over contrasting theoretical orientations, and tensions between different groups on matters of class, gender, ethnicity, language, and sexual orientation would emerge. At times, this would lead to a kind of political paralysis, and little progress would be made in addressing key social and cultural problems. Meanwhile, those on the Right, already at an advantage given the wealth and resources at their disposal, would manage to forge a pragmatic unity despite their differences. Thus, economic liberals and moral conservatives could, in the interests of maintaining their dominant position in a society, work together to secure election victories and achieve other political goals. Freire (1996, 1997a, 1997b) argued for a position of unity in/within diversity, urging others on the Left to value and respect their differences, engage in dialogue with each other, and cooperate in building strong coalitions for progressive change. He pointed out that the different "minority" groups in contemporary multicultural societies were often, collectively, the majority. He also argued that whatever differences exist between groups on the Left, all have a common adversary in the capitalist system. In his earlier work (Freire, 1972a), he had already drawn attention to the destructiveness of "divide and conquer" political policies, and he could see that similar strategies continued to be employed by those intent on retaining power in subsequent decades.

Freire's appeal to a position of unity in diversity might be seen as having some pragmatic merit but is unlikely to win over critics who argue that he lacks an adequate understanding of the complexities of difference and fails to properly address the multiplicity of different layers of oppression. A peasant male may, for example, be oppressed by a landlord but act in an oppressive way in his relations with his wife or children. Freire's use of the overarching categories of "oppressed" and "oppressor" obscures the tensions that can be experienced between and within people who occupy a range of different subject positions

(Weiler, 1991; see also Freire & Macedo, 1993). Freire responded to this line of critique, noting that in his earlier publications he had a particular concern with questions of social class, while also reiterating his commitment to the liberation of all oppressed groups. Indeed, Freire claims that it is "exactly because of my growing awareness over the years concerning the specificities of oppression along the lines of language, race, gender, and ethnicity that I have been defending the fundamental thesis of Unity in Diversity" (Freire, 1997b, p. 310). References to gender and ethnicity certainly appear more frequently in his later books, though neither are discussed in great depth. It is also evident that Freire was seeking to expand his scholarly reach into other bodies of critical work. Mention is made, for instance, of postmodernism, with Freire distinguishing between fatalistic and progressive postmodern positions (Freire, 1994, 1998a). Again, his moves in this direction remained, at the time of his death, underdeveloped. While there was clearly more theoretical work to do, there are lessons from Freire's observations on Left and Right politics that we would do well to heed today. Political history following Freire's death has confirmed the continuing ability of the Right to divide and conquer while also building support among groups that might in the past have voted for parties on the Left. The election of Donald Trump as President of the United States is an obvious example, with the targeting of disaffected working-class voters combining effectively with the active promotion of divisiveness to secure victory.

The global COVID-19 pandemic has also highlighted the importance of some of the key democratic virtues espoused by Paulo Freire (Roberts, 2022). Freire would have stressed the need for rigor in investigating the causes and consequences of the virus and in considering responses to it. Dialogue, with a sense of structure and purpose, is especially important in situations of this kind. The COVID-19 crisis is a problem with multiple dimensions – biological, ethical, political, economic, and educational, among others – and openness and humility are necessary if we are to learn from others who have knowledge and experience in domains other than our own. To date, media coverage of the crisis has relied quite heavily on commentaries from epidemiologists, statistical modelers, and medical professionals. The inclusion of more voices from scholars in the humanities and social sciences could arguably play an important role in deepening and extending public understanding of the virus. We should not shy away from speaking, and indeed can see ourselves as having a responsibility to do so – if we have something helpful to offer that could save or improve lives – but we also need to know how and when to listen. An important test for Freirean democratic principles lies in the twists and turns the COVID story has taken as vaccines have been rolled out across the world in 2021 and 2022. While vaccination rates have been high in many countries, there are also various "anti-vax" movements across the world. In cases where this opposition to vaccination is based on conspiracy theories, it can seem difficult, if not impossible, to build the kind of dialogue Freire had in mind in his democratic ideal. Despite these impediments to dialogue, teachers still have a potentially valuable role in providing a range of peer-reviewed, scholarly sources for students to read and in seeking to foster respectful consideration of competing perspectives on vaccination policies.

Exercising appropriate authority, without being authoritarian, will often be crucial in contexts where widely divergent views are held. Demonstrating pedagogical authority can be essential if discussion is to remain respectful, purposeful, and rigorous. Even in situations where such efforts appear to fail, all is not lost from an educational perspective. Developing a greater awareness of what views are out there and of how they come to be formed can be helpful for teachers in understanding the students with whom they work, in grasping some of the limits of education, and in planning classes in the future.

In continuing to reinvent Freirean ideas in contemporary contexts, we will want to remain open to new approaches to teaching and learning in democratic classrooms. But, if we are to be consistent with Freire's portrait of critical consciousness, we will not want to assume that just because something is new it must be better. Similarly, we must, as Freire suggests, not reject the old just because it is old. The origins of democracy lie in ancient history and there are lessons to be taken from those times that are still relevant today. The same is true of Freire's work. As we have seen in this chapter, Freire's democratic sensibilities were honed among impoverished communities in Brazil. Those experiences were pivotal in shaping the distinctive approach to democracy, education, and humanization that we find in Freirean theory and practice. At the time of his death, Freire was continuing to expand his intellectual horizons, aware that he had more work to do. As he grew older, he did not slow down; he was as restless, energetic, and engaged as ever. There is much that we can learn from his approach to life that can be helpful in educational settings, with learners at all ages and stages of development. The democratic orientation that underpins Freire's pedagogical philosophy is one where we must always be prepared to be unsettled, ever open to the possibility of acting on the basis of critical reflection and dialogue to change the world. This idea has application well beyond school and university classrooms. Democratic states may appear to enjoy periods of relative stability, but stability can be illusory; it can mask deeply oppressive social realities. We must be willing to ask searching questions of any democracy: of our political leaders, of our laws and institutions, and of ourselves as democratic citizens. Living democracy in the manner envisaged by Freire is far from easy but the difficulties we encounter can, in the long run, strengthen our resolve to keep listening and learning, contributing in our own small way to a conversation that will never end.

References

Aronowitz, S. (1993). Paulo Freire's radical democratic humanism. In P. McLaren & P. Leonard, eds., *Paulo Freire: A critical encounter*. London: Routledge, pp. 8–24.

Barros, S. (2020). Paulo Freire in a hall of mirrors. *Educational Theory*, 70(2), 151–69.

Beckett, K. (2018). John Dewey's conception of education: Finding common ground with R. S. Peters & Paulo Freire. *Educational Philosophy and Theory*, 50(4), 380–89.

Bingham, C. (2016). Against educational humanism: Rethinking spectatorship in Dewey and Freire. *Studies in Philosophy and Education*, 35, 181–93.

Chambers, D. W. (2019). Is Freire incoherent? Reconciling directiveness and dialogue in Freirean pedagogy. *Journal of Philosophy of Education*, 53(1), 21–47.

Chen, R. H. (2016). Freire and a pedagogy of suffering: A moral ontology. In M. A. Peters, ed., *Encyclopedia of educational philosophy and theory*. Singapore: Springer, pp. 866–70.

Escobar, M., Fernandez, A. L., Guevara-Niebla, G., & Freire, P. (1994). *Paulo Freire on higher education: A dialogue at the National University of Mexico*. Albany, NY: State University of New York Press.

Espinoza, O. (2017). Paulo Freire's ideas as an alternative to higher education neoliberal reforms in Latin America. *Journal of Moral Education*, 46(4), 435–48.

Farrell, B., Angel, M. C. N., & Vahl, M. (2017). Hope and utopia in "post-truth" times: A Freirean approach. *Revista Brasileira de Alfabetização – ABAlf*, 1(6), 81–97.

Freire, P. (1972a). *Pedagogy of the oppressed*. Harmondsworth: Penguin.

Freire, P. (1972b). *Cultural action for freedom*. Harmondsworth: Penguin.

Freire, P. (1973). *Education for critical consciousness*. New York: Continuum.

Freire, P. (1976). *Education: The practice of freedom*. London: Writers and Readers.

Freire, P. (1978). *Pedagogy in process: The letters to Guinea-Bissau*. London: Writers and Readers.

Freire, P. (1985). *The politics of education*. London: MacMillan.

Freire, P. (1987). Letter to North-American teachers. In I. Shor, ed., *Freire for the classroom*. Portsmouth, NH: Boynton/Cook, pp. 211–14.

Freire, P. (1993). *Pedagogy of the city*. New York: Continuum.

Freire, P. (1994). *Pedagogy of hope*. New York: Continuum.

Freire, P. (1996). *Letters to Cristina: Reflections on my life and work*. London: Routledge.

Freire, P. (1997a). *Pedagogy of the heart*. New York: Continuum.

Freire, P. (1997b). A response. In P. Freire, J. W. Fraser, D. Macedo, T. McKinnon & W. T. Stokes, eds., *Mentoring the mentor: A critical dialogue with Paulo Freire*. New York: Peter Lang, pp. 303–29.

Freire, P. (1998a). *Pedagogy of freedom: Ethics, democracy, and civic courage*. Lanham, MD: Rowman and Littlefield.

Freire, P. (1998b). *Teachers as cultural workers: Letters to those who dare teach*. Boulder, CO: Westview Press.

Freire, P. (1998c). *Politics and education*. Los Angeles, CA: UCLA Latin American Center Publications.

Freire, P. (2004). *Pedagogy of indignation*. Boulder, CO: Paradigm.

Freire, P. (2007). *Daring to dream*. Boulder, CO: Paradigm.

Freire, P., & Faundez, A. (1989). *Learning to question: A pedagogy of liberation*. Geneva: World Council of Churches.

Freire, P., & Macedo, D. (1987). *Literacy: Reading the word and the world*. London: Routledge.

Freire, P., & Macedo, D. (1993). A dialogue with Paulo Freire. In P. McLaren & P. Leonard, eds., *Paulo Freire: A critical encounter*. London: Routledge, pp. 169–76.

Freire, P., & Macedo, D. (1995). A dialogue: Culture, language, and race. *Harvard Educational Review*, 65(3), 377–402.

Freire, P., & Shor, I. (1987). *A pedagogy for liberation*. London: MacMillan.

Guilherme, A., & de Freitas, A. L. S. (2017). "Happiness education": A pedagogical-political commitment. *Policy Futures in Education*, 15(1), 6–19.

Horton, M., & Freire, P. (1990). *We make the road by walking: Conversations on education and social change*. Philadelphia, PA: Temple University Press.

Kee, J. C., & Carr-Chellman, D. J. (2019). Paulo Freire, critical literacy, and Indigenous resistance. *Educational Studies*, 55(1), 89–103.

Kirylo, J. D. (Ed.) (2020). *Reinventing pedagogy of the oppressed: Contemporary critical perspectives*. London: Bloomsbury.

Mayo, P. (1999). *Gramsci, Freire and adult education: Possibilities for transformative action*. London: Zed Books.

Nieto Ángel, M. C., Maciel Vahl M., & Farrell, B. (2020). Critical pedagogy, dialogue and tolerance: A learning to disagree framework. In S. L. Macrine, ed., *Critical pedagogy in uncertain times: Hope and possibilities*. London: Palgrave Macmillan, pp. 139–58.

O'Cadiz, M. D. P., Wong, L., & Torres, C. A. (1998). *Education and democracy: Paulo Freire, social movements and educational reform in Sao Paulo*. Boulder, CO: Westview Press.

Peters, M. A., & Roberts, P. (2011). *The virtues of openness: Education, science, and scholarship in the digital age*. Boulder, CO: Paradigm.

Roberts, P. (2000). *Education, literacy, and humanization: Exploring the work of Paulo Freire*. Westport, CT: Bergin and Garvey.

Roberts, P. (2010). *Paulo Freire in the 21st century: Education, dialogue and transformation*. Boulder, CO: Paradigm.

Roberts, P. (2016). *Happiness, hope, and despair: Rethinking the role of education*. New York: Peter Lang.

Roberts, P. (2022). *Paulo Freire: Philosophy, pedagogy, and practice*. New York: Peter Lang.

Roberts, P., & Freeman-Moir, J. (2013). *Better worlds: Education, art, and utopia*. Lanham, MD: Lexington Books.

Rozas Gomez, C. (2007). The possibility of justice: The work of Paulo Freire and difference. *Studies in Philosophy and Education*, 26, 561–70.

Schugurensky, D. (2011). *Paulo Freire*. London: Continuum.

Suissa, J. (2017). Pedagogies of indignation and the lives of others. *Policy Futures in Education*, 15(7–8), 874–90.

Tan, C. (2018a). Wither teacher-directed learning? Freirean and Confucian insights. *The Educational Forum*, 82(4), 461–74.

Tan, C. (2018b). To be more fully human: Freire and Confucius. *Oxford Review of Education*, 44(4), 370–82.

Tiainen, K., Leiviskä, A., & Brunila, K. (2019). Democratic education for hope: Contesting the neoliberal common sense. *Studies in Philosophy and Education*, 38, 641–55.

Todd, S. (2018). Culturally reimagining education: Publicity, aesthetics and socially engaged art practice. *Educational Philosophy and Theory*, 50(10), 970–80.

Toh, G. (2018). Anatomizing and extrapolating “Do not publish” as oppression, silencing, and denial. *Critical Inquiry in Language Studies*, 15(4), 258–81.

Vahl, M. M., Arriada, E., & Nogueira, G. M. (2021). Autoritarismo e esperança: Costurando fios entre Paulo Freire e José Cardoso Piresmônica. *Revista Práxis Educacional*, 17(47), 1–20.

Veugelers, W. (2017). The moral in Paulo Freire’s educational work: What moral education can learn from Paulo Freire. *Journal of Moral Education*, 46(4), 412–21.

Weiler, K. (1991). Paulo Freire and a feminist pedagogy of difference. *Harvard Educational Review*, 61(4), 449–74.

Weiner, E. J. (2003). Secretary Paulo Freire and the democratization of power: Toward a theory of transformative leadership. *Educational Philosophy and Theory*, 35(1), 89–106.

Wilcock, N. (2020). The incoherence of the interactional and the institutional within Freire’s politico-educational project. *Studies in Philosophy and Education*, 39(4), 399–14.

8

Rabindranath Tagore on Democratic Education

Ratna Ghosh

8.1 Introduction

Rabindranath Tagore was a progressive educational philosopher whose ideas where far ahead of his time but are most relevant to the contemporary challenges of today. Tagore became internationally known when he received the Nobel Prize in Literature in 1913, the first non-European to get that award, and he was largely seen in the West as a mystic poet and universalist. Although his forward-looking, cosmopolitan, democratic ideas and experiments in education were pioneering and have similarities with other influential intellectuals, he is not well-known outside his country, India.

There are many similarities between Tagore's democratic ideas and those of John Dewey, although there is no evidence they met or corresponded with each other, or were even influenced by each other's thinking. By the time Dewey's *Democracy and Education* was published in 1916, Tagore's philosophy of education had taken concrete shape (Mukherjee, 1962). They were contemporaries, born two years apart in different parts of the world: Tagore (1861–1941) in India and Dewey (1859–1952) in the United States. Similarly, Tagore was an intellectual forerunner of Freire (1921–1997), and they had several similar ideas on education, notably their thoughts on critical consciousness and on freedom not only from poverty but from ignorance, prejudice, and oppression. Freire was against "banking education" in which "knowledge" is deposited into the minds of students, and Tagore spoke of the "factory-model" of schooling and thought of education as a process of absorption, not of filling the child's mind with "knowledge" from books. Correspondingly, Tagore's deep concern with the damage done by colonization and all forms of domination to the minds of people were like Franz Fanon's (1925–1961) ideas of the deformation of the mind due to colonial education (Ghosh et al., 2010). While Tagore is not known for his educational ideas and experiments or for his creative genius in the West, Dewey (1916), Freire (1970) and Fanon ([1961] 2004) have influenced educational thinkers around the globe.

A thinker of universal significance, Tagore's image as a mystical poet from the East obscured his educational vision and philosophy. In his Introduction to

Tagore's *Nationalism* (Tagore, 2017), Ramachandra Guha suggests that Tagore's reputation in India and overseas suffered because he was "a parochial possession" of the province of Bengal and wrote his "outstanding" repertoire of poems, songs, plays, and novels largely in Bengali. At one time, the Bengali elite tried to monopolize him. Although he went on cultural missions to forge links with people in Europe and North America in the West, and also to Japan, China, and South-East Asia in the East, as well as Iran in the Middle East and South America, his work is not well known. Amartya Sen (2011) has argued that while much was lost in translation of his poems, the larger reason for the "eclipse of Tagore in the West" was his open-mindedness, his emphasis on reasoning, which led him to reject some aspects of tradition, his fascination with English literature while rejecting British colonialism, and his rejection of narrow nationalism which went against the grain of his contemporaries as well as some who attended his lectures. He warned against Western imperialism but his admiration of the contribution of Western science was contrary to the way he was seen in the West, as a mystic. Tagore's vision was to synthesize the East and the West, and his internationalist views were eloquently expressed in his book *Nationalism* based on lectures he delivered in Japan and North America over 1916 and 1917. Although he was received very enthusiastically in all the places he visited, in the many famous arenas where he lectured and was complimented by journalists, his "criticism of the virulent nationalism he had witnessed in Japan and America was widely denounced in those countries at the time ... [as was] resigning his knighthood in such a dramatic fashion"[1] (Alam, 2006, n.p.) and frequent and persistent criticism of British colonial rule hurt his reputation.

The famous Indian musician Ravi Shankar wrote of Tagore that had he "been born in the West he would now be (as) revered as Shakespeare and Goethe" (quoted by Amartya Sen, 2011). It is likely he was overlooked, as Raewyn Connell has said because "[d]ebates among the colonised are ignored, the intellectuals of colonised societies are unreferenced" (2007, p. 44). This chapter is a modest attempt to briefly bring to a large audience some democratic educational ideas of Tagore, an intellectual giant from the geographical South.

8.2 Context

Countries of the world are facing a crisis. The COVID-19 pandemic has revealed the effects of the global challenges we face and highlighted the major cracks in societies' institutions in every corner of the world. Several global currents are challenging the very idea of democracy, and democratic institutions are increasingly threatened. Rising levels of poverty and inequality, racism, and discrimination, displacement of large numbers of people due to war, natural disasters, and climate change, violence and antidemocratic hate groups are threatening peace and security at the personal and national levels. In the second

[1] Tagore renounced his knighthood in protest at the Jallianwala Bagh massacre. For more details on this, see footnote 6.

half of the twentieth century, many countries, especially those liberated from colonial domination, found liberal democracy appealing. After the threat to democracy in the Second World War, the United Nations committed itself to promoting and defending democratic values (United Nations, 2005). But at the turn of the twenty-first century, challenges to democratic values are increasing, and the world's largest democracies like India and the United States are facing tremendous threats to democratic policies and practices. So, the issue of democratic education is particularly significant at this point in history.

In the West, democratic education can be traced back to the enlightenment era. John Locke in the seventeenth century and Jean-Jacques Rousseau in the eighteenth century, among several others, published their philosophies of education, which emphasized enquiry and questioning as methods of education. In the late nineteenth century, Leo Tolstoy experimented with a democratic school set up by peasant students and teachers. Tagore was widely read and was influenced by the child-centered pedagogies of many Western educators. Among them were Rousseau, Pestalozzi, Froebel, and Maria Montessori with whom he corresponded (O'Connell, 2004) and who appreciated the methods used to educate students in his educational institution when she visited it (Dasgupta, 2020). But the original inspiration for his philosophy of education came from ancient Indian texts, the Upanishads written around sixth century BCE, the ancient Indian Gurukul system of education, his personal experiences as a child and as an Indigenous intellectual under British colonial rule. Though Tagore's ideas are rooted in traditional philosophies and his own life experiences in colonial India, he synthesized his concepts with Western experiments and thoughts (O'Connell, 2004). He did not write down his philosophy of education in any one volume, but his unique ideas on education can be gleaned from his many articles and essays on education, his lectures all over the world, and his novels, dramas, and poems.

8.3 The Foundation of Tagore's Philosophy of Democratic Education

A social theorist whose thoughts were in advance of his times and defied national–imperial and elite–subaltern binaries (Collins, 2012, p. 3), Tagore has been described as "the myriad minded man."[2] He was a pioneering educational thinker and philosopher, although he is primarily known as a literary genius who wrote, as mentioned, mostly in Bengali, his mother-tongue. His literary expressions covered poetry, novels, short stories, and plays. He also wrote on history, linguistics, and spirituality as well as two autobiographies. Being a widely traveled person, his travelogues, lectures, and essays have been published in several volumes. A polymath, he was also a composer and created a genre of songs known as *Rabindra Sangeet*, and in later life he also became a painter. To trace how his life experiences prompted his democratic values and stimulated

[2] Citation of the honorary doctoral degree conferred on Rabindranath Tagore by Oxford University in 1940.

his educational philosophy, we need to look at the intimate connection between his private and public lives.

Tagore was born in 1861 into an enlightened and educated family in Calcutta, India, during British colonial times. There was intense socioreligious transformation during the nineteenth-century Renaissance in Bengal, the base for the East India Company and then the British Raj. Tagore's grandfather, a very successful entrepreneur was well versed in Arabic and Indian music and had been congratulated by Queen Victoria (Bhattacharya, 2010, p. 144). He worked closely with Ram Mohan Roy, the founder of the Brahmo Samaj[3] for reform of Hinduism and supported educational institutions, the arts, and the establishment of a free press (O'Connell, 2003). His father was also involved in social reform and revived the Brahmo Samaj after the death of its founder. A lover of Indian art and literature, he made his home the meeting place of the best and the brightest in India. Rabindranath, the youngest of 13 children, grew up with his brothers, sisters, and cousins in an extended family, hearing discussions and witnessing experiments in drama, poetry, literature, and music. There were in his family "mathematicians, journalists, novelists, musicians, artists . . . leaders in theatre, science and a new art movement" (O'Connell, 2003). In *My Reminiscences* Tagore (2010) wrote, "[T]he atmosphere of our home was permeated with the spirit of creation" (Bandyopadhyaya, 2018, p. 508). His experiences growing up in a such a culturally rich environment provided informal education that was not only exciting but also the source of his cosmopolitan and liberal ideas, and his philosophy of education.

> I was brought up in an atmosphere of aspiration, aspiration for the expansion of the human spirit. We in our home sought freedom of power in our language, freedom of imagination in our literature, freedom of soul in our religious creeds and that of mind in our social environment. Such an opportunity has given me confidence in the power of education which is one with life and only which can give us real freedom, the highest that is claimed for man, his freedom of moral communion in the human world. (Tagore, 1929, p. 73)

Sent to school at the age of four he was unhappy with the strict discipline and was moved to other schools. After experiencing four schools, he dropped out of the formal system when he was 14, the year his mother died. He found the structured routine of school soul killing, for "all of a sudden I found my world vanishing from around me, giving place to wooden benches and straight walls staring at me with the blank stare of the blind" (Tagore, 1933, p. 114). Sitting within the four walls of a classroom was very restrictive and attending school was to him "an unbearable torture" (Banerjee, 2017):

[3] The Brahmo Samaj is a reformist group of the Hindu religion that attempted to eliminate discriminatory practices such as caste. It was a very influential religious movement started in Calcutta by Raja Ram Mohan Roy along with Tagore's grandfather and later his father. It began the Bengal Renaissance, making significant contributions to cultural, social, intellectual, and artistic development.

> I could well realize that my worth in gentle society was gradually falling down. Yet I could never succeed in tying myself to the perpetually revolving machine of the school, which was to me, as it were, a relentless nightmare like a jail or a hospital, completely isolated from the surrounding life and beauty. (Tagore, [1912] 2018, p. 60)

The joy of freedom he felt to be away from the restrictive routines of the formal school system gave him "the urge to teach himself" (Das Gupta, 2006, p. 69) and enabled him to immerse himself in the broad cultural environment of his home where he was exposed to both Western and Indian literature and thoughts (O'Connell, 2002). He was very sensitive to the beauty of nature, which filled him with a sense of wonder and awe. He longed to be out under the blue skies, among the trees and in the fields with flowers of various colors and forms. To him the "highest education is that which does not merely give us information but makes our life in harmony with all existence" (Tagore, 1933, p. 116).

As a child he spent a lot of time alone and in the care of the family servants. His father had a commanding personality and was very engaged in social reform, which involved frequent travel so that he was often away from his family. Although Rabindranath was not close to his father as a small child, their relationship evolved at around age 11 when his father took him on one of his travels and they spent several months together in a town in the mountains. It was his first visit to Shantiniketan, later to become the site of his university; then west to Amritsar where they stopped for a month. He was greatly influenced by the melodious chants in the beautiful Sikh gurdwara, and he wrote "The golden temple of Amritsar comes back to me like a dream" (Tagore, 2010, p. 86). They spent the next few months in the Himalayan hill station of Dalhousie. The influence of his father remained with him even as an adult.

There he "followed a 'rigorous regime' when he would wake up before sunrise to learn his Sanskrit declensions, shower in ice-cold water, hike up the mountain ridges with his father, sing devotional songs for him, and pursue lessons in English, Bengali and Astronomy" (Banerjee, 2017, n.p.). This father demanded obedience but granted his children freedom to explore and fostered independence and individualism in his sons (Sen, 2014). As early as 11 years of age, his father gave him the heavy responsibility to look after his cash-box (Banerjee, 2017). This certainly was a lesson in responsibility, but he was also fully aware that no carelessness would be tolerated. As Tagore himself wrote, his father expected a lot from his children, but "held up a standard, not a disciplinary rod" (Tagore, 1917, p. 96).

Rabindranath was a poet at heart and was around nine when he could write in a rhythmic style. By the time he was 14, he had already translated Macbeth from English to Bengali in blank verse. Away from a formally structured education he had developed a fondness for reading and read whatever he could, from Sanskrit and Bengali literature to books on history, mythology, legend, and social and natural sciences in both his native Bengali and acquired English (Naravane, 1977). Thus, Rabindranath had the richest possible social and cultural capital for an Indian of his times. In 1878, at the age of 16 he was sent to England where he attended a public school in Brighton, after which he briefly read law at University College, London. He preferred to attend lectures in English literature and read Shakespeare. During that trip he was exposed to English social life and introduced to Western music, which he enjoyed. However, he returned to India in 1880 without finishing any degree although his family had hoped he would become a barrister. As O'Connell (2010) points out, his only degrees came later in his life when he received several honorary doctorates, including one from Oxford a few months before he died.

Upon his return to his home, he published many poems, novels, plays, and short stories. In 1883 he got married, and in 1990 he was sent to manage the family estates in the eastern part of Bengal, which is now in Bangladesh. It was also the year he released his famous *Manasi* poems. The years between 1891 and 1895 were his most productive (Thompson, 1926). His time in crisscrossing the terrain of villages on the Padma River brought him close to the villagers, their lives of extreme poverty, their simplicity, their music. His wife and five children joined him in the estates in 1898, but in 1901, he moved to Shantiniketan to set up a school which would be very different from the schools he had attended.

8.4 Tagore's Educational Institutions

Although Tagore did go through a phase of nationalist thinking, he grew out of his "patriotic conservatism" (Das Gupta, 2004, p. 50), realizing that despite its glorious past "India was part of a larger humanity"; he dreamed of a university that would represent his international liberalism (Som, 2009, p. 121). Tagore was very opposed to the individualism and commercialism in the world and believed that children needed to get away from the influences of conventional upbringing to be free from stereotypes and the superstitious practices in society. He founded a school with the aim of serving humanity and chose *Shatiniketan* (abode of peace) modeled on the idea of a *tapoban* (forest retreat) where students would be amidst nature – away from the urban centers. Twenty years later, in 1921, with an agricultural economist called Leonard Elmhirst, he set up *Shriniketan* (abode of prosperity), a school for rural reconstruction in a nearby village. He started a literacy center and library and experimented with programs for the empowerment of villagers.

In the same year, his school *Shatiniketan* became the basis for his vision of a new type of university which he named *Vishwa-Bharati*. Visualized as an international university, *Vishwa-Bharati* was to be the guiding center of Indian studies and the focal point of Asian studies. Realizing that contact with diverse people would develop respect and understanding of differences in geographical regions, religions, and ethnicities, he invited foreign scholars from Europe and East Asia to the university to teach, and introduced diverse international cultural influences, including the artistic traditions of batik from Indonesia and judo from Japan. Tagore insisted that Indian students be taught the essentials of indigenous and traditional Indian learning rather than be forced to study an imported colonial curriculum. He was sensitive to, and keen on advancing, a critical balance between Western education (particularly in the sciences) and traditional perspectives so that young minds would develop a balanced view of the world (Ghosh & Naseem, 2003).

Tagore contributed money from his 1913 Nobel Prize to the university, spent his personal funds (including selling his wife's jewelry), and raised funds through lecture tours in Europe and the Americas. After Independence, *Vishwa-Bharati* was made a Central University[4] in 1951 through an act of the Indian Parliament and remains a small residential liberal arts university.

The distinctive character of Tagore's institutions is in the philosophy on which they are based. Tagore wanted to emulate the ancient Indian way of teaching the whole child and disliked the colonial way of organizing education and its methods of teaching, which he thought instilled material values and made students follow rules but prevented them from being creative and thinking individuals.

Known as *Gurudev* (the great teacher) he aimed to be the traditional Indian *guru* who would give intellectual, emotional, as well as spiritual guidance to inspire students to develop their minds creatively and aesthetically. His method of teaching was unique by enabling the child to remain curious to inquire, discover, and converse. He emphasized the importance of art and culture in the spiritual development of children, while recognizing the significance of science, stating that "modern Science is Europe's great gift to humanity for all time to come" (Tagore, [1922] 2016, ch. 10).

In Tagore's philosophy of education, the role of the teacher is central: "The Tagorean teacher is not oppressive. She does not pour down cauldrons of knowledge on students' heads hoping that some of it will be absorbed" (Ghosh & Naseem, 2003, p. 98). The teacher's task is to help students realize their potential and facilitate learning through self-expression. Most importantly, the teacher does not operate from a position of power.

Tagore has sometimes been criticized as having been against the teaching of science subjects. On the contrary, Tagore recognized the importance of teaching science and the need for the development of technology in India. He was keenly aware that science and technology were crucial to removing poverty by eradicating illiteracy among the masses of people in India and imperative for increasing production for the country. He sent one of his sons to get an agricultural degree in the United States so that he would come back to his school with scientific and technological knowledge of rural reconstruction to help the villages surrounding it. But he was wary of the potential for using science and technology for purposes of exploitation. Furthermore, while he advised students to "receive with alertness of gifts of science and technology" (Salkar, 1990, p. 20), he was strongly opposed to the teaching of science at the expense of, rather than along with, the spiritual development of the child.

[4] Central universities are under the purview of the federal Ministry of Education as opposed to State universities which are run by State governments.

The democratic structure of his school was remarkable given the prevailing hierarchical structure of Bengali society at the time (Malaviya, 2021), but he was sensitive enough to work within the boundaries of the propensities of the Bengali *Bhadrolok* (middle class) and stopped short of having his students do menial tasks such as cleaning toilets. He wanted the school to be not only socially inclusive but also a socially responsive space where students and teachers relate to each other as in an extended family. Faculty and students, young and old, met in the evening to have tea together in a tea club (Neogy, 2010). This encouraged social interaction, eliminated class and caste consciousness, and brought about human fellowship and unity (Cenkner, 1976).

Tagore's dream was to shape Shantiniketan as a self-governing republic where students would be able to realize their potential by developing their capacities of reasoning as well as their abilities in aesthetics and emotions. Tagore believed that it was both artificial and unreasonable to see reason and emotion as dichotomous. Emotions, he thought, were significant in the process of educating and should be developed in children through proper guidance (Salkar, 1990). He had classes out in the open under large shady trees so that students would be in harmony with the sun and the air. Being aware of the poverty he saw during his years in the family estates, he aspired to eradicate the material poverty of the rural people, but equally important to him was wiping out the poverty of the mind and the soul. His idea was to regenerate the spirit of India by maintaining the real values and doing away with the superstitious beliefs, customs, and dogma, which, as for him, was the aim of both Hindu and Muslim reformers in the Bengal Renaissance.

8.5 A Philosophy of Democratic Education

Democratic education implies that democratic values such as freedom, equality, justice, and respect are both a goal and a means or method of learning to achieving that goal. It involves a child-centered approach to teaching so that the child has the freedom to explore through inquiry and discovery.

Tagore established educational institutions where the means to achieve his goals were humanistic and democratic. In his lecture *My School*, Tagore wrote: "I believe that the object of education is the freedom of mind which can only be achieved through the path of freedom – though freedom has its risk and responsibility as life itself has" (Tagore, 1933, p. 147).

Tagore believed strongly in the Sanskrit saying, "Education is that which liberates" (*Sa' vidya' ya' vimuktaye*). He thought the purpose of education is to gain freedom: freedom from ignorance, from prejudice, from dogma, tyranny, and poverty. But he also thought that the means to do this should give freedom to children to nurture their abilities and self-expression for holistic development.

Tagore sought to decolonize the minds of people through his philosophy and practice of education (Mukherjee, 2021). He thought of freedom and liberation at three levels.

8.5.1 Freedom to Learn

One, freedom is one of the basic tenets of democracy, and freedom of expression is one of the most fundamental of all freedoms. But freedom of expression means more than guaranteeing the right to speak (within limits). It means freedom of a child to explore and express themself by doing so. Based on his own experience with schooling, Tagore was a fervent believer in the freedom of a child to explore and learn. In school

> . . . we are made to lose our world to find a bagful of information . . . We rob the child of his earth to teach him geography, of language to teach him grammar. His hunger is for the Epic, but he is supplied with chronicles of facts and dates. He was born in the human world. But is banished into the world of living gramophones, to expiate for the original sin of being born in ignorance . . . [C]hildren are in love with life . . . [A]re we quite sure of our wisdom in stifling this love? (Tagore, 1933, p. 116)

By emphasizing information, he thought colonial education was obsessed with reasoning and this accentuated a break between the intellectual, physical, and spiritual life. For him, education involved a unity of all knowledge and all the activities of our social and spiritual being (Cenkner, 1976). The mission of education, according to Tagore, was bringing out this unity. Having learnt this from his own experience it was later to become central to his educational philosophy. Education should not be "the conscious process of filling but the subconscious process of absorption" (Taneja, 1983, p. 83) so that children develop the curiosity and imagination with which they are born, and which are the two main ingredients of education.

Tagore's thinking on education is illustrated eloquently in "The Parrot's Training" *(Totaar Kahini)* (1964). One of his many short stories, this is a satire on how the system and methods of education kill the curiosity of children in their attempt to educate them. It is an allegory of the prevailing system of schooling in his time and has immense significance today, especially with the unprecedented use of technology. The story is about educating a parrot that belonged to a Raja. The bird flew and sang but could not recite the scriptures and had bad manners. The Raja loved the bird and felt ignorance was a bad thing; he thought that the bird needed to be educated. The Raja's top advisors were summoned, and they felt the bird's surroundings were not good enough and they built him a golden cage. Then they brought books and gradually stuffed him with so many pages that the bird could neither sing nor fly. In the meantime, the Raja made inquiries about the bird's education and was assured that it was fine. The Raja went to see for himself and was so impressed with all the arrangements that he forgot to see the bird itself. One day he was told that the education of the bird was complete, and he asked that the bird be brought to him. He poked the body but there was only the ruffling of pages. The bird had died.

There are several messages in this tale. To begin with, it was a denunciation of the prevailing colonial system of education in which book knowledge was given sole importance. It was also a commentary on the methods and tools (now technology) used in educating children. The point is that physical and material facilities cannot be seen as more important than the learning "space" of the child if there is no motivation to learn. As Martha Nussbaum says:

> The task of education was to avoid killing off that curiosity, and then to build outward from it, in a spirit of respect for the child's freedom and individuality rather than one of hierarchical imposition of information. . . . [E]ducation must begin with the mind of the child, and it must have the goal of increasing that mind's freedom in its social environment, rather than killing it off. (Nussbaum, 2006, p. 393)

In *My School*, Tagore (1933, p. 147) wrote:

> I know it for certain, though most people seem to have forgotten it, that children are living beings . . . and . . . they should not have mere schools for their lessons, but a world whose guiding spirit is personal love.

In his institutions Tagore developed a spirit of hospitality and relations of love and compassion among all – young and old, from wherever they were and whatever religion or ethnicity they belonged to. They nursed each other when sick and looked after each other (Pearson, 1917).

Malaviya (2021) points out that Tagore developed a pedagogy of love long before the concepts of love and compassion were developed. Spirituality for him meant the development of human values of care, love, and generosity.

8.5.2 Freedom from Ignorance and Prejudice

For Tagore, freedom was the raison d'être of education. He wanted that freedom to unite people and develop a cosmopolitan outlook:

> Our real problem in India is not political. It is social. This is a condition not only prevailing in India, but among all nations. Therefore, political freedom does not give us freedom when our mind is not free. (Tagore, 2017, p. 62)

Freedom from prejudices implies a worldview that is inclusive, welcoming of diversity, and having a cosmopolitan outlook. Tagore used literature, especially his plays, short stories, and novels, to educate people about his democratic and revolutionary ideas, which went against conventional norms. What is most remarkable is that he put all these ideas into practice in his experimental educational institutions. He said:

> I try to assert in my words and works that education has its only meaning and object in freedom – freedom from ignorance about the laws of the universe, and freedom from passion and prejudice in our communication with the human world. In my institution I have attempted to create an atmosphere of naturalness in our relationship with strangers, and the spirit of hospitality which is the first virtue in men that made civilization possible. (Tagore, 1929, pp. 73–74)

Tagore lived at the time of the Bengal Renaissance which, as mentioned in Section 8.3, was a sociopolitical movement that primarily questioned the religious dogma and inegalitarian, discriminatory social customs (such as the caste system, dowry, and sati) that had been normalized in society, and advocated societal reform based on rationality, secular ideas, and humanistic values. It challenged colonialism and sought a radical transformation of Indian society through an awakening in a wide range of intellectual and aesthetic inquiry. Generations of the Tagore family were particularly influential in leading this movement and Rabindranath Tagore emerged as one of the most important figures whose influence on culture and intellectual life continues today.

8.5.2.1 Caste and Class

Tagore was very proud of India's glorious traditions and cultures, but he was equally critical of several social practices and religious beliefs sanctioned by society. He disapproved of many traditional customs and advocated a humane and socially just approach (Cenkner, 1976; Salkar, 1990). He wanted to maintain the essentials of Hindu teaching as in the Upanishads but as a "renaissance Indian" he was selective with the scriptures (Cenkner, 1976, p. 20). He rejected the rigid hierarchy of the caste system.

Tagore's ideas on social reform were based on his conception of the degeneration of Indian society from its original Vedic ideals. While he thought of Vedic caste as promoting social integration, it had over time "mutated into a structure of rigid, immutable gradations segregating entire categories of the population from one another" (Basu, 2012, p. 164). Seeing the oppression of the lower-caste peasants by upper-caste landowners during his time in the estates, as well as the tyranny over the lower castes by the upper-caste nationalist leaders, his views on caste changed over the years and he said:

> In India, the real cause of the weakness that cripples our spirit of freedom arises from the impregnable social walls we raise between the different castes. (Tagore, 2007, p. 627)

Although he himself belonged to the upper caste, a Brahmin, his subgroup of Brahmins was stigmatized because a distant ancestor had converted to Islam. He was very critical of the "walls" that caused inequality and divisions in Indian society and his full support of the Inter-caste and Inter-religion Marriage Act of 1919 was a very bold step against Hinduism's basic tenet on preserving the divisions of pollution and purity. He not only supported widow remarriage, which was strictly forbidden by Hindus although it had been practiced in Vedic times, but arranged for one of his sons to be married to a woman who was widowed as a child.

Tagore expressed his ideas of caste clearly in several publications. His famous novel *Gora,* in which the foster-child named Gora gradually gets disenchanted with some aspects of Hinduism such as caste, is an articulation of Tagore's views on social exclusion. In his short story *Samaskar* (1928) and dance drama *Chandalika* (1933) he portrayed untouchability as evil and inhuman. *Chandalika* shows how an untouchable girl is made conscious of the fact that she is a human being and not an object of contempt as an outcast, when a passing Buddhist monk quenches his thirst by accepting water from her hands, which was not socially expected.

The natural beauty of rural Bengal and the mighty Padma River on the one hand delighted his aesthetic senses. On the other hand, he was shocked and deeply affected to witness the exploitation of the rural poor class by the upper classes, particularly the landlords and moneylenders. His rural reconstruction and upliftment scheme was to get the marginalized people out of their extreme poverty and misery by raising their consciousness of their plight through education and cultural development, and by empowering them through modernizing agriculture. He started small hospitals and a bank to give microcredit at a low interest rate and to which he contributed part of his Nobel Prize money. Tagore worked to remove inequality and believed that a strong democratic society would be the way to benefit the poor (Rafique, 2017).

8.5.2.2 Gender

Tagore challenged the conservative ideas of society on gender. He took the bold step of admitting women students to his university, and even had them reside on campus. They were not put in separate classes but joined the male students in class, sports and *mandir* (meditation hall) services. He encouraged women students to take part in theater and dance dramas and even had them travel to many places in India and around the world. Performing arts were associated with women of questionable repute and these radical initiatives were not easily accepted by the Bengali middle-class families at the beginning. As Nussbaum (2006, p. 361) points out, encouraging young women to have independence of mind and to physically express themselves freely "shook convention and tradition to their foundations." Tagore wrote "unexamined blind conservatism is opposed to creativity" (Sarkar, 2003, p. 168).

Tagore's dance drama *Chitrangada* is based on a story from the epic *Mahabharata* which has been interpreted and adapted in many ways. "Tagore's *Chitrangada* is a lyrical expression of love, illusion and conquest and one of the strongest gender statements ever made in Indian literature" (Mitra, 2015, p. 76). Chitrangada falls in love with the warrior Arjuna who is not attracted by her physical beauty and rejects her. The god of Love grants her exquisite beauty for one year and Arjuna is charmed by her, but she decides to shed her facade and assume her original form. Arjuna, fascinated by her personality rather than her beauty, marries her by agreeing to her several conditions:

> *I am the king's daughter*
> *Not a goddess, nor an ordinary woman*
> *Worshipping me and placing me on a pedestal, that is not me, not me*
> *Neglecting me and keeping me behind, that is not me, not me*
> *If you keep me by your side in crisis and in wealth*
> *If you allow me to stand by you in all hardship and strife*
> *You will come to know me truly*[5]

[5] The words in this translation can be found in "Chitrangada: The Warrior Princess," a video by Maya Emporium Darjeeling Tea and Indian Art Gallery, Australia. February 9, 2021. https://www.facebook.com/watch/?v=235020921498784.

8.5.2.3 Diversity

The classical Upanishads influenced the development of universalism and multiple perspectives in Tagore (Cenkner, 1976). His ideas on unity and diversity shaped his vision for his university. He wanted his students to imbibe different cultural influences, and to experience communicating with other cultures and understanding other creeds. He was strongly opposed to chauvinistic nationalism and imagined a world of unity of all peoples. With its motto, "Where the whole world meets in a single nest,"[6] he envisaged his university as the meeting point of many languages, cultures, and religions from countries of the East and of the West.

Himself a spiritual man, he was concerned about spiritual development in his students but kept religious dogma out of his schools. To him, religion was to be lived not taught. Shantiniketan was a place of learning that was universal and international in spirit. He made it clear that his university was a secular institution, but the birthdays of Christ, Buddha, Mohammed, Chaitanya, Ram Mohan Roy, and other great men were celebrated in the special glass *mandir*. He was agonized by communal violence that flared up sometimes and pronounced that "straightforward atheism is preferable to this terrible thing, delusion of religiosity" (Bhattacharya, 2011, p. 137). There was a fusion of Indian tradition and the Western philosophy in Tagore's writing. He was also influenced by Sufism, Buddhism, and folk customs.

As Malaviya (2021, p. 80) points out, "Tagore understood well how conflicts emanated not from the existence of diversity, but from stifling diversity . . . the idea that diversity can be a source of strength and not weakness," and, quoting Tagore, "perfection of unity is not in uniformity, but in harmony." He wanted to send a message of harmony, love, and peace across the globe.

8.5.2.4 Cosmopolitanism

Related to his ideas on diversity is the concept of cosmopolitanism. While he was critical of the colonial system of education as imposing a foreign culture and language at the expense of India's rich heritage, he did not think that his students should not learn about other people, their cultures, religions, and intellectual and literary traditions, science, and technology. He invited many scholars from other parts of India as well as from Europe and eastern Asia to lecture or stay to give courses and interact with his students. He encouraged his students to read world literature to understand how relationships with other people are established and conducted. The internationalism versus nationalism debate is basic to his educational philosophy (Ghosh & Naseem, 2003).

Tagore was a widely traveled man even in those days when journey was by land and sea. He traveled widely in India, and from the age of 17 he made 17 trips outside India to Europe, North and South America, and East Asia. Meeting a diversity of people from different cultures and religions, he developed a feeling of unity among people of the world and saw the oneness of humanity

[6] Tagore selected for the motto an ancient Sanskrit verse, *Yatra visvam bhavatieka nidam*.

and similarities in peoples and cultures. He loved his country and did not think that cosmopolitanism conflicted with patriotism. As he wrote:

> The monsoon clouds generated on the banks of the Nile, fertilize the far distant shores of the Ganges; ideas may have to cross from the East to the Western shores to find welcome in men's hearts and fulfil their promise. East is East and West is West. God forbid that it should be otherwise – but the twain must meet in amity, peace, and understanding; their meeting will be all the more fruitful because of their differences . . . (quoted in Salkar, 1990, p. 8)

For Tagore, the cosmopolitan person was a "universal person" who was grounded in nature (the biosphere), the universe (the spiritual space), and the community (local and global).

8.5.3 Freedom from Domination

Tagore grew up under colonial domination and was deeply affected by relationships of domination. His decolonization efforts were aimed mainly at two concerns. First, what domination does to the minds of people, and second, the imposition of English language and educational content which robbed Indian children of knowledge of their own history and culture.

8.5.3.1 Freedom of the Mind

Colonial education was restricted to upper-class Indians and an effective yet subtle way of creating a class of natives that was, according to Lord Macaulay in 1835, "Indian in blood and color; but English in talent, in opinion, in moral and in intellect" (Rao, 2020, p. 163) The rest of the population was left with no educational opportunities and remained illiterate, which Tagore believed benefited the colonial administration. At the time of Independence, the literacy rate in India was 16%; for females it was 7%. The colonial system of education in India was out of sync with local culture, language, history, and thought. Indigenous education was denigrated and discredited. Tagore worried about what the degradation of Indian culture and religion would do to the minds of the people and was afraid that they would internalize these negative attitudes:

> What I object to is the artificial arrangement by which foreign education tends to occupy all the space of our national mind and thus kills, or hampers, the great opportunity for the creation of new thought by a new combination of truths. It is this which makes me urge that all the elements in our own culture have to be strengthened; not to resist the culture of the West, but to accept and assimilate it. It must become for us nourishment not a burden. We must gain mastery over it and not live on sufferance as hewers of texts and drawers of book-learning (Datta & Robinson, 1997, p. 222)

Afraid of distorting young minds with an imported curriculum, Tagore was eager to revive the ancient values that seemed to have been lost. He was more concerned about the deformation of the mind brought about by colonial education than by colonial rule itself. To him, relationships of domination were harmful for both the oppressor and the oppressed. He did not agree with Gandhi on several means of dealing with the colonial government and rejected violence in any form. While freedom fighters sought territorial freedom, he turned his attention to fighting for freedom from the insular thinking of Indians in his educational institutions. He was very vocal in his critique of colonial exploitation, and he was equally critical about the social ills and hierarchies in Indian society.

Being a proud Indian who was also cosmopolitan in his outlook, he was happy to receive the knighthood bestowed on him in 1915 by the British crown soon after he was awarded his Nobel Prize. But, as we saw in this chapter's Introduction, when the brutal massacre by the British military at Jallianwala Bagh[7] took place in Amritsar in 1919, he did not hesitate to protest and renounce the title. In his letter to the Viceroy, Lord Chelmsford, Tagore wrote:

> The time has come when badges of honour make our shame glaring in the incongruous context of humiliation, and I for my part, wish to stand, shorn, of all special distinctions, by the side of those of my countrymen who, for their so-called insignificance, are liable to suffer degradation not fit for human beings.

8.5.3.2 Language

Tagore disliked the fact that Indian children were learning in a language which was not their own, but also learning content to which they could not relate. That pushed them to learning by rote. He had himself experienced the memorization of literary texts in English and this left little opportunity for creative and innovative thinking. One of his first essays on education, "The Mismatch of Education" (*Shikshar her-fer*), published in 1892 was a scathing critique of the pattern of education that had been established by the British. The ultimate aim of education, he argued, should be the development of the whole child for harmonious living. He stressed the value of and need for learning in the mother tongue.

It is important to point out that Tagore was not against the English language. He loved English literature and understood the importance of English globally, and for science and higher education. But he insisted that children should be taught in the early years in their mother tongue. Recent developments in language learning have established the benefits of mother tongue education, which helps a child's personal, social, and cultural identity and develops their critical thinking and literacy skills (Cummings, 2001).

English as a medium of instruction benefited the colonizers but it removed the colonized children from their roots and made them imitate the colonial masters. He wanted Indian children to be proud of their heritage and confident

[7] At a peaceful public gathering of unarmed people the army was ordered to block all exists and fire. It is estimated that between 379 and 1500 people were gunned down and over 1,200 other people were injured of whom 192 were seriously injured (Committee on Disturbances in Bombay, Delhi, and the Punjab, 1920).

individuals. He despised packaged knowledge that was given to them and killed their curiosity and creativity. He eloquently expressed his ideas in a poem in his Nobel-winning collection, *Gitanjali* (Tagore, 1966, p. 8):

> Where the mind is without fear and the head is held high
> Where knowledge is free
> Where the world has not been broken up into fragments
> By narrow domestic walls
> Where words come out from the depth of truth

Where tireless striving stretches its arms toward perfection

> Where the clear stream of reason has not lost its way
> Into the dreary desert sand of dead habit
> Where the mind is led forward by thee
> Into ever-widening thought and action
> Into that heaven of freedom, my Father, let my country awake

8.6 Conclusion

Tagore saw education as an art. He was a humanist and believed strongly in creative and emotional development.

> We have come to this world to accept it, not merely to know it. We may become powerful by knowledge, but we attain fullness by sympathy.
> (Tagore, 1933, pp. 116–17)

Tagore's theoretical ideas and emancipatory educational philosophy were built on democratic ideas of freedom of the people through decolonization of the mind, and unity of people around the globe. His experiences in life made him sensitive to the complexities of poverty and ignorance, of gender relations and colonial domination, which gave him a yearning for freedom and international friendships. He loved nature and, indeed, his university to this day is in beautiful surroundings. He had remarkable ability to absorb tradition without dogma, cosmopolitanism without crushing one's own culture, humanistic creativity along with a scientific outlook, and an appreciation of technology as more than a mere tool of production. The emancipatory concepts of cosmopolitanism, inclusiveness and quality education, upliftment of the marginalized, love and compassion, and sustainable development not only have profound relevance but an urgency in the postpandemic world.

References

Alam, F. (2006). *Rabindranath Tagore: South Asian writers in English*. eBook. Detroit: Thompson Gale.

Bandyopadhyaya, D. (2018). Rabindranath Tagore – His childhood and creativity from the perspective of a psychiatrist. *Indian Journal of Psychiatry*, 60(4), 507–09.

Banerjee, S. (2017). Through the ages of life: Rabindranath Tagore – Son, father, and educator (1861–1941). *Érudit*, 27. Digital ed. doi: doi.org/10.7202/1054400ar.

Basu, T. (2012). Caste matters: Rabindranath Tagore's engagement with India's ancient social hierarchies. *South Asia: Journal of South Asian Studies*, 35(1), 162–71.

Bhattacharya, A. (2010). Tagore on the right to education for India. In A. Bhattacharya, ed., *Education for the people: Concepts of Grundtvig, Tagore, Gandhi and Freire*. Rotterdam: Sense, pp. 143–59.

Bhattacharya, S. (2011). *Rabindranath Tagore: An interpretation*. New Delhi: Penguin Viking.

Cenkner, W. (1976). *The Hindu personality in education: Tagore, Gandhi, Aurobindo*. New Delhi: Manohar.

Collins, M. (2012). *Empire, nationalism and the postcolonial world: Rabindranath Tagore's writing on history, politics, society*. London: Routledge.

Committee on Disturbances in Bombay, Delhi, and the Punjab (1920). *Report: Disorders inquiry committee 1919–1920*. Available at: https://archive.org/details/ape9901.0001.001.umich.edu/page/XX/mode/2up?view=theater.

Connell, R. (2007). *Southern theory: The global dynamics of knowledge in social science*. Crows Nest, NSW: Allen & Unwin.

Cummings, J. (2001). Bilingual children's mother tongue: Why is it important for education? *Sprogforum*, 7(19), 15–20.

Das Gupta, U. (2004). *Rabindranath Tagore: A biography*. New Delhi: Oxford University Press.

Das Gupta, U. (2006). *Rabindranath Tagore: My life in my words*. New Delhi: Viking.

Dasgupta, S. (2020). Texts of Tagore and Tagore as text: A framework for diversity and inclusion in the twenty-first century. *The International Education Journal: Comparative Perspectives*, 19(1), 7–18.

Datta, K., & Robinson, A. (1997). *Rabindranath Tagore: The myriad minded man*. New Delhi: Rupa & Co.

Dewey, J. (1916). *Democracy and education*. New York: MacMillan.

Fanon, F. (1961/2004). *The wretched of the earth*. Trans. by R. Philcox, foreword by H. K. Bhabha, preface by J.-P. Sartre, New York: Grove Press.

Freire, P. (1970). *Pedagogy of the oppressed*. New York: Continuum.

Ghosh, R., & Naseem, A. (2003). Education is that which liberates: Educational philosophy of Rabindranath Tagore. *Journal of Post-Colonial Education (Special Issue)*, 2(1), 87–100.

Ghosh, R., Naseem, A., & Vijh, A. (2010). Tagore and education: Gazing beyond the colonial cage. In A. Abdi, ed., *Decolonizing philosophies of education*. Rotterdam: Sense, pp. 59–71.

Malaviya, R. (2021). Promoting "maitri" through education: Tagore and education for peace. *Journal of Peace Education*, 18(1), 72–91.

Mitra, S. (2015). The travels of Chitrangada and Tagore's philosophy. *Heritage*. Available at: www.bethunecollege.ac.in/heritagejournal/journals/heritageJournalVolII2015/articles2015/TheTravels-of-Chitrangada-and-Tagore-Philosophy Heritage2015.pdf.

Mukherjee, H. B. (1962). *Education for fullness: A study of the educational thought and experiment of Rabindranath Tagore*. Bombay: Asia Publishing House.

Mukherjee, M. (2021). Tagore's perspective on decolonizing education. In: *Oxford research encyclopedia of education*. Oxford University Press. doi: doi.org/10.1093/acrefore/9780190264093.013.1559.

Naravane, V. S. (1977). *An introduction to Rabindranath Tagore*. New Delhi: MacMillan Co. of India.

Neogy, A. K. (2010). *The twin dreams of Rabindranath Tagore: Santiniketan and Sriniketan*. New Delhi: National Book Trust.

Nussbaum, M. C. (2006). Education and democratic citizenship: Capabilities and quality education. *Journal of Human Development*, 7(3), 385–95.

O'Connell, K. M. (2002). *Rabindranath Tagore: The poet as educator*. Calcutta: Visva-Bharati.

O'Connell, K. M. (2003). Rabindranath Tagore on education. *The encyclopedia of pedagogy and informal education*. https://infed.org/mobi/rabindranath-tagore-on-education.

O'Connell, K. M. (2004). Approaches to holistic education: The Tagore-Montessori correspondence. *Journal of World Education*, 34(1), 12–8.

O'Connell, K. M. (2010). Rabindranath Tagore: Envisioning humanistic education at Santiniketan (1902–1922). *International Journal on Humanistic Ideology*, 2, 15–42.

Pearson, W. W. (1917). *Shantiniketan: The Bolpur school of Rabindranath Tagore*. London: Macmillan.

Rafique, A. (2017). Rabindranath: A successful social reformer. *New Age*. Available at: www.newagebd.net/article/15115/rabindranath-a-successful-social-reformer.

Rao, P. V. (2020). *Beyond Macaulay: Education in India, 1780–1860*. London and New York: Routledge.

Salkar, K. R. (1990). *Rabindranath Tagore: His impact on Indian education*. New Delhi: Sterling.

Sarkar, S. (2003). "Nari" ("Women"), extract translated in "*Ghare Baire* in its Times." In P. K. Datta, ed., *Rabindranath Tagore's the home and the world: A critical companion*. New Delhi: Permanent Black, pp. 143–73.

Sen, A. (2011, June 9). Poetry and reason: Why Rabindranath Tagore still matters. *New Republic*. Available at: newrepublic.com/article/89649/rabindra nathtagore.

Sen, S. (2014). Remembering Robi. In S. Sen, ed., *Traces of empire: India, America and post colonial cultures*. Chennai: Primus Books, pp. 58–74.

Som, R. (2009). *Rabindranath Tagore: The singer and his song*. Delhi: Penguin.

Tagore, R. (1912/2018). *Jiban Smriti or "remembrance of life."* Bengali ed. CreateSpace Independent Publishing.

Tagore, R. (1917). *My Reminiscences*. London: MacMillan (Gutenberg E-Book released in 2007). http://www.gutenberg.org/files/22217/22217-h/22217-h .htm#Page_30

Tagore, R. (1929). Ideals of education. *The Visva-Bharati Quarterly* (April–July), 73(4).

Tagore, R. (1933). My school. In *Personality: Lectures delivered in America (1917)*. London: MacMillan.

Tagore, R. (1964). The parrot's training. In S. R. Das, ed., *Boundless sky*. Calcutta: Visva-Bharati, pp. 84–88.

Tagore, R. (1966). *Gitanjali*. Trans. by W. Cenkner, London: MacMillan.

Tagore, R. (2007). Freedom. In N. Ghosh, ed., *English writings of Rabindranath Tagore: A miscellany*. New Delhi: Sahitya Akademi (original in *Vishwa-Bharati Quarterly 1957*, 4, 627–28).

Tagore, R. (2010). *My reminiscences*. BiblioLife.

Tagore, R. (1922/2016). *Creative unity*. London: Wentworth Press.

Tagore, R. (2017). *Nationalism*. Introduction by R. Guha, Cyber City, India: Penguin.

Taneja, V. R. (1983). *Educational thought and practice*. New Dehli: Sterling.

Thompson, E. (1926). *Rabindranath Tagore: Poet and dramatist*. London: Humphrey Milford, Oxford University Press.

United Nations (2005). *Resolution 60/1 adopted by the General Assembly on 16 September 2005*. World Summit Outcome. New York: Author.

Part Two

Philosophical and Normative Foundations

9

Normative Case Studies as Democratic Education

Ellis Reid and Meira Levinson

9.1 Introduction

Educational ethics as a field aims to help educators, policymakers, parents, educational partners, and all participants in civil society identify, understand, discuss, and make collective democratic decisions that help bring about more ethical educational systems, institutions, policies, and practices. While educational ethics is a broad-based effort, in this chapter, we focus on one key strategy – the normative case study. Normative case studies are "richly described, realistic accounts of complex ethical dilemmas that arise within practice or policy contexts, in which protagonists must decide among courses of action, none of which is self-evident as the right one to take" (Levinson & Fay, 2016, pp. 3–4). Generally short (2,500 words or less) and written in ordinary language, these empirically researched fictional narratives or nonfiction accounts are designed so that they can be read quickly and then immediately discussed by a diverse group of people in a faculty meeting, parent–teacher association evening, professional development session, college class, or community meeting. By focusing on everyday dilemmas in which it is impossible to realize all important values and principles (or all reasonable interpretations of a single value or principle) at once, normative case studies are not written to lead participants to a single correct answer or one specific "aha!" Rather, they aim to help diverse participants engage with one another about real-world ethical challenges, understand others' perspectives and appreciate their insights even if and as they continue to disagree, and deepen their own capacity and inclination for ethical reflection.

The normative case study "Walling Off or Welcoming In," for example, focuses on the (fictional) Jersey City K-8 School Culture Committee as it tries to figure out how to reestablish a positive and inclusive school culture in light of heightened political, racial, and civic divisions following the election of Donald Trump in 2016. Committee members must develop and agree to a plan for responding to a number of incidents revealing how these broader social divisions reverberate within the school. These include three White first-graders building a wall out of blocks to "keep the Mexicans out," a friend group of fourth graders falling out over one child's use of the term "criminal illegals" to refer to undocumented immigrants, and a White seventh grader being shunned by classmates for his parents' support of Trump (Calleja, Kokenis, & Levinson, 2019). As a second example, "Faith in Mr. D" follows a fictional middle school principal in Toronto who is feeling torn about how to support his primarily Muslim students in being able to attend Friday prayer services and return to class (support he is required by the Canadian constitution to offer in some form) – perhaps by enabling the local imam to lead services in the school cafeteria after lunch – without seeming to endorse gender discrimination and other concerning practices. The case raises questions about the meanings and enactment of diversity, equality, and inclusion (DEI) along multiple dimensions in a school context (Bialystok, n.d.). As a final example, the nonfiction normative case study "Eyes in the Backs of Their Heads 2.0" examines school districts' uses of digital surveillance software to monitor student speech and behavior, prompting conversation about how districts balance student safety, legal obligations, autonomy, and civil liberties in democracies worldwide (Levinson & Mitchell, 2019).

Normative case studies such as these are designed to serve three broad roles within the context of educational ethics. First, cases can play a *heuristic* role by providing philosophers, educators, and policymakers an opportunity to test normative principles and theories in authentic contexts. "Walling Off or Welcoming In," for example, offers a real-world stress test of such principles as political nonpartisanship in public schools and zero tolerance for bullying; "Faith in Mr. D" enables educators, policymakers, and parents to gain clarity about what they believe DEI demands. Second, cases can play a *generative* role by identifying contexts or phenomena for which extant theories provide insufficient guidance or conceptual clarity, spurring development of new principles, concepts, or other theoretical resources. In a commentary written about "Eyes in the Backs of Their Heads 2.0," for instance, Carrie James and Emily Weinstein contrast an "app-dependent approach" to student surveillance, in which technologies are used to constrain students' action, with an "app-enabling" process, meaning one that expands and enriches students' capacities, for supporting student safety (James & Weinstein, 2019). In his "Eyes" commentary, Erhardt Graeff expands democratic participatory design theories to discuss the roles that students, educators, parents, and administrators can play in democratizing digital surveillance (Graeff, 2019). Third, normative case studies play a *pedagogical* role by offering opportunities for educators, policymakers, and other interested stakeholders to develop sound moral judgment in ethically fraught, challenging situations. We recently led small group conversations about "Eyes" with about 50 data science professionals from school districts around the United States, during which time they used the case to extrapolate to their own practices and discuss principles that they might apply moving forward. "Walling Off" has similarly been used by groups of educators to help them prepare for and respond to political division in their own classrooms and schools.

Our focus in this chapter is this third, pedagogical role played by normative case studies. We argue that the normative case study approach can be profitably understood as a kind of democratic education by virtue both of its unfolding in the context of democratic relations among learners and of its support for democratic competencies. In other words, normative case studies enable interaction among democratic citizens confronted by a common problem and are oriented toward supporting professionals to develop key democratic skills. In particular, we argue that by reading and engaging in facilitated discussions of normative case studies, participants develop their ethical sensitivity and moral agency, learn to deliberate with others in the face of moral disagreement, and grow in their capacity to work as part of a collective to tackle common problems.

In the rest of this chapter, we elaborate on what it means to understand the normative case study approach as a kind of democratic education. Although normative case studies are used by a wide range of audiences, we focus here on practitioners in light of our focus on the pedagogical role of cases and our belief that supporting the ethical work of practitioners is critical to promoting educational justice. We begin by describing normative case studies in more detail as a genre and a pedagogical tool. In Section 9.3, we outline the ways that this approach supports moral sensitivity and moral agency, paying careful attention to the relationships among moral sensitivity, judgment, and moral agency. In Section 9.4, we shift our attention to the importance of disagreement within democratic life. We argue that centering normative case studies on ethical dilemmas helps participants develop the capacity for sustaining reasonable deliberation across disagreement, which we argue is critical to the kind of collective action necessary to face a range of ethical challenges. Alongside the development of moral agency, then, we contend that supporting the capacity for good disagreement is a second key aim of the normative case study approach. In the final section, we address two interrelated concerns rooted in the recognition that while the normative case study approach relies on participants confronting disagreement to achieve its key ends, groups may instead reach premature consensus thanks to groupthink, power dynamics that elevate some perspectives and suppress others, or rejection of the idea that there is any ethical dilemma at all. We return to cases' construction as a genre and as a pedagogical tool to suggest that careful writing and facilitation can address these concerns, and in fact that they help clarify the value of normative case studies as an approach to democratic education.

9.2 Normative Case Studies as a Genre and Pedagogical Tool

The concept of the "normative case study" was first developed by sociologist David Thatcher in 2006 to describe case studies that "aim to contribute to our understanding of important public values ... by bringing into view situations we had not previously envisioned, since normative reflection about such cases can lead us to rethink the ideals to which we are committed if the ideals advise counterintuitive judgments about the case" (Thatcher, 2006, p. 1632). He focuses on normative case studies as scholarly exercises in theory-building, arguing that they contribute to normative theory development in a manner similar to how causal and interpretive case studies contribute to the development of explanatory theory (Thatcher, 2006, p. 1635). Thatcher illustrates this through analyzing Jane Jacobs' *The Death and Life of Great American Cities*, which is an extended case study of New York's Greenwich Village and other neighborhoods. He shows that Jacobs' work not only develops social scientific concepts such as "street eyes" to explain how informal surveillance works in many city neighborhoods, but also normative arguments about the value of vital public life.

The normative case studies that we are concerned with in this chapter are inspired by Thatcher's conceptualization, but they take a different form than works like Jacobs' book. As we described in the Introduction of this chapter, the normative case studies that we and others have been developing (see, for example, Levinson & Fay, 2016, 2019; Taylor & Kuntz, 2021; Harvard Graduate School of Education, n.d.) are quite short – they are generally able to be read by a native speaker in about 10 minutes – and are written to highlight reasonable but conflicting perspectives about the choices at stake. In "Walling Off," for example, members of the School Culture Committee struggle with how to respond to students who repeat Trump's language. One parent suggests it should be treated as bullying, asking, "How are kids supposed to react when they hear their classmates insinuating that they don't even belong in this country?" The principal warns that educators are mandated reporters for bullying and harassment: "Do we really want to criminalize what should be teachable moments?" A teacher raises developmental considerations – on what grounds should the school distinguish among the speech of first versus fourth versus seventh graders in making these determinations? – while a second parent points out that his own child is feeling excluded and harassed by both students and teachers because of his support for Trump (all quotations from Calleja, Kokenis, & Levinson, 2019). "Eyes," similarly, includes statements and data from a sweeping range of sources including educators, legal briefs and legislation, psychologists, counselors, school administrators, civil liberties advocates, and digital surveillance companies themselves. The cases are thus written to illuminate areas of uncertainty and values conflicts, rather than to make definitive value propositions of the sorts that Thatcher identifies.

By giving voice to multiple reasonable perspectives, normative case studies also enable diverse interlocutors to engage with one another in collective but divergent conversation about hard ethical choices, rather than reinforcing solely convergent viewpoints or best practices. This can happen in many ways. Groups often use a standard discussion protocol to talk through a case, beginning with the question "What are the dilemmas in this case, and for whom?" Discussion participants then move on to considering why these dilemmas arise, what actions might be taken by whom to address one or more of the challenges, and what participating in the case deliberation has revealed to them as participants about their own school community, about their values, or about educational ethics more broadly.[1] When we partner with schools and districts to lead case discussions, we often extend this protocol to give time to participants to draw explicit connections to similar challenges they are experiencing in their own context. By priming people's capacity for disagreement and comfort with uncertainty during the part of the discussion that is focused explicitly on the case, facilitators are more readily able to elicit honest and conflicting ideas from participants about the ethical dilemmas that are arising in their own setting. A second key distinction between our normative case studies and those described by Thatcher, then, is that our cases are written to be discussed.

In the Section 9.3, we explore in more depth both of these key distinguishing features of our approach to normative case studies: (i) the focus on ethical dilemmas and (ii) the importance of discussion.

9.3 Moral Sensitivity and Epistemic Friction

The normative case study approach can be understood as a form of democratic education, first, because it promotes *relations of democratic equality* among discussion participants. By relations of democratic equality, we mean the ways that participants both (i) recognize that their own individual beliefs and understanding are necessarily partial and (ii) value their fellow participants as offering different, potentially enriching perspectives. Through careful facilitation and the use of a structured discussion protocol, our approach encourages participants to enter into relations of democratic equality, allowing them to contribute to one another's development as moral agents. We argue in this section that the democratic form of the normative case study approach, and its concomitant faith in the collective knowledge of education professionals, is critical to promoting moral sensitivity and, ultimately, moral agency. We start by clarifying the connections among sensitivity, judgment, and agency. We then expand on the importance of the democratic form of our approach. We will return to the importance of facilitation in Section 9.5.

One critical goal of the normative case study approach is the development of moral sensitivity among educators and education professionals. By moral sensitivity, we mean an agent's capacity to recognize the morally and ethically salient features of a particular situation.[2] Moral sensitivity is a critical component of moral judgment, since failures of sensitivity ensure that an agent will fail to judge that scenario appropriately irrespective of their capacity for moral reasoning. As Lawrence Blum (1991) has argued:

> An agent may reason well in moral situations, uphold the strictest standards of impartiality for testing her maxims and moral principles, and be adept at deliberation. Yet unless she perceives moral situations as moral situations,

[1] For further guidance about normative case study pedagogies, see Levinson & Fay, 2016, ch. 7; Levinson & Fay, 2019, ch. 10.

[2] Although some philosophers have drawn important semantic and conceptual differences between "ethics" and "morals" or "morality," we treat the terms as interchangeable for the purposes of this chapter.

> and unless she perceives their moral character accurately, her moral principles and skill at deliberation will be for nought and may even lead her astray. (p. 701)

Following Blum, we contend that moral perception is a critical aspect of moral agency. Moral perception involves developing a particular take on a situation that draws one's attention to certain morally salient features of that situation (and away from others), thereby setting the scene for moral deliberation. Agents demonstrate moral sensitivity when they appropriately pick out the morally salient features of a situation.[3] In engaging in discussions of normative case studies, participants are offered structured opportunities to engage with differently situated peers in relations of democratic equality in the service of broadening their moral sensitivity.

An example will help to illustrate the importance of moral sensitivity. In the case study "Stolen Trust," a high school teacher believes her cell phone has been stolen from her purse (Burger & Levinson, 2016). The teacher, Ms. Smith, had checked her phone messages right after school and returned her phone to her purse afterward. She hasn't taken her phone out of her purse since and is certain that her phone had to have been taken some time that afternoon. She had spent that entire time working one-on-one with her student Wesley, and she knows her purse hasn't left her side except for a brief moment when she left her purse and Wesley alone in the room together. Relatively quickly, Ms. Smith comes to believe that the culprit must be Wesley. She then faces the question of whether to report his (apparent) theft to school or law enforcement authorities.

The case offers a number of additional details about the context in which Ms. Smith and Wesley find themselves. Wesley is Black and lives near the school in an economically depressed area. He has not had many strong, lasting connections with adults. Ms. Smith is White, college-educated, and early in her teaching career. The two of them have been working closely together for months, building a strong personal connection and producing significant academic gains for Wesley. Their work together, however, takes place within the context of a zero-tolerance school. "Zero tolerance" in this case means that Ms. Smith is contractually obligated to report all instances of rule-breaking to the school administration and that misbehavior is dealt with severely. As theft plainly violates school rules (and state law), Ms. Smith has a contractual duty to report Wesley's theft. She has good reasons to believe that the school will report the theft to the police and that the state will then prosecute 17-year-old Wesley for felony theft as an adult.

[3] Moral sensitivity, however, should not be understood as some general capacity that inevitably transfers from context to context or that offers a single scale along which we can rank moral agents. Agents, for instance, may well be able to accurately perceive the morally salient features of their professional life, while failing to be similarly sensitive in their home life. Or, an agent may typically demonstrate moral insensitivity in most instances but demonstrate acute moral sensitivity in some particular instance. Alternatively, an agent may generally demonstrate moral sensitivity while regularly failing to perceive some particular feature of the world as being morally salient, even if they would agree that that feature – race or gender come to mind here – is morally significant if it were pointed out to them.

As Ms. Smith considers how to proceed, she could potentially fail to be appropriately morally sensitive in at least two ways: first, by failing to recognize Wesley as a child and, second, by failing to recognize the moral significance of background injustices.

The first possible failure of moral sensitivity is unfortunately common. As a matter of both developmental fact and of law, Wesley is still a child at least for another year or two, and children regularly do stupid, careless things that shouldn't jeopardize their long-term life prospects in light of their diminished moral responsibility. While we must treat children as if they *are* responsible at least some of the time to aid their moral development (i.e., they should experience a sense of responsibility and feel the force of the consequences that flow from this), they should not in fact suffer any lasting negative consequences (see Levinson, 2022). Particularly for Black boys like Wesley, however, educators (often, but not only, White educators) can misperceive these children as adults, changing how they understand and react to their behavior. Through this process of "adultification" taking place within the mind of teachers (and others), poor decisions by a student can come to be read not as childish misbehavior but as a threat demanding serious response and deserving of serious, even life-changing, consequences (Ferguson, 2000, p. 179). If Ms. Smith were to respond to Wesley's theft by immediately thinking he deserved to be charged, prosecuted, and punished as an adult, then she would demonstrate at least one failure of moral sensitivity by failing to perceive Wesley as a child.

Such a response might also signal a second failure of moral sensitivity by Ms. Smith, in the form of misrecognition of or indifference to the significant background injustices at play in this case. Neither Wesley's nor Ms. Smith's race, class, and subjection to zero-tolerance policies are incidental to the case. Low-income Black students are far more likely to be subject to zero-tolerance rules and consequences than are White students, particularly those from middle- or upper-income families; they also are less likely to have access to schools and other organizations that offer consistent, strong adult support networks. Teachers in the United States, by contrast, are disproportionately White, even in schools and districts serving mostly students of color. There are many reasons for this disparity, including systematic discrimination against Black educators and in favor of White educators. Ms. Smith's position of power over Wesley is no historical accident. With these patterns and histories in mind, Tommie Shelby writes in response to the case, "We should, on grounds of reciprocity and civic duty, support and comply with the rules of a just social order. But we don't have an obligation to obey the rules of a seriously unjust society or its basic institutions. This is so even if we have said we would uphold the regulations, as Ms. Smith did when she signed her teaching contract" (Shelby, 2016, p. 79).

Shelby goes on to argue that in light of the weight of the unjust burdens shouldered by Wesley, Ms. Smith has a duty to shield him from the prospect of expulsion and jail time, which would only further compound the injustices he suffers. Whether or not one agrees with Shelby's specific analysis of Ms. Smith's duties in this case, he raises an important second kind of failure of moral sensitivity: namely, the failure to see one's duties as fitting within a broader set of duties to ensure just relations among members of one's political community. We would be concerned by a teacher who was so consumed by her role and responsibilities as a teacher that she failed to perceive the myriad injustices that shape the lives of her students or to recognize these injustices as involving her own moral agency.

Critically, these failures of moral sensitivity typically occur automatically rather than reflectively. Adultification, for instance, is best understood as an instinctive and immediate process wherein a teacher subconsciously sees some children as possessing adult characteristics and responds to these children accordingly. Judgments about role morality and the relevance of structural injustices are also generally made subconsciously and instinctively. As moral sensitivity is typically automatic, failures of sensitivity can doom moral judgment before one can even begin to deliberate about what to do. To quote Blum again, "moral perception comes on the scene prior to moral judgment" (Blum, 1991, p. 702).

However, while these processes may be automatic, they aren't fixed. The discussion protocol we use to lead normative case study discussions, for instance, is premised in part on the belief that professional educators can develop their moral sensitivity through slowing down the process of perceiving and judging the ethical features of educational decision-making. Our protocol starts by asking participants to think about the ethical dilemmas at play in the case and the reasons they're properly considered dilemmas – for instance, because the problems involve tensions among competing values or differing interpretations of some particular value. We usually spend at least 50–60% of the time allocated for the normative case study discussion on these two questions: (i) What are the dilemmas in the case, and for whom? (ii) Why are they dilemmas? We "sit" on these questions precisely in order to slow people's thinking down and expand their moral sensitivity. In starting by investigating the nature of the central ethical dilemmas, and by putting off the moment of decision, we encourage participants to develop their capacity to recognize morally salient features of ethical challenges of professional practice.

Moreover, normative case study discussions invite people to articulate their ideas out loud and deliberate with one another as a group, rather than merely think individually, about what's at stake in the case. In doing so, participants expose their own ideas to (ideally constructive) critical feedback and response from others, as well as gain exposure to other perspectives that they might never have considered. This process forces participants to slow down and consider which considerations are relevant and, in at least some instances, they come to recognize that certain features of the world that may ordinarily escape their notice are critical to good moral judgment. This process stands in contrast to best practices oriented training designed to give educators a toolbox of predefined responses so they can act quickly and be solutions-oriented. While we don't deny that defining and routinizing best practices can be useful, we argue that the pressure to act quickly can be detrimental to contextually sensitive right action and can also discourage professionals from seeking out colleagues to discuss ethically challenging decisions. Normative case study discussions, by contrast, offer education professionals the opportunity to reflect, engage with peers, and develop their capacity to see the full ethical complexity of the challenges they regularly confront in their practice.

This is the first sense in which the normative case study approach constitutes a form of democratic education. Our approach relies, in important respects, on enabling differently positioned professionals to share their situated knowledge so they can independently and collectively develop a deepened ethical sensitivity to the range of considerations that are morally salient. In effect, we rely on a kind of *epistemic friction* that forces participants to compare their beliefs and understandings of the case to others, justify why they take some elements of a case to be critical, and confront why they allow other elements of the case to slide into the background (Medina, 2013, p. 50). The normative case study approach can be understood as democratic as it realizes egalitarian relations among differently situated knowers as part of a commitment to the belief that engagement with diverse perspectives promotes moral agency.

Returning to "Stolen Trust" will help us to illustrate the sort of epistemic friction we have in mind. That case, which was cowritten by one of the two authors of this chapter, describes Ms. Smith as being certain that her phone was stolen by her student, Wesley. She knows her phone was in her purse all afternoon and that her purse was only out of her sight for the brief moment she stepped out of her classroom and left Wesley alone. In discussions of the case, however, we regularly encounter participants who refuse to even consider the idea that Ms. Smith faces any dilemma at all; surely, she's simply wrong about where she last had her phone. We often call responses like this the "magic fairy dust solutions" as they make difficult normative questions disappear by simply redescribing the case.

Other times, however, participants question Ms. Smith's certainty in a way that helpfully forces the group to reconsider not just Ms. Smith's perception of the event but also their own. In his commentary about the case, for instance, David Knight doesn't deny that Wesley may well have taken Ms. Smith's phone, but he nonetheless presses both her and all who engage with the case to challenge "how we choose to see, understand, and imagine our students and their possibilities." He suggests that by interrogating our own biases about who is likely a thief, educators can engage in "acts of critical imagination" that enable them "to exercise agency in an active way that reflects one's ethical commitments rather than in a manner that passively reinforces extant social biases and injustices" (Knight, 2016, pp. 93, 95). In taking up Knight's challenge, normative case study discussion participants support a kind of beneficial epistemic resistance against the credulity of those who may be too quick to accept the suspicions of White people about the wrongdoing of Black people. The friction offered by these alternative positions allows us to reflect on our ethical perception, overcoming possible ethical insensitivities, and also invites us to see ourselves as active ethical agents and "autonomous decision makers (even in highly regulated settings)" (Knight, 2016, p. 93). Central to our conception of moral agency, then, is a democratic commitment to deliberation with differently situated others.

9.4 Ethical Disagreement and Democratic Deliberation

The second sense in which the normative case study approach is democratic shifts our focus from the *form* of our approach to its *content*. We contend that by focusing participants on discussions of ethical dilemmas, the normative case study approach supports participants to develop their capacity to disagree with one another well. That is, in deliberating about practical questions for which there is no clear course of action, participants are encouraged to consider ethical challenges from multiple reasonable perspectives, even shifting perspectives across the course of a single discussion as other participants present new reasons for action or rebut old ones. The normative case study approach can be understood as a form of democratic education because it supports participants in developing the capacity to disagree with one another well about challenging moral issues in education.

Moral disagreement is endemic to democratic life. Being able to sustain reasoned deliberation across disagreement – what we're calling disagreeing well – is therefore a vital democratic skill. As Amy Gutmann and Dennis Thompson have argued, there are at least four drivers of moral disagreement in a democracy. Following David Hume, they identify two of these drivers as the facts of *moderate scarcity* and our *limited generosity*. Together, these two features of the human condition ensure ongoing debate among individuals over scarce resources to which each has some legitimate claim. Gutmann and Thompson further identify *conflicts among fundamental values* and *incomplete human understanding* as two additional drivers of moral disagreement. These two latter sources of disagreement also reinforce one another. The fact of conflicting values ensures that agents will regularly confront practical questions that demand challenging moral judgments about how to negotiate competing considerations, while incomplete human understanding ensures that we will often fail in these situations to find a unique solution (assuming one exists) and find ourselves confronted by disagreement. As Gutmann and Thompson conclude, the pervasiveness and seeming permanence of these four features of our democratic life ensure that "the problem of moral disagreement is a condition with which we must learn to live, not merely an obstacle to be overcome on the way to a just society" (Gutmann & Thompson, 2000, p. 26).

These four sources of moral disagreement are also operative within the field of education, ensuring educators will regularly face challenging ethical dilemmas in their practice. In fact, with respect to scarcity, in many places around the world (including, shamefully, the United States), many educators work in underfunded schools that enforce conditions of more than moderate scarcity – of educational materials, preparation time, space, training, even clean air and buildings – and work with students from low socioeconomic status backgrounds who struggle with significant scarcity in their home lives, too. These two sources of scarcity work together to force difficult moral questions – about how to divide limited resources among particularly vulnerable, unjustly overburdened young people, about the responsibilities of educators already working long hours and, in some cases, doing things like paying for classroom supplies out of pocket. Given the fact of limited generosity – among all stakeholders, including students and teachers alike – these challenging tradeoffs can produce deep disagreements.

Education professionals must also regularly deal with value conflicts. "Stolen Trust" offers an example of what we mean. In case discussions, educators regularly attest to the importance of care in their work. Caring often manifests in what Nel Noddings has called "engrossment" – the effort to feel with the person being cared for, becoming fully receptive to their perspective (Noddings, 1986, p. 30). Educators, however, are responsible not only for the student directly in front of them but for all of their other assigned students as well, and possibly even for those whom they will serve in the future. Doing right by these other students often demands avoiding or at least limiting this sort of engrossment with a particular student, both by widening educators' aperture of care and by sometimes prioritizing values like fairness or consistency instead. In the case of Ms. Smith and Wesley, for example, normative case study discussion participants sometimes point to the tension between caring for Wesley and ensuring consistency in the application of rules, both because consistency may be valuable for its own sake and because such consistency can be critical to helping students feel secure at school. As Elizabeth Anderson puts it in her commentary on the case, "To the extent that strict rules of orderly conduct are needed to create a school environment that promotes learning, they are demanded by justice" (Anderson, 2016, p. 88) – although she also clarifies later, "Justice [also] demands that [Ms. Smith] oppose institutional racism," (Anderson, 2016, p. 90) thus reigniting ethical tensions within the value of educational justice itself. Participants also raise concerns about the impact that Ms. Smith's potentially losing her job would have on the other students she teaches. Even if Ms. Smith were miraculously to land on her feet and secure another teaching job somewhere despite having been fired for failing to adhere to uphold district policy, how would her choice to risk being fired demonstrate care for, or be fair to, the other students in her care? (One might be particularly concerned about Ms. Smith's choosing to prioritize care for Wesley over her responsibilities to her law-abiding students, many of whom are also likely struggling with the impact of racial and economic injustice in their own lives but have not resorted to theft.)

We dwell on these sources of moral conflict and disagreement in order to underscore the range and depth of the ethical challenges educators face. Especially given persistent issues with both underfunding and overpolicing of schools and students, educators are frequently put into positions where they are asked to do justice in situations where doing justice is simply not possible.[4] As one of us has previously written, this impossible demand can lead to moral injury – "the trauma of perpetrating significant moral wrong against others despite one's wholehearted desire and responsibility to do otherwise" (Levinson, 2015, p. 207). This sort of moral injury is both bad in itself and can lead to

[4] Although hyperpolicing of students and the establishment of a "school to prison pipeline" may be most visible in the United States, which is where "Stolen Trust" is set, overpolicing, particularly of youth from historically marginalized communities, is unfortunately prevalent in many national contexts. Examples in Europe, for instance, include PREVENT legislation and associated surveillance, particularly of Pakistani and Bangladeshi communities in the UK (as illuminated by renewed attention to the Trojan Horse Affair; Reed & Sayed, 2021; elevated rates of arrest in the Parisian banlieues and of school exclusions of Muslim students throughout France; policing of Roma students across Central Europe; and excess policing of immigrant, Muslim, and Turkish youth in the Netherlands and Germany.

teachers' feeling demoralized, burning out, and even exiting the profession, which risks further harming students who lose ethically sensitive, veteran teachers (Santoro, 2018). For people who remain in the profession, an opposite harm may occur. In his study of the moral lives of street-level bureaucrats – that is, frontline state workers, including teachers – Bernardo Zacka finds that especially under conditions of scarcity, these service workers may develop reductive moral dispositions to help manage the strain of the conflicting demands placed on them. "Reductive dispositions truncate not only the moral perception of street-level bureaucrats, but also their normative sensibility. Such dispositions fail to do justice to the full range of considerations that frontline workers must remain attuned to" (Zacka, 2017, p. 99).

We recognize that many of the challenges we've named, from immediate values conflicts and experiences of moral injury to the potential downstream consequences of burnout, demoralization, and the development of reductive moral dispositions in large part reflect systemic failings rooted in an unjust basic structure. However, we believe that the essential work of agitating for deeper structural transformations must also be accompanied by strategies that support educators and students in the here and now – and that normative case study discussions can, in fact, support both sets of aims. This is in part because such discussions help educators develop moral imagination and sensitivity, as we discussed in Section 9.3. But it is also because collective action is central to both sets of strategies – near-term and long-term – and learning how to live with moral disagreement is critical to pursuing collective action. The ability to engage in good disagreement supports coalition-building among like-minded, though not fully aligned stakeholders; it also supports good epistemic habits that encourage good collective work.

With respect to coalition-building, the capacity to sustain deliberation across disagreement opens up the possibility of finding collaborators with whom collective action initially seems unlikely. By recognizing the reasonableness of those who disagree with us and the moral status of the reasons from which they act, we manifest an attitude of mutual respect toward our interlocutors that helps to leave open the possibility of finding a mutually agreeable basis for action in the future. As Gutmann and Thompson write, "Mutual respect not only helps sustain a moral community in the face of conflict but also can contribute toward resolving the conflict" (Gutmann & Thompson, 2000, p. 80). They go on to identify a set of capacities and dispositions they argue can help democratic citizens manifest the kind of mutual respect that can help sustain the possibility for collective action (Gutmann & Thompson, 2000, pp. 82–85).

The normative case study approach puts participants in a position where they are likely to confront a range of conflicting views on authentic ethical challenges, and it encourages these participants to approach these views with open-mindedness and respect. Furthermore, by doing so in the context of a case discussion, rather than solely in response to a concrete dispute that must be resolved in real time, participants will arguably be more open to engaging with alternative perspectives and to considering the views of typically opposed stakeholders. Educators feel invested in the dilemmas raised by the case studies, but they also can achieve a kind of emotional and reflective distance that is harder to maintain when debating immediate decisions that will impact one's own students or school district. By working through competing normative principles, conceptions, and standpoints through the relative safety of a case discussion, educators and policymakers may then feel not only better prepared but also more open and empathetic when they confront similar conflicts in the context of a parent–teacher conference, faculty meeting, or school board standoff.

This does not mean, of course, that educators and policymakers should accept any and all normative claims as having equal (or even any) weight, and well-conducted normative case study discussions do not encourage participants to adopt such a stance. Disagreeing well demands that we learn to distinguish between reasonable and unreasonable points of view, and that we be willing to reject the latter even when they are being put forward in good faith by people we otherwise view as democratic equals. This aspect of democratic education brings together the skill of moral sensitivity that we discussed in the Section 9.3 with the disposition to sustain reasonable disagreement that we have been considering in this section. Professionals who lack moral sensitivity risk failing to distinguish between what is normatively reasonable versus unreasonable, potentially sacrificing good disagreement in favor of hollow accommodation, a hunt for agreement simply for agreement's sake; we do not believe this serves democratic aims or upholds democratic values any more than too-quick rejection of reasonable disagreement does.

Normative case studies can support professionals' development of this kind of civic ethical discrimination in two ways. First, they are written to engage educators in deliberation about reasonable dilemmas rather than unreasonable disagreements. For example, "Stolen Trust" focuses on Ms. Smith's dilemma about how to fulfill her obligations given that she is teaching in a zero-tolerance school, rather than on whether the school itself should maintain its zero-tolerance policies, since such policies are in fact empirically and normatively indefensible, even though they remain widespread. Similarly, the principal in "Faith in Mr. D" must confront the existence of Islamophobia in wrestling with how to accommodate his Muslim students' prayer attendance, but the case does not present these Islamophobic beliefs as worthy of respect in a democracy, even if they must be addressed as strategic matter (see Levinson & Geron, forthcoming, for further discussion of these issues).

Second, participants in normative case study discussions often explicitly discuss what views and moral claims deserve to be treated seriously versus rejected out of hand as unreasonable. This very question lies at the heart of democratic deliberation, particularly in democracies that are undergoing rapid norm shifts or facing deepening partisan schisms (Levinson & Reid, 2019). Too often, the failure to negotiate the inevitable disagreements that arise in situations like these is that educators move to excise any and all potentially controversial material from the agenda, whether that means not teaching controversial issues in the classroom, abandoning divisive policies even when they are demonstrably just and equitable, or even banning award-winning books. By bringing the conversation openly into deliberative spaces, however, the normative case study approach can support education professionals' inclinations and capacities to engage with one another about what should be treated as legitimately controversial, and strengthen their commitments to uphold ethical policies and practices in the face of unreasonable challenges.

9.5 The Normative Case Study Approach in Practice

These very features of normative case studies may, however, raise two interrelated concerns about their appropriateness as a form of democratic education: in particular, about how normative case study discussions may suppress rather than enhance both moral sensitivity and practices of good disagreement. The first concern is about the dynamics of normative case study discussions: what is to guarantee that participants in any normative case study discussion will embrace epistemic friction – or even provide any epistemic resistance to one another – rather than engage in mutually reinforcing groupthink? The second concern is about normative case studies' ideological foundations: Why should we expect normative case study authors to be better than anyone else at challenging their own ideological beliefs and blinkered understandings in centering dilemmas that allow for the appropriate range of competing ethical claims rather than welcoming some unreasonable stances while excluding other reasonable viewpoints? Normative case studies are not neutral, so how can we trust that these tools for democratic education will not themselves be exploited for partisan ends?

While we are sympathetic to both concerns, we also believe that two critical features of the normative case study approach – namely, the roles of the discussion facilitator and the case writer – offer some level of protection against both objections. To begin with, a well-crafted case is designed internally to encourage groups to consider novel and challenging perspectives. As we have mentioned, every case includes sympathetic accounts or representations of conflicting beliefs and values. In this respect, critically, the characters themselves can often serve as valuable sources of epistemic resistance. One key principle guiding our approach to writing normative case studies is that characters should be portrayed in their best light. That is, we strive to write cases in which well-intentioned, thoughtful, competent, and ethically sensitive individuals disagree about what to do and about the relevant ethical considerations that ought to drive their action. In doing so, we hope to encourage participants to take seriously the views presented by even those characters whose views they disagree with. We contend that this strategy ensures that, even among like-minded groups, normative case study discussions will always present participants with views demanding careful consideration and response.

Well-trained discussion facilitators can further press participants to articulate and engage with competing perspectives, even in groups that seem initially leery of disagreement or of making themselves vulnerable to critique. Democratic theorists have long recognized that unjust background inequalities regularly assert themselves in deliberative contexts, subverting the ability of the unjustly disadvantaged to press their particular claims or, even, to be taken as people whose claims merit paying attention to (see Mansbridge, 1983; Sanders, 1997).

Simply sitting down to deliberate with others within our present nonideal context, then, isn't necessarily a sound strategy for supporting key democratic commitments, nor does it necessarily manifest mutual respect among differently situated discussants. A capable facilitator, however, can play the critical role of helping to ensure that different viewpoints are listened to, that no one dominates the discussion, and that potentially uncomfortable tensions within a group aren't ignored. While a facilitator is no silver bullet, good facilitation can help support the kind of group deliberation liable to achieve the aims of the normative case study approach.

Facilitators can draw upon multiple strategies to promote sound deliberation. For instance, simply by mentioning to a group that a handful of people have spoken the most, facilitators can help encourage quieter voices to speak up and louder voices to listen. Facilitators can also take on more active roles. They may bring out overlooked character perspectives or remind participants of details from the case that haven't factored into the conversation. Facilitators may also ask discussion participants to explain their reasoning, ask probing questions to uncover a misconception or an unspoken presupposition, rephrase claims to make them more pointed, or even directly challenge a participant's framing of a dilemma or a principle. In this way, the facilitator herself can act as a key source of epistemic resistance, helping ensure the kind of productive friction necessary to good normative case study discussions. More basically, a facilitator can simply encourage a group to follow the discussion protocol, discouraging people from jumping immediately toward what course of action they believe is called for. In this way, facilitators encourage the kind of slow thinking that is critical to supporting moral sensitivity.

Good facilitation is not a panacea, of course. Groups committed to some mistake, moral or otherwise, will be less well served by the normative case study approach than groups who possess greater virtues like intellectual humility or open-mindedness. Furthermore, insofar as normative case studies shape the terrain of reasonable disagreement, ruling out certain views or perspectives even as they welcome in others, some groups will inevitably not find certain cases generative because they reject how those cases are framed. Frankly, this challenge is unavoidable; it applies to every form of democratic education, not just to normative case studies. The literature on controversial issues teaching is helpful here. As education scholars who have written on this topic have noted, to label some issue controversial and bring it into the classroom for discussion implies that there are reasonable positions on multiple sides worthy of student exploration. However, much of what is actually controversial in the public sphere – for example, vaccine safety, election integrity – involves bad faith arguments or failures to properly understand the relevant evidence. Naming an issue controversial, therefore, demands judgment (Hess & McAvoy, 2015).

Something similar is true of crafting normative case studies. Naming something as an ethical dilemma is to assert that reasonable people can defend different sides of the dilemma, whether because they prioritize the relevant values in different ways or because they disagree about what it means to apply some key principle in the particular context of the case. If one horn of the dilemma represents an unreasonable point of view, a normative case study risks promoting the wrong sort of disagreement. Therefore, case authors must draw on their own ethical and professional judgment in framing dilemmas. They cannot simply rely on the fact of public controversy as a reliable guide (Levinson & Reid, 2019). Perhaps unsurprisingly, developing the central dilemma of a case is often one of the most time-consuming aspects of case writing, often being visited repeatedly over the course of the case development process (Levinson & Geron, forthcoming).

While there are certainly limits to what the normative case study approach can accomplish, we believe that these limits shouldn't detract from what it can do. At root, this approach takes seriously the critical capacities of education professionals and aims to put these professionals in the position to develop as moral agents and as democratic citizens. In a pluralistic democracy like ours, we believe this combination of faith and professional support is crucial, and that well-written normative case studies and well-facilitated case discussions can be a powerful tool for providing such support.

References

Anderson, E. (2016). No just outcome. In M. Levinson & J. Fay, eds. Dilemmas of educational ethics: Cases and commentaries. Cambridge, MA: Harvard Education Press, pp. 88–92.

Beachum, L. (2022, February 22). Jewish lawmaker denounces bill banning critical race theory: "I cannot accept a neutral, judgment-free approach." *Washington Post.* Available at: https://www.washingtonpost.com/nation/2022/02/22/wyoming-critical-race-theory.

Bialystok, L. (n.d.). *Faith in Mr. D: Religious accommodations in schools.* Available at: https://www.justiceinschools.org/faith-mr-d.

Blum, L. (1991). Moral perception and particularity. *Ethics*, 101(4), 701–25.

Burger, K., & Levinson, M. (2016). Stolen trust: Cell phone theft in a zero-tolerance high school. In M. Levinson & J. Fay, eds. Dilemmas of educational ethics: Cases and commentaries. Cambridge, MA: Harvard Education Press, pp. 73–78.

Calleja, S., Kokenis, T., & Levinson, M. (2019). Walling off or welcoming in? The challenge of creating inclusive spaces in diverse contexts. In M. Levinson & J. Fay, eds. Democratic discord in schools: Cases and commentaries in educational ethics. Cambridge, MA: Harvard Education Press, pp. 13–18.

Ferguson, A. (2000). *Bad boys: Public schools in the making of black masculinity.* Ann Arbor, MI: University of Michigan Press. https://doi.org/10.3998/mpub.16801.

Gutmann, A., & Thompson, D. F. (2000). *Democracy and disagreement: Why moral conflict cannot be avoided in politics, and what should be done about it.* 3. Cambridge, MA: Belknap Press of Harvard University Press.

Harvard Graduate School of Education (n.d.). *Justice in schools.* Available at: https://www.justiceinschools.org.

Hess, D. E., & McAvoy, P. (2015). *The political classroom: Evidence and ethics in democratic education.* New York: Routledge.

Jacobs, J. (1992). *The Death and Life of Great American Cities.* Reissue ed. Vintage.

James, C., & Weinstein, E. (2019). Seeing eye to eye with students. In M. Levinson & J. Fay, eds. Democratic discord in schools: Cases and commentaries in educational ethics. Cambridge, MA: Harvard Education Press, pp. 127–131.

Knight, D. (2016). In M. Levinson & J. Fay, eds. Dilemmas of educational ethics: Cases and commentaries. Cambridge, MA: Harvard Education Press, pp. 93–96.

Levinson, M. (2015). Moral injury and the ethics of educational injustice. *Harvard Educational Review*, 85(2), 203–28. https://doi.org/10.17763/0017-8055.85.2.203.

Levinson, M. (2022). Theorizing educational justice. In R. Curren, ed., *Routledge handbook of philosophy of education*. London: Routledge, pp. 114–24.

Levinson, M. Action-guiding theory: A methodological proposal (unpublished manuscript

Levinson, M., & Fay, J. (Eds.) (2016). *Dilemmas of educational ethics: Cases and commentaries*. Cambridge, MA: Harvard Education Press.

Levinson, M., & Fay, J. (Eds.) (2019). *Democratic discord in schools: Cases and commentaries in educational ethics*. Cambridge, MA: Harvard Education Press.

Levinson, M., & Geron T. (forthcoming). The ethics of world-building in normative case studies. *Educational Theory*.

Levinson, M., & Mitchell, G. (2019). Eyes in the back of their heads 2.0: Student surveillance in the digital age. In M. Levinson & J. Fay, eds., Democratic discord in schools: Cases and commentaries in educational ethics. Cambridge, MA: Harvard Education Press, pp. 111–117.

Levinson, M., & Reid, E. (2019). Polarization, partisanship, and civic education. In C. M. Macleod & C. Tappolet, eds., *Philosophical perspectives on moral and civic education: Shaping citizens and their schools*. New York: Routledge, Taylor & Francis, pp. 86–112.

Mansbridge, J. J. (1983). *Beyond adversary democracy*. Chicago, IL: University of Chicago Press.

Medina, J. (2013). *The epistemology of resistance: Gender and racial oppression, epistemic injustice, and the social imagination*. Oxford: Oxford University Press.

Noddings, N. (1986). *Caring: A feminine approach to ethics and moral education*. Berkeley, CA: University of California.

Reed, B., & Syed, H. (2021). The Trojan Horse Affair. Serial podcast. *The New York Times*. https://www.nytimes.com/interactive/2022/podcasts/trojan-horse-affair.html.

Sanders, L. M. (1997). Against deliberation. *Political Theory*, 25(3), 347–76. https://doi.org/10.1177/0090591797025003002.

Santoro, D. (2018). *Demoralized: Why teachers leave the profession they love and how they can stay*. Cambridge, MA: Harvard Education Press.

Shelby, T. (2016). The challenge of responding to injustice. In M. Levinson & J. Fay, eds. Dilemmas of educational ethics: Cases and commentaries. Cambridge, MA: Harvard Education Press, pp. 79–82.

Taylor, R., & Kuntz, A. (2021). *Ethics in higher education: Promoting equity and inclusion through case-based inquiry*. Cambridge, MA: Harvard Education Press.

Thatcher, D. (2006). The normative case study. *American Journal of Sociology*, 111(6), 1631–76.

Zacka, B. (2017). *When the state meets the street: Public service and moral agency*. Cambridge, MA: The Belknap Press of Harvard University Press.

10

Moral Education and Democratic Education

Michael Hand

10.1 Introduction

What is the relationship between democratic education and moral education? Should we think of one as a subdivision of the other – and if so, which is the part and which the whole? Should we think of the two as overlapping, with some aims in common and some aims peculiar to each? Or should we think of them as fully separate and distinct endeavors?

Both democratic education and moral education have significant formative components. That is to say, educators in both domains are concerned not only with imparting knowledge and understanding and equipping pupils with skills and competences, but also with cultivating dispositions and attitudes. A central aim of democratic education is to dispose children toward democracy and a central aim of moral education is to make children moral. My particular interest in what follows is in how we should understand the relationship between these two formative projects. Is the cultivation of democratic dispositions and attitudes an exercise in moral formation? Are democratic educators, to that extent at least, also moral educators?

My discussion is divided into five sections. In the first three, I define democracy, address some ambiguities in the term "democratic education," and sketch an account of education in and about democracy. In the fourth, I give an outline of the nature and aims of moral education. And in the fifth, I examine the relationship between the two domains, focusing on their formative components. I argue that none of the core dispositions democratic educators are charged with cultivating ought to be construed as moral. In their formative dimensions, democratic education and moral education are distinct undertakings, albeit complementary ones.

10.2 What Democracy Is

Following Thomas Christiano, I take democracy to be "a method of group decision making that is characterized by a kind of equality among the participants at an essential stage" (Christiano, 2008, p. 81). A group decision is one made by and for a group and intended to be binding on all members of that group. Group decisions are democratic when the decision-making process is designed to give all group members an equal say.

It is clear that many group decisions are not characterized by equality among participants. For example, in family decisions about where to go on holiday or whether to redecorate the house, children typically have less say than their parents, if they are consulted at all. Similarly, in workplace decisions about moving to new premises or changing hours of work, the views of employees rarely carry the same weight as those of employers. Families and workplaces, insofar as their usual arrangements for group decision-making do not give all group members an equal say, are not democracies.

This is not to say that democratic decision-making is uncommon in everyday life. Consider the normal procedure by which a group of friends might go about selecting a restaurant for lunch. Each member of the group is consulted about her dietary restrictions and preferences, and about her previous dining experiences at the restaurants under consideration. Consensus is sought through dialogue and compromise, and if consensus cannot be reached, the matter is settled by a vote. The decision-making process may not be explicitly or self-consciously democratic, but there is tacit recognition that the preferences of each group member should carry equal weight.

And, of course, in democratic polities, it is widely accepted that every citizen should have an equal say in how they are governed. Sometimes citizens are consulted directly on a political decision by means of a referendum (recent referendums in the United Kingdom have asked whether Britain should leave the European Union, whether Scotland should become an independent country, and whether the alternative vote system for electing Members of Parliament should replace the first-past-the-post system). More often, citizens have their say indirectly, by electing representatives to make political decisions on their behalf. The latter still counts as democratic decision-making because there is equality among citizens at an essential stage – the point at which representatives are elected – even if not at the stage of passing laws or deciding public policy.

Note that this account of democracy is purely descriptive. It does not purport to settle the question of whether and when group decisions *ought* to be made democratically. We should, I think, resist the temptation to say that all group decisions should be made in this way: it is perfectly reasonable for parents not to give children an equal say in family decisions because children are not yet competent decision-makers. Nor should we assume too readily that the case for democratic decision-making at the political level is open and shut. One worry here is that governing large and complex societies is extraordinarily difficult and most citizens lack the political understanding to make sensible judgments at the ballot box. Another is that, in groups with millions of members, democratic decision-making affords each individual member a vanishingly small influence: "in a national election, the probability that someone's vote will change the outcome is essentially zero" (Shachar & Nalebuff, 1999, p. 525). Knowing that their vote counts for so little arguably makes it imprudent for citizens to invest significant time and energy in understanding the options before them, and may incentivize them to vote irresponsibly. I shall return to the question of the goodness of democracy shortly.

10.3 The Ambiguity of "Democratic Education"

The term "democratic education" is multiply ambiguous. At the most basic level, the adjective "democratic" can modify the noun "education" in two ways: it can pick out a way of tackling education as a whole (education approached democratically), or it can pick out a specific part of education (education in and about democracy). In the first sense, democratic education is analogous to liberal education, progressive education, and evidence-based education; in the second, it is analogous to civic education, moral education, and environmental education. (Interestingly, the term "religious education" has the same basic ambiguity: it can mean either education approached religiously or education in and about religion.)

When "democratic education" picks out an approach to education as a whole, there is a further ambiguity. Education can be democratic in the sense that decision-making in educational communities (in schools, colleges, universities, etc.) is characterized by equality among the members of those communities. This is the meaning of the term in the democratic schools movement. Alternatively, education can be democratic in the sense that the design of educational systems and policies is guided by democratic deliberation. The thought here is not that educational communities should themselves operate democratically, but that public education in a democratic state should be governed by the will of the people.

A prominent advocate of the idea that schools should themselves be democracies is A. S. Neill. At Summerhill, the school he founded in 1924, Neill sought to give all pupils and staff an equal say in decisions that affected them:

> Summerhill is a self-governing school, democratic in form. Everything connected with social, or group life, including punishment for social offenses, is settled by vote at the Saturday night General School Meeting. Each member of the teaching staff and each child, regardless of his age, has one vote. My vote carries the same weight as that of a seven-year-old. (Neill, 1960, p. 39)

Neill's rationale for democratic self-governance is that it affords the greatest possible freedom to pupils. He contends that children flourish under conditions of freedom and that "you cannot have freedom unless children feel completely free to govern their own social life" (p. 44). He is at pains to distinguish freedom from "license": the "spoiled child" has license to do as she pleases, regardless of the trouble she makes for those around her, while the free child understands that "freedom means doing what you like, so long as you don't interfere with the freedom of others" (p. 80). But children can only be free in this sense when they are equal participants in group decision-making.

The idea that public education should be democratically governed is famously defended by Amy Gutmann. On her view, with respect to the design of educational institutions, we do better to rely on democratic deliberation than on expert judgment:

> The most distinctive feature of a democratic theory of education is that it makes a democratic virtue out of our inevitable disagreement over educational problems. The democratic virtue, too simply stated, is that we can publicly debate educational problems in a way much more likely to increase our understanding of education and each other than if we were to leave the management of schools, as Kant suggests, "to depend entirely upon the judgment of the most enlightened experts." (Gutmann, 1987, p. 11)

Liberal theories of education, says Gutmann, are "profoundly undemocratic" insofar as they call for "a philosopher-king to impose the correct educational policies, which support individual autonomy, on all misguided parents and citizens" (p. 11). In the end, she considers it less important that educational policies are "the right ones" than that they are "enlightened by the values and concerns of the many communities that constitute a democracy" (p. 11).

I draw attention to these influential construals of the term "democratic education" with a view to setting them firmly to one side. My interest here is not in any of the ways of tackling education as a whole that might be picked out by the word "democratic." I wish to focus, specifically and exclusively, on education in and about democracy. I take it that a person may be implacably opposed to the idea that schools should be democracies, and resolutely committed to the view that educational policies should be made by experts, and still hold that the task of equipping pupils for participation in democratic decision-making is central to education.

10.4 Education in and about Democracy

Why should children be educated in and about democracy? The most obvious reason is that participation in democratic decision-making will feature prominently in their lives. They will be members of groups and communities of various kinds and will be involved, to a greater or lesser extent, in decisions made by and for those groups. Not all of the group decisions they are involved in will be made democratically, but some of them will. So children should be prepared by their education to play an active part in democratic decision-making.

Also likely to figure in most people's lives are discussions about which decisions should be made democratically and which should not. It is often a matter of dispute within groups whether a particular decision should be made by all members equally or by only a subset of members – the ones with relevant expertise, for example, or the ones in positions of leadership. So education should equip children to participate not only in democratic decision-making, but also in discussions about when democratic decision-making is appropriate. This means they will need an understanding of the advantages and disadvantages of the democratic method and the ability to form considered judgments about when to use it.

These reasons for educating in and about democracy have force in nondemocratic polities as well as democratic ones. In countries with governments installed by means other than a popular vote, there is still plenty of democratic decision-making in friendship circles, community groups and informal associations. Nevertheless, it is fair to say that the reasons have greatest force in democratic polities. Where the principle of equality among participants is entrenched at the political level, it is especially important that children are prepared by their education for participation in the democratic process and for reflection on its merits.

What, then, does education in and about democracy look like? I suggest that democratic educators seek to facilitate learning of three main kinds: (i) knowledge and understanding of democracy, (ii) democratic skills and competences, and (iii) democratic dispositions and attitudes. Let me say a little about each.

First, democratic education involves imparting knowledge and understanding of democratic theory and practice. Children must come to understand what democracy is and how it works in groups of different shapes and sizes. They need to know which group decisions are normally made by democratic means in their society, and how their society differs from others in this respect. They should be made aware of the principled and pragmatic arguments for and against the democratic method and of the benefits and drawbacks of giving people an equal say in group decisions. And, in democratic polities, children should acquire an understanding of the processes by which democratic governments are elected and held to account, of the rights and responsibilities of democratic citizenship, and of the opportunities for citizens to deliberate together on political questions. In the National Curriculum for England, for example, the citizenship programme of study stipulates that pupils should be taught about:

- parliamentary democracy and the key elements of the constitution of the United Kingdom, including the power of government, the role of citizens and Parliament in holding those in power to account, and the different roles of the executive, legislature and judiciary and a free press
- the different electoral systems used in and beyond the United Kingdom and actions citizens can take in democratic and electoral processes to influence decisions locally, nationally and beyond
- other systems and forms of government, both democratic and non-democratic, beyond the United Kingdom
- local, regional and international governance and the United Kingdom's relations with the rest of Europe, the Commonwealth, the United Nations and the wider world. (DfE, 2013, n.p.)

Second, democratic education involves equipping children with the skills and competences necessary for participation in democratic decision-making. Many democratically made decisions, not least the political decisions made by citizens in democratic polities, are *intellectually demanding*, requiring people without relevant expertise to absorb large quantities of complex information, to work out how it bears on the decision in hand, to take account of biases in the way information is presented, and to form considered judgments on contentious matters. So, a central task of democratic education – one it shares, of course, with education in most other domains – is to foster the skills of disciplined inquiry, critical thinking, and reasoned judgment. But democratically made decisions are also *interpersonally demanding*, requiring people to listen to one another, to see things from one another's point of view, to seek common ground in the face of disagreement, and to stand ready to compromise. To prepare children for participation in democracy, schools must therefore equip them with the skills of communication, cooperation, and compromise. The Council of Europe has recently proposed an eightfold classification of the skill-clusters needed in a culture of democracy:

- autonomous learning skills
- analytical and critical thinking skills
- skills of listening and observing
- empathy
- flexibility and adapatability
- linguistic, communicative and plurilingual skills
- co-operation skills
- conflict-resolution skills (Council of Europe, 2018, pp. 19–21)

And third, democratic education involves cultivating in children a set of democratic dispositions and attitudes. Children should acquire not only an understanding of democratic theory and practice and competence to participate in democratic decision-making, but also some pro-democracy preferences and inclinations. Three dispositions democratic educators can plausibly be expected to promote are: (i) a general preference for the democratic method; (ii) an inclination to participate in democratic decision-making (and, in particular, to vote in democratic elections); and (iii) an inclination to comply with democratically decided rules (and, in particular, to obey democratically decided laws).

For reasons we have already noted, it is not self-evident that a general preference for the democratic method is warranted. There are often good grounds for making group decisions nondemocratically: where some group members are children, for example, or where decisions are straightforwardly technical, it may be sensible to leave the decision-making to the adults or the experts. If, in fact, quite a large proportion of group decision-making is nondemocratic, and reasonably so, it may seem that cultivating in children a general preference for democracy does them no service. But, while considerations of this kind certainly tell against the cultivation of an *overriding* preference for democracy, they have less force against the cultivation of a general or other-things-equal preference. In group decision-making, the democratic method should be the normal or default option. A decision made by and for a group and intended to be binding on all members of that group is one in which all members should have an equal say *unless there is good reason to depart from that norm*. Even if it turns out that good reasons to depart from the norm are rather common, the burden of proof always lies on those advocating the departure. A general preference for the democratic method serves us well because our starting point in group decision-making should be equality among members, regardless of how often it transpires that the introduction of inequalities is justified.

The case for cultivating an inclination to participate in democratic decision-making is fairly intuitive. Where a group to which I belong is deciding between options that will affect me, or between rules that will bind me, and where provision has been made for me to have a say in those decisions, it would be imprudent of me not to participate. Whatever my interests, aspirations, or commitments might be, I reduce my chances of furthering them by opting out of the group decision-making process. Here, too, there will be exceptions: declining to participate is not *always* imprudent. If the costs of participation are high (because, for example, I will need to invest significant time and energy in researching the options and weighing them against each other), and if the benefits of participation are low (because, for example, having my say is unlikely to influence the thinking of other group members or change the outcome of the process), it may be quite rational not to participate. Many people choose not to vote in democratic elections for reasons of exactly this kind. While I think democratic educators have a mandate to encourage full and active participation in democratic decision-making at the national level, they should not pretend that the benefits of participation at this level are as tangible as the benefits at other levels, or that the reasoning of nonvoters is invariably defective. In any case, the fact that prudence does not always demand democratic participation does not count against the claim that it usually does, or against the aim of cultivating in children an inclination to participate in the decision-making of the groups to which they belong.

Finally, the cultivation of an inclination to comply with democratically decided rules is supported by reasons of both self-interest and fair play. The self-interested reason is that group members unwilling to abide by group rules, not least where all members have had an equal say in the formation of those rules, are likely to face sanctions of one kind or another, including the possibility of exclusion from the group. The fair play reason is that those who voluntarily join groups with a view to enjoying the benefits of membership, where those benefits depend on general compliance with group rules, owe it to other group members to follow the rules. As John Rawls has it: "when a number of persons engage in a mutually advantageous cooperative venture according to rules, and thus restrict their liberty in ways necessary to yield advantages for all, those who have submitted to these restrictions have a right to a similar acquiescence on the part of those who have benefited from their submission" (Rawls, 1971, p. 112). Again, these two reasons do not override all other considerations: some group rules, even democratically decided ones, are unjust or ill-conceived or counterproductive and group members are at least sometimes justified in refusing to comply with them. Moreover, and notoriously, there is a serious objection to the fair play argument at the national level: most citizens do not voluntarily join the national communities to which they belong, but are born into them and have no realistic option to leave them. It is unclear whether involuntary group membership still incurs the obligations of fair play. But, notwithstanding the exceptions and even if the fair play argument does not hold for all groups, it remains generally true that there are good reasons of self-interest and fair play for compliance with democratically decided rules, and for promoting such compliance in schools.

10.5 Moral Education

I am aware that the foregoing sketch of the nature and aims of democratic education is highly compressed. The following outline of the nature and aims of moral education is, I fear, more compressed still. In the space available here I can do no more than summarize the key features of what I take to be the most plausible account of moral education – an account I have elaborated and defended in detail elsewhere (Hand, 2018).

Morality consists in a special kind of subscription to standards. A standard specifies something to be done: it is, says David Copp, "anything that is expressible by an imperative" (Copp, 1995, p. 20). To subscribe to a standard is to have a set of interrelated dispositions and attitudes toward it: someone who subscribes to a standard characteristically intends to comply with it, feels good about complying with it and bad about failing to comply with it, and habitually does comply with it. For subscription to standards to qualify as moral, two further attitudes are required. First, the moral subscriber not only intends and inclines to comply with her standards, but also desires and expects everyone else to comply with them too. Second, the moral subscriber endorses penalties for noncompliance with her standards: as J. S. Mill has it, "the idea of penal sanction" is "the real turning point of the distinction between morality and simple expediency" (Mill, [1861] 1962, p. 303). The distinguishing features of moral subscription to standards, then, are that it is *universally enlisting* and *penalty-endorsing*.

Of the many and varied standards to which people morally subscribe, it always makes sense to ask whether their subscription is justified. Purported justifications for moral subscription may be demonstrably sound or demonstrably unsound, or their soundness may be a matter of reasonable disagreement among reasonable people. If moral education is to be rational, and thus to avoid the charge of indoctrination, moral standards must be taught according to their justificatory status. Where moral standards are justified, educators should aim to bring it about that children subscribe to them and believe them to be justified; where moral standards are unjustified, educators should discourage children from either subscribing to them or believing them to be justified; and where moral standards are of uncertain justificatory status, educators should teach them nondirectively, with the aim of equipping children to form their own considered views.

Because much of morality is controversial, much of moral education will be nondirective. But not all moral standards are matters of reasonable disagreement. There are some that enjoy the support of a demonstrably sound justification and to which children's subscription may properly be cultivated. The justification I have in mind rests on two claims. The first is that all human beings, or at least all human beings living alongside others in social groups, are unavoidably confronted with a serious practical problem. Copp calls it the "problem of sociality" (Copp, 2009, p. 22). The second is that human beings can effectively ameliorate this problem by means of universally enlisting and penalty-endorsing subscription to some basic standards of conduct.

The problem of sociality arises from three contingent but permanent features of the human condition, discussions of which are to be found in the writings of many philosophers, including Thomas Hobbes ([1651] 1929), David Hume ([1739] 1896), H. L. A. Hart ([1961] 1994), G. J. Warnock (1971), John Rawls (1971), and J. L. Mackie (1977). These features, sometimes described as the "circumstances of justice," are (i) rough equality, (ii) limited sympathy, and (iii) moderate scarcity of resources. The problem to which they collectively give rise is that there is, in human social groups, a standing propensity to outbreaks of conflict and breakdowns in cooperation.

Under the circumstances of justice, we cannot rely on self-interest and sympathy to keep the peace. We need a supplementary kind of motivation for keeping to cooperative agreements and treating each other in nonharmful ways. We need the kind of motivation that subscription to standards can provide. But note that the problem of sociality will not be ameliorated by subscription to conflict-averting and cooperation-sustaining standards unless *everyone*, or almost everyone, subscribes to them. Indeed, if only some people subscribe, the problem may actually be exacerbated. If some members of a social group commit themselves to prohibitions on theft and violence and other members do not, the former succeed only in making themselves more attractive targets to the latter. What the problem calls for, then, is not just subscription to the relevant standards of conduct, but universally enlisting and penalty-endorsing subscription to them. We must each take responsibility not only for complying with the standards ourselves, but for actively encouraging others to comply and for standing ready to punish them when they do not.

Which standards of conduct are the conflict-averting and cooperation-sustaining ones? They are, unsurprisingly, the basic moral standards to which almost everyone does, in fact, subscribe. They include prohibitions on killing and causing harm, stealing and extorting, lying and cheating, and requirements to treat others fairly, keep one's promises, and help those in need. To deal with the danger to each person of others coming "to dispossesse, and deprive him, not only of the fruit of his labour, but also of his life, or liberty" (Hobbes [1651] 1929, p. 95), there must be standards that afford basic protection to people and their property; and to overcome the distrust that threatens to make us "lose our harvests for want of mutual confidence and security" (Mackie, 1977, p. 111), there must be standards that oblige us to be fair, honest, and reliable in our dealings with each other, and to extend each other a helping hand in times of need.

A central task of moral education, then, is to cultivate in children the dispositions and attitudes that constitute subscription to basic moral standards, alongside an understanding of the problem-of-sociality justification for those standards.

10.6 The Relationship between Democratic Education and Moral Education

In light of these accounts of democratic education and moral education, how might we understand the relationship between the two? It is clear, I think, that neither can be subsumed under the other. Much of the knowledge and understanding of democratic theory and practice imparted by democratic educators is at best tangential to morality, and many of the moral problems and questions addressed by moral educators have little or nothing to do with democracy. The more interesting possibility is that there is an overlap between the two, in particular with respect to the cultivation of dispositions and attitudes. Insofar as democratic educators are charged with promoting the three democratic dispositions identified above (a general preference for the democratic method, an inclination to participate in democratic decision-making, and an inclination to comply with democratically decided rules), are they also, and to that extent, moral educators? To answer that question we shall need to consider each of the dispositions in turn.

What justifies a general preference for the democratic method, I have suggested, is that our starting point in group decision-making should be equality among members. There may be all sorts of good reasons for moving on from this starting point, but until such reasons are presented, we should default to giving all group members an equal say. The appeal of the default position is its *fairness*, and, as we have just seen, treating others fairly is a requirement of basic morality. So moral considerations lend powerful support to a general preference for the democratic method.

But we should not infer from this that a preference for the democratic method is itself moral, or that "use the democratic method" is a standard to which moral subscription is justified. In the first place, moral standards ordinarily regulate the conduct of individuals, not groups. It is individuals who subscribe to standards of conduct, who intend to comply with them, feel good about complying with them and bad about failing to comply with them, and habitually do comply with them. It makes little sense to talk of groups having these intentions, feelings, and habits. But it is groups, not individuals, that use or fail to use the democratic method of group decision-making. Individuals can (and should) prefer that the groups to which they belong default to using the democratic method, but a preference regarding the actions of a group is not at all like a moral obligation to act. In the second place, and insofar as it is within the power of individuals to influence the decision-making methods selected by groups, the reason an individual has to favor the democratic method falls a long way short of a moral duty to promote it. Using one's powers of persuasion to convince fellow group members that a given decision should be made democratically may be warranted by the circumstances and worthy of praise, but it is not morally required: failure to deploy one's persuasive powers to this end is not the sort of omission that should attract moral censure. And in the third place, there are simply too many occasions when giving everyone an equal say is *not* the best way to make a group decision for moral regulation to be appropriate here. Moral requirements and prohibitions only make sense in relation to conduct that is almost always desirable or undesirable. To be sure, no moral rule is exceptionless, but exceptions must be rare for moral regulation to be justified. And group decisions there is good reason to make nondemocratically are not nearly rare enough.

The primary justification for an inclination to participate in democratic decision-making (and, in particular, to vote in democratic elections) is prudential. Whatever interests we seek to further in and through our group memberships, we reduce our chances of furthering them by declining to have our say in group decisions. So an inclination to have our say is generally beneficial to us and the standard "participate in democratic decision-making" is one to which we do well to subscribe. But the kind of subscription justified by this prudential argument is not moral subscription. It is not universally enlisting and penalty-endorsing. The benefit to me of democratic participation does not depend on all other group members participating too: indeed, the fewer participants there are in the democratic process, the greater my own influence on the final decision. Nor are there prudential grounds for penalizing noncompliance. My interest in having my say gives me no reason to coerce others to participate, nor does their interest give them reason to coerce me.

There are other considerations in favor of an inclination to participate in democracy that look more promising as arguments for moral subscription. One is that group decisions have greater legitimacy when all group members have been involved in making them. Another, specific to voting in democratic elections, is that elected representatives are better motivated to serve all members of the electorate when they all show up at the ballot box. According to the Australian Electoral Commission (AEC), for example, compulsory voting in federal and state elections in Australia serves to "encourage policies which collectively address the full spectrum of elector values, because all voters have to be appealed to by government and opposition parties in order to win, and maintain, a majority in Parliament" (AEC, 2006, p. 10). Considerations of this kind have the potential to support moral subscription because they give each of us a proper interest in the participation of everyone else.

The difficulty is that these other considerations are controversial. Why should the legitimacy of group decisions depend on the involvement of all group members, as distinct from the involvement of all group members who wish to have a say? And even if the former confers more legitimacy than the latter, is the difference great enough to warrant the intrusion in people's lives entailed by moral regulation? Does it justify imposing and enforcing a duty to participate? Similar questions are raised by the claim about the motivation of elected representatives. Is it actually true that elected representatives are inclined to serve the electorate more responsibly or fairly when voter turnout is high than when it is low? And even if it is true, is the problem serious enough to warrant the imposition of a moral (or, indeed, legal) requirement to vote? Might there be other, less drastic measures we can take to motivate our elected representatives to attend to the interests of all citizens, not just the ones who vote? The answers to these questions are, as things stand, matters of reasonable disagreement among reasonable people. And because of that disagreement, educators have no mandate to cultivate moral subscription to the standard "participate in democratic decision-making."

Finally, the inclination to comply with democratically decided rules (and, in particular, to obey democratically decided laws) is supported by reasons of self-interest and fair play. It is, in general, a good idea to abide by the fairly chosen rules of the groups to which we belong because (i) rule violations typically incur sanctions we wish to avoid and (ii) we owe it to other group members whose compliance with the rules facilitates the benefits of group membership. The first reason plainly cannot serve as a justification for moral subscription, but perhaps the second can. Perhaps fair play demands universally enlisting and penalty-endorsing subscription to the standard "comply with democratically decided rules."

The burden of proof on anyone wishing to make that case is, however, a heavy one. There is a justified moral requirement to treat others fairly and compliance with democratically decided rules often meets this requirement. But sometimes the requirement to treat others fairly can only be met by violating such rules. Noncompliance with group rules may be morally required because the rules are simply unjust – and the mere fact that a rule has been chosen by democratic means does not license the inference that it is just. Noncompliance may also be morally required because group rules, though well-intentioned and broadly just, nevertheless give rise to various kinds of injustice in practice, at the point of application to the real world. The democratically decided rules by which groups organize their affairs and conduct their business, essential though they are, frequently have unintended consequences, become out of date, fail to allow for particular circumstances, or unfairly exclude people from the benefits of membership. They do not have the authority of moral rules and there is no second-order moral rule that demands compliance with them.

And, as noted above, there is an additional difficulty with attempting to derive a moral duty to obey democratically decided laws from considerations of fair play. Membership of national communities is, for most people, not voluntary in any meaningful sense. There is no freely made decision to join the community with a view to enjoying the benefits of membership and no voluntary submission to the restrictions on liberty that yield those benefits. The involuntariness of the citizen's membership of the democratic polity, in conjunction with the vanishingly small influence she can hope to have on decision-making at the national level, makes the fair play argument for a moral duty to obey the law hard to substantiate.

I conclude that none of the core dispositions democratic educators are responsible for cultivating can properly be construed as moral. There is a sound educational justification for bringing it about that children have a general preference for the democratic method, an inclination to participate in democratic decision-making, and an inclination to comply with democratically decided rules; but there is no justification for doing so in a way that gives these dispositions the form and weight of moral commitments. As candidates for moral subscription, the standards "use the democratic method," "participate in democratic decision-making," and "comply with democratically decided rules" are controversial and should therefore be taught nondirectively in schools.

It follows that, with respect to the cultivation of dispositions and attitudes, there is no overlap between democratic education and moral education. This is not to deny that there are certain questions democratic educators and moral educators will both want to explore in their classrooms. Given that many citizens of democratic polities believe they are duty-bound to vote and to obey the law, open-ended discussion of what there is to be said for and against such duties may feature in classes on democracy and morality alike. But an overlap in the questions democratic educators and moral educators will want to explore does not imply an overlap in the dispositions they are charged with cultivating. Making children moral and disposing them toward democracy are two distinct undertakings.

If there is no overlap between the formative components of democratic education and moral education, the two are at least complementary. The basic moral commitment to treating others fairly is a prime motivator of the democratic preference for giving all members an equal say in group decisions and the democratic inclination to comply with fairly chosen rules. Conversely, the core democratic dispositions furnish moral agents with a powerful template for fair treatment of others in group decision-making contexts. Democratic education should not itself be understood as an exercise in moral education; but it is quite properly seen as an ally and a beneficiary of the project of teaching children morality.

References

Australian Electoral Commission (AEC). (2006). *Compulsory voting in Australia.*

Christiano, T. (2008). Democracy. In C. McKinnon, ed., *Issues in political theory.* Oxford: Oxford University Press, pp. 80–102.

Copp, D. (1995). *Morality, normativity and society.* Oxford: Oxford University Press.

Copp, D. (2009). Toward a pluralist and teleological theory of normativity. *Philosophical Issues*, 19, 21–37.

Council of Europe. (2018). *Reference framework of competences for democratic culture: Vol. 2.* Strasbourg: Council of Europe Publishing.

Department for Education (DfE). (2013). *National curriculum in England: Citizenship programmes of study for key stages 3 and 4.*

Gutmann, A. (1987). *Democratic education.* Princeton, NJ: Princeton University Press.

Hand, M. (2018). *A theory of moral education.* London: Routledge.

Hart, H. L. A. (1961/1994). *The concept of law.* 2nd ed., Oxford: Clarendon Press.

Hobbes, T. (1651/1929). *Leviathan.* Oxford: Clarendon Press.

Hume, D. (1739/1896). *A treatise of human nature.* Oxford: Clarendon Press.

Mackie, J. L. (1977). *Ethics: Inventing right and wrong.* Harmondsworth: Penguin.

Mill, J. S. (1861/1962). *Utilitarianism.* London: Collins.

Neill, A. S. (1960). *Summerhill: A radical approach to child rearing*. New York: Hart.
Rawls, J. (1971). *A theory of justice*. Cambridge, MA: Belknap Press.
Shachar, R., & Nalebuff, B. (1999). Follow the leader: theory and evidence on political participation, *The American Economic Review*, 89(3), 525–47.
Warnock, G. J. (1971). *The object of morality*. London: Methuen.

11

Rawlsian Political Liberalism and Democratic Education

Blain Neufeld

11.1 Introduction

Within contemporary liberal societies, citizens endorse a range of religious, moral, and philosophical views, such as Buddhism, atheism, and utilitarianism.[1] This diversity cannot be eliminated without the exercise of politically oppressive power, something that liberalism's commitment to toleration rules out. Yet such pluralism poses a challenge for the realization of citizens' equal political autonomy. Decisions regarding certain fundamental political issues – for example, what the laws should be concerning abortion, marriage, and education – can involve citizens *imposing* political positions justified in terms of their respective worldviews upon others. If this is so, then many citizens will be subject to laws that are justified by reasons that they cannot accept.

According to John Rawls' account of "political liberalism" (2001, 2005), however, there *is* a form of democratic equality that is realizable by all citizens within pluralist societies.[2] Citizens can be equally politically autonomous if they enjoy equal political power and *justify* the exercise of that power with "public reasons."[3] Political liberalism thus reconciles the ideal of democratic self-government with the principle of toleration. A political liberal education for democratic citizenship consequently would focus on teaching students how to exercise their rights and resources when participating in the political decision-making processes of their society, and how to use public reasons when helping to decide fundamental political questions.

This chapter proceeds in three sections. The core elements of political liberalism are outlined in Section 11.2. The main requirements of a political liberal democratic education are summarized in Section 11.3. I explain that political liberalism's concern with accommodating pluralism means that it is open to diverse educational options for students and families. This accommodation is

[1] These views contain multiple variants: for example, the many denominations of Christianity. They also may combine in various ways: for example, atheists and theists can endorse versions of utilitarianism.

[2] Recent defenses of political liberalism include Lister, 2013; Quong, 2011; Watson & Hartley, 2018.

[3] Rawls claims that "public reason is the form of reasoning appropriate to equal citizens who as a corporate body impose rules on one another by sanctions of state power" (Rawls, 2001, p. 92).

limited, however, by political liberalism's concern for the future political autonomy of students. To illuminate the distinctive way in which political liberalism combines a concern with accommodating pluralism with the goal of securing the future political autonomy of citizens, I outline an alternative view in Section 11.4. The "convergence" account of public justification, like political liberalism, endeavors to accommodate social diversity – but *without* political liberalism's idea of public reason or commitment to political autonomy. Consequently, the convergence account, I explain, fails to respect adequately the interests of students as future citizens. Political liberalism, in contrast, secures these interests *and* accommodates social diversity.

11.2 Political Liberalism: An Overview[4]

11.2.1 The Fact of Reasonable Pluralism

A central claim of political liberalism is that citizens living in societies that respect basic liberal rights, including liberty of conscience and freedom of association, invariably will subscribe to a range of incompatible philosophical, moral, and religious "comprehensive doctrines" (Hinduism, secular humanism, virtue ethics, etc.). Such doctrines apply to most or all aspects of persons' lives.

Importantly, these doctrinal disagreements are not always the result of error, poor reasoning, or ignorance. Rawls employs the idea of the "burdens of judgment" to help explain how disagreements might persist among persons, even when reasoning as well as possible, over which comprehensive doctrine is true. The burdens are among "the many hazards involved in the correct (and conscientious) exercise of our powers of reason and judgement" (Rawls, 2005, pp. 55–56). They include factors like the indeterminacy of many of our moral concepts, and the different kinds of life experiences and social conditions that influence our deliberations about religious and moral issues. Rawls outlines six burdens (pp. 54–57), but his list is not meant to be exhaustive. The diversity that follows from the free exercise of human reason is the "fact of reasonable pluralism" (pp. 36f, 441). Reasonable pluralism can be eliminated only through the exercise of political oppression (p. 37).[5]

11.2.2 The Criterion of Reciprocity and the Liberal Principle of Legitimacy

The fact of reasonable pluralism is a central concern for political liberalism because it poses a challenge for the realization of political relations of *reciprocity* among citizens.

Political liberalism's "intrinsic (moral) political ideal" is the "criterion of reciprocity" (Rawls, 2005, p. xlv). The criterion of reciprocity underpins political

[4] For a more substantial discussion of these ideas see Neufeld, 2022, ch. 1. Excellent overviews of Rawls' political philosophy include Freeman, 2007; Wenar, 2017.

[5] "Unreasonable" pluralism – disagreements caused by poor reasoning, etc. – also clearly exists. But while unreasonable pluralism may potentially be reduced, and ideally eliminated, through better education, public discussion, and the like, political liberalism maintains that *reasonable* pluralism is unavoidable within free societies.

liberalism's account of the legitimate exercise of political power: the "liberal principle of legitimacy." Rawls describes these ideas in the following passage:

> [T]he idea of political legitimacy based on the criterion of reciprocity says: our exercise of political power is proper only when we sincerely believe that the reasons we would offer for our political actions . . . are sufficient, and we also reasonably think that other citizens might also reasonably accept those reasons. This criterion applies on two levels: one is to the constitutional structure itself, the other is to particular statutes and laws enacted in accordance with that structure. (p. xliv; see also p. 137)

Hence a proposal advanced by citizens for a constitutional amendment or law concerning distributive justice (e.g., a guaranteed "basic income" for all citizens) would satisfy the criterion of reciprocity and the liberal principle of legitimacy *if* it were justified by reasons that those citizens think are acceptable to others who adhere to different comprehensive doctrines.

11.2.3 Reasonable Political Conceptions of Justice

To accommodate the fact of reasonable pluralism while respecting citizens' equal standing, Rawls holds that society should be organized by a "political conception of justice." Such a conception satisfies the "basic structure restriction" and the "freestanding condition." According to the basic structure restriction, a political conception of justice applies directly only to society's "basic structure": its main political and economic institutions, understood as an overall system of cooperation encompassing all citizens. "Voluntary associations" like religious institutions may organize themselves internally in other ways (e.g., their governance need not be democratic) but they cannot violate the rights of citizens that are secured by the basic structure, including those of their members. A political conception of justice satisfies the freestanding condition by being formulated in terms of distinctly "political" ideas (concepts, principles, ideals, and values). Such political ideas do not presuppose the truth of any *particular* comprehensive doctrine. Instead, they are construed as implicit within the public political culture of democratic society, namely, the conception of citizens as free and equal, and of society as a fair system of cooperation. Hence a political conception of justice is *compatible* with (and ideally integrated into) the different comprehensive doctrines endorsed by citizens (Rawls, 2005, pp. 11–15, 374–76). (A "comprehensive" conception of justice, in contrast, is based upon a particular comprehensive doctrine – say, a version of utilitarianism – and/or applies directly to areas of life beyond the basic structure.)

A political conception of justice is "reasonable" in virtue of satisfying the criterion of reciprocity. Any such conception meets three conditions.[6] First, it secures equally for all citizens a set of "basic liberties" adequate for free and equal citizenship in a democratic society. Among these liberties will be

[6] In addition to these conditions, all reasonable conceptions satisfy the "basic needs principle" (Rawls, 2001, pp. 47–48; 2005, pp. 7, 166).

(inter alia) liberty of conscience, freedom of association, and the liberties necessary for equal political participation. Second, a reasonable political conception of justice assigns to the basic liberties a "special priority" vis-à-vis other political principles and values (such as efficiency or welfare). Finally, a reasonable political conception of justice guarantees for all citizens adequate resources (e.g., income and wealth) for them to effectively exercise their basic liberties over the course of their lives (Rawls, 2005, p. 450).[7]

11.2.4 Justice as Fairness

The political conception of justice that Rawls defends as the *most* reasonable is "justice as fairness." It consists of two principles, the first of which enjoys "lexical priority" over the second (Rawls, 2001, pp. 46–47). The first principle secures a set of "basic liberties" – freedom of association, the political liberties, freedom of thought, the rights and liberties associated with the rule of law, and "the rights and liberties specified by the liberty and integrity (physical and psychological) of the person" – equally for all citizens within the constitutional structure of society. The second principle consists of two subprinciples (the first of which has priority over the second): (i) the "fair equality of opportunity" principle, which regulates the distribution of unequal social positions of authority within the basic structure and (ii) the "difference principle," according to which social and economic inequalities "are to be to the greatest benefit of the least-advantaged members of society" (pp. 42–43). These principles, Rawls claims, best specify and realize the political ideas of citizens as free and equal, and society as a fair system of social cooperation. (However, other reasonable political conceptions of justice exist.)

11.2.5 Ideal Theory and the Well-Ordered Society

Rawls distinguishes between "ideal" and "nonideal" theory and proposes that in working out which political conception of justice is the most reasonable, citizens should start with ideal theory. A core element of Rawls' version of ideal theory is the idea of the "well-ordered society." The well-ordered society is a "realistic utopia": it is "realistic" in taking certain natural, social, and psychological facts as given, but "utopian" in imagining what, given these facts, a fully legitimate and just society would look like.

Within the well-ordered society, a reasonable political conception of justice (such as justice as fairness) organizes the basic structure, and citizens fully comply with the requirements of justice because there is an "overlapping consensus" on that conception (Rawls, 2001, pp. 32–38; 2005, Lecture IV). In such a consensus, citizens who endorse different comprehensive doctrines *also* support the political conception of justice. They do so by integrating that

[7] Any conception that fails to satisfy all these conditions fails to secure the social conditions necessary for the *ongoing* freedom of citizens (see Weithman, 2011). Hence, "libertarian" views that fail to satisfy the third feature violate the criterion of reciprocity and are "unreasonable."

conception into their broader sets of beliefs and values.[8] A society in which there is an overlapping consensus can be stable "in the right way": through the free allegiance of its members.

The idea of the well-ordered society provides citizens with an exemplar for thinking critically about their own society – that is, for evaluating the justice of existing political institutions and practices. It also provides citizens with a target or goal for political reform: citizens' political activities should aim at reforming the institutions of their basic structure so that their society more closely resembles the realistic utopia of the well-ordered society. The idea of the well-ordered society also plays a role in helping citizens to evaluate different conceptions of justice by enabling them to compare visions of societies fully "well ordered" by those conceptions.[9]

11.2.6 Citizens as Reasonable

A core idea of political liberalism is that of citizens as capable of being *reasonable*. Reasonable citizens acknowledge the fact of reasonable pluralism and share a commitment to satisfying the criterion of reciprocity (Rawls, 2005, pp. xliv, 16, 49–50, 54). To satisfy this criterion, citizens justify their proposals concerning "constitutional essentials" and "matters of basic justice" (pp. 214–15, 227–30, 235) in terms that other citizens – or at least those similarly committed to the criterion of reciprocity (see Lister, 2018) – find acceptable. The reasonableness of citizens expresses itself in what Rawls calls the first "moral power": citizens' capacity to form and act upon a "sense of justice" (Rawls, 2001, pp. 18–19, 196).

11.2.7 Civic Respect and Public Reason

One way to understand how citizens can be reasonable is to see reasonableness as involving a form of mutual respect. Given its political context, this conception of mutual respect can be termed "civic respect" (Davis and Neufeld, 2007; Neufeld, 2022). Civic respect has four features:

1. It requires that citizens acknowledge the fact of reasonable pluralism.
2. It is a form of "recognition respect" (Darwall, 2006). Recognition respect, roughly, is that respect which is owed to persons in virtue of some characteristic that they possess. This characteristic grants such persons a certain *standing* in their relations with others. Civic respect is the form of recognition respect that is owed to persons in virtue of their standing as free and equal *citizens*. One expresses such respect by taking this standing into account when deciding political questions in concert with one's fellow citizens.

[8] For Rawls' account of how this might be achieved, see his "Reply to Habermas" (Rawls, 2005, Lecture IX). (The achievement of such integration may involve revisions to citizens' comprehensive doctrines.)

[9] On ideal theory and the well-ordered society, see Rawls, 1999, pp. 4–5, 7–8, 215–16, 308–09; 2001, pp. 4–5, 13, 65–66. For discussion of Rawlsian ideal theory, see Adams, 2020; Neufeld, 2022, ch. 3; Simmons, 2010; Stemplowska & Swift, 2014. For a defense of ideal theory in the context of education policy, see Brighouse, 2015.

3. It is limited in scope to relations among citizens within the basic structure of society.
4. It requires that citizens decide political questions regarding constitutional essentials and matters of basic justice in a way that satisfies the criterion of reciprocity, that is, in accordance with the idea of "public reason."

"Public reasoning" is the form of reasoning that Rawls maintains citizens should use when deciding fundamental political questions. The idea of public reason should be understood as "part of the idea of democracy itself" (Rawls, 2005, p. 441). The terms of public reason – the particular "public reasons" that make up the content of public reasoning – are provided by the family of reasonable political conceptions of justice endorsed by citizens (including justice as fairness). Public reasons also may include the methods and conclusions of transparent forms of inquiry (such as those of logic and the sciences). Decisions concerning constitutional essentials and matters of basic justice made via public reasoning satisfy the liberal principle of legitimacy.

11.2.8 The Duty of Civility and the Public Political Forum

When citizens use public reasons to decide fundamental political questions, they realize their "duty of civility" (Rawls, 2005, p. 444). This duty applies primarily to public officials within the "public political forum," which is where national political issues are debated and authoritative decisions regarding them are made. It consists of three parts: "the discourse of judges in their decisions, especially of the judges of a supreme court; the discourse of government officials, especially chief executives and legislators; and ... the discourse of candidates for public office" (p. 443). Other citizens, however, are not exempt from the duty of civility: they fulfill it by holding public officials to the idea of public reason when evaluating their performance within the public political forum, especially (though not exclusively) when voting (pp. 444–45).

Political debates need not employ public reasons alone. Reasons drawn from comprehensive doctrines can be introduced in the public political forum, so long as what Rawls calls "the proviso" is satisfied. The proviso is satisfied when "proper political reasons – and not reasons given solely by comprehensive doctrines – are presented that are sufficient to support whatever the comprehensive doctrines introduced are said to support" (Rawls, 2005, p. 462). For instance, a utilitarian legislator could explain her support for a law permitting physician-assisted suicide on utilitarian grounds (e.g., such a law would maximize overall utility), so long as she *also* provided a justification in terms of public reasons (e.g., the law in question best respects citizens' equal freedom to control their lives). Moreover, political debates *outside* of the public political forum – discussions within civil society, what Rawls calls the "background culture" – need not use public reasons (pp. 442–43). Nonetheless, the duty of civility requires sufficient public reason justifications for all *decisions* concerning constitutional essentials and matters of basic justice.

11.2.9 Citizens as Rational

Citizens also are characterized by political liberalism as capable of being *rational*. Citizens' rational nature includes what Rawls terms their "second moral power": the capacity to form, revise, and pursue "conceptions of the good." A conception of the good "is an ordered family of final ends and aims which specifies a person's conception of what is of value in human life or, alternatively, of what is regarded as a fully worthwhile life" (Rawls, 2001, p. 19). Rational persons determine for themselves what kinds of lives have value, and they pursue or revise their life-plans in accordance with those determinations over time.

11.2.10 Citizens' Higher-Order Interests

Citizens' opportunities to exercise their two moral powers – their capacities for conceptions of justice and the good – over the course of their lives constitute their "higher-order interests" (Rawls, 2005, pp. 74–75, 106). These higher-order interests are independent of citizens' various comprehensive doctrines. Moreover, citizens' reasonable nature, their sense of justice, constrains their rational pursuit of their conceptions of the good (see Rawls, 2001, pp. 6–7, 81–82, 191).

This conception of citizens, Rawls stresses, "is meant as both normative and political, not metaphysical or psychological" (Rawls, 2001, p. 19). It is an ideal that most persons with adequate education and resources are *capable* of realizing in their lives (at least well enough to be considered equal citizens). Reasonable political conceptions of justice are formulated with reference to this conception of citizens: acceptable principles of justice are those that citizens can support freely given their higher-order interests (their interests in being able to exercise the moral powers). This normative political conception of citizens, moreover, is freestanding in nature, and hence compatible with different comprehensive doctrines.

11.2.11 Full Political Autonomy

When citizens are committed to interacting with one another in accordance with civic respect, it is possible for them all to enjoy and exercise full political autonomy. Citizens' full political autonomy includes (i) "institutional autonomy" and (ii) "justificatory autonomy."[10]

Institutionally autonomous citizens possess the rights and resources that enable them to take part as (roughly) equal contributors to their society's main political decision-making processes. Citizens exercise institutional autonomy "by participating in society's public affairs and sharing in its collective self-determination over time" (Rawls, 2005, p. 78). Hence, the equal political

[10] Elsewhere, I hold that there is a third element to full autonomy: *shared* autonomy. For the sake of brevity, I focus on institutional and justificatory autonomy here. For discussion of shared political autonomy and its importance for political liberalism, see Neufeld, 2022, ch. 2.

liberties – including the rights to vote, engage in political speech, and run for public office – must be part of any reasonable political conception of justice.

Citizens enjoy justificatory autonomy when fundamental political decisions are made using reasons that they find acceptable in light of their higher-order interests (Rawls, 2005, p. 77). Public reasoning makes possible citizens' justificatory autonomy despite the fact of reasonable pluralism. But although public reasons are acceptable to all, citizens may reach different conclusions concerning political questions. It is to be expected that individuals will give different weights to different public reasons and interpret them in somewhat different ways. "[T]his is the normal case," Rawls observes, "unanimity of views is not to be expected" (p. 479). Even when they disagree over which political positions are the most reasonable, though, citizens possess justificatory autonomy insofar as the positions selected are supported by public reasons. This is because, as Paul Weithman explains, "[t]he fundamental terms of citizens' association are those they would give themselves on the basis of their own freedom and equality" (Weithman, 2017, p. 102). The three conditions that *all* reasonable political conceptions of justice satisfy comprise these "fundamental terms" of political association.

11.3 Education for Democratic Citizenship

11.3.1 Political Liberal Citizenship Education: Reasonableness and Political Autonomy

The adoption and pursuit of political liberal educational goals would help existing liberal democratic societies come to resemble more closely just well-ordered societies. This is because a political liberal citizenship education would cultivate in future citizens the capacity for reasonableness, and thereby enable them to realize full political autonomy.

Reasonable citizens, recall, possess the first moral power: the capacity for a sense of justice.[11] Consequently, students would learn about the political ideas (including the values, principles, and ideals) that underlie liberal democracy. These ideas include those of citizens as free and equal, and society as a fair system of social cooperation. Students also would be taught about the reasonable political conceptions of justice of their society and how to think critically about them. And they would learn how to engage in the public life of their society, namely, how to exercise their political liberties (their right to vote, engage in political speech, etc.).

Cultivating reasonableness in students also involves teaching them how to interact with others on the basis of civic respect. Recall that civic respect applies to citizens' relations within the basic structure of society, and especially the public political forum. It requires (inter alia) that citizens (in order to satisfy the

[11] A political liberal education also would teach students how to be *rational* citizens (capable of exercising effectively the second moral power, the capacity for a conception of the good). Since this chapter focuses on *democratic* education, I leave that dimension of political liberal education aside here. (For discussion of it, see Neufeld, 2022, ch. 5.)

criterion of reciprocity) employ public reasons when helping to decide questions concerning constitutional essentials and matters of basic justice.

If students learn how to interact with one another on the basis of civic respect, it is possible for them to enjoy and exercise full political autonomy as citizens. They would know how to be institutionally autonomous by knowing how to use their rights and resources to take part as equal contributors to their society's main decision-making processes. And by learning how to employ public reasons when helping to decide fundamental political matters, either when participating in the public political forum themselves or when evaluating the performance of public officials, students would learn how to realize justificatory autonomy as citizens.

11.3.2 Comprehensive Autonomy

Rawls distinguishes between political autonomy and comprehensive autonomy – the latter is also referred to as "ethical autonomy" (the terms "ethical autonomy" and "comprehensive autonomy" will be used interchangeably hereinafter). Comprehensive autonomy (inter alia) applies to the whole or most aspects of persons' lives. Although political liberalism "affirms political autonomy for all," Rawls claims that it "leaves the weight of ethical autonomy to be decided by citizens severally in light of their comprehensive doctrines" (Rawls, 2005, p. 78). Democratic citizens are to help determine the main institutions and laws to which they all are subject (their basic structure). The question of whether to value and exercise autonomy in the dimensions of their lives that are not concerned with deciding fundamental political issues is to be determined by citizens for themselves.

Does this distinction between political and comprehensive autonomy have educational implications? Rawls thinks that it does. In *Political Liberalism*, he briefly considers the scope of the "requirements the state can impose" on the education of children belonging to "religious sects [that] oppose the culture of the modern world and wish to lead their common life apart from its unwanted influences." Comprehensive liberal approaches to education, Rawls notes, "may lead to requirements designed to foster the values of autonomy and individuality as ideals to govern much if not all of life." By contrast, "political liberalism has a different aim and requires far less" (Rawls, 2005, p. 199). Because it aims only at political autonomy, which is limited in its scope to society's basic structure, Rawls holds that a political liberal educational system can accommodate the beliefs and practices of the members of the religious sects in question.

There are many conceptions of the concept of autonomy (Rawlsian political autonomy is one conception).[12] When he refers to ethical autonomy, Rawls seems to have in mind something similar to what Gerald Dworkin calls "substantive" autonomy (Dworkin, 1988). A life lived autonomously, in this sense, requires that persons critically reflect on their deepest ends and beliefs and

[12] On the distinction between "concepts" and "conceptions," see Rawls, 1999, p. 5. For discussion of this distinction with respect to autonomy, see Dworkin, 1988, pp. 9–10.

display a kind of "independence" by not deferring (at least not usually) to others, including authorities (e.g., religious or community leaders), on such questions. Substantive ethical autonomy also may involve a willingness to explore, or at least seriously consider, alternative ways of life (projects, life-plans, and the like). According to Rawls, citizens can be politically autonomous even if they are not substantively (ethically) autonomous, say, by accepting their religious views on the basis of faith and community and not through independent critical reflection.

11.3.3 Political Autonomy: Educational Implications

Political liberals acknowledge that teaching students to become politically autonomous might lead some to come to value and exercise a more comprehensive form of autonomy (Rawls, 2005, pp. 199–200). Nonetheless, teaching political autonomy and teaching ethical autonomy are distinguishable: there is a difference, in both theory and practice, between teaching students the political ideas and skills necessary for free and equal citizenship and teaching students a form of comprehensive autonomy.[13]

Classes that aim to teach students how to be politically autonomous teach them about their rights and liberties as citizens, about the political virtues, the main elements of reasonable political conceptions of justice, and how to participate in the political decision-making processes of their society. Such classes differ from those that aim to teach students to be ethically autonomous. The latter kind of classes would encourage students to reflect critically upon their comprehensive beliefs and values, including their religious ones, as well as those of other students.

The following pedagogic strategy can help teach students how to interact on the basis of civic respect, and thereby help them to respect each other's political autonomy.[14] Students would participate in formal debates concerning a range of fundamental political issues. Such issues could be both historical (concerning, say, pivotal constitutional issues in the history of their county) and contemporary (regarding, for instance, physician-assisted suicide, drug legalization, reparations for historical injustices, and the like) in nature. After students are told that they live in a society characterized by persistent reasonable disagreement over a wide range of religious and moral questions, the rules of the debate would be introduced. The key rule would be that students defend their positions concerning fundamental political issues with public reasons. Positions defended without sufficient public reasons would be ruled inadmissible. Students would be encouraged to rise on "points of order" to help them identify arguments that

[13] Culp (2019) similarly distinguishes between political autonomy and ethical autonomy (what he terms "public autonomy" and "personal ethical autonomy"), and argues that teaching the former but not the latter is a legitimate aim of democratic education (see especially chs. 2 and 6). (Culp also holds that the teaching of "personal moral autonomy" is an appropriate aim of democratic education [p. 42f]. Insofar as this idea concerns relations between *citizens* within the basic structure of society, I think that it is part of political liberalism's idea of reasonableness, specifically, the "recognition respect" feature of civic respect.)

[14] An earlier version of this strategy is outlined in Davis and Neufeld, 2007.

violate the duty of civility. For instance, if based exclusively on utilitarian considerations, an argument offered in support of abortion rights would be ruled inadmissible; an argument that appealed to the free and equal status of citizens, in contrast, would be admissible. Through their participation in such debates, students would learn how to employ public reasons when deciding fundamental political questions.

Such practice debates need not exclude comprehensive doctrines altogether. Recall Rawls' "proviso," which permits the presentation of reasons drawn from comprehensive doctrines. What the duty of civility requires is that *sufficient* public reason justifications also be given for any decision concerning a fundamental political question. With respect to teaching students how to interact with other citizens on the basis of civic respect, such additional "comprehensive" justifications may sometimes be helpful in fostering deeper mutual understanding among students from different backgrounds. Hence, students could provide nonpublic reasons for their positions in practice debates – so long as they *also* learn how to provide sufficient public reason justifications. A Catholic argument in support of greater economic equality in society, for instance, could be presented, but the student doing so would have to learn how to present a public reason argument for greater economic equality as well.

Even permitting a role for the proviso, though, such exercises would teach students how to exercise political autonomy without *necessarily* exposing their comprehensive beliefs and values to rational scrutiny. Granted, some students may choose to scrutinize their comprehensive doctrines because of their participation in such debates (and similar educational exercises) and thereby come to value and exercise comprehensive autonomy. Even so, broader critical scrutiny, the exercise of ethical autonomy, is *not* necessary or unavoidable. Students need not introduce reasons drawn from their comprehensive doctrines in class debates if they do not want to, and even when they do, such reasons are not *themselves* subject to critical evaluation (aside from being "ruled" "nonpublic").[15]

Political liberalism's concern with *equal* citizenship provides an additional reason why it would be beneficial to permit students to refrain from presenting their comprehensive views, or evaluate the views of others, in class debates. Unless the comprehensive doctrines of students in classrooms are roughly balanced in terms of representation, it is likely that discussions of issues involving appeals to moral or religious "truths" would generate strong pressure on students with minority perspectives – but likely not those adhering to the majority doctrine – to question their views and, moreover, to come to feel unwelcome in their schools. Pedagogically, promoting civic respect and the ideal of equal citizenship may be more feasible by employing practice debates that focus on public reasons that all can find acceptable, rather than

[15] Nothing within political liberalism *prohibits* classes and other educational activities that encourage students to explore critically different comprehensive doctrines or that assist students in acquiring and exercising a form of ethical autonomy. Such courses and activities, though, cannot be *required* of all students.

encouraging "no holds barred" discussions that draw upon and evaluate students' disparate comprehensive doctrines.[16]

11.3.4 Political Liberalism and the Scope for Educational Choice

Rawls is right, I think, to claim that teaching political autonomy requires "less" than teaching ethical autonomy.[17] Within a political liberal framework, then, there are more ways to satisfy – in terms of pedagogy, curriculum content, and school organization – the requirements of citizenship education than within a comprehensive liberal framework concerned with cultivating ethical autonomy. Moreover, it follows from political liberalism's concern with accommodating the fact of reasonable pluralism that it should be open (ceteris paribus) to permitting schools that draw upon the various comprehensive doctrines endorsed by citizens.[18] Hence, political liberals generally should permit forms of educational choice for families which accommodate citizens' diverse comprehensive doctrines – while also ensuring that *all* students learn how to become reasonable politically autonomous citizens (see Davis & Neufeld, 2007; Ebels-Duggan, 2013; Edenberg, 2016; Wong, 2021).

Even if different kinds of schools are available to students, democratic education may require, at least at the secondary school level, *some* "mixed" citizenship classes. In such classes, students whose families and communities endorse different comprehensive doctrines might participate together in the kinds of practice debates described in Section 11.3.3 (or other similar exercises) to better appreciate the demands of public reasoning within diverse societies. Such classes would involve collaborations among different schools representing different comprehensive doctrines (e.g., students from Catholic, Jewish, and secular humanist schools might engage in public reason debates together).

[16] Thanks to Andrew Lister for discussion of this point.

[17] While a number of political liberals defend Rawls' claim that an education for political autonomy is less demanding than one for comprehensive autonomy (Davis & Neufeld, 2007; De Wijze, 1999; Ebels-Duggan, 2013; Neufeld, 2022, ch. 5), this position has been challenged by both political and comprehensive liberals. Some political liberals maintain that, while teaching political autonomy may differ in theory from teaching ethical autonomy, political liberalism nonetheless requires in practice a form of education for citizenship that is much more demanding than that suggested by Rawls (Costa, 2011; Macedo, 2000). These scholars, though, make this claim with respect to the nonideal circumstances of the United States; hence their conclusions do not affect Rawls' claim regarding education within the well-ordered society, and very well may not apply *outside* of the American context even at the level of nonideal theory (see Neufeld, 2013 and n. 19 in this chapter). Rawls' claim also has been disputed by some comprehensive liberals; they contend that teaching political autonomy invariably amounts to teaching ethical autonomy (Callan, 1996, 1997; Gutmann, 1995). But such claims about the nature and teaching of autonomy, I think, fail to appreciate adequately the distinctiveness, both conceptual and pedagogical, of political autonomy. For my replies to these lines of argument, see Davis & Neufeld, 2007; Neufeld, 2013; Neufeld, 2022, ch. 5.

[18] This justification for certain kinds of "school choice" policies must be distinguished from another justification: that allowing families to choose schools will lead to better school performance overall and hence better educated citizens. By breaking up the "state monopoly" on public schools and allowing market forces to operate within the educational sphere, according to this argument, the quality of schools will improve over time. For the classic statement of this argument, specifically in support of voucher systems, see Friedman, 1955. However, the actual experience of voucher-based school choice programs within the United States over the past few decades has been rather lackluster in terms educational outcomes (Carnoy, 2017). (Other justifications for school choice policies are outlined in Feinberg & Lubienski, 2008.)

Moreover, political liberals acknowledge that in certain social circumstances – say, in societies that are threatened by instability or that suffer from persistent class- or race-based inequality – promoting political justice *may* restrict the scope for educational choice, irrespective of students' wishes or those of their parents (Davis & Neufeld, 2007; Neufeld, 2013). If, for instance, the specific kinds of school choice policies that have been implemented within the United States in recent decades have had generally inegalitarian, and thus unjust, consequences (see Howe, 2008), then political liberals have a reason to oppose such policies. Even if this is so, however, this worry need not apply to all potential systems of educational choice, or to the social contexts of other liberal democratic societies.[19]

11.4 Convergence Public Justification and Education

11.4.1 Convergence Public Justification: An Overview

The "convergence" account of public justification is an alternative to Rawlsian political liberalism that has been developed and defended in recent years by Gerald Gaus and Kevin Vallier (Gaus, 2011; Gaus & Vallier, 2009; Vallier, 2014, 2015, 2019). Like political liberalism, it is an account of how to decide political questions fairly within pluralist societies. Unlike political liberalism, the convergence account eschews any *necessary* role for public reasons.[20] Gaus (2015) criticizes as insufficiently motivated Rawls' duty of civility and its requirement that citizens use public reasons to decide fundamental political questions.

Central to the convergence account is what Gaus and Vallier call the "public justification principle" (hereinafter "PJP"). The PJP states: "*L* is a justified coercive law only if each and every member of the public *P* has conclusive reason(s) *R* to accept *L* as a requirement" (Gaus & Vallier, 2009, p. 53). So long as all "members of the public"[21] have their own sufficient – public *or* nonpublic ("comprehensive") – reasons that "converge" in supporting the political decisions in question, those decisions are legitimate.[22] Political decisions thus can be justified by a

[19] The experiences of non-US educational systems with forms of school choice – for example, the educational systems of Canada (where alternative language schools are available in all provinces, and some provinces [Alberta, Ontario, and Saskatchewan] provide full funding to certain [primarily Catholic] religious schools) and New Zealand (where a nationwide quasi-voucher system has been in place since 1989) – indicate, I think, that greater choice need not invariably have the negative social consequences that some critics assert.

[20] Convergence theorists sometimes refer to their view as a form of "public reason" liberalism (e.g., the title of Gaus, 2011). This is infelicitous, as a key feature that distinguishes the convergence account from political liberalism is that the former *rejects* any necessary role for distinctly "public reasons" (although it permits the use of such reasons). Because of this, and for the sake of clarity, I reserve the term "public reason" for the political liberal view. (For further discussion, see Neufeld, 2022, pp. 6–7.)

[21] The "members of the public" are moderately idealized versions of adult citizens (Gaus and Vallier, 2009, pp. 53–54).

[22] While convergence public justifications draw upon the reasons *of* the public – and such reasons must be "intelligible" to all members of the public – those reasons need not themselves *be* public reasons. Reasons that are merely "intelligible" are *non*public reasons that are understandable by those members of the public who do not themselves hold the relevant comprehensive doctrine(s). (See Vallier, 2014, pp. 28–29.)

range of *incompatible* reasons drawn from the disparate comprehensive doctrines of the members of the public.[23]

The informational demands of the PJP are considerable. As Vallier notes, "justificatory reasons are diverse and dispersed and so hard to discern" (Vallier, 2014, p. 187). Because most citizens are incapable of determining whether political proposals satisfy the PJP, convergence theorists reject "deliberative democracy" (Gaus & Vallier, 2009, pp. 65–70; see also Vallier, 2015).[24] Indeed, Vallier holds that most citizens have *no* duty to try to ensure that their society's laws satisfy the PJP, even when engaging directly in their society's political life, such as when voting. He writes: "My view allows citizens to act on whatever reasons they like" (Vallier, 2014, p. 190).

In contrast to most citizens, though, legislators *are* subject to a duty related to the PJP, what Vallier calls the "principle of convergence restraint for legislators" (PCRL):

> A legislator should not vote for law *L* in order to contribute to *M*'s becoming or remaining law (where *L* may be equivalent to *M*) if he justifiably believes that members of the public lack sufficient reason R_n to endorse *M*. (Vallier, 2014, p. 191; see also Vallier, 2015, p. 154.)

Even with respect to legislators, though, Vallier concedes that the informational demands of this principle are quite strong and so specifies that the PCRL "require[s] that legislators be sensitive to information about public justification *when they encounter it*" (Vallier, 2015, p. 155; my italics).

Instead of advocating an ideal of widespread democratic participation by politically autonomous citizens, convergence theorists recommend relying upon institutional arrangements, such as properly designed constitutional structures, and legislators' compliance with the PCRL, to ensure that the PJP is adequately satisfied by society's laws over time. Nonetheless, Gaus and Vallier claim that their view realizes a kind of autonomy for citizens. Drawing upon their reading of Kant's moral philosophy, they hold that if the PJP is satisfied, then each citizen "is both subject and legislator: each is subject to the law, yet each legislates the law, and so all are free and equal under the law" (Gaus & Vallier, 2009, p. 52). The sense in which citizens "legislate" here, though, is quite passive: the responsibility for ensuring that the PJP is satisfied, as we have seen, does not require *anything* of most citizens. The version of "self-legislation" that Gaus and Vallier rely upon, then, differs significantly from the political liberal ideal of full political autonomy; the latter involves the determination *by* citizens of the laws to which they are subject.[25]

[23] Public reasons can satisfy the PJP. My focus here is on those political decisions that *cannot* be justified via public reasons but *can* be justified via the PJP. I interpret Gaus and Vallier as maintaining that most justified political decisions will have this form.

[24] For criticism of the rejection of deliberative democracy by the convergence account – and defense of political liberalism's commitment to it – see Boettcher, 2020.

[25] For further discussion, see Neufeld, 2022, ch. 2.

11.4.2 Convergence Public Justification and Education

Employing the framework of convergence public justification, Vallier argues for a robust form of school choice (Vallier, 2014, ch. 7). Extensive "school choice respects diversity and reasonable pluralism," he writes, "by allowing each person or group to make her [sic] own choices" (p. 246). Because "citizens' reasons of integrity often involve raising children," parents should be allowed "to make their own decisions about their children's education," including whether to prioritize "their child's salvation *over their democratic citizenship*" (pp. 232, 245, 250; my italics). Nonetheless, "the state could require that schools be accredited in order to guarantee minimal educational quality and civic competence" (p. 244; see also p. 226). It is unclear, though, what guaranteeing "civic competence" involves. According to Vallier, "the Public Justification Principle does not require that they [students] develop complex deliberative capacities to engage one another in public discussion" (p. 230). The convergence account of public justification, then, would *not* mandate that all students learn how to act as reasonable citizens, including how to interact with others on the basis of civic respect (or some similar principle).

The underlying problem with Vallier's view is that it includes no account of the interests of children *separate* from those of their parents. His defense of school choice appeals entirely to the interests of parents. Political liberalism, in contrast, ascribes to all citizens – including children as *future* citizens – a set of higher-order interests. The realization of these interests vis-□-vis children as future citizens cannot be sacrificed or constrained for the sake of parents' preferences. Political liberalism endeavors to accommodate parents' interests in raising their children in accordance with their respective comprehensive doctrines and conceptions of the good – but *only* insofar as this is compatible with securing the higher-order interests of children as future politically autonomous citizens.[26]

The above criticism may strike readers as merely begging the question against the convergence view. Since the convergence account of public justification rejects political liberalism's conception of citizens and ideal of full political autonomy, it is unsurprising that political liberals will find the educational prescriptions of convergence theorists like Vallier inadequate. Yet I think that *any* political theory that fails to have a conception of children's interests *independent* of those of their parents is manifestly flawed. Children are not simply elements of parents' conceptions of the good or life-projects. Rather, children have separate interests that must be respected, including (for the purpose of this discussion) interests in *becoming* free and equal citizens.[27] The fact that the convergence account lacks any conception of children's interests is, I believe, a decisive strike against it. Political liberalism, in contrast, accommodates

[26] My claim here resembles one made in Schouten 2018. A key difference is that Schouten interprets teaching students how to exercise the second moral power (the capacity for a conception of the good) as involving teaching them a form of ethical autonomy (p. 1090f). While I agree with Schouten that parents are not entitled to prevent their children from learning how to exercise the two moral powers, I deny that this requires teaching students a form of ethical autonomy (see Neufeld, 2022, pp. 134–36). (For a broadly similar point, see Culp, 2019, p. 32f.)

[27] Children also have interests in enjoying good childhoods (see Neufeld, 2022, ch. 4).

reasonable pluralism *and* protects the interests of children as future free and equal citizens.

11.5 Conclusion

Teaching students how to become politically autonomous citizens is an educational goal that can be freely supported by reasonable citizens who endorse a wide range of comprehensive doctrines, including doctrines *not* committed to an ideal of comprehensive autonomy. Moreover, the requirements of a political liberal education for citizenship are compatible with a range of different kinds of schools, including those oriented toward particular comprehensive doctrines. Political liberalism, then, is supportive of certain forms of educational choice for families; this follows from political liberalism's concern with accommodating the fact of reasonable pluralism. At the same time, political liberalism holds that *all* schools must ensure that students acquire the skills and knowledge necessary for them to become politically autonomous citizens upon adulthood. This requirement distinguishes the political liberal approach to citizenship education from the approach that Vallier claims follows from the convergence account of public justification. The latter view fails to protect adequately children's interests in becoming free and equal democratic citizens.[28]

References

Adams, M. (2020). The value of ideal theory. In J. Mandle & S. Roberts, eds., *John Rawls: Debating the major questions*. Oxford: Oxford University Press, pp. 73–86.

Boettcher, J. (2020). Deliberative democracy, diversity, and restraint. *Res Publica*, 26(2), 215–35.

Brighouse, H. (2015). Nonideal theorizing in education. *Educational Theory*, 65(2), 215–31.

Callan, E. (1996). Political liberalism and political education. *Review of Politics*, 58 (1), 5–33.

Callan, E. (1997). *Creating citizens: Political education and liberal democracy*. Oxford: Clarendon Press.

Carnoy, M. (2017). *School vouchers are not a proven strategy for improving student achievement*. Washington, DC: Economic Policy Institute. Available at: https://www.epi.org/publication/school-vouchers-are-not-a-proven-strategy-for-improving-student-achievement.

Costa, V. M. (2011). *Rawls, citizenship, and education*. New York: Routledge.

Culp, J. (2019). *Democratic education in a globalized world: A normative theory*. London: Routledge.

[28] My thanks to Julian Culp for helpful comments on an earlier draft.

Darwall, S. (2006). *The second-person standpoint*. Cambridge, MA: Harvard University Press.

Davis, G., & Neufeld, B. (2007). Political liberalism, civic education, and educational choice. *Social Theory & Practice*, 43(1), 47–74.

De Wijze, S. (1999). Rawls and civic education. *Cogito*, 13(2), 87–93.

Dworkin, G. (1988). *The theory and practice of autonomy*. Cambridge: Cambridge University Press.

Ebels-Duggan, K. (2013). Moral education in the liberal state. *Journal of Practical Ethics*, 1(2), 34–63.

Edenberg, E. (2016). Civic education: Political or comprehensive? In J. Drerup, G. Graf, C. Schickhardt & G. Schweiger, eds., *Justice, education, and the politics of childhood*. Dordrecht: Springer, pp. 187–206.

Feinberg, W., & Lubienski, C. (2008). Introduction. In W. Feinberg & C. Lubienski, eds., *School choice policies and outcomes: Empirical and philosophical perspectives*. Albany, NY: SUNY Press, pp. 1–20.

Freeman, S. (2007). *Rawls*. London: Routledge.

Friedman, M. (1955). The role of government in education. In R. Solo, ed., *Economics and the public interest*. New Brunswick, NJ: Rutgers University Press, pp. 123–44.

Gaus, G. (2011). *The order of public reason: A theory of freedom and morality in a diverse and bounded world*. Cambridge: Cambridge University Press.

Gaus, G. (2015). Public reason liberalism. In S. Wall, ed., *The Cambridge companion to liberalism*. Cambridge: Cambridge University Press, pp. 115–40.

Gaus, G., & Vallier, K. (2009). The roles of religious conviction in a publicly justified polity: The implications of convergence, asymmetry, and political institutions. *Philosophy & Social Criticism*, 35(1), 51–76.

Gutmann, A. (1995). Civic education and social diversity. *Ethics*, 105(3), 557–79.

Howe, K. R. (2008). Evidence, the conservative paradigm, and school choice. In W. Feinberg & C- Lubienski, eds., *School choice policies and outcomes: Philosophical and empirical perspectives*. Albany, NY: SUNY Press, pp. 61–78.

Lister, A. (2013). *Public reason and political community*. London: Bloomsbury.

Lister, A. (2018). The coherence of public reason. *Journal of Moral Philosophy*, 25(1), 64–84.

Macedo, S. (2000). *Diversity and Distrust: Civic Education in a Multicultural Democracy*. Cambridge, MA: Harvard University Press.

Neufeld, B. (2013). Political liberalism and citizenship education. *Philosophy Compass*, 8(9), 781–97.

Neufeld, B. (2022). *Public reason and political autonomy: Realizing the ideal of a civic people*. London: Routledge.

Quong, J. (2011). *Liberalism without perfection*. New York: Oxford University Press.

Rawls, J. (1999). *A theory of justice*. Rev. ed. Cambridge, MA: Harvard University Press.

Rawls, J. (2001). *Justice as fairness: A restatement*. Cambridge MA: Harvard University Press.

Rawls, J. (2005). *Political liberalism*. Exp. ed., New York: Columbia University Press.

Schouten, G. (2018). Political liberalism and autonomy education: Are citizenship-based arguments enough? *Philosophical Studies*, 175(5), pp. 1071–93.

Simmons, A. J. (2010). Ideal and nonideal theory. *Philosophy & Public Affairs*, 38(1), 5–36.

Stemplowska, Z., & Swift, A. (2014). Rawls on ideal and nonideal theory. In J. Mandle & D. A. Reidy, eds., *A companion to Rawls*. Oxford: Wiley-Blackwell, pp. 112–27.

Vallier, K. (2014). *Liberal politics and public faith: Beyond separation*. New York: Routledge.

Vallier, K. (2015). Public justification versus public deliberation: The case for divorce. *Canadian Journal of Philosophy*, 45(2), 139–58.

Vallier, K. (2019). *Must politics be war? Restoring our trust in the open society*. Oxford: Oxford University Press.

Watson, L., & Hartley, C. (2018). *Equal citizenship and public reason: A feminist political liberalism*. New York: Oxford University Press.

Weithman, P. (2011). Convergence and political autonomy. *Public Affairs Quarterly*, 25(4), 327–48.

Weithman, P. (2017). Autonomy and disagreement about justice in political liberalism. *Ethics*, 128(1), 95–122.

Wenar, L. (2017). John Rawls. In E. N. Zalta, ed., *The Stanford encyclopedia of philosophy* Spring ed. Available at: https://plato.stanford.edu/archives/spr2017/entries/rawls.

Wong, B. (2021). Let God and Rawls be friends: On the cooperation between the political liberal government and religious schools in civic education. *Journal of Applied Philosophy*, 38(5), 774–89.

12

Social Justice Education and Democratic Legitimacy

Lauren Bialystok

12.1 Are Schools Brainwashing Our Children"?

A 2012 cover story in the popular Canadian general interest magazine, *Maclean's*, provocatively accused schools of brainwashing students (Reynolds, 2012). Stories of young students being encouraged to protest big oil, "explore their sexuality," and criticize the World Trade Organization raised the concern that "social justice" is a moniker concealing a variety of practices intended to recruit young students to progressive causes (Reynolds, 2012). While schools in Canada, as in most liberal democracies, have a mandate to emphasize inclusiveness and anti-oppression (e.g., Ontario Ministry of Education, 2009), it is not always clear when that mandate is exceeded by teachers with political agendas. The scope and application of some educational activities and policies are associated with substantive policy positions that can be easily lined up with the political left-of-center. Indeed, politicians have expressed concern over the ideological bent in public education. The *Maclean's* article notes that a Grade 3 class protest of an oil pipeline elicited fury from Progressive Conservative Member of Provincial Parliament Rob Milligan, who called the teacher's activity "brainwashing" and "an abuse of power" (Reynolds, 2012, p. 22).[1]

Brainwashing – or "indoctrination," as it is more formally called – has been a concern since the earliest recorded works in philosophy of education. Children's vulnerability and need for guidance both necessitates education and automatically introduces the risk of intellectual programming. When parents are given complete authority over their children's upbringing, we worry about the closed echo chamber cutting children off from other views; but when children are sent to common schools, parents may worry about other views crowding out the familial norms in which they should be anchored. Choices about how to induct a generation of young people into a diverse society involve delicate calculations. This has led to voluminous scholarship about teaching controversial issues and politics, promoting common values in education, and negotiating a bevy of hot-

[1] Importantly, the *Maclean's* article conflates questions of age-appropriateness with general questions about what type of political messaging belongs in schools. I point out examples of this in Section 12.5.

button topics such as those referenced in the *Maclean's* article (Hess & McAvoy, 2014; Zimmerman & Robertson, 2017).

Since 2012, antagonism over the politicization of classrooms has only intensified. Events in the United States in particular have further cemented schooling as a battleground for ideological domination (Packer, 2022). While growing numbers of teachers and schools have wrestled with the legacies of slavery and colonialism, state legislatures have been busy passing bills that ban critical race theory in schools (Gabriel & Goldstein, 2021). While young people identify as queer, trans, and nonbinary in record numbers, Florida has passed a bill colloquially known as "Don't Say 'Gay'" that explicitly forbids teaching about lesbian, gay, bisexual, trans, and queer (LGBTQ) inclusion (Sopelsa et al., 2022). Critics on both the left and right contend that schools are being hijacked by partisan forces and students are being groomed as pawns in the culture wars.

American political developments reverberate through Western democracies, and especially its closest neighbor, Canada. Here I suggest that the Canadian example continues to be instructive for parsing out the contours of legitimate political education in a pluralistic democracy. My premise is that whatever we count as "social justice education" (SJE) should have a coherent justification within the political culture. If something taught in public schools is perceived as a form of brainwashing, it is a challenge not only to the individual teachers or administrators involved, but also to the system that claims to deliver an essential public good. Note that my purpose here is broader than staking a claim in the debates over whether and how to raise controversial topics in the classroom (e.g., Hess, 2004); my concern is whether SJE is a defensible approach to education in a pluralistic society. My conclusion is that, even in a liberal democratic culture beset by misinformation and polarization, the tenets of SJE are usually well justified in a way that most opposing political values are not. A deeper examination of the overlap between democratic education and social justice is necessary to respond to allegations of brainwashing, as well as to reinforce objections to actual instances of inappropriate political education or indoctrination.

In this chapter, I offer an outline for the type of philosophical defense that could be deployed in the face of challenges to SJE. I am not interested in policing the use of the term, but rather in providing a refutation of the charge that SJE is inadmissible because it is not politically neutral. In so doing, I will argue for parameters within which educators may teach substantive political views, whether the political content is ostensibly aimed at social justice or not. There are four sections to this argument. First, I show why SJE is an inherently controversial concept that invites the kind of pushback that is chronicled in *Maclean's*. Second, I explain the basic elements of liberal statehood that have come to inform our public institutions and defend a more robust version of liberalism, known as "comprehensive liberalism." Third, I argue that many practices that we wish to protect under the banner of SJE can be defended by appeal to Canada's documented commitments to substantive values of equality and individual rights, even when some politicians and citizens disagree with them. While I do not engage with specific constitutions outside the Canadian context, I take for granted that such commitments are the norm in contemporary Western democracies, and ought to inform the construction of social justice education in any society that sees itself as such. Finally, I suggest five initial criteria for distinguishing between defensible SJE and brainwashing. I demonstrate how these criteria would be applied to some contentious cases mentioned in *Maclean's* and conclude by reflecting on the viability of this approach in the face of more vicious political polarization and attacks on democracy itself.[2]

12.2 Social Justice Education and the Backlash

Arguably, democratic education has always been oriented toward social justice. If democracy is supposed to replace all the oppressive styles of governance that preceded it, then social justice is in its DNA. It is only within an established regime of a nominal liberal democracy that SJE comes to be associated with particular left-leaning causes, especially once major legal reforms are thought to have addressed the remaining vestiges of discrimination in law and institutions. It is out of frustration with the failed promises of liberal equality – as evidenced in persistent pernicious disparities in educational opportunity, socioeconomic status, and life chances along predictable lines of race and other social categories – that advocates demand deeper reckoning with such forces as racism, sexism, and colonialism.

Among many educators and educational researchers, SJE has become not only ubiquitous but also almost untouchable, the apple pie of contemporary education work. This is true despite the great plurality of definitions of SJE among educators (Hackman, 2005; Murrell, 2006; Bull, 2008; North, 2008; Hytten & Bettez, 2011; Sensoy & DiAngelo, 2012). There is no single concept of SJE but rather a constellation of discursive and pedagogical practices that emerge from various intellectual and political traditions. However, from the outside, SJE may appear as more uniform and less unimpeachable. In both Canada and the United States, conservative political and institutional forces have collided with the tide of SJE and sought to stem its momentum. In 2006, the National Council for Accreditation of Teacher Education notoriously removed the term "social justice" from all its documents, calling it "radical" (Wise, 2006).

It is not surprising that a feel-good phrase like "social justice" should spark such controversy. The term is ethically loaded, even outside the context of education. To borrow a coinage from philosopher Charles Stevenson, it is an "emotive" phrase, meaning that it cannot be uttered without any evaluative component – to say that something is socially just is to recommend it. At the same time, identifying a need for social justice, and especially SJE, is an inherently oppositional stance: it implies that there is something that needs

[2] A version of this text was previously published in Bialystok (2014).

rectifying or improving; it criticizes the status quo.[3] This may put political and educational leaders in a defensive position. The very existence of a powerful SJE movement poses a certain challenge to people in power before any demands have even been articulated, and regardless of which political party is in office.

For all the attention to social justice in the education literature, and all the vitriol over education in the public sphere, there has been very little attempt to erect a principled justification of SJE within a democratic framework (but see Applebaum, 2009). It is difficult to insist on the legitimacy of a profoundly divisive practice by merely doubling down on the content that is itself divisive. A philosophical defense would contend with the practice's legitimacy, in addition to or instead of its intrinsic rightness.[4] Such a defense would need to take seriously the irreducible diversity of interests and at times incommensurate rights of different stakeholders. The point would not be to defend any practices that anyone has ever described as SJE, as educators and educational scholars use the term as a broad catchall to characterize their commitments – perhaps too broad to admit of important distinctions. Rather, it would establish principles for politically defensible educational practices in general. We could then assess whether individual practices are legitimate, regardless of which definition of SJE is being employed. I will argue that educational activities can take stances on controversial political issues, including advancing social justice causes, as long as they cohere with certain tenets of coexistence in a pluralistic society – most clearly articulated within liberal theory – and that much of the work usually defined as SJE can live up to this condition.

12.3 Liberal Legitimacy

Political legitimacy is one of the cardinal ideals of liberalism. Jeremy Waldron says that what unites different forms of liberalism is "a certain view about the justification of social arrangements" (Waldron, 1987, p. 128). Specifically, in contrast to political arrangements such as military regimes, in a liberal society "all aspects of the social should either be made acceptable or be capable of being made acceptable to every last individual" (Waldron, 1987, p. 128). This means that if state-sponsored actions such as public education measures are theoretically unacceptable to some group of otherwise reasonable citizens, it should be a cause of concern not just for that group, but for all citizens. While there will never be perfect agreement with every policy the government implements, the liberal vision is of assent to a background set of values or procedures that can be accepted even when they result in policies that citizens disagree with.

However, the degree to which such "overlapping consensus" can realistically be secured in a pluralistic society is contested (Rawls, 1993, p. 134). To be

[3] I will ultimately argue that the defense of SJE appeals to the status quo in terms of laws, national identity, and other aspirational sources for social organization, but criticizes the status quo in terms of how these ideals are presently realized.

[4] I do not address here the ethics of particular teachers' decisions. For an insightful discussion of the macro and micro ethical concerns affecting practitioners of SJE, see Hytten (2015).

somewhat binary, the views can be divided into political liberalism and comprehensive (or perfectionist) liberalism (Waldron, 2004). On the one hand there are political liberals, famously galvanized by Rawls in *Political Liberalism* (1993), who hold out hope that we can agree on a "purely political conception of justice" that avoids trampling on anyone's individual views about what is just, good, or true in other domains. On the other hand, there are liberals who are skeptical about separating political matters from all other kinds of controversial judgments. The differences between these types of liberalism have implications for whether, and how, SJE can be defended.

The first type, political liberalism, requires that political arrangements cannot be logically dependent on adherence to any "comprehensive doctrines" about what makes for a good life or a good citizen; they are "freestanding" (Rawls, 1993, p. 12). A doctrine is "comprehensive" if it "covers not only the political domain but also the domain of human conduct generally" (Nussbaum, 2011, p. 5). Religious doctrines and major philosophical schools of thought count as comprehensive doctrines. Yet the term "comprehensive" is certainly misleading here, because even very partial and nondogmatic theories are unavailable as the basis of political arrangements, according to political liberalism, as long as there is disagreement over them. Political arrangements should be ones that anybody would reasonably endorse in order to ensure their own ability to pursue the good life as they see it (Rawls, 1985, 1993).

On the political liberal conception, the government is to remain *neutral* on any matters that are not directly pertinent to political arrangements. This would include unresolvable, contentious issues, such as the existence of God, or the value of the contemplative life. "Neutral" means that the state should neither take a stance on, nor give preference to those who take particular stances on, such matters. So instead of favoring atheism, contemplation, or other positions, the state endorses the metaview that everyone is entitled to live their lives as they see fit, as long as they display the appropriate political virtues.

Comprehensive liberals are more circumspect about neutrality. They believe that liberalism is itself a kind of view about how the world is and what makes for a good life, albeit one that is characterized by its respect for other views (Berlin, 1969; Raz, 1986). In other words, they think that the political conception *does* logically depend on a comprehensive doctrine of some sort, and is not likely to be the subject of overlapping consensus. This view, known as comprehensive liberalism, "affirms liberal political arrangements in the name of certain moral ideals, such as autonomy, individuality or self-reliance" (Sandel, 1998, p. 189). The crucial departure from political liberalism here is that there is no "purely political" or "freestanding" conception that all reasonable people will assent to, irrespective of what else they believe. Even people interested in fair terms of social cooperation will disagree about political procedures. At least in this respect, therefore, comprehensive liberalism is *not* neutral in aim: individuals who decline to sign on to certain substantive values will not necessarily agree with liberal political arrangements, and may find their views disfavored in social policies.

Indoctrination has been associated with highly illiberal institutions and societies, such as religious cults and fascist regimes. What kind of education is appropriate in a society that nominally aspires to policies that would be reasonably acceptable to everyone? Such societies would be characterized precisely by the freedom to believe in things that may differ from what our parents, community, or elected officials believe. Liberal education is therefore intended to furnish students with skills such as critical thinking that enable them to adjudicate substantive questions of the good for themselves; this facilitates liberalism at the level of the individual. Furthermore, civic education is considered a prerequisite for the sustenance of a democratic society: "education [should] include such things as knowledge of their constitutional and civic rights . . . [and] prepare them to be fully cooperating members of society" (Rawls, 1993, p. 199).[5] Hence any form of education that confines children to specific comprehensive doctrines is a breach of the state's legitimate extent and impedes, rather than nurtures, the development of children into responsible citizens. Moreover, such indoctrination would infringe on the right to privacy; while the state provides common education, it may not unduly interfere with family life (UNCRC, 1990, Article 16). Liberal philosophers have argued that parents should have the ethical scope to inculcate children into their culture, beliefs, ways of thinking, and values, even as the state should endorse broadly liberal goals (Neufeld & Davis, 2010; Brighouse & Swift, 2014). It is easy to see how SJE, when perceived as partisan persuasion, threatens to collide with these basic liberal tenets.

As most teachers know, however, this vision of a politically neutral education is profoundly unrealistic, if not also profoundly undesirable. First, all education is biased – from the choice of the curriculum to the organization of schools to the modes of assessment and evaluation – thus some conceptions of what is "good" or "right," beyond basic respect for pluralism, will seep into students' experiences regardless of the teacher's intentions.[6] To be clear, these conceptions will not always be presented as select reasonable views of which there are many others: they will, at least in lower grades, be susceptible to being viewed as exclusive truths, just as opponents of indoctrination fear. Such an outcome seems unpalatable to political liberals.

Second, and more troublesome for liberal debates about the proper scope of education, children need some reliable structures in which to develop intellectually and emotionally. They need candidates for what is good as well as broad ways of thinking about the world that allow them to make sense of their experiences, or what Charles Taylor calls "frameworks" (Taylor, 1989, p. 25).

[5] By "fully cooperating," Rawls does not necessarily mean "obedient." Indeed, he outlines a theory of civil disobedience in *Justice as Fairness*. "Fully cooperating" here should be understood as being willing to participate in collective social arrangements from which everyone may seek fair rewards, rather than narrowly pursuing one's own interests at the expense of others.

[6] Teachers' own approach to neutrality – that is, their divulging or not divulging their own opinions on controversial issues – is one aspect of the larger political picture. Hess (2004) identifies four approaches teachers can take to addressing controversial issues: denial, privilege, avoidance, and balance (p. 259). For further discussion, and a defense of teacher neutrality as an aim, see Maxwell, Chapter 35 in this volume.

In a climate of vicious partisanship and the politicization of everything from cartoon characters to face masks, students are apt to form normative judgments in the context of kinship and identity, usually starting with their parents. Encountering conflicting, indeed antagonistic, messages between home and school could be seriously disorienting and even lead to crises of allegiance.

Political liberalism is of limited help here, as it assumes that individuals have the ability to choose between competing conceptions of the good, while acknowledging that this is a capacity restricted to rational adults, at best (a premise for which liberalism has also endured resounding criticism). Children are by definition not yet ready to separate their own views of the world from others that are equally reasonable, whichever definition of the latter is preferred; in Rawls' terminology, children cannot yet assume the "burdens of judgment" (1993, p. 54). In education, unlike in much analytic ethical theory, the rational agents who are supposed to make judgments about the good are formed precisely through interactions with particular conceptions of the good. They do not precede such judgments.

The prospect of a truly apolitical education is illusory. So the question becomes, how does education remain legitimate while inevitably favoring certain worldviews over others? In the remainder of this chapter, I attempt to sketch out an answer to this question.

12.4 A Philosophical Defense of SJE

However it is defined and implemented, a defense of SJE that takes seriously the concerns about indoctrination in a liberal democracy can proceed in one of two broad directions. It could either argue that SJE is bound within a strictly political conception of liberalism and only endorses positions on which there is no "reasonable" controversy; or it could acknowledge that it is making claims about the good that are not always subject to overlapping consensus, but are nevertheless justified. If the second route is taken, the account will also need to show why the substantive claims associated with SJE, but not any substantive claims whatsoever, are justified in the education system of a liberal democracy. This is critical: if a teacher can preach that gender is socially constructed and deny the self-regulation of the economy, why can't someone else preach race science and deny the Holocaust? The lines must be drawn carefully so as to be expansive but not undiscriminating.

I think it is fairly clear that attempting to defend SJE within political liberalism is a nonstarter.[7] SJE may vary widely in its parameters and execution, but it features certain common tenets: an emphasis on diversity and anti-racism;

[7] Using Hess's four types of responses to controversial issues in the classroom, a strictly political liberal would endorse either "avoidance" ("The issue is controversial, but . . . I do not think I can teach it fairly") or "balance" ("The issue is controversial and . . . I will try to ensure that various positions get a best case, fair hearing") (Hess, 2004, p. 259). The political liberal would further have to argue that there is relatively little implicit bias in educational choices that do not directly engage with recognizably controversial issues.

inclusive attitudes toward families, sexuality, gender, and relationships; care for the environment; critical perspectives on power and institutions; opposition to all forms of oppression and efforts to make them visible, especially to people with privilege; and critiquing the reach of capitalism, particularly as it interacts with democratic institutions. In practice, these commitments may take the form of more or less radical critiques of existing education and attempts to overhaul the status quo. They feed into positions on such issues as sex education, curriculum design, and values discernment. These have never been "neutral" topics enjoying overlapping consensus, and in contemporary North America, they are positively explosive.

However, while SJE may, depending on how it is taught, be aligned with partisan political perspectives, it also has some solid foundations in Canadian law and political culture.[8] Although the policy landscape is a mixed bag, many precedents are available to practitioners of SJE as democratic justifications of the views they wish to encourage. Above all, the basic rights of all citizens are enshrined in the Canadian Charter of Rights and Freedoms and reinforced through provincial human rights codes. Individuals and organizations that denounce equality in the public realm are not merely unfashionable; they are in contravention of Canadian law. Insofar as SJE seeks to advance and protect the dignity of all people, especially those who remain on the margins of social and political life, it extends this logic and seeks to hold society accountability for its double standards. By contrast, those who support racial hierarchy, seek to discriminate on the basis of sexual orientation, or advance other nonegalitarian agendas will find no explicit succor for their views in any Canadian legislation currently in effect.[9]

Of course, most controversy over SJE, and political disagreement more generally, cannot be resolved through a quick consultation with the Charter or whatever guarantor of equal rights a state has on paper. Views that are more conservative or skeptical of what passes for SJE also have rights and equality in mind. Yet these views can often be shown to be at odds with other goals of the Canadian law and political system.

An example of this type of conflict emerged in Ontario in 2012, the same year the *Maclean's* article was published. The so-called Accepting Schools Act (2012), or Bill 13, provides for protection against sexual harassment, gender-based violence, and homophobia, including allowing students to choose to form gay–straight alliances (GSAs). Some Catholic leaders complained that the bill undermines religious rights by forcing faith-based schools to allow students to describe and validate multiple sexual orientations in a way that chafes against scripture (O'Leary, 2012). For complex historical reasons related to the original terms of Canadian confederation, Catholic schools – but not other faith-based schools – are funded by taxes in Ontario alongside the secular public system, and are generally entitled to teach the curriculum in a manner they deem consistent with the

[8] For a critique of the premise that comprehensive liberalism in fact guides Canadian politics and is therefore normative, see Tanchuk et al. (2021).

[9] I make no comments here about the freedom to express these views (laws regarding hate speech and the like); this argument is confined to what can be taught in schools.

Catholic faith. Some senior administrators in the Catholic school system sought to prohibit the formation of clubs if they were called "gay–straight alliances," recommending the title "respecting difference clubs" instead.

Here we have a situation of mutually exclusive comprehensive doctrines colliding under the auspices of an educational system that is supposed to avoid making pronouncements about the good. Putting aside the question of whether it is defensible for a liberal state to fund faith-based schools,[10] the Government was in a position of having to choose between imposing a gay-positive bill on all schools equally and allowing Catholic schools to rely on their own alternative (Ontario Catholic School Trustees' Association, 2012). In other words, it had to affirm one group's rights over another despite powerful dissent.[11] Cardinal Thomas Collins of the Archdiocese of Toronto even used liberal language to express the view that Catholic doctrines were being sidelined: "Why are Catholics not free to design their own methods of fighting bullying in harmony with the local situation and with their own particular school? . . . We simply ask that diversity be respected in our society" (O'Leary, 2012).

Bill 13 may or may not be regarded as an instance of SJE (indeed, as a top-down measure it may by definition lack the subversiveness that some believe is integral to SJE), but it illustrates the incommensurate views that often surface in debates over educational politics. The protection of sex and gender minorities is a logical extension of the principle of equality, but it remains socially controversial. When SJE is criticized for taking stances on social issues that are challenged by other powerful forces in the educational system, practitioners need to appeal to the higher-order values and laws that support it. Crucially, the atmosphere of antihomophobia that Bill 13 seeks to create is not only consistent with values articulated at the level of the Charter, but also resists the very risk of indoctrination or censorship that some critics of SJE have voiced. The Cardinal-endorsed approach to "respecting difference" states: "the terms 'gay' and 'lesbian' are not used to define people in the Church's official teachings and documents . . . 'gay' and 'lesbian' are often cultural definitions for people and movements that have accepted homosexual acts and behaviors as morally good" (ECDCCCB, 2011, p. 1). If SJE can be criticized for inducting children into an ideological mindset or policing their vocabulary, then this line of argument backfires upon closer inspection: the alternative proposed in Catholic schools would be at least equally restrictive.[12] In contrast, by requiring schools to allow students to form GSAs, but not prohibiting religious education or the formation of other affinity groups within schools, Bill 13 attempts to protect vulnerable students while leaving greater scope for pluralism.

In referring to background political commitments and progressive legislation to justify the goals of SJE, my point is not that we have completed our work in

[10] Many critics, such as the Canadian Civil Liberties Association and the United Nations Human Rights Committee, have decried Canada's selective funding of Catholic schools to the exclusion of other faith-based schools, which is protected in the Constitution.

[11] This is an example of the failure of Rawls' ideal of "neutrality of aim."

[12] For further discussion of SJE and/as ideology, see Applebaum (2009).

achieving the liberal vision of social justice, even on paper. The point is that there is some official commitment to anti-oppression politics and egalitarian values, along with features of the "basic structure" that seek to translate legal equality into something materially meaningful. Legislation is not the end goal of social change, but it can certainly be a sign of progress, and one that educators are well within their rights to build upon. Indeed, some provincial education laws explicitly require teachers to promote respect for these laws and for all human rights.

These examples confirm that the Canadian state and provincial authorities do not observe neutrality of aim (avoiding favoring some comprehensive views over others) or necessarily seek acceptance by all "reasonable" citizens. Some Canadians would not choose to protect as many rights as we in fact do, or they would choose to protect different ones. Some views of the good are certainly more prominent, and afforded more state protection, than others. Nor are these static: as Canadian culture evolves, political values evolve with it. Marriage equality legislation may have been unthinkable 30 years ago. Today, even leaders who may personally disagree with the worldview it reflects know better than to suggest reopening it for public debate.

Armed with this understanding, we are in a position to better defend at least most SJE against charges of illegitimate bias or brainwashing. Regardless of how it is defined, most SJE hangs on the coattails of comprehensive doctrines that have been given greater support in the wider political landscape. We can say that SJE chases the progressive horizon of Canadian politics. The values expressed in defensible SJE reflect and seek to build on concrete achievements in Canadian law and political developments, and to bridge the gap between the promise of these laws and the reality for many Canadians. At its most powerful, SJE exposes the injustice in the status quo by appealing to the justice of the political ideals that we aspire to – for example, invoking the Charter to illuminate cases of rights and freedoms denied in Canada. In this sense, SJE is not only legitimate, but strongly desirable in the Canadian education system.

While it is an open question how much Canada's political culture resembles that of the United States or other so-called liberal democracies, the framework I have presented here builds on the types of background values and foundational documents that are common across such societies. Seeing SJE as substantive – that is, not neutral – and in need of justification presents an opportunity to articulate general terms for the legitimate appearance of politics in a democratic education system. In the Section 12.5, I offer five criteria and illustrate how they would be applied in the Canadian context, before anticipating, in the Conclusion, two important objections.

12.5 Social Justice or Brainwashing? Splitting the Hairs

I am not prepared to suggest that there are universal rules about what forms of education can be defended philosophically, but in what follows I offer a list of criteria that do most of the work needed to meet the brainwashing objection. This is not a definition of SJE; it is, rather, a list of conditions that all educational initiatives should live up to, SJE included. It covers both the form and the content of politicized educational endeavors, providing a guideline for discriminating between brainwashing and legitimate political messaging in schools. While their goal is to protect against indoctrination of any kind, it will be clear that these criteria are generally more compatible with politically progressive views than with more conservative ones, thus corroborating the stereotype that SJE is politically biased. Hence, while not all forms of so-called SJE are immune to charges of brainwashing, and some forms of politicized education that are inconsistent with SJE are still legitimate, we can split hairs in such a way that most SJE will be vindicated against the charges leveled in the *Maclean's* article, as well as many of the more virulent ongoing attacks on progressive education.

Any comprehensive doctrines espoused in mandatory education in Canada must meet the following criteria:

1. **Have legislative backing in the form of such documents as the Charter, human rights codes, and current policy.** This criterion alone rules out most of the comprehensive doctrines that do not belong in an educational setting. Teaching racial hierarchy is thus inadmissible, even if it were not (in addition) indoctrinative; racial equality is legally nonnegotiable. Of course, many historical laws have been explicitly racist or incompatible with human rights and equality, and it may be objected that existing legislation is inadequate or wrong-headed; this is addressed in criterion 4 below.

   The positions that are defensible in education need not be backed by all legislation or policies: indeed, SJE is a prime opportunity to reveal the inconsistencies – in the spirit if not the letter – between some of our codes and statutes. For example, before gender identity and gender expression were added to the Canada Human Rights Act in 2017, teachers could encourage students to ask why sex and sexual orientation were protected, but these forms of identity were not.
2. **Be compatible with reasonable pluralism.** Not all comprehensive doctrines accept the potential reasonableness of their rivals to the same extent. Even where liberalism is comprehensive, it allows for more pluralism of belief than illiberal alternatives. Doctrines that are structurally incompatible with pluralism – whether religious or otherwise ideological – should not be endorsed in mandatory schooling.
3. **Not force engagement in partisan politics or political activism that students do not choose.** There is a critical difference between teaching students to think about the world in such a way that may motivate independent political involvement, and requiring students to defend or oppose particular political parties or policies. The issues debated by politicians should be analyzed in class, even when some positions are bound to emerge more strongly than others. But signing students up for political rallies or marching them down to City Hall to protest a particular bill inhibits students from forming their own conclusions autonomously.

4. **Be connected with developing skills for democratic engagement.** Elaborating on the preceding criterion, while comprehensive doctrines may be taught or endorsed, they should be accompanied by the development of age-appropriate skills such as critical thinking, logic, and media literacy that will help prevent any doctrines from becoming dogma and ensure lifelong reflection about substantive views, including those encompassed by law. This task has become increasingly important, but also increasingly challenging, in the face of growing conspiracy theories and disinformation (Burbules, 2022). I make no claims here about how best to teach such skills; I only stress that it remains the correct goal.
5. **Respect students' freedom to abstain from activities that contravene their own (emerging or tentative) comprehensive doctrines.** When students do come to class with substantive commitments, these need to be respected. We now accept that it is profoundly objectionable to force a student to pray in school or to pledge allegiance to something she rejects. Likewise, it is illiberal to force students to participate in social justice activities that violate their freedom of conscience, even if the activities are otherwise justified. This condition would not, however, require teachers to design alternative lesson plans or let students stay at home when controversial topics are discussed. Students should be exposed to SJE, but entitled to hold their own opinions. Abstention may come into play when the class undertakes some action arising out of the SJE teaching, such as raising money for a particular cause.

These conditions are not dissimilar from some extant articulations of SJE, such as Hackman's: "[SJE] encourages students to take an active role in their own education and supports teachers in creating empowering, democratic, and critical educational environments" (Hackman, 2005, p. 103). My list of criteria takes substance into account, and can thus distinguish between defensible and indefensible applications of comprehensive doctrines. It resists the logical claim that if SJE is allowed, religious fundamentalism or racist ideologies should be as well. In short, SJE is justifiable, not because every citizen endorses the concrete values it represents, but because and only insofar as it reflects a democratic political culture that does.

As a test of these principles, let me return to few examples of alleged SJE that were raised in the *Maclean's* article.

> [Students] brought home student planners marked with the international days of zero tolerance on female genital mutilation [FGM] and ending violence against sex workers. (Reynolds, 2012, p. 20)

Canada has strong legislative and cultural injunctions against gender-based violence and all forms of human rights violations (principle 1 – legislative backing). Bringing these issues to the attention of students in the school system, while difficult, can increase their understanding of current issues (principle 4 – democratic engagement) without taking partisan stances on any policy positions (principle 3 – no forced engagement). There is no concern about principle 2 (reasonable pluralism) or principle 5 (freedom to abstain) because there is no protected space in Canadian society for endorsing these forms of violence.[13]

> The Durham Board of Education in Ontario came under fire for discouraging the terms "wife" and "husband" in class in favour of the gender-neutral "spouse," and the words "boyfriend" and "girlfriend" in favour of "partner." (Reynolds, 2012, pp. 20–21)

Using gender-neutral terms such as "partner" is consistent with Canadian policy and liberal values, even though not everyone is comfortable with them. Changes in vocabulary may be initially awkward but ultimately help bring about social change, as evolutions in acceptable terms for women and people of color over the last half-century demonstrate. The distinction needs to be preserved, however, between politically correct language and first-person authority. If students are punished for choosing to use more conventional terms to describe their own families or imagined relationships, criterion 5 would be violated.

> A Grade 3 class in Toronto took to the streets with signs and an oversized papier mâché oil pipeline to protest the laying of an actual pipeline in western Canada. (Reynolds, 2012, p. 20)

This activity – regardless of the age of the students – violates criterion 3, showing that what passes for (or is regarded as) SJE can tread too far in the direction of indoctrination. Yet there are appropriate ways of teaching about the effects of big oil without violating my criteria, and which may lead to students undertaking the same protest independently. For example, drawing attention to the negative impacts of the pipeline, such as its effects on the environment and on Indigenous communities, is entirely justified by such laws as the Environmental Protection Act (1999) and recent social activism surrounding Indigenous rights in Canada, particularly if accompanied by a critique of the political bias in media and government discussions of the issue, such as television ads promoting Alberta's tar sands.[14]

> OISE [The Ontario Institute for Studies in Education]'s website features a Grade 5 math lesson on government budgets that culminates in students writing letters to MPPs [Members of Provincial Parliament] advocating

[13] It is possible that these awareness days were also objected to on the grounds that students may hail from countries or cultures where such violence is accepted; there may even be girls in the class who have undergone FGM. This "cultural relativism" concern is ruled out on the version of liberalism I have espoused. There is no place in Canada, much less the education system, to talk about FGM as a reasonable culture practice that happens to differ from others that are more common in Canada. Personal experiences of violence, as well as distress over conflicting messages between school and home, need to be dealt with sensitively, but validating FGM so as to "include" these cultures is not consistent with Canadian, or any liberal, values.

[14] These activities would probably fall flat with students in a Grade 3 classroom, suggesting that opposition to the protest was likely also based on concerns about age-appropriateness (indeed, what counts as indoctrination among young children may not count as such among older students with more developed critical thinking skills). Based on my criteria, the mandatory protest of the oil pipeline is not a legitimate activity at any grade level, but older students, such as those in Grades 7–12, could benefit from an exploration of the politics of the pipeline.

> changes in spending priorities. Though not explicitly partisan, it juxtaposes the money spent on the war in Afghanistan with the money spent on poverty—and that does suggest a certain point of view. (Reynolds, 2012, p. 22)

Writing letters to MPPs on a given issue – whether the MPPs targeted are determined by the teacher or the decision is up to the students – transgresses a fine line between democratic education and forced political engagement. Using government budgets to teach math is a great way to incorporate questions of justice into the curriculum, but presenting complex ethical questions as fact is manipulative. Students need to be given the skills and the opportunity to analyze the distribution of government resources (presumably outside of math class) and then choose whether to lobby for different spending priorities.[15] The costs of war, both fiscal and otherwise, as well as the severity of poverty in Canada, can be underscored without forcing students to jump to policy conclusions.

As we can see, not every initiative that has been forwarded as an example of SJE will find full vindication within the criteria I have set out. This is not to say that the initiatives that fail my criteria are not examples of furthering social justice. Rather, they may be examples of social justice that cannot yet be defended coherently to the public at large, and therefore do not belong in the public education system. With greater social change, they may earn their defensibility in time. Likewise, these criteria may allow for philosophically defensible educational moves that social justice educators would balk at, although the most egregious ones have been ruled out. This is to be expected. Liberalism is fundamentally about getting along with people we disagree with.

12.6 Conclusion

I will conclude by anticipating two important criticism of my approach. First, it may be objected, especially from avid practitioners of SJE, that the space I have carved out for the defensible introduction of familiar, left-leaning social justice causes in K-12 is too narrow. After all, I am confining educational activities to (at least some) overlap with precedent. Is this not stagnant, conciliatory, even antithetical to the very activist connotations of "social justice" I outlined? What about the revolutionary function of education?

The discrepancy between what is defensible under the status quo and what we might wish to bring about is not as extreme as this objection presumes. Although SJE should be grounded to some extent in formal political commitments, there is usually a substantial lag between the adoption of certain stances at a legal or macro level and their actualization at a micro level. Indeed, laws and foundational state documents are *aspirational*: they declare what we believe

[15] In a civics class, it would be appropriate to assign students the task of choosing a political issue and writing a letter about it to an MPP of their choice, because this encourages democratic participation and political development without forcing students into a particular partisan stance.

in, not what is actually the case. Discrimination on the basis of sexual orientation is illegal in Canada, but homophobia is still rampant. If such prejudice were nonexistent, presumably we would not need legislative efforts to curb its effects.

Much of the work of SJE lies in these interstices between ideals and practice – for example, in educating students so that they not only obey the law protecting same-sex couples from discrimination, but come to understand and embrace antihomophobia principles in their everyday lives. Progressive education has extensive work to do in protecting and furthering such values, and in reminding the public of its own stated commitment to equality. In addition, through its emphasis on democratic skill development, SJE can facilitate critiques of the law and encourage students to imagine more just social arrangements that we have yet to aspire to. The most progressive interpretations of the current law can give way to better laws in time.

A second and more fundamental objection concerns the viability of defending SJE within a liberal democratic paradigm in an era of precipitous liberal democratic decline – or even being concerned with political legitimacy at all. In the time since the *Maclean's* cover article was published, the norms of liberal democracy have been so eroded, in the United States in particular, that we might wonder whether the effort to abide by public norms is morally or even strategically worthwhile. Why talk about reining in education for social justice out of a concern for democratic legitimacy when a substantial portion of the world's largest putative democracy believes that free and open elections have been "stolen"? The concern for legitimacy, one may object, is hopelessly, even recklessly, naive.

This charge, made more vivid by each successive round of democratic rule-breaking, presents a sobering challenge to defenders of democratic education and the norms of liberal democracy. Abiding by the norms of legitimacy I have set out when one's political adversaries flout them will certainly produce frustration and, sometimes, defeat. In the long run, however, it is inconceivable that a better society will be brought about by resorting to antidemocratic or illiberal tactics in the name of freedom and equality.

I have argued that the background commitments SJE attempts to instantiate – meaningful equality, redress for injustice, and so on – derive from the noblest of the political aspirations that formed our societies, and can be defended in public education. But what is "socially just" is only "democratic" if it is advanced without indoctrination and coercion. As we saw in the Section 12.5, some self-styled SJE is in violation of the democratic criteria I have laid out. This tendency has arguably been amplified in the Trump and post-Trump eras: there is an understandable impulse to jump to the progressive conclusion, bypassing persuasion and dialogue. Aside from the incommensurate backlash this sparks, however, this approach to SJE is pedagogically unsound. Conservative critics are not wrong that some dogmatic approaches to social justice – enforcing allegiance to particular political paradigms and terminology; canceling or silencing dissenting perspectives; reducing all students to a series of social positionalities and ranking levels of oppression – is more doctrinaire than educative. Moreover, in the zeal to communicate the "correct" answers on such complex issues as race, history, power, and identity, social justice educators may minimize the diversity of views within their own ranks, and treat as fixed the discursive borders that are still evolving. Such dogmatism not only makes SJE even more vulnerable to attack; it also stymies the ongoing refinement of political discourse and the development of solidarity among progressives.

To conclude, I have argued that SJE can often be defended within the legislative and political framework of a liberal democracy, using Canada as an example. The Canadian example should be instructive for similar societies grounded in liberal principles and respect for human rights. Where this is not the case, I am not ruling out the ethical view that it would be best, all else being equal, to radically educate all students – even indoctrinate them – into some of the values espoused by practitioners of SJE. Yet education also has an obligation to the public at large. The purpose and transformative potential of public education would be undermined if the curriculum were indeed susceptible to charges of brainwashing. This is something we should care about, even if terms like "brainwashing" are used carelessly in public discourse. The business of changing social policy needs to be pursued in the public arena by autonomous adults. This does not mean, however, that education should be static or resigned. As Callan puts it, "liberal democracy at its best, in education as in other social endeavours, will not leave everything as it is" (Callan, 1997, p. 13).

References

Applebaum, B. (2009). Is teaching for social justice a "Liberal Bias"? *Teachers College Record*, 111(2), 376–408.

Berlin, I. (1969). *Four essays on liberty*. Oxford: Oxford University Press.

Bialystok, L. (2014). Politics without "brainwashing": A philosophical defence of social justice education. *Curriculum Inquiry*, 44(3), 413–40.

Brighouse, H., & Swift, A. (2014). *Family values: The ethics of parent-child relationships*. Princeton, NJ: Princeton University Press.

Bull, B. (2008). *Social justice in education: An introduction*. New York: Palgrave Macmillan.

Burbules, C. N. (2022). Promoting critical thinking in anti-critical thinking times: Lessons from Covid. *Philosophical Inquiry in Education*, 29(1), 5–10.

Callan, E. (1997). *Creating citizens: Political education and liberal democracy*. Oxford: Oxford University Press.

Episcopal Commission for Doctrine of the Canadian Conference of Catholic Bishops (ECDCCCB). (2011). Pastoral ministry to young people with same-sex attraction. http://www.cccb.ca/site/images/stories/pdf/ministry-ssa_en.pdf.

Gabriel, T., & Goldstein, D. (2021, June 1). Disputing racism's reach, Republicans rattle American schools. *The New York Times*. Available at: https://www.nytimes.com/2021/06/01/us/politics/critical-race-theory.html.

Hackman, H. (2005). Five essential components for social justice education. *Equity and Excellence in Education*, 38(2), 103–09.

Hess, D. E. (2004, April). Controversies about controversial issues in democratic education. *PSOnline*, 257–61. Available at: https://people.ucsc.edu/~ktellez/hess.pdf.

Hess, D. E., & McAvoy, P. (2014). *The political classroom*. New York: Routledge.

Hytten, K. (2015). Ethics in teaching for democracy and social justice. *Democracy & Education*, 23(2), 1–10.

Hytten, K., & Bettez, S. C. (2011). Understanding education for social justice. *Educational Foundations*, 25(1–2), 7–24.

Murrell, P. Jr. (2006). Toward social justice in urban education: a model of collaborative cultural inquiry in urban schools. *Equity & Excellence in Education*, 39(1), 81–90.

Neufeld, B., & Davis, G. (2010). Civic respect, civic education, and the family. *Educational Philosophy and Theory*, 42(1), 94–111.

North, C. (2008). What's all this talk about "social justice"? Mapping the terrain of education's latest catchphrase. *Teachers College Record*, 110(6), 1182–206.

Nussbaum, M. (2011). Perfectionist liberalism and political liberalism. *Philosophy and Public Affairs*, 39(1), 3–45.

O'Leary, J. (2012, June 1). Cardinal Collins defends Catholic approach to bullying. *The Catholic Register*. Available at: http://www.catholicregister.org/component/k2/item/14577-cardinal-collins-defends-non-gsa-approach-to-school-bullying.

Ontario Catholic School Trustees Association. (2012, June 25). Respecting difference. A resource for Catholic schools in the province of Ontario. Available at: https://www.ocsta.on.ca/ocsta/wp-content/uploads/2020/04/PDF-RespectingDifference-FINAL-Jan.26.2012.pdf.

Ontario Ministry of Education. (2009). *Ontario's equity and inclusive education strategy*. Toronto.

Packer, G. (2022, March 10). The grown-ups are losing it. *The Atlantic*. Available at: https://www.theatlantic.com/magazine/archive/2022/04/pandemic-politics-public-schools/622824.

Rawls, J. (1985). Justice as fairness: Political not metaphysical. *Philosophy and Public Affairs*, 14(3), 223–52.

Rawls, J. (1993). *Political liberalism*. New York: Columbia University Press.

Raz, J. (1986). *The morality of freedom*. Oxford: Clarendon Press.

Reynolds, C. (2012). Why are schools brainwashing our children? *Maclean's*, 125 (43), 20–23.

Sandel, M. (1998). *Liberalism and the limits of justice*. 2nd ed., Cambridge: Cambridge University Press.

Sensoy, Ö., & DiAngelo, R. (2012). *Is everyone really equal?: An introduction to key concepts in social justice education*. New York: Teachers College Press.

Sopelsa, B., Bellamy-Walker, T., & Reuters (2022, March 8). "Don't Say Gay" bill: Florida Senate passes controversial LGBTQ school measure. *NBC News*. Available at: https://www.nbcnews.com/nbc-out/out-politics-and-policy/dont-say-gay-bill-florida-senate-passes-controversial-lgbtq-school-mea-rcna19133.

Tanchuk, N., Rocha, T., & Krus, M. (2021). Is comprehensive liberal social justice education brainwashing? *Philosophy of Education*, 77(2), 44–59.

Taylor, C. (1989). *Sources of the self: The making of modern identity*. Cambridge, MA: Harvard University Press.

United Nations Convention on the Rights of the Child (UNCRC). (1990). UN Commission on Human Rights, E/CN.4/RES/1990/74. Available at: https://www.refworld.org/docid/3b00f03d30.html.

Waldron, J. (1987). Theoretical foundations of liberalism. *The Philosophical Quarterly*, 37(147), 127–50.

Waldron, J. (2004). Liberalism, political and comprehensive. In G. F. Gaus & C. Kukathas, eds., *The handbook of political theory*. London: Sage, pp. 89–100.

Wise, A. E. (2006). *Accreditation hearing of the National Council for Accreditation of Teacher Education (NCATE) before the U.S. Department of Education's National Advisory Committee on Institutional Quality and Integrity (NACIQI)*. Washington, DC: Government Printing Office.

Zimmerman, J., & Robertson, E. (2017). *The case for contention*. Chicago, IL: University of Chicago Press.

13

Critical Theory, Local Moral Perception, and Democratic Education

Drew Chambers

13.1 Introduction

Sometime in the 1920s, in a pastel yellow building neighbored by colonial sugar factories, sat a young Aimé Césaire wondering why his science grades were so low. Truthfully, Aimé didn't have to wonder – he knew; the pages of his botany books were filled with plants native to France and not one from his home, Martinique (Rowell, 2008). His education at the Lycée Schoelcher – one of "official culture," as he would come to describe it – led him fatefully away from the shores of the Antilles to Paris, the Sorbonne, and literary acclaim. However, Césaire would return to Martinique fractured, confronted with a seemingly unscalable abyss between Paris's cultural gauze and Martinique's apparent disarray. Césaire's famed novel-in-verse, *Journal of a Homecoming*, recounts his struggle upon returning to his native land. He recalls: "After an absence of ten years, [I] found myself assaulted by a sea of impressions and images. . . . I felt a deep anguish over the prospects for Martinique" (2000, p. 81). In Paris, an intense intellectual fervor washed over Césaire, deepening his attachment to the Western canon, and incubating his poetic talents. In Martinique, by contrast, he was confronted with "swamps of rust," funereal heaps of trash and dog cadavers, splintering barrels of rum, and all the thralldom that flowed from colonization; in his own words, what Césaire found upon returning to Martinique was "death in its thousand ignoble local forms" (2017, p. 115). He was a true cosmopolitan patriot, committed to the decolonial project but in love with the humanistic genealogies of Europe, yet who could not look upon his home without seeing anything more than the "abandoned ghastliness of [its] sores" (2017, p. 95). Luckily for Césaire and for Martinique, his inadvertent neocolonial disdain for the island dissipated, or, perhaps more accurately, was epiphanically exorcised. In a moment of clarity portrayed in the *Cahier*, Césaire comes abruptly face to face with the high-brow prejudice his education had wrought within him. For all his presumed righteous nobility, he realizes that he failed to see Martinique authentically.

Where he once saw death, there was actually life; where he once felt disdain, there was now "love, immense, ablaze" (Césaire, 2017, p. 133). Césaire would spend the rest of his life in Martinique, founding literary journals, representing the island to the French assembly, resisting the grotesque grip of Vichy France, and serving as Fort-de-France's democratically elected mayor for 56 years. I began this chapter with Césaire because his story is emblematic of what I hope to show here. As much as his story is one about the costs of "moving up" (Morton, 2019), it is also a story about how to be a better citizen, a better neighbor.

This chapter concerns the relationship between democratic education and critical theory. A chapter like this should attempt to answer two fundamental questions. First, what does democratic education informed by critical theory minimally entail? Second, what does it take for a critical democratic education[1] to succeed? It is not too difficult to answer the first question, largely because of the rich lineages that democratic theory and critical theory possess. The second, however, poses a more substantial challenge. In a political age marked by polarization, de facto segregation, global capitalism, and endemic misinformation, what hope do the critical and democratic projects have? I suggest that Césaire's narrative arc provides a vital insight to the success of those projects. What ended up completing the circuit of Césaire's democratic aspirations and his decolonial ambitions was a certain kind of attention to his native land. What I will argue in what follows is that the circuit breaker for a critical democratic education is, perhaps counterintuitively, attention to one's local context. Insofar as one fails to attend to the particulars of their local setting, the potential of democracy and critical theory lays unrealized.

The remainder of this chapter will proceed as follows. Section 13.2 sets the stage by offering a sketch of both democratic education and critical theory. Section 13.3 draws out a common occluding characteristic of both democratic education and critical education, namely, their preoccupation with national and international scopes. Sections 13.4 and 13.5 draw on the work of Iris Murdoch and John McDowell to argue that cultivating moral attention to one's local setting must be seen as an essential aspect of critical democratic education. The chapter concludes by offering brief educational applications and responses to objections related to objectivity and the threat of parochialism. Ultimately, I hope to demonstrate that attention to one's local context can energize the democratic and critical spirits because, in Murdoch's words, "in so far as goodness is for use in politics and in the market place it must combine its increasing intuitions of unity with an increasing grasp of complexity and detail" (2014, p. 93).

[1] As a shorthand in this chapter, I often use the term "critical democratic education." By that term, I mean an educational approach that is – in some combination – within, for, and through democracy (Sant, 2019), and informed by critical theory. Educational approaches informed by critical theory are often grouped under the blanket term "critical pedagogy." I have no terminological points to parse here and tend to think of "critical democratic education" as "democratic education" with some features, be they ideological or technical, of critical pedagogy.

13.2 Democratic Education and Critical Theory

In this section, I offer a brief sketch of democratic education and critical theory by tracing their contemporary lineages and drawing out each project's key commitments. My gloss of democratic education is that it emphasizes teaching capacities for and commitment to inclusive deliberation as a means toward justice. My gloss of critical theory is that it is a method of social and political theorizing that prioritizes emancipatory justice within the context of history and often against the backdrop of mass culture.

13.2.1 Democratic Education

Democratic education in its contemporary instantiation is most accurately seen as flowing from the proverbial watershed that is John Dewey's work, particularly *Democracy and Education*. Dewey influenced a vast number of his own contemporaries, and his influence remains powerful today. Aside from Dewey, democratic education experienced its fullest bloom around the turn of the century with the work of Michael Apple (1999), Eamonn Callan (1997), Amy Gutmann (1999), and Martha Nussbaum (1997),[2] with Danielle Allen (2016),[3] Sigal Ben-Porath (2006),[4] Gert Biesta (2011), and Meira Levinson (2012) following. To offer a thorough explication of each of these thinkers' views would take an entire volume. Indeed, the present volume will offer the best – and often firsthand – account of their work. Moreover, as Levinson (2014) writes, "To some extent, which of these aims [of "democratic civic education"] rises to the fore depends on one's ideal of democracy itself" (p. 136). Consequently, it would be a mistake to think that theorists of democratic education share a unified conception of what it entails.[5]

That said, there seem to be recurring elements of democratic education theory that rise to the level of being hallmarks of the project. At the very least, even though some of these hallmarks might be contested by certain scholars, the hallmarks are common enough in the literature to qualify as such. Democratic education characteristically aims to accomplish the following: (i) engender a rational support for democracy, (ii) develop certain capacities necessary for the

[2] Nussbaum states that her "model of education for democratic citizenship" relies on cultivating three essential capacities: the capacity for critical examination, an ability to see oneself as a human beings bound to all other human beings, and the ability to think what it might be like to be in the shoes of a person different from oneself (Nussbaum, 2006). In her proposal, it is clear to see that she emphasizes certain civic and epistemic virtues that are commonly thought basic to just democratic behavior.

[3] Allen's project is broader than just democratic education. She is concerned with "democratic eudaimonism," or, in other words, what leading a flourishing life might mean in a democratic context. An aspect of such eudaimonia, however, is civic education vis-à-vis participatory readiness, which itself is supported by "verbal empowerment, democratic knowledge, and a rich understanding of the strategies and tactics that undergird efficacy" (2016, p. 40).

[4] Ben-Porath argues for what she calls "expansive education," which aims at peace building and democracy. She specifically states that a "strong democratic education" would be "committed to promoting the values, attitudes, and behaviors necessary for the preservation of democracy while remaining responsive to the social demands of conflict" (2006, p. 117).

[5] Oftentimes today, democracy is identified with liberal democracy though liberality is not necessarily an essential characteristic of democracy (Bridoux & Kurki, 2014, p. 2).

exercise of democratic citizenship, and (iii) produce certain virtues facilitative of democracy. These three hallmarks of democratic education consistently rely on at least one enduring principle of democratic theory, namely, democracy's rejection of external authority from which stems its contemporary insistence on inclusion. At its core, democratic government is concerned with securing the consent of its citizenry, particularly considering differing positions and beliefs (Crick, 2002).

Gutmann, in her landmark *Democratic Education*, contends that, "Education in character and in moral reasoning are therefore both necessary, neither sufficient, for creating democratic citizens" (1999, p. 51). Her position is aligned not just with Dewey 80 years prior, but also Israel Scheffler 30 years prior. Scheffler writes succinctly, "The function of education in a democracy is rather to liberate the mind, strengthen its critical powers, inform it with knowledge and the capacity for independent inquiry, engage its human sympathies, and illuminate its moral and practical choices" (1997, p. 29). What resounds in accounts of democratic education is a priority on educating people to be good thinkers but with appropriately democratic sympathies including inclusive dialogue (Waghid et al., 2016, p. 12). In sum, democratic education seems to minimally involve educating the citizenry to responsibly and volitionally take up the mantle of their democratic citizenship.

13.2.2 Critical Theory

Critical theory shares a similarly impressive, and perhaps larger, contemporary history. There is the formal Critical Theory that is synonymous with the Frankfurt School, as well as critical theory broadly construed, referring to social criticism generally. The former is often designated as stemming from the work of Theodor Adorno and Max Horkheimer, perhaps most notably in their 1947 coauthored text, *Dialectic of Enlightenment*. After the early and adolescent days of the Frankfurt School came Jürgen Habermas who entered the scene in the 1960s. Following on Habermas's heels came the Frankfurt School's third generation with Axel Honneth, a student of Habermas, and then Rahel Jaeggi, a student of Honneth, accompanied by folks such as Seyla Benhabib and Robin Celikates. Such a brief gloss of the critical theory lineage cannot possibly account for the richness of the tradition, but it provides a dim guiding light of the path for someone unfamiliar with it.[6]

It is difficult to think of as unified any theory or project as expansive as critical theory, especially when the project intentionally resists unification. Even so, it will be helpful for the sake of bridging democratic education with critical theory to draw out some rough perspective of what critical theory typically involves. In

[6] Those not mentioned but perhaps just as influential in the broader field include dozens of names ranging from, of course, Marx and Kant predating the Frankfurt School, to contemporaries of its first instantiation such as Georg Lukács, Walter Benjamin, and Herbert Marcuse, to ancillary and distinct voices like Max Weber and Michel Foucault, to foundational thinkers of offshoots of the project including Derrick Bell, Kimberlé Crenshaw, Nancy Fraser, Kwame Nkrumah, and Gayatri Spivak. This list is still far from replete and there is not the space here to give each thinker a full treatment, but their work ought to be recognized as historically important to the development of critical theory.

Dialectic of Enlightenment, Adorno and Horkheimer describe the basic premise of the book as the following: "That the hygienic factory and everything pertaining to it, Volkswagen and the sports palace, are obtusely liquidating metaphysics does not matter in itself, but that these things are themselves becoming metaphysics, an ideological curtain, within the social whole, behind which real doom is gathering, does matter" (2002, p. xviii). Honneth, contrasting the formal Critical Theory with social criticism, says that the former "insists on a mediation of theory and history in a concept of socially effective rationality" (2004, p. 338). Further, Honneth contends that behind each of the distinct trains of thought emerging from the Frankfurt School one finds "the same idea forming the background of each of the different projects – namely, that social relationships distort the historical process of development in a way that one can only practically remedy" (2004, p. 339).

Christ et al. offer a more programmatic summary of the constitutive elements of critical theory. They write:

> [F]irstly, critical theories are self-conscious of their social embeddedness, more particularly, of their connection to social practices and struggles. Secondly, critical theories give up the pretence of neutrality and are committed to a particular goal, namely the emancipation of all human beings from exploitation, oppression, and domination. Last but not least, they see the theoretical enlightenment that they aim to bring about . . . as itself a contribution to achieving this goal. (2020, p. viii)

Sally Haslanger further illuminates the prongs identified above when she says that "critical theory begins [with] facing entrenched injustice," often draped with ideologies that obscure its presence (2020, p. 36). Consequently, because "the world itself can become distorted, we need a critical vantage point not just on what we believe, but on what is" (Haslanger, 2020, p. 36). The project of critical theory is to manage a theoretical explication of how that vantage point is possible, as well as to manage making that vantage point actionable (Celikates, 2018, pp. 207–8).

13.2.3 Critical Theory, Democracy, and Education

As should be at least somewhat clear already, critical theory and democratic theory have aims that are potentially sympathetic to one another. Arguably the most prominent critical theorist responsible for connecting critical theory to a theory of democracy is Habermas. Habermas's democratic theory champions "the procedures and communicative presuppositions of democratic opinion – and will-formation" (Habermas, 1994, p. 9). Those deliberative procedures "function as the most important sluices for the discursive rationalization of the decisions of an administration constrained by law and statute" (Habermas, 1994, p. 9). In that way, deliberation itself is constitutive of interests in Habermas' democratic society.

Despite his being situated in the critical theory project, Habermas has been criticized for acquiescing too much to preexisting circumstances and prevailing norms in his democratic theory such that it is less critical than it is typically liberal in the Rawlsian tradition (Critchley & Honneth, 1998; Scheuerman, 1999; Shabani, 2003). Regardless of Habermas' own attempts to craft a critical democratic theory, there is a prominent stream of thought that sees the two as compatible. Iris Marion Young goes so far as to say, "Democratic theory, including the theory of deliberative democracy, should understand itself primarily as a *critical* theory, which exposes the exclusions and constraints in supposed fair processes of actual decision making" (2001, p. 688; emphasis in original).[7] While critical theory and various strands of democratic theory may occasion certain theoretical and methodological pitfalls, the two projects share some aims and commitments.

Not many have written on the notion of a *critical* democratic education. Among those who have, Henry Giroux suggests that democratic education as citizenship education should be reformulated by "by situating it within an analysis that explores the often overlooked complex relations among knowledge, power, ideology, class, and economics" (1980, p. 331). In her review of nearly 400 articles published between 2006 and 2017 on democratic education, Edda Sant identifies the key principles of critical democratic education as being "concerned with the deficits of aggregative and liberal systems as they reproduce inequality and existing power relations" and, conversely, defending "a 'thick' normative democracy in which all humans have equal and real opportunities to be agents of social transformation" (2019, p. 674).

13.3 National and Global Consciousness

One shared characteristic of democratic education and critical theory is a preoccupation with national and global consciousness. I will first explain the ways national consciousness shows up in each of these bodies of work, followed by the ways in which global consciousness does.

13.3.1 Democratic Education and National Consciousness

Democratic education has often been understood as education for and within a democratic society. Gutmann, for instance, contends that the prime commitment of democratic education is a commitment to "conscious social reproduction," which more or less entails educating "all educable children to be capable of participating in collectively shaping their society" (1999, p. 39). Underlying Gutmann's point is the apparent truism that in a democratic society, people have different ideas about what it means to live a good life and therefore have different positions on the enactment of laws or whatever else is up for deliberation. Conscious social reproduction is founded on that truism insofar as it recognizes it and takes it as essential to the deliberative project of

[7] For two thorough expositions, each of different lengths, of the relationships between democracy (and particularly the deliberative form) and critical theory, see Rostboll (2008) and Hammond (2019).

democracy. Naturally then, Gutmann's focus in *Democratic Education* is educating a citizenry for democracy within a democracy.

Similar to Gutmann, Levinson's *No Citizen Left Behind* tends to emphasize the domestic orientation of democratic education. While Levinson provides some suggestions oriented toward the importance of local awareness and local contingencies, she, on the whole, thinks of citizenship education as for the sake of public priorities and creating society (2012, p. 264). Democratic education is naturally situated in the context of a democracy, in which a legitimate one will have public support. Consequently, any straightforward theory of democratic education will likely locate the project within the bounds of a democratic society, which is to say a domestic context.

13.3.2 Critical Theory and National Consciousness

Since critical theory's beginnings in the Frankfurt School, it has been dedicated toward uncovering and indicting ills of "mass culture" that "spread like a cataract across the life of society in all its aspects" (Adorno & Horkheimer, 2002, p. 21). In this sense, critical theory is not a positive project with a domestic orientation like that of democratic education, but rather a negative project created in reference to national and international phenomena. The proverbial crosshairs of Adorno and Horkheimer include diseases like nationalism, fascism, industrial capitalism, the so-called culture industry, and forces that would otherwise operate on a societal level to alienate and oppress particularly the middle and lower classes.

13.3.3 Democratic Education and Global Consciousness

Given our increasingly globalized world, some scholars have offered addenda to the established democratic education theories by examining their capacity to inform individual global consciousness (e.g., Aboagye & Dlamini, 2021; Culp, 2019; De Lissovoy, 2011; Misiaszek, 2019). In her epilogue to the revised edition of *Democratic Education*, Gutmann herself offers a supplement to her ostensibly domestic approach when she writes, "Democratic education . . . should not limit its vision to a single society. It should encourage students to consider the rights and responsibilities of both a shared citizenship and a shared humanity with all people, regardless of citizenship" (1999, p. 309).

Julian Culp specifically critiques typical conceptions of democratic education for not being sufficiently globally minded: "[D]emocratic conceptions of democratic education . . . all suffer from a domestic bias. They have as their sole subject matter a democratic society and do not ascribe any importance to considerations that concern cultural, economic, social and political phenomena beyond that society" (2019, p. 89). As an alternative, Culp suggests his theory of global democratic education. Extending from his conception of global democratic justice, Culp contends that democratic education has an obligation to teach for basic structures of justification at international levels. Therefore, for Culp, "democratic citizenship education should not only aim at cultivating and maintaining democratic consciousness domestically, but also transnationally among citizens from different states" (2019, p. 101).

13.3.4 Critical Theory and Global Consciousness

As might be expected, critical theory has also received attention and extension in reference to global issues. White, for instance, criticizes Adorno and Horkheimer's brand of critical theory for espousing critiques that "were so totalized that they have little basis on which to acknowledge differences between societies, both in the sense of types of institutions and in the sense of more or less injustice" (2017, p. 137). Globalization, argues White, is a helpful framing of critical theory for two reasons. First, because globalization is often a motivating factor for state and corporation decision-making. And second, because globalization has the capacity to foment paranoid perceptions of alleged tacit "foreign invasion and attitudes of resentful resistance" in certain individuals throughout the world (White, 2017, p. 4). Adorno, in fact, indicated the same in his searing rebuke of new right-wing extremism in Germany in the 1960s drawing attention to how the propaganda of German nationalists denigrated global democracy (2020, pp. 19–20).

There is no shortage of attempts to globalize critical theory (e.g., Deutscher & Lafont, 2017; Pensky, 2005; Ray, 1993; Rehbein, 2015). These treatments of critical theory arise in an era of political discourse increasingly intent on recognizing the effects of colonialism and interpreting it as a particular instantiation of capitalism and hegemony, therefore of the same ilk that harms people domestically. Critical theory as a method is not restricted by national borders and insofar as contemporary instances of oppression arise from global phenomena, critical theory is beholden to think globally.

13.3.5 The Educational Pitfalls of Expanding Scopes

As the preceding sections suggest, the heart of critical theory is its dedication to revealing the ways that systems of oppression – often capitalistic – marginalize, exploit, and oppress human beings. Such systems operate increasingly on global levels and therefore the harm they perpetuate crosses borders. The findings and methods of critical theory can be powerful educational resources. When put into operation alongside democratic education, students might feel invigorated to exercise the tools of democracy for the sake of their own agency and the betterment of their fellow citizens. It seems manifestly worthwhile for students to get to grips with the ways that economic and political power organizes in their country and leads to their own (often surreptitious) commodification. Furthermore, the capacities that a democracy creates for its citizenry and the demands it extends upon them can aid in efforts to quell injustice.

A critical democratic education like the one I've just sketched can feel exhilarating and even liberating for students. In a social studies or science class, students might learn about, for instance, the dozens of Indigenous frontline struggles against fossil fuel projects across North America, along with accompanying topics like tribal sovereignty, the ecological impacts of pipelines and mines, and various political economic mechanisms used by the oil industry to maintain profit. Learning about the immense power the oil industry wields might feel daunting to students, but likewise learning about successes won by Indigenous tribes from the Carrizo/Comecrudo Tribe of Texas to the Dene Nation in northern Alberta might spark hope in students that injustice is not insurmountable (Brown, 2021). If organizing led by Indigenous groups could lead (and has led) to hundreds of millions upon hundreds of millions of metric tons of annual CO_2 emissions being avoided, then there is still meaningful action to take in an apparently global, and seemingly asymmetric, battle (Goldtooth et al., 2021).

As a historic example of the liberating potential of critical democratic education, we can consider the work of Brazilian educator Paulo Freire, who was an acolyte of the Frankfurt School and the so-called father of critical pedagogy Freire's work on adult literacy education in Brazil and Chile involved engaging low-income adults in discussions of nationalism, development, illiteracy, and democracy alongside teaching those adults how to read and write. Not only were Freire's methods unbelievably successful, but they also led to profound existential growth for his students. Participants of Freire's rural teaching said things like, "Before we were blind, now the veil has fallen from our eyes" (Freire, 1970, p. 223), and "The democratization of culture has to do with what we are and with what we make as people. Not with what they think and want for us" (Brown, 1974 p. 251). To hear one's students say that their learning has lifted a veil and enabled them to resist hierarchical oppression (from literate landowners in the case of Freire's students) must constitute a deeply valuable educational success.

As students grow in their understanding of the problems uncovered and highlighted by critical theory, they naturally develop a host of emotional and intellectual responses. It is true that in the best cases, a critical democratic education can feel liberating, but it can also naturally and easily lead students to increase in empathy for others, experience indignation about injustice, and develop justified mistrust of certain sources of authority. Empathy, anger, and mistrust – rightly oriented – can precipitate students wanting to join the chorus of protestors, TV talking heads, and Twitter pundits in condemning the sources of injustice. Responses like those – protesting, conversing, posting, etc. – to injustice are well and good, and likely a meaningful source of change in today's political landscape (Peeren et al., 2017). At the same time, democratic citizenship involves much more than single-minded attention to large-scale issues or action defined merely in terms of position-endorsement and posting.

When the scope of critical attention and democratic action expands increasingly outward, theories and practices become increasingly abstracted. It is one thing to "think globally," if thinking globally means understanding, to some lesser or greater degree, global topics. But thinking globally in a way that supplants thinking – and seeing – locally is problematic (Cvetkovich & Kellner, 2018). One stated (or unstated) goal of critical theory is to "deparochialize" (Ouziel, 2022, p. 377). Deparochializing is an apt descriptor of much of the way social engagement goes on today: social media incentivizes national and global discourse (Suvojit, 2016), collective social movements across the world are couched in national or global terms (Peeren et al., 2017), and the news topics we hear about and talk about are overwhelmingly nonlocal (Martin & McCrain, 2019; Moskowitz, 2021). It is difficult to say whether drivers of deparochialization are also drivers of abysmally low turnout in local elections, including school board elections, which, despite being an instance of significant and direct political influence, are also left uncontested and unvoted (Cai, 2020). It is not my intent here to valorize local politics and abnegate national politics. Far from rejecting the importance of global issues, I am instead arguing that without genuine attention to local contexts, the value of critical theory and democratic education to global issues will be hamstrung.

To illustrate the necessity of local attention to critical democratic action, we can further examine Paulo Freire's example and return to Aimé Césaire's story. The root of Freire's pedagogy was neither in providing an education in abstract terminology (like, e.g., "mass culture" or "alienation") nor in providing an education in distant-yet-significant political issues. Rather, Freire's approach was rooted directly in the lives of his students. The materials Freire and his team created reflect, literally, a life of farming, hunting, trading, and crafting, which is to say the quotidian experiences of those engaged in the learning. In Freire's own words, his pedagogy concentrates on "familiar local situations – which, however, open perspectives for the analysis of regional and national problems" (1974, p. 51). As the farmers with whom Freire worked learned to read and write and engaged with their local realities dialogically, they also registered to vote and strengthened labor organization efforts (Mies, 1973). Consequently, the local focus of Freire's methods generated more than just local consciousness, but, importantly, vitalized the learners and their immediate communities.

Aimé Césaire's transformative education occurred most dramatically in France. As recounted in this chapter's Introduction, Césaire's elite education at the Sorbonne led him to experience no shortage of internal conflict. In one sense, Césaire had all the trappings of a critical democrat upon his return to Martinique. He easily saw how colonialism had ravaged the world, he despised the racism that persisted even in liberal quarters, and he understood most impressively the corpus of thinkers writing in critical and democratic theories from Hegel to Marx to Margaret Mead (Césaire, 2010). Even with his education and ideals, however, Césaire struggled mightily to effectively operationalize whatever democratic spirit he had. Wherever he looked in Martinique, he grimaced. The source of his grimace was ultimately colonialism, but the literal source in front of his eyes was sadly his own home and people.[8] Without learning to embrace his locality, he would struggle to put his knowledge to use. To put it bluntly, no amount of recognizing injustice or being committed to

[8] It should be noted that Césaire's education and biography are complex. His *Journal of a Homecoming* (2017) represents his story poetically and it is from the *Journal* that I draw my analysis, recognizing that Césaire's thoughts and narrative were likely less stark than the poem makes them out to be.

the decolonial cause was enough to enable Césaire to be the citizen Martinique needed. Rather, hearkening back to Mr. Revert's geography lessons that initially made him love the island as a teen (Clément, 2011), Césaire's true democratic legacy began when he relearned to see the goodness of Fort-de-France intermingling with and persisting alongside the grime of injustice. It was not merely through a global education that Césaire became a cherished mayor, it was just as much, if not more, due to his *local* reeducation. I now turn to explicating what it is about local attention that makes it so vital for critical and democratic education.

13.4 Realizing the Virtues of Democracy and Critical Theory

In this section, I make the case that critical democratic education should emphasize attention to local contexts if it wishes to succeed. As I've indicated, what exactly constitutes critical democratic education is not uniform across accounts of it. However, certain markers do seem to be necessary for each component of such an education: the democratic and critical.

For the sake of simplicity, let us box up these markers as essential critical democratic virtues (hereafter ECDV), comprising essential critical virtues (hereafter ECV) and essential democratic virtues (EDV).

Ben-Porath says of essential democratic civic virtues: "[I]n much of the literature that discusses, analyzes or measures civic virtue, its components include some combination of political knowledge, efficacy, trust, the capacity to communicate effectively and with an open mind (including tolerance and respect), and preparedness for collective action (or solidarity). Autonomy is sometimes discussed, as well as commitment to justice" (2013, p. 112). I contend that EDV entail these virtues in a general sense, which is to say EDV are a set of virtues that are more or less fostering of public discourse in a just, respectful, and informed manner.

There has not been a treatment of virtue in critical theory in the same way that accounts of civic virtues, epistemic virtues, and moral virtues have been developed. That said, it is clear that certain dispositions, behaviors, traits, and inclinations are endorsed by critical theory. Adorno identifies the "need to hold fast to moral norms, to self-criticism, to the question of right and wrong, and at the same time to a sense of the fallibility of the authority that has the confidence to undertake such self- criticism" (2000, p. 169). Similarly in his account of education and the public sphere, Honneth mentions the importance of virtues such as empathy, tolerance, autonomy, cooperation, and "an interest in the political emancipation of the lower orders of society" (2015, p. 18). Therefore, let us think of ECV as encompassing those virtues that generally cultivate "communicative practice that fosters moral initiative and the ability to take up the perspective of others" (Honneth, 2015, p. 28) – moral initiative both in the sense of criticizing authority and in the sense of pursuing justice.

The belief of this contribution is that ECDV, worthwhile though they are, cannot be realized while oriented only toward the national or global. Rather, to have a chance of successfully actualizing ECDV in students, special attention must be given to the local context in which students live and learn. I say this because moral perception of the sort that partially constitutes and motivates ECDV is honed and trained in immediate particulars, or what Iris Murdoch calls "concrete universals." While it is my position that the vast majority of research in critical theory and democratic education does not speak of the importance of local consciousness, I coincidentally find a helpful starting point in an aphorism from Adorno's *Minima Moralia*. Adorno writes:

> Liberality that accords men their rights indiscriminately, terminates in annihilation, as does the will of the majority that ill uses a minority, and so makes a mockery of democracy while acting in accordance with its principles. Indiscriminate kindness towards all carries the constant threat of indifference and remoteness to each, attitudes communicated in their turn to the whole. (2005, p. 77)

By "indiscriminate kindness," I do not take Adorno to be suggesting that we ought not love our enemies, extend kindness to any person regardless of our familiarity with them, or respect individual rights wholesale. Instead, I take him to be targeting a certain mode of embodying those principles. The mode of indiscriminate kindness that he condemns is a mode that treats an ethos of respect as sufficient for civic life. Kindness toward our fellow citizens, if it is to be meaningful, must extend beyond a simple ethos into kind behavior and just engagement with particular others. When a general spirit of virtue persists in generality without particularity, it runs the risk of counterproductively deteriorating into indifference or even, as Father Zosima from *The Brothers Karamazov* admits, an inability to endure time with any actual person (Dostoyevsky, 1998, p. 72).[9] Indifference stalls civic and moral initiative and reduces a person's contact with what is real. A worthwhile critical democratic actor extends kindness indiscriminately, but also exercises that kindness with specific people and in relation to specific issues. It is far easier to say one practices indiscriminate kindness toward all people everywhere than it is to actually practice indiscriminate kindness to the people with whom one comes into contact, whoever they may be. Yet, practicing kindness pointedly in our small spheres of influence is precisely the lifeblood of democracy.

Our tiny spheres of influence are important sites of critical democratic virtue because they are dialectically engaged with those spheres where our influence dwindles. For instance, national corporations crop up in our local lives meaning that their messaging, governance, values, and positions inundate our local spheres. Likewise, as consumers who purchase products from national corporations, we represent, at least in the conglomerate, a vital presence on their national stage. This relationship may seem obvious, but if it is, then it should also be obvious that our practice of critical democratic virtue must be local in character if it is to be national or international in character. To put some flesh

[9] I thank Douglas Yacek for bringing this example to my attention.

on the bones of the argument, I am saying that if one cares about, say, global carbon emissions, they must also care about the way they and their neighbors get to work. I am saying that if, for example, a teacher in the London Borough of Barking and Dagenham wants to help students develop critical engagement with economic forces that shape their lives, they must teach not only about new UK–EU trade relations, but also about the preponderance of food deserts in Barking and Dagenham.

In what follows, I offer three normative reasons for why cultivation of one's local consciousness is helpful to strengthen ECDV in people. I draw these reasons from Iris Murdoch's moral philosophy, which revolves around something she calls "loving attention." Before getting to the reasons, though, I will address three clarificatory questions.

13.4.1 Clarifying Local Consciousness and Loving Attention

First, what is meant by "loving attention"? By "loving attention," Murdoch means a sort of moral perception. Moral perception, explains John McDowell, is a "reliable sensitivity to a certain sort of requirement that situations impose on behaviour" (2002, p. 51).[10] A moral person "knows what it is like to be confronted with a requirement of" moral action, and such a sensitivity to situations "is, we might say, a sort of perceptual capacity" (McDowell, 2002, p. 51). Moral perception, then, is seeing things as morally imbued, and thus the moral life entails seeing things as they morally are. An agent can reason well in moral situations, hold herself to strict principles such as openness and impartiality, and deliberate well with others, but she must still perceive "moral situations *as* moral situations, and [perceive] their moral character accurately" if she wishes to be moral other than by mere accident (Blum, 1994, p. 30; emphasis added). Loving attention is Murdoch's distinct characterization of moral perception, which is to say sensitivity to moral reality.[11]

This explanation, however, does little more than locate loving attention in a family of terms; more is needed to understand what loving attention is as a particular form of moral perception. Starting with the back half, attention is

[10] Note, however, that Murdoch's definition of moral perception has to do with more than behavior since it includes things internal to a person (e.g., thought activity).

[11] My use of terms like "moral reality" and, later, "the Good" may be objected to by certain critical theorists who decry such analysis as antipluralistic or even antiquated. Perhaps, on the one hand, reality is not value laden and so it makes no sense to talk of deriving some sort of moral insight from it. On the other hand, even if there is such a thing as moral reality, perhaps any attempt to get at it will just lapse into ethnocentrism and therefore reify the very injustices that critical theorizing purportedly attempts to identify and dismantle. Of course, however, critical theory and civic action need some reference by which to judge their efficacy. Therefore, putting aside positions that are relativistic in a strong sense, the main qualm is whether my discussion of moral reality problematically reifies arbitrarily reigning moral positions. As I hope will become clear, talk of moral reality and "the Good" is not idle but it is also not dogmatic. Ultimately, what we are after as "critical theorists" is to arrive at "social criticism that is rationally authoritative without being ethnocentric" (Crary, 2018, p. 36). To do so, we are in dire need of looking "at our lives from new evaluative perspectives" (Crary, 2018, p. 36). I am making the case that we do so – that we really *look* at our lives and our neighbors, and do so with the supposition that what we see there might be normatively informative. This is because getting some sense of moral reality "provides the setting in which moral response in its broadest sense takes place" (Blum, 1991, p. 713). If we want to be "good" citizens," if we want to remedy injustice, we have to perceive that our worlds and social arrangements have some ethical valence.

"effort" to keep one's perception fixed upon the real things before us so as "to prevent [our perception] from returning surreptitiously to the self with consolations of self-pity, resentment, fantasy and despair" (Murdoch, 2014, p. 89). If mere perceiving (or looking, as Murdoch says) is the morally neutral word when it comes to moral perception, then attention is the morally good sort of perception (Murdoch, 2014, p. 36). Love is a peculiar word to pair with attention, but Murdoch intends it to counter *self*-love, which she sees as endemic to human psychology and vitiating of attention. Love sustains attention insofar as it can provide "attachment or even passion without sentiment or self" (Murdoch, 2014, p. 87). In other words, love as the "general name of the quality of attachment" is a way to describe what it means to give one's attention to moral reality with a desire to see it as it is (Murdoch, 2014, p. 100). Love can be degraded and cause error, but Murdoch thinks that when refined it functions as "the energy and passion of the soul in its search for Good" (2014, p. 100). In sum, attention is good moral perception and love is attention's enabling condition.

Second, why do I specify that moral perception relies on local consciousness? Cannot one morally perceive national and global realities or even general ideas, such as the notion of civic responsibility or the effects of mass culture? Put another way, if what I am advocating for is attention to particulars, why can't those particulars be national or global? The primary reason has to do with distance. Both Murdoch and McDowell, though their views differ, use metaphors of sight to explain moral perception. Moral perception is a matter of vision. Vision, of course, is affected by conditions that aid or obscure its efficacy. To see something, there must be something there to see. More, without the aid of some instrument, greater distances usually make accurate sight tougher. It is difficult to conceive of what it means to cultivate, let alone embody, ECDV in the context of concerns and concepts at such a great distance as those national or global. It is easier to see one's neighbor in particularity than in the abstract, just as it is easier to "see" an individual member of a class of people than to "see" the class as a whole. I will return to this point again after explaining the function of moral perception from Murdoch's perspective.

13.5 The Value of Attention to Local Particulars

The special facility local contexts have for instilling ECDV will become clearer in what follows as I turn to making the case for local consciousness vis-à-vis moral perception of a Murdochian flavor.[12] I argue that, following Murdoch, moral perception of particulars promotes three consequences: (i) humility, (ii) the acquisition of moral knowledge, and (iii) the deepening of moral concepts, all of which undergird the attainment and exercise of essential critical democratic virtues.

[12] Murdoch herself does not use the phrase "moral perception." That phrase, however, is commonly used by others including those who read, respond to, and interpret Murdoch and her writing. For the most part, when I use "moral perception" in the remainder of this chapter, I mean "loving attention," which itself I take to just be Murdoch's specific take on moral perception. At times I'll be speaking generally about moral perception, but those instances should be clear enough without me having to note them.

13.5.1 Local Attention and Humility

It is difficult to see moral reality. Yet, the critical democratic actor who practices ECDV must, at least in a weak sense, be able to see it. She must be able to see the moral significance of her fellow citizen, the moral significance of her choices as a citizen, and the moral layers of externalities like policies, organizations, and political parties. One reason it is difficult to accurately see moral reality is because internal conditions obscure our attempts to do so. Murdoch targets human psychology as the primary challenge to accurate moral perception. Her view of the psychological self identifies it as "relentlessly looking after itself" (2014, p. 76); to wit, "We are largely mechanical creatures, the slaves of relentlessly strong selfish forces the nature of which we scarcely comprehend" (2014, p. 97). McDowell, following Murdoch, asserts the same when he writes, "If we are aware of how, for instance, selfish fantasy distorts our [moral] vision, we shall not be inclined to be confident that we have got things right" (2002, p. 72).

Given our obscuring ego, "one of the main problems of moral philosophy might be formulated thus: are there any techniques for the purification and reorientation of an energy which is naturally selfish, in such a way that when moments of choice arrive we shall be sure of acting rightly?" (Murdoch, 2014, p. 53). How is it that attention to particulars can somehow surmount the challenge?

A few points are needed to explicate this position. First, Murdoch contends that the Good is probably indefinable and nonrepresentable; McDowell says it is uncodifiable. Drawing on Plato's allegory of the cave from *Republic* VII, if the Good is the sun, then "[w]e do not and probably cannot know, conceptualize, what it is like in the centre" (Murdoch, 2014, p. 97). That said, there's some hope that we can see things illuminated by the sun (as opposed to pathetic imitations of sunlight in the form of a cave fire) and perhaps even the edges of the sun.

Following, the second point is that Murdoch asserts that the Good, part and parcel with perfection, is transcendent in a certain way, which means that it is intimated in our lives even if it is ultimately nonrepresentable or codifiable. How is the Good transcendent in our lives? Murdoch suggests a few ways, but her most consistent example is beauty. Beauty, suggests Murdoch, can (i) refocus our attention from ourselves, (ii) demonstrate detail and unity, and (iii) provoke recognition of perfection. The experience of giving ourselves over to beauty, as it were, "affords us a pure delight in the independent existence of what is excellent. Both in its genesis and its enjoyment it is a thing totally opposed to selfish obsession" (2014, p. 83).

It might be helpful here to offer an illustration. Murdoch describes herself staring out her window but nonetheless "unseeing" the world because her mind is preoccupied with anxiety and resentment, perhaps as a result of her ego having been bruised. She is sitting there brooding, staring out but fixated inwardly when in an instant she catches sight of a hovering kestrel. The bird captures her sight, reflexively, and has succeeded in capturing her attention, too. "The brooding self with its hurt vanity has disappeared. There is nothing now but kestrel" (2014, p. 82). In this example of attention, Murdoch demonstrates the capacity of looking into the world as a means of piercing the veil our greedy ego sets up around reality. Rather than beauty being a moment of "exalted self-feeling," it is moral when it manifests as a "self-forgetful pleasure" (2014, p. 83). The mechanism by which beauty jerks our attention from ourselves is contemplation of something good outside of us and therefore nonabsorbable by our esurient self. When we love something in the attentive, moral way Murdoch describes, we sense the "the tension between the imperfect soul and the magnetic perfection which is conceived of as lying beyond it" (2014, p. 100).

Loving attention begets humility, but humility begets loving attention in such a way that the two are caught in a worthwhile feedback loop. The virtue of humility is facilitatory of critical democratic engagement because it energizes virtues like openness, deliberation, care, and recognition of the goods of others. A trove of empirical and theoretical research has suggested that part of what underlies political polarization is epistemic arrogance and part of what ameliorates polarization is intellectual humility (Bowes et al., 2020; 2022; Hodge et al., 2021; Iyengar et al., 2019; Lynch, 2019; 2021; Porter & Schuman, 2018). When an agent is plagued by epistemic arrogance, they may be resistant to deliberative discourse and dismissive of accounts and positions different than their own, both of which stymy democracy. Conversely, when an agent is intellectual humble, they may loosen their claims of epistemic authority, such that alternative conceptions of, for example, the good life can be taken as legitimate. Further, recognition that one is far from perfection or that one's view of the (especially moral) world had been clouded can spur one to consider the sources of imperfection and misperception. When we consider those sources, we may find ourselves critically engaging with the very forces that dehumanize us and others. The sort of humility that stems from good moral perception is therefore itself likely constitutive and facilitative of ECDV.

Is it not the case, however, that one might attain humility through engagement with things outside one's local settings? I do not preclude that possibility, but I do contend that the more visceral engagement is, the more capacious it is to be humility inducing. There is an obvious and profound difference between seeing a great work of art on one's computer screen and seeing it in the Metropolitan Museum of Art. Likewise, there is an even more profound difference between signing a virtual petition and looking into the eyes of another person while volunteering at a community organization. It is manifestly marvelous that art from around the world can be witnessed without traveling and that support for change can come from anywhere. However, the type of attention that is most likely to cultivate ECDV is a type of attention that thrives on local experience.

13.5.2 Local Attention and Moral Knowledge

The relationship between moral knowledge and moral living is different for Murdoch (and McDowell) than the Kantian notion of it as the substrate of reason that allows us to make at least some sense of the a priori moral concepts that govern us. While Kant suggests that "searching around" in "the space of transcendent concepts known as 'the intelligible world'" is to the great detriment of moral life (2009, p. 87), Murdoch suggests that moral living is necessarily contingent on our sense of the intelligible world as real and morally revealing. McDowell puts it this way: "If there is more than one concern that might impinge on the situation, there is more than one fact about the situation that the agent might, say, dwell on, in such a way as to summon an appropriate concern into operation. It is by virtue of his seeing this particular fact rather than that one as the salient fact about the situation that he is moved to act by this concern rather than that one" (2002, p. 68). The way knowledge is operative in moral life is through having knowledge of facts and being able to truthfully recognize their moral valence. Loving attention aids in knowing the moral reality of a situation.

It is not the case that knowledge is operative in moral life in the same way that scientific knowledge is operative in the scientific method. Instead, by practicing loving attention, we are attempting to gain "a refined and honest perception of what is really the case [and] a patient and just discernment and exploration of what confronts one" (Murdoch, 2014, p. 37). The difference between moral knowledge and certain other sorts of knowledge is that moral knowledge is "impossible to codify in universal terms because moral truths concern individual realities like human beings: beings whose concepts and realities are historical and so individual through and through" (Mylonaki, 2019, p. 593). So moral perception aids knowledge because (i) it involves removing barriers to accurately knowing and perceiving (e.g., our egocentrism), (ii) it provides reasons to act, and (iii) perceptual moral engagement occasions instances of seeing new moral features of the world.

The (i) point is made clear in light of the analysis made about how moral perception cultivates humility; one upshot here is that moral perception is moral because of the very kind of perceiving it entails. The (ii) point is made clear in the analysis of the last two paragraphs about moral action being related to a person being sensitive to the moral features of a situation. The (iii) point deserves some further explication, though it relates to both (i) and (ii).

From Murdoch's perspective, when we manage to engage in accurate moral perception, we stand to gain a clearsighted view of the world. In some instances, as I have discussed, we are able through our perception to think of features about the world as being morally salient and therefore epistemically relevant as a reason for acting a certain way. This is McDowell's point, that moral perception is about sensitivity to reasons for acting. Murdoch, however, has a more expansive understanding of the value of moral perception. Not only, for instance, does moral perception help us see things as morally salient, it also helps us notice things we never had noticed before and helps us to correct things we had previously noticed but had gotten wrong.

As an example of the latter, Murdoch provides a famous example of a mother, M, who comes to think of her daughter-in-law, D, in a positive light after having previously only being able to see her in a negative light (though treating her justly all along). Murdoch's example of M and D demonstrates that since M's activity here is not just external in her behavior but also "in her seeing knowing mind," our moral concepts "set up, for different purposes, a different world" from the "hard world set up by science and logic" (2014, p. 27). Through perceptually attending to D, M gains more accurate knowledge of D.

We might illustrate an example of situational aspects becoming morally salient using an example of a local store being forced out of business, a story common to both small towns and cities. In the example, a small, family-owned hardware store, let's call it Morales Hardware, rents its store space from a large property owner. The property owner is approached by a big-box home improvement chain, let's call it Acme, with an offer to rent the space at a great premium of the current rate. The property owner gives first refusal to Morales Hardware, but the Morales family is unable to afford the new rent and, as a result, they are forced to shutter their doors. A community member, Nathan, may see the situation as morally neutral or even morally positive. In Nathan's mind, the market dictates business survivorship and the arrival of Acme means lower prices, promotions, and rewards programs. Further, Nathan has positive views of Acme because they have shopped in Acme stores before and they like the current TV advertisement series they're running. Lastly, Acme has ensured that more jobs will be created by their opening than Morales Hardware was previously able to provide. All in all, one might be convinced that the forced closure is a good thing for the neighborhood.

That said, there might also be a host of reasons that the forced closure of Morales Hardware and opening of Acme would in fact vitiate the community. Among these reasons, one could be that the Morales family take great pride in their store and see it as a vital organ of the neighborhood, whereas Acme sees the store in purely instrumental terms. The offshoots of the Morales' perspective might include their stocking goods produced by other local businesses, their extending personalized support and financial assistance to community members who shop there, and their sponsoring community endeavors. Nathan weighing whether to support Morales Hardware might miss the details or the moral salience of the Morales' perspective. If he does miss those details, then his position will be substantially less informed than it otherwise could be; we could say that his position would be morally or epistemically thin. Yet perhaps through talking with one of the Moraleses or a store patron, or possibly through spending time in the store itself, Nathan becomes familiar with all the goods the local store offers above and beyond a chain like Acme. Where the question was at first simply a matter of market constraints, the situation takes on new moral depth as unrecognized or unseen features of the situation become morally salient. The experience is one in which features of the world are seen as meriting a moral response due to one's efforts of attempting to see those features firsthand. In the example, deliberation about live political questions is thickened through moral attention. Not only might Nathan organize efforts to save Morales Hardware, but he may also become more sensitized to the moral dimensions of capitalism in a general sense or on a broader scope. It is not a great leap of the imagination to think that Nathan might change his consumer habits, support certain regulatory measures, or vote for policies and candidates that would weaken corporate power. What I mean to demonstrate with the example is that local attention has the capacity to deepen moral knowledge in ways that can make one a better critical democratic actor as both a member of a neighborhood and as a citizen of a nation.

It might be argued from a social justice perspective that Nathan has an obligation to think in terms like "the least well off" or that Nathan's new position is tantamount to expression of a privileged "not in my backyard (NIMBY)" syndrome. If Acme can provide cheaper, fuller healthcare coverage to its employees than the Morales family can provide to their employees is that not reason enough to endorse Acme, given the national discourse around healthcare injustice? Or perhaps it might be said that Nathan should not devote resources (like his time) to getting a clearer picture of some tiny hardware store when there are larger, more significant issues facing the world. To consider these objections, let's bring the case back to the proposed framework. I contend that what we should really want for Nathan as a critical democratic actor is to authentically develop the virtues *of* a critical democratic actor. A citizen embodying virtues of criticality and democracy does not adopt shallow, self-interested NIMBY-based reasoning (because we should think that such reasoning is fundamentally at odds with ECDV). It is of course desirable that Nathan care for the worst off in society, including the worst off in his neighborhood. And if Nathan is sensitized to issues of injustice, then healthcare disparity should grieve him. However, the basis of my argument is that knowing what it means to care for the worst off begins precisely *in* one's backyard, so to speak. The reason Nathan ought to spend his cognitive resources and time to "see" a fuller picture of Morales Hardware is because in doing so, Nathan will be nurturing the ECDV within himself. Doing so will facilitate Nathan exhibiting the practical wisdom necessary to organize against healthcare disparities and exercise civic care for others. As Gibson writes, conflicts about community space must relinquish any sort of "false dream of a rational, expert-controlled technocracy and the possibility of an uncontestable claim to represent the 'civic good'" (2005, p. 399). The decision of whether to support the Moraleses or Acme is not one that can be reasoned a priori, nor is it a decision that is worthless in the grand scheme of political life. Much to the contrary, it is a decision that is best made using firsthand moral perception, and the conflict itself is a uniquely generative site of critical democratic growth.

13.5.3 Local Attention and Moral Concepts

This brings us to the third consequence of moral perception, which relates to our moral concepts. As mentioned in Section 13.5.2, what happens in Murdoch's example of M and D is M gaining greater conceptual clarity about D. Much of the insight Murdoch's moral philosophy provides is related to the way that moral perception deepens and enriches our moral concepts and, relatedly, the language we have at our disposal to conceive of and express moral perception. In loving attention, particularly when we attend to others, we gain familiarity with new concepts, deepen existing concepts, and gain new terms to express old and new concepts. Attention therefore improves our perpetual ability because with new concepts and terms we can now see and express things that we previously could not. This is, in part, possible because certain concepts (if not all, suggests Murdoch) are ideal and, as such, conceptually (though not practically) perfectible and therefore perpetually learnable.

To explain this argument, we can start with the idea that moral concepts are infinitely perfectible. Murdoch thinks that moral endeavors "are characteristically endless not only because 'within', as it were, a given concept our efforts are imperfect, but also because as we move and as we look our concepts themselves are changing" (2014, p. 27). When we try to see a person or situation accurately and with a sense of justice, we confront dynamic circumstances both within and without. Outside of us, we face complexity in the form of changing attitudes, behaviors, and parameters. Within us, we face complexity in the form of new ways of understanding the complexity outside of us and new ways of understanding the concepts and tasks set out before us. My conception of kindness grows over time and, as such, places new demands on me over time. We should think of concepts as undergoing a "deepening process, [or] at any rate an altering and complicating process" (Murdoch, 2014, p. 28).

Murdoch is committed to at least moral concepts like justice being ideals to be learned infinitely, but she teases that perhaps any universal concept could be treated the same way. For instance, she asks, "[w]hy not consider red as an ideal endpoint, as a concept infinitely to be learned, as an individual object of love? A painter might say, 'You don't know what "red" means'" (2014, p. 29). Of course, there is some literally unchangeable feature of things we call red, but really understanding red in all its permutations and applications is perhaps something that perpetually unfolds before us over our lives, if only we are sensitive to the concept of red as a painter might be. Here is another example. What does it mean to be loved? What does it mean to be thankful? In his poem *Catalog of Unabashed Gratitude,* Ross Gay (2015) gives us two examples of thanking another and being loved by another:

> thank you to the man all night long
> hosing a mist on his early-bloomed
> peach tree so that the hard frost
> not waste the crop, the ice
> in his beard and the ghosts
> lifting from him when the warming sun
> told him sleep now; thank you
> the ancestor who loved you
> before she knew you
> by smuggling seeds into her braid for the long
> journey

Do we typically think of thanking the peach farmer who cares for his crop with and against the movements of the natural world? Do the descendants of kidnapped West African women consider having been loved by those ancestors who surreptitiously protected rice grains on the treacherous transport across the Atlantic by hiding them in their hair so that their descendants might survive amidst the injustice of plantation colonies (Carney, 2004)? Perhaps some folks' conceptions of love and gratitude do encompass even these seemingly distant events, but perhaps for others such a notion would be new. If the notion was new, one's conception of love or gratitude may thicken for the long haul, thereby opening, as a matter of cause-and-effect, a host of doors previously unseen or seen but locked.

Gay's poem is an example of how one person's conception of gratitude and love is deep enough to encompass very distant actors, but what is clear from Gay's work and life is that his concepts of gratitude and love were enriched not through intellectual engagement with things distant, but instead embodied engagement with those close by. Because concepts are imbued with language and persist in conceptual schema, we can enrich our conceptual understanding in community with other people. Murdoch assents to the prevailing opinion that language is publicly contingent: public concepts "are in this obvious sense sovereign over private objects; I can only 'identify' the inner, even for my own benefit, via my knowledge of the outer" (2014, p. 14). The obvious public aspect of language means that we share language with one another and are thus able to develop understanding with and from one another. Murdoch writes: "Uses of words by persons grouped round a common object is a central and vital human activity. The art critic can help us if we are in the presence of the same object and if we know something about his scheme of concepts" (2014, p. 31). Together we group around something – "a human being or the root of a tree or the vibration of a colour or a sound" – and oftentimes our conception of that thing is enriched both by attention to it and guidance from another to notice what is there (Murdoch, 2014, p. 64).

Let me return now to Ross Gay in order to consider how his conceptual understandings have become, I would argue, so deep. Gay often writes about two sites of conceptual deepening: a community garden in Indiana and basketball courts in Philadelphia. Here is what Gay writes about the first place:

> Hear ye! hear ye! I am here
> to holler that I have [. . .]
> stood ankle deep in swales of maggots
> swirling the spent beer grains
> the brewery man was good enough to dump off
> holding his nose, for they smell very bad,
> but make the compost writhe giddy and lick its lips,
> twirling dung with my pitchfork
> again and again
> with hundreds and hundreds of other people,
> we dreamt an orchard this way,
> furrowing our brows,
> and hauling our wheelbarrows,
> and sweating through our shirts,
> [. . .]
> and friends this is the realest place I know,
> it makes me squirm like a worm I am so grateful,
> [. . .]

> there is a fence and a gate twisted by hand,
> there is a fig tree taller than you in Indiana,
> it will make you gasp.
> It might make you want to stay alive even, thank you;

What is clear from Gay's description of the garden is that his conception of gratitude is (i) organized around common objects like the fig tree and the spent barley, and (ii) done with other people. I think it would be impossible for Gay to squirm like a worm with gratitude if the gardening were done alone, and the reason the gate matters is *because* it was twisted by hand. Speaking of the community garden, Gay says that his "creative life is really informed by that community gesture, that gesture of 'how do we care for our neighbors?' Which I think is, in a way, the fundamental question of that orchard: how do we care for each other?" (Jewell & Gay, 2019). In the community garden, Gay says he became "abundantly aware that things are other things"; in other words, Gay's notion of the world grew just as M came to realize D was something other than what M had seen before. Gay recounts further that it was specifically working with people whom he didn't know for the benefit of people he may never meet that set his "ethical orientation" on a certain course (Jewell & Gay, 2019). Gay's civic life, including as a Black advocate of racial justice, seems to have been demonstrably enriched by his care and attention to people like the good brewery man.

Gardens are hard to come by for many, but the point I am making (which may be different from the point Gay would make) is not about the garden, but rather the attention. As proof, consider another site of attention about which Gay writes that seems to have also informed his conceptual schemata: the basketball court. The basketball court is ubiquitous in American cities, as the football pitch is in London. Gay says that it was at Seger Park in Center City Philadelphia that he began to understand "a court as a site of care, ball as a practice of care, a kind of constant practice at working it out" (2020). Consider the goings on at Seger, attention to which likely contributed to Gay's conceptual schemata:

> The quick eye contact – a kind of touch – between you and the guard whose name you do not yet know. The big man, whose name you do not yet know, seeing your eyes touch, sliding into a high backscreen to free you up for an oop. A baby who stumbled on the court whisked quickly off by a kid waiting for next. Dude's knee buckled and three people immediately put hands on him. Banging on doors and dragging the youngsters out of bed to the court. Bringing water to share. An old timer taking a kid to the side, teaching her how to use her hands in the post. . . . The whole very busy court paused as a father takes his son and another boy, both of them taller than him, who just got into a quick scuffle, outside the court to work it out.

There is of course no guarantee that these rather mundane interactions would spur development in ECDV, but for Gay the special attention he practices toward them seems to have. What is abundantly clear from Gay's essay on pickup basketball, though, is that no sense of a national or global issue could have adequately captured the conceptual depth present at a local hoop. I don't know that most folks who play pickup sports downtown would contend that, "A good court – maybe this is the definition of a good court – helps you witness the catalog, the encyclopedia, of tendernesses it is" (Gay, 2020). But Gay does, and so perhaps cultivating the sort of attention to our local particulars is a worthwhile endeavor.

I have said repeatedly that my urge to develop loving attention toward our particular contexts whatever they may be is not mutually exclusive with acting virtuously as a national or global citizen. Quite to the contrary, the most important upshot of my argument is that the virtue necessary for democratic citizenship on large scales is dependent on being developed in local situations. As our set of moral concepts grows and our existing moral concepts deepen, we become more adept at analyzing situations in which we might be called to act, including acting as citizens. We can return to the concepts from Gay's poem: gratitude and love. If one's concept of gratitude has been developed such that they are thankful for peach farmers in the Michoacán countryside despite buying their bushel from a supermarket in Mexico City, then perhaps they will be inclined to support policies that combat water shortages affecting farms in Michoacán. If one's concept of love has been nurtured so that they can conceive of loving generations hundreds of years down the line, then perhaps they will reconceive the moral significance of their decisions today thereby prompting support for, say, renewable energy subsidies. These examples illustrate my assertion in this section that having more thoroughgoing concepts at our disposal when confronting civic decisions has the capacity to make us better, or at least more considerate, civic actors at all levels.

13.5.4 Why Attention Must Be Local

I want to return now to the question of local attention. It seems clear, at least to Murdoch, that for moral perception to be effective in producing the three effects I have outlined, one needs to attend to particulars. I asked, though, why those particulars could not just be particulars with a national or global orientation as critical democratic education typically stresses. I suggested in a word that it is easier to see one's neighbor in particularity than in the abstract and to do so one must be with one's neighbor.

In returning to this point, I want to stress the idea of deepening concepts in community. When we are teaching for students to grasp and perhaps embody ECDV, we hope that they will make progress in understanding the concepts embedded in those schemata. "Progress in understanding of a scheme of concepts," writes Murdoch, "often takes place as we listen to normative-descriptive talk in the presence of a common object" (2014, p. 31). Morally perceiving common objects and situations is valuable for its "provision of rich and fertile conceptual schemes which help us to reflect upon and understand the nature of moral progress and moral failure and the reasons for the divergence of one moral temperament from another" (2014, p. 43). In all of Murdoch's analysis of moral development, the consciousness in play is a local one. With others, we talk about people and things in our presence and as a result illuminate, for one another, the possibilities for growth our conceptual schemata have.

As an example of this, consider the grave global state of the environment. Conservation and sustainability are undoubtedly national and global concerns and therefore require national and transnational effort. However, consciousness of what's ecologically at stake in our world can only really be attained through loving attention to one's local context, and loving attention itself will require local action. One does not come to understand how beholden one is to the natural world simply through eco-slogans, even if slogans act as a referent for deeper messages.

The conservationist poet Wendell Berry urged in 1970: "If you are worried about the damming of wilderness rivers, join the Sierra Club, write to the government, but turn off the lights you're not using, don't install an air conditioner, don't be a sucker for electrical gadgets, don't waste water. In other words, if you are fearful of the destruction of the environment, then learn to quit being an environmental parasite" (2019, pp. 21–22). Berry is calling for people to engage in moral perception of their own homes and their own lives rather than just perception at-a-distance of issues in the abstract or endeavors located outside the domains they regularly inhabit. Accurate perception of the natural world and what behaviors help or harm it is achieved in the first person (Elliott, 2007) – it is not just about "them" or "there," but it is also about "me" and "here." As Douglas Yacek points out, "preoccupation with the environment only on a global scale – that is, without a sense of care and concern rooted in the local – may even contribute to the very problem that is creating our climate predicament. If our concerns remain global and abstract, we will have difficulty developing the robust form of love and care for nature that an enduring commitment to preservation and restoration requires" (2022, p. 120).

Of course, just action is not the only upshot of local consciousness; local attention is often the only way we can understand moral situations. Consider the European refugee crisis. To understand the crisis, it is not enough to be told the numbers of migrants attempting to cross Europe's borders, or the countries from which they seek asylum, or the reasons that motivate their migration. To instill motivation to address the crisis, it is likely not enough to see photos of children drowned in the Mediterranean Sea while attempting to flee warzones with their families or to read about the conditions of detention centers where detained asylum-seekers may languish for years. If one has not known or talked to refugees, if one has not recovered bodies from capsized rafts, then the task of accurately apprehending the features of the crisis will be more difficult. From statistics and news reports, one can comprehend a general sense of the crisis, but general senses of moral situations, if I and Murdoch are right, do not a good citizen guarantee. One's best hope of seeing the moral reality of the refugee crisis is experiencing the crisis firsthand. Our second-best hopes include getting as close a firsthand experience as we can acquire and coming to see the situation through firsthand experiences of like situations. Given that our local contexts do not comprise every moral situation for which it might be important for us to perceive accurately, the second-best options might be all many of us have for certain issues. Consequently, our local contexts become all the more important since it is through attending to them that we gather concepts and experiences that facilitate accurately seeing distant contexts.

I have one further point to make regarding local consciousness. One might wonder whether moral perception is an agential experience. Does one *choose* to lovingly attend to others, or rather is it simply something that happens or does not happen? A way to make sense of the question is to consider what Murdoch has to say about facilitating good moral perception. She asks, "[H]ow do we alter and purify that attention and make it more realistic?" (2014, p. 67). By "altering," Murdoch means removing the hurdles that prevent us from accurate moral sight. Willing ourselves to understand and practice ECDV seems nearly a misnomer, so perhaps the will is not the best source of motivational energy in play. Murdoch thinks it is not and instead suggests we cultivate something like secular contemplation, which "is hard to understand and maintain in a world increasingly without sacraments and ritual" (2014, p. 67).

The religious and mystical language of sacrament, ritual, and contemplation seems out of place in a liberal democratic context, but the notion of a sacrament can be easily secularized. A sacrament can be thought of as something that "provides an external visible place for an internal invisible act of the spirit" (Murdoch, 2014, p. 67). Murdoch's concept of a secular sacrament is simply a practice that provides an opportunity to wrest one's focus from oneself and onto their setting and those others who occupy it. In his essay on the concept of sacraments, Andre Dubus explains that sacraments, as a way to attend to others, can exist in mundane routines. Dubus gives a host of examples of sacraments in his own life: making sandwiches for his young daughters, speaking on the phone with a loved one, his doctor bringing over spinach pies and chili dogs to comfort Dubus in a time of sorrow, pounding ice into shards to place onto the dry tongue of his dying father.

Making sandwiches is as plain as any task, but part of what makes it sacramental for Dubus is his particular context:

> Making sandwiches while sitting in a wheelchair . . . can be a spiritual trial; the chair always makes me remember my legs, and how I lived with them. . . . The memory of having legs that held me upright at this counter and the image of simply turning from the counter and stepping to the drawer are the demons I must keep at bay, or I will rage and grieve because of space, and time, and this wheeled thing that has replaced my legs. So I must try to know the spiritual essence of what I am doing. (1998, p. 89)

His analysis evokes both Murdoch's assertion about the allure of the self and her assertion that there are instances where one can overcome the inward gleam by contemplating the particulars of one's place (Greenwood, 2013;. The cognitive and psychosocial benefits of secular meditation have been well established by empirical research (Chang et al., 2022; Donald et al., 2019; Hölzel et al., 2011; Oyler et al., 2021). Among the associated outcomes with mindfulness-based interventions include reduction in outgroup bias and increase in prosocial behavior, which seem to have prima facie import for democratic citizenship

(Mathiowetz, 2016). Similar research exists for place attachment, the likes of which suggest that stronger cognitive–emotional bonds with one's settings and places are associated with numerous psychological benefits (Scannell & Gifford, 2017). The developmental data suggest that place attachment develops through similarly numerous processes, but the processes that show the greatest agential capacity are sensory, narrative, and ideological in nature (Cross, 2015). What the literature in these areas intimates is that intentional practices of an attentional sort have the capacity to nourish democratic citizenship. Consequently, the analysis that Murdoch postulates and the testimony that Dubus provides seem to be bolstered by empirical research.

In answer to the question about how agential moral perception is, it seems that while there are occasions in which we are struck by moral sight (consider Murdoch's kestrel example), there are also instances where we work at it, such as in the case of M actively pursuing a clear-sighted conception of D or Dubus making after-school sandwiches for his girls. McDowell sums up this point well: there is "colossal difficulty [in] attaining a capacity to cope clear-sightedly with the ethical reality that *is* part of our world" but an attempt to do so "may actually work towards moral improvement; negatively, by inducing humility, and positively, by an inspiring effect akin to that of a religious conversion" (2002, p. 73; emphasis in original). There's no guarantee that we will gain any clear-sighted perspective of moral reality, but without trying our chances seem diminished. Bringing, yet again, the foregoing analysis back to critical democratic education, the point is that one does not purely will themself to be a good critical democratic citizen. Instead, they will themself to attend to their localities in hopes that when the time comes to exercise their citizenship, they will do so virtuously, as a result of having been sensitized to the moral features of the world.

13.6 Responses and Applications

In concluding this chapter, I want to take time to address two potential concerns with my position and suss out potential educational implications. Two concerns one might raise to pairing moral perception with critical democratic education are (i) moral perception may not provide enough objectivity to be useful, and (ii) local attention may undermine critical theorizing. These concerns are reasonable, but not insurmountable.

13.6.1 The Argument from Objectivity

Murdoch's account of moral perception involves a great deal of subjectivity. Indeed, the very talk of perception implies a departure from traditional notions of objectivity that suggest our subjective endowments distort access to what is real by presenting us with what only seems (perceptually) to be the case. From that perspective, the only way we can ostensibly be confident that we have got an accurate view of what is real is to abstract from our subjective seemings.

One response suggested by Alice Crary is to question the assumption that we ought to hold such a narrow conception of objectivity. In Crary's view, which I find compelling and believe Murdoch would as well, we lack an understanding of what it would mean to accurately abstract from our subjective endowments and therefore we lack an understanding of what it would mean to satisfy a narrow view of objectivity, particularly in light of a social perspective of reasoning and language. If we can move beyond the narrow view and instead equip a conception of objectivity that allows for subjective qualities to have objective force, then we can judiciously engage with perceptual seemings. In certain cases, qualities we perceive may be "mere appearance," but in other cases, those qualities may be true in an objective sense (Crary, 2010, p. 30).[13] The modest extension I offer here is that insofar as Murdoch's project is founded on making our perception clearer, it is at least germane to investigating what appearances might be objective.

13.6.2 The Argument from Critical Theory

The sort of moral theory I am espousing here might be criticized for being too individualistic or not activistic enough. In the first case, moral perception could be accused of being parochial in its dependence on one's individual standpoint, and therefore might prevent critical engagement with oneself or with social structures. In the second case, it could be argued that the sort of moral perception I've outlined is too focused on perception and introspection at the expense of action. Both concerns are legitimate.[14] Critical education must provide some way to recognize injustice in myriad forms, acknowledge one's complicity in injustice, and participate in remedying injustice to the extent one should. If moral perception is subjective and the moral reality it perceives is uncodifiable then what standard does it provide to critique what one sees? I offer three brief responses here. First, the purpose of moral perception is not seeing oneself in the world. Quite differently, as Murdoch would have it, it is about recognizing the magnetism of the Good and perfection, which gives way to recognizing the limits of one's perception. Self-criticism and skepticism are baked into the endeavor. Second, Murdoch makes clear that moral perception is deepened through engagement with others. Others can broaden our moral vocabulary and nourish our moral concepts, thereby aiding our perception in becoming more accurate. The phenomenon of attention that Murdoch draws is one in which someone is attentive to the moral reality of the other and receptive to the moral insights of the other. Third, overt action is indispensably important to inner experience. Murdoch writes, "Will cannot run very far ahead of knowledge, and attention is our daily bread" (2014, p. 42). Willing oneself to do what

[13] See also Crary (2019) and Crary (2021). In the former, Crary outlines her case for a wider conception of objectivity, while in the latter, she explains how nonneutrality does not preclude access to objectivity.

[14] And both have been addressed by others before. For a defense of Murdoch's moral philosophy being capacious of feminist aims, see Bolton (2022) and Hämäläinen (2015). For a defense of Murdoch's moral philosophy being capacious of criticality generally, see Clarke (2011).

is right has a direct relationship with knowing what is right, and it is through moral perception that we gain knowledge of moral reality. Concerns about this sort of moral perception failing to provide room for essential critical virtues seem unwarranted.

13.6.3 Considering Applications

For teachers, school leaders, and theorists in support of either democratic education or critical education, I argue that whatever virtues – using the term loosely – are constitutive of that educational project require also cultivating moral perception of one's local setting. Moral perception as a way of accessing moral reality is rooted in particulars often best manifest in locality: the places where and the people with whom one lives. A quick rejoinder to my proposal might be that what our democracies really need today is moral perception of people unlike oneself in order to cut across partisan lines and diminish polarization. That is what our democracies need, not just for the sake of democratic deliberation but also for the sake of recognizing injustices and striving to alleviate them. Complicating such an aim is the fact that many democracies are rife with geographic segregation of social groups.[15] Absent schools and communities being integrated – which is to say making local contexts more diverse – is there any hope for critical democracy? While there's no guarantee that attention to local particulars will make someone a better democratic actor or more critical citizen, I think there are two reasons to be hopeful. First, while there is no particular so morally imbued as another creature, nonsentient particulars can foster perception of moral reality as well. Murdoch, at least, is confident that art and nature can facilitate moral knowledge. An especially apt extension here might be documentary films, which can intertwine beauty with focused depictions of reality. In watching documentaries, other localities are still mediated and therefore more dilute, but the particulars of those places – those people and their lives – are still more perceptible in that instantiation than in perhaps any other mediated one. Second, the very heart of attention to particulars is the acquisition of moral knowledge and the reduction of hurdles therewith. By virtue of the nature of knowledge and the value of attitudes like humility, attention to particulars is worthwhile even in light of nonlocal relationality. The argument of this chapter is not that attention to local particulars should supplant a national or

[15] Blum and Burkholder (2021) offer a gripping historical account of efforts to racially integrate American schools, as well as an argument on why racial integration must be an essential aspect of schools in multiracial democracies. Their account, however, is ideal and does not grapple with the nonideal conditions American schools face.

global aspect to critical democratic education, but rather that moral perception of one's local community can energize those very aspects. Helping students pay moral attention to the particulars of their lives does not mean they will become good citizens, but perhaps, echoing Murdoch, it might make them the most likely people of all to become good citizens.[16]

References

Aboagye, E., & Dlamini, S. N. (Eds.). (2021). *Global citizenship education: Challenges and successes*. Toronto: University of Toronto Press.

Adorno, T. (2000). *Problems of moral philosophy*. Ed. by T. Schröder, Trans. by R. Livingstone, Cambridge: Polity Press.

Adorno, T. (2005). *Minima moralia: Reflections on a damaged life*. Trans. by E. F. N. Jephcott, London: Verso.

Adorno, T. (2020). *Aspects of new right-wing extremism*. Trans. by W. Hoban, Cambridge: Polity Press.

Adorno, T., & Horkheimer, M. (2002). *Dialectic of enlightenment: Philosophical fragments*. Ed. by G. S. Noerr, Trans by E. Jephcott, Redwood City, CA: Stanford University Press.

Allen, D. (2016). *Education and equality*. Chicago, IL: The University of Chicago Press.

Apple, M. W. (1999). *Official knowledge: Democratic education in a conservative age*. London: Routledge.

Ben-Porath, S. (2006). *Citizenship under fire: Democratic education in times of conflict*. Princeton, NJ: Princeton University Press.

Ben-Porath, S. (2013). Deferring virtue: The new management of students and the civic role of schools. *Theory and Research in Education*, 11(2), 111–28. doi: https://doi.org/10.1177/1477878513485172

Berry, W. (2019). *Think little*. Berkeley, CA: Counterpoint Press.

Biesta, G. J. J. (2011). *Learning democracy in school and society: Education, lifelong learning, and the politics of citizenship*. Rotterdam: Sense Publishers.

Blum, L. (1991). Moral perception and particularity. *Ethics*, 101(4), 701–25.

Blum, L. (1994). *Moral perception and particularity*. Cambridge: Cambridge University Press.

Blum, L., & Burkholder, Z. (2021). *Integrations: The struggle for racial equality and civic renewal in public education*. Chicago, IL: The University of Chicago Press.

Bolton, L. (2022). Murdoch and feminism. In S. C. Panizza & M. Hopwood, eds., *The Murdochian mind*. London: Routledge, pp. 438–50.

Bowes, S. M., Blanchard, M. C., Costello, T. H., Abramowitz, A. I., & Lilienfeld, S. O. (2020). Intellectual humility and between party animus: Implications for affective polarization in two community samples. *Journal of Research in Personality*, 88, 103992.

[16] I want to thank the editors for their immensely insightful comments on a draft of this chapter, and to express my gratitude to Mark Jonas and Megan Laverty for their generosity as interlocutors and mentors as I grappled with the ideas present in this chapter.

Bowes, S. M., Costello, T. H., Lee, C., McElroy-Heltzel, S., Davis, D. E., & Lilienfeld, S. O. (2022). Stepping outside the echo chamber: Is intellectual humility associated with less political myside bias? *Personality and Social Psychology Bulletin*, 48(1), 150–64. doi: https://doi.org/10.1177/0146167221997619.

Bridoux, J., & Kurki, M. (2014). *Democracy promotion: A critical introduction*. London: Routledge.

Brown, C. (1974). Literacy in thirty hours: Paulo Freire's process. *The Urban Review*, 7(3), 245–56.

Brown, L. M. (2021). The efficacy paradox: Teaching about structural inequality while keeping students' hope alive. In M. E. Kite, K. A. Case, & W. R. Williams, eds., *Navigating difficult moments in teaching diversity and social justice*. Washington, DC: American Psychological Association, pp. 105–18.

Cai, J. (2020). The public's voice: Uncontested candidates and low voter turnout are concerns in board elections. *National School Boards Association*. Retrieved from: https://www.nsba.org/ASBJ/2020/April/the-publics-voice.

Callan, E. (1997). *Creating citizens: Political education and liberal democracy*. Oxford: Oxford University Press.

Carney, J. A. (2004). "With grains in her hair": Rice in colonial Brazil. *Slavery & Abolition*, 25(1), 1–27. doi: https://doi.org/10.1080/0144039042000220900.

Celikates, R. (2018). Critical theory and the unfinished project of mediating theory and practice. In P. E. Gordon, E. Hammer & A. Honneth, eds., *The Routledge companion to the Frankfurt school*. London: Routledge, pp. 206–20.

Césaire, A. (2000). *Discourse on colonialism*. New York: New York University Press.

Césaire, A. (2010). Culture and colonization. *Social Text*, 28(2), 127–44.

Césaire, A. (2017). *Journal of a homecoming / Cahier d'un retour au pays natal*. Trans. by N. G. Davis, Durham, NC: Duke University Press.

Chang, D. F., Donald, J., Whitney, J., Miao, I. Y., & Sahdra, B. K. (2022). *Does mindfulness improve intergroup bias, internalized bias, and anti-bias outcomes? A meta-analysis of the evidence and agenda for future research*. doi: https://doi.org/10.31219/osf.io/5wev3.

Christ, J., Leopold, K., Loick, D., & Stahl, T. (Eds.). (2020). *Debating critical theory: Engagements with Axel Honneth*. Lanham, MD: Rowman & Littlefield.

Clarke, B. (2011). Iris Murdoch and the prospects for critical moral perception. In J. Broackes, ed., *Iris Murdoch, philosopher*. Oxford: Oxford University Press, pp. 227–54.

Clément, V. (2011). Latitude and longitude of the past: Place, negritude and French Caribbean identity in Aimé Césaire's poetry. *Caribbean Studies*, 39(1–2), 171–93.

Crary, A. (2010). Minding what already matters: A critique of moral individualism. *Philosophical Topics*, 38(1), 17–49.

Crary, A. (2018). Wittgenstein goes to Frankfurt (and finds something useful to say). *Nordic Wittgenstein Review*, 7(1), 7–41.

Crary, A. (2019). Objectivity. In J. Conant & S. Sunday, eds., *Wittgenstein on philosophy, objectivity, and meaning*. Cambridge: Cambridge University Press, pp. 47–61.

Crary, A. (2021). Dehumanization and the question of animals. In M. Kronfeldner, ed., *The Routledge handbook of dehumanization*. London: Routledge, pp. 159–72 doi: https://doi.org/10.4324/9780429492464-chapter10.

Crick, B. (2002). *Democracy: A very short introduction*. Oxford: Oxford University Press.

Critchley, S., & Honneth, A. (1998). Philosophy in Germany. *Radical Philosophy*, 89, 27–39.

Cross, J. E. (2015). Processes of place attachment: An interactional framework. *Symbolic Interaction*, 38(4), 493–520.

Culp, J. (2019). *Democratic education in a globalized world: A normative theory*. London: Routledge. doi: https://doi.org/10.4324/9780367136550.

Cvetkovich, A., & Kellner, D. (2018). Introduction: Thinking global and local. In A. Cvetkovich & D. Kellner, eds., *Articulating the global and the local*. London: Routledge, pp. 1–30.

De Lissovoy, N. (2011). Pedagogy in common: Democratic education in the global era. *Educational Philosophy and Theory*, 43(10), 1119–34.

Deutscher, P., & Lafont, C. (Eds.) (2017). *Critical theory in critical times: Transforming the global political and economic order*. New York: Columbia University Press.

Donald, J. N., Sahdra, B. K., Van Zanden, B., Duineveld, J. J., Atkins, P. W., Marshall, S. L., & Ciarrochi, J. (2019). Does your mindfulness benefit others? A systematic review and meta-analysis of the link between mindfulness and prosocial behaviour. *British Journal of Psychology*, 110(1), 101–25.

Dostoyevsky, F. (1998). *The Karamazov brothers*. Trans. by I. Avsey, Oxford: Oxford University Press.

Dubus, A. (1998). *Meditations from a movable chair*. New York: Vintage Books.

Elliott, D. (2007). *Ethics in the first person: A guide to teaching and learning practical ethics*. Lanham, MD: Rowman & Littlefield.

Freire, P. (1970). The adult literacy process as cultural action for freedom. *Harvard Educational Review*, 40(2), 205–25.

Freire, P. (1974). *Education for critical consciousness*. New York: The Seabury Press.

Gay, R. (2015). *Catalog of unabashed gratitude*. Pittsburgh, PA: University of Pittsburgh Press.

Gay, R. (2020). Have I even told you yet about the courts I've loved? On the unlikely tenderness and care of a good pick-up basketball game. *Literary Hub*. Retrieved from: https://lithub.com/ross-gay-have-i-even-told-you-yet-about-the-courts-ive-loved.

Gibson, T. A. (2005). NIMBY and the civic good. *City & Community*, 4(4), 381–401.

Giroux, H. A. (1980). Critical theory and rationality in citizenship education. *Curriculum Inquiry*, 10(4), 329–66.

Goldtooth, D., Saldamando, A., & Gracey, K. (2021). *Indigenous resistance against carbon*. Indigenous Environmental Network, Oil Change International. Retreived from: https://www.ienearth.org/indigenous-resistance-against-carbon.

Greenwood, D. A. (2013). A critical theory of place-conscious education. In R. B. Stevenson, M. Brody, J. Dillon, & A. E. J. Wals, eds., *International handbook of research on environmental education*. London: Routledge, pp. 93–100.

Gutmann, A. (1999). *Democratic education*. Princeton, NJ: Princeton University Press.

Habermas, J. (1994). Three normative models of democracy. *Constellations*, 1(1), 1–10.

Hämäläinen, N. (2015). Reduce ourselves to zero?: Sabina Lovibond, Iris Murdoch, and feminism. *Hypatia*, 30(4), 743–59. doi: https://doi.org/10.1111/hypa.12172.

Hammond, M. (2019). Deliberative democracy as a critical theory. *Critical Review of International Social and Political Philosophy*, 22(7), 787–808.

Haslanger, S. (2020). Taking a stand: Second-order pathologies or first-order critique. In J. Christ, K. Lepold, D. Loick, & T. Stahl, eds., *Debating critical theory: Engagements with Axel Honneth*. Lanham, MD: Rowman & Littlefield, pp. 35–50.

Hodge, A. S., Hook, J. N., Van Tongeren, D. R., Davis, D. E., & McElroy-Heltzel, S. E. (2021). Political humility: Engaging others with different political perspectives. *The Journal of Positive Psychology*, 16(4), 526–35. doi: 10.1080/17439760.2020.1752784.

Hölzel, B. K., Lazar, S. W., Gard, T., Schuman-Olivier, Z., Vago, D. R., & Ott, U. (2011). How does mindfulness meditation work? Proposing mechanisms of action from a conceptual and neural perspective. *Perspectives on Psychological Science*, 6(6), 537–59. doi: https://doi.org/10.1177/1745691611419671.

Honneth, A. (2004). A social pathology of reason: On the intellectual legacy of critical theory. In F. Rush, ed., *The Cambridge companion to critical theory*. Cambridge, UK: Cambridge University Press, pp. 336–60. doi: https://doi.org/10.1017/CCOL0521816602.014.

Honneth, A. (2015). Education and the democratic public sphere: A neglected chapter of political philosophy. In J. Jakobsen & O. Lysaker, eds., *Recognition and freedom*. Rotterdam: Brill, pp. 17–32.

Iyengar, S., Lelkes, Y., Levendusky, M., Malhotra, N., & Westwood, S. J. (2019). The origins and consequences of affective polarization in the United States. *Annual Review of Political Science*, 22, 129–46.

Jewell, J., & Gay, R. (2019). Unabashed gratitude & structures of care, with poet gardener Ross Gay. *Cultivating Place, North State Public Radio*. Retrieved from: https://www.cultivatingplace.com/post/2019/11/28/unabashed-gratitude-structures-of-care-with-poet-gardener-ross-gay.

Kant, I. (2009). *Groundwork of the metaphysics of morals*. Cambridge: Cambridge University Press.

Levinson, M. (2012). *No citizen left behind*. Cambridge, MA: Harvard University Press.

Levinson, M. (2014). Citizenship and civic education. In D. Phillips, ed., *Encyclopedia of educational theory and philosophy Vol. 1*. New York: Sage, pp. 135–38.

Lynch, M. P. (2019). *Know-it-all society: Truth and arrogance in political culture*. New York: Liveright.

Lynch, M. P. (2021). Political disagreement, arrogance, and the pursuit of truth. In E. Edenburg & M. Hannon, eds., *Political epistemology*. Oxford: Oxford University Press, pp. 244–58.

Martin, G., & McCrain, J. (2019). Local news and national politics. *American Political Science Review*, 113(2), 372–84. doi: 10.1017/S0003055418000965.

Mathiowetz, D. (2016). "Meditation is good for nothing:" Leisure as a democratic practice. *New Political Science*, 38(2), 241–55.

McDowell, J. (2002). *Mind, value, and reality*. Cambridge, MA: Harvard University Press.

Mies, M. (1973). Paulo Freire's method of education: Conscientisation in Latin America. *Economic and Political Weekly*, 8(39), 1764–67.

Misiaszek, G. W. (2019). Ecopedagogy as an element of citizenship education: The dialectic of global/local spheres of citizenship and critical environmental pedagogies. *International Review of Education*, 62(5), 587–608.

Morton, J. (2019). *Moving up without losing your way: The ethical costs of upward mobility*. Princeton, NJ: Princeton University Press.

Moskowitz, D. (2021). Local news, information, and the nationalization of U.S. elections. *American Political Science Review*, 115(1), 114–29. doi: 10.1017/S0003055420000829.

Murdoch, I. (2014). *The sovereignty of good*. London: Routledge.

Mylonaki, E. (2019). The individual in pursuit of the individual; A Murdochian account of moral perception. *The Journal of Value Inquiry*, 53(4), 579–603. doi: https://doi.org/10.1007/s10790-018-9675-4.

Nussbaum, M. (1997). *Cultivating humanity: A classical defense of reform in liberal education*. Cambridge, MA: Harvard University Press.

Nussbaum, M. C. (2006). Education and democratic citizenship: Capabilities and quality education. *Journal of Human Development*, 7(3), 385–95. doi: https://doi.org/10.1080/14649880600815974.

Ouziel, P. (2022). Democracies joining hands in the here and now. In J. Tully, K. Cherry, F. Forman, J. Morefield, J. Nichols, P. Ouziel, et al., eds., *Democratic multiplicity: Perceiving, enacting, and integrating democratic diversity*. Cambridge, UK: Cambridge University Press, pp. 374–88. doi: 10.1017/9781009178372.022.

Oyler, D. L., Price-Blackshear, M. A., Pratscher, S. D., & Bettencourt, B. A. (2021). Mindfulness and intergroup bias: A systematic review. *Group Processes & Intergroup Relations*, 1368430220978694.

Peeren, E., Celikates, R., De Kloet, J., & Poell, T. (Eds.). (2017). *Global cultures of contestation: Mobility, sustainability, aesthetics & connectivity*. Cham: Palgrave Macmillan.

Pensky, M. (Ed.). (2005). *Globalizing critical theory*. Lanham, MD: Rowman & Littlefield.

Porter, T., & Schumann, K. (2018). Intellectual humility and openness to the opposing view. *Self and Identity*, 17, 139–62.

Ray, L. J. (1993). *Rethinking critical theory: Emancipation in the age of global social movements*. New York: Sage.

Rehbein, B. (2015). *Critical theory after the rise of the global South: Kaleidoscopic dialectic*. London: Routledge.

Rostboll, C. F. (2008). *Deliberative freedom*. Albany, NY: SUNY Press.

Rowell, C. H. (2008). It is through poetry that one copes with solitude: An interview with Aimé Césaire. *Callaloo*, 31(4), 989–97.

Sant, E. (2019). Democratic education: A theoretical review (2006–2017). *Review of Educational Research*, 89(5), 655–96.

Scannell, L., & Gifford, R. (2017). The experienced psychological benefits of place attachment. *Journal of Environmental Psychology*, 51, 256–69.

Scheffler, I. (1997). Moral education and the democratic ideal. *Inquiry*, 16(3), 27–34.

Scheuerman, W. (1999). Between radicalism and resignation: Democratic theory in Habermas' "between facts and norms." In P. Dews, ed., *Habermas: A critical reader*. Oxford: Oxford University Press, pp. 155–77.

Shabani, O. P. (2003). *Democracy, power, and legitimacy: The critical theory of Jürgen Habermas*. Toronto: University of Toronto Press.

Suvojit, B. (2016). Transcendence through social media. *Journal of Media and Communication Studies*, 8(3), 25–30.

Waghid, Y., Waghid, F., & Waghid, Z. (2016). *Educational technology and pedagogic encounters: Democratic education in potentiality*. Leiden: Brill.

White, S. K. (2017). *A democratic bearing: Admirable citizens, uneven injustice, and critical theory*. Cambrige: Cambridge University Press. doi: https://doi.org/10.1017/9781316717394.

Yacek, D. W. (2022). Anxiety, guilt and activism in teaching about climate change. In J. Drerup, F. Felder, V. Magyar-Haas, & G. Schweiger, eds., *Creating green citizens*. Berlin/Heidelberg: J. B. Metzler, pp. 115–34.

Young, I. M. (2001). Activist challenges to deliberative democracy. *Political Theory*, 29(5), 670–90.

14

Democratic Deliberation in the Absence of Integration

Michael S. Merry

14.1 Introduction

Democratic deliberation minimally describes the capacity to engage with others on matters of social and political import in a respectful manner, exhibiting a give-and-take that recognizes both the significance and seriousness of other points of view, and where the aim is to achieve greater mutual understanding. Democratic education is the seedbed for the cultivation of this noble ideal. Though it has many aims, at its core lies the commitment to deliberation between differently positioned, thinking, and contributing individuals of equal moral and political standing. Yet for deliberative interactions in educational settings to fruitfully occur, certain favorable conditions must also obtain.

In this chapter, I chiefly concern myself with one of these putative conditions, namely that of *school integration,* strongly implied by liberal models of democratic deliberation and debatably necessary for consensus-building and legitimate decision-making. It is in integrated educational settings, the argument runs, that liberal democratic societies are best able to ensure equal status, recognition, and opportunity among participants, but also where substantive interactions across difference can occur. In and through these interactions we might reasonably hope to challenge prejudices and stereotypes that so often cause misunderstanding, distrust, and intolerance. Seen in this way, school integration ought to work in tandem with democratic education insofar as it entails bringing together young people from different backgrounds, experiences, and perspectives in order to learn with, and from, one another. And in learning with and from one another, the expectation is also that students might collectively foster a number of civic virtues.

Inconveniently, however, around the globe high segregation and stratification indices within and between countries, regions, provinces, cities, and even neighborhoods present a number of challenges to this attractive ideal. Nowhere is this more evident than in the educational domain. Indeed, if we take school integration – minimally understood to imply spatial mixing – to be the most favorable facilitative educational condition for democratic deliberation, then this condition is often, if not typically, absent. What, then, do these realities portend for democratic deliberation, or for the cultivation of civic virtue? What indeed do such realities portend for democracy itself?

The structure of this chapter is as follows. In Section 14.2, I describe, in broad strokes, what I understand the aims of democratic deliberation to be. I then delineate a number of civic virtues educators hope to cultivate through deliberation, but I restrict much of my attention to the baseline virtue of toleration. Whatever else deliberation is supposed to do, it is reasonable to expect that it minimally ought to assist in fostering *this* virtue. Accordingly, I adopt a substantive definition that entails an ability and willingness to listen and learn from differences, and further to use this information to reflect upon one's own present beliefs and understandings. Following this, I recapitulate the argument that integration is the ideal educational condition necessary for the kinds of substantive interactions democratic deliberation ought to facilitate. In Section 14.3, I provide an assessment by considering a number of difficulties with this idealistic account. I will demonstrate that liberal versions of democratic deliberation predicated on integration as a facilitative educational condition are puzzlingly inattentive both to the inevitability of segregation, as well as the inequities occasioned by integration, thus rendering their account untenable. In Section 14.4, I probe the possibilities for democratic education in the absence of integration. I argue that neither the possibilities for deliberation nor the cultivation of civic virtue turn on an environment being "integrated." Indeed, some kinds of segregation may be more conducive to fostering both deliberation and civic virtue.

14.2 Democratic Deliberation

The notion of deliberative democracy is meant to capture a robust exchange of ideas involving multiple perspectives from which everyone involved can learn, and through which legitimate decision-making can occur. It welcomes debate on matters of substantive disagreement. Where principled differences frustrate consensus, a deliberative approach stresses the importance of finding a common ground necessary for consensus-building. Indeed, it is the common ground of shared belief and practice in the public sphere that establishes both the rule of law and the legitimate exercise thereof. Integration that can facilitate deliberation therefore seems imperative precisely because many beliefs and practices are so disparate.

Notwithstanding the importance of local attachments, citizenship articulated as "shared fate" (Williams, 2003) requires that persons engage one another from time to time in order to address and find acceptable solutions to the challenges facing fellow citizens. It further entails a capacity for enlarged thought, the ability to see oneself bound up in relations of interdependence with others, and the capacity to reshape the practices and institutions of one's environment. In short, citizenship-as-deliberation requires the capacity for communicating with others, under conditions of social equality, and forging paths of social cooperation.

These deliberative habits require educational development. Democratic deliberative theorists (Gutmann & Thompson, 2004; Macedo, 2000; Satz, 2007) insist that it is in the state school where young people are most likely to acquire the relevant knowledge, skills, dispositions, and virtues necessary for this important work. Paula McAvoy and Diana Hess even go so far as to say that "schools are the institution that can transform the political climate" (2013, p. 43). Echoing that sentiment, Amy Gutmann and Sigal Ben-Porath (2015) opine that "recommitting primary and secondary education to the value of democratic citizenship could reduce [the] democratic deficit." They write:

> Citizenship education at its best addresses those differences by educational practices that cultivate tolerance and open-mindedness, address controversial issues in a mutually respectful way, and develop an understanding of different cultures that is compatible with toleration and mutual respect. These educational practices not only support the core values of a liberal democracy, they also enable students to practice them in a way that will position them as civic equals in their democratic society . . . schools that cultivate the capacity of citizens to respect each other and engage with each other beyond differences and to view each other as civic equals may be a democratic citizenry's best hope for the future of democracy. (p. 5)

Here we discern a number of necessary conditions for deliberation to do its work. One condition is its public character. By "public" we are meant to understand both the space in which deliberations occur, and to which all participants have access; but "public" is also taken to mean the kinds of allowable reasons in these interactions. In other words, participants ought not to have recourse to arguments or evidence deemed unreasonable or inaccessible to other participants. Another condition is the importance of epistemic diversity in these deliberations, where differences among participants in terms of sex and gender, ethnicity/race, culture/religion, social class, and political commitment are taken as salient proxies for different points of view worthy of discussion. In other words, the integration ideal is strongly implied, for a more homogenous school or classroom would presumably yield fewer divergent perspectives, without which deliberation cannot meaningfully occur. These different backgrounds, identities, and experiences are understood to inform different ways of knowing and understanding. Moreover, it is through deliberative exchanges with different others that young people are to be socialized into the kinds of dispositions and habits they later will need as adult citizens operating in a pluralistic society.

14.2.1 Deliberative Virtues

The educative route to deliberation requires that certain virtues be cultivated. Among the virtues, we hope to see patience, honesty, a sense of fairness, and the moral courage needed to be challenged by ideas we find unpleasant or unfamiliar. We also hope to find a willingness to listen, intellectual humility, self-reflection, and a capacity for discernment, truth, and understanding of complex social and political matters, many of them controversial. Finally, we hope to develop the communication skills and etiquette required for conducting a respectful discussion in which core beliefs may be challenged, principled disagreement can be expected, and thus also during which emotional reactions are likely to be charged.

Whether or not this grocery list of educational aims is remotely feasible in most classrooms is a question I will bracket for the time being. For now, I merely focus on one of the items the authors mention more than once: *toleration.* I do so for two reasons: first, toleration will strike many readers as the bare minimum that we ought to expect from deliberation; I therefore will treat it as a baseline civic virtue. Second, given both the currency that toleration continues to have in civic discourse, as well as the conviction many espouse that our world is increasingly becoming *less* tolerant, toleration may nevertheless signal an achievement of sorts if its substantive cultivation augurs greater possibilities for peace, cooperation, and more democratic decision-making.

Substantive toleration necessitates meaningful interaction with others espousing opposing views. Meaningful interaction denotes an openness to others, where the aim is to listen and learn from differences, but also to prioritize truth, which entails that we (i) acknowledge that the relevant evidence will likely support some views more than others; and (ii) that a moral vocabulary in any case will be needed in order to adjudicate between competing normative claims. In other words, not every view (e.g., "women are inferior to men") is worthy of serious consideration. Notice, too, that toleration implies respect, at least insofar as genuine listening and learning also signals a willingness to change one's mind.

And so, in an educational setting, tolerance will minimally require that young people come into meaningful contact with others of different background and persuasion on terms of equal status and recognition. But meaningful interaction, like a meaningful relationship, signals neither a shared point-of-view nor mutual understanding. It may entail difficulty, misinterpretation, unease and even distress, even if it sometimes also yields positive emotions and outcomes. These presumably difficult substantive encounters with others will assist in cultivating the capacity not only for toleration, but also critical reflection upon one's own beliefs and assumptions, an openness to challenge, and the intellectual humility required to change one's mind on the strength of the best reasons and evidence. We might also hope that these encounters will produce the cultivation of attitudes and dispositions necessary for constructing, maintaining, and participating in democratic decision-making.

14.2.2 Integration as Facilitative Condition

If a healthy liberal democracy describes a system of mutual social cooperation, then segregation would seem to pose a threat to the extent that citizens fail to identify with, let alone empathize with, different others, thus rendering cooperation impossible. Moreover, given that demographic concentrations often inversely correspond to opportunity structures, officeholders (who typically hail from the more privileged strata) often know too little about their less advantaged constituents. This lack of knowledge impedes both the cultivation of competence and the understanding needed to write policy that is more responsive to their needs and concerns. Accordingly, if elected officials of democratic political institutions are supposed to be both responsive and accountable to their citizens, then the fact that some citizens are able to leverage their concentrated resources and political influence in ways that wittingly or unwittingly disadvantage those with minority views results in both widespread distrust and an absence of legitimacy.

Now, if it is true that segregation causally inhibits both equal participation and opportunity, then integration does indeed seem to be the most sensible tonic. Particularly in integrated schools many hope to find opportunities for intermingling that will grant the disadvantaged access to the cultural and social capital of the better off, while simultaneously providing the privileged exposure to the less fortunate that will yield greater empathy and understanding. Such an integrated environment, first in the school and later in the workplace, will presumably lead to persons relaxing around each other, having fewer stereotypical views of others different from themselves, and sharing information and networking strategies that make power-sharing possible. In short, school integration not only will assist in removing barriers to social mobility; it also will provide the foundation for a common project of "living together democratically" so that citizens move away from tribalism and identity politics and instead embrace mutual identification.

Though incomplete, this short sketch describing integration-for-democratic deliberation will suffice. In Section 14.3, I move to assess these claims by addressing several unarticulated assumptions before turning my attention to some empirical difficulties with both integration and deliberation.

14.3 Assessment

Many of the ideas in democratic theory mentioned in Section 14.2 are so widely shared among political scientists and philosophers that a number of unspoken assumptions escape closer scrutiny. Perhaps the most important of these is that *the state is uniquely responsible* for preparing children for democratic citizenship, and relatedly, that state-funded and managed schools are *ideally suited* to this important work. A corollary assumption is that the precepts of democracy – for which constitutional principles are a proxy – are themselves self-evidently true, and hence can be coercively inculcated without objection onto a captive audience of young people. And because these beliefs are too often taken for granted, democratic theorists concern themselves much too little with questions concerning the legitimacy of this coercive endeavor (Merry, 2020).

But liberal democratic theorists also rarely concern themselves with a bevy of practical difficulties. Here are but two. The first concerns what it is reasonable to expect from teachers charged with facilitating these deliberations. It is not unreasonable to conjecture that in most countries both direct instruction and rote learning remain the standard pedagogy. Moreover, even when there is the will to do things otherwise – for example to foster dialogue in the classroom – relatively few teachers possess adequate time, patience, or knowledge and skills to facilitate discussions of the kind deliberation theorists have in mind, particularly those involving contentious subject matter, and perhaps most especially in divided societies (Johnson & Johnson, 1988; Nystrand et al., 1997; Pace, 2019; Quaynor, 2012; Zembylas & Kambani, 2012). And even when teachers *do* make the time or broach controversial topics for discussion, it is not a foregone conclusion that things will go according to plan. For example, contrary to the expectation that minoritized others in the classroom are eager to deliberate with their majority peers on contentious subject matter, many will prefer to remain silent – if they are not first actively silenced – and disengage from the conversation altogether, rather than risk the frustration and fatigue of trying to educate the others in the classroom who routinely ignore or express skepticism about ideas and experiences with which they are unfamiliar (Berenstain, 2016; Fine, 2018).

Yet even if some students are fortunate enough to have highly skilled teachers capable of facilitating classroom deliberations, the next difficulty is even more daunting. This concerns likely tension with parents and the local community. A vivid, but by no means unique, illustration is the decision taken by hundreds of school districts throughout the United States during the 2020–2021 academic year to introduce critical race theory (CRT) into primary and secondary school curricula. School board meetings, once mind-numbingly dull affairs attended by almost no one, quickly became public spectacles, with livid parents demanding that school officials retract their decision. Nor is the irony lost on parents, who are repeatedly told to be "involved in their child's education," until of course that involvement impugns the professional authority of the school staff (Bæck, 2010). Importantly, too: the pushback from parents – whether concerning racial injustice or any other sensitive issue – is just as likely to come from minority parents over concerns about the ignorance or insensitivity of the teacher or other students in the classroom (Hailey, 2022; Merry & Schinkel, 2021). Indeed, many minority parents justifiably object to their children being portrayed as pitiable victims.

None of these difficulties is trivial, but in this chapter, I will set these aside in order to assess how well the argument for democratic deliberation manages on its own terms, in particular with respect to the conviction that integration is a key facilitative condition for deliberation, out of which we can expect certain civic virtues to emerge.

14.3.1 Integration Revisited

The belief that integration is a facilitative condition for democratic deliberation must confront numerous difficulties. First, it is dubious to suggest that segregation per se threatens democracy. Arguably, any or all of the following impediments pose a far more serious threat: (i) xenophobic nationalism endemic to most societies, including liberal democracies; (ii) massive wealth disparities; (iii) rigidly tracked education systems; (iv) a dearth of proportional voting; (v) quid pro quo campaign contributions and corporate lobbying; (vi) the plethora of political candidates beholden to party interests; (vii) judicial appointments by political fiat; (viii) a deplorable corporate media in many countries that fails to inform the public about matters of substance; and, last but certainly not least, (ix) the algorithmic design of social media platforms that rapidly disseminates misinformation and exacerbates the polarization of voter sentiments.

Second, there is plenty of evidence that segregation obtains even in the absence of pernicious efforts to impose it. The habit of clustering with others sharing the same history, culture and language, dialect and religion, or myriad other habits and customs governing daily life, is as old as human civilization. Liberal democratic values also aid in facilitating segregation to the extent that citizens are free to associate with those whose company they prefer; indeed, in free societies voluntary association is both a moral and constitutional right. Further, constitutional guarantees in many countries give parents ultimate decision-making power concerning the education their child receives, even if the wealthy inevitably have more – and often better – options available to them. In any case, the idea that liberal democratic governments ought to dictate to citizens where they should live, or which school one's child is required to attend, is anathema precisely because this would necessitate a draconian curtailment of inviolable constitutional liberties.

To merely delineate these facts is not to endorse the status quo; nor is it to suggest that the playing field is level; nor, finally, does it mean that one ought to take a casual attitude vis-à-vis historical injustice, some of which undoubtedly has produced invidious forms of segregation. In other words, one can agree that all forms of involuntary segregation are wrong, and even endorse the notion that integration under favorable conditions and with the relevant kind of resources in play is ideally better suited to facilitating deliberative interactions. Be that as it may, in the absence of social and political arrangements capable of providing these resources and facilitating these conditions, mere *spatial* integration does not typically bring about more deliberation, let alone voluntary social interaction, greater toleration, and equitable treatment. And the difficulties with the integrationist defense do not merely concern improbable efforts to socially engineer neighborhood, school, and even classroom composition. Indeed, the greater difficulties concern reconciling such a rosy view with more than half a century of empirical scholarship on school segregation.

To be sure, some of that evidence suggests that school integration *has* provided some disadvantaged students access to certain objective goods, for example, a safer learning environment; greater teacher retention and staffing stability; a more demanding curriculum; access to higher tracks; and a bevy of extracurricular activities. Much of the time, however, the benefits of integration are hypothesized rather than demonstrated. Fundamentally, the problem is that successful integration depends on more than physical access to spaces with certain kinds of material resources. It also will depend very much on the design of the school system, not to mention how one is perceived and treated once in the building. Countless studies – ironically including many studies produced by integration advocates – document time and again that young people from stigmatized minority backgrounds face innumerable institutional and psychological hurdles in "integrated" settings (e.g., Conger, 2005; Diamond, 2006; Lewis et al., 2015; Santiago-Rosario et al., 2021; Tyson, 2011). These integration failures are so common that they also routinely appear in fiction. "What is the school for?" asks a character in J. M. Coetzee's *Age of Iron*. "It is to make us fit into the apartheid system" (1990, p. 67). "John was a trailblazer," Sherman Alexie notes with cruel irony, "a nice trophy for St. Francis, a successfully integrated Indian boy" (1996, p. 19). And in Richard Wright's *The Outsider*, we find this poignant description:

> She had attended a racially mixed school in her adolescence and the snubs and ostracism had branded her with a deep sense of not belonging and a yearning to have her status as an outsider cleared of shame. (1953, p. 66).

Examples like these can be effortlessly multiplied. And because these phenomena are so ubiquitous, abundant, and consistent across many societies where similar empirical research has been done, it will suffice to illustrate these observations by alluding to one recent example of qualitative empirical work.

Sociologist Simone Ispa-Landa notes many ways in which an integrated school works well, including for many minorities. But things go less well for those often believed to be the primary beneficiaries of school integration. Basing her conclusions on wide-ranging observations and interviews in a spatially integrated high school, she found the following:

> All the suburban students I interviewed liked the *idea* of offering urban minorities spots in "their" schools ... However, they felt that suburban schools should try to recruit (in their words) "better," more "hardworking," or "more intelligent" black students ... Thus nested within the discourse about the black students' supposed under-achievement was another discourse, one that questioned the black students' presence and/or "deservingness" to a suburban education. (2013), pp. 224–25[1]

Ispa-Landa's research elsewhere (Ispa-Landa & Conwell, 2015) concerning transfers of stigmatized minority students into white majority neighborhoods and schools further captures the racially charged schooling experiences that many can expect to have. Among her findings we see the usual litany of involuntary features, familiar to readers of sociology of education research. These include: (i) a faith in the credibility of high stakes standardized tests to measure or predict intellectual aptitude; (ii) teacher mismatch and bias, in particular as it concerns low expectations concerning the intellectual ability of stigmatized minority students; (iii) these expectations correlate strongly with disproportionate referrals for special education, discipline, and suspension; (iv) these patterns also simultaneously reinforce a belief in meritocracy *and* social ostracism, othering,

[1] While her research concerns black urban students in a predominantly white suburban high school in the United States, similar findings involving different stigmatized minority groups are also well documented in other countries.

and containment, but also more generally regarding what teachers believe is a suitable academic level for stigmatized minority students. Paradoxically, too, these patterns operate in tandem with good intentions.

The last item merits further comment. In countless situations Ispa-Landa observed that many school staff were "eager to help" and went out of their way to lavish condescending praise ("good job!") on black students. Curiously, however, similar academic success was rarely advertised or openly celebrated as it concerned white majority students, let alone other, minority students (e.g., of Asian or Jewish background), from whom academic success was simply expected.[2]

Significantly, however, even in the absence of overt discriminatory treatment, the following are consistently observed: low expectations; disparities with respect to standardized test scores; patterns of clustering, centered around shared background, experience and interest. Indeed a great deal of empirical evidence suggests that also in highly mixed school settings the influence of peer groups tends to foster segregation (McPherson et al., 2001; Moody, 2001), only sometimes in order to navigate hostile spaces as visible minorities (Anderson, 2021; Hussain, 2021). In other words, *neither historical nor structural explanations of segregation suffice to explain its common occurrence*. That cohorts of diverse background and opinion exist – whether in school or anywhere else – is not the issue; instead, the question is whether it is common.

The reader will recall that "shared fate" theorists would have us communicate with others, under conditions of social equality, and together forge paths of mutual cooperation. Yet the shared fate variant operates on the presumption that students will attend the same schools or the same classes, pursue the same extracurricular activities, or enjoy a social life together outside of school, an arrangement far removed from the segregated reality in most countries. And even when classrooms *are* mixed in all the ways that matter, other problems inescapably arise.

14.3.2 Deliberation Revisited

The various difficulties discussed in Section 14.3.1 matter not only in terms of educational opportunity or academic achievement. They also clearly gesture at a number of problems where democratic deliberation in the school is concerned. The story goes that deliberation will position participants as civic equals, thereby assisting to repair deep misunderstandings and mistrust, and further aid in bringing young people together to engender harmony and understanding. Remember, too, that the integration ideal is assumed to be a facilitative educational condition, where the aim is not only to mitigate stereotyping and

[2] When gender is factored into the equation, elsewhere Ispa-Landa (2013) also found that certain features of black (male) identity and behavior were fetishized owing to positive stereotypes related to athletics and hip hop culture; black boys in white majority schools, *even when tracked low*, were often viewed as "popular" and even high status in terms of social standing. The same did not hold true, however, for black girls, whose attitudes or behaviors (described as "loud" or "difficult") were often constructed as problematic, even deviant.

prejudice but also one of working to leverage salient differences for joint decision-making and a more legitimate pursuit of the public good. Yet as appealing as all of this sounds, several difficulties come into view.

One almost certainly concerns the rules of engagement. Liberal proponents of democratic deliberation typically insist on publicly available reasons and reliable methods of inquiry as prerequisites. The difficulty is that many varieties of human experience are categorically *not shared*, creating hermeneutical gaps, the likes of which impose additional burdens on those whose experiences are difficult to convey using publicly available reasons. Moreover, if deliberation requires a reserved, nonconfrontational communication style, where the reliable methods of inquiry stipulate that emotional responses (such as anger) are discouraged, then the game of deliberation is already rigged in favor of those with mild temperaments, or else who have been socialized into a middle-class etiquette of "acceptable" school behaviors – something that deliberative theorist John Dryzek (2000, p. 63) has described as "oppressive self-control" – in addition to ideas and beliefs that more closely correspond to conventional norms. Thus, intended or not, the net result is the exclusion of perspectives from consideration that do not meet these criteria. Stanley Fish describes what is almost certain to happen to those deemed to have "incorrect" views in such deliberations:

> [If] he has reasons they are unaccompanied by evidence; if he has evidence it is the wrong kind; if he has the right kind, it is not as good as the evidence we have. You know that [proponents of democratic deliberation] could go on forever in this vein because all they are doing is negotiating a very small circle that begins and ends with their own prior conviction and a vocabulary made in its image. The key word in that vocabulary is "reasonable", but all that is meant by the word is what my friends and I take to be so. (1999, p. 91)

Many liberal philosophers and political theorists narrowly interpret "unreasonable" views to refer to religious fundamentalists who appeal to conscience or the authority of a sacred text. No doubt this worry applies to some individuals. But plenty of other nonshared personal experiences and perspectives viewed as unreasonable from the standpoint of the (idealized) deliberation are unlikely to be permitted as well. Most of these do not lean on supernatural claims but rather a multitude of unpleasant experiences – condescension, harassment, discrimination, microaggression, etc. – that typically (i) are not experienced by many of one's (more popular or advantaged) peers, and (ii) whose effects are aggravated by the institutional norms of the school itself. The not infrequent result is to have one's experience denied or dismissed as hyperbole by those unable to comprehend what many individuals contend with as a matter of routine.

The difficulties of facilitating these conversations are made even more improbable in light of the fact that the official school narratives informing these discussions typically omit minority perspectives that could inform the matter at hand. The upshot, as philosopher Ian Shapiro (1999, p. 32) discerningly observes, is that deliberation is just as likely to "unearth new irreconcilable differences, with the effect that the relationship [among participants with different experiences and beliefs] worsens and perhaps even falls apart in acrimony." Such an outcome is even *likely* to happen if and when teachers themselves lack the relevant knowledge and skill, but also virtues (inter alia, patience, empathy, moral discernment) necessary to facilitate heated discussions.

14.3.3 Toleration

But surely, one anticipates a critic saying, even with these difficulties in mind, we can at least expect more, rather than less, toleration? Perhaps. But much will depend on whether or not participants share the same understanding of what toleration means or requires. It almost certainly is the case that many persons understand toleration to mean something more closely approximating resigned acceptance of difference for the sake of peace, or a kind of reluctant moral stoicism concerning the fact that others have rights to believe and behave in ways one finds disagreeable (Walzer, 1997). Indeed, it is a routine feature of staged debate – both in media and in schools – to have opposing sides to a controversial issue, where the ostensible aim of such exercises (if not simply to entertain) is that listeners tolerate all views expressed during the allotted time. Even civic educators who exhort teachers to "teach the controversy" also insist that they should refrain from partisan proselytizing and instead facilitate the airing of different points of view.

It is also questionable whether promoting toleration is a commendable educational aim. Indeed, surely there are many things (e.g., bullying, dishonesty, racism, cruelty) that we should *not* tolerate, whether in school or anywhere else. Left to itself, "tolerating differences" – sometimes couched in terms of "multiperspectivity"' or "learning to disagree" – lends itself to a moral relativism that consists in little more than an exchange of opinions. And this is precisely how "toleration" in the classroom works much of the time, where opinions concerning matters of substance are effectively treated as matters of taste, not unlike a preference for arthouse cinema or football. *This* kind of toleration stops well short of substantive civic virtue, effectively rendering it as nothing more than a hollow performance.

14.4 Segregation and Democratic Deliberation

To recap an important point: segregation that either is imposed or that correlates strongly with structural disadvantage is prima facie morally problematic. But three caveats follow. First, whether or not segregation per se is problematic will depend on the background conditions – opportunity structures, choice sets and social networks – attending the segregation. Even when historical injustice correlates strongly with some instances of segregation, it is far from obvious whether compulsory "integration" is a remedy. Provided the right enabling conditions are in place, integration may facilitate certain benefits. Yet when integration either implies enforced assimilation, or merely reduces to spatial mixing within unaltered institutional structures, we are just as likely to see patterns of inequality unabatedly continue.

Second, while the structural factors of segregation cannot be overlooked, there are also voluntary cultural and individual processes at work. Even members of stigmatized minority groups do not cluster simply as a defensive reflex against racism or social exclusion. Persons also gravitate to areas where they are able to be in close proximity to similar others, where communication and cultural norms are understood, and where they may profit from living with others who share similar lifestyles, social networks, and cultural needs. In other words, spatial concentrations can supply resources of solidarity often unavailable in more mixed settings, particularly when that mix is tilted in favor of the dominant group. Third, and more pragmatically articulated: so long as entrenched patterns of segregation – in particular among society's most privileged members – seem unlikely to change, then it is not contrary to reason for minority groups to turn existing segregation to advantage. Not unlike how stigmatized identities can be reappropriated, segregated spaces, too, can also be redefined, reclaimed, and redirected to better serve the interests of their members (Merry, 2013, 2021).

In sum, while much harm undoubtedly coincides with some forms of segregation, these facts alone do not remove voluntary reasons for preferring to live, work, or recreate with others like oneself, however one wishes to define "like oneself." And notice that "like oneself" for those who live with stigma also provides additional reasons to prefer the company of similar others if this ensures greater protection from exclusionary harm. Put another way, some spatial concentrations may indeed be sites of deprivation and stigma; but many spatial concentrations also serve as sites of *reprieve* from deprivation and stigma; indeed, they may supply opportunities to relax, to be nourished by the company of similar and congenial others, and even to convalesce from the unremitting stress of "integration." bell hooks (1995, p. 109) has further argued that segregation can help "to maintain oppositional worldviews and standpoints to counter the effects of racism and to nurture resistance."

On this reading, many (though not all) segregated spaces, including neighborhoods and schools, do not merely describe spatial concentrations of a particular group; rather, they may serve as spaces in which persons are able to rejuvenate identities, celebrate the importance of marginalized lives, and even experience greater freedom of expression without fear or concern about misunderstanding, rejection, or being silenced. However, it is not my contention that segregation only serves to buffer stigmatized persons from harm, or accommodate a desire to be with similar others. Indeed, some kinds of segregation may actually aid in fostering important civic virtues.

14.4.1 Segregation and Civic Virtue

When fair channels of deliberation under integrated conditions are either hostile, or, more likely, simply not available, we should not be surprised if some communities reject deliberation that is exclusively defined, delineated, and imposed by others. As Dryzek has it, "Reasoned agreement as an operating principle may be easiest to achieve in locality-specific disputes and problems with a relatively small number of identifiable participants who can meet in face-to-face interaction" (2000, p. 50). Indeed, when spatial concentrations can assist in mobilizing around shared interests and aims, then we begin to approximate what Nancy Fraser (1997, 2021) has called "counter-publics."

Counter-publics often provide a more efficacious means of securing parity of participation in deliberation, as well as in facilitating the bonds of solidarity against structural barriers of discrimination (Brown & Davis, 2001; Stull et al., 2015; Wane, 2009), than policies adopted through formal channels, and for which integrated settings are believed to be an imperative condition. To be sure, gay/feminist/disability/tribal minority rights campaigns may, at times, opt to work in alliance with members of majority groups. Indeed there inevitably will be times when *all* minorities must build bridges if fundamental change to mainstream institutional structures and attitudes is ever to materialize (Merry et al., 2016). But those causes do not mean that there is no value in maintaining nonintegrated spaces and institutions for the benefit of those who prefer the company of similar others.

The same logic of turning segregation to advantage extends to the cultivation of civic virtue. Counter-publics allow for group solidarity that reinforces a position of strength from which to engage with the wider public. As the need arises, members of a counter-public can formulate their own interpretations of their interests and needs and advance these for public hearing, where neither public nor civic virtue depends on integration. Certain political obligations – basic rights and responsibilities – may compel our attention, and our identities may incorporate political characteristics. But civic virtue does not reduce to political behaviors, such as political organizing or voting. Nor should it be conflated with republican notions of citizenship that accentuate national over communal attachments and their attendant expressions of common good.

Counter-publics can even more effectively galvanize our efforts in responding to others in need. Indeed, attachments to specific communities often supply persons with the substance of belonging that makes more expansive notions of cooperation both possible and meaningful (Bernal, 2006; Gandin, 2006; Martinez, 2006). As such, some kinds of segregation can have a direct and positive impact both on community solidarity and on local politics; associational membership often is an antecedent, if not the impetus, to other forms of civic virtue. Cities and neighborhoods with spatial concentrations also have better facilitated political inroads for aspiring politicians, who in turn can be more responsive to the concerns of the local citizenry. The denser the associational network is, the more civic virtue and political trust one often can expect. This trend cuts across demographic lines and exists in neighborhoods across many societies (Merry, 2013; Baldassarri & Diani, 2007; Jacobs et al., 2004).

Further, many spatial concentrations open up opportunities for entrepreneurship and other forms of service provision, such as clothing and cultural accessories, skin and hair products, markets and grocery stores, books and newspapers, community centers, and job networks. These lead to an institutionalization of networks and services that not only increases the attractiveness of the neighborhood in question (whatever its drawbacks and liabilities) but also contributes to the maintenance of a subculture many find attractive and hence are keen to cultivate and sustain. The upshot is that while it is certainly true that some types of segregation are irredeemably harmful, this is often not the case. As the foregoing paragraphs illustrate, segregation may coincide with many tangible benefits.

14.4.2 Segregated Schooling?

Now, even if proponents of democratic deliberation reluctantly acknowledge these things to be true, they still are likely to resist the suggestion that the same should be said about education. And indeed, empirical researchers have marshaled powerful evidence showing that many segregated majority-minority schools often lack the monetary resources necessary to provide more challenging academic tracks, smaller class sizes, and greater staff retention. Or they may point to the concerning parallel between certain minority concentrations and poverty. Integrationists are right to be worried about these injustices when and where they occur. But two points must be underscored.

First, we have already seen that the empirical evidence often points away from the integrationist thesis as it concerns equitable treatment of those who ostensibly stand to benefit from it. Most integrationist "success stories" concern relatively small numbers of individuals whose physical presence poses little threat to the usual state of affairs, and may even provide false reassurance to school staff and parents that their school is more inclusive than it actually is. Second, it is doubtful whether most majority-minority schools always have fewer monetary resources at their disposal. Weighted pupil funding to compensate for poverty and disadvantage is the norm in many countries. However, monetary resources alone are rarely sufficient to close achievement gaps. This is because nonmonetary resources arguably matter more.

Indeed, an abundance of empirical research (e.g., Carter & Merry, 2021; Frost, 2007; Hattie, 2002; Veenman, 1996) suggests that class composition matters far less – both as it concerns educational achievement and expectations to graduate from a four-year university course – than the following resources, any one of which is difficult to finance and scale up: (i) rigor of the curriculum; (ii) quality of instruction; (iii) high teacher expectations; (iv) strong school leadership; (v) shared academic goals; (vi) a cohesive, value-centered learning environment; (vii) empathic care; (viii) positive role-modeling and mentoring, and (ix) a sense of shared community among peers. Ideally, we want to see schools have *both* kinds of resources; unfortunately, however, policymakers typically find it easier to increase investment without addressing the ways in which the institutional norms of state school systems perpetuate inequality. As a result, the status quo is rarely altered.

Again, many readers will grudgingly concede these points – including the importance of counter-publics – but still worry about the implications of homogenous classrooms for democratic deliberation. Surely, they will insist, more homogenous educational spaces simply fail to provide the necessary tension for such fruitful interactions to occur? Yet even some rather outspoken champions of democratic deliberation take a more nuanced view vis-à-vis classroom composition. For instance, political philosopher Debra Satz wisely acknowledges that "not all forms of de facto segregation threaten the ideal of relations among equal citizens. The social context of that segregation matters" (2007, p. 636). Moreover, and despite their commitment to "teaching the controversy," McAvoy and Hess, too, are reluctant to view homogeneity in the classroom as inherently problematic. They write:

> Even in classes that appear to be extremely homogenous, students consistently reported that they are able to recognize and appreciate the ideological diversity in their midst if their teachers included discussions of controversial issues in the curriculum. Many students stated that the range of opinions expressed in their classes was far wider than in their homes, in part because there were simply more participants, and therefore a greater diversity of viewpoints. (2013, p. 40)

As these observations make clear, the challenges faced in a more homogenous (read: segregated) classroom are just as real in terms of divergent viewpoints present, the importance of equitable treatment, or the need to establish rules of communication, listening, and respect. In other words, there is no reason to presume that segregation per se produces a famine of perspective, that is, less epistemic diversity.

Liberal democratic educators may lament that the gaps separating individuals in terms of experience and opinion may not be as wide as that which an integrated classroom might provide. On the other hand, if the gap between perspectives is less extreme, this may bode well for the deliberative process. Indeed a more "segregated" classroom in terms of culture, gender or ethnic/racial differences may in fact serve as a pedagogical convenience to both teachers and students, perhaps attempting to grapple with controversial topics for the first time. In other words, circumscribed diversity in a classroom may help to ease inevitable frictions that surface during deliberative interaction.

Nor, finally, does a more segregated classroom necessarily mean that a substantive understanding of toleration is out of reach. Remember that a substantive definition denotes an openness to others, an ability and willingness to listen and learn from differences, and to reflect upon one's own present beliefs. On this understanding of toleration, even students in a more segregated setting can develop a moral vocabulary necessary to adjudicate between competing normative claims. They also can learn the importance of using evidence to assess the reliability of some views over others. Finally, students also can develop a capacity to critically reflect upon one's beliefs and assumptions, and cultivate the intellectual humility necessary to alter one's point-of-view.

14.4.3 Final Worries

No doubt some liberal democratic theorists may still worry that these virtues will be self-contained, that is, that what may work well for members within one's community will not facilitate the civic virtues necessary to engage with those outside of one's community. They bid us to reconsider integration as an imperative for achieving these aims. Integration, the reasoning goes, is the ideal, and hence to 'settle' for democratic deliberation in segregated settings is defeatist. But rejoinders are available.

First, as we have seen, even in societies where legal mandates have been wielded to coercively foster integrated schooling, the outcomes in most cases have done little to address the structural inequalities endemic to school systems, ones that correlate strongly with race and social class (Carter & Merry, 2021). Though we may find this lamentable, most societies remain highly segregated, even if patterns of mixing in many domains continues to occur (Merry, 2021). Second, it is not defeatist to insist that we take seriously what the empirical evidence says, and to be open to pragmatic alternatives when that evidence consistently points *away* from integrationist dogma. Moreover, if and when de facto conditions of segregation can be turned to advantage, such that one's circumstances are pragmatically redefined, reclaimed, and redirected to serve the collective interests of self-determination, then this should be read as *resisting* defeat, not accommodating it.

Third, community-centered civic virtues facilitated by local attachments need not eclipse more remote concerns. Indeed, our links to strangers are rarely as remote as we may think. Local communities also function within broader polities, and even nations operate within international alliances. There is no reason to suppose that civic virtues – if they are in fact virtues rather than contentious political rhetoric concerning "shared values" – will be restricted to specific locations; indeed, they often have what economists call powerful externalities. To paraphrase Robert Putnam (2000), inward-looking (*bonding*) virtues do not exclude outward-looking (*bridging*) virtues. Indeed, the concentrical effects of civic virtue will be cultivated first with those one already knows before ever reaching beyond to less familiar contexts. That is more or less how the homophily principle works. Any civic virtues sewn in Guyanese or Columbian classrooms would presumably suffice until a mass exodus of refugees escaping political repression and famine in Venezuela would test the mettle of those virtues; the same presumably would be true of Indonesian Muslims in Aceh prior to the arrival of Rohingya refugees from Myanmar, or Jordanian hospitality shown toward Syrian and Palestinian refugees, or Liberians doing the same for those fleeing the Ivory Coast.

Without romanticizing these encounters, notice that each of these illustrations share a number of things in common, quite apart from suffering on a massive scale: each concerns neighboring countries where cultural, religious, and even linguistic similarities more readily facilitate the bridging. Where proximity is absent, as in the Rohingya case, religious brotherhood (*ummah*) aids in compensating. Either way, if circumstances that permit such bridging are missing, that in itself is no tragedy. Similarly, the benefits of a deliberation within a segregated classroom or school can later serve one well in very different environments, even if new skills and understandings inevitably will be required with those whose differences we may find less familiar. In any case, all classroom deliberations are but rehearsals, not unlike how attorneys "play" at prosecuting a case in law school before ever entering an actual courtroom, or how army platoons "play war" with one another before – if ever – encountering enemy forces.

In short, neither the integrity nor the possibility for deliberation and cultivation of civic virtue turn on an environment being integrated. Indeed, the cultivation of civic virtue within an appropriately structured homogenous environment, one also capable of facilitating a sense of belonging associated with attachments to a particular group, is a powerful precursor for the more expansive expression of social trust. Moreover, as we have seen, it is often under segregated conditions that students feel themselves freer to discuss, imagine, and pursue what civic virtue means when there are possibilities for parity of participation. If and when segregation is reconceived and reclaimed as a counter-public, it may be likely that participants have recourse to arguments that others cannot dismiss so quickly as unreasonable.

In any case, students do not need to be thrown into the deep end as it were, grappling with every conceivable difference before the relevant civic virtues begin to emerge. Indeed, the *absence* of certain kinds of diverse experiences in the classroom (e.g., incomprehension, silence, denial, antagonism) is almost certain to mitigate unnecessary unpleasantness that so often inhibits students from cultivating both the relevant civic virtues, as well as the skills necessary for deliberation. And if that is right, then in many cases the convenience of a homogenous classroom may be even more significant for those not likely to fare as well in a school in which their minoritized identities prove to be a liability.

References

Alexie, S. (1996) *Indian killer*. New York: Grand Central.

Anderson, E. (2021). *Black in white space: The enduring impact of color in everyday life*. Chicago, IL: University of Chicago Press.

Bæck, U. D. K. (2010). "We are the professionals": A study of teachers' views on parental involvement in school. *British Journal of Sociology of Education*, 31(3), 323–35.

Baldassarri, D., & Diani, M. (2007). The integrative power of civic networks. *American Journal of Sociology* 113 (3): 735–780.

Berenstain, N. (2016). Epistemic exploitation. *Ergo*, 3(22), 569–90.

Bernal, D. D. (2006). Rethinking grassroots activism: Chicana resistance in the 1968 East Los Angeles blowouts. In M. Apple & K. Buras, eds., *The subaltern speak: Curriculum, power and education struggles*. New York: Routledge, pp. 141–62.

Brown, M. C., & Davis, J. E. (2001). The historically black college as social contract, social capital and social equalizer. *Peabody Journal of Education*, 76(1), 31–49.

Carter, P., & Merry, M. S. (2021). *Wall to wall: Examining the ecology of racial and educational inequality with research*. White paper. The Spencer Foundation.

Coetzee, J. M. (1990). *Age of iron*. London: Penguin.

Conger, D. (2005). Within-school segregation in an urban school district. *Educational Evaluation and Policy Analysis*, 27(3), 225–44.

Diamond, J. (2006). Still separate and unequal: Examining race, opportunity, and school achievement in "integrated" schools. *The Journal of Negro Education*, 75 (3), 495–505.

Dryzek, J. (2000). *Deliberative democracy and beyond: Liberals, critics, contestations*. Oxford: Oxford University Press.

Fine, M. (2018). Silencing and nurturing voice in an improbable context: Urban adolescents in public school. In E. B. Hilty, ed., *Thinking about schools*. New York: Routledge, pp. 337–55.

Fish, S. (1999). Mutual respect as a device of exclusion. In S. Macedo, ed., *Deliberative politics: Essays on democracy and disagreement*. Oxford: Oxford University Press, pp. 88–102.

Fraser, N. (1997). *Justice interruptus: Critical reflections on the "postsocialist" condition*. New York: Routledge.

Fraser, N. (2021). *Rethinking the public sphere: A contribution to the critique of actually existing democracy*. New York: Routledge.

Frost, B. F. (2007). Texas students' college expectations: Does high school racial composition matter? *Sociology of Education*, 80(1), 43–65.

Gandin, J. L. (2006). Creating real alternatives to neoliberal policies in education: The citizen school project. In M. Apple & K. Buras, eds., *The subaltern speak: Curriculum, power and education struggles*. New York: Routledge, pp. 217–42.

Gutmann, A., & Ben-Porath, S. (2015). Democratic education. In M. T. Gibbons, ed., *The encyclopedia of political thought*. London: John Wiley & Sons.

Gutmann, A., & Thompson, D. (2004). *Why deliberative democracy*. Princeton, NJ: Princeton University Press.

Hailey, C. (2022). Racial preferences for schools: Evidence from an experiment with white, black, Latinx and Asian parents and students. *Sociology of Education*, 95(2), 110–32.

Hattie, J. (2002). Classroom composition and peer effects. *International Journal of Education Research*, 37, 449–81.

hooks, b. (1995). *Killing rage: Ending racism*. New York: Henry Holt.

Hussain, S. (2021). Ethnic segregation and "resegregation" in northern English schools. *Ethnicities*. doi: 10.1177/14687968211044016.

Ispa-Landa, S. (2013). Gender, race, and justifications for group exclusion: Urban black students bussed to affluent suburban schools. *Sociology of Education*, 86(3), 218–33.

Ispa-Landa, S., & Conwell, J. (2015). "Once you go to a white school, you kind of adapt": Black adolescents and the racial classification of schools. *Sociology of Education*, 88(1), 1–19.

Jacobs, D., Phalet, K., & Swyngedouw, M. (2004). Associational membership and political involvement among ethnic minority groups in Brussels. *Journal of Ethnic and Migration Studies* 30 (3): 543–559.

Johnson, D. W. & Johnson, R. T. (1988). Critical thinking through structured controversy. *Educational Leadership*, 45(8), 58–64.

Lewis, A., Diamond, J., & Forman, T. (2015). Conundrums of integration: Desegregation in the context of racialized hierarchy. *Sociology of Race and Ethnicity*, 1(1), 22–36.

Macedo, S. (2000). *Diversity and distrust: Civic education in a multicultural democracy*. Princeton, NJ: Princeton University Press.

Martinez, G. (2006). "In my classroom they always turn things around, the opposite way": Indigenous youth opposition to cultural domination in an urban high school. In M. Apple & K. Buras, eds., *The subaltern speak: Curriculum, power and education struggles*. New York: Routledge, pp. 121–40.

McAvoy, P., & Hess, D. (2013). Classroom deliberation in an era of political polarization. *Curriculum Inquiry*, 43(1), 14–47.

McPherson, M., Smith-Lovin, L., & Cook, J. (2001). Birds of a feather: Homophily in social networks. *Annual Review of Sociology*, 27, 415–44.

Merry, M. S. (2013). *Equality, citizenship and segregation*. New York: Palgrave.

Merry, M. S. (2020). *Educational justice*. New York: Palgrave.

Merry, M. S. (2021). Is faith in integration bad faith? *On Education: Journal for Research and Debate*, 4(11), 1–7.

Merry, M. S., Harris, R., & Manley, D. (2016). Community, virtue and the white British poor. *Dialogues in Human Geography*, 6(1), 50–68.

Merry, M. S., & Schinkel, A. (2021). What is an appropriate educational response to controversial historical monuments? *Journal of Philosophy of Education*, 55(3), 484–97.

Moody, J. (2001). Race, school integration, and friendship segregation in America. *American Journal of Sociology*, 107(3), 679–716.

Nystrand, M., Gamoran, A., Kashur, R., & Prendergast, C. (1997). *Opening dialogue*. New York: Teachers College Press.

Pace, J. (2019). Contained risk-taking: Preparing preservice teachers to teach controversial issues in three countries. *Theory and Research in Social Education*, 47(2), 228–60.

Putnam, R. (2000). *Bowling alone: The collapse and revival of American community*. New York: Simon & Schuster.

Quaynor, L. J. (2012). Citizenship education in post-conflict contexts: A review of the literature. *Education, Citizenship and Social Justice*, 7(1), 33–57.

Santiago-Rosario, M. R., Whitcomb, S. A., Pearlman, J., & McIntosh, K. (2021). Associations between teacher expectations and racial disproportionality in discipline referrals. *Journal of School Psychology*, 85, 80–93.

Satz, D. (2007). Equality, adequacy, and education for citizenship. *Ethics*, 117(4), 623–48.

Shapiro, I. (1999). Enough of deliberation: Politics is about interests and power. In S. Macedo, ed., *Deliberative politics: Essays on democracy and disagreement*. New York: Oxford University Press, pp. 28–38.

Stull, G., Spyridakis, D., Gasman, M., Samayoa, A., & Book, Y. (2015). Redefining success: How tribal colleges and universities build nations, strengthen sovereignty and persevere through challenges. *Center for Minority Serving Institutions*. Available at: https://repository.upenn.edu/gse_pubs/345.

Tyson, K. (2011). *Integration interrupted: Tracking, black students, and acting white after Brown*. New York: Oxford University Press.

Veenman, S. (1996). Effects of multigrade and multi-age classes reconsidered. *Review of Educational Research*, 66(3), 323–40.

Walzer, M. (1997). *On toleration*. New Haven, CT: Yale University Press.
Wane, N. (2009). Indigenous education and cultural resistance: A decolonizing project. *Curriculum Inquiry*, 39(1), 159–78.
Williams, M. (2003). Citizenship as identity, citizenship as shared fate, and the functions of multicultural education. In W. Feinberg & K. McDonough, eds., *Education and citizenship in multicultural societies: Teaching for cosmopolitan values and collective identities*. Oxford: Oxford University Press, pp. 208–47.
Wright, R. (1953). *The outsider*. New York: Harper.
Zembylas, M., & Kambani, F. (2012). The teaching of controversial issues during elementary-level history instruction: Greek-Cypriot teachers' perceptions and emotions. *Theory and Research in Social Education*, 40(2), 107–33.

15

Education and Democratic Citizenship: Capabilities and Quality Education

Martha C. Nussbaum

15.1 Education: Two Contrasting Pictures

I begin with two descriptions of education in India. First, a typical example of education for the rural poor, as conducted by one of the countless nongovernmental organizations (NGOs) that work on this issue – the Patna- centered NGO Adithi, created and run by the dynamic activist Viji Srinivasan, before her tragic premature death in 2005. Infrastructure in Bihar is so bad that it took us two days, even in a jeep, to get to this district near the Nepalese border. When we arrived, we found very meager facilities. Teaching mostly went on outside on the ground, or under the shade of a barn (in which rats ran around, occasionally across our feet). Students had very little paper, and only a few slates that were passed from hand to hand. Nonetheless, it was creative education. The literacy program for adult women, called "Reflect," began the day by asking the 20 or so women to draw (on a large sheet of rough wrapping paper) a map of the power structure of their village. We then discussed the map together, as the women identified possible points of intervention that might change the deal they have from the landlords for whom they currently work as sharecroppers. Everyone was animated; the prospect of criticizing entrenched structures of power had obviously led these women to attach great importance to the associated task of learning to read and write. At the end of the meeting we all joined in a song that is a staple of the women's movement here. It began, "In every house there is fear. Let's do away with that fear. Let's build a women's organization." It went on to sing the virtues of education, as an antidote to fear.

Next, I visited the literacy program for girls, housed in a shed next door. The girls of the village, goatherds by day, were beginning their school day around 4 p.m. About 15 girls in all, age 6–15, come to this single "classroom" for three hours of after-work learning. There are no desks, no chairs, no blackboard, and

This chapter was first printed in the Journal of Human Development, 7(3), November 2006, pp. 385–96. doi: 10.1080/14649880600815974.

only a few slates and bits of chalk. Nonetheless, it all seemed to work, through the resourcefulness and passion of the teachers, themselves poor rural women who have been assisted by Adithi's programs. Proudly the girls brought in the goats that they had been able to buy from the savings account they have jointly established in their group. Mathematics is taught in part by focusing on such practical issues. After that, the girls performed for us a play that they had recently performed for their village. It was about dowry, and the way this institution makes female lives seem to be of lower value to parents than male lives. Playing both male and female roles themselves, the girls told a story of how one young woman refused to be given in marriage with dowry. Her parents were shocked, and the father of the prospective groom became extremely angry. After much discussion, however, including a description of the way in which dowry is linked to the malnutrition and death of girls and the murders of adult women, the groom himself decided to refuse a dowry. He stood up proudly against his father – and the tall girl playing the groom stood up all the more proudly. Eventually, even the two sets of parents agreed that the new way is better. The marriage took place, and no money changed hands. Teachers told us that the whole village came to the play, and they think it did some good. Meanwhile, the girls giggled with pleasure at the subversive entertainment they had cooked up.

There are many points of interest in this scene, which I have seen replayed with small variations in many different parts of rural India (Nussbaum, 2004). But let me mention a few only: first, the close linkage between education and critical thinking about one's social environment; second, the emphasis on the arts as central aspects of the educational experience; third, the intense passion and investment of the teachers, their delight in the progress and also the individuality of their students.

Now I turn to another generic story, a story of government schools. This is a story I have heard again and again, in many different regions: from West Bengal's Pratichi Trust (organized by Amartya Sen), which has done an extensive study of primary education in several districts of West Bengal (Pratichi Trust, 2002); from the rural activists whose nongovernmental work I have just described, as they contrast their work with government schooling; from students in Indian universities, when I asked them about their prior education; from parents who send their children to government schools; and from many Indian-Americans, when I ask similar questions. It is not a universal story. But it is depressingly common (Nussbaum, 2005).

First, teachers often do not show up to teach at all. Second, when they do show up, they often do little real teaching, because they are waiting to offer "private tuition," when the richer families hire them for after-school instruction. This lucrative employment would be drastically undercut if they really did good teaching in the classroom. Third, my central concern in this lecture, even when responsible teaching is done in the classroom, it is still primarily focused on rote learning, as students are crammed with facts and routinized answers for the various examinations they are going to sit. Students report that the experience is quite deadening. It stimulates neither imagination nor critical thinking.

Students who have gone on to have some independence of mind typically credit this achievement either to an elite private school (but many of these also stress rote learning) or to a family that worked to keep the mind alive and growing. The one exception is science and technology, where national self-interest has produced generally high-quality education.

Nothing could be more crucial to democracy than the education of its citizens. Through primary and secondary education, young citizens form, at a crucial age, habits of mind that will be with them all through their lives. They learn to ask questions or not to ask them; to take what they hear at face value or to probe more deeply; to imagine the situation of a person different from themselves or to see a new person as a mere threat to the success of their own projects; to think of themselves as members of a homogeneous group or as members of a nation, and a world, made up of many people and groups, all of whom deserve respect and understanding. So it is not surprising that education has been so emphasized in recent political debates in many developing and developed countries.

Much of this debate, however, has been taking place on a very narrow terrain, that of basic literacy and numeracy, and that of scientific and technological education. To the extent that other subjects, such as history, are vigorously debated, the debate typically focuses on the content of required textbooks (Nussbaum, 2007). There is no doubt that scientific and technological education is important, and there is also no doubt that good textbooks are important. It is indeed important that young people read a complex and nuanced version of Indian history, one that stresses the agency and interaction of many different groups and presents an accurate picture of these interactions – as opposed, for example, to the simplistic picture of Hindu purity and Muslim rapacity purveyed by some educators on the Hindu right. In the light of the whole huge question of how to develop the minds of young children who are going to grow up to be democratic citizens, however, the twin emphasis on technology and textbooks seems extremely narrow. Not only India, but many other modern nations, are ignoring issues of great urgency. I shall argue that abilities connected with the humanities and the arts are crucial to the formation of citizenship. They must be cultivated if democracies are to survive, through educational policies that focus on pedagogy at least as much as on content.

15.2 Education for Freedom: Three Abilities

Let me begin with the model of education for democratic citizenship that I elaborated in my book *Cultivating Humanity* (Nussbaum, 1997). It has affiliations with the ideas of the progressive educationists John Dewey in the United States and Rabindranath Tagore in India.

Three capacities are essential to the cultivation of democratic citizenship in today's world. First is a capacity stressed both by Tagore and by Jawaharlal Nehru (whose daughter Indira attended Tagore's Santiniketan school): the capacity for critical examination of oneself and one's traditions, for living what, following Socrates, we may call "the examined life." This means a life that accepts no belief as authoritative simply because it has been handed down by tradition or become familiar through habit, a life that questions all beliefs, statements, and arguments, and accepts only those that survive reason's demand for consistency and for justification. Training this capacity requires developing the capacity to reason logically, to test what one reads or says for consistency of reasoning, correctness of fact, and accuracy of judgment. Testing of this sort frequently produces challenges to tradition, as Socrates knew well when he defended himself against the charge of corrupting the young. But he defended his activity on the grounds that democracy needs citizens who can think for themselves rather than simply deferring to authority, who can reason together about their choices rather than just trading claims and counterclaims. He compared himself with a gadfly on the back of a noble but sluggish horse: he was stinging the democracy to wake it up, so that it could conduct its business in a more reflective and reasonable way. Modern democracies, much as ancient Athens – but even more so, given the nature of modern media – are prone to hasty and sloppy reasoning and to the substitution of invective for real deliberation. We need Socratic teaching to fulfill the promise of democratic citizenship.

Critical thinking is particularly crucial for good citizenship in a society that needs to come to grips with the presence of people who differ by ethnicity, caste, and religion. We will only have a chance at an adequate dialogue across cultural boundaries if young citizens know how to engage in dialogue and deliberation in the first place. And they will only know how to do that if they learn how to examine themselves and to think about the reasons why they are inclined to support one thing rather than another – rather than, as so often happens, seeing political debate as simply a way of boasting, or getting an advantage for their own side. When politicians bring simplistic propaganda their way, as politicians in every country have a way of doing, young people will only have a hope of preserving independence if they know how to think critically about what they hear – testing its logic and its concepts, and imagining alternatives to it.

Students exposed to instruction in critical thinking learn, at the same time, a new attitude to those who disagree with them. Consider the case of Billy Tucker, a 19-year-old student in a business college who was required to take a series of liberal arts courses, including one in philosophy (Nussbaum, 1997, ch. 1). Interestingly enough, his instructor, Krishna Mallick, was an Indian-American originally from Kolkata, familiar with Tagore's educational ideal and a fine practitioner of it. Students in her class began by learning about the life and death of Socrates; Tucker was strangely moved by that man who would give up life itself for the pursuit of the argument. Then they learned a little formal logic, and Tucker was delighted to find that he got a high score on a test in that: he had never before thought he could do well in something abstract and intellectual. Next, they analyzed political speeches and editorials, looking for logical flaws. Finally, in the last phase of the course, they did research for debates on issues of the day. Tucker was surprised to discover that he was being asked to argue against the death penalty, although he actually favors it. He had never understood, he said, that one could produce arguments for a position that one does not hold oneself. He told me that this experience gave him a new attitude to political discussion: now he is more inclined to respect the opposing position, and to be curious about the arguments on both sides and what the two sides might share, rather than seeing the discussion as simply a way of making boasts and assertions. The following year he took another course from Mallick, not part of his requirement, on Gandhi and the philosophy of nonviolent resistance.

This transformation is precisely what Socrates, and Tagore, had in mind. The idea that one will take responsibility for one's own reasoning, and exchange ideas with others in an atmosphere of mutual respect for reason, is essential to the peaceful resolution of differences, both within a nation and in a world increasingly polarized by ethnic and religious conflict. Tucker was already a high school graduate, but it is possible, and essential, to encourage critical thinking from the very beginning of a child's education. The girls in Bihar had this experience. Their entire education developed their critical and self-critical capacities. This freedom is of particular urgency for women, who are so often encouraged to be passive followers of tradition.

But now to the second part of my proposal. Citizens who cultivate their capacity for effective democratic citizenship need, further, an ability to see themselves as not simply citizens of some local region or group, but also, and above all, as human beings bound to all other human beings by ties of recognition and concern. They have to understand both the differences that make understanding difficult between groups and nations and the shared human needs and interests that make understanding essential, if common problems are to be solved. This means learning quite a lot both about nations other than one's own and about the different groups that are part of one's own nation.

The international part of this ability is particularly difficult to cultivate in the United States, since Americans are so resistant to serious learning about any other country. Because of America's size, wealth, and power, they feel perfectly able to go through life without this learning. People in most other nations are less likely to sustain a comparable degree of ignorance. A non-US teacher begins with an advantage; but that is not to say that a great deal of work does not have to be done to make understanding of other nations and cultures complex and nuanced, rather than based on fear and prejudice.

Still more delicate, perhaps, is the related task of understanding differences internal to one's own nation. An adequate education for living in a pluralistic democracy must be a multicultural education, by which I mean one that acquaints students with some fundamentals about the histories and cultures of the many different groups with whom they share laws and institutions. These should include religious, ethnic, social, and gender-based groups. Language learning, history, economics, and political science all play a role in pursuing this understanding, in different ways at different levels. Awareness of the history of cultural, economic, religious, and gender-based differences is essential in order to promote the respect for another that is the essential underpinning for dialogue. There is no easier source of disdain and neglect than ignorance and the sense of the inevitable naturalness of one's own way.

This is where good textbooks are indeed important. A good textbook will convey fact in a balanced and accurate way and will give all the narratives their due. It will reveal the complexity of the nation, both past and present, and it will help students understand the internal complexities of groups (Muslims, Christians, the rural poor) that might easily be viewed in too simplistic and monolithic a way. This task includes showing students how and why different groups interpret evidence differently and construct different narratives. Even the best textbook will not succeed at this complex task unless it is presented together with a pedagogy that fosters critical thinking, the critical scrutiny of conflicting source materials, and active learning (learning by doing) about the difficulties of constructing a historical narrative.

This brings me to the third part of my proposal. As the story of the dowry play in Bihar indicates, citizens cannot think well on the basis of factual knowledge alone. The third ability of the citizen, closely related to the first two, can be called the narrative imagination. This means the ability to think what it might be like to be in the shoes of a person different from oneself, to be an intelligent reader of that person's story, and to understand the emotions and wishes and desires that someone so placed might have. As Tagore wrote, "We may become powerful by knowledge, but we attain fullness by sympathy . . . But we find that this education of sympathy is not only systematically ignored in schools, but it is severely repressed" (Tagore, 1961, p. 219).

The narrative imagination is cultivated, above all, through literature and the arts. Reliance on the arts was the most revolutionary aspect of Tagore's and Dewey's proposals, which used theater, dance, and literature to cultivate the imagination. Through the imagination we may attain a kind of insight into the experience of another that it is very difficult to attain in daily life – particularly when our world has constructed sharp separations, and suspicions that make any encounter difficult.

The arts offer children opportunities for learning through their own creative activity, something that Dewey particularly emphasized. To put on a play about dowry (or a play about racism in the United States) is to learn about it in a way that is likely to seem more meaningful to a child than the reading of a textbook account. Learning about hardship and discrimination enters the personality at a deeper level.

The arts are also crucial sources of both freedom and community. When people put on a play together, they have to learn to go beyond tradition and authority, if they are going to express themselves well. And the sort of community created by the arts is nonhierarchical, a valuable model of the responsiveness and interactivity that a good democracy will also foster in its political processes. When I talk to Amita Sen, who danced in Tagore's dance-dramas, first in Santiniketan and then in Kolkata, I see the revolutionary nature of what Tagore had done for young women in particular, urging them to express themselves freely through their bodies and to join with him in a kind of profoundly egalitarian play. The scandal of this freedom, as young women of good family suddenly turned up on the Kolkata stage, shook convention and tradition to their foundations. So too with the dowry play: to have young teenage girls get up in front of their entire village to perform that play was a deeply subversive act of social criticism.

Finally, the arts are great sources of joy – and this joy carries over into the rest of a child's education. Amita Sen's book about Tagore as choreographer, aptly entitled *Joy in All Work*, shows how all the "regular" education in Santiniketan, which enabled these students to perform very well in standard examinations, was infused with delight because of the way in which it was combined with dance and song. Children do not like to sit still all day; but they also do not know automatically how to express emotion with their bodies in dance. Tagore's expressive, but also disciplined, dance regime was an essential source of creativity, thought, and freedom for all pupils, but particularly for women, whose bodies had been taught to be shame-ridden and inexpressive (Sen, 1999).

There is a further point to be made about what the arts do for the spectator. As Tagore knew, and as radical artists have often emphasized, the arts, by generating pleasure in connection with acts of subversion and cultural criticism, produce an endurable and even attractive dialogue with the prejudices of the past, rather than one fraught with fear and defensiveness. The great African-American artist Ralph Ellison, for example, called his novel *Invisible Man* "a raft of perception, hope, and entertainment" that could help the American democracy "negotiate the snags and whirlpools" that stand between it and "the democratic idea" (Ellison, 1992, Introduction). Entertainment is crucial to the ability of the arts to offer perception and hope. Similarly, the village in Bihar found the girls' dowry play delightful, rather than deeply threatening.

At the heart of all three of the Tagorean capacities is the idea of freedom: the freedom of the child's mind to engage critically with tradition; the freedom to imagine citizenship in both national and world terms, and to negotiate multiple allegiances with knowledge and confidence; and the freedom to reach out in the imagination, allowing another person's experience into oneself. Many politicians the world over do not like educational freedom: they seek the imprisonment of children within a single "correct" ideology. This fearful curtailment of freedom can be found in recent attempts by India's Hindu right to "saffronize" the curriculum; it can also be a property of Left-wing conceptions, which sometimes also prefer solidarity and correctness to the possibility that someone might choose another way. It is only the risky idea of critical and imaginative freedom that offers democracies lasting strength, as they face an uncertain future.

15.3 The Bird Nobody Noticed

These ideas have roots in many traditions, old and new. But there is no more wonderful depiction of what is wrong with an education based on mere technical mastery and rote learning than Tagore's sad story "The Parrot's Training":

> A certain Raja had a bird whom he loved. He wanted to educate it, because he thought ignorance was a bad thing. His pundits convinced him that the bird must go to school. The first thing that had to be done was to give the bird a suitable edifice for his schooling: so they build a magnificent golden cage. The next thing was to get good textbooks. The pundits said, "Textbooks can never be too many for our purpose." Scribes worked day and night to produce the requisite manuscripts. Then, teachers were employed.

> Somehow or other they got quite a lot of money for themselves and built themselves good houses. When the Raja visited the school, the teachers showed him the methods used to instruct the parrot. "The method was so stupendous that the bird looked ridiculously unimportant in comparison. The Raja was satisfied that there was no flaw in the arrangements. As for any complaint from the bird itself, that simply could not be expected. Its throat was so completely choked with the leaves from the books that it could neither whistle nor whisper."
>
> The lessons continued. One day, the bird died. Nobody had the least idea how long ago this had happened. The Raja's nephews, who had been in charge of the education ministry, reported to the Raja:
>
> "Sire, the bird's education has been completed." "Does it hop?" the Raja enquired. "Never!" said the nephews. "Does it fly?" "No." "Bring me the bird," said the Raja. The bird was brought to him, guarded by the kotwal and the sepoys and the sowars. The Raja poked its body with his finger. Only its inner stuffing of book-leaves rustled. Outside the window, the murmur of the spring breeze amongst the newly budded asoka leaves made the April morning wistful. (Tagore, 1994)

This wonderful story hardly needs commentary. Its crucial point is that educationists tend to enjoy talking about themselves and their own activity, and to focus too little on the small tender children whose eagerness and curiosity should be the core of the educational endeavor. Tagore thought that children were usually more alive than adults, because they were less weighted down by habit. The task of education was to avoid killing off that curiosity, and then to build outward from it, in a spirit of respect for the child's freedom and individuality rather than one of hierarchical imposition of information.

I do not agree with absolutely everything in Tagore's educational ideal. For example, I am less antimemorization than Tagore was. Memorization of fact can play a valuable and even a necessary role in giving pupils command over their own relationship to history and political argument. That is one reason why good textbooks are important, something that Tagore would have disputed. But about the large point I am utterly in agreement: education must begin with the mind of the child, and it must have the goal of increasing that mind's freedom in its social environment, rather than killing it off.

15.4 Democracy in the Balance

To what extent has education for freedom, as I have described it, become a reality in the world today? Tagore's actual influence has not been widespread. Several reasons can be found for this: the relatively narrow reach of the Bengali language and the poor quality of many English translations of Tagore's work; Tagore's own personal charisma and artistic distinction, which made it difficult to convert Santiniketan into a mass movement; and his distaste for bureaucracy, which meant that, unlike Dewey (who was not a creative artist but who was a capable entrepreneur), he did not try to have a mass movement. Even in Santiniketan today, education is routinized; even the dance performances contain little creativity. Dewey, by contrast, has had widespread influence. In every primary school in the United States, and in many other nations that are aware of his influence, one will see at least some of Dewey's ideas realized, as young children learn by doing rather than by rote learning, as they use drama and literature to probe difficult historical and global issues. NGOs the world over use such ideas very creatively, knowing that their task is not to stuff their pupils with facts, but to produce minds that seek out learning on their own. The fact that NGO education is purely voluntary makes them seek out techniques that enliven curiosity.

Science and technology are important, and nations are surely right to focus on the prosperity that they promise to bring. It would be disastrous, however, if the other parts of a liberal education were short-circuited in the process, producing nations of smart engineers who have little capacity for empathetic imagining and for critical thinking. Such impoverishment of mind would nourish the politics of obtuseness and hatred, all over the world. Progressive education – emphasizing critical thinking and imaginative learning – exacts higher financial and human costs than education that allows rote learning to dominate in history and the humanities. One cannot teach my three abilities with a pupil: teacher ratio of 50:1, which was what Amartya Sen's Pratichi Trust found in primary education in West Bengal. But its importance for the health of democracy is out of all proportion to these costs. Furthermore, both pupils and teachers come to school eager for the day when the day is spent in lively interaction, rather than rote learning: thus progressive education holds out hope of stemming the tide of teacher and pupil absenteeism, a chronic problem, also well documented in Sen's report.

I do not believe that Tagore's experiments work only in the presence of a charismatic leader like Tagore. The imagination is a hardy plant. When it is not killed, it can thrive in many places – as it thrives in Bihar, as it thrives in similar projects I have observed in other regions. If NGOs that have no equipment and no money, only heart and mind and a few slates, can accomplish so much, there is no excuse for government schools the world over to lag behind. I can best summarize my wish for the future of education in today's world with a poem of Tagore's addressed to his country:

Where the mind is without fear
And the head is held high,
Where knowledge is free;
Where the world has not been broken
Up into fragments by narrow domestic walls;
Where words come out from the depth of truth;
Where tireless striving
Stretches its arms towards perfection;
Where the clear stream of reason
Has not lost its way into the
Dreary desert sand of dead habit;
Where the mind is led forward
By thee into ever-widening

Thought and action –
Into that heaven of freedom,
My Father,
Let my country awake. (From Gitanjali, translation by the author)

References

Ellison, R. (1992). *Invisible man*. New York: Random House (originally published 1952, introduction added 1981).

Nussbaum, M. C. (1997). *Cultivating humanity: A classical defense of reform in liberal education*. Cambridge, MA: Harvard University Press.

Nussbaum, M. C. (2004). Women's education: A global challenge. *Signs*, 29, 325–55.

Nussbaum, M. C. (2005). Education and democratic citizenship: Beyond the textbook controversy. *Islam and the Modern Age*, 35, 69–89. (A slightly different version published as "Freedom from dead habit". *The Little Magazine*, 6, 18–32).

Nussbaum, M. C. (2007). *The clash within: Democracy, religious violence, and India's future*. Cambridge, MA: Harvard University Press.

Pratichi Trust (2002). *The Pratichi education report 1*. New Delhi: TLM Books.

Sen, A. (1999). *Joy in all work* (Translation of Ananda Sarbakaje). Kolkata: Bookfront Publication Forum.

Tagore, R. (1917). My school. In *Personality: Lectures delivered in America*. London: Macmillan, pp. 111–50.

Tagore, R. (1961). *A Tagore reader*. Ed. by A. Chakravarty, Boston, MA: Beacon Press.

Tagore, R. (1994). A parrot's training. In V. Bhatia, ed., *Rabindranath Tagore: Pioneer in education*. New Delhi: Sahitya Chayan.

Part Three

Key Topics and Concepts

16

Educational Justice and Democratic Education

Stefan Gosepath

16.1 Introduction

What are the purposes or aims of education in general and of democratic education in particular? And what are the appropriate ways and means of such an education? This chapter offers an overview of some of the more important approaches to these questions in contemporary, mostly anglophone, conceptions of educational justice in primary and secondary education. Section 16.2 starts with some provisions of some important goals of education. Section 16.3 turns to educational justice in gerneral. Section 16.4 asks about the spheres of educational justice: Is it education and socialization in general, or the school system in particular? Section 16.5 distinguishes three different levels of education: (i) basic education for all; (ii) the cultivation of individual talents and capacities; and (iii) selection for higher education and the job market. Section 16.6 outlines the differences between five principles of justice and equality in the field of education: (i) strict equality, (ii) a conception of fair equality of opportunity, (iii) a conception of luck-egalitarian equality of opportunity, (iv) a prioritarian conception of educational justice, and (v) democratic adequacy as a conception of educational justice. Section 16.7 concludes the chapter.[1]

16.2 The Purpose of Education

A theory of education loses sight of its central philosophical questions if it is concerned only with the appropriate means of education and does not ask about its purpose. The determination of the purpose of education should not, however, be seen solely in terms of its functional significance for the overall welfare of society or for individual economic success, wellbeing, or individual economic success, because this would place the importance of education for human life in general and social life in particular in too limited a focus (Meyer, 2009, pp. 6, 169).

[1] This chapter is a partial replication and further development of the arguments made in Gosepath (2014). I also draw on Culp (2020b).

Rather, the purpose of education must be further defined by the extent to which education is something good for those to be educated; that is, it contributes to their respective individual good lives (Meyer, 2009, p. 99) and good for society, its social cohesion, and interactions. Furthermore, a functional definition of the purpose of education is too one-sided, because it cannot be used to assess how the canon of education that is common today, which is not merely geared to economic success, is to be evaluated. Aesthetic and cultural education, in particular, cannot be reduced to its functional role of contributing to the achievement of educational goals, such as the promotion of creativity or the acquisition of mathematical skills (Meyer, 2009, p. 74).

One can find four common purposes or aims of education, which are often put forward. There are certainly more generally recognized aims of education, but for the purpose of this chapter, these might be regarded as the most relevant.

The first purpose is that education should promote autonomy or at least help people to lead self-determined lives. In the field of education, the focus should thus be on the enablement of an autonomous or self-determined way of life. To reach this goal, educational institutions should contribute to the possibilities for trainees to act; ensure that adolescents are enabled to reflect critically on their goals and values; and enable students to subject their opinions and acquired knowledge to critical examination (Meyer, 2009, ch. 2).

The second aim of education is that it should open up exposure to objects or content that provide valuable experiences. This is especially true of educational objects that are conducive to the promotion of autonomy, but also to the experience of acquiring knowledge in general. The purpose of education is accordingly to make valuable experiences possible (Meyer, 2009, ch. 3).

A third objective of education is that it should promote at least those valuable functions and capabilities that are recognized by most people as conducive to a good life (Nussbaum, 1992, 2000; Meyer, 2009, ch. 4). In this regard, education has, first of all, the fundamental task of enabling the acquisition of competencies that make it possible to satisfy basic needs. In addition, education should provide a broad spectrum of valuable experiences so that adolescents can learn about different standards for evaluating experiences as well as critically reflect on their life plans in the context of their culture.

A fourth objective of education in modern times is that it prepare people to participate in collective self-determination in a democratically governed political system (Dewey, [1916] 1980; Gutmann, 1987; Culp, 2019). If citizens are to live up to the democratic ideal of sharing political sovereignty, they must learn not just to behave in accordance with democratic values but also to understand and think critically about them. Society and its educational system must thus cultivate democratically the kind of character and intellect that enables people to choose rationally and autonomously among different ways of life. It also requires the state to cultivate the capacity for rational deliberation together with others. Certain political capabilities have to be cultivated to enable citizens to fully participate in a democracy. These include, among others, the capabilities to rationally deliberate with others, to form one's own opinion and justify it, to comprehend what is at issue, to vote, to hold office, to assemble, to petition the government, to speak freely, and so forth. Education that is defensible according to a democratic ideal should prepare children so that they are capable of assuming the rights and correlative responsibilities of equal citizenship. In short, democratic education must enable future citizens to participate in society-wide, political decision-making processes, and should both express and develop the capacity of all children to become equal citizens.

16.3 The Right to Education and Educational Justice

Due to the values of these purposes of education, it is commonly accepted that pupils, trainees, and students have educational entitlements regardless of whether their education contributes to the overall welfare of society. International human rights law (see Universal Declaration of Human Rights, Article 26; International Covenant on Economic, Social, and Cultural Rights, Articles 13 and 14) recognizes the human right to access to free and compulsory primary education of good quality that is suitably adapted to the societal context

Given this generally ackknowledged right to education, a society has to decide how to provide for such a right. Should it leave the distribution of education within its population to market mechanisms alone? Should it aim for everyone to be educated equally well? Should it be concerned simply to ensure that everyone's education is good enough; if so, good enough for what? Should it try to maximize the educational level of the worst off, or, perhaps, to distribute education so as to help the worst off in some other way? Whatever principles guide policymakers, to what lengths should they be willing to go to achieve them? (We will return in section 16.4 to possible answers to these questions.)

There should be no doubt – and there is much supporting data – that the school system has an enormous influence on the future lives of its students. Because it decisively shapes all of our lives and, in particular, our opportunities in later life, education and the school system are an essential field of application of justice. Justice, in turn, should be the fundamental ideal of a normatively value-oriented policy. In the education system, which is concerned with the development of certain mental and physical abilities made possible by means of school education, educational justice should therefore prevail. "Educational justice" is thus not just one of the many new (fashionable) hyphenated justices, but an old question and demand of justice. As is well known, justice demands according to the old formula *suum cuique* (to each his own), that is, to each according to his/her justified claims (Plato, [380 BCE] 1991: 433a). An action is fair when it gives everyone what they deserve. All justice seems to be related to what is appropriate. Justice then refers to the totality of reciprocal claims and obligations, or moral rights and obligations, that people have against each other from the standpoint of impartiality. This definition is very formal because it leaves open the crucial question of who gets what. The formula or general concept of justice contains several variables that must be answered in order to arrive at specific conceptions of justice.

Clearly, not everyone can be promoted in the way they imagine to be ideal. The point of *suum cuique*, after all, is precisely that the (justified) demands of each person (in the relevant field) should be adequately met. In all cases where the extent of satisfaction of a particular person's claims competes with the extent of satisfaction of the claims of other persons – and that is almost always the case – considerations of justice force us to compare the different claims and to weigh them against each other. If there are no relevant differences between persons (in the relevant respect), persons are to be treated equally, because they have the same dignity and, as citizens of the community, also the same status (Gosepath, 2015).

16.4 The Sphere of Educational Justice

Here, as everywhere else, one should first ask what is or should be the appropriate domain of justice for which a criterion of justice is sought. What may be just in one area or sphere of justice is therefore by no means just in another area (Walzer, 1983). A theory of justice cannot be monistic, that is, it must not represent only one single criterion of justice for all spheres of application, but must do justice to the complexity of life in its application reference and thereby recognize a multiplicity of criteria of justice, different ones depending on the sphere. In this context, it is also essential how these areas or spheres of justice are (re)constructed.

What, then, is the appropriate sphere of justice where education is concerned? Education and socialization in general? Or the school system in particular? Schooling is only one factor among many that affect an individual's later economic and social status and educational achievements. The most important factor is likely to be the individual's family background – its size, income, and wealth; the parents' social and especially educational status; their personal traits, class, race; and so on. Other factors, such as teachers' and friends' backgrounds, can also be important. If this is the case, it raises the question of whether the school system is really the proper focus for egalitarian concerns and public action. Should we not rather focus on education in a broader sense of the term, thus including the influence that factors such as family background or socialization as a whole have on educational outcomes?

Moreover, people cannot be educated fairly in an unjust society because their everyday experiences would always refute the intentions of the educator. As Schleiermacher ([1826] 2000) pointed out, teaching is imparted not only through "intentional education" – the deliberate, goal-directed intentions of the educator – but, also and more importantly, when it comes to values and to shaping a life, through "functional education;" that is, in and through social and personal relations. If this is true, it means that to aim at justice in the educational domain certainly demands that we broaden its scope. In this respect, one cannot meaningfully ask about the justice of a school system or a type of school without also considering the justice or, in most cases, injustice of the conditions of socialization.

Nevertheless, the scope of educational justice is ultimately limited. Its sphere of application is public, not private life. Where to draw this line is of course controversial. Liberals take it as a basic right that the family, or the parent, has primary responsibility for the upbringing of a child. Since the family is regarded as private, the state should regulate education within the family as little as is necessary. But since education within the family probably has the farthest-reaching effects on life prospects in almost all respects (comparable only to a person's genetic endowment), justice requires that the effects of family backgrounds are counterbalanced with respect to education without infringing on the basic rights of parents.

A society that establishes and maintains a public school system already goes some way toward providing all its members with basic knowledge and capabilities and some opportunity to develop skills that will enable them to succeed. The same can be said of a society that enforces minimum standards of child welfare. Such standards may include healthcare, an adequate diet, mastery of one's mother tongue and the language of one's place of residence, and the bases for adequate intellectual and emotional development. One can imagine a society that is organized even more in accordance with this spirit. Finally, justice in education is also affected by inequalities in other spheres that have a massive impact on life prospects, such as the economy. By trying to reduce inequalities in these other relevant spheres, more egalitarian policies would ideally counterbalance the influence of many of the factors relevant to a person's family background.

16.5 Three Different Levels of Education

Putting this broad construal of education and socialization to the side for the moment, this section now turns to the question of what good is to be justly distributed in the narrower domain of primary and secondary school education. The suggestion is, as outlined in this chapter's Introduction, that we should distinguish between at least three levels of school education, corresponding to three primary purposes: (i) basic education for all; (ii) the cultivation of individual talents and capacities; and (iii) selection for higher education and the job market. Each of these levels requires a different kind and metric of equality. In the following, the three levels will be discussed in turn.

16.5.1 First Level of Education

The first and most important task of a fair school system is basic education in the broadest sense of the term, centering on basic knowledge and skills, but including the acquisition of cultural resources and even personality development as well. It is essential for a number of reasons that this kind of basic education should be mandatory and universal. First of all, it has a quasi-transcendental value: without at least minimal education and knowledge, we would not be able to live our own lives. It is thus to be regarded as the most important resource for coping with the challenges of everyday life. Second, it has additional pragmatic values. Since it is a precondition of other higher ideals, such as private and public autonomy, education affords an opportunity to live a *good* life. An adequate education is important since it enables individuals to enjoy the culture of their society and take part in public affairs. Third, it has intrinsic value: a great deal of people value and appreciate education, in the sense of *Bildung*, in its own right.

Since basic education is essential in these three ways, we want all children to be adequately educated for life within their society. Education is therefore considered a human right. Western societies grant this human right by providing universal access to school and, even more importantly, by making it mandatory up to a certain age. The kind of equality that should be demanded on this level from the viewpoint of justice is equality of outcome. Its metric is basic capacities or capabilities, such as literacy, numeracy, and basic knowledge of the natural sciences and humanities. The application of a metric of equality of opportunity would be off-target here. Since everybody has a right and duty to go to school up to a certain level, the idea of merit implied by the concept of equality of opportunity does not apply. Equality of opportunity is normally a component of a moral theory of justified social *in*equality. On this first level, however, access to education should vary as little as possible. Here, we aim for equal outcomes: all members of society should acquire the same basic capacities.

16.5.2 Second Level of Education

The second task of education is the cultivation of talents. A society provides too little scope for opportunity, personal development, and autonomous choice if it fails to provide for the recognition, development, and exercise of a wide range of (worthy) human talents. Society is thus obliged to offer a range of educational opportunities that give everyone the chance to develop their talents to at least some extent. This obligation arises first from the idea that in order to have real choices, one needs a broad range of desirable options to choose from. Second, society should also cultivate a wide range of worthy human talents for the reason that these may turn out to be socially or economically useful. Third, every person should have the right and chance to develop their talents and abilities in accordance with their ideas unless this will infringe on the rights of others. In a market economy ruled by supply and demand, one cannot know in advance which talents will be needed. It thus seems wise to have a broad pool of developed talents at hand in case demand shifts. Since, as far as we know, society cannot effectively plan its economy, it should not attempt to plan the cultivation of talents entirely, but rather leave the development of skills partly up to the choices and motivation of individuals. This, at the same time, helps reveal the diversity of talents and their worth. What qualifies a person as talented or untalented (or for that matter as able or not able) is not simply a function of their natural attributes, but rather the intersection of these attributes with values and demands resulting from the organization of society.

On this second level, justice demands that access to education and success in school should not vary according to differences in social background or other arbitrary characteristics. Education should be provided for everyone regardless of their background, and a concerted effort should be made to develop all talents. This calls for a school system that is insensitive to background and at the same time sensitive to endowment and ambition. The cultivation of talents should, according to this logic, be meritocratic and proportional to students' aptitude and readiness to learn. This will of course lead to inequalities of outcome, but these may be economically useful, if not, strictly speaking, necessary. If we then go on to stipulate that the development of especially valued talents works to everyone's advantage, including that of those who are worst off, then inequalities of trained talents would be justified. These prima facie justifiable inequalities can create problems, however, that turn them into unjust inequalities. For if certain talents and the corresponding jobs or social roles are valuable, no doubt special advantages and rewards will be attached to them. Inequalities in trained talents will thus lead to inequalities of positions and income. And bestowing special advantages on people on the basis of unchosen endowments such as talents seems unfair from the point of view of most egalitarian conceptions of justice. (We will return to the difficulty in finding a just solution to this problem).

16.5.3 Third Level of Education

Let us finally turn to the third level of education. This third level is entirely competitive. At this level, high school can be seen as the first of many playing fields on which competition for higher learning, better jobs, higher income, and superior positions in the social hierarchy takes place. From the point of view of social justice, the opportunities which prove relevant to any consideration of justice are above all opportunities for a certain income and certain assets in the economic sphere as well as opportunities for specific positions, offices, and professions in society, and for social status. Since at this third level, as in a race, inequality of outcome is simply inevitable, it can be regarded as the proper domain of equality of opportunity.

16.6 Principles of Justice and Equality in the Field of Education

But there is quite a philosophical debate about the right principles of justice and equality in the field of education. Principles of equality that are usually advocated in philosophical discussions are some versions of equality of opportunity, adequacy, and priority. All of these views are united in rejecting strict equality of outcome. This section, as described in this chapter's Introduction, outlines the differences between five principles of justice and equality in the field of education: (i) strict equality, (ii) a conception of fair equality of opportunity,

(iii) a conception of luck-egalitarian equality of opportunity, (iv) a prioritarian conception of educational justice, and (v) democratic adequacy as a conception of educational justice.

16.6.1 Strict Equality

It is generally regarded as unacceptable and impractical that positions and offices should be equally distributed in any strict sense. It is unacceptable from a normative point of view, because general civil rights guarantee every person a free choice of occupation. Therefore no person should be obliged prima facie to practice a particular occupation or to do a particular job. Basic and civil rights also entail every person's right to develop their own talents and abilities in accordance with their own ideas. If, moreover, we assume that individuals can be made responsible for their individual achievements, on condition that they start off with equal opportunities, then they should be entitled to the fruits of their free, autonomous occupation. The strictly equal distribution of positions and offices seems impractical because it would undermine the efficient social organization of the division of labor, which is directed toward the goal of obtaining those candidates for socially necessary or desirable occupations who, on account of their abilities and previous achievements, are the best suited for them. Hindering this mechanism of selection for socially desirable occupations would be extremely unwise from the point of view of those directly or indirectly affected by the occupation in question. Organizing a society in this way would ultimately damage all members of that society; free-market production would become less efficient, and goods that are in demand would be quantitatively and qualitatively worse. This would in turn detract considerably from the quality and quantity of the total amount of distributable goods, so that the productive inefficiency would also have an indirect effect on the justice of the social setup as a whole. In order to take into account these prudential arguments and arguments based on civil rights, the distribution of positions and offices should not be strictly equal.

16.6.2 Conception of Fair Equality of Opportunity in Education

Contrary to the conception of strict equality of results, the idea of equality of opportunity for positions, offices and income does not – either normatively or descriptively – assume purely static social relations with a fixed system for the distribution of material goods. Instead, on the one hand, it takes into account social dynamics as a social fact; on the other hand, it gives voice to the normative conviction that social mobility is also necessary for just social development.

The object of any principle of equality of opportunity is not equal chance of success, but a legitimately unequal chance of success. It can apply to power, positions, rights, wealth, etc. Equality of opportunity is introduced in political discussion (see Williams, 1973, pp. 366–97) when the distribution of goods is at issue – goods that are, firstly, wanted by many people; secondly, said to be "deserved" or "earned"; and thirdly, in short supply, so that not everyone can have them, either by nature or for contingent reasons. They are available to everyone who fulfills certain conditions, but not everyone fulfills the conditions (above all, personal abilities, professional qualifications, and personal motivation).

When we talk about equality of opportunity in connection with education, social dynamics, and, in particular, the potential for upward mobility, there is, however, general disagreement as to what is necessary for the realization of equality of opportunity in practice (Jencks, 1988, p. 518). In the philosophical debate, one distinguishes between at least two more demanding versions of equal educational opportunity: fair equality of educational opportunity and luck-egalitarian educational opportunity (Brighouse & Swift, 2014a).

Fair equality of educational opportunity is regarded as a fair means for the chances to reach higher and unequal income and wealth later in life (Brighouse, 2000; Brighouse & Swift, 2014a). Equality of educational opportunity to access jobs, plus meritocracy in organized market societies, are thus supposed to justify distributive outcomes with unequal levels of income and wealth. In a liberal society, social and economic inequalities are to be arranged so that both are reasonably expected to be to everyone's benefit and attached to positions and offices open to all (Rawls, 1999, p. 53).

One might argue that the rule of equality of opportunity in the sphere of education and socialization, with its emphasis on responsible agency within a field of social competition, is preparing young people for adult life: The playing field is leveled when the influence of unchosen individual circumstances on success is counterbalanced so that the game of life is not tilted by morally arbitrary factors such as socioeconomic status and cultural background. This understanding of fair educational opportunity demands a meritocratic conception of educational equality: "An individual's prospects for educational achievement may be a function of that individual's talent and effort, but they should not be influenced by her social class background" (Brighouse & Swift, 2014a, p. 15).

Careers should be open on equal starting conditions to all those who are competent and able. This is known as the principle of fair equality of opportunity (see Rawls, 1999, pp. 73–78). Competition for positions can offer formal equality of opportunity; nevertheless, some people have better starting opportunities while others are prevented from even developing their talents in the first place as a result of their social environment or background. Such unequal starting opportunities in the competition for positions are recognized and accounted for by the principle of fair equality of opportunity. It is directed against the actual preferential treatment of those that are already socially and materially better off. The children of poor parents should not be prevented by school or university fees from receiving an adequate education, nor should prejudice prevent women from receiving an adequate education, especially since it is education which constitutes the crucial starting point in the competition for higher-level positions.

The principle of fair equality of opportunity justifies excluding any advantage or disadvantage based on morally irrelevant criteria such as gender, appearance, or social and ethnic background, and instead making success or failure depend solely on one's own achievements. It should be "earned" or "merited," rather than being "inherited" or awarded based on social position, gender, or background. Justice requires, among other things, that "there should be a fair competition among individuals for unequal positions in society," and that in this competition successes (and failures) ought to be determined by qualifications only (Fishkin, 1983, p. 19). "The basic meritocratic norm says that each selector ought to fill the position she is charged to fill with someone who is no less well qualified for that position than any other candidate" (Lippert-Rassmussen, 2013, p. 286).

Applied to the social sphere of education, fair equality of opportunity demands that society be organized in such a way that everyone has equal rights to advantageous social positions, that all careers are open to those who are capable, and that all people are guaranteed equal social starting opportunities. Next to legal structural conditions, fair equality of opportunity also demands comprehensive sociopolitical measures which must work toward dismantling existing forms of social disadvantage and discrimination. In addition, they must also create the material conditions necessary for all equally talented and motivated people to enjoy equal opportunities, regardless of the social inequality that exists between them. This latter point means that all people, regardless of their social background, should be able to receive education, further education, and support (e.g., for disabled people) which should, if necessary, be made available to them by publicly financed educational institutions. In normative terms, this is all the more important, as it means that the value of education and qualification ought not to be regarded from a purely economic point of view. Education makes cultural views accessible to persons and enables them to participate to an increased extent in social life, thus providing them with a secure sense of self-esteem (see Rawls, 1999, p. 87). Education can enrich the personal and social life of an individual; for that reason alone it should be available to everyone.

16.6.3 A Conception of Luck-Egalitarian Equality of Opportunity in Education

On the whole, the principle of fair equality of opportunity nowadays receives widespread recognition. However, convincing though it may be, the basic idea does, according to some more egalitarian views, not go far enough; it meets with both moral and practical difficulties. The idea of fair equality of opportunity misses out on an important respect in which human fate is influenced by factors which the person concerned cannot "help" – the effects of which are thus "undeserved:" if social circumstances are indeed not the responsibility of individuals and if the resulting inequalities are therefore unfair, then the same must be true of natural talents. We can call this the conception of substantive equality of opportunity. If we accept that natural factors are also a morally arbitrary influence on the distribution of goods, then the popular concept of merit does not hold. In fact, it becomes clear that what we regard as our own achievement is by no means entirely based on what is our own, but depends instead on endowments we just happen to find ourselves with. According to the so-called luck-egalitarian principle of liberal-egalitarian responsibility, it is unjust if one person is less provided for than others (in terms of her shares of resources) unless it is as a result of conditions for which she herself is responsible, that is, her own voluntary decision or a mistake she could have avoided (Arneson, 1989; Cohen, 1989, p. 922; Rakowski, 1991; Dworkin, 2000; Gosepath, 2004, V.1.2; for the prominent critique, Anderson, 1999). In these instances of unjust inequality, the persons concerned are, from an egalitarian point of view, entitled to compensation. This principle holds that persons are indeed themselves responsible for certain instances of inequality resulting from their own voluntary decisions, and – apart from minimal provision in an emergency (Gosepath, 2004, V.1.5) – they do not deserve compensation. Individuals can reasonably be held responsible for the choices that determine their potential positions in the social hierarchy only if the social arrangements in society, like the educational system, are endowment-insensitive and ambition-sensitive (Dworkin, 2000). According to the luck-egalitarian position, pure equal opportunity is insufficient because it does not compensate for unequal innate gifts. What applies for social circumstances should also apply for such gifts, both of these factors being purely arbitrary from a moral point of view and requiring adjustment. In the educational field, this means, according to Brighouse Swift (2014a, p. 17): "An individual's prospects for educational achievement may be a function of that individual's effort, but it should not be influenced by her social class or her level of talent."

If one accepts the argument of the moral arbitrariness of talents, the commonly accepted criteria for merit (like productivity, working hours, or effort) are clearly relativized. Motivation or effort that students show could possibly themselves be explained by their social background and natural talents; that is, by factors for which students cannot properly be held responsible (Brighouse & Swift, 2014a, p. 17). This might be seen as (highly) problematic. Objections to all versions of "brute-luck egalitarianism" come from two sides. Some authors criticize its, in their view, unjustified or excessively radical rejection of merit: the egalitarian thesis of desert only being justifiably acknowledged if it involves desert "all the way down" (Nozick, 1974, p. 225) not only destroys the classical, everyday principle of desert, since everything has a basis that we ourselves have not created. If society, with its educational system, would remedy inequalities in students' efforts, this would effectively amount to seeking equal educational achievements for all students and undermine the idea of equal educational opportunity by decoupling students' educational achievements from their choices (Brighouse & Swift, 2014a, p. 18). In the eyes of some critics, along with the merit principle, this argument also destroys our personal identity, since we can no longer accredit ourselves with our own capacities and accomplishments (Pojman & McLeod, 1998; Olsaretti, 2003). In addition, students' prospects for educational achievement should not depend on the level of motivation that they display, given that, at least young students have not yet fully developed the capacity for responsible agency (Stojanov, 2016).

16.6.4 A Prioritarian Conception of Educational Justice

Against an educational analogue of Rawls' fair equality of opportunity, the harming-the-less-advantaged objection suggests an educational analogue of the difference principle. As Harry Frankfurt puts it: "The fundamental error of egalitarianism lies in supposing that it is morally important whether one person has less than another regardless of how much either of them has" (Frankfurt, 1987, p. 34). Parfit distinguishes between egalitarianism and prioritarianism. Parfit's (1997) priority view calls for focus on improving the situation of society's weaker and poorer members and, indeed, all the more urgently the worse off they are, even if they can be less helped than others in the process. According to prioritarians, benefiting people is more important the worse off those people are. This prioritizing will often increase equality, but they are two distinct values, since in an important respect, equality is a relational value while priority is not. However, egalitarians and prioritarians share an important feature in that both hold that the best possible distribution of a fixed sum of goods is an equal one. It is thus a matter of debate whether prioritarianism is a sort of egalitarianism or a (decent) inegalitarianism.

Schouten (2012) has argued for such a prioritarian principle in school education. Reforms should be designed to prioritize to a very great extent the prospects for flourishing of those whose prospects are worse. For the most part, in practice and in our social environment, this will require reforms that improve educational provision for the less academically successful; but it also helps explain why investment in those who are more successful is not unimportant. In particular, severely cognitively disabled children, at a certain point, may benefit more from marginal resources in people who will become carers and developers of new, life-enhancing technologies.

One crucial problem is that unequal academic achievement generally begets unequal life prospects in a highly stratified society like ours. If academic achievement, financial rewards and positions and life prospects were decoupled in a society, egalitarians would be much less troubled by unequal academic performance due to natural differences. But if one has to take that link as given, what does justice require in this nonideal situation? According to Schouten, justice does not require the mitigation of the natural talents' effect on academic performance. The problem, from the viewpoint of justice, is rather that society highly rewards academic success in terms of economic and wealth prospects so that the naturally less talented students are likely to enjoy lives that are less flourishing than those of their peers who are naturally more talented. Therefore, according to Schouten (2012, p. 479): "We can understand our prioritarian obligation to naturally disadvantaged students as an obligation to benefit them generally, where that benefit may take the form of a direct investment in their future prospects that bypasses the mechanism of improved academic outcomes." As one can see, this brings one back to question the spheres of educational justice; namely, do they entail just the school system or society and its distribution of life prospects as a whole? As Schouten (2012, p. 487) sees it: "The ultimate goal of education is not to impart some narrowly defined academic skills or knowledge; rather, it is to enable students to lead good lives. Academic skills and knowledge are merely vehicles by which the ultimate goal is conventionally attained." Another question about prioritarian views such as this is always whether the prioritarian principle (here, of educational justice) should only supplement or substitute the principle of fair (educational) opportunity and what would be more plausible from the viewpoint of justice. Not harming the less advantaged may be seen as a more urgent and weighty principle than educational equality, but, as Schouten acknowledges, that does not mean educational equality does not matter.

16.6.5 Democratic Adequacy as a Conception of Educational Justice

There is an alternative conception of educational justice which states that all citizens have a right to a democratically adequate education. This principle should ensure not that children have equal educational resources, opportunities, or prospects, but rather that everyone is educated well enough so that they can meet all others as equals, or peers, in the public domain. Everyone should receive an education adequate for them to do or be X. Versions of the adequacy principle differ in their specification of X (Brighouse & Swift, 2014a, p. 27). X can be the adequacy of functioning in the economy (Tooley, 1996) or individual, social, and democratic life, etc. The two prominent versions, those by Anderson (2007, 2010) and Satz (2007), define adequacy in terms of the education needed to develop the capabilities to function as a peer in public social interactions. Their view goes back to Dewey, ([1916] 1980), who already defends the importance of schooling for creating democratic subjects. Gutmann (1987) also ties adequacy to the developed capacity to participate as an equal in political life and the capability to function effectively in the political decision-making process.

Anderson's and Satz' views are based on their rejection of the principles of fair and luck-egalitarian equality of educational opportunity. Anderson (1999) has instead endorsed generally a principle of sufficiency as the core commitment of a theory of social justice, which is in turn grounded in a very extensive critique of equality as a general principle of justice. Anderson forcefully argued against thinking of equality as an essentially distributive value; that is, as a matter of what pattern of distribution qualifies as an equal one. On the alternative model, which she and others favor, equality is understood in terms of an ideal society in which persons relate to one another as having the status of equals. Instead of being a matter of identifying a "currency" to be equalized, (Cohen, 1989) equality should be, "a matter of how people regard one another and how they conduct their social relations" (Miller, 1997, p. 224). The latter view has become known today largely as the relational egalitarian position (Schemmel, 2021), although Anderson (1999, 2007) herself calls it democratic equality, and others, social equality (Fourie et al., 2015). The point of social/relational equality is to avoid injustices (following Young, 1990) such as marginalization (i.e., having no access to useful social participation), powerlessness (i.e., having access only to social roles that excessively restrict autonomy), cultural imperialism (i.e., having one's culture rendered invisible or represented by derogatory stereotypes), or domination (i.e., subjection to arbitrary power; Pettit, 1997). The view holds that the eradication of certain pernicious social hierarchies, such as those of domination, status, and caste is a key demand of justice (see Anderson, 1999; Fourie et al., 2015; Schemmel, 2021). For example, we may have egalitarian duties to eliminate systemic racism by restructuring our culture and institutions, or even to eliminate social class by severely restricting the intergenerational transmission of economic inequality and educational advantage. In this light, Anderson (2010) has further expanded her analysis of social integration with particular emphasis on racial discrimination in the United States. She therefore advocates an integrationist conception of democratic education and citizenship, which emphasizes "cooperation and communication across group lines, for the purposes of forging shared norms and goals of the democratic polity as a whole and to that extent forging a shared identity of citizens" (Anderson, 2010, p. 110). Democratic or relational equality also requires the development of certain social conditions and personal skills that enable people to assume an equal position in society. For example, citizens need adequate food, shelter, clothing, education, and medical care. Thus, although relational equality focuses primarily or sometimes exclusively on just social relations and not on the distribution of goods per se, it may also provide intrinsic and instrumental reasons of justice to care about more distributive equality in socially produced goods (Schemmel, 2011).

Besides their general objections against equality, Satz and Anderson also provide specific critiques of the conception of equal educational opportunity. They argue that realizing equal educational opportunity would result in a natural aristocracy, since the naturally most talented would enjoy the greatest chances of success (Satz, 2007, p. 630). In addition, the conception of equal educational opportunity would prohibit inequality of educational opportunity even if such inequality benefited the least well off. This is the so-called leveling down objection (Nozick, 1974, p. 229; Raz, 1986, ch. 9, pp. 227, 235; Temkin, 1993, pp. 247–48). Sometimes inequality can only be ended by depriving those who are better off of their resources, rendering them as poorly off as everyone else. But would it be morally good if, for example, in a group consisting of both blind and seeing persons, those with sight were rendered blind because the blind could not be offered sight? That would, in fact, be morally perverse. Doing away with inequality by bringing everyone down contains – thus, the generally accepted objection – nothing good. Such leveling down objections would of course only be valid if there were no better and equally egalitarian alternatives available; and nearly always, there are such. More concretely, to avoid the leveling down objection, one would have to allow inequality of educational opportunity with the aim of higher productivity and output from those with more educational opportunities, if those who have become more productive would share these additional resources with the least well off (Kotzee, 2013). Defenders of equality of opportunity in education are most likely pluralist, accepting more than one principle of justice. They might accept the prioritarian view that benefiting someone matters more the less well-off that person is (Brighouse & Swift 2009; 2014a) and thus avoid the leveling down objection.

In addition, Anderson (2004, p. 104) and Satz (2007, pp. 633–34) point out that their conception of democratic educational adequacy is compatible with parental educational liberty. It allows differential parental educational investments that entail unequal educational opportunity among equally talented and motivated students as long as all students meet the threshold of a democratically adequate education. Fair or luck-egalitarian equality of educational opportunity would, however, in their view violate parental educational liberty. Parental liberty and its possible infringement for the sake of equality of opportunity is a controversial point in the educational debate. One needs an account of what can be considered as legitimate partiality and what cannot. Where should the boundary be between where the state should respect parent–child interactions that generate unfairness and where it need not? Based on their account of familial goods, Brighouse and Swift (2014b) argue that the exercise of parental partiality is unjustified if it violates equal educational opportunity and if it is not essential for realizing the value of the family.

Anderson and Satz want to derive the nature and content of educational adequacy from the requirements for full membership and inclusion in a democratic society of equal citizens (Satz, 2007, p. 636). One problem is of course the indeterminacy of this criterion. Another, in the eyes of the critics, is that it is – even through a very demanding understanding of it – not enough. This has to do with the sufficientarian view underlying the conception. The doctrine of sufficiency says "What is important from the moral point of view is not that everyone should have *the same* but that each should have *enough*. If everyone had enough, it would be of no moral consequence whether some had more than others" (Frankfurt, 1987, p. 21). Suppose that all children in a given society have an adequate, that is, sufficient, education. No matter how high the standard of adequacy may be, there still remains the question of what to do with resources and opportunities that may be left once the adequacy standard is met. Should their distribution be left to chance, the market, parental partiality, or the "right of the strongest"? The principle of adequacy makes no comment at all on this. "Sufficientarian principles do not constrain inequalities in educational access above the sufficiency threshold" (Anderson, 2007, p. 615). The possible high inequality above the threshold and the privileging of the talented and well educated seems counterintuitive to more egalitarian leaning persons.

There is a possible solution to this problem; namely, again, pluralism, that is, allowing other principles of justice as well. Just as other principles of justice can be invoked to rescue equality of opportunity conceptions against the leveling down objection, so can adequacy theorists rely on additional principles of justice to make their case more plausible. Some philosophers have suggested that the two conceptions of educational justice could also be viewed as complementary. Reich (2013) makes this proposal with a division of spheres in mind: he proposes that equality should be regarded as the appropriate ideal for regulating the private benefits that students derive from education, whereas adequacy is the appropriate ideal for regulating the education that students should receive in order to maintain democratic relationships. Culp (2019, ch. 3; 2020a) suggests prioritizing democratically adequate education whenever this is necessary to achieve a democratic order and to leave it to the democratic process to decide upon the relative importance of further principles of educational justice, such as fair or luck-egalitarian educational opportunity or parental educational liberty.

16.7 Conclusion

As we have seen, more general theories of justice such as luck-egalitarianism, prioritarianism, and sufficientarianism (Gosepath, 2021) tend to inform the more specific conceptions of educational justice (Culp, 2020b). The question remains whether a full theory of educational justice will not be pluralist and, as such, recognize several values. Thus, it would most likely acknowledge the importance of familial life, embody appropriate concern for the prospects of the less advantaged, accept the urgency of ensuring that all have adequate educations in unjust circumstances, and incorporate a principle of educational equality of opportunity (Brighouse & Swift, 2014a, p. 30).

References

Anderson, E. (1999). What is the point of equality? *Ethics*, 109, 287–337.

Anderson, E. (2004). Rethinking equality of opportunity: Comment on Adam Swift's how not to be a hypocrite. *Theory and Research in Education*, 2(2), 99–110.

Anderson, E. (2007). Fair opportunity in education: A democratic equality perspective. *Ethics*, 117(4), 595–622.

Anderson, E. (2010). *The imperative of education*. Princeton, NJ: Princeton University Press.

Arneson, R. (1989). Equality and equal opportunity for welfare. *Philosophical Studies*, 56, 77–93.

Brighouse, H. (2000). *School choice and social justice*. Oxford: Oxford University Press.

Brighouse, H., & Swift, A. (2009). Educational equality versus educational adequacy: A critique of Anderson and Satz. *Journal of Applied Philosophy*, 26(2), 117–28.

Brighouse, H., & Swift, A. (2014a). The place of educational equality in educational justice. In K. Meyer, ed., *Education, justice and the human good. Fairness and equality in the educational system*. London: Routledge, 14–33.

Brighouse, H., & Swift, A. (2014b). *Family values*. Princeton, NJ: Princeton University Press.

Cohen, G. A. (1989). On the currency of egalitarian justice. *Ethics*, 99, 906–44.

Culp, J. (2019). *Democratic education in a globalized world. A normative theory*. London: Routledge.

Culp, J. (2020a). Bildung und Gerechtigkeit. *Zeitschrift für philosophische Forschung*, 74(2), 296–309.

Culp, J. (2020b). Educational justice. *Philosophy Compass*. e12713. https://doi.org/10.1111/phc3.12713.

Dewey, J. ([1916/1980). Democracy and Education. In J. A. Boydston, ed., *The Middle Works, 1899–1924, vol. 9 of the collected works of John Dewey*. Carbondale: Southern Illinois University Press, pp. 1882–953.

Dworkin, R. (2000). *Sovereign virtue. The theory and practice of equality*. Cambridge, MA: Harvard University Press.

Fishkin, J. (1983). *Justice, equal opportunity, and the family*. New Haven, CT: Yale University Press.

Fourie, C., Schuppert, F., & Wallimann-Helmer, I. (Eds.) (2015). *Social equality: On what it means to be equals*. New York: Oxford University Press.

Frankfurt, H. (1987). Equality as a moral ideal. *Ethics* 98, 21–42.

Gosepath, S. (2004). *Gleiche Gerechtigkeit*. Frankfurt: Suhrkamp.

Gosepath, S. (2014). What exactly does equality in education mean? In K. Meyer, ed., *Education, justice, and the human good. Fairness and equality in the education system*. Oxford/New York: Routledge, pp. 100–12.

Gosepath, S. (2015). The principles and the presumption of equality. In C. Fourie, F. Schuppert,, I. Wallimann-Helmer, (eds.), *Social equality: On what it means to be equals*, Oxford: Oxford University Press, pp. 167–85.

Gosepath, S. (2021). Equality. *The Stanford encyclopedia of philosophy*. Edward N. Zalta, ed., https://plato.stanford.edu/entries/equality.

Gutmann, A. (1987). *Democratic education*. Princeton, NJ: Princeton University Press.

Jencks, C. (1988). Whom must we treat equally for educational opportunity to be equal? *Ethics*, 98, 518–33.

Kotzee, B. (2013). Educational justice, epistemic justice, and leveling down. *Educational Theory*, 63(4), 331–49.

Lippert-Rassmussen, K. (2013). *Born free and equal? A philosophical inquiry into the nature of discrimination*. Oxford: Oxford University Press.

Meyer, K. (2009). *Bildung*. Berlin: de Gruyter

Miller, D. (1997). Equality and justice. *Ratio*, 10, 222–37.

Nozick, R. (1974). *Anarchy, state, and utopia*. New York: Basic Books.

Nussbaum, M. (1992). Human functioning and social justice. In defense of Aristotelian essentialism. *Political Theory*, 20, 202–46.

Nussbaum, M. (2000). *Women and human development: The capabilities approach*. Cambridge: Cambridge University Press.

Olsaretti, S. (ed.) (2003). *Desert and justice*. Oxford: Clarendon Press.

Parfit, D. (1997). Equality and priority. *Ratio*, 10, 202–21.

Pettit, P. (1997). *Republicanism: A theory of freedom and government*. Oxford: Clarendon Press.

Plato. (380 BCE/ 1991). *The Republic*. 2nd ed., New York: Basic Books.

Pojman, L. P. & McLeod, O. (eds.) (1998). *What do we deserve? A reader on justice and desert*. Oxford: Oxford University Press.

Rakowski, E. (1991). *Equal justice*. Oxford: Clarendon Press.

Rawls, J. (1999). *A theory of justice*. 2nd rev. ed., Cambridge, MA: Harvard University Press.

Raz, J. (1986). *The Morality of Freedom*. Oxford: Oxford University Press.

Reich, R. (2013). Equality, adequacy, and K-12 education. In D. Allen and R. Reich, eds., *Education, justice and democracy*. Chicago, IL: University of Chicago Press, pp. 43–61.

Satz, D. (2007). Equality, adequacy, and education for citizenship. *Ethics*, 117, 623–48.

Schemmel, C. (2011). Why relational egalitarians should care about distributions. *Social Theory and Practice*, 37, 365–90.

Schemmel, C. (2021). *Justice and egalitarian relations*. New York: Oxford University Press.

Schleiermacher, F. (2000). Grundzüge der Erziehungskunst (Vorlesung 1826). In M. Winkler and J. Brachmann, eds., *Schleiermacher, Texte zur Pädagogik. Kommentierte Studienausgabe Bd. 2*. Frankfurt am Main: Suhrkamp.

Schouten, G. (2012). Fair educational opportunity and the distribution of natural ability: Toward a prioritarian principle of educational justice. *Journal of Philosophy of Education*. 46(3), 472–91.

Stojanov, K. (2016). Social justice and education as discursive initiation. *Educational Theory*, 66(6), 755–67.

Temkin, L. (1993). *Inequality*. Oxford: Oxford University Press.

Tooley, J. (1996). *Education without the state*. London: IEA

Walzer, M. (1983). *Spheres of justice. A defence of pluralism and equality*. New York: Basic Books.

Williams, B. (1973). *Problems of the self. Philosophical papers 1956–1972*. Cambridge: Cambridge University Press.

Young, I. M. (1990). *Justice and the politics of difference*. Princeton, NJ: Princeton University Press.

17

Global Justice and Democratic Education

Krassimir Stojanov

17.1 Introduction

During the last two decades or so, we have been witnessing a vivid and fairly controversial discourse on global justice in political theory and philosophy. Within it, we can distinguish between two main parties, which stand in strong opposition to each other. We can call the first one the "cosmopolitan" party. I would like to label the second party as the one of "state-centered nationalism" (which is to be distinguished from "ethnic nationalism" or "nativism"). While most proponents of both parties agree that all individuals should have equal basic human rights regardless of their citizenship, they disagree about whether or not the state should privilege its citizens over noncitizens in the distribution of socioeconomic goods and opportunities, or whether inequalities between citizens and noncitizens are unjust, in the same way as inequalities among citizens are. Of course, this does not mean that there are not authors who takes a mid-stance between the parties of the "cosmopolitans" and the "statists."[1] But it is the opposition between both parties which determines the structure, that is to say, the coordinate system of the discourse on global justice.

It is remarkable, that up to now this controversy has only rarely and rather superficially touched upon education in general and educational justice in particular.[2] One reason for that could be the fact that, unlike economic

[1] A good example of an attempt to take a mid-stand between both parties is David Miller's "political philosophy of immigration" in which he combines a "weak cosmopolitanism" with "national self-determination." While the former requires respecting the human rights of immigrants and giving them reasons for decisions that concern them, the latter ascribes a right to domestic citizens to decide which and how many immigrants their country should admit and how the immigrants should integrate in the country (Miller, 2018, pp. 213f.). Yet Miller's self-description of his position as "communitarian" indicates that in fact it is much closer to the statist party than to the cosmopolitan one (Miller, 2018, p. 161).

[2] To be sure, a quite intensive and elaborate debate on the content and the scope of the right to education as a (universal) human right that is spelled out in international conventions such as the International Covenant on Economic, Social and Cultural Rights (ICESCR), is in place in international law studies and in legal theory (see Coomans, 2007 for a good overview of this debate). However, the debate remains largely detached from the *philosophical* discourse on educational justice in domestic and global contexts. More importantly, the legal debate barely addresses the question as to whether (and to what extent) the human right to education (as well as further socioeconomic rights) allows states to allocate different educational resources and opportunities to citizens and noncitizens (see Coomans, 2007, pp. 203–7). I believe that this is a genuine

enterprises, institutionalized education takes place almost exclusively within nation-states.[3] There is no significant distribution of educational goods and opportunities besides nation-states: there are only a few supranational educational organizations, and their contribution to the production and distribution of educational goods is rather marginal.

However, even at the level of national educational systems the question of the justifiability of an unequal treatment of citizens and noncitizens occurs – and it occurs here mostly as a question of whether (and, if yes, under which conditions) educational inequalities between autochthone and immigrant children could be justified. In other words, the question here is which – if any – educational inequalities between both groups of children due to their different nationalities are morally legitimate, and which inequalities are definitely unjust?

In the following sections, I try to find a convincing answer to that question. In Section 17.2, I briefly recapitulate the controversy between the cosmopolitan and the state-nationalist approaches. I focus on the topic of assumed special obligations we supposedly have to our fellow citizens; a topic that is at the heart of that controversy. In Section 17.3 I elaborate on the question of whether such special obligations to a privileged treatment of cocitizens over noncitizens apply to institutionalized education. At the end of that section I make the claim that the answer to that question depends on how we understand education – whether we spell it out as a traditionalist-authoritarian, or as democratic social practice. In Section 17.4, I argue that democratic education necessarily implies moral universalism. It implies not only the recognition of the equal moral status of all students, but also the inclusion of their individual experiences, worldviews, and ideals, regardless of their nationalities, or ethnic or cultural backgrounds, in an open and diverse-friendly ethical discourse that should be established in every classroom. This inclusion is a matter of social esteem, which together with further recognition forms of moral respect and empathy builds up the core not only of a democratic, but also of a just education. In the concluding section, I argue that since the latter is necessarily cosmopolitan in its essence, it should also be institutionalized (and perhaps primarily) at a supranational level. However, this appears to be a demand for the not-so-near future.

philosophical question, insofar as its answer depends on how one determines the basic principles of distributive and relational justice.

[3] As Julian Culp states, philosophical extrapolations on educational justice have an overwhelmingly domestic focus. These discussions are in most cases restricted to the question of which rights to education cocitizens of a nation-state should ascribe to each other; they largely neglect the educational challenges of globalization and transnational migration (Culp, 2020, pp.9f; 2022) Culp himself significantly contributed to overcoming that deficit by developing a profound theory of "global democratic educational justice" (Culp, 2019, esp. pp. 54–86). While Culp's conception of global educational justices aims mostly at the determination of global educational adequacy that consists in the enabling of all students to partake in transnational political discourses, in this chapter I firstly address a different question, namely, whether ascribing unequal educational resources and opportunities to citizens or noncitizens should be rendered unjust (and under which conditions). In my view, this question remains open (and morally urgent), even if we assume that all students (citizens and noncitizens) reach the threshold of (global) democratic participation.

17.2 The Controversy over Global Justice

With Thomas Pogge, we can state that global justice means that all persons should be subjected to the same moral principles and fundamental moral norms. These principles and norms do not allow *arbitrarily* to privilege or disadvantage some persons or groups in the assignment of rights, claims or duties, or in the distribution of goods and recourses (Pogge, 2008, pp. 359–62).

This account of global justice does not imply that the privileged treatment of certain persons or groups is always morally wrong. For example, it is not morally wrong, but rather a special moral obligation, to care for the needs of our own children to an extent that we could not afford for other children, and to support the development of our children in particular ways that we, as parents, apply only to them. Analogically, a state surely has some particular obligations with regard to the wellbeing of its citizens.

The point of global justice is, however, that the privileging or disadvantaging of persons or groups should itself be justified by moral principles that themselves claim universal validity. This demand for moral justification is at odds with what Pogge calls "dogmatic contextualism" which characterizes the usual way in which citizens of Western countries rationalize the huge inequalities in the global economic order and the life-threatening poverty in many non-Western countries that are parts of that order (Pogge, 2008, p. 370). "Dogmatic contextualism" means to restrict the validity of fundamental moral principles only to "our (Western) culture" and to postulate that offenses against them are not morally inacceptable in other cultural contexts. It is dogmatic, because the postulation of a cultural-contextualist determination of moral norms is normally not subject to argumentation – and, strictly speaking, it cannot be such a subject for the simple reason that the culturalist worldview also denies universal or transcontextual standards of argumentation. Thus, moral norms are taken as self-evident within a cultural context, and not as a matter of deliberations or disputes.

Dogmatic contextualism helps the citizens of rich countries to avoid having a bad conscience with respect to citizens of poor countries, since it ascribes a different moral status of inequalities "at home" and "abroad." While most former citizens would renounce extreme inequalities between the rich and the poor in their home country immoral, they easily justify the fact that their incomes are several times higher than those of the inhabitants of the so-called Global South (as well as the fact that many of the latter suffer life-threatening poverty), by referring to supposed "cultural differences." These are postulated not only as reasons for international socioeconomic inequalities, but also as something that would make extreme poverty allegedly more acceptable in the context of the Global South, or of the Third World. In a similar, culturalist manner, many Western politicians tolerate or even support violations of human rights in Latin American or Asian countries, or institutional corruption in Africa or in Eastern Europe; violations and corruption that they find morally inacceptable in their home countries. These politicians postulate, at least implicitly, that the validity of human rights and the moral wrongness of corruption are given only in the Western cultural context and do not apply in the South or in the East. Thus, they do not need to feel guilty when they tolerate or support despotic or corrupt regimes, and when they show no solidarity with human rights or anticorruption activists within these regimes, who are repressed by these regimes.

However, there are also more sophisticated attempts to justify the different moral status of socioeconomic inequalities as well as the different validity of moral norms at home and abroad; attempts that do not necessarily resort to the dogmatic contextualism. Thomas Nagel offers a detailed argument for his claim that certain moral norms could be valid only within the framework of the nation-state – regardless of its particular cultural context (Nagel, 2008). This applies, according to Nagel, even to Rawls' fundamental principles of justice, that is, the equal liberties principle, the principle of equality of opportunities, and the so-called difference principle, which ultimately demands a distribution of socioeconomic goods in favor of the least advantaged (Nagel, 2008, pp. 421–23; see also Rawls, 1999, pp. 65, 266). For Nagel the equality of opportunities principle and the difference principle regulate exclusively what he calls "associative obligations," which exists only within separate nation-states (Nagel, 2008, p. 421). According to Nagel, only persons who share a common set of institutions and rules to which they are on one hand subjected, but which on the other hand depend upon their agreement and which can be democratically changed by them, should have equal liberties and opportunities – and only within that set of institutions and rules (see (Nagel, 2008, p. 425).

This applies, says Nagel, in particular to socioeconomic justice. It "[d]epends on positive rights that we do not have against all other persons or groups, rights that arise only because we are joined together with certain others in a political society under strong centralized control. It is only from such a system, and from our fellow members through its institutions, that we can claim a right to democracy, equal citizenship, nondiscrimination, equality of opportunity, and the amelioration through public policy of unfairness in the distribution of social and economic goods" (Nagel, 2008, p. 424). In other words, the principles of justice and especially of equality of rights and opportunities arise from a structure in which "we are both putative joint authors of the coercively imposed system, and subject to its norms" (Nagel, 2008, p. 425). Accordingly, these principles are restricted to a social "system" that coercively enforces norms, which at the same time should be eligible to be freely accepted by those who are subjected to the norms, even when they run against personal preferences of some members of the system (even of the majority of them) (see Nagel, 2008, p. 425). Under the current conditions, only the nation-state is such a system that can impose norms – and this only on its citizens who are its "putative joint authors."

The point of Nagel's argument is that moral principles (at least the Rawlsian ones) are meant to evaluate and legitimize the fairness of governmental measures, which impose the redistribution of goods and equality of positive (socioeconomic) rights, and which might be at odds with the individual interests of some members of the society – especially those of the wealthier ones. Without the existence of governmental institutions that have the power to enforce such measures, those principles are meaningless. Since such institutions do not yet exist at the global level, the principles in question apply only to the nation-state and its citizens.

From that perspective, the equality of liberties and the fair equality of opportunities are not necessarily moral demands for the treatment of immigrants, as long as they do not possess the citizenship of the "guest-country", that is, as long as they do not have the "status of putative joint authors" of the norms which the state imposes. Common practices in several Western and non-Western countries of restricting the access of immigrants to the labor market or to social benefits, as well as of privileging a country's citizens over immigrants in the employment of candidates for attractive offices seem to be fully in accord with the state-nationalist understanding of justice.

But what about discriminations between domestic citizens and immigrants with regard to school education? Do they have the same moral status as these discriminations in the labor market, or in social policy? It is remarkable that up to now this question has been barely discussed in the controversy over global justice: even authors like David Miller (Miller, 2018), who explicitly write on the ethics of immigration, do not systematically elaborate on whether unequal treatment of immigrants in education could be justified in the same way as their unequal access to other social, economic, and cultural rights.[4]

17.3 Are Educational Inequalities Due to Citizenship and Origin Unjust?

I believe that most of us would share the intuition that discrimination between citizens and immigrants in education cannot be morally justified – even if one might otherwise hold that discrimination in the labor market or in social policy is legitimate. In other words, even the proponents of the statist account of justice might find it problematic when immigrant children receive fewer educational resources and opportunities than the children of the domestic citizens.

Why is this? Regardless of their citizenship status, children in general cannot be seen as putative authors of the norms and rules of the given state – and they are only partly subjected to the state enforcement of these norms. The purpose of school education is rather to *develop* the abilities of the children to function as coauthors of society`s norms and to take responsibility in cases where they violate the norms. Both domestic and (most) immigrant children are equal in that that they are prospective citizens of the state in which they grow up and

[4] Miller's rather fragmented remarks on education in *his Strangers in Our Midst* spell out education of immigrants almost exclusively in terms of preparation for citizenship; the remarks barely address education as a *practice of social relations*, in which immigrants often experience institutional discrimination (see Miller, 2018, pp.127f., 136f.)

On the other hand, authors who tends to the cosmopolitan party, for example, Lindsey Schwartz, ascribe on one hand a duty to democratic states to bring immigrant students to a threshold of educational adequacy that is needed for political participation. But on the other hand, they largely leave the question aside about the moral legitimacy of educational inequalities above the threshold between domestic and immigrant students (Schwartz, 2020, pp. 83 f.)

therefore should have equal access to education and equal educational opportunities. This is so even from the state-nationalist perspective.

However, from that perspective two complications occur. First, only the children of immigrants with settled long-term legal status can be seen as prospective citizens of the state in which they live. So, what about the children of undocumented immigrants, or of asylum-seekers, who probably will be forced to leave the country after a limited period of time?

Second, educational equality is not only (and perhaps not primarily) about distribution of recourses and goods, but also about an equal treatment of the students themselves by the teachers and by the school curricula. If all students are to be prepared for the citizenship of the country, in which they go to school, it appears from the statist perspective that they should be initiated by the teachers and the curriculum in the dominant culture and way of life in that country. The other side of that demand is that schools might ignore the alternative beliefs and life-experiences of immigrant children and that, because of their origin, they could generally be seen as "alien" to the dominant culture, and therefore less educable than the domestic children. In addition, normally, schoolteachers are representatives of the sociocultural majority. Thus, it might be more difficult for them to understand and to care for the experiences, the worldviews, the interests, and the specific problems of immigrant children as they can for the children from domestic middle-class families.

With regard to the first point, we should note that several countries, in fact, firmly restrict the access to education of children of supposedly temporary immigrants such as refugees and asylum seekers who have no realistic prospects of receiving permanent immigrant status. For example, in Germany these refugees and asylum seekers are gathered in specific camps (the so called Anker-centers) with no access to the regular school system. Instead, the children receive only very limited and basic classes in the camps themselves. The education that the children receive in the camps is by no means comparable with that of the public schools and it is far below the quantitative and qualitative standards of school education in Germany (see Mittler, 2018).

From the perspective of the state-nationalist position, this kind of educational segregation might appear morally justified, since the children concerned will probably never become citizens of the country in which they recently started to live. However, these children should still be prepared for political and social participation and for active citizenship – regardless of whether this participation and this citizenship are expected to take place in the country in which they currently live, or in some other country.[5] Being enabled to participate in a political community is a precondition for the exercising of one's rights, because this exercising is barely possible without membership of such a community, or without active citizenship. In this sense, the right to education is a kind of "metaright"; in any case, it is a fundamental human right. Even according to the

[5] In a similar vein, Culp (2019) argues for a global scope of the fundamental rights to "democratically adequate education" that should enable citizens to partake in domestic and international political discourses, which shape the processes of decision-making (p. 77).

proponents, like Nagel, of the statist view on justice, fundamental human rights have an equal validity for all persons, regardless of their nationality or ethnic origins (see Nagel, 2008, pp. 426–27). Hence, all infants have an equal right to education, whatever their citizenship or immigration status. Granting equal access to education is independent of the question of how socioeconomic goods and positions of state should be distributed among citizens and noncitizens. Rather, it is a fundamental human right.

However, it is far from clear what the right to equal education actually means. With regard to the point of complication concerning the notion of educational equality, one might doubt that educational equality could be reduced to an equal access to a curriculum that mirrors the dominant culture and way of life of the country, thus neglecting particular worldviews and beliefs of immigrant groups and other minorities. In this case, the children who are born into this dominant culture, and raised within it, would be educationally privileged over the ones who are not. For the former children, it will be easier to internalize the contents of that curriculum, while the latter would appear as having a quasi-natural distance to education caused by their birth into a family outside the sociocultural mainstream. This would lead to a stigmatization of immigrant children as being capable to reach only the lower, nonacademic levels of the educational system.

To understand why granting equal access to the school curriculum (and distributing resources in a way that will enable this access for all children) is not the whole story about educational justice; a distinction introduced by Rainer Forst between two different pictures of justice is helpful. According to the first picture, individuals are passive recipients of goods that are distributed to them by state institutions. The question here is who gets what, and whether or not what she gets is fair or justified with regard to what the others get, or with regard to her essential needs (Forst, 2014, p. 4). In contrast, according to the second picture of justice, it is not about the passive receiving of goods from the state, but about the intersubjective (power) relations and structures, within which the production of the goods takes place. The key issue of justice here is not "[w]hat you have but how you are treated" in those relations and structures (Forst, 2014, p. 6).

From this perspective immigrant students are treated unjustly when their beliefs, worldviews, and biographical experiences count less than those of their domestic counterparts in the classroom, or when no epistemic worth and educational relevance is given to these beliefs, worldviews, and experiences. In this case, immigrant children are subjected to what Miranda Fricker calls "epistemic injustice" (see Fricker, 2007). It occurs when less credibility is given to the (potential) knowledge, as well as to the beliefs and experiences to certain groups of persons (for example, immigrant children) due to their ethnic, social, or cultural origins, or when these beliefs and experiences are not included in the processes of production of publicly validated knowledge.[6]

[6] I discuss the concept of epistemic injustice and its implications for institutionalized education in greater length in Stojanov, 2018a, pp. 42–43.

However, a proponent of the state-nationalist view on justice might argue that children's initiation in the dominant culture of the country in which they live, that is, in its founding traditions, in its values and customs, is crucial for the preparation for citizenship; a preparation that is the main task of school education. Given the limited time school education has at its disposal, it should focus, according to this view, on that dominant culture, and it ought to put to one side the alternative cultural traditions and beliefs of immigrants. Even immigrant children who are not supposed to remain in the country might greatly benefit from their initiation in its national culture, because through it they could grasp how the citizenship in a state is culturally founded. If the price for that initiation is some forms of epistemic injustice – so the proponent of the state-nationalist view might argue – this price is worth paying, as citizenship is the precondition for equality.

However, one can question whether a state is necessarily grounded in a dominant national culture, and whether one's effective citizenship in the state presupposes one's initiation in that culture. This is particularly disputable with regard to liberal-democratic states, since liberal democracy is characterized by a cultural pluralism and by individuals' right to commit to any kind of religions and worldviews they might find true or attractive. The social cohesion of the modern liberal-democratic state is not granted by common beliefs and values that originate from a shared tradition, but by institutionalized procedures and principles for cooperative decision-making and consent-finding between actors who might have very different values, cultural identities, and interests.[7] As I have argued elsewhere, participation in the processes of democratic decision-making and consent-finding requires one's initiation in pluralistically structured practices of discursive deliberation – and not in a particular cultural canon (see Stojanov, 2010, pp. 168–70).

This discursive initiation is the main task of democratic education. As I will argue in Section 17.4, it implies moral universalism, which is the founding principle of global justice.

17.4 Moral Universalism as Core Dimension of Democratic Education

It is worth noting that John Dewey's conception of democratic education, which he presented in his *Democracy and Education* more than a century ago, still remains the most influential one in the field. This conception starts from the assumption that democracy is not only (and not primarily) a system of government, but rather a form of social life, "[a] mode of associated living, of conjoint communicated experience" (Dewey, 1916, p. 101). This lifeform is distinguished by the "[b]reaking down of those barriers of class, race, and national territory which kept men [sic] from perceiving the full import of their activity" (Dewey, 1916, p. 101). In other words, democracy means a diversity of individual

[7] I refer here, of course, to Jürgen Habermas' conception of discourse ethics whose principles correlate with and at the same times make possible liberal democracy (see Habermas, 1991, p. 12; Habermas, 1992, pp. 15–32).

experiences, which the actors communicate to each other in ways that mutually enable their personal growth, that is, the permanent enrichment of their activities and their relations to the world and to their own selves. As is well known, for Dewey education *is* personal growth, and thus education flourishes at best in a democratic lifeform. On the other hand, democratic education anticipates that lifeform, and so enables the students actively to participate in it.

The democratic-educative ways of communicating individual experiences in their diversity is incompatible with what Dewey calls "subordination" of the individuals to a state that is meant to be grounded in an institutionalized "organic" culture (Dewey, 1916, p. 110). Instead, democratic education is genealogically linked to a Kantian "individualistic cosmopolitanism" (Dewey, 1916, p. 111), which, however, must be spelled out in terms of educational institutions and social interactions that take place within them (see Dewey, 1916, pp. 113, 116). The educational "individualistic cosmopolitanism" means that, first, the primary goal of education is the unlimited growth of the abilities of the individual, and especially of her abilities to rational self-determination, and second, that this growth presupposes that the individual develops as member of the universal community of the whole humanity – and not of a particular state (Dewey, 1916, p. 111). In other words, institutionalized education, especially schooling, should not serve the political, economic, or cultural purposes of the state, but the perfection of the individual that leads to the perfection of humanity as such.

Although Dewey is obviously sympathetic to the (Kantian) individualistic cosmopolitanism, he rightfully states that it lacks an account as to which institutional agency should implement it – and by which kinds of governmental arrangements and educational policies. He notes that for Kant and his pedagogical followers, education appears as a matter of "private" interactions between students and teachers who act free from institutional regulations and arrangements – or at least the Kantian educational individualism and cosmopolitanism remain vague with regard to such arrangements (see Dewey, 1916, pp. 111–13).

However, one can direct a similar critique at Dewey himself: his descriptions of the social interactions that should enable individual growth are often vague themselves, and the reconstruction of the norms underlying these interactions remains underdeveloped. It is not enough to state that school interactions should stimulate rich experiences simply by their inner diversity that enable encounters and cooperation between individuals with different social and cultural backgrounds. Rather, one should describe under which conditions and on the grounds of which moral norms these interactions could be realized without reproducing exclusion or oppression of students from underprivileged or marginalized families. A systematic reconstruction of these underlying norms is missing in the work of Dewey. Rather, at that point we have to resort to other conceptions s of communicative action, such as discourse ethics and recognition theory.

One obvious normative condition for the kind of inclusive educational interactions that accommodate social and cultural diversity is respect. It would appear to be something of a truism that students should be treated with respect at schools. However, the triviality disappears the moment in which we begin to reflect on what respect in general, and what respect for infants in the context of education, actually means. Then we face a number of difficult questions. For example, given the epistemic and social immaturity of children, should they be respected in the same way and to the same extent as adults? Or, does respect at schools mean "only" to tolerate the beliefs, the worldviews, and the biographical experiences of the students, or does it require actively to address these beliefs, worldviews, and experiences in the classroom?

Generally speaking, we can distinguish between a broader and a narrower understanding of respect. More than five decades ago R. S. Peters defined respect, in a broad sense, as follows:

> In general respect for persons is the feeling awakened when another is regarded as a distinctive centre of consciousness, with peculiar feelings and purposes that criss-cross his institutional roles. It is connected with the awareness one has that each man [sic] has his own aspirations, his own viewpoint on the world; that each man [sic] takes pride in his achievements, however idiosyncratic they may be. (Peters, 1966, p. 59)

To respect a person as a "distinctive centre of consciousness" means to recognize her origin of unique perspectives and beliefs. However, it does not necessarily require taking up these perspectives or to having dialogues about these beliefs. According to this understanding of respect, a teacher should, for example, properly acknowledge the right of her students to hold religious beliefs that are different from her own or from those of the majority, but she might just see these beliefs as "idiosyncratic," and she would not be morally obligated to try to address them in her teaching. Furthermore, the teacher should assume that the students might have good reasons for their beliefs, but she is not required to try to understand these reasons and to encourage the students to articulate and to deliberate on them in the classroom.

A quite a different picture follows – at least indirectly – from a narrower conception of respect; a conception that is often regarded as Kantian. Harvey Siegel refers to this conception when he spells out respect as the recognition of all persons as "free rational beings" (Siegel, 2018, p. 317) who are capable of rational self-determination through reasoning. The highest moral task of school education is to cultivate the ability to reason through which rational self-determination can take place, since this cultivation is a demand of (prospective) respect for the potential of all children to develop as free rational beings (see Siegel, 2006, pp. 307–8).

This cultivation essentially includes the enabling of children to articulate their own needs, preferences, and beliefs in an argumentative way and to judge them in order to determine and rationally to communicate their own life goals and plans. Therefore, a teacher who respects their students should not simply tolerate their particular ideals and worldviews. In addition, he should attempt to address them in his teaching, to bring them to argumentative articulation in his classroom.

In order to do so, the teacher has to put himself in the students' shoes, to take their individual perspectives to the world and to themselves. In other words, he has to be *empathetic* to the students. In addition, the teacher has also to be able to recognize the possible worth of students' beliefs, ideals, and experiences, their potential to enrich the value horizon of the community. That is to say, that he should treat the students also with *social esteem*.[8]

Ultimately, democratic education requires caring for the worldviews and experiences of all students in their diversity, to include these worldviews and experiences in the school teaching at its starting point in order to bring them to rational and discursive articulation, and to explore the potential worth of these worldviews and experiences for the entire society. As I have argued elsewhere, the institutional realization of the recognition forms of empathy, cognitive respect, and social esteem in schools is what essentially makes up educational justice (Stojanov, 2018a, pp. 42–43). This is especially the case if the latter is understood primarily in relational and not in distributive terms, that is, as referring to the question, of how one "counts" in social relations – and not what one receives from state institutions (see Forst, 2014, pp. 6, 8). Insofar as democratic education, as argued earlier in this section, implies the equal inclusion of the diverse perspectives and the experiences of all students, regardless of their particular social, ethnic, or cultural backgrounds, it requires not just educational justice, but *global* educational justice. That is to say that democratic education requires equal empathy, respect, and social esteem not only toward the children from the domestic community or citizenry, but to all children, insofar as they are (or should be) addressees of institutionalized education.

In reality, educational systems even of liberal-democratic states are still a long way from implementing these central forms of educational justice. A number of surveys and many biographical testimonies of concerned persons in Germany suggest that students with a so called "immigration background" (that is, children or even grandchildren of immigrants) are subjected to specific practices of disregard which can be summarized as follows: even if these students perform very well in the elementary school, their teachers select them for nonacademic professional secondary schools, whose diplomas, according to the German educational systems, do not license for higher education. The reason for this is that most teachers ascribe to these students a "remoteness" from education, that is, from the school curriculum because of their supposed "foreign" cultural identity, and because of them having a first language other than German (see Metzker, 2018). However, not only (and not primarily) teachers should be blamed for portraying students from immigrant families as being remote from

[8] I refer here to Axel Honneth's well-known distinction between love, respect, and social esteem as the main sources of self-development and as the central forms of intersubejctive recognition that are interrelated in their difference to each other (see Honneth, 1995, pp. 95–130). However, unlike Honneth, I prefer to use "empathy" instead of "love" because I think that the term "love" could be misleading in the context of institutionalized education. On one hand, "empathy" is a kind of emotional concern, which, unlike love, could be deliberative cultivated and used as a "tool" in professional action in pedagogical or therapeutic settings. On the other hand, "empathy" stresses more clearly than "love" the practice of the taking the perspective of the other, while at the same time recognizing the other person in her otherness, that is, as a distinctive person whose interests, beliefs, views, or ideals are different from those of myself (see Ilien, 2005, pp. 142–46).

education because of their ethnic origin. Rather, this is a widespread pattern seen in the educational discourses in the country; a pattern which is largely endorsed and disseminated by influential opinion-makers and educational politicians (see, for example, Lenzen et al., 2007, pp. 12, 57, 136).

This pattern of perception and treatment of students "with an immigration background" violates all three norms of educational justice (empathy, respect, and social esteem) that are crucial for democratic education. It is *nonempathetic* because it neglects the individuality of perspectives, experiences, abilities, and life-goals of the concerned students by reducing these personal features to mere accidents of a constructed collective cultural identity, which is labeled as educationally deficient. In addition, it is blind to the suffering that this disregard of the individuality and autonomy causes the persons concerned.

The disregard to the (potential for) rational individual autonomy of the concerned students is itself a form of *disrespect*. It consists in perceiving and treating these students as being determined by their ethnic or cultural origin. In contrast, recognizing the students as "free rational beings" essentially entails the assumption that the individual reflects on the traditions and worldviews in which she is being raised and enculturated, and evaluates their rationality; and that she could transcend their limitations, that she is able to develop her own individual traits and values (which might or might not resort to the traditions of her ethnic or cultural background), and that she is able to support them with reasons and arguments.

Finally, the students with "an immigration background" are institutionally subjected to a *lack of social esteem* for their particular competences and experiences. This concerns, for example, their polylingual abilities. While most students from immigrant families spontaneously switch between different languages and language games, this capability of polylingual communication and self-articulation is normally seen, not as potential enrichment for education and for the entire society, but rather as educational deficit. It should be overcome by requiring the students to use only the German language not only in the school, but also in their private sphere – this is the demand of some leading voices in the area of education policy (see Lenzen et al., 2007, pp. 35, 146).[9]

The situation in Germany regarding educational injustice is only an example of the global structural problem that the experiences, beliefs, and abilities of children from socially or culturally underprivileged families count less in the institutionalized education than those of children from middle-class autochthone families. The outcomes of the Program for International Student Assessment (PISA) studies show that in all of the almost 80 participating countries there is a more or less strong correlation between the sociocultural background of the students and their educational prospects (see Schleicher, 2019,

[9] A further form of social disregard toward the students from immigrant families is their treatment as passive receivers of the values of a supposed German "leading culture" that they are required to internalize through specific educational programs. In this way, the educational institutions totally neglect (and do not bring to articulation) the already existing individual values and ideals of the concerned students as well as their particular life experiences, which stand behind these values and ideals (see Stojanov, 2018b).

pp. 5, 18–31). An obvious reason for this is that the curricula of school education are predominately oriented toward the cultures of the domestic middle and higher classes, thus structurally neglecting the experiences and the potentials of students with lower sociocultural status like those from immigrant families. This indicates that most national educational systems only insufficiently accommodate both moral universalism and sociocultural diversity, and therefore they are falling short of providing a real democratic education. These systems discriminate between educational "insiders" and "outsiders" on the ground of their origin and supposed ethnic or cultural background. Educational insiders are the students, who have been socialized or enculturated in their families in a way that has adjusted their minds to the curricular contents, so that these contents can be easily transferred in their heads. In contrast, educational outsiders have not experienced this kind of socialization and enculturation in their preschool time – or they are still not experiencing it in their social milieus.

Ultimately, the described structural discrimination in institutionalized education originates from what Paulo Freire calls a "banking concept of education" (Freire, [1996] 1970, pp. 52–54) in its application to a homogeneous national culture. According to this conception, the contents of that culture – a package of facts, values, rites, skills, etc. – is to be transferred into the minds of the students and banked there. This can be done more easily with students who were born into and have been raised in the national "lead culture," while the others will appear less educable and will have lower prospects and opportunities to succeed within the educational system. Hence, the banking concept of education cements the inequalities and the borders between the social and ethnic groups, and thus counters the basic demand of democratic education to break down these borders and inequalities.

An institutionalized education that aims to overcome the banking concept with its unjust and undemocratic implications would depart not from a national canon, but from the experiences, beliefs, and ideals of the students themselves. In addition, it would bring these experiences, beliefs, and ideals to a discursive articulation by mediating them with academic contents with universal validity. In Section 17.5, I shall show that this approach would be a revival of what Dewey called "individualistic cosmopolitanism" in education as a conceptual foundation for both democratic education and global educational justice.

17.5 Individualistic Cosmopolitanism and Global Educational Justice

Let us recall that for Dewey "individualistic cosmopolitanism" – if socially and institutionally grounded – is the founding feature of democratic education. "Individualistic cosmopolitanism" basically means here that education is focused on the growth of the individual (and not on the reproduction of a particular state or nation), and that the direction of this growth is the individual becoming a member of the whole humanity, or more precisely, member of the universal community of "free rational beings."

At the time in which Dewey wrote his *Democracy and Education* , many of Georg Wilhelm Friedrich Hegel's writings on education were still unknown. Hence, Dewey was not able to see that Hegel's conception of education not only endorses "individualistic cosmopolitanism," but also gives it a social, even a "materialistic" turn. Hans-Georg Gadamer offered probably the most synthetic and pointed description of Hegel's conception of education as the self's "elevation to universality" (Gadamer, 1986, p. 136). The demand of and the driving forces for this self-universalization are inbuilt in the interaction modes and institutions of modern civil society itself, but they also require support by formal schooling that should facilitate individual's transition from the family to the civil society, a transition which triggers the very process of her education.

According to Hegel, the lifeform of civil society is best understood as the negation of the one of the family (and also of the extended family of an ethnos, of a *Volk*). For him the family and the *Volk* are expressions of the unmediated natural spirit, within which there are no separated singular persons but rather an unmediated identity between them; persons figure only as parts of the whole (Hegel, [1822] 2005, pp. 158–60). In contrast, civil society, which includes the economic and the political spheres of the society, is organized upon the principle of autonomous individuals. They are particular ends in and for themselves and are distinguished by their subjective wills, that is, by their unique needs, interests, beliefs, values, and life-goals (Hegel, [1821] 1986, pp. 177–82; Hegel, [1822] 2005, pp. 339–46).

However, a second principle is also constitutive for civil society, and this is the principle of the interrelation between particular citizens through the "form of universality" (Hegel [1821] 1986, p. 339). In order to satisfy her needs, the particular person has to collaborate with her fellow citizens, and so has to (indirectly) work for the common wealth (Hegel [1821] 1986, p. 340). But to be able to collaborate in this way, the person has to make her individual needs and desires accessible and understandable for others who are particular persons themselves with their own particular needs and free wills, as well as specific worldviews and knowledge. That is why the person has to articulate her needs, wishes, and beliefs in a rational, nonparticularistic way. In short, the person has to articulate the elements of her subjective will conceptually, which includes that she has to provide her beliefs, values, and goals with reasons and to include them in discursive practices of argumentation. Ultimately, education should be understood as a process of conceptual self-articulation.[10]

The conceptual self-articulation in question requires a mediation between individual's subjective beliefs, ideals, and experiences on one hand, and academic contents of the sciences, humanities, and arts, which claim objective and universal validity and have supranational relevance, on the other. Studying the arts helps the individual to express his experiences, desires, and corresponding feelings, while studying the humanities enables him to develop a rich vocabulary for these experiences, desires, and feelings and to converse about them;

[10] I reconstructed the neo-Hegelian "education" or "Bildung" as conceptual self-articulation in Stojanov, 2018c (pp. 81–91).

studying the sciences enables him to understand concepts and arguments in their inferences and to apply them to his experiences, desires, and feelings (see also Stojanov, 2018c, pp. 90–92, 106–12). Those tree disciplinary fields, brought together, make the assertion of the human self as a "distinctive centre of consciousness" (Peters, 1966) in the real or virtual communication with all other selves, that is, centers of consciousness. However, sciences, humanities, and arts can fulfil this function only if they are taught at schools as vehicles for students' conceptual self-articulation – and not as elements of a canon that must be transferred into the heads of the students for the canon's own sake or for the sake of the preservation and continuation of a national state or national culture.

If the considerations in this section are right, then educational justice consists in the equal considering of the perspectives, experiences, and ideals of the students in their diversity as departing points of institutionalized education that mediates these perspectives, experiences, and ideals with academic contents with universal validity. This is possible only if institutionalized education incorporates the recognition forms of empathy, cognitive respect, and social esteem. These forms are also the founding features of democratic education.

Just *and* democratic education can probably be best achieved when the nationalities of the students are mixed and the schools understand themselves as supranationally oriented institutions. On one hand, symmetric diversity is a precondition not only for democratic but also for just education, insofar as it overcomes the widespread division between "native" and "non-native" students with the marginalization of the perspectives and experiences of the latter. On the other hand, nationally institutionalized education tends to focus on a canonized national culture – which leads, as described in Section 17.4 – to a structural discrimination of the students who were not raised in accordance with that culture.

Nowadays, schools are so closely tied to the national state that their transforming to supranational institutions with international students and cosmopolitan curricula and educational aims might appear rather utopian. But it could be a very useful and liberating utopia – as the utopias of a just society or of a wholly democratic society are.

17.6 Conclusion

In this chapter, I have argued that educational inequalities between citizens and noncitizens or between natives and non-natives due to their legal or social status are unjust. This applies, even if one otherwise views the unequal distribution of social and economic benefits by a state in favor of its fellow citizens legitimate. Unlike social justice, educational justice is founded in moral universalism; hence, it can only be global justice. Even more important than the unequal *distribution* of educational resources is the disadvantageous *treatment* of students with non-native origins, because of the focus of educational systems in most states on a canon of a traditionally constructed national culture. The postulated remoteness from that culture of the students concerned structurally generates disrespect, as well as lack of empathy and social esteem for them.

The focus in education on a canonized (and thus homogeneous) national culture is also not compatible with democratic education, since it endorses individuality and diversity. Contemporary democratic education requires individualistic cosmopolitanism as the founding principle of schooling, which should depart from the experiences, perspectives, and ideals of the students in their diversity, and mediate these experiences, perspectives, and ideals with academic content that has universal validity. This task is best achieved when schools function as supranational institutions.

References

Coomans, F. (2007). The content and scope of the right to education as a human right and obstacles to its realization. In Y. Donders & V. Vladimir, eds., *Human rights in education, science and culture*. Paris/Aldershot: UNESCO/Ashgate, pp. 153–82.

Culp, J. (2019). *Democratic education in a globalized world. A normative theory*. London: Routledge.

Culp, J. (2020). Educational justice. *Philosophy Compass*, 15(12), 1–12.

Culp, J. (2022). Global educational justice. In R. Curren, ed., *Routledge handbook of philosophy of education*, London: Routledge.

Dewey, J. (1916). *Democracy and education: An introduction to the philosophy of education (Twenty-Eight Printing 1955)*. New York: The Macmillan Company.

Forst, R. (2014). Two pictures of justice. In R. Forst, ed., *Justice, democracy and the right to justification. Rainer Forst in dialogue*. London: Bloomsbury Collections, pp. 3–26.

Freire, P. (1996/1970). *Pedagogy of the oppressed*. London: Penguin Books.

Fricker, M. (2007). *Epistemic injustice: Power & the ethics of knowing*. Oxford: Oxford University Press.

Gadamer, H. G. (1986). Bildung. In J. E. Pleines, ed., *Hegels Theorie der Bildung. Band II (Kommentare)*. Hildesheim: Olms, pp. 133–43.

Habermas, J. (1991). *Erläuterungen zur Diskursethik*. Frankfurt.: Suhrkamp.

Habermas, J. (1992). *Faktizität und Geltung*. Frankfurt: Suhrkamp.

Hegel, G. W. F. (1821/1986). *Grundlinien der Philosophie des Rechts (G. W. F. Hegel Werke 7)*. Frankfurt: Suhrkamp.

Hegel, G. W. F. (1822/2005). *Die Philosophie des Rechts. Vorlesungen von 1821/22*. Ed. by Hansgeorg Hoppe, Frankfurt: Suhrkamp.

Honneth A. (1995). *The struggle for recognition. The moral grammar of social conflicts*. Cambridge: Polity Press.

Ilien, A. (2005). *Lehrerprofession. Grundprobleme pädagogischen Handelns*. Wiesbaden: VS Verlag.

Lenzen, D., Blossfeld, H.-P., Bos, W., Müller-Böling, W., Oelkers, J., Prenzel, M., & WöÔmann, L. (Eds.) (2007). *Bildungsgerechtigkeit. Jahresgutachten 2007*. Wiesbaden: VS Verlag.

Metzker, J. (2018). Schluss mit der Meinungsmache! So machen wir aus #MeTwo eine echte Rassismus-Debatte, *Perspective Daily, 7. August 2018*. Available at: https://perspective-daily.de/article/589/probiere.

Miller, D. (2018). *Strangers in our midst: The political philosophy of immigration.* Cambridge, MA/London: Harvard University Press.

Mittler, D. (2018). Flüchtlingskinder wird Regelunterricht verweigert, *Süddeutsche Zeitung, 12. September 2018.* Available at: https://www.sueddeutsche.de/bayern/ankerzentrum-manching-fluechtlingskindern-wird-regelunterricht-verwehrt-1.4126395.

Nagel, T. (2008). The problem of global justice. In T. Brooks, ed., *The global justice reader.* Oxford: Wiley-Blackwell, pp. 416–38.

Peters, R. S. (1966). *Ethics and education.* London: Allen & Unwin.

Pogge, T. (2008). Moral universalism and the global economic justice. In T. Brooks, ed., *The global justice reader.* Oxford: Blackwell Publishing, pp. 358–82.

Rawls, J. (1999). *A theory of justice.* Rev. ed. Cambridge, MA: The Belknap Press of Harvard University Press.

Schleicher, A. (2019). *PISA 2018 – Insights and interpretations.* Paris: OECD.

Schwartz, L. (2020). International educational justice: Educational resources for students living abroad. *Global Justice: Theory Practice Rhetoric,* 12(1), 78–99.

Siegel, H. (2006). Cultivating reason. In R. Curren, ed., *A companion to the philosophy of education.* Oxford: Wiley-Blackwell, pp. 305–19.

Siegel, H. (2018). Justice and justification, *Theory and Research in Education,* 16(3), 208–329.

Stojanov, K. (2010). Overcoming social pathologies in education: On the concept of respect. In R. S. Peters & A. Honneth, *Journal of Philosophy of Education,* 43(S1), 161–72.

Stojanov, K. (2018a). Educational justice and transnational migration, *Journal of Global Ethics,* 14(1), 34–46.

Stojanov, K. (2018b). Gemeinsame Wertebildung statt "Wertevermittlung" an Migrant/innen, *ÖDaF-Mitteilungen,* 1(2018), 64–72.

Stojanov, K. (2018c). *Education, self-consciousness and social action. Bildung as a Neo-Hegelian concept.* London/New York: Routledge.

18

Debate and Deliberation in Democratic Education

Jane Lo and Paula McAvoy

18.1 Introduction

At the heart of democratic societies is pluralism – the notion that people will disagree about how to live life well. As suggested by Arendt, all of humanity is the same in the sense that we are all different: "Plurality is the condition of human action because we are all the same, that is, human, in such a way that nobody is ever the same as anyone else who ever lived, lives, or will live" (Arendt, 1958, p. 8). We have different understandings of the world, different perspectives on what *should* be done, and different ways of articulating how the world could be. Because pluralism and its disagreements manifest through the gathering of different ideologies, a democratic society will inevitably result in myriad conflicts. Within democratic education, there is a tradition of helping young people learn to deal with these differences of opinions through discussion. While there are many different types of talk in democratic education, in this chapter we focus on two of the most popular: debate and deliberation. While both help young people see different perspectives through talk, they provide different affordances and challenges for teachers and students in the classroom. Of course, these are not the only two ways for students to explore similarities and differences between their worldviews, so we end this chapter by providing a few other examples of discussions in the classroom that can help preserve and elevate pluralistic thinking.

18.2 Clarifying Discussion

We categorize debate and deliberation as two types of classroom discussion that activate different skills associated with democracy. Research consistently finds that discussion in any form is a difficult strategy for teachers to master and is relatively rare in US classrooms (Kohlmeier & Saye, 2019; Nystrand et al., 2003; Reisman, 2015; Reisman et al., 2019). Over the course of years of professional development work with teachers, we have learned that teachers often hold three misconceptions about discussion. The first is that discussion is an activity in which students talk to the teacher. This most often looks like what Hess and McAvoy (2015) have described as "interactive lecture" (p. 71). In these moments teachers pause lectures to check for understanding by inviting questions or reactions from the class. Sometimes these are questions that are open for interpretation and the exchange looks like a short moment of discussion between the teacher and one or two students. At other times, interactive lecture looks like a verbal quiz, with the teacher asking recall questions to reinforce the content. These are both examples of student talk that does not fall into the category of *actual* discussion.

The second misconception comes from teachers who only envision discussion as a whole-class activity in which, with a single opening question from a teacher, students enthusiastically and respectfully engage in a free-flowing exchange of ideas. In this view of discussion, the instructor believes that students know how to participate and ought to be willing to participate with little prodding. It is possible to engage students in what is essentially a seminar-style discussion, but this is a skill that must be explicitly taught (see Parker & Hess, 2001).

The third misconception is thinking about discussion as a set of individual contributions – who spoke and who didn't – rather than seeing discussions as a collaborative activity. As Laden (2012) argues, reasoning *together* about an issue – be it be two people deciding what movie to watch or a class deliberating about whether the state minimum wage should be increased – requires a different set of skills and dispositions than when we simply decide for ourselves. When we reason together, it requires us to listen and to be responsive to the views of others. The social aspects of discussion also require students to reflect on the views of others to think, for example, "How should I respond to that?" or "I've never thought of it that way; I might need to adjust my view." Students must also engage in the art of furthering the discussion, by being curious about what others say, making room for others to speak, asking questions, and offering ideas. Classroom discussions do not happen when students simply weigh in on a question by stating individual opinions; they happen when students are working through their competing ideas with each other and under the guidance of a teacher.

So then, what is discussion? We define classroom discussion as an activity in which students are talking through their views about a question for which there is disagreement. We differentiate *classroom discussion* from discussion generally. As Bridges (1979) notes, "The central function of [classroom] discussion is the improvement of knowledge, understanding and/or judgment on the matter which is under discussion" (p. 14). For Bridges (1979) classroom discussion is a type of collective inquiry into a question, and it is the act of inquiry that facilitates learning. Within classrooms, students may be invited into a number of different disciplinary disagreements, including literary interpretation, scientific questions, historical controversies, and moral and political issues.

In this chapter, we look at deliberation and debate as two strategies that engage students in discussions of contemporary political issues. As we show, both strategies are designed to unearth different points of view and then engage in reason-giving and argumentation; in other words, they help students to recognize pluralism. When done well, both strategies are also student-centered. That is, students give reasons to each other and share in the responsibility of maintaining the norms embedded in each activity. They also each model inquiry; both deliberation and debate are designed so that students deepen their understanding about the issues being investigated. They are also different in important ways. We show how the adversarial aspect of debate engages a different set of democratic skills than the more collaborative approach of deliberation. These differences require teachers to make judgments about how best to use these strategies in the classroom.

18.3 Debate

Protagoras of Abdera is cited as the man who popularized the profession of Sophists in Ancient Greek society and therefore is often seen as the man who popularized debate as an educative activity in Europe and the Western tradition. Sophists were teachers who focused on teaching wisdom through the tools of rhetoric and reasoning (i.e., making arguments about issues in society). At the same time, Plato famously critiqued the Sophists for prioritizing the art of persuasion rather than using debate as engagement directed at truth-seeking. In other words the Sophists were interested in demonstrating cleverness of argumentation and Plato was interested in identifying epistemic truths. Debate follows a combination of these same processes where individuals provide oral arguments on rationales for particular positions in issues. Since debate and democracy have intertwining beginnings, it is easy to surmise that debate is an integral part of democratic society. Ehninger and Brockriede (1978) are credited with publishing a seminal book in 1963 that showcased the cooperative learning and educative qualities of debate. Their work propelled argumentative studies into a new era where scholars began to study how debates can be leveraged as a teaching strategy (see Colburn, 1972; Kruger, 1968; Moore, 1967). By the mid-1980s, debate as a teaching strategy came to be linked with both student-centered learning and critical thinking (e.g., Colbert & Biggers, 1985; Gruner et al., 1971; Huseman et al., 1972). Nowadays, debate is widely used as a teaching strategy from nurse practitioners (Garrett et al., 1996) to counseling courses (Gervey et al., 2009) and as a liberation pedagogy (Davis et al., 2016).

Debate in the classroom is typically set up with students assigned to two opposing sides of a particular position statement, thesis, or question. Students then research their position, create evidence-based arguments for their side, and present this information to the other side, a judge, and/or a jury. After a predetermined number of cross-examination rounds, where one side can ask questions of the other and provide responses, the judge or jury makes a decision on which side made the most convincing argument based on warranted evidence. Key attributes of a debate are: (i) two opposing sides, (ii) warranted arguments based on evidence, and (iii) a winning side at the end. Proponents of debate suggest this process helps increase student engagement (there is desire to win), fosters critical thinking (warranted arguments), as well as promotes flexible thinking (dealing with cross-examinations) (e.g., Bonwell & Eison, 1991; Jagger, 2013; Zare & Othman, 2013).

In the public realm, debates are generally seen during election season, with candidates debating with one another in public on various important issues in a bid to convince voters to choose their side. One of the most well-known public debates that eventually led to its own format is the Lincoln–Douglas debates of 1858 – also known as The Great Debates of 1858. These were a series of seven debates between Abraham Lincoln, the Republican Party candidate for the United States Senate from Illinois, and the incumbent, Stephen Douglas, who was seeking a third term. As part of the critical attributes of debates, in the end there was a winner. And while Douglas won the election, the debates raised Lincoln's profile and eventually helped him win the United States Presidential Office in 1860. Since then, the Lincol–-Douglas debate format (which emphasizes ethics, logic, and philosophy because the original debate focused on the issue of slavery) has been widely used as a competitive debate format, especially in secondary school settings.

Outside of competitive debates, teachers often use classroom debates as a way to engage with controversial topics or public issues (e.g., Fournier-Sylvester, 2013; Tessier, 2010). Under different formats (e.g., mini-debates, team debates), debates can be used to help students quickly consider different perspectives on a topic before developing arguments around them. Furthermore, the National Council for the Social Studies lists debate as a best practice of social studies teaching that can help promote democratic thinking, argumentation, and perspective taking (NCSS, 2013).

Even though debate is widely used as a pedagogy for critical thinking and seen as a best practice of social studies education, scholars have argued that it may not necessarily be the best format to promote democratic values (e.g., Johnson & Johnson, 1985; Tumposky, 2004). Specifically, debates often set up complex issues as dichotomies, which can limit students' engagement with nuances in controversial topics (Tumposky, 2004), while other forms of discussions (e.g., structured academic controversies) may help foster dialogue and discussion about various nuances of issues (e.g., Johnson & Johnson, 1985, 2011; Johnson et al., 1996). If a goal of democratic education, as suggested at the beginning of this chapter, is to help students engage with the pluralistic nature of existing among people who are different from you, then debate can help people see different sides of public issues, albeit only two opposing sides. Similarly, Tumposky (2004) argued that the competitiveness of debates limits its equitable reach since classroom competitions may unintentionally privilege white male students who may gravitate toward competitive rhetorical tasks (see Kohn, 1986).

Debate continues to be a well-known pedagogical technique used across various educational contexts. Typically touted for its utility in supporting critical thinking and argumentation, debate is often seen as a best practice of democratic education (Gingold, 2013; Kawashima-Ginsberg, 2013). At the same time, because of its presentation of issues in dichotomous ways, debate can limit how students think about complex issues of democracy (i.e., justice, equity, and fairness) (Tumposky, 2004), and may produce more polarized views within participants (McAvoy, P. & McAvoy, G., 2021. In Section 8.4, we contrast debate with deliberation practices, which can help students engage more deeply with democratic values and issues.

18.4 Deliberation

Current conceptions of classroom deliberation are rooted in the values, aims, and dispositions associated with deliberative democratic theory. This theory became popular in the 1970s and 1980s among theorists who began to investigate what makes a democratic decision legitimate, given that people have a plurality of preferences and experiences. Rather than think of democracy as decision-making among adversaries that was primarily fought through the ballot box and interest groups, political theorists such as Benjamin Barber (1984), Joseph Bessette (1980), and Jane Mansbridge (1983) as well as philosophers such as Joshua Cohen (1989), Jürgen Habermas (1989), and John Rawls (1971) sought a path to democratic legitimacy through the *process* of decision-making. A decision is legitimate, in this view, when the public has been given the opportunity to engage in a free exchange of ideas. Deliberative theorists view reason-giving as essential to the creation of legitimacy. Gutmann and Thompson (1996), for example, define deliberative democracy as:

> a form of government in which free and equal citizens (and their representatives) justify decisions in a process in which they give one another reasons that are mutually acceptable and generally accessible, with the aim of reaching conclusions that are binding in the present on all citizens but open to challenge in the future. (p. 7)

Important in this theory is the deliberative space. Participants must recognize each other as political equals and discuss with the intention of finding a (consensus) position that furthers the common good. Participants bring arguments into a deliberation, but they ought to be open to hearing and incorporating the concerns of others as they work collaboratively to find agreement about a policy proposal. This outcome changes the aim of argumentation from identifying the objectively "best" position or winning; instead, the purpose of deliberative argumentation is to understand the views of others and serves as a means toward reaching an agreed upon position. This change of aim also requires participants to offer reasons that promote the common good and avoid reasoning from pure self-interest.

Deliberative theory sets a high bar for the deliberative experience. Some have critiqued this view for not being sufficiently attentive to social inequality and the ways in which people are not viewed as political equals based on identities such as race, gender, or social class (Gibson, 2020; Sanders, 1997; Young, 2002). Indeed, in a study of classroom discussions of controversial political issues, Hess and McAvoy (2015) find that social inequalities in the classroom create a less than ideal deliberative space in which students from higher social class backgrounds can dominate discussion and intimidate others (p. 175). Others have argued that the aim of consensus or seeking common ground does not sufficiently recognize deep ideological divisions that reflect fundamentally different views about what a good society looks like (Lo, 2017; Mouffe, 1999).

In practice, no deliberative space is "ideal" and when deliberation is introduced into the classroom, teachers should be attentive to the ways in which classrooms are "unusual political spaces" (Hess & McAvoy, 2015, p. 9). In addition to unequal power dynamics, classrooms contain participants who are compelled to be there, are often being graded for their participation, and are deliberating for the purpose of learning the skill of deliberation and about the issue being considered. Because students are not usually engaged in deliberations that result in *actual* decisions that bind the community, Levine (2018) argues that classroom deliberations about policy issues "are better described as simulated deliberations, in which the students pretend to be deciding on behalf of the United States" (p. 2).

Given that classroom deliberations about public policy issues are designed to be learning experiences for novices, teachers often employ a number of different strategies to develop students' skills. For example, teachers may have students engage in a simple "turn and talk" with a partner to exchange their views about whether there should be stricter gun policies in their state. Alternatively, teachers might engage students in more elaborate strategies that move students from small group discussions into whole-class discussions (some of these are discussed in Section 18.5). If these strategies are to fall into the category of "deliberation," then they ought to have particular characteristics, including: (i) an open policy question (e.g., Should the school dress code be abolished? Should our state require an ID to vote?); (ii) materials and format that bring in competing points of view about the question; (iii) student-to-student talk; (iv) norms that promote collaboration and a willingness to change one's mind or modify a view; and (v) a design that ends in a decision (e.g., vote or consensus). When making these design choices, teachers also need to be attentive to power relationships within the classroom and beyond the classroom. Using strategies that require students to take turns talking, draw upon common materials, and practice listening for understanding (rather than listening for the purpose of rebutting) are helpful for equalizing the discussion space.

Research on classroom deliberations shows that while there are many ways to structure deliberations, there are some common democratic outcomes. The *Civic Mission of the Schools Report* (Carnegie Corporation of New York, CIRCLE, 2003), for example, names engaging students in legislative simulations in which they deliberate proposed bills as one of its "Six Proven Practices." Researchers have found that legislative simulations can help students become more open to competing points of view, more interested in politics, and more willing to politically participate in the future (Hess & McAvoy, 2015; Levy et al., 2019; Lo, 2015). The Structured Academic Controversy (SAC) developed by Johnson and Johnson (1979) is another model whereby small groups of students are assigned one of two positions of a public policy proposal, which they then read about and present. In the final stage, students drop their roles and deliberate to find a consensus position that all members can endorse. Research on high school students using the SAC model has shown that it improves their ability to take perspectives (Avery et al., 2014). Studies also find that when students are asked to deliberate to find a consensus position, their views about the issues tend to converge from pre to post surveys (Avery et al., 2014; McAvoy & McAvoy, 2021). This research provides empirical support for the idea that deliberation produces a more collaborative approach to engaging students' differing views.

18.5 Beyond Debate and Deliberation

Even though this chapter focuses specifically on debate and deliberation as two well-known and beloved approaches for teaching students to share and exchange ideas, we would be remiss not to mention that there are limitations to both of these approaches. For example, scholars have criticized debate for being too focused on winning, which can dilute complex issues into simple arguments and take away from the depth of inquiry (e.g., Kohn, 1986; Tannen, 1998; Tumposky, 2004). And while deliberation takes more stock of the nuances of arguments, some argue that the deliberative process does not do enough to elevate emotive and emancipatory rationales behind arguments (e.g., Lo, 2017; Mouffe, 1999; Ruitenberg, 2009).

As an example of both concerns, consider a current political issue in the United States: Should states require voters to show a photo ID to receive a ballot? The voter ID movement became popularized following the Supreme Court ruling *Shelby County v. Holder* (2013). In effect, the ruling struck down a section of the 1965 Voting Rights Act, which required states that had engaged in suppressing the Black vote to get Congressional approval to change voting laws. Following the *Shelby* decision, 15 states passed Republican-sponsored voter ID laws making it harder for people, particularly young voters and poor people of color, to access the ballot box (Brennan Center, 2019). Voter ID laws ought to be considered within the legacy of voter suppression in the United States and the ideology of white supremacy. When teachers introduce this as a topic for debate without teaching students about the larger ideological and historical context, then the activity encourages students to offer specious arguments about voter fraud or to stay focused on evidence related to the availability of IDs. Similarly, to deliberate this issue invites students to seek compromises that likely still suppress the vote, such as broadening what counts as an acceptable ID or offering a need-based waiver to acquire an ID. These compromises overshadow the ideological intention behind the laws. Further, African American students likely understand and feel the urgency of these laws differently than white students, and these emotions and histories may be crowded out if the discussion stays focused on the issue itself.

This case of voter ID laws illustrates the complex set of judgments that teachers must make when introducing issues and engaging students in civil discourse. A 2021 report on civic reasoning in schools produced by the US

National Academy of Education challenges teachers to wade into this complexity:

> Civic learning should include a focus on the development of empathy for others, appreciation for multiple points of view, willingness to explore compromises that are informed by democratic values, and awareness of how pre-existing attitudes and emotions can influence perceptions and decision making. (Lee et al., 2021, p. 4)

Given these critiques and challenges, it is important to note that other forms of discussions exist within democratic education that can help promote students' acumen for exchanging ideas and information in productive ways. As mentioned elsewhere in this chapter, discussion is a broader conceptual category under which debate and deliberation can fall. And even though debate and deliberation continue to be the two most well-known forms of discussion pedagogy used in democratic education, there are many others to draw from (see Lo, 2022 for more examples of discussions). Here we briefly highlight three examples.

Philosophical Chairs (Seech, 1984) loosely follows a team debate format, except the aim is to cultivate a willingness to change one's mind when presented with better reasons and arguments. This is done by encouraging students to switch teams or move into an "undecided position" if they find themselves doubting their original view. Unlike traditional debate, Philosophical Chairs allows students to interrogate an issue, and the associated arguments on either side of the issue, with the goal of seeking the most reasonable reasons and positions in mind. In this way, Philosophical Chairs acts as a middle ground between debate and deliberation by helping students to understand the complexities of a particular issue without being distracted by the goal of winning. However, even Philosophical Chairs does not avoid the critique faced by deliberation when it comes to crowding out emotive and emancipatory rationales.

Agonistic deliberation builds on the deliberative model but foregrounds students' emotions and emotive responses to issues (Ruitenberg, 2009). By allowing students to draw on emotions and reactions to an issue, agonistic deliberation takes up the challenge of helping students face emotions associated with particular topics instead of avoiding them. For example, when deliberating the issue of abortion, rather than sticking specifically to legal arguments, agonistic deliberation allows for the discussion of moral and emotional reaction. Put another way, if teachers wish to engage students in an agonistic deliberation on the voter ID example provided at the beginning of this section, they might first ask students to take stock of their feelings on the issue, giving them space to air their ideas and grievances. But then in small groups, have students look at pertinent contextual and historical information, dissect the facts together, while listening and taking notes on differing perspectives of the issue. Then finally, have students decide for themselves what an appropriate course of action is, after taking into account their feelings, the feelings of other students, as well as the facts of the situation. This process would not necessarily yield a consensus among the students, but it does help them see different perspectives and consider viable actions for moving forward. Knowing full-well that drawing on these kinds of reasonings may lead to confrontations and hurt feelings, teachers engaging in agonistic deliberation will need to take appropriate measures to first lay down ground rules that humanizes students, helps students learn to forgive one another, and creates a safe environment for discussion (e.g., Lo, 2017, 2022).

And still, these types of discussions might not be emancipatory in nature; meaning, they do not help students better understand, examine, or dismantle power structures created by colonialistic domination. To ask a discussion activity to be emancipatory may seem lofty, yet, intergroup dialogue is one form of discussion that seeks to enact powerful change through talk (Ford, 2017). In intergroup dialogue conversations, the goal is not just the exchange of ideas about a proposed policy; instead, it is a collective interrogation of social power through the sharing of one's identities and experiences. Unlike deliberation and debate, which focuses mainly on reasoned arguments, intergroup dialogue focuses on personal experiences within structures of power. By understanding that all humanity have shared (and disparate) experiences, intergroup dialogue draws participants into relationship building through conversion, which leads to potential changes in one's own understanding not just of others but also of oneself. This type of discussion is not focused on "solving" an issue, it is a conversation about people and experiences. Its emancipatory power comes in the form of changes in the mindsets of people who participate in such dialogue. Unlike a debate where changing one's mind is discouraged, and unlike a deliberation where there is possibility of views changing, intergroup dialogue challenges all participants to be changed through conversation.

While we have highlighted three other forms of discussions that can contribute to democratic education in this section, we recognize that there are many other modes of discussion that teachers use to help support democratic aims in the classroom. Ultimately, the goal of these discussion pedagogies, alongside that of debate and deliberation, is to ensure the exchange of pluralistic ideas and experiences so that our democracies can continue to represent the various voices and positionalities that they serve.

References

Arendt, H. (1958). *The human condition*. Chicago, IL: University of Chicago Press.

Avery, P. G., Levy, S. A., & Simmons, A. M. M. (2014). Secondary students and the deliberation of public issues. *PS – Political Science and Politics*, 47(4), 849–54. doi: https://doi.org/10.1017/S1049096514001164.

Barber, B. R. (1984). *Strong democracy: Participatory politics for a new age*. Berkeley, CA: University of California Press.

Bessette, J. (1980). Deliberative democracy: The majority principle in Republican government. In R. A. Goldwin & W. A. Schambra, eds., *How democratic is the constitution?* Washington DC: American Enterprise Institute for Public Policy Research, pp. 102–16.

Bonwell, C. C., & Eison, J. A. (1991). Active learning: Creating excitement in the classroom. *ERIC Clearinghouse on Higher Education*. Available at: https://eric.ed.gov/?id=ED336049.

Brennan Center for Justice. (2019, November 19). *New voting restrictions in America*. Available at: https://www.brennancenter.org/our-work/research-reports/new-voting-restrictions-america.

Bridges, D. (1979). *Education, democracy and discussion*. Lanham, MD: University Press of America.

Carnegie Corporation of New York, CIRCLE. (2003). *The civic mission of schools*. Available at: https://www.carnegie.org/publications/the-civic-mission-of-schools.

Cohen, J. (1989). Deliberation and democratic legitimacy. In A. P. Hamlin & P. Pettit, eds., *The good polity: Normative analysis of the state*. New Jersey: Blackwell, pp. 17–34.

Colbert, K., & Biggers, T. (1985). Why should we support debate? *Journal of the American Forensic Association*, 21(4), 237–40.

Colburn, C. W. (1972). *Strategies for educational debate*. Holbrook: Holbrook Press.

Davis, K. A., Zorwick, M. L. W., Roland, J., & Wade, M. M. (2016). *Using debate in the classroom: Encouraging critical thinking, communication, and collaboration*. London: Routledge.

Ehninger, D., & Brockriede, W. (1978). *Decision by debate*. 2nd ed., New York: Harper and Row.

Ford, K. (Ed.) (2017). *Facilitating change through intergroup dialogue*. London: Routledge.

Fournier-Sylvester, N. (2013). Daring to debate: Strategies for teaching controversial issues in the classroom. *College Quarterly*, 16(3). Available at: https://eric.ed.gov/?id=EJ1018000.

Garrett, M., Schoener, L., & Hood, L. (1996). Debate: A teaching strategy to improve verbal communication and critical-thinking skills. *Nurse Educator*, 21(4), 37–40.

Gervey, R., Drout, M. O., & Wang, C.-C. (2009). Debate in the classroom: An evaluation of a critical thinking teaching technique within a rehabilitation counseling course. *Rehabilitation Education*, 23(1), 61–73. doi: doi.org/10.1891/088970109805059209.

Gibson, M. (2020). From deliberation to counter-narration: Toward a critical pedagogy for democratic citizenship. *Theory & Research in Social Education*, 48(3), 431–54.

Gingold, J. (2013) *Building an evidence-based practice of action civics: The current state of assessments and recommendation for the future*. (CIRCLE Working Paper #78). Available at: https://civicyouth.org/wp-content/uploads/2013/08/WP_78_Gingold.pdf.

Gruner, C. R., Iluseman, R. C., & Luck, J. I. (1971). Debating ability, critical thinking ability, and authoritarianism. *Speaker and Gavel*, 8(3), 63–65.

Gutmann, A., & Thompson, D. F. (1996). *Democracy and disagreement*. Cambridge, MA: Belknap Press of Harvard University Press.

Habermas, J. (1989). *The structural transformation of the public sphere: An inquiry into a category of bourgeois society*. Cambridge, MA: MIT Press (original work published 1962).

Hess, D. E., & McAvoy, P. (2015). *The political classroom: Evidence and ethics in democratic education*. London: Routledge.

Huseman, R., Ware, G., & Gruner, C. (1972). Critical thinking, reflective thinking, and the ability to organize ideas: A multi-variate approach. *Journal of the American Forensic Association*, 9(4), 261–65.

Jagger, S. (2013). Affective learning and the classroom debate. *Innovations in Education and Teaching International*, 50(1), 38–50. doi: doi.org/10.1080/14703297.2012.746515.

Johnson, D. W., & Johnson, R. T. (1979). Conflict in the classroom: Controversy and learning. *Review of Educational Research*, 49(1), 51–69. doi: https://doi.org/10.2307/1169926.

Johnson, D. W., & Johnson, R.T. (1985). Classroom conflict: Controversy versus debate in learning groups. *American Educational Research Journal*, 22(2), 237–56. doi: doi.org/10.3102/00028312022002237.

Johnson, D. W., & Johnson, R. T. (2011). Constructive controversy. In D. J. Christie, ed., *The encyclopedia of peace psychology*. Malden, MA: Blackwell Publishing, pp. 246–51. Available at: http://onlinelibrary.wiley.com/doi/10.1002/9780470672532.wbepp062/abstract.

Johnson, D. W., Johnson, R. T., Smith, K. A., & ERIC Clearinghouse on Higher Education (1996). Academic controversy: Enriching college instruction through intellectual conflict. *ASHE-ERIC Higher Education Report*, 25, (3). Graduate School of Education and Human Development, The George Washington University.

Kawashima-Ginsberg, K. (2013). Do discussion, debate, and dimulations boost NAEP civics performance? *CIRCLE Facts Sheet*. Available at: extension://efaidnbmnnnibpcajpcglclefindmkaj/viewer.html?pdfurl=https%3A%2F%2Fwww.miciviced.org%2Fwp-content%2Fuploads%2F2018%2F10%2Fcircle_naepbechtelfactsheetapril30.final_.pdf&chunk=true.

Kohlmeier, J., & Saye, J. (2019). Examining the relationship between teachers' discussion facilitation and their students' reasoning. *Theory & Research in Social Education*, 47(2), 176–204.

Kohn, A. (1986). *No contest: The case against competition*. Boston, MA: Houghton Mifflin.

Kruger, A. (1968). *Counterpoint: Debates about debate.*, Lanham, MD: Scarecrow Press.

Laden, A. S. (2012). *Reasoning: A social picture*. Oxford: Oxford University Press.

Lee, C. D., White, G., & Dong, D. (Eds.) (2021). *Executive summary. Educating for civic reasoning and discourse*. Committee on Civic Reasoning and Discourse: National Academy of Education. Available at: https://3e0hjncy0c1gzjht1dopq44b-wpengine.netdna-ssl.com/wp-content/uploads/2021/04/NAEd-Educating-for-Civic-Reasoning-and-Discourse-Exec-Summary.pdf.

Levine, P. (2018). Deliberation or simulated deliberation? *Democracy and Education*, 26(1), 1–4.

Levy, B., Babb-Guerra, A., Batt, L. M., & Owczarek, W. (2019). Can education reduce political polarization? Fostering open-minded political engagement during the legislative semester. *Teachers College Record*, 121(5), 1–40.

Lo, J. C. (2015). Developing participation through simulations: A multi-level analysis of situational interest on students' commitment to vote. *The Journal of Social Studies Research*, 39(4), 243–54.

Lo, J. C. (2017). Empowering young people through conflict and conciliation: Attending to the political and agonism in democratic education. *Democracy and Education*, 25(1), 1–9.

Lo, J. C. (Ed.) (2022). *Making classroom discussions work: Methods for quality dialogue in the social studies*. Columbia, NY: Teachers College Press.

Mansbridge, J. J. (1983). *Beyond adversary democracy*. Chicago, IL: University of Chicago Press.

McAvoy, P. & McAvoy, G. E. (2021). Can debate and deliberation reduce partisan divisions? Evidence from a study of high school students. *Peabody Journal of Education*, 96(3), 275–84. doi: 10.1080/0161956X.2021.1942706.

Moore, W. E. (1967). *Creative and critical thinking*. Boston, MA: Houghton Mifflin.

Mouffe, C. (1999). Deliberative democracy or agonistic pluralism? *Social Research*, 66(3), 745–58.

National Council for the Social Studies (NCSS) (2013). *The College, Career, and Civic Life (C3) Framework for Social Studies State Standards: Guidance for Enhancing the Rigor of K-12 Civics, Economics, Geography, and History*. Available at: https://www.socialstudies.org/sites/default/files/c3/C3-Framework-for-Social-Studies.pdf.

Nystrand, M., Wu, L. L., Gamoran, A., Zeiser, S., & Long, D. A. (2003). Questions in time: Investigating the structure and dynamics of unfolding classroom discourse. *Discourse Processes*, 35(2), 135–98.

Parker, W. C., & Hess, D. (2001). Teaching with and for discussion. *Teaching and Teacher Education*, 17(3), 273–89.

Rawls, J. (1971). *A theory of justice*. Cambridge, MA: Belknap Press of Harvard University Press.

Reisman, A. (2015). Entering the historical problem space: Whole-class text-based discussion in history class. *Teachers College Record*, 117(2), 1–44.

Reisman, A., Cipparone, P., Jay, L., Monte-Sano, C., Kavanagh, S. S., McGrew, S., & Fogo, B. (2019). Evidence of emergent practice: Teacher candidates facilitating historical discussions in their field placements. *Teaching and Teacher Education*, 80, 145–56.

Ruitenberg, C. W. (2009). Educating political adversaries: Chantal Mouffe and radical citizenship education. *Studies in Philosophy & Education*, 28(3), 269–81. doi: doi.org/10.1007/s11217-008-9122-2.

Sanders, L. M. (1997). Against deliberation. *Political Theory*, 25(3), 347–76.

Seech, Z. (1984). Philosophical Chairs: A format for classroom discussion. *Teaching Philosophy*, 7(1), 37–41.

Tannen, D. 1998. *The argument culture: Stopping America's war of words*. New York: Random House.

Tessier, J. T. (2010). Classroom debate format. *College Teaching*, 57(3), 144–52. doi: doi.org/10.3200/CTCH.57.3.144-152.

Tumposky, N. R. (2004). The debate debate. *The Clearing House: A Journal of Educational Strategies, Issues and Ideas*, 78(2), 52–6. doi: doi.org/10.3200/TCHS.78.2.52-56.

Young, I. M. (2002). *Inclusion and democracy*. Oxford: Oxford University Press on demand.

Zare, P., & Othman, M. (2013). Classroom debate as a systematic teaching/learning approach. *World Applied Sciences Journal*, 28, 1506–13. doi: doi.org/10.5829/idosi.wasj.2013.28.11.1809.

19

Agonistic Democracy and the Question of Education

Gert Biesta

19.1 Introduction: Democratic Education as Strong Socialization

In August 2021, a new education law came into effect in the Netherlands. The law was intended to clarify what all schools should do with regard to democratic citizenship. The official language around the law was that of "clarification" (in Dutch: *verduidelijking*), but much of the discussion used the phrase "sharpening up" (in Dutch: *aanscherping*). There were a number of reasons behind the introduction of the law, ranging from concerns expressed by the school inspectorate about practices of citizenship education in schools, concerns about the relative position of Dutch students in the IEA's (the International Association for the Evaluation of Educational Achievement) International Civic and Citizenship Education Study, and concerns about antidemocratic tendencies in society and the explicit rejection of democratic values by some (young) people. Within the unique Dutch educational landscape in which schools have a constitutional "freedom of education," the introduction of the law required quite a lot of political maneuvering by the government in order to satisfy parties across the political spectrum.

From a rather minimal and, one might say, relaxed approach in the old law – in which it was argued that schools should work on the assumption that students grow up in a pluriform society, that schools should contribute to the promotion of active citizenship and social integration and should make sure that students have knowledge of and the opportunity to encounter different backgrounds and cultures of fellow-students – the new law contained a much more explicit program for what schools should do. Under the new law, schools are required to promote active citizenship and social cohesion in focused and coherent ways. Schools should ensure that students develop respect for and knowledge of the basic values of democratic society as specified in the constitution, and the universal fundamental rights and freedoms of human beings, where schools also need to ensure that everyone in the school acts according to and in line with these values. Schools should also ensure that students develop social and societal competencies that allow them to take part in and contribute to the pluriform democratic Dutch society. The new law also specifies that schools should ensure that students acquire knowledge about and respect for differences in religious views, in worldviews, in political preferences, in origins (the law doesn't use the word ethnicity), in sex, handicap, or sexual orientation, while also ensuring that equal cases are treated equally. In addition, school administrators are required to create a school culture that is consistent with the values in the law, and in which students are stimulated to practice with these values. The school administrators are also required to ensure an environment in which students and staff can feel safe and accepted, irrespective of the differences mentioned in the law.[1]

The law in the Netherlands is but one example of an ongoing trend in contemporary policies for democratic citizenship education. At European level there is a similar recommendation that puts a strong emphasis on promoting 'common values, inclusive education, and the European dimension of teaching.'[2] And a more extreme version of this line of thought is the so-called Prevent strategy, which tasks all educational institutions in England, Scotland, and Wales with the duty to help prevent individuals from being drawn into terrorism.[3] What unites these approaches is that they see democracy as a community of (common) values that do not just need to be known, but also need to be respected and internalized. What also runs through these approaches is that education for democratic citizenship is seen as a form of what we might call "strong socialization" where the ambition is that all students will adopt the values of the democratic community.

This may sound attractive, both as a conception of democracy and as an educational program, but on closer inspection there are a number of problems and contradictions. One contradiction has to do with the fact that that the very point of democracy lies in the liberty it seeks to ensure for all citizens. The idea that democracy is a community of values, seems to suggest that there is little space for individual freedom – you either adopt the values or you are "out." And this contradiction repeats itself in the educational idea of strong socialization, as students – at least in a democratic society – can never just be seen as objects that need to be socialized into a particular set of values. Students are subjects in their own right, with agency and freedom, which also entails the possibility that they reject the educational program offered to them. Of course, politicians – and teachers – can continue to insist that students should do as they are told, they can try to clarify and sharpen up what schools should do, but as educators we know all too well that if we just keep telling our students how they should behave, we quickly end up in rather unproductive cycles.

In this chapter, I seek to engage with these issues through a discussion of the work of Chantal Mouffe and Jacques Rancière, who have both contributed to what, with a term from Mouffe (see, e.g., Mouffe, 2000, 2013), might be called an "agonistic" understanding of democracy. I will show how their ideas help in

[1] See the Law on Primary Education (WPO), ch. 1, article 8, items 3 and 3a. https://wetten.overheid.nl/BWBR0003420/2022-04-01#Hoofdstukl.

[2] https://eur-lex.europa.eu/legal-content/EN/TXT/?uri=CELEX%3A32018H0607%2801%29..

[3] https://www.gov.uk/government/publications/prevent-strategy-2011.

getting a different understanding of what constitutes the democratic community and how such communities are constituted. This, in turn, will allow me to raise questions about the idea of democratic education as a form of strong socialization. With the help of Mouffe and Rancière I will lay the groundwork for a different approach in which the question of democratic subjectification plays a central role. My ambition with this chapter is not to resolve all problems regarding democratic education and education for democratic citizenship, but rather I hope that my discussion will raise some new questions and will point toward new ways of engaging with these questions.

In all this, it should be noted that the idea of strong socialization is linked to the idea that the democratic community – or any political community for that matter – is a community of common values, so that the educational work in relation to this is to ensure that "newcomers" become members of such communities by adopting fully the values of the community. In what follows, I will raise questions about such an understanding of the democratic community and in precisely this way I raise questions about the idea of civic education as strong socialization into such a community. This does not imply that from the agonistic perspective I will present in this chapter that there is no role to play for civic education – on the contrary – but it can no longer be a matter of socializing newcomers into a community of common values.

19.2 What Is a Political Community?

One could argue that democracy relies on the existence of a well-defined community within which democratic policies and practices can take place. In her interesting book *Political Theory and the Displacement of Politics*, Honig (1993), argues that it is actually the establishment of such communities that is the most important and perhaps also most difficult aspect of democratic politics. She argues that when democratic politics is restricted to those who already agree on the basic rules of the political process, the whole question of how such an agreement comes about is left out of the picture. This not only means that it is left out of our *understanding* of the dynamics of democratic politics, but also that it runs the risk of being *beyond the reach* of democratic contestation. Her thesis about the displacement of politics is precisely aimed at the suggestion that democratic politics is only for like-minded people – those who subscribe to a basic set of rules and values – because that suggestion makes it impossible to see where such a consensus may come from, how it is enforced, and who is and who isn't able to play a role and have a voice in this.

Honig published her book during the heyday of the discussions between liberalism and communitarianism. While liberals and communitarians often claimed to have radically different views, Honig's intervention brought into focus the view that with regard to the underlying conception of the nature and character of the political community, they actually rely on a similar idea, namely that the construction of a political community is seen as something that *precedes* actual politics and thus remains outside of it. While communitarians have, in a sense, been quite open about this – they see the political community as a community of shared values and principles – Honig showed, particularly by discussing the early work of John Rawls, that liberalism operates in a similar way. This has to do with the so-called entry conditions for political participation. In Rawls' early work, before the publication of *Political Liberalism* (1996), these entry conditions – a minimum level of rationality and a minimum level of morality – were considered to be natural and prepolitical rather than being seen as articulating particular *political* values.[4]

Chantal Mouffe's contribution to this discussion not only lies in the fact that she has exposed the political nature of such entry conditions by highlighting how they include some and exclude others and thus do important political work (see, for example, Mouffe, 1993). She also made the case that we should be explicit about such exclusions because it is only from such a vantage point that it becomes possible to understand that those who are outside of the political community are not there because they lack rationality or morality, but because their *political* values differ from the ones held by those on the inside. Mouffe disagrees with some forms of liberalism and, to a lesser extent, some forms of communitarianism about how we should understand the political community and its constitution. But she does acknowledge that democratic politics requires stability and order. Her main point is that any construction of such an order is always a *political* act and also that such a construction should always be up for contestation and revision. A political "hegemony" (Laclau & Mouffe, 1985) is necessary for politics to be possible, but such a hegemony should never be beyond contestation.

One author who has developed a less orderly account of politics and the political community is Jacques Rancière. In his work on democratic politics (for example, Rancière, 1995a, 1999, 2003) he relies on an interesting distinction between *police* (or *police order*) and *politics*. "Police" refers to "an order of bodies that defines the allocation of ways of doing, ways of being, and ways of saying, and that sees that those bodies are assigned by name to a particular place and task" (Rancière, 1999, p. 29). It is an order "of the visible and the sayable that sees that a particular activity is visible and another is not, that this speech is understood as discourse and another as noise" (Rancière, 1999, p. 29). Police should not be understood as the way in which the state structures the life of society because "[t]he distribution of places and roles that defines a police regime stems as much from the assumed spontaneity of social relations as from the rigidity of state functions" (Rancière, 1999, p. 29).

Policing is therefore not so much about "the 'disciplining' of bodies" as it is "a rule governing their appearing, a configuration of *occupations* and the properties of the spaces where these occupations are distributed" (Rancière, 1999, p. 29; emphasis in original). The point Rancière is making here is that *police* refers to the particular way in which a society is ordered, so to speak, which also means that within a particular police order everyone has a place, role, position, and

[4] In later work, Rawls did acknowledge that the underpinnings of liberalism are not that neutral and natural as he initially envisaged.

identity. This is not to say – and this is the important point of Rancière's distinction – that everyone takes part in the running of the order, but just that everyone has a place. After all, women, children, slaves, and immigrants had a clear place and identity in the city state of Athens, but as those who were not allowed to take part in political decision-making. In precisely this respect, then, every police order can be said to be all-inclusive.

The notion of "politics," on the other hands, refers to "the mode of acting that perturbs this arrangement" (Rancière, 2003, p. 226) and that does so – and this point is often overlooked in readings of Rancière's work – with reference to the idea(l) of *equality*. Politics, for Rancière, refers to "an extremely determined activity antagonistic to policing: whatever breaks with the tangible configuration whereby parties and parts or lack of them are defined by a presupposition that, by definition, has no place in that configuration" (Rancière, 2003, pp. 29–30). This break manifests itself through actions "that reconfigure the space where parties, parts, or lack of parts have been defined" (Rancière, 2003, p. 30). Political activity is therefore about "whatever shifts a body from the place assigned to it" (Rancière, 2003). "It makes visible what had no business being seen, and makes heard a discourse where once there was only place for noise" (Rancière, 2003). Politics thus refers to the event when two 'heterogeneous processes' meet: the police process and the process of *equality* (see ibid.). For Rancière politics understood in this way is always and necessarily *democratic* politics. He explicitly denies, however, that democracy can ever be "a regime or a social way of life" (Rancière, 2003, p. 101). Democracy is not and cannot be part of the police order, but should rather be understood "as the institution of politics itself" (Rancière, 2003, p. 101). Every politics is democratic *not* in the sense of a set of institutions, but in the sense of forms of expression "that confront the logic of equality with the logic of the police order" (Rancière, 2003). Democratic politics, for Rancière, is therefore always a "claim" for equality. It is a claim for more equality but often also a claim for a different equality.

Rancière and Mouffe both bring into view that political communities are not natural identities but that their constitution is fundamentally political itself. Whereas Rancière seems to think that politics only exists in those moments where a particular police order is interrupted in the name of equality – after which, we might say, a different, potentially better but never totally perfect police order will emerge – Mouffe acknowledges that the political community can have a more stable form, as long as it is not forgotten that this form is constituted hegemonically and hence politically, and is not based upon natural or neutral values or identities. What both deny is that the political dimension of democratic politics can be completely contained within a particular order. Rancière would say that this can never be the case – and in this sense his conception of politics can be characterized as "anarchic." Mouffe would say that if we only focus on the democratic order and forget how this order has been brought about, we miss a crucial aspect of democratic politics. What Mouffe and Rancière therefore bring to the table is the claim that the democratic community can not be understood as a stable community with a positive identity. This then begins to undermine the idea that the only job to be done by education is the socialization of newcomers into such a community, not because strong socialization may not be possible – although there is the question whether it is a desirable modus operandi for education – but because the very community in which newcomers are supposed to be socialized may actually not exist.

19.3 Drawing the Borders of the Political Order

The question of the political community is not only a matter of this community itself (what it looks like from the inside), but also has to do with the status of its borders (what it looks like from the outside). As I have made clear in Section 19.2, according to some conceptions of liberal democracy the borders of the democratic order are understood in terms of rationality and morality. Or, to put it more crudely and directly: those who are on the inside of the democratic order are there because they are committed to acting in rational and moral ways, which can only mean that those on the outside are there because they are unable to act in a rational and moral way. This inability can either be structural – think of those who are considered to be mad or amoral, but also think of children who are not yet entirely rational and moral. But the outside of the democratic order is also populated by those who reject the standards of rationality and morality that characterize the democratic order, which, whether we like it or not, is what individuals and groups can do. In strong versions of liberalism the borders are seen as natural, and thus as uncontested and incontestable – a bit like "you are either with us or you are a terrorist." In weaker or more political versions of liberalism there is an awareness of the political character of the borders and the border control that is going on.

In one sense, Mouffe's work has affinity with the more political understanding of liberalism. She doesn't deny that democratic politics needs order, but her main concern is about the ways in which such an order is understood and represented and also about the ways in which the borders around this order are established. Mouffe emphasizes that she doesn't advocate a "pluralism without any frontiers" because she does not believe "that a democratic pluralist politics should consider as legitimate *all* the demands formulated in a given society" (Mouffe, 2005, p. 120; emphasis added), particularly not if, in the name of the values and principles of a particular hegemony, this hegemony is being undermined. (Think of those who use their own freedom to restrict the freedom of others.) She thus argues that a democratic society "cannot treat those who put its basic institutions into question as legitimate adversaries" (Mouffe, 2005, p. 120). But she emphasizes that such exclusions should be envisaged "in political and not in moral terms" (Mouffe, 2005, p. 120). This means that when some demands are excluded, it is not because they are evil, "but because they challenge the institutions constitutive of the democratic political association" (Mouffe, 2005, p. 121).

Mouffe adds, however, that "the very nature of those institutions" should also be part of the debate. This is what she has in mind with her idea of a "conflictual consensus," which she describes as a "consensus on the ethico-political values of liberty and equality for all, [but] dissent about their interpretation ... A line should therefore be drawn between those who reject those values outright and those who, while accepting them, fight for conflicting interpretations" (Mouffe, 2005, p. 121). What do liberty and equality mean? Whose liberty and whose equality should be considered? Should this consideration only include human beings or should it encompass a wider circle? These are all questions that need ongoing debate, according to Mouffe. This also means – and I tend to think that this is key to Mouffe's message – that "our allegiance to democratic values and institutions is not based on their superior rationality" (Mouffe, 2005, p. 121) Liberal democratic principles "can be defended only as being constitutive of our form of life" (Mouffe, 2005, p. 121). They are not the expression of a universal morality or rationality, but are thoroughly "ethico-political" (Mouffe, 2005, p. 121) and thoroughly historical.

With regard to the question of borders and bordering, this brings Mouffe's views closer to those of Rancière, in that both highlight the political nature of such border-work. For Rancière, however, democratic politics *only* occurs in the redrawing of the borders of a particular police order, and only when such redrawing is done with reference to the idea of equality. There are, after all, also redrawings of the political order that aim for a decrease of equality or, with a slightly odd formulation: equality for the few, not for the many (see Biesta, 2020a). This explains why for Rancière democracy is necessarily *sporadic*. It only occurs from time to time in very particular situations and can never become a normal state of affairs (see Rancière, 1995a, pp. 41, 61; see also Biesta, 2009). This not only implies, as I have shown, that the essence of politics cannot be captured if we only look at what happens *within* a particular order. It also means that there is a need to account for the work that happens at the borders of the democratic order including, if we follow Rancière, the work that happens at the very moment at which orders are being redrawn in the name of equality – if, that is, we wish to have a conception of citizenship that is sensitive to the political significance of these dynamics. All this has important implications for what it might mean to be a democratic citizen and also for what it might mean to education for democratic citizenship.

19.4 The Dynamics of Democratic Politics

So far I have discussed different understandings of political communities and their constitution, including questions about how borders are constituted, policed, and challenged. Yet for a full picture of the dynamics of democratic politics, it is also important to look at democratic processes and practices themselves, that is, how they occur within the political community. Whereas simple conceptions of democracy tend to see democracy entirely in quantitative terms – democracy as majority rule – the main contribution made by proponents of the idea of deliberative democracy, is that rather than just taking all preferences from voters at face value, an important part of the democratic process is the deliberative *transformation* of the preferences of individuals and groups. Under the deliberative model, democratic decision-making is seen as a process which involves "decision making by means of arguments offered *by* and *to* participants" (Elster, 1998, p. 8) about the means *and* the ends of collective action.

As Young explains, deliberative democracy is not about "determining what preferences have greatest numerical support, but [about] determining which proposals the collective agrees are supported by the best reasons" (Young, 2000, p. 23). The reference to "best reasons" indicates that deliberative democracy is based upon a particular conception of deliberation. Dryzek, for example, acknowledges that deliberation can cover a rather broad spectrum of activities but argues that for *authentic* deliberation to happen the requirement is that the reflection on preferences should take place in a *non-coercive* manner (Dryzek, 2000, p. 2). Such a requirement "rules out domination via the exercise of power, manipulation, indoctrination, propaganda, deception, expression of mere self-interest, threats ... and attempts to impose ideological conformity" (Dryzek, 2000, p. 2). This resonates with Elster's claim that deliberative democracy is about the giving and taking of arguments by participants "who are committed to the values of rationality and impartiality" (Elster, 1998, p. 8) and with his suggestion that deliberation must take place between "free, equal and rational agents" (Elster, 1998, p. 5).

The deliberative turn thus moves away from a purely aggregative understanding of democracy, toward one that acknowledges that democracy can never simply be a matter of counting of preferences, but also needs to involve the weighing of preferences in light of what we might call the common good or public interest; the *res publica*. Democracy thus always involves and entails the translation of "private troubles" into "collective issues" (Bauman, 1999), which is one of the key functions of the public sphere (see Habermas, 1989; Marquand, 2004; see also Biesta et al., 2013; Biesta, 2014). I am inclined to think that one limitation of some of the work that goes on in discussions about deliberative democracy is that it is based on the assumption that deliberation is only open to those who meet certain 'entry conditions, such as, in the formulation of Elster, rationality and impartiality.[5] This also assumes – a point I will return to later in this section – that the (political/civic) identities of those who take part in the deliberation are assumed to be shaped *before* the deliberation starts, rather than that they "emerge" from participation in the deliberation.

Mouffe makes a similar point when she criticizes deliberative democracy for the fact that it sees power as a disturbing factor in democratic politics, something that we need to get rid of if democracy is to work well or is to work at all. For Mouffe, the idea that democratic politics is about "the free and unconstrained public deliberation of all on matters of common concern" (Benhabib, quoted in Mouffe, 2000, p. 10) is mistaken because relations of power are *constitutive* of the social (Mouffe, 2000, p. 14). The question for democracy, therefore, "is not how to eliminate power but how to constitute forms of power more

[5] I deliberately refer to *some* of the work within the deliberative tradition, as there are other voices within this tradition that have argued for a broader and more encompassing conception of deliberation – see particularly the work of Iris Marion Young (2000).

compatible with democratic values" (Mouffe, 2000, p. 14), that is, how to use and mobilize power to support rather than undermine democratic processes and practices.

This is where Mouffe positions her "agonistic pluralism,'" which she sees as an alternative to deliberative democracy. Agonistic pluralism is based on a distinction between *the political*, by which Mouffe refers "to the dimension of antagonism that is inherent in human relations" (Mouffe, 2000, p. 15), and *politics*, by which she refers to "the ensemble of practices, discourses and institutions which seek to establish a certain order and organize human coexistence in conditions that are always potentially conflictual because they are affected by the dimension of 'the political'" (Mouffe, 2000, p. 15). For Mouffe politics thus aims at the creation "of a unity in a context of conflict and diversity" (Mouffe, 2000, p. 15). This always entails the creation of a distinction between "us" and "them." Mouffe argues, however, that the "novelty of democratic politics is not the overcoming of this us/them opposition – which is an impossibility – but the different way in which it is established" (Mouffe, 2000, p. 15).

What Mouffe is arguing for here is the need for transforming *antagonism* into what she refers to as *agonism*, so that the "them" in democratic politics is no longer perceived and approached as an enemy that has no right to exist and should be destructed, but is seen as an *adversary*. Mouffe defines an adversary as a "legitimate enemy, one with whom we have some common ground because we have a shared adhesion to the ethico-political principles of liberal democracy: liberty and equality" but with whom "we disagree on the meaning and interpretation of those principles" (Mouffe, 2000, p. 15). While antagonism is the struggle between enemies, agonism refers to the struggle between adversaries, which is why Mouffe concludes that "from the perspective of 'agonistic pluralism' the aim of democratic politics is to transform *antagonism* into *agonism*" (Mouffe, 2000, p. 16; emphasis in original; see also Mouffe, 2013).[6]

If my reading of Mouffe's work is correct, then I believe that the task of the transformation of antagonistic relationships into agonistic relationships is not only at stake in the *construction* of a particular political order – or in Mouffe's terms: the construction of politics – but is also an important element of the modus operandi of political orders so constructed. It is not as if all problems disappear as soon as a particular democratic hegemony is established. Questions about how to engage with different opinions and values are likely to permeate democratic processes and practices, and the task of transforming antagonism into agonism so that we do not see our adversaries in moral terms of good versus bad or rational versus irrational but in political terms, that is, as pursuing a

[6] A helpful way to understand the difference between antagonism and agonism is through sport (and the very concept of agonism actually has its origin in sports). While different football teams, for example, are keen to win from their adversaries – one could say that that is the ultimate point of football – they do not want to destroy their adversaries because in that case they would destroy the very possibility of playing football in the first place. It also explains why everyone who is interested in playing football should not just have a concern for their own team, but should also have a concern for the very conditions – such as the quality of the playing field, the rules and regulations, the arbiters and referees – that make it possible to play football. While antagonistic relationships destroy the very possibility to play football, agonistic relationships share a common concern and interest, without making all teams the same or without giving up on the idea that winning matters.

different *political* agenda within a broader adhesion to the principles of liberty and equality, is an ongoing one.

All this seems to suggest that, for Mouffe, there is important democratic work to be done with the domain of politics, that is, within a particular political order. Rancière seems to deny this possibility, perhaps first and foremost because he locates the essence of democratic politics somewhere else, namely in the contestation of a particular political order in the name of the principle of equality – not just the search for more equality or equality for more people but again and again a search for a different equality, so to speak. This is why he holds that every politics is democratic *not* in the sense of a set of institutions, but in the sense of forms of expression "that confront the logic of equality with the logic of the police order" (Rancière, 2003, p. 101). One of Rancière's helpful examples is around voting rights for women. While one could see this as a struggle for women to be included into the group of those who can vote, Rancière's point is that within a settlement in which women have no right to vote, the very idea that one can be a woman and have the right to vote is an absurdity. The very category of a women-with-the-right-to-vote simply doesn't exist and doesn't make sense. The struggle is therefore not one of being included in an existing order but of the transformation of that order so that the idea of being a woman with the right to vote *makes sense* (see also Biesta, 2019).

In Rancière's own words, political activity is therefore always "a mode of expression that undoes the perceptible divisions of the police order by implementing a basically heterogeneous assumption, that of a part of those who have no part, an assumption that, at the end of the day, itself demonstrates the sheer contingency of the order [and] the equality of any speaking being with any other speaking being (Rancière, 2003, p. 30). This dispute, which Rancière identifies as the proper "form" of democracy (for this expression, see Rancière, 2003, p. 225) – is not the opposition of interests or opinions between social parties. This, in turn, means that for Rancière democracy is "neither the consultation of the various parties of society concerning their respective interests, nor the common law that imposes itself equally on everyone. The *demos* that gives it its name is neither the ideal people of sovereignty, nor the sum of the parties of society, nor even the poor and suffering sector of this society" (Rancière, 2003). The political dispute rather is a conflict "over the very count of those parties." (Rancière, 1999, p. 100) It is a dispute between "the police logic of the distribution of places and the political logic of the egalitarian act" (Rancière, 1999, p. 100).

This is why Rancière argues that politics is "primarily a conflict over the existence of a common stage and over the existence and status of those present on it" (Rancière, 1999, pp. 26–27). This is why the essence of democracy/politics for Rancière is not a matter of consensus but of what he refers to as *dissensus* (see Rancière, 2003, p. 226; see also Rancière, 1999, pp. 95–121). But dissensus has a very precise meaning in Rancière's work. It is not the "opposition of interests or opinions . . ., but the production, within a determined, sensible world, of a given that is heterogeneous to it" (Rancière, 2003, p. 226). This, then, is the democratic work that emerges from Rancière's attempt to articulate the essence of the political. While it might be tempting to say that this work occurs outside of the existing police order, this outside, in Rancière's thinking, does not denote the location of those who are excluded – after all, as I have argued, for Rancière everyone is in a sense always included in any police order. It is rather an outside that denotes a way of acting and being that cannot be conceived within the particular police order and in that way does not yet exist as a possible identity or way of being and speaking.

19.5 The Subject of Politics

I have indicated that liberal and communitarian views about the political community seem to start from the assumption that political identities are formed *before* democratic politics itself takes place and can take place. This has to do with the ideas that in order for democratic politics to occur – for example in the form of democratic deliberation – those who wish to take part in the process need to meet certain entry conditions such as, in the case of Elster's version of deliberative democracy, a commitment to the values of rationality and impartiality or, in the case of communitarian conceptions of politics, the adoption of and adherence to particular values which are often referred to as "common" values.

On such a set-up, there is a very clear task for education which we can describe as that of making newcomers – not just children and young people but also those who arrive from different countries, societies, or political cultures – ready for their participation in democratic politics, either by instilling the qualities of rationality and impartiality or by instilling a particular set of common values. Education thus appears as a form of strong socialization which, in a sense, makes education both the guarantor and gatekeeper of democratic politics. Or in a less utopian way of thinking: it puts the burden for making democratic politics work on educators and the education system. This helps to explain why, when democratic politics fails to work in the way it ought to work – for example, because of the rise of extremism and antidemocratic tendencies – education comes under pressure to do what it allegedly is supposed to do (without asking the question whether education is able to perform this task). Hence the sharpening up, the need for teaching common values across Europe, and for Prevent strategies.

The value of Rancière's insights is that he comes to democracy and democratic politics from the other end of the spectrum. For him, as mentioned, democratic politics is precisely *not* about "the opposition of interests or opinions between social parties" (Rancière, 2003, p. 225); it is precisely *not* "the consultation of the various parties of society concerning their respective interests" (Rancière, 2003, p. 225) in order to come to some kind of more or less "successful" consensus. It is not that such processes are not important or don't exist, but for Rancière they take place within the existing police order, whereas democracy – and perhaps it is better to refer to it as (sporadic) moments of democratization – always take place when the existing order is interrupted with reference to the idea(l) of equality.

One interesting implication of this view is that democratic politics is not dependent upon the availability of a particular kind of political subjectivity. Rather, Rancière argues that democratic interruptions of the police order generate new political subjectivities. This is the reason why Rancière writes that a political subject "is not a group that 'becomes aware' of itself, finds its voice, imposes its weight on society" (Rancière, 1999, p. 40), because establishing oneself as a subject does not happen before the "act" of politics but rather in and through it. Rancière thus characterizes a political subject as "an operator that connects and disconnects different areas, regions, identities, functions, and capacities existing in the configuration of a given experience – that is, in the nexus of distributions of the police order and whatever equality is already inscribed there, however, fragile and fleeting such inscriptions may be" (Rancière, 1999, p. 40). Rancière gives the example of Jeanne Deroin who, in 1849, presented herself as a candidate for a legislative election in which she couldn't run. Through this "she demonstrates the contradiction within a universal suffrage that excludes her sex from any such universality" (Rancière, 1999, p. 41). It is the staging "of the very contradiction between police logic and political logic" that makes this into a political act (Rancière, 1999, p. 41), and it is in and through this act that political subjectivity is established.

Politics itself thus becomes a process of subjectification; a process in and through which political subjectivity is generated or, to be more precise, a process in and through which new ways of doing and being come into existing. Subjectification here refers to "the production through a series of actions of a body and a capacity for enunciation not previously identifiable within a given field of experience, whose identification is thus part of the reconfiguration of the field of experience" (Rancière, 1999, p. 35; see also Rancière, 1995b).

Two things are important in this definition of subjectification, and they hang closely together. The first is the supplementary nature of subjectification (see Rancière, 2003 pp. 224–25), that is, the insight that subjectification is different from identification (see Rancière, 1995a, p. 37). Identification is about taking up an *existing* identity, that is, a way of being and speaking and of being identifiable and visible that is already possible within the existing order – or, to use Rancière's phrases, within the existing "perceptual field" or "sensible world" (Rancière, 2003, p. 226). Subjectification, on the other hand, is always "disidentification, removal from the naturalness of a place" (Rancière, 1995a, p. 36; see also Ruitenberg, 2010a). Subjectification "inscribes a subject name as being different from any identified part of the community" (Rancière, 1995a, p. 37). It is, in other words, about saying "no" to the existing police order, and to say "no" with reference to the idea(l) of equality.

When Rancière uses the notion of "appearance" in this context, it is not in order to refer to "the illusion masking the reality of reality" (Rancière, 2003, p. 224). Subjectification is about the appearance – the "coming into presence," as I have called it elsewhere (Biesta, 2006) – of a way of being that had no place and no part in the existing order of things. Subjectification is therefore a *supplement* to the existing order because it adds something to this order; and precisely for this reason the supplement also *divides* the existing order, that is, the existing "division of the sensible" (Rancière, 2003, pp. 224–25). Subjectification thus "redefines the field of experience that gave to each their identity with their lot" (Rancière, 1995a, p. 40). It "decomposes and recomposes the relationships between the ways of *doing*, of *being*, and of *saying* that define the perceptible organization of the community" (Rancière, 1995a, p. 40; emphasis in original).

On Rancière's account, then, democratic politics does not require a particular kind of political subjectivity that is firmly established before the political process itself can take place. The political subject, according to Rancière, emerges in and through the act of politics. The political subject, to put it differently, is not the producer of consensus but the product of dissensus. Or in more mundane language: the political subject is the one who causes trouble in the name of equality. On this account, it is no longer education that needs to turn individuals into political subjects; it is rather that through engagement in democratic politics – which is always sporadic – democratic subjectness emerges. Rancière thus seems to turn the traditional way to think about the relationship between education and democracy on its head, which may have significant implications for democratic education.

Whereas Rancière's views about democratic politics are fundamentally anarchic, which means that there is never a stable "identity" waiting for individuals to step into, and whereas liberal and communitarian views are fundamentally "archic" as they do assume that the democratic citizen has a stable and a positive identity, that is, an identity that can be articulated and spelled out, Mouffe seems to occupy a middle position. What Mouffe shares with liberalism and communitarianism is an acknowledgment that democratic politics requires a degree of stability, continuity, and form. What she challenges is the suggestion that such a democratic hegemony is nonpolitical or prepolitical. What she also challenges is the suggestion that there is only one ideal form of the democratic political community. In both cases she highlights the importance of ongoing contestation, albeit within the confines of what she refers to as "a shared adhesion to the ethico-political principles of liberal democracy" (Mouffe, 2000, p. 15).

One could say, therefore, that the kind of political subject "needed" in Mouffe's political universe, is the person who is committed to the principles of liberty and equality and, more generally, to the political project of democracy (which also means a person who understands that democracy is a *political* project to begin with). This is not only a more open kind of political subjectivity than what is assumed in approaches to democratic education that see it as a form of strong socialization. It is also a much more political kind of subjectivity and not a prepolitical or nonpolitical rational being who, because of his or her rationality would automatically choose democracy. That, after all, is very unlikely to happen.

To think of the democratic subject as one who is *committed* chimes well with Mouffe's suggestion that what is key here is to ignite a *passion* for democracy. After all, if the key dynamic of democratic politics "is to transform *antagonism* into *agonism*" (Mouffe, 2000, p. 16), this requires, according to Mouffe, that we provide "channels through which collective passions will be given ways to express themselves over issues, which, while allowing enough possibility for identification, will not construct the opponent as an enemy but as an adversary" (Mouffe, 2000, p. 16). This, in turn, means that "the prime task of democratic politics is not to eliminate passions from the sphere of the public, in order to render a rational consensus possible, but to mobilize those passions toward democratic designs" (Mouffe, 2000, p. 16; see also Ruitenberg, 2009; 2010b). This is also why, recently, Mouffe has made a case for what she refers to as a "left populism," so as to channel the populist passions, which are real, in the direction of democracy (see Mouffe, 2018). This suggests that the democratic subject is the one who is driven by a *desire* for democracy or, to be more precise, a desire for engagement with the ongoing experiment of democracy (see also Biesta, 2010, 2011, 2021).

19.6 Conclusion: Democratic Education Beyond Strong Socialization

In this chapter, I have tried to argue that the essence of democratic politics cannot be captured adequately if we think of democracy *only* as a stable political order. Although order is important for the everyday democratic conduct of our lives, we should not forget that any political order can only exist because of a division between inside and outside. With Mouffe, I believe that this division is itself a fundamental political "event." To suggest that the border of the democratic order is natural, not only masks the political character of the division between inside and outside, but also forecloses the possibility to question how the borders are being drawn and therefore forecloses the possibility for a redrawing of the borders. The redrawing of such borders is not just a quantitative matter – it is not just a matter of bringing more individuals into a particular order. With Rancière, I believe that the most significant redrawings of the borders of the political order are those that are *qualitative*, that is, that generate new political identities and subjectivities – where the category "women-with-the-right-to-vote" makes sense and where the category "slave" no longer makes sense.

Taken together, these ideas form a significant departure from the conventional way in which education, citizenship, and democracy are connected, as they challenge the idea that political subjectivities and identities *can be* and *have to be* fully formed before democracy can take off. The formation and ongoing transformation of political subjectivities rather *is* what engagement in democratic politics is about. The difference I have been trying to articulate in this chapter is therefore not between differing conceptions of what a good citizen is – in which case the underlying assumption that we can first decide what a good citizen is and then work on its "production" through education and other means would remain in place – but between different ways in which we understand the relationships between citizenship, democracy, and education.

What is valuable about Mouffe's agonistic pluralism is her insistence that democracy is a political and historical project – not something rational and eternal but a very particular way in which we, as human beings, try to live our lives together, not just with the recognition that there is plurality, but also with the recognition that such plurality should, in principle, be valued and secured. The "in principle" remains important, because any voice that uses its own freedom to destroy the freedom of others, undermines the possibility of living together in plurality. Here there is an obvious limit, and one could argue that all policies for democratic citizenship education that argue that all differences deserve "respect" – itself a moral category – are hugely naive, as those who seek to undermine the very possibility of living together in plurality do not deserve respect at all (and neither should they feel "safe and accepted," as the Dutch law on citizenship education suggests).There is, to put it in Mouffe's terms, an antagonistic "limit" to pluralism, and the language of respect misses this limit in a number of ways.

Rancière's contribution is helpful because he keeps reminding us to think of democracy as "sporadic," as something that happens from time to time when the existing police order – which may not be bad, or may at least be a bit better than how things used to be – encounters the principle of equality which, in more everyday language means that democracy happens at those moments when someone raises the question of whether the equality we have is the best equality or whether we can envisage a different equality. We have rather big examples of historical shifts that, in hindsight are often referred to as processes of emancipation, and what is emancipatory about them is not that those in power let others in – in which case we might say that the ones who were in power remained in power. The bigger historical shifts actually interrupt the whole "distribution of the sensible," the whole sociopolitical setup, so that new identities became possible and new subjectivities emerged.[7] Some of these historical shifts are violent – they are antagonistic. But others turn out to be agonistic and "prove" that a different "distribution of the sensible" is a real possibility, although not one that is achieved easily.

Agonistic democracy is not a simple solution for the complex questions surrounding democracy, and also not for the complex questions that are at stake in democratic education and education for democratic citizenship. But I do think that the work of Mouffe and Rancière can help us to remain suspect of calls for strong socialization and work toward more meaningful, more difficult, and more political alternatives.

References

Bauman, Z. (1999). *In search of politics*. Cambridge: Polity Press.

Biesta, G. (2006). *Beyond learning: Democratic education for a human future*. Boulder, CO: Paradigm Publishers.

Biesta, G. (2009). Sporadic democracy: Education, democracy and the question of inclusion. In M. Katz, S. Verducci & G. Biesta, eds., *Education, democracy and the moral life*. Dordrecht: Springer, pp. 101–12.

[7] The case of Rosa Parks remains an impressive example of this dynamic (see Biesta, 2020b).

Biesta, G. (2010). How to exist politically and learn from it: Hannah Arendt and the problem of democratic education. *Teachers College Record*, 112(2), 558–77.

Biesta, G. (2011). Citizenship education reconsidered: Socialisation, subjectification, and the desire for democracy. *Bildungsgeschichte. International Journal for the Historiography of Education*, 1(1), 58–67.

Biesta, G. (2014). Making pedagogy public: For the public, of the public, or in the interest of publisness? In J. Burdick, J. A. Sandlin & M. P. O'Malley, eds., *Problematizing public pedagogy*. New York: Routledge, pp. 15–25.

Biesta, G. (2019). Transclusion: Overcoming the tension between inclusion and exclusion in the discourse on democracy and democratisation. In G. Biesta, ed., *Obstinate education: Reconnecting school and society*. Leiden: Brill, pp. 97–111.

Biesta, G. (2020a). Perfect education, but not for everyone: On society's need for inequality and the rise of surrogate education. *Zeitschrift für Pädagogik*, 66(1), 8–14.

Biesta, G. (2020b). Can the prevailing description of educational reality be considered complete? On the Parks-Eichmann paradox, spooky action at a distance, and a missing dimension in the theory of education. *Policy Futures in Education*, 18(8), 1011–25.

Biesta, G. (2021). Regaining the democratic heart of education. In M. Soskil, ed., *Flip the system US: How teachers can transform education and strengthen American democracy*. New York: Routledge, pp. 32–38.

Biesta, G., De Bie, M., & Wildemeersch, D. (Eds.) (2013). *Civic learning, democratic citizenship and the public sphere*. Dordrecht/Boston: Springer Science+Business Media.

Dryzek, J. (2000). *Deliberative democracy and beyond: Liberals, critics, contestations*. Oxford: Oxford University Press.

Elster, J. (Ed.) (1998). *Deliberative democracy*. Cambridge: Cambridge University Press.

Habermas, J. (1989). *The structural transformation of the public sphere: An inquiry into a category of bourgeois society*. Cambridge, MA: The MIT Press.

Honig, B. (1993). *Political theory and the displacement of politics*. Ithaca, NY: Cornell University Press.

Laclau, E., & Mouffe, C. (1985). *Hegemony and socialist strategy*. London: Verso.

Marquand, D. (2004). *Decline of the public*. Oxford: Polity Press.

Mouffe, C. (1993). *The return of the political*. London: Verso.

Mouffe, C. (2000). *Deliberative democracy and agonistic pluralism. Political Science Series 72*. Vienna: Institute for Advanced Studies.

Mouffe, C. (2005). *On the political*. London/New York: Routledge.

Mouffe, C. (2013). *Agonistics: Thinking the world politically*. London/New York: Verso.

Mouffe, C. (2018). *For a left populism*. London/New York: Verso.

Rancière, J. (1995a). *On the shores of politics*. London/New York: Verso.

Rancière, J. (1995b). Politics, identification, and subjectivization. In J. Rajchman, ed., *The identity in question*. New York/London: Routledge, pp. 63–70.

Rancière, J. (1999). *Dis-agreement: Politics and philosophy*. Minneapolis, MN: University of Minnesota Press.

Rancière, J. (2003). *The philosopher and his poor*. Durham, NC: Duke University Press.

Rawls, J. (1996). *Political liberalism*. New York: Columbia University Press.

Ruitenberg, C. (2009). Educating political adversaries. *Studies in Philosophy and Education*, 28(3), 269–81.

Ruitenberg, C. (2010a). Queer politics in schools: A Rancièrean reading. *Educational Philosophy and Theory*, 42(5), 618–34.

Ruitenberg, C. (2010b). Conflict, affect and the political: On disagreement as democratic capacity. *In Factis Pax*, 4(1), 40– 55.

Young, I. M. (2000). *Inclusion and democracy*. Oxford: Oxford University Press.

20

Punishment and Democratic Education

Bryan R. Warnick and A. C. Nikolaidis

20.1 Introduction

The success of liberal democracy is premised on the capacity of citizens to govern themselves and coexist harmoniously with others. Of course, not all societies we call "democratic" fully enable or allow such functioning, and perhaps none do so perfectly. We consider, however, the endorsement of democratic values and the cultivation of relevant capabilities of citizens to be necessary for any democracy to maintain its stability and legitimacy in the long run. Any healthy democracy must implement democratic principles at both a political and interpersonal level. At a political level, democracy is manifest as a polity that codifies the rule of the people into law. At an interpersonal level, it exists as a mode of association and communication (Dewey, 1916) where members of a community recognize their mutual interest in the viability of their democracy and cooperate to ensure that everyone's interests are considered, no one's interests are unduly privileged, and all are reasonably satisfied by the state of affairs.

The interpersonal character of democracy renders education – a fundamental component of any stable society – an especially important institution of democratic societies. Democratic education must ensure that citizens are not only able to participate in the political process, but that they are able and inclined to engage with other citizens in exercising collectively their right to self-governance and individually their right to lead flourishing lives without infringing on others. Democratic societies must, therefore, make concerted efforts to provide an education that supports the virtues and capabilities necessary for democratic citizenship.

While democratic education is typically associated with specific classes in civics or history (in the United States, with K–12 Social Studies or Advanced Placement Government and Politics), the important values and relevant capabilities of democracy extend beyond civic content knowledge to all forms of school relationships. Democratic capabilities can be developed in any class or school situation that indirectly cultivates collaborative skills, attentive listening, or respect for others' ideas and contributions. These skills are particularly necessary when there is social conflict and thus school discipline becomes particularly important from a democratic perspective. There are forms of discipline and punishment, in fact, that work against the cultivation of democratic capabilities and some that are more compatible. As such, we suggest that all schools committed to the cultivation of basic democratic skills and civic competence ought to enact discipline policies and practices that align with, or at least do not impede, the school's democratic mission. This, we contend, requires a general shift from a retributive justice model to a restorative justice one. While in some circumstances retributive forms of punishment align with the democratic mission of schools, the tenor of retributive justice conflicts with the development of important democratic capabilities.

20.2 Punishment and Education

Normative inquiries into the intersection of punishment and education have gained renewed visibility in recent years despite the relative dearth of literature on the subject (Thompson & Tillson, 2020). In exploring such conceptual and normative considerations, scholars have debated the educational value of punishment (e.g., Hobson, 1986; Marshall, 1984), investigated the necessity of punishment in educational settings (e.g., Hand, 2020), and argued for certain forms of punishment in education over others (e.g., Curren, 2020).

Such developments notwithstanding, few scholars who engage in conceptual and normative work have specifically explored the connection between punishment and democratic education and even fewer the connection between restorative justice and democratic education, as we will do in this chapter.[1] Those who have explored the connection between punishment and democratic education suggest an alignment between democratic education and restorative practices – e.g., the need for punishment to be adjusted to the community-building purpose of democratic education (Gathercoal, 1998) – but fall short of naming restorative justice as the punishment paradigm that best aligns with the aims of democratic education. Those who explicitly address the connection between restorative justice and democratic education do so in the context of highlighting the alignment of restorative justice and education in general, which, among other things, is charged with promoting fundamental democratic values and civic purposes (Warnick & Scribner, 2020).

This inattention to the theoretical connection between restorative justice and democratic education is unsurprising, since arguments for restorative justice approaches have generally been limited to considerations of equity. This focus is the result of concerns about zero-tolerance discipline policies and exclusionary

[1] Notably, three comprehensive reviews of theoretical scholarship on democratic and citizenship education that span the last three decades make no reference to discipline and punishment as relevant areas for consideration in democratic education policy and practice. Instead, they limit their scope to primarily curricular (the content of teaching), pedagogical (the method of teaching), and jurisdictional (the administrative organization of teaching) considerations (see Knight Abowitz & Harnish, 2006; Osler & Starkey, 2006; Sant, 2019).

forms of punishment, like suspensions and expulsions, common in the United States since the 1980s (Fronius et al., 2016). As evidence continues to accumulate that zero-tolerance policies and exclusionary punishment disproportionately impact students of color and students with disabilities (United States Government Accountability Office, 2018) – and are at least partially responsible for maintaining the persistent achievement gaps that education policymakers have been struggling to curb for more than half a century (Gregory et al., 2010) – the promise that restorative justice could decrease educational inequities has understandably determined much of its value as a possible alternative.

Since social justice and equity are features of democracy, any approach that produces more just and equitable outcomes is undoubtedly valuable for democratic societies. There is, however, more to consider. Education for democracy is distinct from and irreducible to features of democracy wherein democratic education takes place (Levinson, 2011). This brings up the question of whether restorative justice is directly valuable to democratic education, apart from its value for democratic societies. A comprehensive account of punishment and democratic education ought to consider the full scope of democratic education, whether punishment as a general practice appropriately fits within this scope, and, if it does, how restorative justice as a specific form of disciplinary practice meets the standards that render punishment an acceptable, and perhaps even desirable, aspect of democratic education. In the remainder of this chapter, we provide such an account, arguing that a commitment to democratic education necessitates a commitment to restorative justice.

20.3 Democratic Capabilities

Scholars of democratic education have extensively discussed the values that democratic education ought to instill in students and the capabilities that all citizens must have for a democratic system to operate at its full potential. Following this scholarship, we discuss how the current retributive system of punishment often hinders the development of certain capabilities that we consider to be especially important while a restorative system supports it. We focus on six essential democratic capabilities: autonomy, reciprocity, trust, tolerance, deliberation, and epistemic virtue.[2] In this section, we describe these capabilities and their centrality to democratic education.

20.3.1 Capability for Autonomy

In representing the rule of the people, democracy is a form of self-governance and, as such, presupposes that citizens are responsible agents who can make their own decisions about, and can pursue, what is valuable in life (Rawls, 1993). For this reason, democracy requires that citizens have, at the very least, a

[2] While some of these capabilities, like reciprocity, are widely espoused (see Rawls, 1993), others, like autonomy and deliberation, remain controversial (see Brighouse, 1998; Galston, 1991; Gutmann & Thompson, 1996, 2004; Levinson, 1999; Macedo, 1999; Sanders, 1997). Given the limited scope of this chapter, we avoid addressing these debates.

minimal capacity for autonomy such that they are capable of making and assuming responsibility for those decisions. Of course, not all citizens choose to lead autonomous lives nor does the status of a democracy depend on them doing so. For genuine self-rule, however, a democracy must enable citizens to autonomously scrutinize the basic laws and institutions of their society. Only then is the government legitimate and only then are its laws and decisions binding on the public (Brighouse, 1998). Autonomy requires, on some level, the ability to make independent choices, to understand how actions have consequences, and to take responsibility for one's actions.

20.3.2 Capability for Reciprocity

To ensure social cooperation, it is important that democracies are characterized by reciprocal relations and that rules and laws are mutually beneficial and justifiable. Those who contribute to the good of society must fairly benefit from this cooperation such that it is reasonable for someone to cooperate and do their part in sustaining the cooperation that democracy demands (Rawls, 1993). Reciprocity requires an ability to compromise, yield to the perspective of others, and adjust one's actions to accommodate others. It requires that grievances be appropriately redressed to restore social cooperation (Allen, 2020) and that decisions made can be justified to everyone regardless of differences in beliefs and values (Gutmann & Thompson, 1996). Being capable of reciprocity, then, requires that one is able and disposed to reciprocate benefits they receive, compromise with others, redress grievances that arise, and justify their decisions to others in mutually acceptable terms.

20.3.3 Capability for Trust

As a system of social cooperation, democracy requires trust in others and their ability and likelihood to act in ways that advance the common good (Putnam, 1993). Social trust is associated with functional democratic institutions and democratic stability (Rothstein & Stolle, 2008). Fostering social trust in diverse societies requires that people are capable of showing trust and being trustworthy (Vallier, 2018). Showing trust presupposes that one can reasonably expect others to abide by social norms, meet social expectations, and reciprocate benefits. When norm violations occur, trust is restored by holding wrongdoers accountable. Being trustworthy presupposes knowledge of the social norms one is expected to abide by, which is acquired through learning, socialization, modeling, and reminders of social expectations. Democratic education must prepare students to be trusting and trustworthy so as to cultivate trust among members of society.

20.3.4 Capability for Tolerance

As a form of governance by the people, democracy involves tensions between persons and groups with different beliefs, experiences based on identity, and understandings of what a valuable life entails. For this reason, democratic citizens must be capable of tolerating reasonable differences in belief, cultural practices, and lifestyles, to avoid repression that compromises democratic values and ensure that shared citizenship is possible (Scanlon, 2003). Though tolerance may be restricted to protect the integrity of a democratic state (Galston, 2017), it is essential that democratic citizens are capable of accepting the right of others to hold different beliefs or values, pursue different lifestyles, and influence the shaping of their state. Tolerance requires a knowledge that differences in beliefs and values exist, a familiarity with what the major differences are in belief systems, and an understanding that democracy requires giving people space to live these differences.

20.3.5 Capability for Deliberation

While tolerance is necessary for harmonious coexistence in democracy, it is not sufficient. Common ground must be found to enact policy that is mutually acceptable. In democracies this process takes place through deliberation, namely, discussing and evaluating different courses of action for the purpose of solving a common problem (Hess & McAvoy, 2014). Deliberation is important for democracy because the rule of the people precludes the possibility of executive decisions being made by an unaccountable authority. It prompts decision-making that is premised on reasons that are readily available to, accessible by, acceptable by, and legitimately binding for all democratic citizens (Gutmann & Thompson, 2004). For decision-making to be the product of democratic deliberation, all citizens must be capable of participating to avoid the effective exclusion of certain portions of the population which would compromise the legitimacy of democratic decision-making.

20.3.6 Capability for Epistemic Virtue

Finally, because democratic deliberation can be epistemically and culturally biased against marginalized groups (Levinson, 2003), it is important that citizens develop a capacity for epistemic virtue. We focus on three relevant virtues: testimonial justice, epistemic humility, and open-mindedness. Testimonial justice enables dominantly positioned listeners to cultivate a critical awareness of the epistemic implications of social location such that they understand how prejudices might impact their judgment about marginalized speakers' credibility and take corrective measures (Fricker, 2007). Epistemic humility and open-mindedness enable dominantly positioned knowers to accept the inadequacy of their epistemic resources in accounting for the significance of oppression on marginalized groups and to grasp the significance of marginalized epistemic resources that may be incomprehensible through a dominant epistemic lens (Dotson, 2012; Medina, 2013).

20.4 Punishment and Democratic Education

Given this vision of democratic education, the question for educators is how punishment and disciplinary practices align with democratic aims and purposes. We begin by examining whether *any* form of punishment or disciplinary practice is compatible with democratic education. Some disciplinary practices are compatible with democratic education, we argue, but not all. After rejecting practices that are incompatible with democratic education, we turn to the model that aligns more successfully, restorative justice.

There is a case to be made that no form of punishment is compatible with democratic education. The reason is that punishment is the imposition of one person's will over another through force rather than persuasion. This seems like a direct violation of the spirit of democracy which, as John Dewey (1916) suggests, "repudiates the principle of external authority" (p. 101). Punishment is perhaps the external imposition of authority par excellence – it is used to coerce people to do things that they would otherwise not do. Most punishment practices require no participation or cooperation. The aim is simply to make people submit. With this dynamic of force-and-submission, there is little in the experience of punishment that leads to the building of democratic capabilities and dispositions: no building of trust or tolerance, no opportunity for reciprocity or mutual understanding, and certainly no deliberation. If we want to educate students for democracy, it appears, educators would be better advised to use reason and dialogue with students, rather than mete out punishments.

There is much that is correct in this argument. A preference for reason and persuasion over brute force should be a guiding principle of democratic education. Student interest and engagement should triumph over external imposition of rules and punishments. No educator who believes in democracy will act as a despotic tyrant of their classroom – acting as judge, jury, and, as it were, executioner. Importantly, part of the reason why punishment is deemed necessary in schools is because students are often understandably unmotivated. They become apathetic or rebellious because of neglected and understaffed classrooms, overburdened and uninspired pedagogues, and crumbling school buildings. In such cases, democratic educators and policymakers should look reflexively inward at the flawed institutions of which they are part, instead of reaching for ever more stringent tactics of control and domination.

While the conflict between democratic education and punishment is considerable, one need not preclude the other. Consider the following case. A teacher collaborates with students to create a set of rules and expectations that will govern the classroom community as well as determine the consequences for violating those rules. In this deliberative process, all students have a voice and are trusted to take responsibility as members of the classroom community. The deliberative process, moreover, continues until all students consent to the social contract of the classroom.[3] Maybe an adopted rule would be that students should respect the classroom space or that they should not steal or damage

[3] Given age-dependent developmental constraints in students' ability to account for all relevant considerations and to consent to necessary provisions that they are not fully capable of grasping at a young age, there are limits to how democratic such a deliberative process can be in practice. Depending on the age of students, the teacher's better understanding of measures that are necessary for protecting students from physical or emotional harm may legitimately restrict the deliberative process described.

the property of other students. If a student is found culpable of violating this rule, an agreed upon social consequence is given to them. The student might be asked to, say, clean up the mess, repair the damage, or apologize to those who were hurt.

This case is very different from situations where teachers enforce their will through the brute force of autocratic forms of punishment. Students are active participants in shared community life and the punishment meted out to wrongdoers is justifiable in terms that are acceptable by all, including the wrongdoers themselves. In establishing the punishment, moreover, students experience a learning environment that cultivates democratic capabilities including trust, reciprocity, and deliberation. The punishment, such as cleaning up the mess or repairing the damage, would also be "symbolically adequate" to the harm that was done. To be symbolically adequate, Christopher Bennett (2008) writes, a punishment must ask offenders "to undertake the sort of reparative action that they would be motivated to undertake were they genuinely sorry for what they have done" (p. 9). Symbolically adequate punishment sends the message that there is a connection between the action and the social consequences, and that the punishment is indeed democratically warranted, rationally consistent, and not some arbitrary whim of those in power.

Another way of thinking about punishment and democratic education is to clarify the purpose of punishment. The purpose might be retribution, to simply give people "what they deserve" for their past behavior, or it might be deterrence, to dissuade people from doing harmful things in the future. Some have argued that an adequate theory of punishment must include both retributive (past-looking) and deterrent (forward-looking) elements (Hart, 2008).

Thinking in terms of these theories can be helpful, but the picture becomes more complex in schools. Retribution – giving people what they deserve – assumes an environment of morally competent and responsible agents who understand the connection between actions and consequences and who can thoughtfully regulate their emotions and desires. Even if it is true that adults can be morally responsible in this way, children and youth have not yet fully developed these capacities. Retribution, then, is often an inappropriate purpose of punishment in schools, especially in the case of younger children. This is particularly true if the retribution is enacted with the spirit of vengeance.

To question the full moral accountability of children is not to say that the idea of moral responsibility is irrelevant in schools, never to be mentioned with children. On the contrary, schools can and should talk about students taking responsibility, respecting prior agreements, keeping their word, and so forth. In schools, though, moral responsibility needs to be understood developmentally, as something that schools are working on, rather than a fully formed capacity meriting complete moral accountability. A discourse of taking responsibility can be seen as part of a process of moral education and community healing. One way to develop responsibility, in fact, may be to act *as if* students have moral agency.[4]

[4] We are indebted to the thoughtful comments of the volume editors for this insight.

We will see that punishment, when properly structured, can help students learn to take responsibility, which will then help them to develop moral capacities relevant to democracy. The sort of responsibility-taking we have in mind is part of a larger project of moral education, however, and not a justification for retribution.

Deterrence is more defendable justification for punishment. There are certain actions – bullying, cruelty, racism, theft, and more – that schools justifiably want to deter and designating them as punishable infractions seems appropriate for this reason. The question then becomes whether punishment is an effective deterrent. After all, only some punishments deter and only some of the time. This becomes an empirical question and a contextual judgment for educators.

While there is room for deterrence as a purpose of punishment in schools, there is another purpose: communication or expression. The expressive function of punishment is closely related to the purpose of punishment as a kind of moral education. Punishment, in this sense, is not retribution or deterrence so much as an initiation of students into a moral realm of conduct (Hand, 2018). This initiation occurs through what scholars have called "the expressive function of punishment": communicating to an offender the gravity of a harm that has occurred and the moral community's negative view of that action (Feinberg, 1965). Punishment serves to condemn the action, communicating its disapproval to both the offender and the larger community.

Philosophers who see value in the expressive function of punishment argue that speech alone is sometimes not enough to send the appropriate message – to respond to sexual assault merely with a verbal response, a strongly worded letter, for example, would greatly minimize the harm that has occurred. It would trivialize the action to both the offender and the community. There are some things that words alone are unable to capture, so action is necessary to send the appropriate message. These philosophers seem correct, from our perspective: sometimes actions speak louder than words. Punishment can be a communicative act when words alone are inadequate to the task of condemnation.

At its best, punishment can promote dialogue between an offender and the community. The expressive function of punishment need not, and should not, be a one-way expression of condemnation. Condemnation provides an opportunity for certain forms of response by the offender that are (again) impossible with words alone. In response to the community's expression of disapproval, for instance, the offender can willingly accept a punishment and use it as a statement of remorse. Antony Duff (2001) writes:

> Sometimes. . .a (mere) apology is not enough. If I have done a serious wrong to another person, I cannot expect to settle or resolve the matter merely by apologizing to him: something more than that is due to him and from me. This is not because a serious wrong is likely to involve some material harm for which compensation must also be paid. Some such wrongs (serious betrayals of a friendship or a marriage, for instance) involve no such harm,

> while some harms (the harm involved in a rape or in a fraud committed by a friend, for instance) cannot be made good by material compensation. The point is rather that the victim cannot reasonably be expected to forgive me, to treat the matter as closed, merely on receipt of a verbal apology, however sincere, and that the wrongdoer cannot reasonably expect to close the matter thus. The wrong goes too deep for that. It goes too deep for the victim. . .It also goes too deep for the wrongdoer, whether or not she realizes it. To think that she could just apologize, and then return to her normal life, would be to portray the wrong as a relatively trivial matter that did not seriously damage the victim or their relationship. (p. 95)

Accepting a punishment can allow an expression of remorse to "go deep." It allows offenders to show that they take responsibility for the harm that has been caused and, with this response, comes the possibility for community reconciliation. As part of a process of reconciliation, people are changed – they are better able to see and hear those around them. They participate in various levels of dialogue and, in doing so, develop democratic capabilities.

Of course, not all punishment in society is structured or contextualized to promote this sort of dialogue, reconciliation, and democratic engagement. Indeed, the criminal justice system is often structured such that offenders seek to minimize both their responsibility and the harms that they have caused. Meanwhile, existing forms of punishment (monetary fines, imprisonment, death sentences) do little to promote reflection or productive remorse. The same holds true of existing forms of school discipline. Many traditional school disciplinary practices ask very little moral work of students. They ask little in terms of reflection, dialogue, or responsibility-taking. For a true punishment-response-reconciliation dynamic to occur, the punishment needs to occur in a larger context of communication, between victims, offenders, and community members.

To further help us distinguish these productive and unproductive forms of punishment, a distinction can be made between "primary" and "secondary" expressions of punishments. The primary expression of punishment is, simply, moral condemnation. It is the voice of the community registering its condemnation of both the action and the perpetrator. Secondary expressions are more variable and concern particular punishments. A specific type of punishment sends its own message beyond moral disapproval. It communicates the nature of an action, how social power functions, and the place of the offender in the moral community. Secondary expressions of punishment can work with or against democratic ideals and channels of democratic education.

Consider two school punishments that do not align with democratic education: corporal and exclusionary punishment. Corporal punishment is no longer a common practice in American schools – it is practiced by approximately 3% of the nation's schools (roughly 4,000 out of 130,000 schools) – but it is worth mentioning (Sparks & Harwin, 2016). Like many traditional forms of school punishment, corporal punishment asks very little of students. Paddling, for instance, does not ask students to think about their wrongdoing or consider the effects of their actions on others. The unreflective, individualistic nature of paddling renders it unable to make a positive contribution to democracy. What is worse, the secondary expressions of corporal punishment actively work against democratic capabilities and dispositions. Paddling sends the message that physical force is an appropriate way to solve problems and that those who are physically stronger or in positions of authority should assert their will over others. Social science research supports this worry by showing that students who experience corporal punishment are more likely to be violent themselves (Ohene et al., 2006). Paddling legitimizes coercive violence in human affairs and, in doing so, not only fails to foster democratic capabilities but actively undermines their cultivation.

While corporal punishment is relatively rare, exclusionary punishment – suspensions and expulsions – is a common feature of American schools. Like corporal punishment, exclusionary punishment asks little of students in terms of democratic engagement. In fact, exclusionary punishment removes students precisely from the place where the moral dialogue is likely to occur: the school and classroom communities that set the original context for the behavior. These types of punishment certainly *seem* more benign than corporal punishment. They send a less troubling message about physical violence and may be justified if a student presents a clear and present danger to other students. At the same time, the negative effects of exclusionary practices are well-documented in the literature. The American Academy of Pediatrics, for instance, notes that exclusionary punishment seriously damages student progress and learning, decreases the likelihood of graduation, increases the likelihood of involvement in the juvenile justice system, and has a lasting impact on future employment and earnings (Council on School Health, 2013). For our purposes, we note that the secondary expressions of exclusionary punishment send messages about membership (or lack thereof) in the school community. They express the idea that certain students are not welcome at school: "You do not belong here." In a democratic community, in contrast, the ethos of inclusion runs deep – the ideal in democracy is to work through differences rather than excise those who diverge. The enduring message from schools ought to be one of inclusion, and attempts should be made to repair broken relationships through dialogue rather than to separate and silence.

Another reason to be wary of corporal and exclusionary punishments is how connected they are to racial inequality. A study from the United States Government Accountability Office (2018) found that, although Black students account for only 15.5% of all students they account for 39% of all students suspended from school (pp. 12–15). This is true across different types of schools and income levels, suggesting that the phenomenon is grounded in racial attitudes rather than differences in class-based behavioral expectations. For the same infractions, it has been shown that Black students are punished more harshly than White students (Okonofua & Eberhardt, 2015). It has also been shown that White students are often suspended for "objective behaviors" (e.g., cutting class), whereas Black for "subjective behaviors" (e.g., being disrespectful) where implicit racial biases can influence an educator's judgment (Skiba et al.,

2002). Aside from being unjust, such disparities delegitimize the democratic order. They send their own messages about who is valued and who is a second-class citizen.

20.5 Restorative Punishment and Democratic Capabilities

Punishment and democratic education, then, are not fundamentally opposed. Democracy is about social cooperation and communication that facilitates such cooperation, but verbal communication alone can symbolically fail to capture the depth of our moral lives. Punishment can communicate the gravity of misconduct to offenders and to communities when words alone cannot. When well-constructed, punishment can also enable offenders to accept responsibility and show remorse, allowing for reconciliation and, hopefully, some degree of healing that can restore trust and facilitate social cooperation. These features of punishment make it potentially useful in preserving a democratic way of living among diverse persons and groups. Yet the ability of punishment to facilitate such processes depends on its secondary expressions and the context of communication within which it is embedded.

Since corporal and exclusionary punishment work against democracy, what kind of punishment might better align with democratic ideals? The answer, in part, is a restorative justice approach to discipline and punishment. The first key principle of this approach is that "crime" causes a breach of social relationships. One party causes harm to another by violating norms of community trust and reciprocity. The second principle is that the goal of discipline and punishment is to restore the relationship and to rebuild community ties. The third principle is that participation and communication, in the form of active dialogue between affected parties, are necessary for restoring relationships.

Dialogue allows victims to explain how they have been harmed by an action. Only when the offender understands the harm they caused, after all, can a sincere apology be offered and full responsibility be accepted. Offenders, for their part, are also given a chance to explain the situation from their perspective. The goal is to create mutual understanding and move toward a restored relationship – that is, to agree about what happened, who bears responsibility, and what actions are required to redress the harm done. As part of accepting responsibility, the offender might be asked to show remorse and repair damages incurred. They may be asked to return or replace items, clean up messes, pay restitution, or perform community service. Restorative justice, therefore, asks much of offenders and infuses reparative actions with greater meaning: it asks for their presence, engagement, attention, considered response, responsibility, and true remorse often expressed through actions.

Restorative justice practices are similar to indigenous practices worldwide. In Western democracies, they were originally implemented in criminal justice programs and only later found their way into education. Research on the effectiveness of restorative justice programs among juvenile offenders has been quite promising, for example, in reducing rates of recidivism (Sherman & Stang,

2007). Such programs are now becoming more popular in schools, where restorative approaches take the form of "restorative circles" where students, teachers, and community members meet and discuss problems. The approach is new and experimental, and empirical research on the "effectiveness" of existing approaches in schools is mixed (Acosta et al., 2019; Augustine et al., 2018; Fronius et al., 2016; Katic et al., 2020).

One important feature of restorative justice is that it asks participants to take responsibility. While this is most important for the offender, all participants are expected to reflect and be open about what happened and what role they may have played. According to Canton's (2017) description of restorative justice "the roles of 'offender' and 'victim' are not necessarily pre-determined when the attempt at conflict resolution begins and indeed deciding who was in the wrong may matter less than achieving an outcome that sufficiently commands everyone's confidence" (p. 152). Schools, like other social institutions, cocreate the behavior of their members. Rigid and poorly designed school policies and practices influence student behavior. Educators must recognize the role that schools, and larger social structures, play in encouraging misconduct. They should listen to students, be open to changing their minds, and accordingly make adjustments to school policies and practices. What seems like misconduct in some cases might even be a justified response to unfair circumstances (Nikolaidis & Thompson, 2021). In such cases, the focus must be placed on transforming the circumstances of students.[5]

Note that the secondary expressions of restorative justice approaches to school discipline are superior to retributive approaches. Where corporal punishment sends the message that human relationships are based on physical and institutional power and that problem-solving requires physical violence, restorative justice views human relations as dialogical and communicative. Instead of "might makes right," the focus is on relationships, understanding, and reason-giving. Similarly, where exclusionary punishment sends a message of rejection and severance from the community, restorative justice seeks to reintegrate students into school life and social cooperation. Instead of exclusion, the focus is inclusion. In other words, the secondary expressions of restorative justice point toward democracy. Consider the democratic capabilities we described in Section 20.3 and how they relate to restorative justice:

Capability for autonomy. The focus on taking responsibility, an integral part of restorative justice approaches, asks students to see themselves as agents who can make decisions and whose actions matter in the world. The message is on owning up to what one does. The ultimate outcome is a shared decision, allowing the participants to act as collective agents in determining their

[5] Indeed, any meaningful conception of restorative justice must have a transformative component. A parallel commitment to "transformative justice" entails a recognition that there are fundamental problems with our social institutions (including education) that render restoration of de facto relations both illusory and undesirable. Relations ought to be changed such that those who are marginalized and victimized by an unjust system are the ones who are neither disproportionately punished for their infractions nor prompted by that very system to engage in infractions out of necessity (Morris, 1995).

futures. It also helps participants understand the social consequences of their actions, the effects of their actions on others, and the harms that have been done. This sense of causal connection – actions and consequences – is a prerequisite for autonomy.

Capability for reciprocity. Restorative justice is an act of cooperation as participants seek to restore relationships. Participants are asked in the beginning to listen and respond to each other in mutually justifiable terms, in an initial act of reciprocation. They are asked to attend to the concerns of others and adjust their actions accordingly. All participants are asked to take responsibility for their contributions to a situation, leading the way to redressing grievances and reconciling fractured relations. This often involves compromise and adjustment on both sides of a dispute or situation. Importantly, restorative justice provides an opportunity for schools to show that they are also able and willing to reciprocate by abandoning unfair policies and practices and transforming their institutional processes.

Capability for trust. In restoring community relations, restorative justice ultimately rebuilds bonds of trust. Unlike retributive justice, it assumes that all human beings are valued and can be trusted to cooperate and achieve mutual understanding. It casts human beings as trustworthy and works toward building greater trust moving forward. Moreover, restorative approaches facilitate trust by teaching students trustworthiness. Through open discussion, those who were wronged can express why they feel that their trust was betrayed while offenders can learn what expectations they ought to meet to be considered trustworthy, and they are provided with a chance to change and restore conditions of trust in the school community. Building trust among students and teachers also increases trust in the school as an institution.

Capability for tolerance. In eliciting authentic communication between diverse persons, restorative justice alerts students to the presence of conflicting value systems that until that point may have been concealed. It foregrounds the conflicting values that may cause problems or tensions between members of the school community, and it affords students and teachers the opportunity to understand when conflicting values are reasonable and ought to be tolerated. On a more practical level, restorative justice practices enable students to raise questions regarding what conduct should be tolerated in a democratic community and what should be discouraged. It demands that members of the community find mutually acceptable ways to move forward following conflict.

Capability for deliberation. When it comes to democratic education, deliberation is where restorative justice shines. It brings students together to communicate and deliberate about a common problem, to consider various solutions to the problem, and to collectively agree on a course of action that is acceptable by all involved parties. Restorative justice requires a genuine exchange of perspectives. It asks students to *listen* to others, to understand what they have done and how they view the situation. At the same time, it also encourages students to *speak*, to explain their reasons and motivations, their hopes and frustrations. In doing so, it is inclusive in a way that autocratic distribution of punishment can never be, especially given the cultural mismatch between teachers and students which results in the privileging of white middle-class norms and the disproportionate punishment of marginalized students.

Capability for epistemic virtue. We discussed the virtues of testimonial justice, epistemic humility, and open-mindedness. Restorative justice is particularly useful in demanding that schools *listen* to marginalized students, rather than ignoring their complaints and imposing consequences ex cathedra. It requires that participants in deliberation give due credibility to all their interlocutors including, and most importantly, to voices that have been historically silenced. Moreover, by fostering an environment where all have an opportunity to state their perspectives without prior judgment and where everyone's position must be seriously considered, restorative justice is conducive to the development of epistemic humility and open-mindedness. It presents opportunities – on the part of both students and schools – to realize that their previous interpretations of events were likely misguided. Getting the chance to practice engaging with people in such profound ways is critical to developing these deep-seated democratic virtues moving forward.

In short, restorative justice fosters rich educational moments that prioritize listening and cooperation. This is the type of experience that prompts students to become democratically minded. Where corporal punishment seeks to impose rules through force, and exclusionary punishment seeks to sever students from the moral community, restorative justice seeks to restore relationships through reconciliation and mutual understanding and to rebuild community ties that have been broken. By giving all students a greater voice, it encourages resistance against the racial inequalities that are prominent in other forms of punishment. Restorative practices are a way of thinking about punishment that aligns with democratic education.

Some might question whether restorative justice is properly conceived as a paradigm of punishment rather than just a mode of collective problem-solving. To be sure, restorative justice is not a view of punishment per se. If a student does something wrong, however, and is asked to participate in a restorative circle, the student may consider this to be a type of burden, thus a punishment (ideally, it becomes more than that through the process of discussion). At the same time, restorative justice legitimates other forms of punishment. Indeed, after a restorative justice circle, it may be decided that students must do something to right a wrong that has been committed, something symbolically adequate to the harm that was caused. Students, as we have discussed, may be asked to clean up a mess, write a letter of apology, replace stolen items, or be subjected to other forms of punishments that schools are familiar with. However, the punishment is connected to a process that deepens its social meaning for offenders, victims, and the community. Victims can describe the harm and, with this description, offenders can offer more meaningful apologies through words and actions. At the same time, offenders can explain their actions and schools can learn what they can do better. Restorative justice presents opportunities to rethink punishment and transform school practices, highlighting how past practices may have been illegitimate.

Admittedly, this is an idealized picture of what restorative justice can accomplish in terms of democratic education. Often, both students and teachers are reluctant to engage for many reasons – suspicion of the process and (on the part of teachers) lack of time, training, and resources. Productive conversations and authentic communication can be hard to achieve under the best of circumstances. Some point to examples of schools that successfully implement restorative justice programs and to research indicating its potential (Jain et al., 2014), while others point to resistance on the part of teachers and research showing more negative effects (Eden, 2019). Giving up on restorative justice, however, is in some sense giving up on democracy. Democracy is an ideal that often does not work in practice as it is supposed to work in theory. Still, the ideal of democracy seems worthy of pursuit, even under nonideal circumstances. At the very least, restorative justice exemplifies a mindset of engaging with students that all educators can realistically strive toward: more listening to students, more care for community relationships, more cooperation with students as moral beings to collectively solve classroom problems. This is the mindset of teachers who respect and support democracy.

20.6 Conclusion

As citizens of a democratic society, we have an obligation to uphold principles of democracy and live by the democratic values that provide our society stability and legitimacy. Educators have a similar duty to instill in future generations the values and capabilities that they need to participate meaningfully in that society. They have an obligation to provide students with an education that helps them flourish in life, without sacrificing the democratic ideals that are a precondition for such flourishing to materialize. Punishment, we believe, has a place in such democratic education, but it must be used in ways that align with democratic principles.

It is possible to construct a democratic ethic of school punishment. Based on what we have presented here, we believe such an ethic is grounded on four principles. First, classroom and school rules should be constructed cooperatively with students, with the goal that students freely consent to the norms of conduct. Second, when problems arise with student behavior, a process of dialogue and mutual understanding should be undertaken, as exemplified by restorative justice approaches. Third, any corrective and restorative actions growing out of the dialogue should be symbolically adequate to the harm that was caused – they should relate in some way to the harm and their secondary expressions should align with democratic ideals. Fourth, educators should be open-minded and reflective and adjust their attitudes and practices based on what grows out of the dialogue. When punishment is framed correctly, it becomes an act of collective problem-solving within an authentic community. In this, it is not only compatible with democratic education; it becomes an act democratic education.

References

Acosta, J., Chinman, M., Ebener, P., Malone, P. S., Phillips, A., & Wilks, A. (2019). Evaluation of a whole-school change intervention: Findings from a two-year cluster-randomized trial of the restorative practices intervention. *Journal of Youth and Adolescence*, 48(5), 876–90.

Allen, D. (2020). A new theory of justice. In D. Allen & R. Somanathan, eds., *Difference without domination: Pursuing justice in diverse democracies*. Chicago, IL: The University of Chicago Press, pp. 27–57.

Augustine, C. H., Engberg, J., Grimm G. E., Lee, E., Wang, E. L., Christianson, K., & Joseph, A. A. (2018). Can restorative practices improve school climate and curb suspensions? An evaluation of the impact of restorative practices in a mid-sized urban school district. RAND Corporation. Available at: https://www.rand.org/pubs/research_reports/RR2840.html.

Bennett, C. (2008). *The apology ritual: A philosophical theory of punishment*. Cambridge: Cambridge University Press.

Brighouse, H. (1998). Civic education and liberal legitimacy. *Ethics*, 108(4), 719–45.

Canton, R. (2017). *Why punish? An introduction to the philosophy of punishment*. London: Palgrave Macmillan.

Council on School Health. (2013). Out-of-school suspension and expulsion. *Pediatrics*, 131(3), e1000–07.

Curren, R. (2020). Punishment and motivation in a just school community. *Theory and Research in Education*, 18(1), 117–33.

Dewey, J. (1916). *Democracy and education: An introduction to the philosophy of education*. New York: Macmillan.

Dotson, K. (2012). A cautionary tale: On limiting epistemic oppression. *Frontiers*, 33(1), 24–47.

Duff, A. (2001). *Punishment, communication, and community*. Oxford: Oxford University Press.

Eden, M. (2019). Restorative justice isn't working, but that's not what the media is reporting. The Fordham Institute. Available at: https://fordhaminstitute.org/national/commentary/restorative-justice-isnt-working-thats-not-what-media-reporting.

Feinberg, J. (1965). The expressive function of punishment. *The Monist*, 49(3), 397–423.

Fricker, M. (2007). *Epistemic injustice: Power and the ethics of knowing*. Oxford: Oxford University Press.

Fronius, T., Sutherland, H., Guckenburg, S., Hurley, N., & Petrosino, A. (2016). Restorative justice in U.S. schools: A research review. WestEd Justice and

Prevention Center. Available at: https://jprc.wested.org/wp-content/uploads/2016/02/RJ_Literature-Review_20160217.pdf.

Galston, W. A. (1991). *Liberal purposes: Goods, virtues, and diversity in the liberal state*. Cambridge: Cambridge University Press.

Galston, W. A. (2017). Why liberal tolerance, rightly understood, is coherent and defensible. *San Diego Law Review*, 54(2), 199–216.

Gathercoal, F. (1998). Judicious discipline. In R. E. Butchart & B. M. Landau, eds., *Classroom discipline in American schools: Problems and possibilities for democratic education*. Albany: SUNY Press, pp. 197–216.

Gregory, A., Skiba, R. J., & Noguera, P. A. (2010). The achievement gap and the discipline gap: Two sides of the same coin? *Educational Researcher*, 39(1), 59–68.

Gutmann, A., & Thompson, D. (1996). *Democracy and disagreement*. Cambridge, MA: Harvard Belknap.

Gutmann, A., & Thompson, D. (2004). *Why deliberative democracy?* Princeton, NJ: Princeton University Press.

Hand, M. (2018). *A theory of moral education*. New York: Routledge.

Hand, M. (2020). On the necessity of school punishment. *Theory and Research in Education*, 18(1), 10–22.

Hart, H. L. A. (2008). *Punishment and responsibility: Essays in the philosophy of law*. 2nd ed., Oxford: Oxford University Press.

Hess, D., & McAvoy, P. (2014). *The political classroom: Evidence and ethics in democratic education*. New York: Routledge.

Hobson, P. (1986). The compatibility of punishment and moral education. *Journal of Moral Education*, 15(3), 221–8.

Jain, S., Bassey, H., Brown, M. A., & Kalra, P. (2014). *Restorative justice in Oakland schools: Implementation and impacts*. Oakland Unified School District. Available at: http://www.instituteforrestorativeinitiatives.org/uploads/1/6/3/2/16320200/exec_summary_-_rj_ousd_report_2014.pdf#:~:text=Restorative%20Justice%20in%20Oakland%20Schools%20In%202005%2C%20 OUSD,students%20coming%20from%20the%20juvenile%20justice%20system.%201.

Katic, B., Alba, L. A., & Johnson, A. H. (2020). A systematic evaluation of restorative justice practices: School violence prevention and response. *Journal of School Violence*, 19(4), 579–93.

Knight Abowitz, K., & Harnish, J. (2006). Contemporary discourses of citizenship. *Review of Educational Research*, 76(4), 653–90.

Levinson, M. (1999). *The demands of liberal education*. Oxford: Oxford University Press.

Levinson, M. (2003). Challenging deliberation. *Theory and Research in Education*, 1 (1), 23–49.

Levinson, M. (2011). Democracy, accountability, and education. *Theory and Research in Education*, 9(2), 125–44.

Macedo, S. (Ed.) (1999). *Deliberative politics: Essays on democracy and disagreement*. Oxford: Oxford University Press.

Marshall, J. D. (1984). Punishment and moral education. *Journal of Moral Education*, 13(2), 83–89.

Medina, J. (2013). *The epistemology of resistance: Gender and racial oppression, epistemic injustice, and resistant imaginations*. Oxford: Oxford University Press.

Morris, R. (1995). Not enough! *Mediation Quarterly*, 12(3), 285–91.

Nikolaidis, A. C., & Thompson, W. C. (2021). Breaking school rules: The permissibility of non-compliance in an unjust educational system. *Harvard Educational Review*, 91(2), 204–26.

Ohene, S. A., Ireland, M., McNeely, C., & Borowsky, I. W. (2006). Parental expectations, physical punishment, and violence among adolescents who score positive on a psychosocial screening test in primary care. *Pediatrics*, 117(2), 441–47.

Okonofua, J. A., & Eberhardt, J. L. (2015). Two strikes: Race and the disciplining of young students. *Psychological Science*, 26(5), 617–24.

Osler, A., & Starkey, H. (2006). Education for democratic citizenship: A review of research, policy and practice 1995–2005. *Research Papers in Education*, 21(4), 433–66.

Putnam, R. D. (1993). *Making democracy work: Civic traditions in modern Italy*. Princeton, NJ: Princeton University Press.

Rawls, J. (1993). *Political liberalism*. New York: Columbia University Press.

Rothstein, B., & Stolle, D. (2008). The state and social capital: An institutional theory of generalized trust. *Comparative Politics*, 40(4), 441–59.

Sanders, L. M. (1997). Against deliberation. *Political Theory*, 25(3), 347–76.

Sant, E. (2019). Democratic education: A theoretical review (2006–2017). *Review of Educational Research*, 89(5), 655–96.

Scanlon, T. M. (2003). The difficulty of tolerance. In T. M. Scanlon, ed., *The difficulty of tolerance: Essays in political philosophy*. Cambridge: Cambridge University Press, pp. 187–201.

Sherman, L. W., & Stang, H. (2007). *Restorative justice: The evidence*. Smith Institute. Available at: https://www.iirp.edu/pdf/RJ_full_report.pdf.

Skiba, R. J., Michael, R. S., Nardo, A. C., & Peterson, R. L. (2002). The color of discipline: Sources of racial and gender disproportionality in school punishment. *The Urban Review*, 34(4), 317–42.

Sparks, S. D., & Harwin, A. (2016, August 23). Corporal punishment use found in schools in 21 states. *Education Week*. Available at: https://www.edweek.org/leadership/corporal-punishment-use-found-in-schools-in-21-states/2016/08.

Thompson, W. C., & Tillson, J. (Eds.). (2020). Pedagogies of punishment [Special issue]. *Theory and Research in Education*, 18(1).

United States Government Accountability Office. (2018). *K–12 education: Discipline disparities for Black students, boys, and students with disabilities*. Available at: https://www.gao.gov/assets/gao-18-258.pdf.

Vallier, K. (2018). *Must politics be war? Restoring our trust in the free society*. Oxford: Oxford University Press.

Warnick, B. R., & Scribner, C. F. (2020). Discipline, punishment, and the moral community of schools. *Theory and Research in Education*, 18(1), 98–116.

21

Children's Rights and Democratic Education

Colin M. Macleod

21.1 Introduction

Invocation of children's rights in the context of education is now a ubiquitous feature of political discourse. This is true even though there are significant philosophical disagreements about the precise nature and justificatory basis of children's rights as well controversies about the substantive content of children's rights. Some hold that children's rights are indispensable to the protection of the fundamental interests of children, others express concerns that a discourse of rights is corrosive to healthy relations between adults and children, and still others deny that children are even bearers of moral rights at all on the grounds that children lack the full agential capacities requisite to being a holder of rights (Griffin, 2002).[1] Despite these philosophical disputes about children's rights, there is near universal acceptance of the idea that all children have a justice-based entitlement to education. Even those who are skeptical that children are, strictly speaking, bearers of moral rights do not doubt that the provision of education to children is a key requirement of a just democratic community. So, there is agreement that all children[2] are entitled to an education that equips them with essential skills of literacy and numeracy and provides them with basic knowledge in a variety of standard areas – for example, science, history, art, literature, and politics. Moreover, there is general consensus that education should be conducive to preparing children to be capable participants in democratic processes and communities (Gutmann, 1999). Education is partly about "creating citizens" (Callan, 1997). This is tantamount to accepting that children are rights bearers and that their rights play an

[1] See Macleod (2018) for a critical review of different forms of skepticism about the attribution of rights to children.

[2] Some children with significant cognitive impairments may not be able to become fully literate or numerate. So, some of the standard aims of education need to interpreted with due sensitivity to the needs of children with cognitive disabilities. Expressly democratic components of education also need to be interpreted with such children in view. Since schools are arguably partly a site of democracy and since people with cognitive disabilities are full members of the democratic community, there are reasons to provide children with such disabilities access to schools with their peers even if they cannot meet the academic goals that are reasonably set for students without disabilities. However, proper examination of this important topic goes beyond the scope of my discussion. For discussion of issues of inclusion in the context of special education see Ladenson (2003).

important role in determining the appropriate character and content of democratic education. However, against this backdrop of broad agreement about the core aims of education and its broad democratic mission, there are many areas of theoretical and practical controversy. There is contestation both about the basic principles that should animate a conception of democratic education and what institutional arrangements and policies are required to give effect to ideals. In what follows, I shall distinguish a set of broad issues and provide a brief overview of some key fault lines in debates about democratic education. I will indicate how sometimes competing visions of children's rights are implicated in these debates. The partition between issues is not always sharp, since how a matter should be resolved in one domain often turns on considerations that are salient in another domain.

With that caveat in place, five broad areas of debate can be identified. First, there are questions about the appropriate content of democratic education and the associated conception of democratic values that should inform democratic education. Second, there are issues about the access that children have to democratic education. At stake here are considerations of distributive justice and whether or to what degree inequalities in the caliber of education available to children are permissible. Do children have a right to equally good education? Third, issues arise about who has authority to control at least some facets of children's education. Here there is contestation about the degree to which parents may influence the educational environment enjoyed specifically by their own children. May parents tailor education with a view to authoritatively fixing their children's identities? Are parents morally permitted to confer special educational advantages on their own children when doing this is disadvantageous to other children? To what extent do children's rights constrain the rights of parents? Fourth, there are questions about the degree to which schools themselves should be sites of democratic activity in which students, at a suitable age and stage, exercise control over features of their schools. Do children, within the context of schools, have rights to democratic self-determination? Finally, there is a host of issues about the institutional design of schools for the advancement of ideals of democratic education. Many of these issues are highly context specific and reflect features of the political landscape and history of particular communities. In Canada, for instance, the terrible injustices generated by the residential school program give rise to questions about how schools and educational policies should be shaped so as to address the unjust disadvantages faced by Indigenous communities.[3] In the United States, special attention is devoted to the challenge of overcoming the legacy of racist segregation of schools and ongoing racial inequalities in the provision of education.[4] In what follows, I will focus primarily on the background theoretical and normative issues that inform debates about policies and institutional design.

[3] The report of the Truth and Reconciliation Commission of Canada (2015) included 11 calls to action in the domain of education.

[4] See, for instance, the contrasting views of Anderson (2010) and Merry (2013) as to whether racial integration of schools is the best strategy for addressing racism.

21.2 The Content of Democratic Education

As I have noted, democratic education has a key preparatory objective: it seeks to equip children with the skills, knowledge, and dispositions they need to meaningfully participate in the civic and political life of a community. The content of education suitable to that general objective depends on features of the political community to which children belong, the interpretation of basic democratic values, and the fundamental rights that are ascribed to children. Although there are many ways of partitioning content issues in relation to these factors, I will review four areas of contestation: (i) the character of education for toleration in the wake of pluralism; (ii) the character of education suitable for democratic participation; (iii) education and autonomy facilitation; and (iv) the promotion of civic virtue.

21.2.1 Pluralism and Toleration

The background context for many debates about the appropriate content of democratic education involves recognition of the pluralism that characterizes most democratic communities (Macedo, 2000). The citizens of democratic states, though broadly committed to the legitimacy of democratic processes for crafting state policy and resolving differences between people, hold diverse moral, political, religious, and aesthetic views. They also differ in the ethnic, linguistic, cultural, and sexual identities they embrace. An important general challenge for democratic politics is to negotiate this pluralism in a manner that displays respect for people despite their differences and disagreements about important matters. Given pluralism, the virtue of toleration is important to democracy and part of democratic education is focused on cultivating an understanding of and commitment to toleration on the part of students. But since the ideal of toleration is itself contested, there are rival views about what suitable cultivation of toleration requires (Forst, 2013). Here we can draw a rough distinction between thin and robust conceptions of toleration education. On a thin conception, toleration education consists primarily in alerting students to the fact that society is characterized by pluralism and that people have rights, subject only to the limitations prescribed by law, to give expression to their views and commitments in the choices they make about how to lead their lives. Here, mastering toleration is primarily a matter of properly acknowledging the civil liberties that people have along with their associated rights to nondiscrimination. In cultivating this conception of toleration, there is no requirement that students be provided with education about the beliefs, practices, and history of other people (e.g., the content of different faiths, the cultural practices of different ethnic groups, or the nature of diversity in gender identity or sexual orientation). Similarly, toleration of this variety does not require that education be oriented toward facilitating a sympathetic appreciation of diversity or a recognition that the commitments of others with respect to religion, sexuality, or culture may be reasonable and possibly worthy of adoption or admiration.

By contrast, on a more robust conception of toleration, it is important to cultivate not only a commitment to respecting the basic rights of members of the community but also a respect for other members of the community that is grounded in an informed understanding of the nature of their important beliefs, practices, and commitments. For instance, within the realm of religion education for toleration includes teaching children about different faith traditions as well as atheism and agnosticism so that students can sympathetically appreciate the rituals, modes of dress, and social norms that others view as important to their sense of self (Macleod, 2010). This form of toleration grounded in mutual understanding does not require encouraging students to believe that all faiths or conceptions of the good are equally credible or valuable. But it does encourage a degree of humility about one's own commitments and a willingness to acknowledge that other people can reasonably adhere to vastly different practices or commitments.

In terms of curriculum content, the thin view of toleration is associated with minimal education about the way diversity expresses itself in communities, and avoidance of subjects such as religion and sexuality in which students might be exposed to pedagogical materials that pose challenges to the deeply held convictions of students or their parents. The robust conception of toleration does not steer away from such materials, instead it welcomes pedagogical content that explores diverse and even controversial positions concerning religion and sexuality. Through consideration of such topics, misperceptions and biases may be corrected and students can ground their assessment of the diversity that surrounds them on facts rather than ignorance. Of course, in political communities marked by partisan division successfully addressing controversial subjects in the classroom can be extremely challenging (Hess & McAvoy, 2014).

21.2.2 Democratic Participation

As prospective participants in the democratic processes and practices of their communities, children have a right to an education that adequately prepares them for meaningful participation in democracy (Gutmann, 1999). However, the content of education appropriate to that participatory objective depends itself on the conception of democratic politics that is adopted. Here there is a rough division between broadly aggregative and deliberative conceptions of democracy. In aggregative conceptions of democracy, democratic legitimacy is mainly grounded in the operation of procedurally fair electoral processes. In deliberative conceptions of democracy, legitimacy requires good faith efforts on the behalf of citizens to exchange reasons in a respectful fashion. Aggregative conceptions of democracy adopt a somewhat passive view of citizenship in which participation in democratic politics is both optional and driven primarily by the concerns that citizens have to advance their own interests. Appropriate democratic conduct requires only that citizens respect the basic rights of others and that they abide by the fair procedures through which political outcomes are determined. By contrast, deliberative conceptions adopt a more expansive ideal of citizen engagement in which active participation in democratic politics is valorized and in which citizens seek, through reasoned, respectful debate and discussion to persuade fellow citizens of the merits of the political positions and policies they espouse. The common ground between these views is that a decent democratic education must provide students with a basic knowledge of the political history, constitutional structure (including protected political rights), and main procedures (e.g., electoral systems) of the political community to which they belong. But whereas the aggregative conception views the provision of such an education as sufficient preparation for meaningful and appropriate democratic activity, the deliberative conception holds that students should acquire the skills of critically reasoning that are requisite for reasonable and respectful political debate and discussion. Moreover, students should be encouraged to adopt the dispositions of open-mindedness, honesty, and humility that are conducive to engaging one's fellow citizens in dialogical processes of rational discussion aimed at persuasion. Democratic education, on this view, seeks to facilitate democratic activity that is less sullied by the shallow, partisan hackery that characterizes so much contemporary politics and that many find distasteful and alienating. But the noble aspirations of a deliberative democratic education are difficult to realize and can be seen to reflect a naïvely utopian ideal of politics.

21.2.3 Autonomy Facilitation

Democratic societies are characterized by value pluralism: citizens hold a wide variety of conceptions of the good and they differ, consequently, in the projects they pursue and the activities they value. With respect to their own lives, adult citizens have the right to make their own decisions about what conception of the good they embrace and what life plans to pursue. At the same time, many parents and communities seek to raise children in a way that leads children to embrace a particular conception of the good that they favor. For instance, religious parents frequently try to secure their children's adherence to a particular faith by sending them to parochial schools and by insulating them from educational influences that might challenge the religious views favored by the parents. The central issue that arises here is whether children have a right to an autonomy facilitating education. Since the precise nature of autonomy is itself a contested matter, the exact content of a right to an autonomy facilitating education is open to some interpretation (Levinson, 1999, pp. 22–35). However, autonomy is generally understood as a capacity that permits a person to deliberate about a range of possible ends, to select among available ends, and to pursue the ends that the person views worthy of adoption.

Autonomy has various social and material conditions and education figures prominently in developing the moral and psychological capacities requisite to deliberation about ends. It also plays a crucial role in providing people with knowledge and understanding about the plurality of ends that they might adopt. Since democratic communities protect the liberty of adult citizens to form and pursue their own conceptions of the good, it seems reasonable for childhood education to play an essential role in furnishing children with knowledge about the plurality of (reasonable) ends that people view worthy of adoption. Similarly, education can play a large role in developing deliberative capacities such that people can critically examine different commitments and make their own decisions about what conceptions of the good to pursue. The democratic basis for claiming that children have a right to autonomy facilitation has two main components. First, meaningful exercise of the key liberty rights that lie at the heart of democracy arguably depends on citizens being robustly autonomous. So, an autonomy facilitating education is essential to providing children proper access to rights to self-determination that democracies safeguard (Levinson, 1999). Second, since it is not legitimate in a democracy for some citizens to impose a conception of the good on others, it is not democratically legitimate for parents or communities to control education of children in the service of advancing certain conceptions of the good and impeding other views. In short, parents lack the authority to attempt to secure their children's adherence to a particular conception of the good.[5] On this view, a democratic education is not, for instance, compatible with attempts at religious indoctrination or even denying students with an unbiased understanding and appreciation of the plurality of reasonable conceptions of the good within the democratic community.

Skeptics about children's right to autonomy facilitation claim that fidelity to democratic ideals can be achieved without robust autonomy (Galston, 1991). On these views, the core requirement of democratic citizenship is only a basic understanding of and respect for democratic processes along with acknowledgement of the rights of citizens. Democratic education can adequately prepare students simply by providing instruction about the basic functioning of democratic institutions (e.g., the electoral system, the role of courts) and about the main rights that members of the democratic community have. Although this entails some education about the existence of pluralism within democratic communities, it does not require the cultivation of capacities for meaningful contemplation of diverse views, and it is compatible with giving parents enormous latitude to control and shape the conceptions of good held by their children.

Theorists in this broad camp offer varying accounts of the capacities and dispositions that are requisite to democratic activity and differ consequently on the required facets of democratic education. Those who adopt a broadly deliberative conception of democratic legitimacy typically endorse an education that secures development of the two moral powers that play a central role in Rawls' theory: a capacity for a conception of the good and a sense of justice (Rawls, 2001, pp. 18–19). Having these powers is held to be important to the possibility of participating in mutually respectful exchanges of reasons on

[5] Defenders of children's right to autonomy facilitation differ about the degree to which autonomy facilitation is compatible with parents adopting approaches to education in which one view of the good is favored over others. Some hold that any systematic favoring of conceptions of the good in the raising of children is illegitimate and should be avoided as much as possible (Clayton, 2006). Others allow that it is permissible for parents to provisionally privilege a particular conception of the good in raising children providing that such privileging does not encumber the capacity of children to learn about and reflectively consider other views (Macleod, 1997).

which democratic legitimacy is said to depend.[6] Sparser conceptions of democracy in which democratic legitimacy only requires the operation of fair aggregative processes yield correspondingly thinner conceptions of the required content of democratic education. A suitable democratic education need only provide instruction about the basic constitutional structure and the rights protected in that structure. Here, there is no requirement that students be provided an education that enables them to engage their fellow citizens in informed democratic discussion and debate. Instead, the aim is simply to cultivate a commitment to abiding by the laws of the democratic community. Those who are skeptical about autonomy facilitation typically grant parents and communities strong prerogatives to shape the ends of their children. On this approach, children have no right to an "open future" or even a future in which a wide diversity of ends remain open to children to contemplate or pursue. Instead, the rights of parents to pursue their own conceptions of the good is thought to ground the entitlement of parents to tightly control and shape the conceptions of the good of their children. Children are, in effect, treated as ingredients in the implementation of parental plans and if parents embrace a narrow, sectarian conception of the good then they have a right to control educational influences with the aim of inculcating that view in their children. On this view, children's rights to autonomy are extremely weak at best.

21.2.4 Promoting Civic Virtue

A content issue that is somewhat orthogonal to the previous content issues concerns the degree to which democratic education should be oriented to the promotion of civic virtues of various kinds. Although what is at stake here clearly has connection to content issues, part of the focus is on the role of education in cultivating dispositions and attitudes toward possible democratic ideals. The health of democracies depends not only on citizens having knowledge of democratic processes and the capacities requisite to negotiate them successfully, but also active participation. So, the question arises as to how and to what degree education should valorize and encourage active participation in democratic politics. This is different than merely preparing children to participate in democracy. Instead, it involves developing dispositions in children that encourage fulsome engagement in democratic politics.

According to a broadly Aristotelian strain of civic republicanism, active participation in politics is a richly rewarding form of human activity through which true human flourishing can be advanced (Oldfield, 1990). Since it seems reasonable that the state should facilitate genuine flourishing by citizens, and since children will not always come to recognize the value of civic engagement,

[6] The kind of education that facilitates development of the moral powers might be hard to distinguish from an education that facilitates autonomy but those who follow Rawls on this point insist that people with adequately developed moral powers need not be robustly autonomous. However, Rawls allows that even though education cannot expressly aim at cultivating autonomy, it is not objectionable if education for the moral powers has the effect of facilitating autonomy (Rawls, 1996, p. 200).

it is appropriate for schools to actively promote democratic participation as a conception of the good. Here civic virtue is valorized on the grounds it has a special, perhaps unique role, in human flourishing. However, the perfectionist stance of the Aristotelian approach is troubling to democratic theorists who emphasize pluralism about the good life and the importance of permitting citizens to determine for themselves what ends make their lives go best. Even if it is granted that civic participation is a great good for many people, it is doubtful that it is an essential facet of human flourishing for all people. If there is a plurality of routes to flourishing, then the state acts wrongly if it uses the educational system to recruit children to a specific and controversial conception of the good. Although alerting students to the possible value of civic participation for their own good is reasonable, the decision about whether to pursue civic life in the name of flourishing is something best left to individual citizens.

A different strategy for defending the importance of cultivating civic virtue is to emphasize the responsibilities, grounded in justice, that citizens have to contribute to the maintenance of healthy democratic institutions. If the maintenance of the very institutions that secure the basic rights of a person requires a significant degree of civic engagement then fostering that engagement via the cultivation of civic virtue in education can be defended without an appeal to perfectionism (Kymlicka, 2002, p. 299). This approach treats the cultivation of civic virtue as instrumentally important to justice rather than as a vehicle for flourishing.

The difference in the justificatory strategies employed by these approaches for cultivating civic virtue is important, but it is less clear what difference this justificatory difference makes to the appropriate content of education aimed at promoting civic virtue. Here dilemmas arise about whether the cultivation of patriotism or nationalism contribute appropriate civic virtue. Although patriotism and nationalism can motivate valuable civic participation and solidaristic commitment to the common good, patriotic and nationalist sentiments can blind citizens to injustices faced by marginalized and historically disadvantaged groups. Since some of the most egregious injustices in supposedly democratic communities involve denying children fair access to even minimally decent education, it is especially important that efforts to cultivate civic virtue via nationalism or patriotism are critically assessed with a view to guarding against their exclusionary and oppressive tendencies.

21.3 Children's Rights to Access Education

As I have noted, education plays an important role in preparing children for participation in processes of democratic self-government but it also prepares children for participation in various social and economic facets of civil society. But in most communities, there are vast inequalities in the quality of education to which children have access. These inequalities greatly influence the overall social and economic character of a democratic community and the life prospects that children will have access to as adults. So, addressing the rights of children to democratic education requires attention to the distribution of educational resources and opportunities among children from different family backgrounds. Despite the long and ugly history of racist and sexist discrimination in the provision of education to children, there is now near universal agreement that considerations of race, sex, and ethnicity should not influence the caliber of education to which children have access. Boys are not entitled to better education than girls, and racial or ethnic majorities are not entitled to better education than racial or ethnic minorities. The fact that there are still enormous educational inequalities grounded in race and ethnicity is a huge problem that requires urgent attention. Of course, it is a familiar fact that objectionable educational inequalities rooted in race or ethnicity are often closely tied to educational inequalities that are rooted in social and economic class. Nonetheless, there is less consensus among theorists as to whether considerations of economic class should, once stripped of their connection to racist exclusion, be permitted to influence children's access to education.

Many egalitarians who hold that just institutions should extinguish or mitigate as far as possible differences in people's life prospects that are grounded in morally arbitrary characteristics hold that all children should enjoy equal access to (excellent) education (Brighouse & Swift, 2009; Macleod, 2012). Even if justice permits differences in the income, wealth, and social standing of adults in virtue of the choices they make about how to pursue opportunities for economic and social advancement, children's access to essential goods such as education should not be influenced by the wealth or social standing of their parents. After all, children do not choose their parents and their fundamental life prospects should not be held hostage to the wealth of their parents. Eliminating class-based educational inequalities is a requirement not only of so-called luck-egalitarianism in which there is an express commitment to extinguish the ill-effects of brute luck on people's life prospects but also of the principle of fair equality of opportunity famously defended by Rawls. As Rawls says "those who have the same level of talent and ability and the same willingness to use these gifts should have the same prospects of success regardless of their social class origin, the class into which they are born and develop until the age of reason" (Rawls, 2001, p. 44).

The claim that children have a fundamental right to equal access to education has, however, been resisted by some relational egalitarians. These relational egalitarians argue that fidelity to the ideal of fundamental equality that animates justice does not require extensive distributive equality in the domain of education (Anderson, 2007; Satz, 2007). For such theorists, an attractive ideal of fundamental equality is principally concerned with regulating the social relations that obtain between people in a democratic community. Social institutions and practices should be designed not to ensure that people enjoy reasonably equal life prospects; rather the aim is to ensure that citizens of a democratic community can "interact with one another on terms of equality and respect and are not vulnerable to oppression by others" (Anderson, 2007). In the realm of education, the ideal of relational equality requires only that children have access to primary and secondary education of a sort that adequately prepares them for entry into the labor market and meaningful participation in democratic processes. The quality of education to which all children are entitled must also be sufficiently good to give them the opportunity to access post-secondary education. However, beyond such a threshold of sufficiency the educational resources and opportunities open to children may be extremely unequal. Wealthy parents are, for instance, permitted to send their children to elite, advantage conferring private schools and to lavish other advantages on their children that are beyond the means of poor families. Although the sufficientarian conception of educational justice adopted by relational egalitarians provides a basis for criticizing many educational inequalities that currently plague most democratic communities, it denies that children have an equal right to education that is violated by a system of class hierarchy in the provision of education.[7]

21.4 Control Issues

The special relationships that obtain between parents and their children generate some issues about how authority over children's education is conceived. Although children have, as we have seen, rights to education along various dimensions, they do not exercise full authority over the content and character of their education. Most obviously, education for children is compulsory and children, especially young children, have very few prerogatives to determine what kind of schools they will attend and what curriculum they will learn. These decisions are made by adults with authority over children. There are clearly some dimensions of education over which parents do not exercise authority. Parents are not, for instance, free to deny their children access to education or to indoctrinate them with racist or antidemocratic ideology. Democratic states thus exercise an important measure of control over education and set curriculum objectives that are mandatory for all students. Nonetheless, parents are widely perceived to enjoy some nontrivial prerogatives in shaping facets of their children's education. Parents often wish to shape the religious, cultural, linguistic, and ethical identities of their children by transmitting their own conceptions of the good to their children, and they also frequently wish to enrich their children's educational experiences by supplementing education provided by schools[8] with private instruction of various sorts (e.g., music lessons, athletic coaching, subject tutoring). We can distinguish three dimensions of

[7] There are some parallels between the sufficientarian view of educational justice embraced by relational egalitarians and the approach to education adopted by contemporary republican theorists for whom the animating value of political community is an ideal of freedom as nondomination (Pettit, 1997; Skinner, 1998; Laborde, 2008). Although very few republican theorists expressly address matters of distributive justice in relation to children, it is clear that ensuring that all children have access to an education that "brings children to the minimum level of independence essential for republican citizenship"(Laborde, 2008, p. 159) is imperative. Since republican theories generally reject comprehensive egalitarian distributive ideals, it is likely that republicanism also endorses a sufficientarian position (Macleod, 2015).

[8] Some parents wish to opt out of formal schools and provide education to their children via homeschooling. Whether homeschooling is a permissible exercise of parental educational prerogatives is an important question (Dwyer & Peters, 2019).

control issues that bear upon the authority that parents have over education of their children. The first dimension concerns the degree to which parents may undertake educational efforts to promote a conception of the good to their children by securing an educational environment that is expressly oriented to a sectarian conception of the good. Religious parents, for instance, may want their children to receive special instruction about their faith tradition, such as doctrinal commitments, ritual practices, and associated social norms. Second, parents may wish to insulate their children from educational materials that they view as objectionable or corrosive to the conception of the good they have. Conservative parents, for instance, often seek to prevent their children from accessing materials and instruction about human sexuality or science (e.g., evolutionary biology) that are at odds with their religious outlook. Note that although control issues of promotion and insulation can overlap, there is an important distinction between them in that promotion need not entail insulation. Teaching children about traditional Christian views of sex within marriage does not preclude teaching children about the diversity of competing views regarding acceptable forms of sexual conduct, etc. Third, in a less ideological vein, we must determine the degree to which parents may enrich their children's education by furnishing them with supplemental private educational resources.

Unsurprisingly, the way in which these control issues are appropriately resolved will depend greatly on the way issues we have already broached are resolved. For instance, if children have a right to autonomy facilitation, then the authority of parents to promote ideals or insulate children from controversial material will be constrained by our understanding of educational strategies that are conducive to autonomy. Similarly, the degree to which parental prerogatives to enrich children's education are permissible will depend on our views about justice in the distribution of education. Sufficientarians will, for instance, be less concerned about parental efforts at educational enrichment than egalitarians.

I will not attempt to resolve these debates here, but it is worth noting two different ways in which articulation of the educational rights of children are relevant to them. First, children's rights affect the way parents must be sensitive to the interests of their own children. Some restrictions on the control prerogatives of parents are grounded in a concern to protect the interests of the children over whom parents do have a degree of legitimate authority. But children's rights also function in a second way to constrain the authority of parents by requiring parents to be suitably sensitive to the interests of children that are not theirs and over whom they do not have authority. For example, parents who enrich their own children's education by providing special tutoring are not violating the rights of their own children, but they could be violating the rights of other children by conferring unfair advantages on their own children. In practical terms, this facet of respect for the rights of children has an important bearing on whether parents are justified in sending their children to elite private schools (Swift, 2003). Similarly, children often have a large stake in what other children are taught about matters such as sexuality and religion. For instance, a parental decision to insulate their own children from sexuality education can result in other children who are gay or queer being treated with contempt or intolerance. The general point here is that suitable recognition of children's rights can constrain the exercise of parental control over education of their own children in multiple ways.

21.5 Schools as Sites of Democracy

A fundamental feature of democratic communities is that citizens together exercise rights of collective self-determination. The people, via their participation in various democratic processes, govern themselves by deciding how institutions should be shaped and which policies should be adopted. Schools are not only institutions for the preparation of citizens, they are also sites of democratic activity. And although children do not enjoy the full democratic rights of adult citizens, they arguably have some interests, especially as they become adolescents and develop mature agential capacities, in exercising democratic influence over the character of the educational institutions they are required to attend. Children's rights to democratic self-determination within the context of education are limited in various ways. Students cannot, for instance, vote to abolish school or eliminate key parts of the curriculum. Nonetheless, affording students the opportunity to exercise some nontrivial control over features of their schools is arguably important for two reasons. First, although students at secondary school are not fully autonomous in the sense that they enjoy all capacities and knowledge requisite to exercise full authority over the direction of the lives, they are not mere wantons who are pushed around by raw desires. Instead, they are maturing agents who can reflectively regulate many elements of their lives and who may be held responsible for decisions they make. Respect for the agential capacities of adolescents arguably requires permitting students to have a say in the governance of the schools they attend. Second, permitting students to exercise rights of democratic self-determination via participation in student governance arguably plays a valuable role in the cultivation of skills and dispositions that are important to participation in the broader democratic community as adults. In this way, school student councils may function "as seedbeds of civic virtue" (Maxwell & Tanchuk, 2019, p. 113). Interestingly, evidence about the efficacy of student governance in promoting civic virtue suggests that the effect is strongest when students are permitted to influence school policy about reasonably weighty matters. When student governments only exercise control over trivial matters the impact on the cultivation of civic virtue seems very modest at best (Maxwell & Tanchuk, 2019).

21.6 Institutional Design

The foregoing discussion has focused primarily on various theoretical dimensions concerning the nature and content of children's rights in relation to ideals of democratic education. It is clear that there is normative disagreement about these matters and different positions will yield different, and often sharply divergent, implications about the kinds of educational institutions and policies that both respect children's rights and advance ideals of democratic education. Moreover, different democratic communities will face different challenges that reflect specific features of their political circumstances and history. For instance, the sharply polarized political environment in the United States generates special pedagogical challenges about how schools should broach controversial topics concerning race, sexuality, and religion.[9] The long history of including religious education and worship in English public schools provides a very different context for addressing the place of religion in education than, say, in France with its orientation to an ideal of laïcité. Nonetheless, by way of conclusion it is worth observing that some credible depictions of the rights of children imply that most contemporary democracies are falling well short of meeting the rights of all children. Very few children receive the robust kind of civic education that is arguably a prerequisite for effective and meaningful participation in democratic processes. The widespread ignorance about political matters on the part of citizens along with cynicism about and alienation from politics that are so common today provide evidence that schools are failing in their democratic mission to children. The distribution of educational resources and opportunities in most democratic communities is extremely unequal and falls well short of meeting even modest sufficientarian standards let alone egalitarian standards. Meaningful recognition of children's equal rights education, as democratic citizens, requires dramatic improvements in the provision of education to poor and marginalized children. It might even require the abolition of advantage conferring private schools. Similarly, respecting children's rights to autonomy facilitation would almost certainly require significant limitations on the educational measures that parents can deploy to shape their children's religious identity and beliefs. This could include severe limits on the permissibility of strongly parochial schools or schemes of homeschooling. Finally, recognition of children's rights to a degree of democratic self-determination within their schools would radically alter the character of most high schools. Of course, the conceptions of children's rights that I have highlighted here are contested and more conservative interpretations of the democratic rights of children are easier to reconcile with the educational status quo in many communities. But it is doubtful that any sincere attempt to take children's rights seriously is compatible with only minor tinkering with the design of current educational institutions.

References

Anderson, E. (2007). Fair opportunity in education: A democratic equality perspective. *Ethics*, 117, 595–622.

Anderson, E. (2010). *The imperative of integration*. Princeton, NJ: Princeton University Press.

[9] See Hess and McAvoy (2014); Levinson and Reid (2019).

Brighouse, H., & Swift, A. (2009). Educational equality versus educational adequacy: A critique of Anderson and Satz. *Journal of Applied Philosophy*, 26(2), 117–28.

Callan, E. (1997). *Creating citizens: Political education and liberal democracy*. Oxford: Oxford University Press.

Clayton, M. (2006). *Justice and legitimacy in upbringing*. Oxford: Oxford University Press.

Dwyer, J., & Peters, S. (2019). *Homeschooling: The history and philosophy of a controversial practice*. Chicago, IL: University of Chicago Press.

Forst, R. (2013). *Toleration in conflict. Past and present*. Trans. by C. Cronin, Cambridge: Cambridge University Press.

Galston, W. (1991). *Liberal purposes: Goods, virtues, and diversity in the liberal state*. Cambridge: Cambridge University Press.

Griffin, J. (2002). Do children have rights?. In D. Archard & C. Macleod, eds., *The moral and political status of children*. Oxford: Oxford University Press, pp. 19–30.

Gutmann, A. (1999). *Democratic education: Revised edition*. Princeton, NJ: Princeton University Press.

Hess, D., & McAvoy, P. (2014). *The political classroom: Evidence and ethics in democratic education*. New York: Routledge.

Kymlicka, W. (2002). *Contemporary political philosophy: An introduction*. Oxford: Oxford University Press.

Laborde, C. (2008). *Critical republicanism*. Oxford: Oxford University Press.

Ladenson, R. (2003). Inclusion and justice in special education. In R. Curren, ed., *A companion to the philosophy of education*. Oxford: Blackwell Publishing, pp. 525–39.

Levinson, M. (1999). *The demands of liberal education*. Oxford: Oxford University Press.

Levinson. M., & Reid, E. (2019). Polarization, partisanship, and civic education. In C. Macleod & C. Tappolet, eds., *Philosophical perspectives on moral and civic education: Shaping citizens and their schools*. New York: Routledge, pp. 86–112.

Macedo, S. (2000). *Diversity and distrust: Civic education in a multicultural society*. Cambridge, MA: Harvard University Press.

Macleod, C. (1997). Conceptions of parental autonomy. *Politics and Society*, 25(1), 117–40.

Macleod, C. (2010). Toleration, children and education. *Educational Philosophy and Theory*, 42(1), 9–21.

Macleod, C. (2012). Justice, educational equality and sufficiency. In C. Macleod, ed., *Justice and Equality*. Calgary: University of Calgary Press, pp. 151–75.

Macleod, C. (2015). Freedom as non-domination and educational justice. *Critical Review of International Social and Political Philosophy*, 18(4), 456–69.

Macleod, C. (2018). Are children's rights important? In E. Brake & L. Ferguson, eds., *Philosophical foundations of children's and family law*. Oxford: Oxford University Press, pp. 191–208.

Maxwell, B., & Tanchuk N. (2019). School councils as seedbeds of civic virtue? Liberal citizenship theory in dialogue with educational research. In C. Macleod & C. Tappolet, eds., *Philosophical perspectives on moral and civic education: Shaping citizens and their schools*. London: Routledge, pp. 113–34.

Merry, M. (2013). *Equality, citizenship, and segregation: A defense of separation*. New York: Palgrave Macmillan.

Oldfield, A. (1990). *Citizenship and community: Civic republicanism and the modern world*. London: Routledge.

Pettit, P. (1997). *Republicanism: A theory of freedom and government*. Oxford: Oxford University Press.

Rawls, J. (1996). *Political liberalism*. New York: Columbia University Press.

Rawls, J. (2001). *Justice as fairness: A restatement*. Cambridge MA: Harvard University Press.

Satz, D. (2007). Equality, adequacy and education for citizenship. *Ethics*, 117, 623–48.

Skinner, Q. (1998). *Liberty before liberalism*. Cambridge: Cambridge University Press.

Swift, A. (2003.) *How not to be a hypocrite: School choice for the morally perplexed*. London: Routledge.

Truth and Reconciliation Commission of Canada (2015). *Truth & reconciliation: Calls to action*. Manitoba: University of Manitoba.

22

Education, Trust, and the Conversation of Democracy

Anthony Simon Laden

22.1 Introduction

Is education the remedy for democratic ills? Educators and democrats alike tend to think so, and quote with approval lines like this, from a letter that Thomas Jefferson wrote to William Jarvis on September 28, 1820:

> I know no safe depository of the ultimate powers of the society, but the people themselves: and if we think them not enlightened enough to exercise their controul with a wholsome discretion, the remedy is, not to take it from them, but to inform their discretion by education. This is the true corrective of abuses of constitutional power. (Jefferson, 1820)

But what if, under certain conditions, this sentiment is wrong? What if education sometimes makes it harder rather than easier for the people to govern themselves democratically? This chapter explores that thought. I argue that certain essential features of education can undermine a society's members' ability to interact with each other in the ways necessary for democracy to flourish. The upshot is not that we need less education or less democracy, but that we need to think more carefully about the relationship between the two.

Here is the basic idea: the democratic nature of a democratic society depends on its citizens talking with one another, not merely at or to one another. Citizens can only talk with one another if they share enough basic reference points to not find one another inscrutable, however. This requires that citizens occupy overlapping trust networks: that they accept as trustworthy some of the same sources of information. Whether or not our trust networks overlap is a function of the topography of what might be called the epistemic landscape. One of the main effects of education is to shape the trust networks a student inhabits. But an educational system that focuses on improving the epistemic standing of individual students may have no or no good effects on the epistemic landscape. In a society where various communities occupy distinct trust networks, inhabiting various epistemic islands, education aimed at individual epistemic improvement will often relocate students in the epistemic landscape without altering the overall landscape. This reshuffling of who stands where fails, on its own, to bridge the divides that isolate some on epistemic islands. Moreover, it may increase the epistemic distance between those on various islands by giving at least some of them reason to distrust the educational system that is creating divides between them and their children. When some citizens charge educational institutions with indoctrinating their students or cutting them off from their home communities, this is the source of their unease. Seeing how this can happen will also suggest some solutions to the problem.

The chapter proceeds in stages. Section 22.2 lays out the sense in which democratic citizens need to be able to talk with one another. Section 22.3 introduces the idea of a trust network as a kind of epistemic environment each person occupies, and argues that talking with one another requires occupying overlapping trust networks. Section 22.4 then explores the role of education in shaping trust networks, and how that process can create or fail to bridge epistemic islands. Section 22.5 then looks at solutions.

22.2 Democratic Conversations

While democracy is often understood as a form of government, and thus a theory of state institutions, we can also approach democracy as a social form: societies can be democratic or not. While democratic societies are likely to have democratic governments, the mere presence of a democratic government is not sufficient to make the society democratic. A society is democratic in virtue of how its members interact: how they solve the problem of how to live together under conditions of pluralism. Democratic societies solve this problem by enabling the members of the society to work out together the terms on which they live together.

This characterization of a democratic society relies on a distinction between living and doing things *together* and merely doing them *side-by-side*: a less robust form of interaction that involves mere coordination (including coordination by procedures to which each has an input) (Laden, 2012, pp. 20–32). We successfully act or live side-by-side when we coordinate our lives or actions so that we do not run into one another or get into irresolvable conflicts. But such coordination can occur without there being anything that *we* see as *our* action. In contrast, when we act and live *together*, we undertake a more robust form of sharing, where we not only coordinate our actions but understand those actions as *ours*, as what *we* are doing (together) that is not reducible to what each of us does. Acting together in this sense can be facilitated by sharing a set of values, norms, or goals, and so it is sometimes thought that insisting on such robust interaction has communitarian implications. People who are united by a single faith or worldview or mission can rely on it to generate a common sense of what they are doing and why. But acting and living together does not require forming a community in this sense. What is necessary is that our action can be intelligible to us as our action (as what *we* are doing).

We can then think of democracy as the activity that people who wish to live together and yet do not share a robust set of values, norms, or goals engage in together. That activity is to work out together the terms under which they will live together. To genuinely work out together those terms, people need to treat one another as free and equal: no one can impose her terms on others. And this, in turn, generates a surprising result. In order for citizens[1] to continue to accept what they do as done in their name, they always need to have a way of challenging and criticizing the terms on which they live together. If someone is prohibited from raising concerns and criticisms of what her fellow citizens are doing, or these concerns and criticisms are not taken normatively seriously,[2] then that person is no longer working out with others how to live together. The democratic quality of their interaction has broken down. But of course, this also means that if others are not open to hearing and taking seriously the criticisms and concerns their fellow citizens raise, then they are not engaging democratically with them. So, on this picture, the activity of working out together the terms on which we live together requires continual openness to criticism, challenge, and contestation. In fact, it is this constant remaining open to criticism, challenge, and contestation that comprises, in large part, the activity of working out together the terms on which democratic citizens live together.

Democratic citizens preserve this openness by sustaining an ever-shifting pluricentric conversation, where we engage with different people in different situations and for different purposes, but where any of us can raise challenges and criticisms, and have them taken normatively seriously. So, in a flourishing democracy, citizens have to be able to talk with one another in this sense: to engage in these ongoing pluricentric conversations. What is essential to doing so is not coming to agreement or endorsing each other's positions but being able to understand each other and being open to being moved or changed by what our fellow citizens say, in particular when they challenge or criticize an established or emerging consensus. It is not necessary that every citizen understand or appreciate every other citizen's position (that is part of the force of the description of the conversation of democracy as pluricentric). But it is necessary that no group of citizens is completely cut off from the wider conversation, stuck only talking to and being understood by others in their group. The networks of understanding and mutual intelligibility that map out which citizens can successfully talk with which other citizens must be fully interconnected. There can't be any islands.

Trust turns out to play two important roles in securing the conditions under which citizens can engage in these democratic conversations. First, we need to trust our fellow citizens enough to be vulnerable before them. Engaging responsively in conversation means being open to being changed by that conversation,

[1] I use the term "citizen" to refer to anyone who engages in the democratic work of living together, rather than to people who have a particular legal status. For fuller discussion of this "civic" notion of citizenship, and its contrast with a perhaps more familiar legal or "civil" notion, see Tully (2014).

[2] I mean here to distinguish cases where citizens take a protest movement or its tactics seriously by straining to grasp its criticisms and appreciate their normative force from those where they take the movement seriously because it poses a threat to their comfort or security and so needs to be dealt with in either the positive or negative sense of that phrase, even though they do not think of it as addressing them in a legitimate way. In the first case, citizens take the movement normatively seriously. In the second case, they do not.

which is to say being changed by what others say and think. That openness is a form of vulnerability, and so it demands a certain level of trust in our fellow citizens. Second, it requires that we have some common reference points, that we, for instance, accept overlapping sets of sources of information. As I argue in Section 22.3, that turns out to be a function of who and what each of us trusts.

22.3 The Need for Overlapping Trust Networks

Consider two familiar reactions to the requirement developed in Section 22.2 that citizens be able to talk with one another. The first starts from the assumption that for people to engage in the sorts of conversation described, they need to share sets of values. Even if we accept that people can act together without sharing a complete set of comprehensive values, this line of thought goes, they will still need to share a set of political or liberal values to do anything more than act side by side. This assumption can motivate criticisms of an overly thin, purely procedural liberalism that doesn't commit itself to a set of shared values, but also a skepticism about the possibility of any genuine form of multiculturalism that is not just a form of perfectionist liberalism.[3] In both cases, it can be the basis for an argument favoring a view of democratic education as inculcating a particular (generally liberal) set of civic values and virtues. Such an approach sets the bar of unity too high, however, requiring agreement rather than mutual intelligibility to sustain democratic conversations.

The second accepts that people can engage in genuine conversations across differences in values, as long as they can agree on the facts. This view leads easily to a recommendation for more basic education: if citizens are working with alternative sets of facts, that is because at least some of them are mistaken about what the facts are, and this can be corrected by teaching them the facts and the skills to uncover them. This approach goes wrong by relying on an overly simplistic epistemology. While it may be true that conversations are aided by an agreement about what the facts are, there is no way for us to have unmediated access to most of the facts that matter to us in our interactions with our fellow citizens. Educating those who are mistaken about the facts can only be a reasonable strategy to the failures of conversation if there is already some agreement about who has access to the facts and who doesn't. Since there is no incontrovertible way to just point to the facts that are going to matter for important democratic conversations, insisting that education teach the facts either gives no real guidance or ends up demanding that the educational system train citizens to accept dominant and mainstream views of what the facts are.

We can accept that our access to facts is almost always mediated by various complex social practices without denying that there are facts that hold independent of those social practices. By suggesting that we need a more sophisticated epistemology that pays attention to how social practices mediate our

[3] On the first, see, for instance, Taylor (1994). On the second, see, Fish (1997).

access to facts, I do not mean to endorse a view that holds that there are no facts or that there can be alternative sets of facts. Nevertheless, once we pay attention to how we come to know things about the world, especially the sorts of complex things that are of most importance when we are trying to work out how to live together, we can see how much of our knowledge is shaped by our patterns of trust.

Consider the sense in which I normally trust my senses to provide information about the physical world. I accept their deliverances directly into my thinking, treating what they tell me as the truth about the world. I adopt what C. Thi Nguyen calls "an unquestioning attitude" (Nguyen, 2003). I also adopt this attitude of trust toward other sources of information. As I go about my day, I believe what my watch says about the time and what my search engine says about where to find things on the internet. I typically follow the directions of a stranger in an unfamiliar city without hesitation or consulting my map.

Trust of this form also plays an outsized role in the kinds of knowledge taught in schools, colleges, and universities, and on which all sorts of policy debates turn. My knowledge of US history or theoretical physics comes from reading books or listening to people talk, whether in classes, lectures, documentaries, or reports. Most of those sources in turn rely on other, perhaps more specialized, sources that also rely on additional sources. Further knowledge mediates even conclusions drawn from basic archival and experimental evidence. Experiments often rely on machinery whose workings the scientist may not understand or question, or on other experimental work that supports taking this as evidence for that. Treating an archival document as evidence involves accepting processes of authentication and continuity of storage. Trust in the sense above links these chains of support and makes the information at their ends usable. Because I trust my sources of knowledge who trust their sources of knowledge and so on, their information directly informs my further thinking.

Chains of trust then intersect and work together to form broad trust networks that shape what we know and how we add to this knowledge. If I believe a newspaper report about the rate of economic growth in the US in the last quarter, it is not because I personally know and trust the reporter or that I have independent grounds for believing the figure. I accept what is reported because I trust in a complex background network of institutions and practices: those that hire, educate, and confer credentials on reporters, fact checkers, and editors, as well as those that collect data and develop theories for interpreting it. In all these cases, watchdog agencies that call attention to mistakes along the chain of transmission and determination bolster my trust. I believe that there are no such mistakes because I have not been alerted to any. If other people do not have confidence in the figure the newspaper reports, it is likely not because they do not believe in facts, but because they do not trust some of these institutions.

Trusting of this sort is an unavoidable feature of human life: we are limited cognitive creatures and so need to rely in this unquestioning way on all sorts of sources of information, no matter how critical and well-informed we are. We thus all inhabit trust networks. In this regard, a college graduate trained in critical thinking who relies on government agencies, scientific bodies, and university expertise occupies and relies on a certain trust network no less than does a person without such training who relies on social media, neighbors, family members, and religious authorities. They differ in who and what they trust, not in how much they trust. The trust networks they rely on may be more or less trustworthy, however, and this, rather than the extent of their trust, will determine their particular epistemic standing: Who is in a better position to know what is actually the case?

Our various trust networks do not only shape what and how we know, however. They also shape our social ties. Trusting offers others direct and unmediated access to our thinking process, thoughts, and psyche. Like other forms of intimacy, trusting leaves us vulnerable to mistakes, bad judgments, and manipulation, among other things. This connection between trust and intimacy goes both ways. We trust those in our social networks and by extension what and whom they trust, giving these people an outsized influence on the shape of our trust networks, and thus our beliefs and our attitudes toward various sources of knowledge. But also, and as important, the shape of our epistemic trust networks determines who can be in our social networks. Two people with vastly divergent trust networks will have difficulty talking with one another or relating in ways that foster and sustain community. They won't just disagree; we can disagree with those with whom we have close social ties. Rather, they will find each other inscrutable because each works from a different set of accepted facts.

Thus, our ability to be intelligible to one another and to be able to take seriously their criticism and challenges rests on our having some shared sense of what sources of information or knowledge production are trustworthy. That is to say that citizens can only engage in the democratic activity of working out together how to live together if some of their trust networks overlap. It isn't that every citizen must occupy the same networks, or even that there be some networks that all citizens occupy. Since the democratic conversation is pluricentric, it can continue even if one group of citizens cannot effectively talk with some other group of citizens, as long as there is a chain of communication and interaction that links them together. In other words, what is needed is not a shared set of facts or values or even a common trust network, but the elimination of any epistemic islands: groups of people who occupy a trust network that has no overlap with the trust networks of any other of their fellow citizens.

Epistemic islands are, however, not uncommon, and one reason for that is the close connection between our trust networks and our social ties. Communications theorists and epistemologists describe certain trust networks as echo chambers (Capella & Jamieson, 2008; Nguyen 2020).[4] Echo chambers limit the extent of their occupants' trust networks, and thus what they believe, in ways that make it hard to change their beliefs. People in an echo chamber are

[4] Nguyen argues that Jaimeson and Cappella fail to distinguish echo chambers from epistemic bubbles and so refines the concept. I follow his refinement here, though I go on to make a further refinement by contrasting echo chambers with epistemic nests.

primed to distrust or reject new sources of information that might contradict their beliefs. New contrary evidence presented to them often has the seemingly paradoxical effect of strengthening their original beliefs. Cults and conspiracy theories create echo chambers, and some scholars argue that conservative media in the US does as well. By fostering a shared trust network among its occupants, echo chambers foster community, and occupants are often uninterested in escaping an echo chamber because they value the community it provides. But those inside an echo chamber will, at least with regards to the topics it governs, live on an epistemic island. There will be no way, short of undoing or escaping the echo chamber, for those outside to have their challenges and criticisms taken seriously by those inside, or vice versa.

Though echo chambers provide stark and somewhat sinister examples of epistemic islands, close-knit communities can generate epistemic islands in a more seemingly benign fashion, by setting up what might be called epistemic nests. Whereas echo chambers work by cultivating distrust of outside sources, nests provide positive social incentives to trust only insiders, or trust them to a much higher degree. Epistemic nests rely on the connection trust networks create between our beliefs and our social ties. The positive social incentives provided by occupying an epistemic nest come via the value of belonging to its community. Communities can form epistemic nests without engaging in the abusive practices that mark echo chambers or by threatening to expel members who stray from a particular orthodoxy. The process can be more subtle: those who have left the nest no longer share the same assumptions and reference points with those still inside, making interaction and conversation more difficult. At the limit, those in the epistemic nest live on an epistemic island, and while people can leave an epistemic nest, doing so only changes their placement in the epistemic landscape. The landscape and its islands remain.

22.4 Education as the Shaping of Trust Networks

If what we know and think we know about the world is mediated by all sorts of social practices and institutions and thus depends on the nature of the trust networks we inhabit, then it would not be surprising if education served to change those networks as those being educated developed new knowledge and skills of knowledge acquisition. But it turns out that the shaping of student trust networks is not just a by-product of education. It is one of the main ways in which education works to improve students' capacities as knowers, what might be called their epistemic standing.

Consider, for instance, three routinely articulated aims of a college education that also play a role in primary and secondary education:

1. *Development of disciplinary fluency.* Education that is not merely aimed at amassing a body of facts aims to make students familiar with the methods and standard sources of particular disciplines. College students may learn to read a discipline's academic journals or conduct research with its methods, but

even high school students learn how to absorb the material it takes as evidence, and work with its distinctive tools. Primary school students will learn to handle the basic blocks out of which such specialized knowledge is ultimately developed. Using these methods and sources fluently involves taking an unquestioning attitude to them, or at least to the background network that brings them to light. It makes otherwise inscrutable material legible, and thus allows students to access new sources of information directly. Fluency adds nodes to a student's trust network, expanding it to include new sources of information.

2. *Development of critical thinking.* While fluency grows one's trust network, critical thinking prunes it. The habits and skills of critical thinking lead students to question previously unquestioned sources, and thus to remove them from the student's trust networks, at least temporarily. Critical thinking can prune a student's trust networks without necessarily altering her beliefs or values: she may still accept the same facts and values as before, but not in the same trusting way. It can, of course, also lead to changes in those beliefs or values.
3. *Development of new social ties and erosion of old ones.* Schools and colleges are themselves social environments, and even an institution as geographically and socially constrained as a neighborhood elementary school will expand the range of people a student interacts with and the sorts of interactions that they have with this wider network. It is impossible for children to go to school with only the friends and acquaintances they have met through their families unless they are homeschooled: so attending school expands a child's social network.[5] In addition, the time spent in school is time not spent with family or their social network, and so it erodes the ties a child has to that network. Since social ties and trust networks shape one another, by changing where and with whom students spend time, schools and colleges further change whom and what these students trust. And as this third pathway makes clear, the effect of educational institutions on the trust networks of their students is not merely a result of what happens in classrooms.

   The social effects of education increase the higher up the educational ladder a student climbs: high schools will draw from a wider region and mix a larger variety of students together than elementary schools, and colleges will take this a step further. And while residential colleges and boarding schools provide the most intense form of this effect, it happens at every level and stage. Moreover, through their extracurriculum, almost all educational institutions work to increase the time and variety of situations in which students can interact with one another away from home.

The effects that a particular educational institution has on the trust networks of its students are not haphazard. A given education is designed to help its students occupy particular trust networks for particular reasons. Those

[5] This will of course be less true for students who attend schools narrowly designed to educate only members of a tight-knit community or public schools that draw on a geographical region whose population forms such a community (as some rural schools do, and some urban schools in highly segregated cities can). Nevertheless, even such schools broaden a child's social network beyond what is available from home.

designing the curriculum may think of the trust networks they help their students inhabit as more trustworthy or epistemically effective. They may think of them as sanctioned by a given community or moral or social authority. What is important to note for my purposes here is that even a purely academic, epistemically oriented education is developing habits that lead its students to occupy certain trust networks and not others. And these effects are not neutral.

We can now see how a certain mundane form of education might be a hindrance rather than a help to a democratic society. Imagine a society in which not insignificant numbers of its members occupy epistemic islands, perhaps on the basis of close and insular community ties, perhaps on the basis of shared religious or cultural beliefs or practices, perhaps as a result of distrust that results from systematic mistreatment and disregard by the dominant society. Two kinds of schools are likely to develop in such a society. First, there will be local, parochial, and community schools that are designed to teach members of given communities in ways that strengthens their ties to that community. Such schools can have the effect of reinforcing the echo chambers and epistemic nests that students occupy, thus reinforcing their separation on epistemic islands. Where there is also a fairly robust form of geographical sorting into epistemic islands, local public schools can evolve into playing a similar function. The second type of school will be a comprehensive or common public school that is designed to take students out of their epistemic nests and get them off their epistemic islands, and place them, along with their classmates, on the broad plain of the epistemic mainland. It turns out, however, that even such schools can serve to exacerbate the problem that the presence of citizens who inhabit epistemic islands pose to democratic conversations.

Although common public and nonsectarian private schools aim to provide a neutral and nonsectarian education, they often do so by training students to inhabit mainstream and elite trust networks. If this work is done without any sensitivity to the costs involved, or the nature of the transformation students undergo who come from communities who do not inhabit or reject these trust networks, then it is likely only to rearrange who is on what epistemic landmass, not to reconfigure the underlying geography. To put this point less metaphorically, a successful common public school education will often aim to train all its students to occupy a set of trust networks that are incompatible with the trust networks of those on various epistemic islands. It will do this in the name of improving each of their epistemic standings. That will serve to take these students out of one set of trust networks and place them in another. But it will leave behind those in the student's original trust networks, and do nothing, on its own, to bridge the divides between the student's family's network and the student's newly acquired one. While such institutions will make it easier for their students to talk with one another and ultimately to participate in the wider range of interactions with those outside of their home communities, this can come at the cost of making it harder for some students to talk with their own families and communities back home. Moreover, by shaping students' intellectual habits and skills to fit well within a particular set of trust networks, an educational system may make them less open to being moved by what those outside of those networks say, including those they were previously close to. The more easily I occupy a set of trust networks, the less I have a sense that my knowledge is shaped by them, the more invisible they are to me, and the less I notice their effects on how I think and what I take seriously. And so, as much as an education is designed to foster open-mindedness and a willingness to listen to and take seriously alternative points of view, it also winds up making some positions (those that emerge on epistemic islands that one is not or no longer a part of) increasingly inscrutable.

The upshot of this is that in a society already characterized by epistemic islands, even a common school can serve to widen the gap between citizens, even as it changes who inhabits which epistemic space. This can lead to a backlash among people on the epistemic island in which they are moved to develop and defend their own schools to prevent having their children removed, epistemically speaking, from them. When a school devoted to reproducing community values is seen as a defense against the indoctrinating effects of common and nonsectarian schools, it is even more likely to educate its students in a way that serves to further deepen and widen the gaps between its epistemic island and everyone else. If education has this effect, it will undermine a society's ability to maintain its democratic conversations across these divides, and the remedy will not be more of such education, not even more education in common schools.

22.5 Solutions

How, then, should a democratic society and its education system respond? It helps to see the problem under a somewhat different description by distinguishing two important educational goods at stake here. The first is the epistemic standing of individual students. This is, arguably, not merely an educational good, but the good of education itself. Successful education makes students better knowers. The second is the epistemic landscape of the society: the situation and relationship among the trust networks occupied by the members of society. What I have suggested is that an education system that successfully pursues the first of these goods can turn out to have a negative effect on the second insofar as it improves the epistemic standing of individual island dwellers by simply removing them from their islands. And yet it is the second good, even more than the first, that is essential to sustaining a society's democratic character. If this is right, then it may be that the solutions designed to realize the second good will have to accept trade-offs in their ability to realize the first good. Note that I say it *may* involve trade-offs, not that it *must*. For there can be epistemic benefits to one's individual standing as a knower in being able to occupy a range of trust networks and see the value in looking at the world from the perspective they enable. But there is nothing to guarantee that changing the epistemic topography of the society will have such benefits, and the democratic value of doing so is not contingent on it also improving our standing as knowers. And so, even if improving the epistemic topography does not always involve the trade-offs mentioned, it is the possibility of such trade-offs that make the problem difficult. Moreover, since the first good is an individual good and the second a social one, we need to also pay attention to *who* is being asked to sacrifice this educational good for the sake of the democratic health of the society.

If democracy suffers when there are epistemic islands, then it flourishes when those islands can be reintegrated into the epistemic mainland. To do so in ways that respect the freedom of those who occupy the trust networks that form those islands, the society needs to build the equivalent of land-bridges out to those islands, to reconnect them without absorbing them. What can serve as such bridges? People who can occupy sets of trust networks that form otherwise separate islands. When a person can genuinely occupy otherwise isolated trust networks, then the pluricentric democratic conversation can flow through them, providing, for instance, ways for the objections that arise in one epistemic community to make their way into otherwise nonoverlapping ones. The more people who can do so, the stronger the bridge and the easier it will be both for those who act as a bridge to continue to and for the democratic conversation to include those on the island in question: for them to hear and take seriously challenges to their positions and for their challenges and criticisms to be taken seriously by others. An educational system that helped students become such bridges would thus serve to improve the epistemic landscape of the society without merely eliminating or assimilating the isolated trust networks into those occupied by the people on the epistemic mainland.

To see how that might be done, consider three broad strategies of bridge-building between disconnected trust networks. The first is conceptual: sometimes there is a way to frame various issues or systems of beliefs that unify them, despite their seeming disconnection or even incompatibility. Adopting such a frame or perspective then makes it possible to simultaneously occupy what previously seemed like distinct trust networks and thus act as a bridge between them. This approach is not always available, and it has its dangers, as it can lead to seeing the more marginalized trust network as merely a simple or na□ve version of the more mainstream one, and so absorbing, rather than building a bridge to, the island. Nevertheless, being able to engage in this strategy requires a set of intellectual skills, which can be taught just as much as the skills of critical thinking. These include an ability to think charitably about unfamiliar positions, look for commonalities or connections between seemingly distinct or opposed positions, and resist intellectual arrogance and judgmental attitudes. It can also be aided by the attitudes of both teachers and thought-leaders in the society. It is harder to develop and deploy the conceptual abilities to find common ground between positions being staked out, developed, and defended by people who insist on being dismissive to those who disagree or who do not implicitly trust one's sources. It is easier to imagine doing this kind of work if one thinks of it as knitting together disparate trust networks rather than reconciling established facts with misguided delusions, or ideologies with hard truths. The conceptual work that would allow an educational system to help students develop into bridges via this strategy has to happen outside of classrooms as well as in them.

The second is translational: even when there is no way to knit together trust networks into a seamless whole, it is sometimes possible to learn to translate from one to the other. Those adept at code-switching, literal translation, and careful but creative reformulation can serve as ferries, if not bridges, between distinct epistemic communities, lessening their isolation. All of these activities involve costs to the one moving between the islands, and so part of enabling students to act as ferries in this way is to not only teach them the necessary skills but to help them deploy them in ways that are not overly costly.[6] As with the ability to conceptually reframe, the abilities required for this solution need not only to be taught but to be socially valued. Translation and code-switching are difficult work and can place special burdens on those who do it. Fostering a set of social attitudes that sees those skilled at these tasks as doing valuable and necessary social labor, rather than as hypocrites or lacking in integrity or authenticity, can make that work easier to undertake and at least remove some of the burdens faced by those who do it.

The third is personal: recall that trust networks situate us socially as well as epistemically. We can connect to another person's trust networks by coming to accept and trust the sources they do, by aligning ourselves epistemically with them. But we can also connect to their trust network by trusting them, not directly their trust network. Learning to trust another or maintain a trusting relationship with someone can be a social act: like maintaining a friendship across geographical or cultural distance. People who forge and maintain genuine friendships and relationships can bridge distinct epistemic trust networks by giving the ideas and positions developed within one a genuine and sympathetic hearing by someone occupying the other.[7] As with the other two strategies, this one requires a set of skills, resources, and social support. Friendships across difference are difficult to foster and hard to sustain and require particular kinds of care and nurturance. A variety of social skills – of patience, of suspension of certain habits of judgment or thought, of openness and flexibility, of humility and a willingness to sacrifice – is necessary for this work. And it takes time and access: to spend time together, to keep in touch, to pursue shared interests or activities or projects. Finally, it is aided by supportive social attitudes: that returning to one's home community is not a failure, and that venturing from it is not a threat; a willingness to welcome someone's new or old friends into a new environment; and an acceptance of the code-switching and compartmentalizing that maintaining old and new ties sometimes require. All of these can be supported within an educational system: directly through teaching or encouraging the development of the necessary social skills, and indirectly, by making available the necessary resources, including time away from school and schoolwork, and by modelling and supporting the necessary attitudes.

[6] Morton (2019) provides helpful discussion of how this might be done and the issues involved.

[7] For one articulation of this thought in the context of intersectional feminism, see Lugones and Spellman, (1990). See also Nguyen, (2020).

Many, if not all, of the actions listed above may involve trade-offs with the main good of education: improvement in the epistemic standing of individual students. In some cases, these trade-offs are direct and obvious. Giving students more time to maintain relationships with family members and friends both in and outside of their home communities means having them spend less time at school, doing schoolwork or only fostering and nurturing relationships with those who might help them escape echo chambers and leave epistemic nests. In other cases, the trade-offs will be more subtle and easier to miss. The capacity to take a charitable attitude toward an unfamiliar doctrine, position, or belief might be seen as a central epistemic and intellectual virtue (it is generally prized by philosophers, for instance), but it is also true that a disposition to treat unfamiliar ideas charitably may get in the way of decisively rejecting views that deserve such rejection. (As the old quip goes: His mind was so open that his brain fell out.) Sometimes there will be democratic value in connecting communities who are clearly misinformed or mistaken or who cherish antidemocratic values, even if there would be epistemic value in soundly rejecting their trust networks as flawed. In still other cases, the trade-offs may be ambiguous, and the nature of the trade-off may be quite context sensitive. While it is true that the time and energy devoted to code-switching is energy that is not being devoted to developing fluency in a single system, there can be intellectual and epistemic as well as social value in being multilingual and multicultural. And while it is true that the time and energy devoted to becoming a bridge is time and energy not devoted to being a fully rooted and solid member of a given epistemic community, which of those projects is of more epistemic value is going to vary from case to case.

Nevertheless, becoming and succeeding at being an epistemic and social bridge is a costly endeavor and, more importantly from a democratic standpoint, it is a cost that is unlikely to be borne by all or all equally. If there is indeed a social benefit in encouraging and training people to become such epistemic bridges, then it is important that the costs of doing so are also socially distributed and properly recognized. It can be easy to miss this point as well as at least one way of addressing it equitably, however. For those citizens who occupy trust networks that situate them comfortably on the epistemic mainland, it is easy to imagine that the epistemic landscape, if fractured, features a large central continent perhaps surrounded by small offshore islands inhabited by the ignorant and misguided. If that is your picture of the democracy-threatening epistemic landscape I have been describing, then anything that an educational system does to remove students from the islands and bring them ashore is bestowing a benefit on them. Thus, if the price for that is to also tax them with the work of becoming bridges, that is not going to seem like an unfair system. Moreover, you are likely to think the best result would be to depopulate the islands completely, thus removing the need for bridges and ferries, and restore the democratic conversation that way. In that case, allowing students who grew up within an island's epistemic nest a chance to retain their ties to their home communities is not asking them to perform a necessary service for their fellow citizens (for which we might think they are owed compensation or at least gratitude). It is a concession to their social and emotional needs (and so to be borne at their own expense if possible). Finally, it can be easy to think that, if the populations isolated on islands remain small and relatively powerless, the threats they pose are only to themselves and not to the well-functioning of democratic conversations happening on the mainland. Note that the outlook being described here grows out of comfortably occupying trust networks centrally located on the mainland. As such, it is likely to be at least in the background of the perspectives of those who are influential and authoritative in the fields of knowledge production and transmission that shape how education is designed and carried out.

But that perspective is blinkered in important ways and discerning how to see past it will suggest an outlook that would lead to better cost-sharing. Rather than see epistemic threat in the sorts of marginalized and discounted outlooks found on epistemic islands, we might see such communities as offering an antidote to dangers of intellectual and epistemic conformity and complacency brought on by being insulated from radical challenge.[8] From this perspective, the urgency of bridge-building is not merely to build connections in from the islands, but to build connections out to them. Building and maintaining connections from the mainland out to the epistemic communities that are separate from it provides a way for the dominant society to keep itself honest and its arrogance in check by putting itself in a position to take normatively seriously the challenges and criticisms that come from further afield. It thus can serve not only democratic ends but epistemic ones for those stuck in and blinkered by mainstream outlooks. And even when the trust networks found on the island are epistemically weaker than those found on the mainland, learning to appreciate how they work and what apparent value they have to those who inhabit them can help deparochialize the perspectives of those who become outbridges.

Seeing the epistemic landscape this way suggests two remedies to the maldistribution of costs. First, if the building of epistemic bridges is a project of connecting out rather than connecting in, then it is much more clearly something that those who reside comfortably on the mainland need to be taught how to do. The sorts of bridge-building skills discussed in this chapter are then ones to teach to all students and not just those who grow up on epistemic islands. In fact, those most in need of such skills might be the students who otherwise appear to be epistemically privileged and whose education involves the least radical transformation of their trust networks, just as those most in need of second-language instruction are those who grow up in a monolingual family who speak the dominant language of instruction in the society. So, for instance, rather than think of the fostering of social ties as a technique for allowing members of marginalized and excluded epistemic communities to hold on to their ties to home, we can think of it as a technique for helping those in the center foster new ties with those in the marginalized and excluded communities.[9] Alternatively, we can think about how to design an education system

[8] One of the main lessons of Mill's "On liberty" (Mill, 1989).

[9] This is the "use" of friendship emphasized by Lugones and Spelman (1990).

that works as hard to immerse students who grow up in communities connected to the epistemic mainland in the worldviews and trust networks on various epistemic islands as it does the reverse. An example of this strategy with respect to the effects of linguistic islands would be to increase access to and the perceived social value of Spanish-language immersion programs for monolingual English speakers in the US as a means to bridging the isolation of predominantly Spanish-speaking communities.

Second, if the social value of building and maintaining people's capacities to become epistemic bridges accrues to the inhabitants of the mainland as much as to those on various islands, then it is easier to see those who start on islands and may sacrifice personal advancement to foster and maintain epistemic bridges as doing socially necessary and beneficial work: not only preserving democracy but protecting the mainland against epistemic threats. It is thus easier to see why they need to be given compensation and extended gratitude and generally supported with the necessary resources to do this work.

Democratic societies have the unfortunate habit of tasking their schools with solving many social problems that the schools neither caused nor are well-positioned to solve. I hope to have at least made plausible that the breakdown of democratic conversations is not one of these: not only can our schools help nurture, sustain and even restart democratic conversations if they make it their aim to do so, but in doing so, they would be addressing a problem for which they also bear some responsibility. They might also serve to lower some of the social costs they otherwise impose on students from communities who form epistemic islands. That said, I don't mean my analysis of the relationship between education and democracy to be reduced to a discussion of the role of schools in democracy. Schools are only one of the institutions that play an educative role in a democratic society, and professional teachers are only some of the citizens whose work and action serves to educate others and shape their trust networks. In one way or another, all the institutions of a democratic society play an educative role and all its citizens are teachers, whether they mean to be or not. That means that all of us bear some responsibility when the democratic conversation breaks down, and all of us can play a positive role in reviving it.

References

Capella, J. N., & Jamieson, K. H. (2008). *Echo chamber: Rush Limbaugh and the conservative media establishment*. Oxford: Oxford University Press.

Fish, S. (1997). Boutique multiculturalism, or why liberals are incapable of thinking about hate speech. *Critical Inquiry*, 23(2), 378–95.

Laden, A. S. (2012). *Reasoning: A social picture*. Oxford: Oxford University Press.

Lugones, M., & Spelman, E. (1990). Have we got a theory for you! In A. Al-Hibri & M. A. Simons, eds., *Hypatia reborn*. Indianapolis, IN: Indiana University Press.

Jefferson, T. (1820). From Thomas Jefferson to William Charles Jarvis, 28 September 1820. *Founders Online* (National Archives). Available at: https://founders.archives.gov/documents/Jefferson/98-01-02-1540.

Mill, J. S. (1989). On liberty. In *"On liberty" and other writings*. Cambridge: Cambridge University Press.

Morton, J. (2019). *Moving up without losing your way: The ethical costs of upward mobility*. Princeton, NJ: Princeton University Press.

Nguyen, C. Thi. (2020). Echo chambers and epistemic bubbles. *Episteme*, 17(2), 141–61.

Nguyen, C. Thi. (2023). Trust as an unquestioning attitude. In T. Szabó Gendler & J. Hawthorne, eds., *Oxford Studies in Epistemology: Vol. 7*. Oxford: Oxford University Press, pp. 214–44.

Taylor, C. (1994). *Multiculturalism: Expanded paperback edition*. Princeton, NJ: Princeton University Press.

Tully, J. (2014). *On global citizenship: James Tully in dialogue*. London: Bloomsbury.

23

Patriotism and Democratic Education

Richard Dagger

23.1 Introduction

To take a stand on the value of patriotism for democratic education is to enter thrice-contested terrain. Not only is patriotism the subject of much scholarly dispute, but so too are democracy and education. To be sure, few scholars doubt that democracy and education are in general good things, and both have been largely free from the suspicion and scorn sometimes directed against patriotism. Beyond this general agreement, though, there is much disagreement about exactly what counts as democracy or education, and the question of how to realize the worthy aims of each is also highly contentious. Other contributors to this volume will explore these matters, however, and their efforts will allow this chapter to concentrate on the part of the contested terrain that bears most directly on the question of whether patriotism has a valuable part to play in democratic education. My task, in short, is to make a case for the value of patriotism for democratic education, taking "democracy" and "education" to be, for the most part, well-understood and uncontroversial terms.

The argument takes this form. First, democratic societies are not frictionless devices or machines that will run of themselves. On the contrary, they face many challenges and they require much effort, including the support of their citizens, in order to survive and prosper. Second, this support must be more than passive acquiescence, for democracy is a regime in which the people in some sense rule themselves. For the people to rule, they need an education that prepares them for the self-government of democratic citizenship. Among the many elements of such an education is the encouragement of patriotism. The conclusion, then, is that patriotism does indeed have a valuable part to play, through democratic education, in the preservation of democratic society.

In developing this argument, I shall proceed from the idea of democracy as a cooperative venture. Ventures or practices of this kind cannot rely entirely on the spontaneous cooperation of their participants, but neither can they survive without a high degree of uncoerced cooperation. Coercion has a part to play in a democracy, in other words, but it cannot be an overwhelming part. Like other cooperative practices involving more than a few people, democracies require rules to provide the reasonably clear expectations necessary to coordinate public activities, and rules do not enact or enforce themselves. Like other cooperative practices, moreover, democracies face collective-action problems. For these reasons, democracy requires the rule of law. If patriotism is a valuable reinforcement to a democratic society, it will be in large part because patriotism, properly understood, reinforces the rule of law.

23.2 Democracy

To speak of democratic society is to indicate that democracy is as much a way of life as it is a form of government. This twofold conception of democracy is what Tocqueville had in mind when he declared, in the Introduction to *Democracy in America*, that a "new political science is needed for a world itself quite new"; for this new world would be dramatically different from the ancien régime of France and Europe (Tocqueville, 1969, p. 12). The hallmark of this new world – a hallmark he took to be most evident, albeit imperfectly realized, in the United States – was "the equality of conditions," which Tocqueville saw as a "basic fact" that exercised "dominion over civil society as much as over the government" by creating opinions, giving birth to feelings, suggesting customs, and modifying "whatever it does not create" (Tocqueville, 1969, p. 9). Democracy, as the Greek origin of the word indicates, is thus a polity in which the people rule themselves, but this they can do only when there is a high degree of both social and political equality.

Underpinning both kinds of equality is what Robert Dahl called the "principle of intrinsic equality," a fundamental conviction that holds, "We ought to regard the good of every human being as intrinsically equal to that of any other" (Dahl, 1998, p. 65). Establishing democratic relationships in society and government is the best way to act on this principle, according to Dahl. In the case of political equality, he identified five defining features of democracy, understood to be the rule of political equals: (i) equal opportunity for *effective participation* in policy-making; (ii) *voting equality* in decision- making; (iii) equal and effective opportunities to gain an *enlightened understanding* of relevant policy alternatives; (iv) equal opportunity to exercise *final control* over the public agenda; and (v) the *inclusion of all*, "or at any rate most, adult permanent residents" in the matters covered by the first four features (Dahl, 1998, pp. 37–38; emphasis in original). Sustaining a polity that meets these criteria, however, is a challenging task. It requires a citizenry that is willing not only to engage in political activity but to set aside differences, overcome disagreements, and regard one another as equally entitled to have a say in the direction of the polity. That is, they must exhibit a high degree of cooperation among themselves and accept the need for an occasional resort to coercion on the part of their government.

This is to say that a democracy is a cooperative practice secured by the rule of law. But what is a cooperative practice? And how does it relate to the rule of law?

To begin with the former, we may discern four basic aspects to a cooperative practice (Dagger, 2018, ch. 2). The first is that there must be some sense in which the cooperation is both beneficial and burdensome to those who engage in it.

Two gladiators who are fighting to the death are not engaged in a cooperative activity, for they are not cooperating to achieve some mutually beneficial end. A group of musicians must cooperate if they are to play a song or symphony together, but their playing will not constitute a cooperative practice or enterprise if it is all benefit to them and no burden. There must be some hardship to bear – at least some restriction of the participants' liberty, in H. L. A. Hart's terms (Hart, 1970, p. 70) – that is necessary to the achievement of the goal or benefit that the participants hope to achieve. In the case of the musicians, there must be occasions on which one or more of them would rather not play a certain piece or would prefer not to rehearse so often or so long. Something similar is true of all cooperative practices.

A second feature is that cooperative practices are ongoing. They may begin with spontaneous activity, but they will need rules or laws if they are to continue. In some cases, these rules are nothing more than informal and perhaps unspoken norms. In a very small group, when the point of the activity and the need for cooperation are obvious, the rule may be nothing more than "you do your part, I'll do mine, and no shirking." In larger groups, and especially when the cooperation is supposed to extend well into the future, formal rules that specify the nature of the required cooperation will be necessary.

A third element of a cooperative practice is that it will produce one or more public goods that leave it susceptible to collective-action problems. Public goods such as clean air and national defense are indivisible, nonexcludable, and nonrival, which is to say that one person's enjoyment of the good does not deprive another of an equal opportunity to enjoy it. Indeed, non-cooperators often may enjoy the public good or benefit as fully as those whose cooperative efforts produce the good in question. This leaves cooperative practices vulnerable to free riders who hope to reap the benefits of others' cooperative labors and sacrifices without bearing those burdens themselves. That is why coercive measures are typically necessary to discourage free riding and ensure the survival of the cooperative endeavor.

Coercion or some other means of discouraging free riders thus speaks to the fourth key aspect of cooperative practices, which is the need for assurance. The point is not that everyone is always seeking to be a free rider at the expense of others. On the contrary, the point is that even people who are willing to make cooperative sacrifices will be foolish to do so when their sacrifices will be futile. For that reason, cooperative practices must find some way to assure those who would willingly cooperate that their cooperation will not be in vain. They must have security, in other words, against those who would take unfair advantage of their cooperative good nature. Coercion, in the form of preventive measures and punishment, is thus necessary to provide that security and assurance.

Conceiving of democracy in this way reveals that democracy, in both its social and political aspects, rests on the willingness of its citizens to cooperate with one another, but this cooperation itself requires the assurance afforded by the threat of coercion. Another way to put the point is to say that democracy relies in two ways on the rule of law. In order to rule themselves as a cooperative body, citizens need the guidance of laws that establish expectations and clarify norms.

Indeed, in a democracy, the principal way in which the people rule is through their cooperation in the enactment of laws, whether this is done directly by the citizens themselves or through the actions of their elected or appointed officials. Once laws are enacted, then civic cooperation continues in the form of law abidance, which must be secured by the coercive force of law.

There is, of course, much more involved in the rule of law, which stands, according to one commentator, "in the peculiar state of being *the* preeminent legitimating political ideal in the world today, without agreement upon precisely what it means" (Tamanaha, 2006, p. 4; emphasis in original). Nevertheless, three themes seem fundamental to the rule of law, beginning with the conviction that government must be limited by law. That is, the duty of government is to serve the people by protecting their rights and interests, which entails that the authority of those in government must be confined within established bounds. Those who hold power must act in accordance with public reasons and recognized procedures. From the democratic point of view, such reasons and procedures must be in some way enacted and enforced by the people themselves, for if the government is to protect their rights and interests, it must answer to them.

The second theme is legality, a term legal scholars use to indicate that certain formal conditions must be met before the elements of a legal system are truly lawful. According to John Rawls, for instance, one of the key precepts of the rule of law is that similar cases are to be treated similarly; another is that there is no offense or crime without a law (Rawls, [1971] 1999, sec. 38). Rawls acknowledges the influence of Lon Fuller here, as do many others who trace their conceptions of legality to the eight principles Fuller elaborated in chapter two of his *The Morality of Law* (1969). As conveniently condensed by John Finnis, Fuller's principles hold that:

> A legal system exemplifies the Rule of Law to the extent that . . . (i) its rules are prospective, not retroactive, and (ii) are not in any other way impossible to comply with; that (iii) its rules are promulgated, (iv) clear and (v) coherent one with another; that (vi) its rules are sufficiently stable to allow people to be guided by their knowledge of the content of the rules; that (vii) the making of decrees and orders applicable to relatively limited situations is guided by rules that are promulgated, clear, stable, and relatively general; and that (viii) those people who have authority to make, administer, and apply the rules in an official capacity (a) are accountable for their compliance with rules applicable to their performance and (b) do actually administer the law consistently and in accordance with its tenor. (Finnis, 1980, p. 270)

As Finnis's summary indicates, some scholars take legality to be the sum and substance of the rule of law. This, however, is to overstate its importance. To be sure, we need to know what counts as law before we can count on the rule of law; but we also need to know something about the kind of ruling that will take place under the rule of law. For that reason, it would be a mistake to allow the second theme, legality, to eclipse the first – that is, limited government – or the third, which I shall call "impersonality."

There are at least three reasons for using this term. The first is that law is supposed to be impersonal in the sense that it is no respecter of persons. Like the blindfolded image of Lady Justice, the aim of law is to serve and protect equally all those who come before it regardless of their wealth, power, connections, or social status. That this is an ideal seldom attained is a reason for striving harder to ensure everyone an equal standing before the law, not to grant exemptions or privileges to some without a justification grounded in the common good. Second, the rule of law is impersonal because it rejects the rule of autocrats, their families, and the factions to which they give rise. By assuming the arbitrary right to hand down the rules, autocrats place themselves above the law. They may profess to live under the "laws" they have made, just as everyone else in the regime must do, but they will retain the authority to revise and rescind laws at their discretion. Moreover, they are likely to hold those who serve within their administrations to the standard of personal loyalty and, in so doing, to ignore the distinction between personal interest and public duty. Such conduct is inimical to the rule of law.

Livy's classical formulation of the rule of law as "the empire of laws and not of men" is in effect a compressed statement of these last two themes, legality and impersonality (Sellers, 2003, p. 29). Taken together, they imply the first theme, limited government. Taking all three together, they form the basis for a democratic society as a cooperative practice of self-government secured by coercion. Law can have no empire, however, if it has no place in the hearts and minds of the men and women it is supposed to rule impersonally. Personal loyalty to autocrats and would-be autocrats is surely contrary to the rule of law, but there must be loyalty or fidelity to the law itself and to the polity it is supposed to govern. This form of impersonal loyalty is, in Gerald Postema's words, "the animating soul of law's commonwealth." It is loyalty to other persons, in a way, for "fidelity is owed by individuals *not to laws or government*, but *to each other*, that is to fellow members of law's commonwealth" (Postema, 2014, p. 20; emphasis in original). Fidelity to law is thus a kind of loyalty that individuals owe to one another as citizens – a kind of civic loyalty that opposes the insistence on personal loyalty that undermines the rule of law. To appreciate the importance of civic loyalty is to grasp the third reason for thinking that impersonality is one of the basic features of the rule of law.

There is, however, a further implication to this way of thinking about democracy and law, and it sounds a cautionary note. If a democratic polity is a cooperative practice that depends on the assurance secured by the rule of law, as I have claimed, and if the rule of law itself depends on the civic loyalty or fidelity of the citizenry, as Postema argues, then we must be deeply concerned with the good health of "the animating soul of law's commonwealth." The most promising way to address this concern is likely to be through education. To see why, it will help to turn again to Tocqueville.

23.3 Education

In the paragraph preceding his call for a new political science for a new world, Tocqueville proclaims that the "first duty" of those who direct society is "to educate democracy" (Tocqueville, 1969, p. 12). By this curious phrase, he means that the people who are to assume democratic power must be prepared for a life of social and political equality. This would be less a matter of training, however, than of education in the original sense of the word. That is, "education" derives from the Latin *educere*, which means to lead or draw out and from which we retain, in English, "educe." Originally, then, education involved drawing out or developing the potential within a person – or, for that matter, within other animals (Peters, 1973, p. 53). Tocqueville believed that people in general have the potential to live democratically, but he also believed that this potential must be drawn out of them. In particular, the people must learn to be self-governing in order to forestall the tyranny of the majority. Hence the need "to educate democracy."

Tocqueville's concern, in effect, is that a polity may meet Dahl's fivefold criteria for democracy without cultivating the civic qualities necessary to a successful and stable democracy. That is, democracy does indeed involve political equality and popular sovereignty, which entails some form or degree of majority rule, but it also requires protection against arbitrary rule. Just as the rule of law protects the people against the arbitrary rule of despots, so too must it protect against the reckless rule of an impulsive, short-sighted populace. Better still, though, is to educate the people so that they will be willing and able to govern themselves. Citizens must be prepared to govern themselves, that is, not only by exercising their political equality through effective participation in policy-making and control of the public agenda, among other things, but also by recognizing the need to curb their impulses and enthusiasms. Recognizing this need will lead them to consider carefully the likely consequences of various policies, listen to those who disagree with them, and generally act as responsible citizens concerned to promote the common good. The majority must be heeded, but it must also heed those who disagree with it.

Educating democracy in this sense is not only the responsibility of schools. In fact, Tocqueville says relatively little about the formal education of children. He directs his attention, instead, to activities that take place among adults within civil society, such as those involving voluntary associations and a free press, and to activities that straddle and elide the distinction between civil society and official government, such as juries and town meetings. Such activities presuppose some prior education, of course, in so far as they assume some degree of literacy. But they also serve an educative purpose by drawing out and informing the capacities necessary for democratic self-government. For Tocqueville, one might say, democracy is in some ways a matter of learning by doing. The same point holds for one of Tocqueville's earliest admirers, John Stuart Mill, who praised representative government that involves extensive civic participation as the "ideally best" form of government because of its promotion of "active character" (Mill, [1861] 2015, ch. 3). Giving the individual "something to do for the public," he argued, "supplies, in a measure, all [the] deficiencies" of the routine and narrowly circumscribed work to which most people are subject. Serving on juries and in "parish offices" must make people "very different beings, in range of ideas and development of faculties, from those who have done nothing in their lives but drive a quill or sell goods over a counter. Still more salutary," Mill adds,

> is the moral part of the instruction afforded by the participation of the private citizen, if even rarely, in public functions. He is called upon, while so engaged, to weigh interests not his own; to be guided, in case of conflicting claims, by another rule than his private partialities; to apply ... principles and maxims which have for their reason of existence the common good ... He is made to feel himself one of the public, and whatever is for their benefit to be for his benefit. (Mill, [1861] 2015, pp. 223–24)

As this discussion of "the moral part of the instruction" indicates, Mill has in mind something approaching the cooperative-practice conception of democracy, according to which the individual members of the public are engaged in a mutually beneficial enterprise that requires everyone to look beyond their individual interests. The same is true of Tocqueville, who deplored the tendency of "individualism" to dispose "each citizen to isolate himself from the mass of his fellows and withdraw into the circle of family and friends" (Tocqueville, 1969, p. 506). To combat this isolating individualism, he argued, it is necessary to turn to the doctrine of "self-interest properly understood," which may not "inspire great sacrifices, but every day it prompts some small ones; ... its discipline shapes a lot of orderly, temperate, moderate, careful, and self-controlled citizens" (Tocqueville, 1969, pp. 526–27).

In large part, then, educating democracy amounts to encouraging engagement in public affairs in order to foster cooperative dispositions among "self-controlled citizens." But that is not to say that formal schooling has no part to play in this endeavor. On the contrary, formal education has a preparatory, an informative, and a reinforcing role in the cultivation of cooperative citizens. It has a preparatory role because participation in public affairs requires literacy and other basic skills; it has an informative role because it helps students understand the workings of democracy; and it has a reinforcing role because it contributes to the development of the critical and analytical skills that are vital to effective public participation. As a cooperative practice, moreover, democracy is an ongoing enterprise, and schooling is essential to its maintenance. John Dewey put the point this way: "Democracy has to be born anew every generation, and education is its midwife" (Dewey, [1916] 1993, p. 122).[1]

As many have recognized, formal schooling is important to democratic education as much for *how* students are taught as for *what* they are taught. Preaching the virtues of democracy to the young will do little to cultivate democratic citizenship if the way they are taught – what is sometimes called the "hidden curriculum" – encourages them to be passive consumers of knowledge and followers of authority. Education, according to this view, must proceed democratically if it is to promote democracy. Whether this view requires schools only to include modest elements of democratic government, such as election of class

[1] See Crittenden (2002) for an extended reflection on the implications of this way of thinking about democracy and education.

officers and student councils, or whether it demands a thoroughly democratic curriculum (Crittenden, 2002, ch. 6), or something somewhere between these poles, is a matter of much debate – and a subject best left to the other contributors to this volume.

The question of particular importance here is whether attempts to teach patriotism are a proper part of schooling that aims to support democracy understood as a cooperative practice secured by the rule of law. Is a patriotic education necessary, in other words, to the health of Postema's "animating soul of law's commonwealth"?

23.4 Patriotism

Whether patriotism is a virtuous sentiment to be praised and promoted or a vicious one to be deplored and discouraged is a matter of much dispute among scholars. In this respect, as noted in the Introduction of this chapter, it differs dramatically from democracy and education. To some, patriotism is clearly a virtue, at least when it is distinguished from jingoism or chauvinistic nationalism. Prominent examples in this category are Alisdair MacIntyre's "Is Patriotism a Virtue?" (1995), Maurizio Viroli's (1995) *For Love of Country*, and Steven Smith's (2021) *Reclaiming Patriotism in an Age of Extremes*. To others, though, patriotism is a dangerous "mistake" (Kateb, 2000)), a kind of "bad faith" (Keller, 2005), and even akin to racism (Gomberg, 1990). Those who fall into the latter camp will have no desire to entertain the possibility that patriotism may have an important role to play within democratic education.

But what is patriotism? On two points there is widespread agreement. The first is that patriotism is the love of one's country – Thompson (2008) and Gilbert (2009) are rare exceptions – and the second is that patriotism is not to be identified with nationalism (e.g., Dietz, 1989; Smith, 2021, pp. 106–22). The difficulty, though, lies in the words "love" and "country," each of which covers a vast swath of vaguely bounded conceptual ground. With regard to "love," perhaps the best we can say is that patriotism is a sentiment – in particular, a form of affection – that is rooted in familiarity, gratitude, and "above all," according to Steven Smith, loyalty (2021, p. 12). But what of country?

Responses to this question tend to interpret "country" in one of three ways.[2] The first interpretation takes one's country to be one's fatherland or ancestral home; the second takes it to be one's nation, a term that usually carries ethnic and/or cultural connotations; and the third takes it to be the polity or political society of which one is a citizen. These three lines of interpretation are not altogether distinct from one another, but they do mark significantly different points of emphasis in the understanding of patriotism. According to Viroli, for instance, all authentic patriotism falls into the third category, which he calls "republican patriotism," and he insists on the need to forswear the

[2] The following paragraphs draw on Dagger (2020).

interpretation that regards patriotism as fundamentally the love of one's nation. Etymology, he suggests, is telling in this regard:

> Latin authors made a clear distinction between the political and cultural values of the republic and the non-political values of nationhood; in fact, they used two different words: *patria* and *natio*. Which of the two was considered more important is rather obvious. The bonds of citizenship, as Cicero put it in *De Officiis* (I.17.53), are closer and more dignified than the bonds of the *natio*. (Viroli, 2000, p. 268)

One might observe, of course, that the appeal to the origins of "patriotism" in the Latin *patria* and beyond that in the Greek *pater*, could speak in favor of the understanding of patriotism as love of one's fatherland. And so it might, Viroli says, as long as we conceive of this sentiment in essentially political terms; for love of the fatherland "is a specific affection for a specific republic and its citizens. It is found especially among citizens of free republics who share many important things – laws, liberty, public councils, public squares, friends and enemies, memories of victories and defeats, hopes and fears" (Viroli, 2002, p. 80). For republican patriots, at least, the claims of one's nation and one's forebears must be understood in almost exclusively civic terms.

This desire to keep patriotism free of the taint that nationalism brings with it, particularly in view of its association with Nazism and ethnic cleansing, is understandable and widely shared, as I have noted. Nevertheless, the distinction Viroli would have us draw between *patria* and *natio* is too sharp. His attempt to confine the ancestral aspect of patriotism largely to its political features is also suspect. In fact, there is evidence in the passage Viroli cites from *De Officiis* to cast doubt on his strictly political understanding of patriotism. Cicero does indeed proclaim in this passage that the bonds "of race, nation [*nationis*] and language" are among "man's closest," but "closest of all is that of city [*civitatis*], for fellow-citizens have many things in common." He soon insists, however, that "above all these it is between members of the same family that the greatest bonds are to be found"; and familial bonds lie "at the root of every city," where they form, "as it were the seedbed of the state [*rei publicae*]." Indeed, "[b]lood relationship then is the prime factor in uniting men in bonds of love and goodwill" (Cicero, 1967, p. 58).[3]

Whatever Cicero's intentions may have been, it seems clear that Viroli overstates the point when he claims that Cicero took "the bonds of citizenship" to be "closer and more dignified than the bonds of the *natio*." At this point, however, it is enough to note how the three ways of interpreting the "country" in "love of country" may be distinct analytically yet nevertheless blend together in powerful appeals to patriotism. Abraham Lincoln's Gettysburg Address provides a dramatic example of their connection in its opening sentence, in which Lincoln evokes all three senses of "country": "Four score and seven years ago *our fathers* brought forth on this continent, a new *nation*, conceived in *Liberty*, and

[3] For related evidence from other works of Cicero, see Dagger, (2020), sec. 3.

dedicated to the *proposition* that all men are created *equal*" (emphasis added throughout). That so respected a republican as Lincoln could intertwine appeals to ancestry and nationality with the civic ideals of liberty and equality reveals that the force of patriotism extends beyond its narrowly political or civic aspect. So, too, does Lincoln's invocation, in the conclusion to his first inaugural address, of the "mystic chords of memory, [which] stretching from every battlefield and patriot grave, to every living heart and hearthstone, all over this broad land, will yet swell the chorus of the Union, when again touched, as surely they will be, by the better angels of our nature."[4]

Beyond the interpretations of love of country as love of fatherland, nation, or polity lies a fourth but less often appreciated sense or aspect of "country".[5] This fourth aspect is country in the geographical sense of landscape, terrain, and inhabited space. In this case, one's country is a visible thing, or a vast set of visible things that can never be seen all at once. This love of country as countryside figures, alongside other senses of "country," in well-known poetic tributes to patriotism. John of Gaunt's speech in Shakespeare's *Richard II* (Act II, Scene 1) is a case in point, with its celebration of England as "this sceptered isle, this earth of majesty . . ., This other Eden, demi-paradise . . ., This precious stone set in a silver sea which serves it in the office of a wall or as a moat defensive to a house . . ., This blessed spot, this earth, this realm, this England . . . ." Another example is Canto Six of Walter Scott's *Lay of the Last Minstrel,* which begins with the minstrel asking, "Breathes there the man, with soul so dead, Who never to himself hath said, This is my own, my native land!" Then after consigning any such dead souls to "the vile dust . . . Unwept, unhonour'd, and unsung," the poet goes on to yearn for his own native land: "O Caledonia! Stern and wild, Meet nurse for a poetic child, Land of brown heath, and shaggy wood, Land of the mountain and the flood, Land of my sires! What mortal hand Can e'er untie the filial band, That knits me to thy rugged strand!"

To be sure, neither Shakespeare's Gaunt nor Scott's minstrel speaks only of the country as countryside. The minstrel's apostrophe to the land of his sires, with its "filial band," clearly invokes the ancestral aspect of "country," and John of Gaunt's troubled apprehension of the fate of the England he has loved – "This land of such dear souls, this dear, dear land, Dear for her reputation throughout the world" – contains traces of a conception of a country as nation in the sense of a people apart from others. Even so, the notion of one's country as a physical place or territory carries a distinctive force in these poetic expressions of patriotism. This is a force not only worth remembering but also, perhaps, of reinforcing through patriotic education.

Before turning directly to patriotic education, however, there are two further conceptual matters to consider. One concerns adjectives and the other morality.

Adjectives are significant in this context because patriotism comes in various forms and degrees, and its scholarly defenders typically want to make clear what they are – and perhaps more often, are not – defending. In his survey article in

[4] See Smith, (2021, pp. 149–56), for further thoughts on Lincoln's conception of patriotism.

[5] Nussbaum, (2013), is an important exception; see, for example, pp. 14, 209, 238.

The Stanford Encyclopedia of Philosophy, Igor Primoratz (2020) distinguishes among four degrees of patriotism, ranging from "extreme," which he associates with Machiavelli, to "robust" (MacIntyre, 1995), "moderate" (Baron, 2002; Nathanson, 1989), and "deflationary," which covers attempts to justify patriotism not in itself but only in so far as it follows from gratitude, fairness, the good consequences it produces, or some other independent ground (Primoratz, 2020, sec. 2.2). Other varieties include what Primoratz calls "ethical patriotism" (Baron, 2002), what Jürgen Habermas and others have called "constitutional patriotism" (Habermas, 1996, Appendix II; Müller, 2007), Viroli's (2000) previously noted "republican patriotism," and Steven Smith's "enlightened patriotism" (Smith, 2021, ch. 5). Smith is in some ways typical of those who think it wise to use a qualifying adjective when advocating patriotism, for he is well aware of the simplistic "love it or leave it" caricatures to which patriotism is often reduced and of the horrors committed by nationalists who have been mistaken for patriots. In fact, Smith argues, patriotism stands as an Aristotelian mean between two extremes, nationalism and cosmopolitanism, with nationalism being "an excess of patriotism" and cosmopolitanism its "deficiency" (2021, pp. 106–7). Contrary to its caricature, moreover, patriotism "can be self-correcting"; rather than "blind obedience," it "entails judgment and discrimination" (Smith, 2021, p. 41). Genuine patriotism, in a word, is enlightened.

Whether Smith has hit upon the right adjective is not my concern here, but the larger point is. That is, some qualification of this kind is necessary to make it clear that patriotism is not an unquestioning commitment to "my country right or wrong." But what, then, is the nature of the patriotic commitment? In particular, is it a moral commitment?

There is disagreement on this point. On the one hand, many who defend patriotism clearly believe that it has moral value, or that the only defensible form of patriotism is one that "makes compatible the demands of national loyalty and the requirements of universal morality" (Nathanson, 1989, p. 551). On the other hand, some commentators believe that patriotism is devoid of moral content. In Amy Gutmann's words, "patriotism is a sentiment rather than a moral perspective" (Gutmann, 1999, p. 312). Lad Sessions agrees when he states that patriotism "as such is *a*moral, neither morally right nor morally wrong in all cases," however morally worthy or reprehensible it may be in particular cases (Sessions, 2010, p. 105; emphasis in original). He goes on, though, to make the following general claim: "Without patriotic loyalty, countries survive (and do not thrive) only by use of coercion, threat or bribery, a tenuous project for the long term" (Sessions, 2010, p. 111). This claim bears directly on the argument of this chapter. It bears, that is, on the relationship of patriotism to the cooperative-practice conception of democracy. For if patriotic sentiment is widespread, so that citizens are confident that their fellows generally are willing to bear the burdens of a polity secured by the rule of law – that they are willing to do what they regard as their patriotic duty – then social trust will reduce the need to rely on coercion to provide the assurance that one's cooperative efforts will not be wasted. Patriotism in this sense encourages citizens to meet their moral responsibilities to one another. Put more broadly, patriotism has a moral dimension in so far as it takes people outside of themselves and leads them to think and act less as self-absorbed individuals and more as people concerned with the wellbeing of their compatriots.

To this claim about the moral dimension of patriotism, the critics have an obvious reply. Patriotism may overcome the individual's partiality for their particular interests, they can say, but concern for the wellbeing of one's country and compatriots itself falls short of the impartiality that morality demands. Morality is a matter of doing what is right or just, in other words, and it respects no political or geographical boundaries. This obvious reply, however, is not obviously compelling, for it may rest on too simple or narrow a conception of morality. The nature and definition of morality are matters too complicated to try to settle here, but it should suffice to say that David Hume, Adam Smith, and other important philosophers have found room for sentiments, sympathy, and local attachments within their conceptions of morality. Steven Smith's understanding of patriotism as a mean between nationalism and cosmopolitanism is worth considering in this light, as are the essays of Marcia Baron (2002) and Stephen Nathanson (1989), which make the case for the importance of patriotism within liberal morality. They and other authors give us reason to believe, in short, that patriotism is a moral disposition, and thus no reason to dismiss it from the outset as an immoral attitude at odds with a democratic education.

23.5 A Patriotic Education?

The opposition of patriotic partiality to moral principles has its counterpart in recent debates over the teaching of patriotism in schools. These debates are frequently framed as a contest between patriotism and autonomy, or sentimental attachment versus critical reasoning, with William Galston's *Liberal Purposes* (1991, ch. 11) and Amy Gutmann's *Democratic Education* (1999) cast as leading representatives of the opposing sides. In an oft-quoted passage, Galston puts the case for teaching patriotism forcefully:

> Few individuals will come to embrace the core commitments of liberal society through a process of rational inquiry. If children are to be brought to accept these commitments as valid and binding, the method must be a pedagogy that is far more rhetorical than rational . . . Civic education . . . requires a nobler, moralizing history: a pantheon of heroes who confer legitimacy on central institutions and are worthy of emulation. It is unrealistic to believe that more than a few adult citizens of liberal societies will ever move beyond the kind of civic commitment engendered by such a pedagogy. (1991, pp. 243–44)

As this statement indicates, Galston's focus is on the teaching of history, and the ongoing debate has continued to concentrate on the wisdom of teaching patriotic history. There is also the challenging question of whether history can be taught both patriotically and truthfully. The practical problem, as one critic says, is "how to encourage patriotic identification while teaching history with integrity" (Costa, 2009, p. 108).

There are, I think, two responses to this challenge. One is to note that the focus on history is reasonable, but it should not divert our attention from the possibility of fostering patriotism in other parts of the curriculum, including the so-called hidden curriculum. The second response is to give due attention to the gradual nature of formal education.

Regarding the first response, David Archard has argued that "the way forward" – that is, the way to resolve the debate between an education for patriotism or for autonomy – "lies in recognising that we should not teach patriotism because *we do not need to*" (Archard, 1999, p. 167; emphasis added). After all, he says, "we are members of our *patria* in advance of our education," and "any education must be particularistic in ways that, without explicitly teaching it, favour the acquisition of patriotism" (1999, p. 167). There are, in other words, numerous aspects of every child's environment, even before schooling begins, that contribute to the formation of a national identity and thereby foster an attachment to one's country. In school, moreover, children are almost certain to find "a national, though not a nationalist, curriculum," and they will find it not only in history classes but in those focused on the geography, language, literature, and culture more generally of their own country (1999, p. 168).[6] Archard's observations are well founded, but do they support his claim that "we should not teach patriotism because we do not need to"? Is it perhaps more accurate to say that our schools are teaching patriotism whether they intend to do so or not? If so, is it perhaps possible that they could do a better job of teaching patriotism if they gave more careful thought to the task?

This possibility probably explains why the debate concentrates so often on history, for it is there that the question of intention – to cultivate patriotic attachment or critical thinking – seems most obvious. This controversy has proceeded, however, without due attention to what I called the gradual nature of formal education. The contrasting views of Robert Fullinwider and Harry Brighouse help to make my point. In his "Patriotic History," Fullinwider takes the "core idea" of such a history "to do not with *pride* but with *duty*: what projects over time, begun by others, am I duty-bound to take on (or resist)? Our answers to that question fix our moral identities" (Fullinwider, 1996, p. 222; emphasis in original). To support his argument, Fullinwider draws on examples from textbooks written for American students in the eighth grade (that is, 12 or 13 years old). In his rebuttal, "Should We Teach Patriotic History?," Brighouse (2003, p. 174) supports his argument – that "the primary attention of liberal authors of textbooks should not be on directly encouraging identities in, or teaching values to, readers, but on teaching them what happened and teaching them the skills essential to figuring out why" – by referring to books written for high school students (that is, 16 to 18 years old). What is appropriate for students at one age, however, may not be appropriate for students at the

[6] As Archard notes (1999, p. 162), one of Galston's critics, Eamonn Callan, believes that the study of literature may be more valuable as a form of civic education than "'conventional historical scholarship'" (citing Callan, 1997, p. 123).

other. This point is especially important in view of the fact that the teaching of history typically begins at a much earlier age than either Fullinwider or Brighouse considers in their examples. In general, we should expect that Galston's "pantheon of heroes" approach may have its place in the elementary grades, but it should gradually give way to a more critical approach to the history of the students' country as they grow older.

Smith's invocation of G. W. F. Hegel as a philosopher who made significant contributions to the understanding of patriotism is also valuable in this context. "Hegelian patriotism," Smith says, "is a form of *Bildung* or moral education that may begin as a matter of trust and habit, but it gradually passes over into rational self-awareness" (Smith, 2021, p. 52). Smith himself believes that patriotism is something that can and should be taught, and he maintains that "the best teachers are old books." In the case of American patriotism, these "old books" include Locke's *Second Treatise*, Montesquieu's *The Spirit of the Laws*, *The Federalist*, Tocqueville's *Democracy in America*, Frederick Douglass's autobiography, "and Lincoln's great speeches and letters" (Smith, 2021, pp. 188–89). These are not works we can expect young children to read, of course, and they are likely to prove challenging even to those in their teenage years. The challenge, though, is not inimical to patriotism, and it is certainly something that a democratic education should encourage students to confront in appropriate ways at appropriate ages.

To be sure, not everyone will accept Smith's contention that old books are, at least in the American context, the best teachers of patriotism. Nor will everyone agree that he has identified the right set of books, whether old or new. In our postcolonial times, for instance, some surely will object to holding up such supporters of colonialism as Locke and Tocqueville as exemplars of a proper patriotism. But there are at least two responses to this kind of concern. The first is that removing a book or two – in this case, Locke's and Tocqueville's – from the reading list will create space for the reading and discussion of other valuable works. There may be a place, for instance, for an exploration of the anticolonial words and deeds of Mohandas Gandhi, of whom Martha Nussbaum maintains that there "was no more canny creator of critical patriotism" than he (Nussbaum, 2013, p. 242) The second response is to note that finding something objectionable in an author's writings is no reason to dismiss everything they have to say. On the contrary, learning to distinguish the valuable insight from the wrong-headed conclusion and the biased assumption is an ability we should want a democratic education to cultivate.

Reading old books can be helpful also when they are seen as rising out of or relating to historical controversies, as would be the case with most of the items on Smith's list and many others we could include, new as well as old. Not only can such texts help to inform historical understanding, but reading them can illustrate the importance of preparing for life in a society in which deep disagreements among the people must be addressed and accommodated. To the extent that patriotic history can help people to meet these demands of democratic citizenship, it has a vital role to play in democratic education. We must remember, though, that an education in patriotism must proceed gradually, and the reliance on old books will be appropriate, at best, only in its later stages.

23.6 Conclusion

> We need scarcely say that we do not mean [by the principle of nationality] a senseless antipathy to foreigners; or a cherishing of absurd peculiarities because they are national; or a refusal to adopt what has been found good by other countries. In all these senses, the nations which have had the strongest national spirit have had the least nationality. We mean a principle of sympathy, not of hostility; of union, not of separation. We mean a feeling of common interest among those who live under the same government, and are contained within the same natural or historical boundaries. We mean, that one part of the community shall not consider themselves as foreigners with regard to another part; that they shall cherish the tie which holds them together; shall feel that they are one people, that their lot is cast together, that evil to any of their fellow-countrymen is evil to themselves, and that they cannot selfishly free themselves from their share of any common inconvenience by severing the connection. (from J. S. Mill, *A System of Logic*; quoted in Viroli, 1995, p. vi)

Maurizio Viroli chose the passage above from Mill's *System of Logic* as the epigraph for his own *For Love of Country*, a book that extols the merits of patriotism, and particularly of republican patriotism. Evidently Viroli saw a close connection between Mill's "principle of nationality" and patriotism, even though Mill did not refer to "patriotism" in the passage. Not only was he right to do so, in my view, but Mill's words are even more appropriate to the argument I have advanced – that patriotic education can provide vital support to a democracy conceived as a cooperative practice secured by the rule of law. Some sense of being part of a polity must be nourished if people are, as Mill said, to "feel that they are one people" from whom some sacrifice is rightly required – even if it is only the sacrifice of paying taxes or devoting some of one's time to participation in elections or other forms of civic self-rule. Without this sense of being part of a polity in which burdens are to be borne for the common benefit, we must expect that individuals, again in Mill's words, will "desire selfishly to free themselves from their share of any common inconvenience by severing the connection." If appeal to patriotism as love of one's ancestral homeland, or countryside, or nation, will supplement the educative force of participation in collective self-government, and thus enhance the sense of membership in a cooperative endeavor, then such appeals are to be encouraged.

The final question is whether patriotism is truly necessary to the solution of this "civic motivation problem," as Ian MacMullen calls it (2015, pp. 149–56). The problem is genuine, according to MacMullen, and some "sense of connection to one's polity" is required to overcome it (2015, p. 156). But that sense of connection is afforded by civic identity, which avoids the unpleasant associations attached to appeals to patriotism. For similar reasons, Victoria Costa also regards "civic identity" or "civic identification" as a superior alternative to patriotism (Costa, 2009, pp. 109–10). But how strong a sense of connection is needed to provide the civic motivation that a democracy understood as a cooperative practice requires? There is no obvious answer to this question, in part because there is no clear line of demarcation between civic identity and patriotic devotion. MacMullen and Costa believe that civic identity is a cooler and less emotional attachment to a polity than patriotism is, but whether that is an advantage is not obviously true. After all, one need not be an extreme or even robust patriot, in Primoratz's terms, to believe that an abiding love for one's country is a far safer response to the problem of civic motivation than relying on the less intense civic identification. For one may well doubt the capacity of such identification to provide "the animating soul of law's commonwealth." Patriotism, even in its moderate and critical forms, may be a deep and abiding emotion, but it is valuable to democracy for precisely that reason. For "patriotic emotion," as Nussbaum has observed (2013, p. 207), "can be a necessary prop for valuable projects involving sacrifice for others." Paramount among such projects is the maintenance of the cooperative practice of democracy.

References

Archard, D. (1999). Should we teach patriotism? *Studies in Philosophy and Education*, 18, 157–73.

Baron, M. (2002). Patriotism and "liberal" morality. In I. Primoratz, ed., *Patriotism*. Amherst, NY: Humanity Books, pp. 59–86.

Brighouse, H. (2003). Should we teach patriotic history? In K. McDonough & W. Feinberg, eds., *Citizenship and education in liberal-democratic societies*. Oxford: Oxford University Press, pp. 157–75.

Callan, E. (1997). *Creating citizens: Political education and liberal democracy*. Oxford: Oxford University Press.

Cicero (1967). *On moral obligation [De Officiis]*. Trans. by J. Higginbotham. Berkeley, CA: University of California Press.

Costa, M. V. (2009). Justice as fairness, civic identity, and patriotic education. *Public Affairs Quarterly*, 23, 95–114.

Crittenden, J. (2002). *Democracy's midwife: An education in deliberation*. Lanham, MD: Lexington Books.

Dagger, R. (2018). *Playing fair: Political obligation and the problems of punishment*. Oxford: Oxford University Press.

Dagger, R. (2020). Patriotism and republicanism. In M. Sardoc, ed., *Handbook of patriotism*. Switzerland: Springer, pp. 87–104.

Dahl, R. (1998). *On democracy*. New Haven, CT: Yale University Press.

Dewey, J. (1916/1993). *The political writings*. Ed. by D. Morris & I. Shapiro. Indianapolis, IN: Hackett.

Dietz, M. (1989). Patriotism. In T. Ball, J. Farr & R. Hanson, eds., *Political innovation and conceptual change*. Cambridge: Cambridge University Press, pp. 177–93.
Finnis, J. (1980). *Natural law and natural rights*. Oxford: Oxford University Press.
Fuller, L. (1969). *The morality of law*. New Haven, CT: Yale University Press.
Fullinwider, R. (1996). Patriotic history. In R. K. Fullinwider, ed., *Public education in a multicultural society: Policy, theory, critique*. Cambridge: Cambridge University Press, pp. 203–28.
Galston, W. (1991). *Liberal purposes: Goods, virtues, and diversity in the liberal state*. Cambridge: Cambridge University Press.
Gilbert, M. (2009). Pro patria. An essay on patriotism. *Journal of Ethics*, 13, 319–46.
Gomberg, P. (1990). Patriotism is like racism. *Ethics*, 10, 144–50.
Gutmann, A. (1999). *Democratic education*. Rev. ed., Princeton, NJ: Princeton University Press.
Habermas, J. (1996). *Between facts and norms: Contributions to a discourse theory of law and democracy*. Trans. by W. Rehg, Cambridge, MA: MIT Press.
Hart, H. L. A. (1970). Are there any natural rights? In A. I. Melden, ed., *Human rights*. Belmont, CA: Wadsworth, pp. 77–90.
Kateb, G. (2000). Is patriotism a mistake? *Social Research*, 67, 901–24.
Keller, S. (2005). Patriotism as bad faith. *Ethics*, 115, 563–92.
MacIntyre, A. (1995). Is patriotism a virtue? In R. Beiner, ed., *Theorizing citizenship*. Albany, NY: State University of New York Press.
MacMullen, I. (2015). *Civics beyond critics: Character education in a liberal democracy*. Oxford: Oxford University Press.
Mill, J. S. (1861/2015). Considerations on representative government. In M. Philp & F. Rosen, eds., *On liberty, utilitarianism, and other essays*. Oxford: Oxford University Press, pp. 179–405.
Müller, J. W. (2007). *Constitutional patriotism*. Princeton, NJ: Princeton University Press.
Nathanson, S. (1989). In defense of "moderate patriotism". *Ethics*, 99, 535–52.
Nussbaum, M. (2013). *Political emotions: Why love matters for justice*. Cambridge, MA: Harvard University Press.
Peters, R. S. (1973). Further thoughts on the concept of education. In R. S. Peters, ed., *The philosophy of education*. Oxford: Oxford University Press.
Postema, G. (2014). Fidelity in law's commonwealth. In L. M. Austin & D. Klimchuk, eds., *Private law and the rule of law*. Oxford: Oxford University Press, pp. 17–40.
Primoratz, I. (2020). Patriotism. In E. N. Zalta, ed., *The Stanford encyclopedia of philosophy*. Available at: https://plato.stanford.edu/archives/win2020/entries/patriotism.
Rawls, J. (1971/1999). *A theory of justice*. Cambridge, MA: Harvard University Press.
Sellers, M. N. S. (2003). *Republican legal theory: The history, constitution, and purposes of law in a free state*. Basingstoke: Palgrave Macmillan.
Sessions, W. L. (2010). *Honor for us: A philosophical analysis, interpretation and defense*. New York: Continuum.
Smith, S. B. (2021). *Reclaiming patriotism in an age of extremes*. New Haven, CT: Yale University Press.

Tamanaha, B. (2006). *On the rule of law: History, politics, theory*. Cambridge: Cambridge University Press.

Thompson, J. (2008). Patriotism and the obligations of history. In I. Primoratz & A. Pavkovic, eds., *Patriotism: Philosophical and political perspectives*. London: Routledge, pp. 147–59.

Tocqueville, A. de. (1969 [1834, Vol. I; 1840, Vol. II). *Democracy in America*. Trans. by G. Lawrence, Ed. by J. P. Mayer, New York: Doubleday Anchor.

Viroli, M. (1995). *For love of country: An essay on patriotism and nationalism*. Oxford: Oxford University Press.

Viroli, M. (2000). Republican patriotism. In C. McKinnon & I. Hampsher-Monk, eds., *The demands of citizenship*. London: Continuum, pp. 267–75.

Viroli, M. (2002). *Republicanism*. Trans. by A. Shuggar, New York: Hill & Wang.

24

The Voice of Poetry in Cultivating Cosmopolitan and Democratic Imagination

David T. Hansen and Yuval Dwek

24.1 Introduction

The terms cosmopolitan and democracy derive from the ancient Greek, though their enactment in various forms and degrees can be found across time in numerous places on the globe. *Kosmopolit□s* translates literally as "citizen of the world." It can also incorporate the notion of "inhabitant of the world," a meaning that conjures ethical and ecological commitment to all life on the planet. *Demokratia* fuses *demos* – the people – and *kratos* – power or rule, thus denoting "power of the people." Both concepts and their associated practices emerged almost in the same moment in ancient Athens. That independent city-state was a site of democratic experiments in governance that have had a lasting influence down to the present day. Its port, the Piraeus, was a cosmopolitan crossroads of traders, exiles, visiting politicians and scholars, travelers, and more. Diogenes (c. 390–323 BCE), an exile from a Greek city-state on the Black Sea, haunted public buildings and quarters in Athens, declaring to anyone who asked that he "came from the world" and was "a citizen of the world." The term he bequeathed us, cosmopolitan, continues to have a vivid life.

Our purpose in this chapter is to illuminate the relationship between cosmopolitan and democratic imagination and education. To do so, we draw upon what the philosopher Michael Oakeshott (1991) calls "the voice of poetry" in the human drama of fashioning a meaningful home on the planet. Home, in this instance, refers to more than a physical location and such things as food, water, and shelter. Home also has a deep moral, aesthetic, social, and spiritual meaning, with "spiritual" rooted not in an established religion but in a fundamental quest for belonging. As we will see, to belong in the world is to have a voice in how humans dwell together as social beings. It is to learn how to keep one foot in local values and commitments, and the other foot in larger, shared human values and concerns. This task, and this invitation, is never a simple educational accomplishment, but it is more than a mere ideal. Our core claim is that poetry is irreplaceable, as its own singular form of expression, for cultivating the cosmopolitan and democratic imagination that can fuel this orientation toward belonging. The primary company we will keep is with the American poet Walt Whitman (1819–92), whose voice both exemplifies and describes that same orientation.

24.2 Conceptual Preliminaries

Our core terms are democracy, education, cosmopolitanism, poetry, and imagination. Democracy has been extensively treated elsewhere in this volume, so here we attend to the other concepts.

24.2.1 Education

Education differs from socialization or what is also called enculturation. Socialization is an essential, formative process. A person literally cannot enter the social world without it. They must be *formed* such that they can participate in that world, and in their infancy and early years lack the wherewithal to accomplish this themselves. This reality does not imply a coercive process, but it does demand intervention on the part of adults. Socialization is fundamentally *additive* in nature. The child adds the ability to ride a bike to their skill set. They add the fact that 2 + 2 = 4 to their knowledge bank.

We understand education as a *transformative* experience, however microscopic a given change may be in comparison with the whole panoply of experience. The child learning arithmetic may also learn to think logically in a manner that, over time, transforms their modes of thinking as a human being. They may discover that riding a bike develops a sense of geography and direction that will serve them well their entire life. In general, if socialization gives us our feet to move in society and culture, education positions us to stand with one foot outside our community and to adopt a reflective outlook toward it. This task requires imagination, another core concept in our chapter.

Formal institutions such as schools and universities are the first things that come to mind when people consider education. Such institutions have proven to be crucial both for socialization and education. Through the numerous subjects they offer, from art through zoology, they position people to understand the local and larger world, to appreciate the histories behind current events and concerns, to develop the skills and knowledge to pursue aims and to collaborate with others, and more. However, education is not reducible to formal institutions. Education is a common feature of ongoing experience for people, who sometimes find themselves in situations – many of them unplanned and unanticipated – that provoke them to reflect, to question, to wonder, to inquire, to be critical. Through the cultivation of habits of perceiving attentively and thinking reflectively, life itself can become a continuous educational experience.

24.2.2 Cosmopolitanism

Philosophical and educational traditions which originate in the Mediterranean Basin have articulated the cosmopolitan idea in its most developed written forms. However, these forms have never been self-contained (or "purely" Western, whatever that could mean), nor are they at all points the most influential in the world today. For one thing, the Mediterranean has always been a cultural mélange, ranging historically from the Moorish, Christian, and Jewish milieu of medieval Spain in the west to the multilingual, multicultural ethos of the Levant in the east, not to mention the Phoenician, Carthaginian, and Maghrebian cultures of North Africa and the Greek and Roman cultures of southern Europe. For another thing, cosmopolitan motifs of hospitality and tolerance appear in numerous philosophical lineages deriving, for example, from the South Asian *Upanishads* (first millennium BCE) and Confucius' *Analects* (sixth century BCE). Contemporary scholars have articulated cosmopolitan themes in these and other longstanding traditions. They have made plain that the movement in cosmopolitan ideas has sometimes been, in global terms, east to west and south to north. Important cosmopolitan-minded thinkers (some of them famed artists as well), such as Aimé Césaire, Octavio Paz, and Rabindranath Tagore, attest to the continuity over time of this truth (cf. Slate, 2012).

As mentioned, the term cosmopolitanism derives from the Greek *kosmopolit□s*, usually translated as "citizen of the world." There are indices of it in Socrates' eagerness to learn from persons from anywhere. We can also discern a cosmopolitan attitude in the practices of the traveling Sophists, Socrates' contemporaries who were itinerant educators and among the very first persons in Western culture who were paid for their educational services. The idea reaches its apogee in the ancient Mediterranean world among the Hellenistic and Roman Stoics, who in various ways suggested it was possible to devote oneself to both local and larger human concerns. They sought to frame practical ways of life in which one could be attuned both to particularized obligations and to the needs and hopes of humanity writ large. Writers as varied as Cicero, Seneca, Epictetus, and Marcus Aurelius ventured cosmopolitan ideas throughout their texts. Later, in the wake of the fourteenth-to-fifteeenth century Renaissance, with its rediscovery of these ancient sources, writers such as Desiderius Erasmus and Michel de Montaigne put forward portraits mirroring those of the Stoics about the importance of tolerance and mutual exchange. They sought an ecumenical approach that could reduce the religious strife prevalent at the time, even as they respected human differences in culture, in the arts, and more.

Commentators during the Enlightenment of the eighteenth century rooted their cosmopolitan claims, in part, in the view that because human beings are capable of reason and moral agency, they must be treated with respect. They are not "things" with a merely economic or cultural value, but are singular beings with dignity. They are creative rather than merely created creatures. They are ends in themselves rather than mere means to others' ends. This outlook led cosmopolitan thinkers, in contrast with some of their Enlightenment confreres, to condemn war, slavery, and imperialism. Immanuel Kant eclipsed his own cultural biases in showing that moral respect – deriving from the German *Achtung*, which can also be rendered as "awe" or "reverence" – translates into the duty to make possible for all people an education that positions them to shape the course of their lives while contributing to the well-being of others.

Kant gave the cosmopolitan idea an enduring boost through his moral philosophy and through his oft-cited argument for how to generate peace among states and communities. (For a critique of Kant's outlook, see Valdez, 2019; for defenses of that outlook, see Kleingeld, 2011, and Muthu, 2003; for discussion of Kant's cosmopolitan perspective on education, see Cavallar, 2015, and Munzel, 2017.)

Cosmopolitan studies as an interdisciplinary, scholarly field, has mushroomed in recent years. Researchers attend to moral, cultural, aesthetic, political, economic, educational, and environmental issues viewed through a cosmopolitan prism. The literature features considerable debate regarding the remit of cosmopolitanism as well as arguments for and against its contemporary pertinence (for discussion and extensive references, see Beck, 2004; Delanty, 2019; Hansen, 2011; Nussbaum, 2021). As the brief overview we have given suggests, cosmopolitanism has historically taken two directions that can be called, for heuristic purposes, the universal and the rooted. For the former, the unit of analysis and concern is humanity writ large. Individuals and local communities matter, but in this outlook the primary moral commitment must be to humanity. This commitment must inform local moral relations and practices.

In contrast, rooted cosmopolitanism begins from the ground – from the individual and local community. People do need to cultivate moral regard and respect for those outside their circle, but what is of concern to people within that circle must be given comparable moral weight, especially if they are subject to violence and oppression. Moreover, the circles in which humans dwell are, save in instances of extreme physical isolation, permeable and subject to endless influence from without, which vitiates any pretense to cultural purity or essences. This fact sheds light on the oft-cited identity politics characteristic of our time, which sometimes features dogmatic, essentialist self-accounts that wall people off from one another. However understandable this impulse may be given particular human circumstances, such a move intensifies polarization and antagonism. The extensive literature on cosmopolitanism documents that persons with these very same identities can manifest them in imaginative, peaceful, and interactive fashion – out of love for what they have inherited, one might say, rather than out of fear, resentment, or anger toward others. This cosmopolitan practice may necessitate institutional and educational support. But it can be, and has been, enacted in the here and now (cf. Aciman, 1994; Anderson, 2011; Diawara, 1998; Tuan, 1996; Wardle, 2010).

In brief, cosmopolitanism has been pursued as a universal philosophy that accents a common humanity as well as institutions to support worldwide human wellbeing and rights. Its rooted version emphasizes cultural and everyday life on the ground: how human beings from diverse backgrounds and origins can not only interact peacefully but also cooperate and learn from one another. The extensive literature on what can be summarized as rooted cosmopolitanism has effectively dissolved damaging, stereotypical images of the cosmopolitan as a footloose, fancy-free elitist enjoying a smorgasbord of the world's cuisines, clothing styles, music, and the like. There is nothing inherently wrong with such pleasures, but they do not in themselves imply a cosmopolitan outlook. The literature has demonstrated that a multilingual taxi driver, operator of a laundry business, or waitress in a local diner, can have a more multifaceted cosmopolitan disposition than the most well-heeled global traveler. Like democratic habits, a cosmopolitan outlook grows from the ground up in one's everyday interactions with people and the world. We illuminate this point in what follows.

A final remark is that cosmopolitanism, as understood here, is not a new identity that would supplant extant local identities. Rather, the orientation invites people everywhere to reimagine how they hold and express their identities and values. Across history, as already alluded to, the latter has sometimes been done dogmatically, fearfully, and/or violently. At other moments, including in the very same locales, people have held, cherished, and enacted their identities and values in peaceful, mutually respectful fashion. Indeed, the latter phenomenon attests to why cosmopolitanism pushes beyond tolerance alone. A person can tolerate another individual or culture without learning anything from them. But in a cosmopolitan dispensation, one's experience of the world is educational in an ongoing, dynamic manner. Imagination plays a central role in making this orientation possible.

24.2.3 Poetry

Poetry is as old and universal as culture, and emerges alongside religion, philosophy, other art forms, and science – all millennia old as well. There are countless expositions of the nature of poetry that cut across the world's cultures. Moreover, poets such as Whitman, Rainer Maria Rilke, Emily Dickinson, Countee Cullen, Wallace Stevens, and others routinely comment on poetry, if not in so many words, within the space of their poems. The particular conception of poetry we bring to bear in this chapter is deeply influenced by our reading of Whitman's "Song of Myself," which we discuss in Section 24.3. Our outlook can be characterized as follows.

For one thing, we believe poetry is not an alternative to prose, nor a second-best mode of expression compared with prose. For another thing, it is not an alternative to philosophical, theoretical, scientific, or theological attempts at explanation. Poetry explains nothing, nor does it aspire to. Its entire focus is on meaning, or its absence, in the affairs of humanity and nature. The poet grasps the fact that explanations are inert until people derive meaning from them. Put another way, people live by meaning, not by explanations considered in themselves (cf. Polanyi & Prosch, 1975). Meaning denotes *interested activity*. Moreover, poetry has no autocratic or dogmatic aspirations. Nor does it harbor a top-down outlook; the poet is not an all-knowing, Olympian spectator. The poet works horizontally, alongside the world. The poet listens to the world, and sees the world, in a richer, deeper form than is customary in everyday life. The poet is at home, even if that "home" is a perennial search for home.

The poet does not mechanize any of this. Rather, the poet readies themselves for it through a patient, nongrasping mode of waiting. They wait for the right image to emerge which will launch their composition. In this respect, the poet does not reach out for inspiration and truth but waits, and hopes, to be reached by a truth that will come in the form of an image. It may be a truth about what it means to suffer, to love, to learn, to remember, to forget, to die, to live, or to write poetry. The poet is all reception, and becomes a conduit, a handperson, a vehicle for the truth they receive. "Through me the afflatus surging and surging," Whitman declaims in "Song of Myself" (Stanza 24). Afflatus is Latin for "blowing or breathing on," and it also denotes a divine inspiration or imparting of knowledge. The world breathes on the poet, metaphorically speaking, and this breath of truth surges through him and, thanks to his artistry, lands on the page.

The poet is both detached and engaged. The poet is a witness, which we take to be an ethical term denoting a fusion of wonder and concern (Hansen, 2021; Hansen & Sullivan, 2022). Many witnesses have composed in prose rather than in poetry, as did Whitman himself in his moving account (2004) of visiting and nursing wounded Union soldiers during the American Civil War.[1] The *poet-witness* is not an actor or activist, as such. But their poetry is a mode of action in its own right; the poet is not a mere spectator. The poet adds something that was not there before, namely, their composition and the truth, reality, wonder, and questioning it evokes. Nor is the poet, *in* the work they put forward, cynical, jaded, or nihilistic; the poem as creative act contradicts such empty postures. The poet's orientation may not be one of optimism, but it is one of faith and hope: faith in the power of poetry to express truth, however redeeming or harsh it may be, and faith, for some, in what they regard as the inextinguishable beauty, truth, and good in the world. They hope that these realities will triumph over the realities of injustice, violence, greed, indifference, and all the other self-inflicted ills of society.

Here is how the poet and translator Michael Hamburger (1973) summarizes these points:

> Whatever I may have done or known in my life, my poetry came out of a kind of wonderment whose other side – the left hand – is a sense of outrage . . . In general, too, this capacity to wonder, and to feel outrage, strikes me as a distinguishing attribute of poets, and a condition of their persistence in [what T. S. Eliot called] the mug's game [i.e. a seemingly quixotic venture] . . . . Ultimately, though, it is not my business to ask why or how I go on, how or why my work appeals or does not appeal to those who read such work . . . nor even whether it will prove durable enough to have been worth the price paid for doing it. *What matters to me now is the durability of that for which it was a receptacle and conductor.* My business is to remain true to the wonderment and outrage as long as they recur, always unexpectedly, always a little differently, always in a way I can neither plan nor choose; and to keep quiet when there is nothing that wants to use me to make itself heard. (p. 333, italics added; see also Hamburger, 2022)

[1] Mark Edmundson (2019) writes: "While he was in Washington [DC] at what he called 'my hospitals', I think Whitman effectively completed 'Song of Myself'. He became a version of the person his poem prophesied. He engaged his soul, 'clear and sweet', as he called it. His soul became his mode of connection with the sick and wounded and dying men. His imagination allowed him to see who they were, what they were feeling, and how he could best help them" (p. 107).

For Hamburger, the poet receives and responds, metabolizing what has come to them and taking pen (or computer) in hand. Images flow one after the other, though getting them right can be taxing in a highly singular way, just as it can be distinctively difficult – sometimes impossible – to find the right word in philosophy, the right shape in sculpture, or the right light in a film. But if the images and words come, so does the poem.

24.2.4 Imagination

Image, imagine, imagination: these familiar terms differ markedly from fantasy, invention, or wishful thinking. As we understand it, imagination does not mean making things up out of whole cloth. It does not point to some special genius or inspiration. The poet knows the absolute truth in the novelist Gustave Flaubert's remark that, when it comes to art, "genius is [nothing but] hard work" – though not quite pure and simple. Rather, as we have implied, poetry is hard work of a distinctive kind, and requires practice, resolve, and contemplation in an equally special way.

As we picture it, the poet imagines in at least three ways.

1. They imagine – that is, they bring images into form – of portions and districts of reality to which persons are normally blind. Most persons, most of the time, are too preoccupied with their concerns, obligations, and interests to pay much attention to their surroundings, which in time tend to blur into an undifferentiated background. Though all too understandable given human needs and limitations, this habit constitutes an immeasurable moral, aesthetic, social, political, and personal loss. It fosters a habit of inattentiveness and indifference that undermines, if not impoverishes, people's capacity to pay attention with imagination and tenacity to things that profoundly matter: from caring for loved ones and strangers, to grander realities such as democracy, justice, and the wellbeing of all entities in the world. The point is not that persons must be attentive 24/7; that posture would be exhausting and might interfere with the necessity of practical action. But it does imply cultivating a habit of stepping regularly outside the stream of action and routine, even if for a millisecond, to see truly what is there.
2. The poet imagines what could be, in a manner captured by the nineteenth-century orator, writer, and abolitionist Frederick Douglass: "Poets, prophets, and reformers are all picture makers," he writes, "and this ability is the secret of their power and of their achievements. They see what ought to be by the reflection of what is, and endeavor to remove that contradiction" (in Slate, 2012, p. 253). Again, the poet does not generate images out of nothing. They must wait for reality to come to them. But their waiting is intensely active, as they think, as they recall and connect things seen and heard, as they begin to experiment with words. Often (always?) to their surprise, possibilities of what could be – of what could be more just, more meaningful, more good, truthful, and beautiful – emerge on printed page. Moreover, this what-could-be is never based on a hatred of reality no matter how harsh and unjust it has been.

To hate anything is to spurn a part of the world, when the precise task is to love the world so much that the person, through their works and days, counters the hate and the conditions that give rise to it. The poet does so not by building institutions and leading causes. Through their capacity to wait, they do so by seeing what could be.

3. The poet imagines what people have long known but are apt to forget and to neglect, sometimes at great cost. Karl Marx perceived this forgetfulness in the emergence of capitalist modes of production and consumption in the nineteenth century, a process in which, as he worried, "all that is solid melts into air" – his poetic image for what can be seen in today's globalization, namely, a nonstop commodification of seemingly every value people hold. The image parallels concerns that educators have expressed regarding pressures to instrumentalize what they do, that is, to render educational practice into a mere means to economic ends. Educators around the world have been pushing against this reductionist view, putting forward neglected educational values such as reflective and critical thinking, the cultivation of minds and bodies rather than mere 'human capital', the deepening of aesthetic, moral, and intellectual sensibility, and more. Their commitment echoes apprehensions that, because of the instrumentalizing influence of economic globalization, many persons today appear to regard democracy as simply a name for economic mobility and money-making juxtaposed with after-hours entertainment, with actual participation in local or larger affairs *as a citizen* at a bare minimum (perhaps remembering to vote). Russell Hanson (1985) remarks: "Insofar as open discourses are vital stimuli for a vivid democratic imagination, they keep alive democratic possibilities. Should our discourses, and hence our imaginations, become impoverished, so too democratic vistas as they recede beyond our ability to recall them". (p. 52)

The poet's imaginative remembrance does not smack of nostalgia or a conservative inwardness. Quite the contrary. Poetry can be an act of remembrance of the very first order of what justice, care, love, hope, community, and much more have long meant to human beings, and can continue to mean if people invest themselves in sustaining them.

Reality, possibility, remembrance: such is the work of imagination in poetry. We turn now to Walt Whitman's remarkable "Song of Myself" – part of his larger work, "Leaves of Grass" – which sheds helpful light on what we will call democratic and cosmopolitan imagination.

24.3 Whitman and the Place of the Poet in Cosmopolitan and Democratic Life

Whitman published "Song of Myself" in 1855. He had been writing poetry for some time, and for a living worked in New York City in various jobs associated with the printing business, while also taking up posts from time to time as a teacher and journalist. He self-published the initial printing of his longer

"Leaves of Grass." He lived a life as uncontainable, varied, and unpredictable as the nation he evokes in "Song of Myself." Because of space limitations, it will not be possible here to portray either his storied life, including his extensive oeuvre of published work (see Loving, 2000; Miller, 2010), or his multifarious influence on poets and thinkers from around the world (Allen & Folsom, 1995).[2]

We draw upon Whitman's original edition of 1855 (Whitman, 1986 [published by Penguin]) rather than the numerous revised editions of the poem he later produced – the latter a compositional process that seems to mirror his philosophy of democracy itself, namely, that nothing remains still, and people need to keep themselves open to new experience and learning. We refer to the "poet" more than to "Whitman" because we understand the poem to be far more than autobiographical, though it encompasses numerous motifs from his life experience. We see the poem as "outrunning" the poet, in a manner of speaking. That is, the poet points to a democratic and cosmopolitan sensibility that for him as much as for the reader is never a permanent accomplishment. We are concerned with what Whitman has bequeathed us, which is something far larger and other than "just himself" – a claim in keeping with his conception of the self as a porous being in ongoing, reciprocally influential contact with the world around them. In brief, our reading of the poem will be philosophical in the natal sense of that term. We ask: What is the wisdom in this extraordinary poem for the conduct of cosmopolitan and democratic life?

We will use square brackets to mark the particular stanza to which we refer in the Penguin edition. In the direct quotes that follow, the reader will note the repeated ellipses of four dots inserted by the poet. They appear to have multiple functions. They slow the reader down, giving the reader time to pause and to think with the poet or, better, to imagine with him. The reverse holds as well: the poet, too, benefits from pauses and moments of contemplation, especially important given the momentous tasks he has accepted to imagine what is, what could be, and what has been but lies forgotten or buried. Perhaps, too, in light of those tasks, the ellipses are the poet's way of signaling "I can't say what I can't say." Sometimes language fails the poet, as it does every person, and no words or formulations work for what he imagines in his mind's and heart's eye. The poet is not divine, though many ancient peoples would say poets are divinely inspired. The poet does not enjoy limitless imagination. But the poet can at least mark the moments where what cannot be said resides invisibly within the interstices of the said, thereby helping to hold things together.

[2] Consider the testimony about Whitman by the award-winning poet and essayist, June Jordan:

> "This great American poet of democracy as cosmos, this poet of a continent as consciousness, this poet of the many people as one people, this poet of diction comprehensible to all, of a vision insisting on each, of a rhythm/ a rhetorical momentum, to transport the reader from the Brooklyn ferry into the hills of Alabama and back again, of line after line of bodily, concrete detail that constitutes the mysterious, the cellular tissue of a nation indivisible but dependent upon and astonishing in its diversity. . . . I too am a descendant of Walt Whitman. And I am not by myself struggling to tell the truth about this history of so much land and so much blood, of so much that should be sacred and so much that has been desecrated" (2002, pp. 244, 247).

24.3.1 The Poet's Address

I celebrate myself,
And what I assume you shall assume,
For every atom belonging to me as good belongs to you. [1]

So the poem begins. It is an address to himself ("I," "myself") and to the reader or listener ("you"). In due course, the poet confounds these pronouns such that it becomes difficult to sort out the addressor and the addressee. It sometimes appears, in a manner that recalls Michael Hamburger's remark, that the poet has become a vehicle or conduit for something speaking through him. At other times, the poet asserts his singular identity directly and boldly, for example in stanza 24 where he appears to leap out of the poem, for a moment, by stating "Walt Whitman, an American . . ." At the close of the poem, the reader circles back and realizes that the very first word of the poem, "I", mirrors the very last word of the poem, "You" [52]. In naming I, myself, and you at the start, the poet in that very instant collapses them into one. He says: the poet's self, and the self of every other person, is fundamentally permeable and porous. He says: the self is not self-contained – "every atom belonging to me as good belongs to you." The poet echoes the laws of physics that demonstrate how permanently connected everything is down to the atomic level. But in his vision, atoms transform from particles to be measured and analyzed into entities that are shared; they become "democratic entities." The poet transfigures the biological reality that humans are of the very same species.

The poet also points, in a cosmopolitan spirit, to what he regards as the moral unity of humanity. He does so by referring to a celebration: "I celebrate myself." We soon learn he is celebrating *us*. "To celebrate" variously means to acknowledge, to recognize, to name, to esteem. It has an air of seriousness but also of joy – all can sing the song. It evokes a ritualized undertaking (Christians "celebrate" Mass). The poet celebrates the particularity of each human being and the universality of what it is to be human. Every person "bears the whole form of the human condition," wrote the sixteenth-century, cosmopolitan-minded Michel de Montaigne (1991, p. 908), whose writings constitute the forerunner of the essay form and which Whitman evidently knew (at least through his close reading of Ralph Waldo Emerson). The poet portrays Montaigne's claim by composing one image after another of humans at work, at play, in love, in friendship, in loneliness, in joy, in sorrow, in closeness, in separation, with each image highly singular and unique, yet also "speaking" of all and to all.

The poem apparently begins as a venture into the interiority of the poet and of the world that has given rise to him. However, as the venture proceeds, borders between interior and exterior, between persons, between humans and nature, between poet and poem, all begin to dissolve. The upshot is that the poet realizes he is "not contained between my hat and boots" [7] and, moreover, he cannot be summarized or captured through any definition or explanation that exists or ever will exist:

I know I have the best of time and space – and that I was never
measured, and never will be measured.
I tramp a perpetual journey. [46]

Everyone takes that "journey," the poet implies: every person leads a life. So does humanity writ large since the very dawn of the human race.

But that journey is perpetually messy and uncertain, and human beings are both vulnerable and fallible, though not in the same ways or to the same degree. People are inconstant; they will never remain entirely fixed in nature, however microscopic each alteration may be as they encounter the world 24/7. This fact implies, in turn, that if we look carefully enough at ourselves and at others, we will time and again discover that we humans are inconsistent and contradictory, a condition the poet fully embraces as he has no interest in mechanistic perfection (more properly described as a nightmare). Humans simply do gyrate unpredictability between happiness and sadness, irritability and calm, gentleness and roughness, trust and suspicion, and all the rest. They may say or believe something now, only to change their minds tomorrow, and perhaps change them back the day after. As the poet observes:

Do I contradict myself?
Very well then . . . . I contradict myself;
I am large . . . . I contain multitudes. [51]

These famous lines point again to how "myself" encompasses a shared or common self, an "ourself" that reflects the mark upon all persons of the human condition, even as every person influences that condition however infinitesimally. Every person contains, participates in, and contributes to the "multitudes" of the world. That world would not exist without their presence (the cosmos collapsing if a single butterfly were to escape it).

It is true that, as the poet shows, a one-of-a-kind, irreplaceable light goes out with every death, and that a one-of-a-kind, irreplaceable light turns on with each newcomer. Yet the poet evokes a deeper continuity, framing an extraordinary, primordial image of where he and every human being began:

Rise after rise bow the phantoms behind me,
Afar down I see the huge first Nothing, the vapor from the nostrils
of death,
I know I was even there . . . . I waited unseen and always,
And slept while God carried me through the lethargic mist,
And took my time . . . . and took no hurt from the foetid carbon.
Long I was hugged close . . . . long long.
Immense have been the preparations for me,
Faithful and friendly the arms that have helped me.
Cycles ferried my cradle, rowing and rowing like cheerful boatmen;
For room to me stars kept aside in their own rings,
They sent influences to look after what was to hold me.
Before I was born out of my mother generations guided me . . .
All forces have been steadily employed to complete and delight me,
Now I stand on this spot with my soul. [44]

For the poet, soul stands for the source of what animates the mind, the heart, the body. He reaches beyond (or behind) physics, biology, and culture to an image of moral verticality. That is, our being mirrors not just our chronological, horizontal socialization and enculturation, as well as our biochemical hardwiring. Rather we, all of us, have been "guided" by generations across time. The aesthetic, moral, intellectual, and spiritual preparations for each of our respective appearances on this earth have been "immense." It is not so much that we owe a debt to nature and to our ancestors, the poet avers, as that we *are* nature and our ancestors *as well as* what we each are, singularly speaking. We are, indeed, multitudes. The verticality, the sheer unfathomable depth, of past, present, and future buoys persons on "the perpetual journey." They can experience the "delight" to which the poet refers, a term he transforms from something that may sound shallow to a heightened consciousness of being alive fused with a profoundly deep, enduring gratitude for that fact (cf. Oakeshott, 1991, p. 540). For the poet, the sense of gratitude motivates and motors their poetic eros: that is, their calling to speak of what is, of what can be, and of what has been forgotten.

Let us summarize.

- The singularity of each person. The poet says: "Now I stand on this spot with my soul."
- The we-ness of each person. Earlier the poet writes: "We found our own my soul in the calm and cool of the daybreak." [25]

What may strike the reader as a grammatical error – the phrase "our own my soul" – transforms into a single entity. Like the self, the soul is singular. But like the self, the soul is universal, is shared. It is not a private possession any more than is the self. The poet addresses us, and himself, in wonder: What would life be like if we remembered all this, this all?

24.3.2 Democratic Imagination

> I speak the password primeval . . . . I give the sign of democracy;
> By God! I will accept nothing which all cannot have their counter-
> part of on the same terms. [24]

Per our discussion thus far, the poet has provided an indirect gloss on why he deploys the term "primeval." It connotes the primordial, that which has existed since the start of time. Primeval denotes earliest, ancient, and first. It conjures images of the primal, the primitive, the most basic of things. On its part, a password is a secret, sometimes secretly shared between persons. What is "the" (not "a") password to which the poet refers? Why is it needed? Why does the poet have it but, apparently, not us? Or is it lying before us in plain sight, like any number of clues to the human condition if we could learn to see the way the poet sees? To recall again the notion of remembrance, is the poet triggering a memory of truths that lie at our feet if we would but turn our gaze from fantasy and wishing – where we look *away* from life with all its precarity, confusions, and promise – *toward* lived experience on the ground?

Time and again, the poet contrasts nature and everyday experience with theory, theology, science, and philosophy. He distinguishes attempts to explain from a quest to be at home in the world. Put another way, he does not need to explain home to be in it. Like Socrates, it appears the poet, in his youth, had sought out final answers: "Backward I see in my own days where I sweated through fog with/ linguists and contenders" [4]. Unlike Socrates, he does not aim to burrow deeper into what we can know and justify philosophically or scientifically, valuable as that is in its proper place. Nor does he seek to supplant or dismiss the effort of a Socrates:

> I have no mockings or arguments . . . . I witness and wait. [4]
> You are also asking me questions, and I hear you;
> I answer that I cannot answer . . . . you must find out for yourself. [46]

The poet aspires to come nearer to the truths of felt and lived experience, just as it is, which he perceives link rather than separate people and the events of the world. For the poet, this linkage is a core image of democracy itself.

In short, the poet is not anti-intellectual, only anti-alienation, anti-isolation, anti-objectification. He offers a poem rather than a diatribe or exhortation:

> Logic and sermons never convince,
> The damp of the night drives deeper into my soul. [30]
> Oxen that rattle the yoke or halt in the shade, what is that you express in your eyes?
> It seems to me more than all the print I have read in my life. [13]
> To walk up my stoop is unaccountable . . . . I pause to consider if it really be,
> That I eat and drink is spectacle enough for the great authors and schools,
> A morning-glory at my window satisfies me more than the metaphysics of books. [24]

The poet is no skeptic or doubter of reality in all its multiplicity and diversity:

> Writing and talk do not prove me,
> I carry the plenum of proof and every thing else in my face,
> With the hush of my lips I confound the topmost skeptic. [25]

All the theories and categorizations in the world can never "prove" – that is, explain – a human being. And no amount of skeptical doubt, suspicion, or cynicism can deny the truth of our human presence to one another and to ourselves. That truth helps constitute the password toward a genuinely democratic life.

Rather than seeking elusive, terminal explanations of what is, which would abstract him from reality, the poet responds with a wonder that deepens the longer he looks, contemplates, and composes:

> Apart from the pulling and hauling stands what I am . . .
> Both in and out of the game, and watching and wondering at it. [4]
> And I know I am solid and sound,
> To me the converging objects of the universe perpetually flow,
> All are written to me, and I must get what the writing means. [20]

We might conclude that the whole poem embodies "the password primeval." That is, the poet does more than deliver it. He "*speaks*" the password (italics added), not just "about" it. He enacts the truths incorporated in his ongoing address. "I am less the reminder of property or qualities, and more the/ reminder of life" [23].

These suggestions shed light on the "sign" of democracy which the poet "gives." A sign can be a pointer toward something, a symbol or indicator, a source of direction. It can also be a manifestation or enactment of that same something – in this case, democracy. Recall the original Greek meaning of that term: rule by the people. The poet goes far beyond the question of governance, because – in anticipation of the likes of John Dewey – he perceives that democracy is more than a form of government but constitutes a way of perceiving, an approach toward human affairs, even a way of life (Dewey, 1985, p. 93; Dewey, 1988). For the poet, democracy as a way of being is *everywhere* if persons look with care. He devotes whole stanzas, one after the other [e.g., 31–33], to painstakingly naming natural creatures and forces. They all belong in the house of the poem, and in the house of democracy. They all have an absolute right of being – thus, the mode of primordial-sounding naming and describing in which the poet engages, as if we humans have simply forgotten the equal right to existence of all beings and entities and, educationally, have forgotten all that they can teach us and inspire in us (the cow's deep eyes, the morning-glory's glory). Nothing in nature is unnatural. Nature rejects nothing, though everything may be continuously evolving. Nature has been democratic from the start.

There are many more stanzas, again like a rolling train across the land, where the poet lists in fine-grained detail Americans of all stripes and persuasions doing what they do in their quotidian lives. They include blacksmiths, tanners, teachers, children, farmers, escaped slaves and freedmen, indigenous people, married people, single people, gay people, tall and short people, happy people, angry people, coachmen, soldiers, pedestrians, swimmers, and much more [e.g., 7–13, 15–16]. The poet wheels all of them, too, into the house of the poem, and the house of democracy. The forms of mutual- and self-isolation that are so damaging to democracy – which the poet has also witnessed – cannot gain a foothold in the poem's tightly knit pattern of connections and connections on top of connections. "Every condition promulges not only itself . . . . it promulges what/ grows after and out of itself" [45]. The poet shows that none of the connections he repeatedly draws out are forced or arbitrary. As a witness, he records them, or, better, transcribes them into the composed poem. To return to an earlier motif, in an important sense he does not write the poem. He is the parchment upon which the world writes, the world he has let in, for which he gives himself over as a receptable, conduit, vehicle. "Through me the many long dumb voices" [24], he writes, referring to all those fellow Americans kept in silence ("dumb") because they were not given a platform to speak. "Through me the forbidden voices" [24], he adds, spotlighting in barely disguised terms gays and lesbians, and by extension others who reject dehumanizing convention yet in ways unharmful to others or to the polity itself, with the latter understood, again, as more than governmental institutions alone but as encompassing the constitution of actual human relations.

As the poet notes, he has no "mockings or arguments." He witnesses and waits. He does not set himself up as a judge of anything or anyone. He does not approve or disapprove of anything or anyone. The poet's radical, democratic inclusivity comes to the fore when he describes his endeavor as

> . . . the meat and drink for
>   natural hunger,
> It is for the wicked just the same as the righteous . . . . I make
>   appointments with all,
> I will not have a single person slighted or left away,
> The keptwoman and sponger and thief are hereby invited . . . . the
>   heavy-lipped slave is invited . . . . the venerealee is invited,
> There shall be no difference between them and the rest. [19]
>
> What blurt is it about virtue and about vice?
> Evil propels me, and reform of evil propels me . . . . I stand
>   indifferent,
> My gait is no faultfinder's or rejecter's gait,
> I moisten the roots of all that has grown. [22]

For the poet, all persons have a "natural hunger" for meaning and purpose, however smothered or distorted this impulse may be. The poet's office, in part, is to honor and respond to that hunger. But the poet's inclusive solidarity, combined with the unabashed sensuality of many of his images, rendered "Song of Myself" highly controversial in its time. Whitman was widely condemned and was fired from a government position when his superiors got hold of the poem. He may well have anticipated this outcome. For example, his deep sympathies for gay and bisexual people, who were forced to keep their identities hidden at the time (and still are in parts of the world today), are evident both in and between the lines.

Thus, the poet speaks directly to the shocked, worried, or confused reader:

> Do you guess I have some intricate purpose?
> Well I have . . . . for the April rain has, and the mica on the side of
>   a rock has.
> Do you take it I would astonish?
> Does the daylight astonish? or the early redstart twittering through
>   the woods?
> Do I astonish more than they? (19)

The poet's democratic sensibility fuses with his cosmopolitan temperament. He evokes a well-known aphorism from the Roman poet and playwright, Terence (second century CE): "*Homo sum humani nil a me alienum puto*; I am a human being; therefore nothing that is human is foreign to me." The poet makes plain that nothing human, or in nature, is alien to him. And nothing should be foreign to *us*, the poet implies. We should ban the term foreigner from our lexicon. As already mentioned, this orientation means accepting the manifold diversity of humanity as part of reality, as part of every person. It does not imply approval or disapproval, but it does help ground fair-minded judgment.

On his part, the poet is careful not to condemn anything outright. But he does not say to the reader: do not judge. Citizens in a democracy must judge between the better and the worse; and they must determine what is better and worse. Nobody else can or should do this for them. The poet reminds them: judge not lest ye be judged. That is, judge always mindful of the full reality of other persons and communities, that they resemble you at least as much as they differ from you. Judge through refined perception, and through awareness of how all touches all, democratically, and that from your judgments waves of ramification will flow to all sides, and then back to you.

While the poet's role is not to judge, there is one thing he will not tolerate. "By God!," as we heard him say, "I will accept nothing which all cannot have their counter-part of on the same terms" [24]. In one sense, this declaration implies he rejects everything, for the radical egalitarianism he evokes does not exist. As he knows, the nation is marked by egregious inequalities and inequities. But as discussed, for the poet a radical equality is the very form of the world, including humanity. Everything and everyone always already have an absolute existence and a right to that existence. The world needs everything and everyone in order to be whole. Humanity alone, the poet makes clear, is the only species to rupture continuities and connections through a will to power not shared by anything else known. It is a will that isolates one entity from another, that separates causes from effects despite the fact that any given cause is only the effect of another cause, and vice versa, such that the very terms cause and effect are exclusively of heuristic value (a real value for some practical purposes) but do not name anything isolatable or discrete in nature. The same holds for all entities. All things touch all things in one way or another.

A change in perception and orientation will not in itself reduce injustice in the nation. But there can be no diminishment of injustice without a sensitive perceptivity and a democratic commitment. In this respect, purposeful perception is not willful but will-less in the sense of being marked by receptivity rather than by a desire to control. At one of many dramatic moments in the poet's "perpetual journey," he imagines:

> I am the hounded slave . . . . I wince at the bite of the dogs,
> Hell and despair are upon me . . . . crack and again crack the
> marksmen,
> I clutch the rails of the fence . . . . my gore dribs thinned with the
> ooze of my skin,
> I fall on the weeds and stones,
> The riders spur their unwilling horses and haul close,
> They taunt my dizzy ears . . . . they beat me violently over the head
> with their whip-stocks. . .

He continues:

> Agonies are one of my changes of garments;
> I do not ask the wounded person how he feels . . . . I myself
> become the wounded person,
> My hurt turns livid upon me as I lean on a cane and observe. [33]

Like any number of democratic-minded people, the poet is profoundly "agonized" by others' suffering. He needs a "cane," metaphorically speaking, to keep him upright as a witness.[3] But his sensibility opposes the supposed moral priority of empathy. He does not pretend to stand in the desperate slave's place or in the place of the painfully wounded person. Such a move is impossible literally and spiritually. The poet is endeavoring *to see* the reality of those who surround him in the fullness of their pain, their joy, their very *existence*. This seeing is prior to all empathy and sympathy, and can discipline them from becoming patronizing or sentimental. It is a direct, clear seeing not easy to achieve or sustain. It will be unsettling as often as comforting or reassuring. But once enacted for the first time, it becomes ever possible, to the point where it can inform an entire way of life. It involves learning to see, if not to cognize in formal terms, the diversity in unity, and the unity in diversity, that marks the web of life, including human life. The poet's incessant describing and redescribing as he regards his fellow Americans, now from this angle, now from that, fuels the image that one of the most doable, and crucial, acts of a citizen is to pay attention to others *in the moment*, to be mindful of how varied, distinctive, maddening, amazing, astounding, repellent, attractive, comforting, frustrating, inspiring, and more, our fellow citizens are. This seeing in the moment resides at the core of a democratic imagination.

24.3.3 Cosmopolitan Imagination

> Whoever degrades another degrades me . . . . and whatever is done or
> said returns at last to me,
> And whatever I do or say I also return. [24]

As we have seen, the theme of reciprocity saturates "Song of Myself" (of Ourself). The poet bears witness to the play of the particular and the universal, of the individual human being and the world. These connections illuminate how the poet's vision is not only democratic through and through – in the poet's vivid sense of democracy – but also cosmopolitan. The poet's cosmopolitanism, built upon his monist view of the cosmos, is not homogenizing. On the contrary, it renders distinctions and particularities in a much more powerful and dynamic manner than can be done from a presumption of the "many" vs. the "one." For the poet, the presumption that the world is composed of discrete, untouching entities, including human beings and cultures, betrays a failure of perception brought about by a will to power. "*This* is us, *that* is you, full stop": this all-too-familiar claim is the inevitable consequence of seeing things atomistically rather than reciprocally or relationally. For the poet, the one is many, the many is one. But the atomistic view preessentializes self and other, and thus hamstrings perception from the very start.

In contrast with this damaging prejudice, the poet's cosmopolitan view shows us that humans can come closer and closer apart all the time (cf. Hansen, 2011,

[3] The poet's shaken condition, as he faces the reality of violence and injustice, calls to mind the emotional and spiritual costs of bearing witness. For example, W. G. Sebald's extraordinary witness in *The Rings of Saturn*, his epic book on various travails of history, opens with the narrator in a hospital, having suffered a moral, psychological, and spiritual collapse from all the suffering and turmoil that he has witnessed. The narrator lacked a cane.

pp. 3–5, passim). If persons make the effort, fueled through their education (rather than just their socialization), to engage different people, different ideas, different values, and different practices, they come closer to them in a spatial-temporal-moral sense. But they are in fact coming closer and closer *apart* from them because it is the very experience of closeness that draws out their differences. That which is truly distinctive and unique about other persons, ideas, practices, values, and so forth, can finally come into clearer view. It is then that people experience something unforgettable: namely, what it is like to appreciate critically and sympathetically that which is different. This experience is one of broadening, deepening, and enriching their humanity. That is, the experience is much more than adding new information about the world, valuable as that can be. It has to do with the kinds of persons people are transforming into through this every experience: persons who see the diversity in the world as a source of wonder, beauty, and concern, rather than as a source of fear, indifference, or violence.

This cosmopolitan orientation, in turn, makes possible the other side of the equation. As persons move closer and closer apart, they can move further and further *together*. Through their ongoing education and experience, people can perceive the always immanent connectedness and continuity, for good and for ill, that marks the human condition, where ruptures themselves, in time, come to be understood as continuities. People can learn to communicate about all the things that matter, which creates grounds for them to collaborate and cooperate. People can move further and further together even as they recognize and acknowledge their differences through moving closer and closer apart. The poet's cosmopolitanism generates an image of a universal culture, marked not by the homogeneity relentlessly manufactured by global capitalism, nor by the suzerainty of any subculture, but by an ever-transforming, ever-refining, ever-unfathomable diversity. These "new forms of cultural diversity" in the world, writes Wolfgang Welsch (1999), "are *more* complex because they are *less separate* than ever before" (p. 203).

24.4 Conclusion: The Necessity of the Poet for Democratic and Cosmopolitan Education

> Unscrew the locks from the doors!
> Unscrew the doors themselves from their jambs! [24]

"Song of Myself" is not a treatise, manual, speech, argument, travelogue, blueprint, diary, sermon, essay, or report. It does what none of these forms can do or need do. Put another way, theory, philosophy, theology, science, and the broad realm of practical matters each has its distinctive claim to being necessary in and for the sake of democratic life. The poet's particular office has to do with imagination. Oakeshott (1991) writes: "[T]he word 'democracy' for some people represents a quasi-scientific image, for many it signifies a practical image (the symbol of a condition desired and to be approved), for de Tocqueville it stood for an historical image, but for Walt Whitman it was a poetic image" (518).

As we have seen, the poet attends in a whole-souled manner to the present moment. That orientation constitutes a marked contrast with the usual human habit of being preoccupied either with the future or the past, thereby rendering routine much of everyday life. The poet illuminates what is, but is unseen. Their images reveal that the present moment can be not fleeting but full. The poet also responds to images of the possible, of that which *could be* but is not yet. These images are not the stuff of fantasy or wishful thinking; they do not come from nowhere. They result from the very same attentiveness to the present moment which holds the germ of what the next moment could be like, with "moment" now dissolving fixed quantitative time. Other images the poet presents trigger remembrance of values, ideas, connections, and more that people have let fall into the shadows. The poet becomes a resuscitator, breathing life back into what has been forgotten but is not (or perhaps ever) out of date, such as the deep good in paying care-full attention to the world.

The poet's gesture is also generous. He evokes a poetics of humane life: images of communicating, appreciating, criticizing, sustaining proximity – ways, in short, of coming closer and closer apart and further and further together. The poet does not judge but waits receptively for truth to reach him. The poet knows that *we* must judge, a task that is part of the very definition of being a citizen. We cannot wait; we must act. By putting forward provocative, truthful images, the poet assists us in this ever-challenging task, made all the more complicated and sometimes confounding by the laser-quick mobility of lies, misinformation, violent images, personal attacks, and corruption of all kinds enabled by social media in our time. The poet helps us to freeze time, metaphorically speaking, and thereby give ourselves the essential moments needed for contemplation and reflection. The poet also brings us joy, an experience far more profound than pleasure or happiness.

At the same time, the poet calls upon the imagination of readers and listeners. "Song of Myself" has the sound of a poet never satisfied with the current image in view. There is always a larger one, a more beautiful one, a more compelling one, a fresher one, a truer one, just over the horizon of present imagination. So it is with people's fondest images of democracy and of a cosmopolitan world: they must not be content with these, or so the poet implies. "What is known I strip away .... I launch all men and women/ forward with me into the unknown" [44]. Democracy and cosmopolitanism are not possessions, nor are they fixed in form or trajectory. They are continuously responsive to the moment, however difficult it is to discern this dynamic (the poet waits for their expression to come in the form of an image). To get outside their most beloved pictures of justice and of a humane life – which, unawares, can harden imagination and vision – people can consider expressions of democracy and of cosmopolitan life from other places and times.[4]

[4] We are grateful to Rob Popik and Rebecca Sullivan for their insightful comments both on our manuscript and on Whitman's great poem. Thanks to Rob, too, for his bibliographic assistance. We also appreciate the helpful comments from the editors.

References

Aciman, A. (1994). *Out of Egypt: A memoir*. New York: Picador.

Allen, G. W., & Folsom, E. (1995). *Walt Whitman and the world*. Ames, IA: University of Iowa Press.

Anderson, E. (2011). *The cosmopolitan canopy: Race and civility in everyday life*. New York: W. W. Norton.

Beck, U. (2004). The truth of others: A cosmopolitan approach. *Common Knowledge*, 10(3), 430–49.

Cavallar, G. (2015). *Kant's embedded cosmopolitanism: History, philosophy and education for world citizens*. Berlin: De Gruyter.

Delanty, G. (Ed.) (2019). *Routledge international handbook of cosmopolitan studies*. 2nd ed., London: Routledge.

Dewey, J. (1985). *John Dewey, the middle works 1899–1924: Vol. 9, Democracy and education*. Ed. by J. A. Boydston, Carbondale, IL: Southern Illinois University Press (original work published in 1916).

Dewey, J. (1988). Creative democracy: The task before us. In *John Dewey, the later works, 1925–1953: Vol 14, 1939–1941*. Ed. By J. A. Boydston, Carbondale, IL: Southern Illinois University Press, pp. 224–30 (original work published in 1939).

Diawara, M. (1998). *In search of Africa*. Cambridge, MA: Harvard University Press.

Edmundson, M. (2019). Walt Whitman's guide to a thriving democracy. *The Atlantic*, 323(4), 100–10.

Hamburger, M. (1973). *String of beginnings: Intermittent memoirs 1924–1954*. London: Skoob Books.

Hamburger, M. (2022). *The truth of poetry: Tensions in modern poetry from Baudelaire to the 1960s*. New York: Routledge (original work published in 1982).

Hansen, D. T. (2011). *The teacher and the world: A study of cosmopolitanism as education*. New York: Routledge.

Hansen, D. T. (2021). *Reimaging the call to teach: A witness to teaching and teachers*. New York: Teachers College Press.

Hansen, D. T., & Sullivan, R. (2022). What renders a witness trustworthy? Existential and curricular notes on a mode of educational inquiry. *Studies in Philosophy and Education*, 41(2), 151–72.

Hanson, R. L. (1985). *The democratic imagination in America: Conversations with our past*. Princeton, NJ: Princeton University Press.

Jordan, J. (2002). *Some of us did not die: New and selected essays of June Jordan*. New York: Basic/Civitas.

Kleingeld, P. (2011). *Kant and cosmopolitanism: The philosophical ideal of world citizenship*. Cambridge: Cambridge University Press.

Loving, J. (2000). *Walt Whitman: The song of himself*. Berkeley, CA: University of California Press.

Miller, M. (2010). *Collage of myself: Walt Whitman and the making of Leaves of Grass*. Lincoln, NE: University of Nebraska Press.

Montaigne, M. (1991). On repenting. In *The Essays of Michel de Montaigne*. Trans. and Ed. by M. A. Screech. London: Penguin (original work published in 1595).

Munzel, G. F. (2017). *Kant's conception of pedagogy: Toward education for freedom.* Evanston, IL: Northwestern University Press.

Muthu, S. (2003). *Enlightenment against empire.* Princeton, NJ: Princeton University Press.

Nussbaum, M. C. (2021). *The cosmopolitan tradition: A noble but flawed ideal.* Cambridge, MA: Belknap Press.

Oakeshott, M. (1991). The voice of poetry in the conversation of mankind. In M. Oakeshott, ed., *Rationalism in politics and other essays.* Indianapolis, IN: Liberty Press, pp. 488–541 (original work published in 1959).

Polanyi, M., & Prosch, H. (1975). *Meaning.* Chicago, IL: University of Chicago Press.

Slate, N. (2012). *Colored cosmopolitanism: The shared struggle for freedom in the United States and India.* Cambridge, MA: Harvard University Press.

Tuan, Y-F. (1996). *Cosmos and hearth: A cosmoplite's viewpoint.* Minneapolis, MN: University of Minneapolis Press.

Valdez, I. (2019). *Transnational cosmopolitanism: Kant, Du Bois, and justice as a political craft.* Cambridge: Cambridge University Press.

Wardle, H. (Ed.) (2010). A cosmopolitan anthropology? *Social Anthropology*, 18(4), 381–506 (Special Issue).

Welsch, W. (1999). Transculturality: The puzzling forms of cultures today. In M. Featherstone & S. Lash, eds., *Spaces of culture.* London: Sage, pp. 194–214.

Whitman, W. (1986). *Leaves of grass: The first (1855) edition.* New York: Penguin.

Whitman, W. (2004). *Memoranda during the war.* Oxford: Oxford University Press (original work published in 1875).

25

Disability and Democratic Education

Franziska Felder

25.1 Introduction: The Link Between Inclusion, Education, Democracy, and Disability

With respect to disability in education, few ideals have so transformed the world of educational theory, policy, and practice as that of inclusion (Ainscow, 2020; Thomas, 2013; UNESCO, 2000). In the educational context, the idea of inclusion was intended to replace that of integration. The latter concept was criticized not only for focusing solely on disability or special needs rather than on diversity in general, but also for emphasizing one-sided adaptation to existing social structures rather than on efforts to change them (Jones & Danforth, 2015).

Given the emphasis that inclusion places on human heterogeneity and changing social structures, we should not be surprised that inclusion – rather than integration – is often regarded as a democratic principle par excellence. We might even go so far as to say that every theory of democracy is at some point based on a theory of inclusion (Calder, 2011). Iris Marion Young (2000, p. 5f.), for instance, writes the following in the introduction to her seminal work *Inclusion and Democracy*: "The normative legitimacy of a democratic decision depends on the degree to which those affected by it have been included in the decision-making processes and have had the opportunity to influence the outcomes."[1]

There is clearly a close link between democracy and inclusion, in at least two respects. First, inclusion is instrumentally important for modern, liberal, and democratic societies, inasmuch as modern democracies rely on the inclusion of their citizens in order to function. Second, inclusion is also one of democracy's aims, since democratic participation is used to involve citizens in the formation of collective political will. Democracy and democratic results are achieved through inclusion.

[1] In the course of her book, Young defends a model she calls "deep democracy." This model of deliberative democracy implies a strong notion of inclusion and political equality as well as a deep understanding of the reality of exclusion – different social groups in society should be able to contribute their voices on an equal footing, so the particular situation of different individuals and social groups should be addressed in order to solve collective problems that arise through these differently situated positions.

In both respects, disability can be a challenge. On the one hand, there are people with disabilities who are largely excluded from democratic decision-making processes due to cognitive or mental impairments (Barclay, 2013). One might say that they are excluded because they do not meet the individual requirements for democratic participation. On the other hand (and linked to the first point), disabled people's interests are often not sufficiently taken into account precisely because of their absence in societal discourses and their general marginalization in society. In other words, neither they nor society benefit from a field of learning and activity in which democratic participation can actually be exercised.

Education can play an important role with regard to these (and other) forms of exclusion from democratic decision-making and democratic processes: first, because education enables individuals to take their destiny actively into their own hands and to participate as citizens in society; and second, because education can strengthen civic spirit, and thus empathy for others' life circumstances. The latter achievement is crucial for educational institutions such as elementary schools because future citizens can be empowered through education to think not only for themselves in the context of their own life situations, but also from the perspective of those whose lives are subject to differing and perhaps greater limitations and/or difficulties when it comes to active participation in society.

One author who understood the connection between inclusion (or participation), education, and democracy in a particularly original way was John Dewey, whose classic work *Democracy and Education* remains as timely as ever, even after the 100-year anniversary of its publication in 2016. Although Dewey never directly addresses the topic of disability (Danforth, 2008) and certainly does not focus his theory of democratic education on the problems just mentioned, his work can help us think more deeply about the connection between inclusion, education, and democracy, especially with regard to the issue of disability. I therefore base my reflections in the following at least partly on Dewey's theory of education and democracy.

In Section 25.2, I outline the key points of Dewey's theoretical framework before turning, in Section 25.3, to the issue of disability and the specific risks it entails for democratic life in general and democratic participation in particular. In Section 25.4, I explore the question of whether Dewey's pragmatist understanding can be used to make progress (at least in thinking about the risks of exclusion) for disabled people's education. In that section, I particularly show that the issue of disability highlights tensions and dilemmas that democratic, inclusive education cannot escape, not even in Dewey's theories. Finally, my conclusion draws together the key points discussed, and explores some of the future challenges for democratic, inclusive education.

25.2 Dewey's Understanding of Democracy and Education

In the mid-1920s, Dewey witnessed the ascendancy of capitalism, which he believed threatened democracy due to an enormous accumulation of wealth alongside the exacerbation of poverty. Based on his observations and concerns, Dewey envisioned a society in which people would be included in a different way, not least through education, and would learn the individual and social skills necessary for social coexistence. In *Democracy and Education* (MW 9, p. 105),[2] he writes about this vision of a democratic, inclusive society and the education it requires: "A society which makes provision for participation in its good of all its members on equal terms and which secures flexible readjustment of its institutions through interaction of the different forms of associated life is in so far democratic. Such a society must have a type of education which gives individuals a personal interest in social relationships and control, and the habits of mind which secure social changes without introducing disorder."

Dewey, in his work, conceives of democracy as a zone of cooperative, practical, and transformative action. His conception of democracy is characterized by the ideal of social cooperation, which is not limited – as for instance in political liberalism – to the political sphere in the narrow sense. Rather, cooperative forms of interaction pertain to society as a whole. Specifically, Dewey sets out a vision of a reflexive-experimental democracy. In his view, democratic forms of association enable the growth of experience. The growth of individual human beings can be understood (at least in part) as a process of character formation in which individuals develop abilities to deal with an expanding range of challenging situations. Growth also typically enhances our awareness of the nuances of existence, and sometimes even the aesthetic qualities of our lives. To grow is to learn, and indeed to learn in ways that contribute to human flourishing.

Dewey cites both philosophical and epistemic reasons for this. First, on philosophical grounds, Dewey believes that the goal of human nature is the growth of individual experience. His epistemic reasons, meanwhile, rest on his belief that cooperation and open discourse are superior to all other forms of will formation. According to Dewey, the growth of experience can only be realized socially, through collective action. Both the character and desires of an individual can thus only emerge and develop in coexistence with other people. This assumption is underpinned by Dewey's naturalistic understanding of human development: a human is a thoroughly social being, and the character, needs, and interests of each person develop in the context of a shared social life. The more democratic these forms of shared social life are, the greater the opportunities for individuals to develop (Wilson & Ryg, 2015). And the more democratic the social spheres involved, the greater the opportunity for all individuals to grow as they engage with the experiences of their fellow human beings.

This focus on growth has a great influence on Dewey's understanding of democracy. First, as already mentioned, Dewey defines democracy more holistically than most (Abowitz, 2017). According to him, it is "more than a form of government; [rather, it is] a mode of associated living, of conjoint communicated experience" (MW 9, p. 93). Second, and connected to the first point: Dewey presents democracy as a social ideal, not one that is (narrowly) political in

[2] Throughout this chapter, MW and LW refer to Dewey's Middle Works (Dewey, 2008a) and Later Works (Dewey, 2008b), respectively.

nature. This latter point has implications for his understanding of democratic education. Namely, instead of viewing education as a purely interindividual process in which a teacher teaches a student, Dewey sees education as a social process with wider implications. He writes (MW, p. 15): "We never educate directly, but indirectly by means of the environment" (MW 9, p. 23). He also notes that the term "environment" means "something more than surroundings which encompass an individual" (MW 9, p. 15).

This distinction is crucial because it illustrates Dewey's fundamentally interactive understanding of education and learning. He argues that the "environment consists of the sum of conditions which are concerned in the execution of the activity characteristic of a living being" (MW 9, p. 26). An important part of educative environments consists of the individuals with whom a person interacts through communication and participation. Dewey observes that the social environment "consists of all the activities of fellow beings that are bound up in the carrying on of the activities of any one of its members. It is truly educative in its effect in the degree in which an individual shares or participates in some conjoint activity" (MW 9, p. 26). This is Dewey's understanding of all educative processes in society, starting with more informal ways of learning through direct participation in the activities of social groups, communities, and institutions in the contexts of daily living.[3] Dewey insists that more formal ways of learning – for instance in schools – should always be continuous with the broader informal contexts. Formal school education and informal learning are connected in complex ways. The institution of formal school education, on the one hand, is a function of social developments and conditions that affect all social life. Social conditions, on the other hand, are dynamic, as the needs and interests of persons, groups, and institutions constantly take new forms, in conjunction with the emergence of new groups, forms of life, institutions, and kinds of identity. As a result, for a democracy to be inclusive and participatory, it must constantly recreate itself and empower individuals to take part in the reconstruction of social meanings and values (Obelleiro, 2017).

The democratic nature of our daily lives, in Dewey's understanding, is tied to objective conditions in our environment as well as subjective dispositions, which means that it aligns with both internal and external elements. Our subjective dispositions are the result of our interaction with the physical and social environment. This understanding leads Dewey to the program of an education for democracy, in which these dispositions, which are important for democratic coexistence, can be enacted and practiced. In school, students learn and develop subjective dispositions, and they also learn to express and reflect on their needs and interests. On the social level, the inclusion and participation of all members of society – the goal of inclusive, democratic schooling – is practiced, expressed, and lived out. The school is a site, among others, where interests are formed, and are not merely articulated, as in Rawls (Wilson & Ryg, 2015). School is thus the key setting where people are able to learn and practice the habits of problem-solving,

[3] In *The Public and Its Problems*, Dewey later observes, "Democracy must begin at home, and its home is the neighborly community" (LW 2, p. 368).

while also gaining a sense of the benefits of collaboration and participation. According to Dewey (MW1, p. 19), the goal of education is consequently "to make each one of our schools an embryonic community life, active with types of occupations that reflect the life of the larger society, and permeated throughout with the spirit of art, history, and science."

In *Democracy and Education*, Dewey provides two criteria by which any kind of social cooperation can be evaluated, including that found in democratic, inclusive schools.[4] The first criterion is the question: "How numerous and varied are the interests which are consciously shared?" (MW 9, p. 89). This criterion "signifies not only more numerous and more varied points of shared common interest, but greater reliance upon the recognition of mutual interests" (MW 9, p. 92). Dewey's second criterion is the question: "How full and free is the interplay with other forms of association?" (MW 9, p. 89). This criterion yields his second standard of democratic life, which means "not only freer interaction between social groups [. . .] but change in social habit [or cultural custom] – its continuous readjustment through meeting the new situations produced by varied intercourse" (MW 9, p. 92). The more numerous and varied the forms of association that human beings enter into, the more fully they are able to realize their potential. Among many other aspects, Dewey's understanding of "the social" as inclusive philosophic concept serves to broaden our understanding of his pluralistic criteria for a healthy democratic society.

Nevertheless, for Dewey the individual is not completely absorbed in the social. Rather, the two are intimately connected. Thus, individual and collaborative learning are constitutively related, as Richard Pring remarks:

> To live and to grow within community requires a great deal of reciprocity, readiness to seek opinions, openness to criticism, access to relevant information. Schools and school systems, therefore, need to be so organized as to encourage their members to engage in discussion and to learn from differences in order to create a richer learning community. That is the essence of democratic living, and such democratic openness is essential for growth of knowledge within both the individual and the surrounding community. The interconnection between community and individual is essential for the growth of both. That is why Dewey favors the common, inclusive school, organized democratically, which reflects the population and the activities of the community in which it is situated. (2017a, p. 347)

For the same reason, individuals are never simply observers in Dewey's view; they are always participants and agents (Garrison et al., 2017).

Likewise, heterogeneity or difference among people and social groups, on the one hand, and democracy on the other, are not conceived of as mutually exclusive in Dewey's theory, but as constitutively related to one other. It furthermore follows that Dewey's idea of democracy is not (and must not be!) limited to

[4] Dewey used the terms "social life" and "community" interchangeably. He used both in a descriptive and a normative sense. He derives normative conditions for social groups from what he considers characteristic of them, namely that they share interests and that exchange and cooperation exist within and between social groups.

the formation of political will, but should encompass the whole of life in all its spaces of experience. As already mentioned, Dewey understands democracy as a form of experience, a way of life. For him, democracy and difference are two sides of an ethical-social understanding of democracy that is centered on the idea of individual growth as well as collective experience. Consequently, "growth is in principle open not only to the lucky few; it is not restricted to members of the intellectual elite. Rather, growth is a fundamental feature of life" (Rogach Alexander & Kitcher, 2021, p. 62). For Dewey, therefore, the plurality of human ways of life is not simply a necessary evil of modern, liberal societies, but, on the contrary, represents the very lifeblood of democracy.

Nevertheless, it should not be forgotten that there are ways of life and forms of heterogeneity within society that are associated with great challenges for inclusion, democracy, and education. People with disabilities, along with those from a migrant background and those who are socioeconomically disadvantaged, poor, or ill, often suffer from severe social prejudice, marginalization, and exclusion. In Section 25.3, I discuss the specific disadvantages and risks that people with disabilities face, before considering in Section 25.4 the extent to which Dewey's understanding of education and democracy might succeed in countering these risks of disadvantage, marginalization, and exclusion.

25.3 Risks of Disadvantage, Marginalization, and Exclusion for Disabled People

Inclusion and participation are not only important aspects and aims of democracy, but also great problems that democracy faces (Castel, 2002).[5] Since its very beginnings, democracy has grappled with the inclusion and participation of groups and individuals (Held, 1987). People have been excluded time and again, for example, because they are not considered "fit" for democracy. This is either because they are not deemed to possess the capacities considered crucial for participation in the political process (e.g., rationality or reason), or because, it is claimed, they do not subscribe to the core values of democracy (e.g., civil rights and liberties). Furthermore, theories of epistemic justice have repeatedly highlighted an additional source of disadvantage, marginalization, and exclusion in democracies, namely, instances in which people's experiences and perspectives are not taken seriously, are considered subordinate, or are silenced altogether. Epistemic injustice arises, according to Miranda Fricker (2007), when people are wronged in their capacity as knowers, and, as a consequence, are ignored as contributors to a society with their knowledge, perspectives, and experiences.[6]

[5] In modern societies, individuals are included in various social subsystems: in the economic system, for example, through their profession or as the consumers of goods and services; in the legal system, as the bearers of individual rights or as legal persons; in the political system, as voters, representatives or other politically active parties; via the healthcare system, as patients or medical providers; and finally also through the educational system, as students and teachers (Parsons, 1967).

[6] Fricker distinguishes two forms of epistemic injustice. First, there is testimonial injustice: devaluation of the testimony of members of a particular group in virtue of their membership of that group, and thus we display prejudice against members of that group as knowers in giving them, for example, less credibility than others. Second, there is hermeneutical injustice:

Such epistemic forms of disadvantage, marginalization, and exclusion occurring in and through (democratic) regimes do not always mean that people fall out of society, so to speak. Often, we do not even observe externally produced disadvantage, exclusion, or marginalization, for they are internal and mostly indirect. In other words, they are not a direct social intention, but are indirectly expressed through the results of democratic expressions of will, in which, for example, the concerns and interests of disabled people are often overlooked or ignored. They are indirect because the persons affected do not have any effective means of influencing the decision-making processes of other citizens, *even if* they might formally have access to the forums and procedures used for decision-making. The people concerned do not drop out of society, therefore, but are excluded from the reciprocity of societal relationships of recognition (including from a moral-legal perspective). As a consequence of these forms of exclusion, or the refusal or failure to grant recognition, those affected cannot partake of the opportunities and reciprocal social relationships and institutions within their society, even though they remain part of that society.[7]

These more subtle forms of disadvantage, marginalization, and exclusion may occur, as already mentioned, when people are not heard or believed, or when their perspective is not taken seriously, which has major consequences for their individual democratic participation and for the democratic community. Iris Marion Young describes the experiences of epistemological marginalization and exclusion as follows:

> [O]thers ignore or dismiss or patronize their statements and expressions. Though formally included in a forum or process, people may find that their claims are not taken seriously and may believe that they are not treated with equal respect. The dominant mood may find their ideas or modes of expression silly or simple, and not worthy of consideration. They may find that their experiences relevant to the issues under discussion are so different from others' in the public that their views are discounted. (2000, p. 6)

Such processes of internal, epistemological exclusion are far more difficult to apprehend and describe than are explicit disadvantage, marginalization, or exclusion, as produced, for instance, via a lack of resources. In the experience of the persons affected, these processes often take the form of uncertainty about one's own position and status.

People with disabilities are particularly affected by instances of epistemic exclusion, and not just by resource poverty and a lack of social recognition, even though both are undoubtedly reflected in, and reflect upon, epistemic

this occurs when as a result of a social structure rendering social group X powerless, members of this groups lack the cognitive resources to adequately make sense of their social powerlessness. It thus harms people by obscuring aspects of their own experience. They cannot understand part of their own experience specifically because they have been hermeneutically marginalized.

[7] And at this point we can perhaps already note that this, of course, first of all concerns the democratic participation and the democratic community of adult people. However, the foundations for this are laid in childhood and, among other things, at school. Children who attend a special school, for example, are not physically and epistemically part of the majority of children who attend a regular school. This also has an impact on their later position in society.

exclusion. Paradoxically, it is also the case that the decreasing social segregation of disabled people since the late twentieth century (for example, via the mainstreaming of disability in education) has resulted in people with disabilities becoming more isolated and unable to share their epistemic knowledge with others who are affected, as Jackie Leach Scully notes:

> [O]ne consequence of mainstreaming is that it is now less common for disabled people to be part of a physical community of others, or even to know another person, with the same or similar impairments. Again, there are many reasons this is generally better for those individuals and for the wider communities in which they now have the opportunity to play a fuller role. However, it also means it is harder for disabled people to find the kind of network that holds minority knowledge about living with a particular impairment. (2018, p. 114)[8]

Social inclusion and participation, in turn, are both a precondition for and a result of participation in various social subsystems, from family to education to work and leisure. In this context, disability is a mechanism by which – or, depending on your point of view, an expression of the way in which – the obligations and entitlements of citizenship are negotiated (Heffernan, 2020). Education in particular has a dual function here. It is both a source of social esteem (which means that a lack of education represents a major determinant of social inequality and social disesteem in today's societies) *and* an expression of entitlement to citizenship. The social disadvantage faced by people with disabilities in modern societies is shown, among other things, by the fact that they have lower education levels and rates of employment, fewer household resources, and poorer health than people without disabilities (Shandra, 2018).

In terms of democratic living, such forms of exclusion and marginalization have major implications, especially for people with cognitive and mental impairments, precisely *because* of the exceedingly strong focus on cognitive and mental abilities in democracies, where certain cognitive and mental abilities (decisions or opinions) are both the result of deliberative democratic processes and a precondition for them. This creates what Olson (2008) calls a "paradox of enablement", which occurs when and because equally able citizens are both presupposed by deliberation and are its intended product. As Olson (2008) rightly points out, we here encounter an epistemological problem concerning the voices of the marginalized, who will not be heard simply because they are not already equipped to participate on an equal footing. And such problems are starkest when they prevent people from making claims about their own (epistemic) exclusion. Here, marginalization is not simply a violation of parity. It also deprives people of the means for demanding inclusion: first, in the

[8] A particular striking example is the Deaf community. Because it is not only the experience as a deaf person in a world with majority hearing people that is important to acquire epistemic knowledge, to share it with others and to participate in society also in a confident and strong way. Especially for the signing Deaf it is enormously important to be able to be in a community with other signing Deaf. The skills learned and practiced in signing are a prerequisite for social and democratic participation. One could even go as far as to say that separation is a necessary means for inclusion and participation.

sense of individuals' orientation toward the polity in which they live, and second in terms of the scope of that polity's active membership.

Again, disability can be a problem in both respects: first, because – especially in the case of people with severe cognitive impairments or certain mental illnesses – the ability to participate in democratic decision-making may be limited; second, because the needs and interests of disabled people do not become the focus of democratic deliberations, in part because some of them lack the skills required to actively engage in discourse themselves, but also because the issue of disability is usually marginalized in society.

25.4 Another Look from Dewey's Perspective

The question naturally arises as to how education should, in general, handle these epistemic issues so relevant for democracy, and in particular, how possibilities within education might be used for constructively dealing with, or even preventing, the exclusion of people with cognitive and mental disabilities. I do not mean to suggest that this is an easy task, or that there is a perfect solution to this dilemma, which is inherent in democracy and democratic deliberation itself, and which also pertains to people other than those with disabilities (for example, people who do not speak the language(s) of the country in which they live). However, despite these issues, Dewey – as a highly vocal supporter of the possibilities for education to improve not only schools, but also democracies – believed that it is possible to better reveal and nurture individual talents through instructional arrangements without first identifying intellectual superiors and inferiors (Danforth, 2008). This opens a door for Dewey's theory of education and democracy, and foregrounds the question of how he would deal with these problems and dilemmas (especially epistemic exclusion, as well as the "paradox of enablement"). In this context, Dewey's vision of education, which is at least able to deal constructively with disability in the sense of a comprehensive lifeworld disadvantage, is of particular importance, since Dewey's work represents the idea that democracy and democratic skills (in the sense of subjective dispositions) ultimately can and must be learned in a reflexive, experimental setting that is democratic and open by design. In such schools and educational systems, as Richard Pring (2017b, p. 13) remarks, knowledge is always "practical, provisional and open to further reconstruction . . . [It] requires respect for the learners as practically engaged with the world, constantly enlarging their way of seeing the world. The teacher's job is to encourage such active learning, introducing new situations, new experiences, new and more profitable ways of seeing the way ahead through the understandings (referred to as the different forms of knowledge) which we have inherited" (Pring, 2017b, p. 13). Education understood in this way is comparable to an ongoing conversation:

> The metaphor of "conversation" is an important one, because it entails the social context in which the individual learner's experience is enriched – conversation with the traditions of thought we have inherited and

> conversations with one's co-learners as one is introduced to different perspectives and criticisms. And through the group or social context the learner acquires the norms of appropriate behaviour – whether those be the rules of playing a game, the standards of scholarly research, or the precepts of the community's morality. All experience has a social and practical dimension. (Pring, 2017b, p. 15)

Dewey's focus offers five critical features for rethinking democracy and education as well as the related challenge of disability:

First, Dewey emphasizes that learning does not happen exclusively (or even particularly) in school. Rather, we educate through the environment, which does not exist only in school. The assumption that we educate through the environment implies, firstly, that Dewey does not have a narrow concept of learning, and secondly, that he does not have a concept of education that is exclusive to school. This is significant in that school opportunities for learning are actually more restricted for some children (particularly those with cognitive impairments) simply because these children face internal limitations. However, this does not mean that social learning is not possible for them, as they may participate in many fields of communication and exchange that are also relevant for democracy, such as the playground, the leisure club, the sports club, the church, or the library. Moreover, Dewey's theory "sheds light on possible ways to reconstruct the environments that currently prohibit and discourage individuals with disabilities from achieving that needed to participate in democratic citizenship" (Mullins, 2019, p. 4).

Second, and related to the above point, democratic learning in schools is a way of life for Dewey, who does not draw any artificial distinction between academic and social learning. But the idea in many approaches to inclusion and democracy is that the two should be considered as completely separate. Often, then, the social aspect is viewed as "a nice add-on" to the real core of school and teaching, which is academic progress and school learning. And of course, it is the case that we go to school to learn to read, write, and do arithmetic (to name just a few skills we acquire). But if that is all we learned, and on top of that we found ourselves in a cold environment where no one cared about us and where we had no common ground, we certainly would not call that a good school. Moreover, we could assume that the motivational and emotional foundations of successful (academic) learning would be compromised. Academic and social learning are thus intimately linked. And even though we should be careful here not to instrumentalize children with disabilities (in the sense that they might be used, for example, to learn how to be a good, understanding person), it is certainly the case that both children with and without disabilities can benefit from learning together, both academically and socially.

Third, in Dewey's work, individual learning is not contrasted with collaborative learning. They are considered interrelated. In schools, children learn in communities, which means that individual learning is embedded in collective learning. But it is also the case that individual learning – unless subject to manipulation or indoctrination – always has community learning as its content and, where appropriate, as its consequence. In the best-case scenario, learning relevant for democracy is based on empathy for the life situations of others, and does not only serve the acquisition of democratic knowledge or individual character traits. This point also illustrates the importance of inclusive schooling, understood as the joint education of children with and without disabilities. The school represents a learning field in this respect, for both the acquisition and the practice of such skills and social situations.

Fourth, Dewey assumes that democratic education promotes the growth of both individuals and entire communities. It also seems clear that education as an institution has socializing effects not only on children and young people, but also on entire societies, in that educational qualifications classify individuals and their knowledge (and thus make them employable, for example) and open up access to valuable social positions (while of course also influencing these social positions themselves). Furthermore, "education is a central element in the public biography of individuals, greatly affecting their life chances. It is also a central element in the table of organization of society, constructing competencies and helping create professions and professionals" (Meyer, 1977, p. 55). A democratic theory of education of the kind that Dewey defends is focused on what Amy Gutmann (1999, p. 14) calls the function of "conscious social reproduction," that is, "the ways in which citizens are or should be empowered to influence the education that in turn shapes the political values, attitudes, and modes of behavior of future citizens." Because the democratic ideal of education is that of deliberate social reproduction, democratic theory also focuses heavily on practices of deliberate instruction by teachers and on the educational influence of institutions of education formed at least in part for that purpose. Here, precisely in the transition from integration to inclusion, the importance of conscious social reproduction becomes apparent in comparison to quasi-natural social reproduction, in which social values and traditions are not questioned at all, or only to a limited extent. For, in inclusion, at least ideally, the heterogeneity of students is taken as a positive starting point for change, which means that education advances the processes of both accommodation and assimilation.

Fifth, since Dewey's ideal of democratic education is social and not narrowly political, there is no risk of equating democratic education with political socialization, for – according to Gutmann (1999, p. 15) – "it is easy to lose sight of the distinctive virtue of a democratic society, that it authorizes citizens to influence how their society reproduces itself." It is precisely this emphasis on social reproduction, or more precisely on social growth, that makes Dewey's theory so unique. For Dewey, individuals and communities learn in a constant process of growth. Growth thus includes individual experiences as well as cooperative learning. The diversity and plurality of ways of life (disability being one expression or form of diversity) is not simply an evil to be dealt with, but rather a constitutive and integral part and starting point of shared learning. Dewey rightly observes "that the relation between democracy and education is a reciprocal one, a mutual one, and vitally so" (LW 13, p. 294). He further claims, "[s]ince education is the keystone of democracy, education should be truly democratic" (LW 9, p. 393). Thus, in my view, Dewey's idea of democracy based on principles of diversity and participation offers a philosophical foundation for establishing and sustaining inclusive environments in education and social life today. Ultimately, Dewey's approach provides the opportunity to link the man-made concept of democracy with the naturally occurring processes of growth and development.

Here, we furthermore have to consider the question of how realistic Dewey's vision is, and what implications follow from his proposals, especially with regard to the subject of disability, which he never addressed in any concrete way. Yet, I argue that Dewey's work sets out the conceptual possibilities for thinking of education differently, namely in truly inclusive terms. I share the view of Richard Pring (2017a, p. 344), who notes: "The failure to introduce young people to shared experiences within a community, through which they develop practical capability and dispositions to resolve differences and participate in social and political thinking, inevitably leads to a diminution of democratic modes of working." The positive conclusion from this statement also points to the normative significance of inclusive education for democratic education, understood as shared problem-solving within education as a way of life.

Above all, such a view broadens our imagination as to what school education could be, but currently is not. Here, we encounter a paradoxical situation:

> On the one hand, we find relatively solid institutional frameworks like tight educational bureaucracies and hierarchies; the closed and quadrangular classroom; the uniform rhythm of time management and disciplinary structure of contents; the uniform use of materials, textbooks, and methods; standardized measurement and grading; and studying for examinations. These represent the still-extant and often dominating attitude of "one sizes fits all" in local as well as global educational contexts. On the other hand, we encounter a social world characterized by diversity, flexibility, and individual responses to life conditions in liquid society. The solid structures in education often seem to restrict the abilities of learners to respond to more liquid life conditions. (Kricke & Neubert, 2020, p. 55f.)[9]

Perhaps – in order not to be incapable of action in the face of this paradoxical situation – we need to become aware of the little democratic moments lurking around every corner in education: democratic moments can arise where teachers and students are exposed to each other as equals in relation to something (a book, a text, or a mathematical puzzle, for instance). Democracy, then, is not only about who is empowered and how, or who relates to whom and how, but also about what objects are engaged with, and in what ways. This reality in turn requires a general recognition of the role of institutions in creating just conditions for the realization of rights, as well as specific consideration of what such conditions would entail, and how they might be achieved and sustained.

[9] In addition, the desire for bonds in communities must be balanced with the desire for individual freedom. Community ties are always changeable, linked to different life projects and a multitude of changing ties; they are – to use Zygmunt Bauman's (2000) words – liquid and fragile, no longer stable and clearly graspable.

Moreover, this kind of theorization calls for clarity about the nature of injustice in these contexts, what it entails, and how it is enacted and sustained.[10]

All these aspects taken together go beyond the conceptual solution that Dewey provides. This is not least because Dewey is rather hesitant about the vision of a just society and the role that wellbeing plays in education, and avoids committing himself to fixed aims in education. We must also remember that there are relatively narrow limits to the implementation of democratic, inclusive education. First, this is because it is not fundamentally possible to avoid hierarchies and dominance in the school context, and also because the argument that relationships should take place on an equal footing requires at least two important qualifications: Compulsory education inevitably implies a certain relationship of dominance, namely that of the state over its future citizens. Additionally, school relationships between teachers and students are always characterized by a power imbalance between the two groups. The teacher has a deontic position that the students do not have, accompanied by certain rights and duties to which students are not entitled, but which also are not expected of them. Second, a democratic, inclusive school can, of course, enshrine a different approach to diversity and heterogeneity, among other things by teaching moral values and norms of coexistence. It does this by showing both that such heterogeneity exists, and that it is possible to deal successfully with different lifestyles. It thus succeeds in transforming difference into equality. However, schools also create difference through their structures and organizational actions. In forms of selection (like the awarding of grades, or praise and reprimand in the classroom), this formation of difference has an impact even in the microarea of school instruction. These double, dilemmatic aspects cannot be resolved, since the antinomies of equality and difference are deeply embedded in pedagogical action and events. Thus, even Dewey with his approach to thinking differently – and, above all, more democratically and socially – about schooling cannot solve all of the problems posed here. In summary, we can say that even a democratic school that includes disabled children and young people to the highest possible degree will produce exclusion and marginalization. It would be a mistake at this point to overestimate the power and influence of schools on a prosperous, democratic coexistence.

25.5 Conclusion

Publications on citizenship, democracy, and disability tend not to focus on education, but rather on the labor market, the political system, assistance and support, and so on (Halvorsen et al., 2017). The same holds true in reverse. Democracy in relation to education and schooling is often discussed in two ways: First, it is debated in terms of schooling that offers the possibility of preparing young people for democracy, for example by giving them skills or by creating spaces in which they can learn and practice democratic habits. Second, it is discussed in terms of its

[10] Even if it is too far to go into this now, it should be noted that perhaps the most exemplary scholarship on these aspects of the indeterminacy problem has been done by the political philosophers Iris Marion Young (1990, 2000) and Nancy Fraser (2000), and the legal scholar Martha Minow (1985, 1990).

contribution to greater equality among various social or cultural groups within society, and thus toward greater social cohesion in general (Masschelein & Simons, 2010). Disability is not treated with specific interest in this context.

A complex gap is thus created within the debate. The thematic trinity of education-democracy-disability is discussed in very few publications, which means that many questions are left open. Dewey is no exception here. But Dewey's understanding of education and democracy helps us better understand what it actually means to become a political subject: "Becoming a political subject is at the same time a creation of the world and being exposed to each other as such (as a singularity) and as equals. This exposition confronts us with the question of living-together and doing justice to each and all" (Masschelein & Simons, 2005, p. 135). Dewey's theory also provides a corrective to a relatively narrow discourse of inclusion that is often solely concerned with gaining a new perspective on human diversity (apart from disability) and in which inclusion and democratic education are related to schools and classrooms alone. Here, Dewey provides a much broader focus. The task is then the following, according to Kricke and Neubert, who concur with Dewey in this respect:

> To make inclusion in a broader sense successful in education as well as in society as a whole, educational communities, like schools, must take pains to establish as many and complex relations as possible to all relevant social and cultural contexts. An inclusive school must be an open school that entertains a wide, diverse, and continual interplay with the local neighborhood, families, social services, cultural workers, institutions of civil society, representatives of business and vocational life, agents in media, politics, and administration as well as many other partners on a local, regional, and global levels [sic] including international cooperation. In the best sense, the school itself becomes a mediator and multiplier for the intercommunication between these often relatively isolated areas or compartments of social life. (2020, p. 64)

In general, whether or not we follow Dewey in our reflections on this context, it is important to note that

> communities are always part of the larger *dispositifs* in societies including complex power relations. Inclusion cannot be won against society. It is, first of all, a social and political task and function, grounded in human rights. It stands against discrimination and undemocratic practices on all levels of society. Inclusive educators therefore must never conceive of their own community or school as an "island of bliss", on which they perform their own isolated *Robinsonade*" (ibid., p. 64).

Democratic schools and democratic education do not resolve the "paradox of enablement", nor do they remedy the social marginalization to which people with cognitive and mental impairments are specifically exposed. At best, however, they raise awareness of a number of important social issues and problems of justice, and expand our capacity for empathy beyond the environment immediately surrounding us. They may not do more than this, but it is to be hoped that they accomplish no less.

References

Abowitz, K. K. (2017). “A mode of associated living”: The distinctiveness of Deweyan democracy. In L. J. Waks & A. R. English, eds., *John Dewey's Democracy and Education: A centennial handbook*. Cambridge: Cambridge University Press, pp. 64–72.

Ainscow, M. (2020). Promoting inclusion and equity in education: Lessons from international experiences. *Nordic Journal of Studies in Educational Policy*, 6(1), 7–16.

Barclay, L. (2013). Cognitive impairment and the right to vote: A strategic approach. *Journal of Applied Philosophy*, 30(2), 146–59.

Bauman, Z. (2000). *Liquid modernity*. Cambridge: Polity Press.

Calder, G. (2011). Inclusion and participation: Working with the tensions. *Studies in Social Justice*, 5(2), 183–96.

Castel, R. (2002). *From manual workers to wage laborers: Transformation of the social question*. New Brunswick: Transaction.

Danforth, S. (2008). John Dewey's contributions to an educational philosophy of intellectual disability. *Educational Theory*, 58, 45–62.

Dewey, J. (2008a). *The middle works, 1899–1924*. Ed. by J. A. Boydston. Carbondale, IL: Southern Illinois University Press.

Dewey, J. (2008b). *The later works, 1925–1953*. Ed. by J. A. Boydston. Carbondale, IL: Southern Illinois University Press.

Fraser, N. (2000). Rethinking recognition. *New Left Review*, 3, 107–20.

Fricker, M. (2007). *Epistemic justice: Power and the ethics of knowing*. Oxford: Oxford University Press.

Garrison, J., Neubert, S., & Reich, K. (2017). The social as the “inclusive philosophic idea” of democracy and education: Some constructivists' reflections. In L. J. Waks & A. R. English, eds., *John Dewey's Democracy and Education: A centennial handbook*. Cambridge: Cambridge University Press, pp. 290–303.

Gutmann, A. (1999). *Democratic education (with a new preface and epilogue)*. Princeton, NJ: Princeton University Press.

Halvorsen, R., Hvinden, B., Bickenbach, J., Ferri, D., & Guillén Rodriguez, A. M. (2017). The contours of the emerging disability policy in Europe: Revisiting the multi-level and multi-actor framework. In R. Halvorsen, B. Hvinden, J. Bickenbach, D. Ferri, & A. M. Guillén Rodriguez, eds., *The changing disability policy system – Active citizenship and disability in Europe. Vol. 1*. Abingdon: Routledge, pp. 215–34.

Heffernan, A. K. (2020). *Disability: A democratic dilemma*. Chicago, IL: University of Chicago.

Held, D. (1987). *Models of democracy*. Cambridge: Polity Press.

Jones, P., & Danforth, S. (2015). From special education to integration to genuine inclusion. In P. Jones & S. Danforth, eds., *Foundations of inclusive education research*. Bingley: Emerald, pp. 1–21.

Kricke, M., & Neubert, S. (2020). Inclusive education as a democratic challenge – Ambivalences of communities in contexts of power. In M. Kricke & S. Neubert, eds., *New studies in Deweyan education: Democracy and Education revisited*. London: Routledge, pp. 49–69.

Masschelein, J., & Simons, M. (2005). The strategy of the inclusive education apparatus. *Studies in Philosophy and Education*, 24(2), 117–38.

Masschelein, J., & Simons, M. (2010). The hatred of public schooling: The school as the mark of democracy. *Educational Philosophy and Theory*, 42(5–6), 666–82.

Meyer, J. W. (1977). The effects of education as an institution. *American Journal of Sociology*, 83(1), 55–77.

Minow, M. (1985). Learning to live with the dilemma of difference: Bilingual and special education. *Law and Contemporary Problems*, 48(2), 157–211.

Minow, M. (1990). *Making all the difference – Inclusion, exclusion, and American law*. Ithaca, NY: Cornell University Press.

Mullins, R. (2019). Using Dewey's conception of democracy to problematize the notion of disability in public education. *Journal of Culture and Values in Education*, 2(1), 1–17.

Obelleiro, G. (2017). Democracy without telos: Education for a future uncertain: On chapter 5: Preparation, unfolding and formal discipline. In A. R. English & L. J. Waks, eds., *John Dewey's Democracy and Education: A centennial handbook*. Cambridge: Cambridge University Press, pp. 46–53.

Olson, K. (2008). Participatory parity and democratic justice. In K. Olson, ed., *Adding insult to injury – Nancy Fraser debates her critics*. London: Verso, pp. 246–72.

Parsons, T. (1967). *Sociological theory and modern society*. New York: The Free Press.

Pring, R. (2017a). Philosophy of education. In L. J. Waks & A. R. English, eds., *John Dewey's Democracy and Education: A centennial handbook*. Cambridge: Cambridge University Press, pp. 340–48.

Pring, R. (2017b). Educational philosophy of John Dewey and its relevance to current dilemmas in education. *Education in the North*, 24(1), 3–15.

Rogach Alexander, N., & Kitcher, P. (2021). Educating democratic character. *Moral Philosophy and Politics*, 8(1), 51–80.

Scully, J. L. (2018). From "she would say that, wouldn't she?" to "does she take sugar?" Epistemic injustice and disability. *International Journal of Feminist Approaches to Bioethics*, 11(1), 106–24.

Shandra, C. L. (2018). Disability as inequality: Social disparities, health disparities, and participation in daily activities. *Social Forces*, 97(1), 157–92.

Thomas, G. (2013). A review of thinking and research about inclusive education policy, with suggestions for a new kind of inclusive thinking. *British Educational Research Journal*, 39(3), 473–90.

UNESCO. (2000). *Inclusion in education: The participation of disabled learners*. Paris: UNESCO.

Wilson, T., & Ryg, M. (2015). Becoming autonomous: Nonideal theory and educational autonomy. *Educational Theory*, 65(2), 127–50.

Young, I. M. (1990). *Justice and the politics of difference*. Princeton, NJ: Princeton University Press.

Young, I. M. (2000). *Inclusion and democracy*. Oxford: Oxford University Press.

Part Four

Challenges

26

Wealth Stratification in US Higher Education and Democratic Education, 1890s–2020s

Bruce A. Kimball and Sarah M. Iler

26.1 Introduction

Higher education advances democracy by deepening students' understanding of democratic citizenship and strengthening their capacity to participate in a democratic polity, as well as by producing and disseminating knowledge about social and political issues and cultivating public debate (Daniels, 2021). In the United States, higher education has also strengthened democracy by fostering social mobility. In this regard, a college or university degree provides students the opportunity to advance themselves and to become social and political leaders.[1]

Yet, higher education requires abundant resources to produce these democratic benefits, and acquiring that revenue has entangled higher education in ironic and contravening relationships with democracy. Starting in the 1890s, American colleges and universities introduced new, so-called democratic, tactics to increase their revenue and accumulate endowment, that is, financial capital. For most of the twentieth century, these novel tactics were applauded as necessary and justified. At the same time, higher education enjoyed widespread esteem in the United States, while colleges and universities became stratified by endowment size and, concomitantly, by prestige.

Then, in the 1980s and increasingly thereafter, Americans' esteem for higher education began to wane. In particular, the seemingly insatiable need of colleges and universities for more revenue and financial capital, especially those with the largest endowments and most prestige, sparked resentment. By the end of the twentieth century, the financial stratification of higher education had widened into a yawning "wealth gap," and this manifestly inequitable

[1] Further discussion and documentation on points in this chapter can be found in Kimball and Iler (2023).

concentration of wealth in the richest stratum of colleges and universities contributed to the decline in public esteem (Waldeck, 2009, p. 1795).

In addition, student debt mounted nationwide. This growing indebtedness obstructed, and even undermined, the social mobility that higher education had long fostered. In fact, scholars have documented the financial strain and emotional stress that student debt imposed on middle-class families, who were becoming "downwardly mobile" and watching their children's career prospects erode (Pinsker, 2019; Zaloom, 2019; Kuper, 2021).

Furthermore, the discordance between the student debt and the mammoth growth of endowments of the wealthy colleges and universities intensified resentment about the decline in mobility (Waldeck, 2009, p. 1795). Finally, the wealth stratification in US higher education became intertwined with the expanding and clearly undemocratic wealth inequality in the US population. The richest individuals and the richest colleges and universities seemed to mutually reinforce their elite and privileged positions in American society in the early twenty-first century.

This historical chapter explains the ironic and contravening influence on democracy entailed by the pursuit of revenue and endowment in higher education. In particular, the chapter reveals how the stratification of wealth emerged in higher education and then widened into the huge wealth gap among colleges and universities. Not only did this yawning gap seem inequitable within higher education, but the skyrocketing student debt impeded the social mobility through which higher education had long fostered democracy. Finally, the chapter argues, the wealth concentration of higher education and the wealth inequality in the US population are deeply interrelated, and this interrelationship weakens democracy today.

26.2 The Fundraising Triad: 1890–1930

Beginning in the colonial period, American colleges and universities supplemented tuition by raising funds through occasional lotteries and subscription campaigns, usually upon their founding or when facing a crisis. Leaders of these schools also made discreet appeals directly to wealthy patrons, and this approach persisted in higher education fundraising to the present day. Meanwhile, between 1890 and 1930, two new modes of fundraising were introduced and widely adopted. Every college and university in the United States now employs these two modes as regularly as they hold commencement. The first is the annual appeal to alumni for donations. The second is the national, multi-year fundraising campaign administered by paid staff. Ironically, both were labeled "democratic" by the elite institutions that introduced them between 1890 and 1920 (Kimball, 2015).

These two innovations at colleges and universities resonated with two developments in the larger society. On the one hand, between 1890 and 1920, enthusiasm for "democracy" rose dramatically, and this term became one of the keywords in American social and political discourse. During that era, labeling something "democratic" conferred an aura of legitimacy and dignity (Williams, 1985, pp. 15–17). On the other hand, a related phenomenon known as "mass giving" or "people's philanthropy" emerged in the United States (Cutlip, 1965, pp. 110, 203–4). Various associations dedicated to social welfare, such as the Young Men's Christian Association, the Knights of Columbus, and the Red Cross, developed new tactics to appeal to the public for donations. Above all, the national drives to support disaster relief and to sell US Liberty Loan bonds during World War I made mass fundraising commonplace in American life (Zunz, 2012, pp. 44–75).

Both the democratic ethos and people's philanthropy led colleges and universities to adopt the two fundraising innovations. One might expect that the first to do so would be the new, public, land-grant universities founded under the Morrill Act of 1862 that proudly called themselves the "people's institutions" and bastions of democracy (Ross, 1942; Nevins, 1962; Cutlip, 1965, pp. 53, 110). But it was the old, private, elite institutions, particularly Yale and Harvard, that pioneered mass giving in higher education, although their presidents preferred the traditional, discreet appeals to wealthy donors and did not lead the way. Instead, independent groups of alumni initiated two modes of mass fundraising that departed from the customary approach at their alma maters. It was a "democratic" revolution of fundraising within elite colleges and universities.

As at other universities, the longstanding reliance on a small coterie of wealthy donors at Yale and Harvard was sustained by the social norms of privilege: large gifts implied dependence on the donor and deference from the recipient. For this reason, appealing to wealthy donors was often mocked as "begging," a jesting term that expressed the price of dependence and deference paid for the gifts (Allen, 1912, pp. 151–52). As the Secretary of Yale warned, "constant personal begging on the part of a university is apt to be undignified" and to cost the university its "reputation for fearless educational independence" (Stokes, 1914, p. 45).

This entailed privilege meant that an alumnus who could afford to give only a small donation to his alma mater would feel presumptuous and ashamed to do so. The gift would suggest that he was an imposter putting on airs and trying to act like a member the wealthy elite. Conversely, presidents asking or receiving such small gifts would feel embarrassed – as though the college actually depended on penurious alumni. As a result, "no Yale graduate ever thought of giving five or ten dollars or any inconsiderable sum to the college, all appeals for money having been made for contributions of considerable amounts, usually from rich men" (Holt, 1917, p. 529).

It was therefore revolutionary when a few graduates in the Yale Alumni Association proposed in 1890 that "men who could afford to give but little" would be "glad to make a small annual contribution if a proper fund of that kind were properly organized and established" (Holt, 1917, p. 529). This proposal to institute a new, legitimate method for regular giving by small donors immediately faced two problems. First, the approach resembled the new national phenomenon known as "mass giving" or "people's philanthropy." How could Yale, an elite college, elevate and distinguish its innovation above the plebian practice of appealing to the "masses" for donations? Second, the new appeal gave the impression of begging for money. How could the college dignify its innovation and differentiate it from asking for charity?

Amid the growing enthusiasm for "democracy" in America in the late nineteenth century, Yale alumni solved both problems by describing their appeal as "democratic giving" (Holt, 1917, p. 529). Yale Alumni Fund (YAF) leaders distinguished between "the large gifts from wealthy individuals" and the "'democratic' contribution" of "gathering in annually the smaller gifts, though collectively large" (Deming, 1911, p. 635). Mindful of the traditional relationship between privilege and deference, YAF declared as its central rationale "that no graduate need feel excluded from giving to the University because he could not afford to give largely" (Yale Alumni University Fund, 1915, p. 3).

Delighted by the new revenue stream, Yale executives echoed the rhetoric of democracy in their justifications of the new practice. In 1901, the President stated, "A college that is democratic in its aims and principles cannot expect its income to be furnished by larger endowments exclusively . . . It must look to the loyalty of its former members for support" (Hadley, 1902, p. 21). In 1911, the Yale Secretary urged YAF "to double the number of its subscribers during the next quarter century" (Stokes, 1911, p. 430). Annual income "coming regularly" from "the rank and file of the graduates would be a continual guarantee of the reliability and democratic character of the University's constituency" (Stokes, 1912, p. 80).

In the 1890s and 1900s, YAF began conducting annual comprehensive solicitations through a network of agents from the classes of graduates. Other institutions soon followed this lead. By 1925, at least 20 colleges and universities had established similar alumni funds. Over the next decade, a hundred more colleges and universities established annual alumni funds or regular alumni giving programs, including the state universities of Buffalo, California, Illinois, Kansas, Kansas State, Michigan State, Michigan, North Carolina, Ohio State, Pennsylvania State, Rutgers, Vermont, and Virginia (Arnett, 1922, p. 17; Curti & Nash, 1965, p. 202; Johnson, 2013, pp. 337–40).

Meanwhile, alumni at Harvard University inaugurated a second fundraising mode that also proliferated throughout higher education in the 1920s. This innovation was the national, multiyear, public fundraising campaign: the Harvard Endowment Fund (HEF), which ran from 1915 to 1925. HEF also resembled mass giving. The campaign borrowed several tactics from the people's philanthropy, including paid staff, orchestrated publicity, convening and training volunteer leaders, a whirlwind final push, and the incessant cry of poverty that was formerly seen as an embarrassment by elite colleges and universities (Kimball, 2014, 2015).

These borrowed tactics heightened the need to dignify the HEF and distinguish it from the mass campaigns that were perceived as begging for charity. While planning their pathbreaking campaign in 1915 and 1916, HEF leaders read YAF annual reports, and decided to make democracy a prominent theme of the Harvard campaign. The HEF executive committee voted to make their drive "as democratic as it possibly could be and . . . in no sense . . . a 'rich man's' fund"

(Duncan, 1916). In 1917, HEF prominently publicized "the decision to carry a wide-spread, democratic appeal to all its graduates and friends" in major newspapers (*New York Times*, 1917).

YAF leaders felt that HEF had stolen their democratic thunder and, perhaps, undermined their appeals in the financial centers of Boston and New York. Within a few weeks, they responded, asserting their stronger claim to democratic fundraising. In a full-page announcement in the *Yale Alumni Weekly* (1917), YAF boldly proclaimed itself "THE MOST DEMOCRATIC ENDOWMENT OF ANY UNIVERSITY."

Continuing to track the progress of YAF, the HEF leaders then tried to reclaim the democratic mantle. They reaffirmed that HEF would announce "Harvard's needs to every living Harvard man and ... will, therefore, be a widespread democratic appeal" (Saltonstall, 1917, p. 313). The HEF Chairman emphasized in speeches and correspondence that, "Our idea is to democratize this fund, ... every one of the forty thousand ... living men who have been connected with Harvard ... ought to contribute according to his means, be the amount large or small" (Lamont, 1917). Later in 1917, YAF responded with "a greater effort at Yale publicity" (Yale Alumni University Fund, 1917, p. 3).

This ironic jousting between two elite universities for the singular honor of being the "most democratic" fundraiser then subsided. The fundraising competition appeared unseemly after the United States entered World War I on April 6, 1917 to make the world "safe for democracy," in the famous words of US President Woodrow Wilson (Wilson, 1917).

Following the war, hundreds of colleges and universities launched drives modeled on the widely publicized HEF (*New York Times*, 1920). At the same time, "discontent with democratic institutions" surfaced in Europe and the United States (Bryce, 1921, vol. 1, p. 5). By the late 1920s, many cautioned that "democracy faces a perilous situation" (Sait, 1929, p. v). Indeed, "democracy may still be called a popular idea in the sense that everybody talks about it, but ... it is very largely discredited," political theorists observed (Brown, 1926, p. vii).

By that point, the leaders of YAF and HEF had already abandoned the rhetoric of democracy, while hundreds of other colleges and universities across the country launched annual alumni funds and national, multiyear fundraising campaigns. The discursive legitimation of "democracy" was no longer necessary because the additional income alone provided sufficient justification in the accelerating competition for revenue and endowment in higher education. Nevertheless, democratic discourse had provided the gateway through which these two novel, and now commonplace, modes of fundraising entered higher education between 1890 and 1925.

Over the next century, these two new modes of fundraising – along with the traditional discreet appeal to wealthy donors – formed the standard triad of fundraising employed by colleges and universities competing for wealth and prestige (see Figure 26.1). Indeed, the schools with the most financial capital were those that embraced the new modes of fundraising in the 1920s, listed in the Appendix 1 of this chapter. The stratification of higher education by wealth was already emerging at that point due, in part, to the innovations in fundraising.

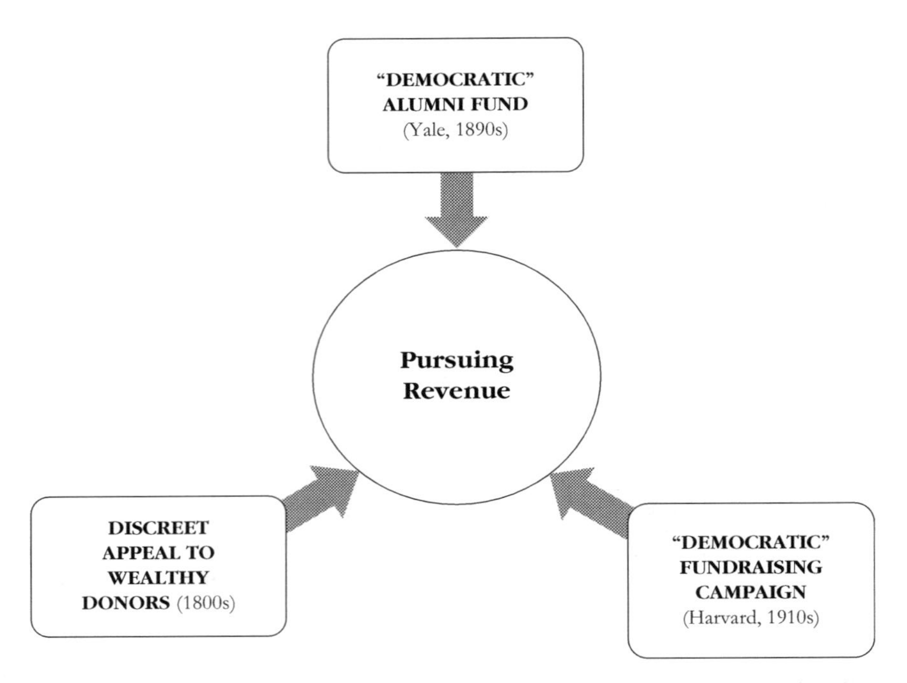

Figure 26.1 Fundraising triad of higher education, 1800s–1910s. Source: Kimball and Iler (2023), 95.

The annual alumni fund provided a continuous stream of supplementary revenue for current operations, while the discreet solicitations of wealthy donors alternated cyclically with publicized, national fundraising drives. Together, these three modes constituted an incessant, ubiquitous cycle of fundraising. But the most productive tactic proved to be the traditional solicitation of wealthy patrons. This undemocratic approach reinforced the interrelation between wealthy Americans and elite colleges and universities because it remained true that about 90 percent of the proceeds of fundraising drives in higher education came from 10 percent of the donors (Drezner, 2011, p. 7; Joslyn, 2019, p. 4).

26.3 Aggressive Investment Strategies: 1950s–2000s

During the Great Depression of the 1930s, fundraising and philanthropy slowed, and the competition for revenue and endowment in US higher education abated. The lull continued in the 1940s due to the upheaval wrought by World War II and the influx of returning veterans funded by the Servicemen's Readjustment Act (1944). This "G.I. Bill" greatly expanded access to higher education and its contribution to social mobility and democracy. In addition, the torrent of funding for veterans brought prosperity to virtually all colleges and universities, forestalling the competition for revenue and financial capital. When the flood of veterans ebbed in 1951, the feverish competition resumed, initiating a golden age in US higher education (Freeland, 1992).

In the 1950s and 1960s, two new, important sources of revenue emerged: mammoth federal grants and aggressive investing of endowment portfolios. The former provided operating income but did not contribute to increasing the financial capital of colleges and universities. The latter was the key to growing endowments and fostering stratification by wealth. In the second half of the twentieth century, three new modes of aggressive investing supplemented the three modes of fundraising that had become customary in the first half of the century.

Since the colonial period, college trustees and treasurers had maintained three distinct aims when investing their endowments: maximize earnings, ensure stable income, and safeguard the principal. Emphasizing the latter two aims, colonial colleges invested their permanent funds conservatively in mortgages, promissory notes, and real estate amid the financial vagaries before 1800. Early in the nineteenth century, the conservative investment strategy persisted, although fixed-income bonds began to replace promissory notes and real estate because they were easier to trade, and their value could be determined with more precision (Cabot and Larrabee, 1951, pp. 628–29).

Through the nineteenth century, most private colleges and universities gradually shifted their investments to government and corporate bonds, along with a small amount invested in relatively risky corporate stocks, especially in railroads, utilities, and banks. In the first three decades of the twentieth century, the fraction invested in corporate stocks expanded somewhat, but rarely reached 20 percent, even in the most aggressive portfolios. Meanwhile, public colleges and universities, especially land-grant institutions, remained more conservative, investing predominantly in long-term bonds and mortgages (Klein, 1930, pp. 86–122, p. 258; King, 1950, p. 108; Williamson, 1993, p. 76, p. 110).

The stock market crash in 1929 and ensuing Great Depression naturally made treasurers and trustees more cautious about investing in equities. Nevertheless, studies of endowments, first appearing in the 1930s, identified financially inequitable trends already emerging in higher education. The new studies found that schools with larger endowments had higher rates of return, which expanded their lead over less-endowed colleges and universities and further stratified higher education institutions by wealth (Seass, 1937, pp. 3–9; Sattgast, 1940, pp. 2–10, pp. 71–89). The greater return on investment was generally attributed to "more competent investment service and advice enjoyed by the boards of trustees" (Eells, 1936, p. 477). The rich could access and afford better advice.

Between 1950 and 1970, the US economy expanded rapidly, and the stock market boomed. Wealthier institutions continued to receive better investment expertise and advice, prompting them to invest more aggressively in equities than had ever been the case in American higher education (Twentieth Century Fund, 1975, pp. 4–19). The aggressive approach to endowment investing during these critical two decades resulted in even higher rates of return that further widened the wealth stratification in higher education. Here again, the university with the largest endowment led the way.

Paul C. Cabot, who had opened the first operating mutual fund in the country in the 1920s, became treasurer of Harvard University in 1948. Starting in that year, he rapidly boosted the equities portion of Harvard's endowment to 60 percent and reduced the fraction of fixed-income securities to 40 percent. At the time, this unprecedented 60/40 strategy seemed extraordinarily aggressive and risky. Few colleges and universities followed Cabot's lead, preferring to invest primarily in bonds, partly because schools with less financial capital could not afford to assume the risk (Putnam, 1953; Williamson, 1993, p. 76; Fishman, 2014, p. 207).

But Cabot's innovation enabled Harvard and other universities that were wealthy enough to assume the risk and replicate the strategy, to benefit from the booming stock market between 1950 and 1965. Over that period, one general index of common stock prices rose 380 percent, while Harvard's common stock portfolio rose 473 percent (Harris, 1970, pp. 351–70). In this way, the 60/40 standard of portfolio management emerged in US higher education and gradually became the predominant approach to "sound investing" over the next four decades (Cabot & Larrabee, 1951, p. 629; Putnam, 1953, p. 629; Lapovsky, 2007, p. 102; Redd, 2015, p. 1).

After the soaring stock market reached its peak in the late 1960s, the United States slipped into a recession in the early 1970s, as the enormous cost of the Vietnam War and the Great Society programs of President Lyndon B. Johnson (1963–69) dragged on the domestic economy. Then followed a decade of stagflation, that is, stagnant growth and steep inflation coupled with high unemployment. Amid this economic malaise, the Ford Foundation sponsored a series of studies proposing another, more aggressive approach to endowment investing, even as the great majority of colleges and universities balked at adopting the 60/40 rule (Twentieth Century Fund, 1975).

The new Ford-sponsored strategy came to be called "total return" investing. Total return treats capital gains, along with dividends and interest, as part of the investment return of an endowment. The 60/40 rule had prescribed investing 60 percent of a portfolio in common stocks of well-established companies that provided high dividends. These dividend-earning "value" stocks had a lower prospect of increasing their price than did the "growth" stocks of small new companies, which paid little or no dividends but offered much greater return in capital appreciation over time if the company did well. Although growth stocks were volatile and therefore risky (at least in the short run), the total-return approach effectively prescribed including them prominently in an endowment portfolio (Welles, 1967, pp. 52–54; Williamson, 1993, pp. 75–76).

Here again, the novel, aggressive innovation in investing benefited wealthy colleges and universities, which could afford to assume the risk and to obtain the best advice to select the growth stocks. The vast majority of schools, having small endowments, fewer resources, and lower capacity to tolerate risk, held back. The richer schools therefore grew richer, and the financial inequity among colleges and universities widened during the late 1970s and 1980s.

Meanwhile, competition for endowment size accelerated after the *Chronicle of Higher Education* published its very first list of the largest endowments in 1970.

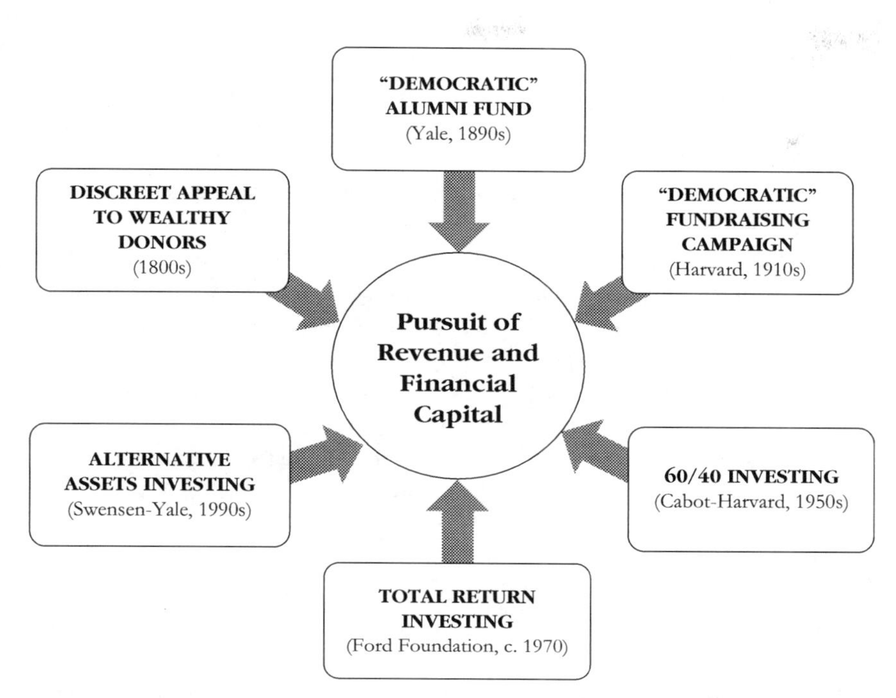

Figure 26.2 Six modes of building wealth in higher education, 1870–2020. Source: Kimball and Iler (2023), 216.

The *Chronicle* genteelly listed the colleges and universities in alphabetical order, rather than by endowment size or return on investment. Nevertheless, that inaugural list signaled the start of a public race for endowment rank in subsequent decades.

Following the introduction of the 60/40 rule and total return, the third critical innovation of endowment investing occurred in the 1990s, when David Swensen, the Chief Investment Officer of Yale University, famously pioneered the strategy of investing heavily in "alternative assets." These highly volatile, nontraditional assets fall into three classes: absolute return, private equity, and real assets. "Absolute return" means "exploiting inefficiencies in pricing marketable securities," often involving corporate mergers, distressed companies, short selling, futures, and derivatives, as hedge funds do. Exploiting such inefficiencies requires complicated financial instruments, highly sophisticated mathematical techniques, and extremely robust and timely data. "Private equity" includes venture capital investments in small, infant companies as well as buying and selling underperforming companies. "Real assets" consist of material assets, such as real estate, petroleum, timber, and other natural resources (Swensen, 2009, pp. 7–8, 54, 76–77, 112–17, 180–82, 245–46). Figure 26.2 summarizes the the development of the six fundraising and investment modes that became conventional in American higher education during the twentieth century.

Whereas the 60/40 rule seemed unconventional in the 1960s and total return appeared very risky in the 1970s and 1980s, alternative assets looked downright dangerous to most colleges and universities in the 1990s. Often leveraged with borrowed money that multiplies gains and losses dramatically, alternative assets yield "uncomfortably idiosyncratic investment portfolios" that appear extremely risky according to "conventional wisdom," observed Swensen (Swensen, 2009, pp. 7–8). Only schools with the biggest endowments could afford both the great risk and the highly expensive investment advice required to invest profitably in alternative assets.

Those that did so after embracing both the 60/40 rule and total return, enjoyed "seemingly limitless gains" from endowment investment during the 1990s and 2000s (Ryan, 2016, pp. 161–62). And Yale, under Swensen, led the pack. As of 2007, Yale's endowment had outperformed virtually all others over the previous five-, ten- and twenty-year periods. Even during the dot-com bust in 2001 and 2002, Yale's "risky" portfolio had posted a mean, positive return of 5 percent, while the average annual return on all college and university endowments was almost negative 5 percent (Swensen, 2009, pp. 1–2). Alternative assets thus triumphed in the best of times and the worst, ushering in yet another golden age for endowment in higher education. Some said that Swensen and his pioneering investment strategy in alternative assets had contributed "more to strengthen our educational and cultural institutions than anyone else on our planet" (Ellis, 2009, p. xvi).

The Great Recession of 2008–9 caused endowments, especially the largest that were heavily invested in volatile alternative assets, to fall precipitously. But they also recovered rapidly. By 2011, endowments in higher education had climbed out of the chasm to their prerecession value of fiscal year 2006. After a small setback in 2012, endowments made up their lost gains due to strong returns in 2013 and 2014. Overall, in the four decades since the advent of total return – from 1974 to 2014 – the mean of the average annual return of endowments was nearly 12 percent (Redd, 2015, table 1). These were the best forty years of portfolio performance in the history of US higher education. Although some critics recommended moderating risk in the future, they also conceded that aggressive investing in alternative assets produced much greater returns than had previous approaches to portfolio management (Fishman, 2014, pp. 201–29; Ryan, 2016, pp. 164, 180–84). But only the richest schools could afford to play the game.

26.4 Wealth Stratification and Financial Inequity

As colleges and universities widely adopted and perfected the fundraising triad and, to a lesser extent, aggressive investment strategies, the financial inequity – stratification of higher education by endowment size – widened between 1980 and 2020. The phenomenon had been observed at least as early as the 1920s (Ward, 1930, p. 4; Eells, 1935). But the "wealth gap" expanded tremendously after 1980 due to the new aggressive investing strategies employed at schools with the most financial capital (Waldeck, 2009, p. 1795). By 2020, 99 percent of the endowed funds in US higher education belonged to about 700, or 18 percent, of all the 4,000 degree-granting colleges and universities in the United

States and Canada. And about 80 percent of the endowed funds belonged to 2.5 percent, or 100, of the total schools (NACUBO, 2021).

Furthermore, academic prestige and reputation were highly correlated with financial capital. The endowments of all 63 members of the Association of American Universities (AAU), the most prestigious and exclusive academic association in North America, ranked among the top 100 endowments of colleges and universities in the United States and Canada (AAU, 2019; NACUBO, 2021). Similarly, the proliferating institutional rankings appearing in popular publications, launched by the *U.S. News & World Report* in 1983, employed measures of academic excellence and reputation that were highly correlated with financial capital (Solarzano & Quick, 1983).

Membership in the elite caste of colleges and universities also endured because the best-endowed colleges and universities retained their lead in financial capital. Nearly all institutions in the wealthiest 3 percent of schools in 1930 (numbering 31) remained in that rank a century later, as shown in Appendix 1. As the total number of colleges and universities grew over time, the absolute number in the wealthiest 3 percent naturally increased, amounting to about 120 in 2020. And new members rarely fell out of that tier once they had joined. The rich remained rich, due not only to the talent and hard work of their faculty and staff, but also to certain advantages conferred by wealth. Indeed, in the 1930s, scholars began to note reasons for the endurance of the highest caste, and those reasons have persisted and multiplied during the past century (Ward, 1930, p. 4; Eells, 1935; Arnett, 1939, p. 84).

First, large endowments could tolerate greater risk and more aggressive investment and therefore consistently earned higher rates of return than small endowments. In addition, wealthy schools normally received more expert advice, both because they could afford it and because their trustees often had contacts in financial circles (Lapovsky, 2007, pp. 100–2; Swensen, 2009, pp. 126–27; Fishman, 2014, pp. 209, 301; Redd, 2015, pp. 4–5; Ryan, 2016, pp. 169, 183). Magnifying the higher rate of return, the bigger size of large endowments increased the absolute return even more than that received by small endowments.

Second, if well-endowed schools suffered a financial setback, their prestige and capital facilitated borrowing to repair the damage. For example, during the Great Recession of 2008–9, Harvard could not sell its large illiquid, alternative assets without taking huge losses. The university therefore issued bonds for $2.5 billion to fund its current operations and uphold its contractual obligations (Munk, 2009; Groll & White, 2010; Humphreys, 2010, pp. 37–38, 54). In contrast, historically black colleges and universities (HBCUs) paid more in underwriting fees to issue tax-exempt bonds, compared not only to elite wealthy schools like Harvard but also to all predominantly white schools (Dougal et al., 2016). Their greater capacity to recover from downturns compounded the financial advantage that elite schools with larger endowments earned from higher rates of return over the past century.

Third, schools with large endowments had more success in fundraising. Over the past century, 90 percent of donations to higher education have usually come from about 10 percent of donors; and wealthy individuals, who could afford large gifts, have generally graduated from the wealthier schools. Hence, endowment size has been strongly correlated with annual revenue from gifts (Joslyn, 2019). One study in 2008 found that each additional $100 million of endowment is associated with an additional $2 million of increased donations annually (Weisbrod et al., 2008, p. 123).

Prosperous donors gave to their alma mater, not only out of altruism or gratitude, but also because "the donor benefits in some way from the act of giving" to a wealthy alma mater, economists have argued. Wealthy alumni of elite institutions burnished their personal brand by keeping their alma mater financially strong. They also improved the chances of admission for their children or grandchildren, and gained public recognition and accolades, often including their name on a building or center (Holmes, 2009, p. 19). Nouveau riche nongraduates who sometimes donated to wealthy, elite schools received some of these same benefits.

These factors also explain the remarkable finding that wealthy schools spent less per-dollar-raised to attract donations than did less-endowed schools (Ehrenberg, 2000, p. 46). In addition, well-endowed schools directed a larger share of gifts to their endowment. Not living hand to mouth, rich schools could afford to solicit donations for either unrestricted permanent funds or a permanent restricted fund that "poses no real restrictions on the institution" (Ehrenberg & Smith, 2003, p. 227).

In sum, wealthy schools received more donations, spent less to obtain them, and allocated more of them to endowment. These benefits increased their financial capital, which they invested more aggressively and expertly to earn larger rates of return on their large portfolios. All these factors explain the financial advantage of the wealthiest schools, their enduring membership in the highest caste, and the growing financial inequity in higher education between 1980 and 2020.

26.5 Impeding Social Mobility and Democracy

By the 1970s, higher education enjoyed widespread esteem in the United States, because its development over the prior century had brought tremendous benefits to the nation. Noted scholars celebrated the resulting economic expansion, technological advancements, educated citizenry, and socioeconomic mobility, relative to other nations, and came to view US higher education as the best in the world (Trow, 1988; Freeland, 1992, p. 419). Through the 1970s, Americans even cheered the growing revenue and financial capital of higher education. The incessant fundraising drives, annual appeals to alumni, and competition for the largest endowment, recorded annually by the *Chronicle of Higher Education*, were widely applauded. Nevertheless, esteem for higher education declined during the 1980s. By the end of that decade, observers said that higher education was rapidly catching "the health care system" as the institution most "criticized by the public today" (Langfitt, 1990, p. 8). Public resentment burned hotter in the 1990s and 2000s, as higher education came under attack on multiple fronts.

One legion marched under the banner of populist anti-elitism, which motivated attacks on colleges and universities by politicians and their supporters during the administration of President Ronald Reagan (1981–89). Another legion of academic and social critics reviled "the commercialization of higher education" and the growing focus on accumulating revenue and financial capital that apparently provided diminishing benefit and increasing waste (Bok, 2003; Newfield, 2003). These critics also assailed the longstanding and worsening "administrative expense bias" that directed much of the accumulating resources to enlarging the administration rather than to improving the educational operations of colleges and universities (McMahon & Strein, 1979, pp. 1–2; Bowen, 1980, p. 140). According to these critics, the pursuit of revenue and financial capital contravened fundamental values that colleges and universities had long espoused, values that had justified the pursuit of wealth to begin with.

Nevertheless, widespread resentment against higher education stemmed fundamentally from the discordance between mounting student debt and growing institutional wealth accompanied by the widening wealth stratification in higher education (Waldeck, 2009, p. 1795). Although elite, wealthy colleges and universities were the prominent targets, the animus extended to the entire system because the most prestigious schools were considered exemplars of higher education. Furthermore, public resentment intensified because the financial inequity in higher education seemed to resemble and reinforce the increasing wealth inequality in the US population, and vice versa, between 1980 and 2020. This interrelationship had two important aspects.

On the one hand, the national wealth inequality was implicated in the rising student debt, because that indebtedness resulted from the stagnation of incomes of the middle or working class. After a century of robust economic growth, the US economy began to slow in the 1970s and remained sluggish through the 2010s. In the four decades after 1980, the income of middle-class families plateaued in constant dollars and trailed increases in the cost of living (Gordon, 2016, pp. 522–25). Middle-class families and students then had to borrow ever larger sums to pay for higher education. By 2020, the nation's cumulative student debt had risen steeply to more than $1.5 trillion, and some experts project that if current trends continue, student debt will reach $3 trillion by the end of the next decade (Collier, 2019; Looney et al., 2020).

Middle-class parents and students who assumed this staggering debt naturally concluded that "American higher education system is a gigantic debt-producing machine" (Carey, 2020). But the overall, per-student cost of higher education did not rise faster than the cost of living. The debt problem resulted from the stagnant income of the middle-class, which lagged behind the cost of living, and reflected the nation's growing wealth inequality.

Despite the slower economic growth in the decades after 1980, rich Americans increased their wealth faster than the middle-class. This increase came from massive tax cuts and from the returns on their invested capital, which historically grew faster than the wages of the middle-class, who owned relatively little invested capital (Piketty, 2014, pp. 304–76). This long-term trend worsened during the 2010s when American corporations spent more than $6 trillion to buy back their own shares, sharply driving up the price of equities. The stock-owning wealthy grew richer, widening the gap between themselves and the wage-earning middle class (Price & Edwards, 2020, pp. 1–11). Wealth became ever more concentrated in the upper 10 percent, especially the top 1 percent, of the population, while the middle-class, whose wages stagnated, assumed debt to pay for higher education.

On the other hand, the growing wealth inequality in the American population also seemed interwoven with the concentration of endowment and wealth stratification of colleges and universities. In the same way that the invested capital of the rich grew while middle-class wages stagnated, so too did the schools with large endowments reap larger investment returns. These institutions had a greater capacity to tolerate higher levels of risk and afford more aggressive investing, as already discussed, leaving the rest of colleges and universities straggling behind.

Furthermore, the richer schools ran mammoth fundraising campaigns, constantly extolling their successive drives as "the largest fundraising endeavor in the university's history" or "the largest ever in higher education" (Ohio State, 2012; Powell, 2013). Indeed, the proportion of donations coming from "mega-gifts" to colleges and universities also rose in the 2010s, while the fraction coming from smaller alumni gifts fell. Fundraising drives became more ambitious and succeeded spectacularly, but a rising proportion of the money came from a shrinking fraction of donors (Scutari, 2017; Joslyn, 2019). In the early twenty-first century, fundraising became less "democratic," reversing the developments of a century earlier.

These trends were perfectly demonstrated by Michael Bloomberg's donation of $1.8 billion to Johns Hopkins University in 2018. The single largest gift ever made to one school, the contribution came from a multibillionaire, went to his alma mater, and was designated for the endowment. Notwithstanding its positive impact, Bloomberg's enormous gift cost him less than the annual income earned from his net worth of some $59 billion in 2020. Bloomberg's gift therefore fortified Johns Hopkins' place within the top 1 percent of endowed schools, without jeopardizing Bloomberg's place within the top 1 percent of wealthiest Americans, while polishing his own pedigree and providing him with large tax deductions (Hauptman, 2019; Basken, 2021). Bloomberg's gift thus exemplified how higher education stratification is closely entwined with wealth inequality in the United States.

In fact, between 1990 and 2020 the endowment concentration in higher education exceeded the capital concentration in the United States population. In 1990, the wealthiest 1 percent of colleges and universities owned about 58 percent of the total endowments of American higher education, while the wealthiest 1 percent of American households owned about 42 percent of all households' invested capital. Between 1990 and 2020, the concentration of household capital approached, but did not catch that of endowment in higher education. In 2020, the wealthiest 1 percent of colleges and universities owned about 54 percent of the total endowment of American higher education, while the wealthiest 1 percent of American households owned about 53 percent of households' total invested capital, as seen in Appendix 2 of this chapter.

By that point, the primary vehicle of social mobility for middle-class youths for the prior 130 years had become, for many, an albatross around their necks that plunged them deeply into debt. Meanwhile, a small number of gilded academic citadels admitted a few, select students into membership in the top 1 percent of American society (Haselby & Stoller, 2021). The scandals of wealthy parents buying admission to elite schools that came to light in 2019 epitomized the situation (Thelin, 2019). "The country's best colleges are an overpriced gated community whose benefits accrue mostly to the wealthy," critics said, with good reason (Carey, 2019). In this way, the century-long pursuit of revenue and wealth that had vastly benefited and improved American higher education came to impede the social mobility that had long contributed to American democracy.

Appendix 1

Largest endowments of US colleges and universities among top 3 percent of degree-granting institutions in 1920 and their rank in 2020 (in millions of nominal dollars)

Top 3% of endowments in 1920			Rank among endowments in 2020	
RANK	INSTITUTIONS	MILLIONS	RANK*	MILLIONS
1	Harvard	44.6	1	40,575
2	Columbia	39.6	12	11,257
3	Stanford	33.3	4	28,948
4	Chicago	28.4	16	8,204
5	Yale	24.0	2	31,202
6	Cornell	16.0	19	7,219
7	Massachusetts Institute of Tech.	15.0	6	18,496
8	Princeton	10.3	5	26,559
9	Carnegie Institute of Tech.	9.6	38	2,671
10	Johns Hopkins	9.1	21	6,750
11	Washington University, St. L.	9.1	15	8,420
12	University of Pennsylvania	9.0	7	14,877
13	*University of California*	7.3	11	12,142
14	*University of Washington*	6.3	33	3,076
15	Northwestern University	5.5	13	10,927
16	University of Rochester	5.2	47	2,330
17	Amherst College	4.4	41	2,565

(*cont.*)

Top 3% of endowments in 1920			Rank among endowments in 2020	
RANK	INSTITUTIONS	MILLIONS	RANK*	MILLIONS
18	Dartmouth College	4.3	23	5,975
19	Bryn Mawr College	4.2	129^	888
20	Clark University	4.2	213#	446
21	Western Reserve University	4.1	61	1,851
22	Tulane University	4.0	76	1,446
23	Vanderbilt University	3.9	20	6,917
24	*University of Minnesota*	3.9	29	3,872
25	*University of Oklahoma*	3.7	56	1,950
26	Tufts College	3.5	59	1,889
27	Barnard College	3.5	236#	357
28	Brown University	3.2	26	4,377
29	Wellesley College	3.2	49	2,285
30	Williams College	3.2	36	2,841
31	Smith College	3.2	58	1,907

* In 2020, top 3% included 120 institutions.
^ Ranked in top 4%
# Ranked in top 6%
Note: Names of public institutions are italicized.
Source: Kimball and Iler, 2023, tables 1.1 and 1.2

Appendix 2

Top tier of endowment in higher education and capital of US households (in nominal dollars)

	ENDOWMENT*			HOUSEHOLD CAPITAL**		
Year	Total ($billions)	$billions owned by richest 1%	Percent owned by richest 1%	Total ($trillions)	$trillions owned by richest 1%	Percent owned by richest 1%
1990	59.9	34.6	58	5.2	2.2	42
2000	241.2	134.2	56	13.9	6.3	45
2010	327.8	187.4	57	18.6	8.8	47
2020	647.5	349.5	54	46.6	24.8	53

* Not including Life Income Funds, which would likely increase the percentage.
** Investments in corporate equities, mutual funds, and private businesses, but not real estate, which would likely increase the percentage.
Source: Kimball and Iler (2023, table 11.1).

References

Allen, W. H. (1912). *Modern philanthropy: A study of efficient appealing and giving.* New York: Dodd, Mead, and Company.

Arnett, T. (1922). *College and university finance.* New York: General Education Board.

Arnett, T. (1939) *Trends in current receipts and expenditures . . . of endowed universities and colleges.* New York: General Education Board.

Association of American Universities. (2019, November 6). *Three leading research universities join the association of American universities* [Press Release].

Basken, P. (2021, April 29). US colleges' billion-dollar question: Is philanthropy worth the cost? *Times Higher Education.* Available at: https://www.timeshighereducation.com/features/us-colleges-billion-dollar-question-philanthropy-worth-cost (Accessed: December 21, 2021).

Bok, D. (2003). *Universities in the marketplace: The commercialization of higher education.* Princeton, NJ: Princeton University Press.

Bowen, H. R. (1980). *The costs of higher education: How much do colleges and universities spend per student and how much should they spend?* New York: Jossey-Bass.

Brown, I. J. C. (1926). *The meaning of democracy.* 2nd ed., Oxford: Richard Cobden-Sanderson.

Bryce, J. (1921) *Modern democracies.* 2 vols., New York: Macmillan.

Cabot, P. C., & Larrabee, L. C. (1951). Investing Harvard money. *Harvard Alumni Bulletin,* 53(12 May), 628–34.

Carey, K. (2019, April 1). The creeping capitalist takeover of higher education. *Huffington Post.* Available at: https://www.huffpost.com/highline/article/capitalist-takeover-college (accessed: December 20, 2021).

Carey, K. (2020, November 18). What about tackling the causes of student debt? *New York Times.* Available at: https://www.nytimes.com/2020/11/18/upshot/student-debt-forgiveness-biden.html (accessed: December 10, 2021).

Chronicle of Higher Education. (1970, May 4). College endowment funds: Their performance in 1969, p. 8.

Collier, L. (2019). College costs. *CQ Researcher.* Available at: http://library.cqpress.com/cqresearcher/cqresrre2019102500 (accessed: 10 December 2021).

Curti, M., & Nash, R. (1965). *Philanthropy in the shaping of American higher education.* New Brunswick, NJ: Brown Book Company.

Cutlip, S. M. (1965). *Fund raising in the United States: Its role in America's philanthropy.* New Brunswick, NJ: Rutgers University Press.

Daniels, R. J. (2021). *What universities owe democracy.* Baltimore, MD: Johns Hopkins University Press.

Deming, C. (1911, March 17). Yale's Larger Gifts. *Yale Alumni Weekly,* 634–35.

Dougal, C., Gao, P., Mayew, W. J., & Parsons, C. A. (2016, February 4). What's in a (school) name? Racial discrimination in higher education bond markets? *University of Houston Law Center Institute for Higher Education Law and Governance Publication.*

Drezner, N. D. (2011). Philanthropy and fundraising in American higher education. *ASHE Higher Education Report,* 37(2), 1–16.

Duncan, R. F. (1916, November 24). *Notebook of the secretary of the Harvard endowment fund.*

Eells, W. C. (1935). Endowments in American colleges and universities. *School and Society*, 41(February, 23), 263–72.

Eells, W. C. (1936). Income from endowments. *The Journal of Higher Education*, 7(9), 475.

Ehrenberg, R. G. (2000). *Tuition rising: Why college costs so much*. Cambridge, MA: Harvard University Press.

Ehrenberg, R. G., & Smith, C. L. (2003). The sources and uses of annual giving at selective private research universities and liberal arts colleges. *Economics of Education Review*, 22(3), 223–35.

Ellis, C. D. (2009). Foreword. In D. F. Swensen, ed., *Pioneering portfolio management: An unconventional approach to institutional investment*. New York: Free Press, pp. ix–xvi.

Fishman, J. J. (2014). What went wrong: Prudent management of endowment funds and imprudent endowment investing policies. *Journal of College and University Law*, 40(1), 199–246.

Freeland, R. M. (1992). *Academia's golden age: Universities in Massachusetts 1945–1975*. New York: Oxford University Press.

Gordon, R. (2016). *The rise and fall of American growth*. Princeton, NJ: Princeton University Press.

Groll, E. J., & White, W. N. (2010, January 9). Harvard to borrow $480 million to fund capital projects and refinance debt. *The Harvard Crimson*. Available at: https://www.thecrimson.com/article/2010/1/9/harvard-debt-rating-last (accessed: December 21, 2021).

Hadley, A. T. (1902). *Annual report of the president of Yale university 1900–1901*. New Haven, CT: Yale University.

Harris, S. E. (1970). *Economics of Harvard*. New York: McGraw-Hill.

Haselby, S., & Stoller, M. (2021, May 28). It's time to break up the Ivy League cartel. *Chronicle of Higher Education*. Available at: https://www.chronicle.com/article/how-meritocracy-became-trickle-down-education (accessed: December 21, 2021).

Hauptman, A. M. (2019, January 17). Bloomberg's gift and the role of endowments. *Inside Higher Education*. Available at: https://www.insidehighered.com/views/2019/01/17/michael-bloombergs-gift-johns-hopkins-raises-questions-about-role-endowments (accessed: December 21, 2021).

Holmes, J. (2009). Prestige, charitable deductions, and other determinants of alumni giving: Evidence from a highly selective liberal arts college. *Economics of Education Review*, 28(1), 18–28.

Holt, G. C. (1917, February 2) The origin of the Yale alumni fund. *Yale Alumni Weekly*, 529–30.

Humphreys, J. (2010). *Educational endowments and the financial crisis: Social costs and systemic risks in the shadow banking system*. Boston, MA: Tellus Institute.

Johnson, B. A. (2013). *Fundraising and endowment building at a land grant university during the critical period, 1910–1940: The failure of Ohio State*. PhD dissertation. The Ohio State University.

Joslyn, H. (2019). Campaign fever: Fundraising drives are getting bigger and more numerous. *The Chronicle of Philanthropy*, 31(6), 8–17.

Kimball, B. A. (2014). The first campaign and the paradoxical transformation of fundraising in American higher education, 1915–1925. *Teachers College Record*, 116(7), 1–44.

Kimball, B. A. (2015). "Democratizing" fundraising at elite universities: The discursive legitimation of mass giving at Yale and Harvard, 1890–1920. *History of Education Quarterly*, 55(2), 164–89.

Kimball, B. A., & Iler, S. M. (2023). *Wealth, cost, and price in American higher education, A brief history*. Baltimore, MD: Johns Hopkins University Press.

King, S. (1950). *A history of the endowment of Amherst college*. Amherst, MA: Amherst College.

Klein, A. J. (1930). *Survey of land-grant colleges and universities*. Washington, DC: U.S. Department of the Interior.

Kuper, S. (2021, April 29). How the middle class became downwardly mobile. *Financial Times*. Available at: https://www.ft.com/content/9101fc2c-c342-4a3b-897a-26c44e6c10cc (accessed: April 25, 2022).

Lamont, T. W. (1917, January 8). *Letter to E. B. Dane*.

Langfitt, T. W. (1990). The cost of higher education: Lessons to learn from the health care industry. *Change: The Magazine of Higher Learning*, 22(6), 8–15.

Lapovsky, L. (2007). Critical endowment policy issues. *New Directions for Higher Education*, 140, 99–110.

Looney, A., Wessel, D., & Yilla, K. (2020, January 28). Who owes all that student debt? And who'd benefit if it were forgiven? *Policy 2020 Brookings Institution*.

McMahon, W. W., & Strein, C. T. (1979). *The university as a non-profit discretionary firm*. Urbana, IL: University of Illinois Press.

Munk, N. (2009). Rich Harvard, poor Harvard. *Vanity Fair*, 51(8), 106.

National Association of College and University Business Officers (NACUBO). (2021). *Endowment Study 2020*.

Nevins, A. (1962). *The state universities and democracy*. Urbana, IL: University of Illinois Press.

New York Times. (1917, January 26). Average Harvard pay $1,840... endowment committee says, p. 10.

New York Times. (1920, February 8). Universities ask over $200,000,000. E1.

Newfield, C. (2003). *Ivy and industry: Business and the making of the American university, 1880–1980*. Durham, NC: Duke University Press.

Ohio State University. (2012, October). *Ohio State launches $2.5 billion dollar fundraising effort* [Published pamphlet].

Piketty, T. (2014). *Capital in the twenty-first century*. Trans. by A. Goldhammer. Cambridge, MA: Belknap Press.

Pinsker, J. (2019, September 3). Why college became so expensive and what that has meant for America's middle-class families. *Atlantic*. Available at: https://www.theatlantic.com/education/archive/2019/09/college-cost-indebted-zaloom/597181 (accessed April 25, 2022).

Powell, A. (2013, September 21). Harvard kicks off fundraising effort. *Harvard Gazette*. Available at: https://news.harvard.edu/gazette/story/2013/09/harvard-kicks-off-fundraising-effort (accessed December 21, 2021).

Price, C. C., & Edwards, K. (2020). *Trends in income from 1975 to 2018*. RAND Education and Labor Working Paper. Available at: https://www.rand.org/pubs/working_papers/WRA516-1.html (accessed December 21, 2021).

Putnam Jr., G. (1953, May 9). Sound investing: A brief comparison of the financial policies of five eastern universities. *Harvard Alumni Bulletin*, 55, 628–30.

Redd, K. E. (2015, November, 1–6). Forever funds. *Business Officer Magazine*,

Ross, E. D. (1942). *Democracy's college: The land-grant movement in the formative stage*. Ames, IA: Iowa State College Press.

Ryan, C. R. (2016). Trusting U: Examining university endowment management. *Journal of College and University Law*, 42(1), 159–212.

Sait, E. M. (1929). *Democracy*. New York: The Century Company.

Saltonstall, R. M. (1917, March). Harvard's new endowment. *Harvard Graduates Magazine*, 313–16.

Sattgast, C. R. (1940). *The administration of college and university endowments*. PhD dissertation. Teachers College, Columbia University.

Scutari, M. (2017, April 10). Mega-gifts are rising and alumni giving is shrinking, which means what exactly? *Inside Philanthropy*. Available at: https://www.insidephilanthropy.com/home/2017/4/10/mega-gifts-universities-fundraising (accessed December 21, 2021).

Seass, A. R. (1937). *Endowment income and investments, 1926–35*. Washington, DC: The American Council on Education.

Solarzano, L., & Quick, B. E. (1983). Rating the colleges. *U.S. News & World Report*, 41–43.

Stokes, A. P. (1911, January 20th). Yale's financial future. *Yale Alumni Weekly*, 430–31.

Stokes, A. P. (1912). *Annual report of the secretary of Yale university 1910–1911*. New Haven, CT: Yale University.

Stokes, A. P. (1914). *Annual report of the secretary of Yale university 1912–1913*. New Haven, CT: Yale University.

Swensen, D. F. (2009). *Pioneering portfolio management: An unconventional approach to institutional investment*. Rev. ed., New York: Free Press.

Thelin, J. R. (2019). An embarrassment of riches: Admission and ambition in American higher education. *Society*, 56(4), 329–34.

Trow, M. (1988). American Higher Education. *Educational Researcher*, 17(3), 13–23.

Twentieth Century Fund. (1975). *Funds for the future: Report of the task force on college and university endowment policy*. New York: McGraw-Hill.

Ward, A.N. (1930). Making provision for the college of liberal arts; the small college. Being a revision and enlargement of the article printed December 10, 1929. Westminster, MD: Unknown.

Waldeck, S. E. (2009). The coming showdown over university endowments: Enlisting the donors. *Fordham Law Review*, 77(4), 1795–836.

Weisbrod, B. A, Ballou, J. P., & Asch, E. D. (2008). *Mission and money: Understanding the university*. New York: Cambridge University Press.

Welles, C. (1967). University endowments: Revolution comes to the ivory tower. *Institutional Investor*.

Williams, R. (1985). *Keywords: A vocabulary of culture and society*. Rev. ed., New York: Oxford University Press.

Williamson, J. P. (1993). *Funds for the future: College endowment management for the 1990s*. 2nd ed., Westport, CT: The Common Fund in cooperation with the American Governing Boards of Universities and Colleges and NACUBO.

Wilson, W. (1917). *Address of the president April 2, 1917, 65th Congress of the United States, 1st session*. Washington, DC: Government Printing Office.

Yale Alumni University Fund (1915). *Twenty-fifth annual report of the board of directors*. New Haven, CT: Yale University.

Yale Alumni University Fund (1917). *Twenty-seventh annual report of the board of directors*. New Haven, CT: Yale University.

Yale Alumni Weekly. (1917, February 2). Alumni make it possible to secure great teachers for Yale, p. 535.

Zaloom, C. (2019) *Indebted: How families make college work at any cost*. Princeton, NJ: Princeton University Press.

Zunz, O. (2012). *Philanthropy in America: A history*. Princeton, NJ: Princeton University Press.

27

Mentoring and Instructional Duties of Professors

Harry Brighouse

27.1 Introduction

Colleges and universities have duties to the public as well as to the undergraduate students who attend them. Crudely speaking, their duty *to the public* is to produce professionals and leaders who are more skilled and knowledgeable, and more inclined to turn their talents, knowledge, and skills to the public good, than they otherwise would be. This duty has two dimensions: making graduates more economically productive than they would otherwise be, and preparing them to be highly skilled at deliberating carefully and responsibly with their fellow citizens about political matters. Graduates are relatively privileged, vote at higher rates than, and are in other ways more influential than, nongraduates: their being skilled at deliberating responsibly in democratic decisions and inclined to do so is vital for the public good. Equally crudely speaking, colleges' and universities' duty *to the students* is to equip them with knowledge and skills, and foster the attitudes and dispositions, that support them living good lives, and to insure them against various harms that might befall them while they are in the undergraduate program.

I shall elaborate on these duties shortly. We have good reasons to think that universities enact these duties suboptimally, to put it kindly. As I'll argue in Section 27.2, even setting aside issues about funding, and issues about the structure of elementary and secondary schooling, the structure of the academic profession makes it highly unlikely that they come close to optimality.

Of course, appropriate and well-implemented reforms could improve matters. But that is not my focus here.[1] Instead, my primary interest is how individual professors should change their own behavior *as long as reform is not forthcoming*. I argue that individual professors should change their behavior substantially in response to the prevailing order; in particular, that they should, regardless of the incentive structure, take undergraduate teaching and the mentoring of undergraduates considerably more seriously than most currently do, and allocate their time, energy, and attention accordingly. I'll explain what "taking more seriously" means.

[1] I focus on reform in Brighouse (2022a).

27.2 Why Teaching and Mentoring Are Suboptimal

The case that teaching and mentoring in colleges and universities is suboptimal is rather simple. First, both teaching and mentoring well involve the exercise of complex cognitive and affective skill sets that can only be developed through purposeful engagement in a learning infrastructure. But few college level instructors purposefully engage in any learning infrastructure around teaching, and hardly any do so around mentoring.

Most university-level instructors have gone through, or are currently in, disciplinary advanced degree (usually PhD) programs. Those programs train them as practitioners of their discipline. They do coursework, and often original research, in a program lasting five or more years. Most have *no training at all* in teaching during that time. In the competitions for tenure-line and permanent instructor positions, hiring committees have only thin, cursory, evidence about their quality or potential as teachers, evidence that, in research-oriented institutions, is mostly ignored anyway. Once they are in the door, they have few structured opportunities to observe colleagues who have a track record as excellent teachers; and colleagues rarely observe or give systematic feedback to them on how to improve their practice. This might make sense if teaching were easy: if it just required already having the knowledge one wants the students to have, standing in front of them, and saying things to them.

But teaching isn't easy. Getting students to learn how to do calculus, developing the close-reading and analytical skills taught in some of the humanities, getting them to succeed in organic chemistry, are all difficult tasks. They involve a complex set of skills. One has to be able to engage everyone in a room of 15, 25, 80, or 300 students, motivate them to pay attention to the problems at hand and motivate them to prepare carefully and well for class. One also has to know how to use time in the classroom with them in a way that optimizes their learning of the content and skills at hand. College teachers do not have the kinds of classroom management problems that kindergarten or 9th grade or 12th grade teachers have. But students are frequently distracted by their own anxieties or thoughts, by the other students in the room, and, at least in current conditions, by the difficulty of disciplining themselves in their relations to the communications devices in their possession. Given these facts, it would be very surprising if most college teachers could not improve significantly with the right kind of seriousness.

At least teaching is treated as part of their job: the number of courses they teach is *counted*, and rewarded, even though the quality of their teaching is largely unknown.

Suboptimal as college teaching *generally* is, it may be even more suboptimal when it comes to teaching the skills and dispositions associated with responsible democratic citizenship. Despite institutional promises to render students "citizens and citizen-leaders for our society" and the like, instructors, who have enormous latitude in what and how they teach, are typically enculturated into the norms of their disciplines and their pedagogical aims reflect that. They are interested in getting students to learn to do philosophy, history, or linguistics, not in making them into responsible citizens. At best, civic skills and dispositions will be unintended outcomes.[2] More realistically, unless they they are straightforwardly included in a set of disciplinary learning objectives, or are systematically developed by the extracurriculum, they're unlikely to be produced (see Brighouse, 2022b, for a detailed discussion of what is involved in teaching college-age students for responsible citizenship).

Now let's turn to mentoring. Mentoring isn't even formally accounted for; it is treated as an optional activity for which, again, there is no professional learning infrastructure. Again, this would not matter if mentoring were unimportant or easy. But it does seem to be important: there is considerable evidence that students who feel connected to at least one faculty member are less likely to quit school, and more likely to succeed than students who do not (Johnson, 2016). And it is not easy. High quality mentorship requires knowing how to make oneself approachable, how to respond to the various needs one's mentee has, and how to induce them to access resources that one cannot provide oneself. An example of the latter: as we'll see in Section 27.3, mental health problems are endemic in college. Identifying that a student probably has a mental health problem takes insight and skill. Finding a way to talk with them about it without shame or anxiety requires sensitivity. And inducing them to seek professional help in the face of stigma that, though much weaker than in the past, persists especially in some populations, is often extremely challenging. Finally, there is a problem of distribution. Who gets to be mentored by whom is, generally, haphazard. Unless one is purposeful and self-conscious about whom one is mentoring, the tendency to mentor the more confident students with whom one has affective or cultural affinities is strong. This leaves students who lack the confidence or inclination to seek out mentorship at a disadvantage. And there are reasons to think that those for whom college is not a cultural second home, especially those from working class or poor backgrounds, are overrepresented in this category. How to build the kind of relationships with these students that might lead to mentorship is something that, for most professors, is not something they enter academia knowing how to do. It has to be learned.

27.3 Undergraduate Education and the Risks to Students

Suboptimal teaching and mentoring is costly. It has costs to the students, and costs to the public good. Let's start with the students. Students take on varying degrees of various risks by coming to college, and the professors are in a position to mitigate some of those risks. I'll focus on three such risks:

1. Risk of mental ill-health
2. Risks associated with academic failure of various kinds (these include dropping out, failing to learn very much, doing badly in classes that are gateway classes for professions to which the students aspire)

[2] For excellent discussions, see Bok (2008), chs. 2, 7, and 9 .

3. Risks associated with going into debt.

Think about the risks of mental ill health. Different methodologies produce different estimates concerning the rates of mental illness among college students, but estimates vary between 10 and 44%. The 2016 National College Health Assessment shows 19% of students surveyed as having been diagnosed or treated for some kind of mental health disorder in the previous 12 months, and 6.2% as having been diagnosed or treated for *both* depression *and* anxiety. Also, 68% reported having experienced one or more of the following in the past 12 months as being "traumatic or very difficult to handle": academics (48.4%); career related issue (26.5%); death of a family member or friend (16.2%); family problems (28.6%), intimate relationships (30.4%); other social relationships (27%); finances (34.1%); health problem of family member or partner (19.7%); personal appearance (28.6%); personal health issues (21.2%) and sleep difficulties (30.1%). The same report finds that in the previous 12 months 38.2% had at some point "felt so depressed that it was difficult to function," 66% had" "felt very sad," and 10.4% had "seriously considered committing suicide"(see ACHA, 2016, pp. 13–16).

Late adolescence is exactly when many mental illnesses begin to be exhibited, and the environment of a residential campus is especially unconducive to dealing well with mental ill-health. Students are surrounded almost exclusively by other 18–24-year-olds. Few have the maturity to recognize many of the signs of mental ill-health, let alone to support those who suffer it. Under considerable social pressure to self-present as young, energetic, happy, enthusiastic, and optimistic, sufferers of depression and anxiety can feel isolated and overwhelmed; as can students who do not suffer mental ill health, but are giving emotional support to those who do.

Think, now, about the risks associated with academic failure. Failing a *course* is costly in a number of ways: one has to pay for another course, one has the experience of having failed, and one has foregone other opportunities (either for learning in other courses, or for income by working, or for enjoyment of leisure time). Failing *out of college* is *more* costly in the same ways: one has the experience of having dropped out of college; the connection with one's social network is loosened, and one has foregone income or other opportunities for learning. For many students, even in the kinds of institution I am concerned with, if they drop out, they also carry debt, which is not compensated for by the enhanced earning power that a degree would have brought.[3]

These risks, which all students bear to some extent, are nevertheless unevenly distributed, and their distribution is connected with social class background. Five-year and six-year graduation rates for African-American students, for Hispanic students, and for Pell-eligible students are generally lower than for the student population as a whole, even at most elite institutions.[4] A student from a disadvantaged background is more likely than the average student to have

[3] Having some college education, but no degree, does seem to enhance one's earning power relative to not going at all, but the credential adds earning power, compared with having the same amount of schooling and no credential.

[4] For example, UC Berkeley lists its six-year graduation rate for all students as 91%, but for Pell-eligible students as 81%, for African-American students as 70.1% and for Hispanic students as 88.7%; the rates for U of Michigan, Ann-Arbor are 91.7%

received poor quality instruction in high school, and less likely to have received compensatory tutoring from her parents or from personal tutors. If the university assigns highly skilled and experienced instructors, invested in the student's success, to teaching the required basic math classes she will learn more math, is more likely to pass and more likely to pass with a better grade, and is significantly less likely to drop out of college. If, however, her teacher is not skilled in teaching students like her, and either has little investment in her success, or has limited opportunities to improve through professional development (or both), the probability of her getting a worse grade, learning less, and dropping out is higher. The lower the level of the class, the more vivid the equity issues.

Consider, finally, the risks of debt. In recent years some journalists and politicians have claimed the existence of a "college debt crisis." In fact the evidence suggests that it is worth going into considerable debt to get a college degree, and that the large debt loads referred to by journalists are mostly borne by students who have graduate degrees that further enhance their earning capacity (Baum, 2016). But *failure* in college – whether dropping out, or failure to learn – affects the post hoc cost-benefit analysis of going into debt. A student who drops out, or learns suboptimally, is less competitive in the labor market than she would be if she had completed or learned more, so the risk of taking on debt paid off less well than if she had graduated, and in some cases the payoff is negative. When instruction is low quality, disadvantaged students are more likely to fail. Among students who do fail, furthermore, disadvantaged students are more vulnerable to debt. Their parents have been able to pay less of the costs of college, are less able to support them in their failure, and are less equipped to help them manage whatever debt they do incur. If, as I conjecture, instructional quality influences student success, and benefits disadvantaged students more than advantaged students, then improving instruction helps to reduce the gap in risks between more and less advantaged students.

27.4 Undergraduate Education and the Costs to the Public Good

What do I mean by saying that suboptimal teaching and mentoring exact a cost to the public good? First let's get a bit more precise about the idea of "the public good," a concept which is much disputed. John Rawls suggests a natural interpretation, which I am going to adopt for the purposes of my argument: the extent to which some action or institution contributes to the public good is the extent to which it contributes to the prospects for wellbeing of the less advantaged members of society (Rawls, 1971). Rawls offers a definition of distributive justice, one component of which is the principle that social and economic inequalities can be justified insofar as they work to the benefit of the least advantaged. The intuitive idea is that unless the inequalities benefit the least advantaged people, we cannot say that they benefit *all* members of society. But, if they do benefit the

for the general population. 81.5% for Pell-eligible students, 79.8% for African-American students, and 88.7% for Hispanic students.

least advantaged then, since everybody else is (by definition) better off than the least advantaged, none of them have grounds for complaint. Rawls' reasoning for his principle suggests a parallel interpretation of the public good: we can only say that something benefits *the public* as a whole if it benefits the least advantaged; if it does benefit the least-advantaged, then others at least have no grounds for complaint. Some readers may find the idea that the public good is indexed to the good of the *least* advantaged unduly strict. So the interpretation of the idea of the public good I will deploy is just this: when judging whether the overall activity of some individual or institution contributes to the public good, a central question is whether the activity benefits the less advantaged. In the case of elite colleges and universities the question is whether and to what extent the activity benefits those whom they exclude, weighing the good of the most disadvantaged most, that of the next most disadvantaged next, and so on.

One way that the undergraduate mission of colleges and universities contributes to the public good is by enhancing the productivity of the students, and orienting the students to direct their productive abilities appropriately. What undergraduate programs do, to an extent that can be increased or reduced by the behavior of the leaders, staff, and faculty, is educate students bound for positions in which they can serve, to a greater or lesser degree, directly or indirectly, the interests of the less advantaged. Different institutions play different roles, but overall undergraduate programs produce nurses, physicians, K-12 teachers, social workers, early childhood workers, counseling psychologists, military recruits, psychiatrists, correctional officers, police officers, public defenders, public prosecutors, human resources managers, etc. How humane they are, how competent they are, and how they balance and successfully reconcile their own private interests with public service, all affect how well the interests of the less advantaged are served. Good – that is, *highly skilled and well-motivated* – teachers and school district leaders, social workers and county social work department leaders, hospital administrators and nurses, human resources managers, urban planners, city managers, etc. benefit the less advantaged by doing their jobs better, more imaginatively, and with greater commitment. Universities contribute to the public good, thus mitigating the costs of social closure, by enhancing the human capital of their students and orienting them to work for the public good.

Colleges and universities are not mere builders of the capabilities of students who go on to do what they would have done – better or worse – anyway. They also play a role in ambition formation. Some students have made a career choice before they enter, and that choice never changes. But for most, their career preferences evolve, partly in response to the influences they encounter in higher education. And even those who have an occupation in mind can change their minds about what they will do within it. Higher education plays a nonnegligible role in orienting the way that the human capital they develop is built. This is done partly through formal advising and suggestions – telling a student what careers are a good fit with their inclinations and abilities. It's also done in informal and probably sometime unconscious ways. The informal status hierarchy on a campus – in which Law, Engineering and Medical Schools have higher prestige than Education and Nursing Schools – typically reflects the status hierarchy beyond academia. Both the institution and the individuals within it can, to some extent, decide whether to reinforce or deflate those status hierarchies by word, attitude, and deed. The public good, even on the Rawlsian interpretation I have given, is complex. High-level computational and analytical skills appear to be important for the operation of capital markets. But it is not fantastical to imagine that at least some of the massive social investment that currently goes into the large percentage of Harvard graduates who go to work on Wall Street being reoriented toward social work, policing, and teaching (including, perhaps, math teaching). One way of reorienting the investment would be to do it directly: we could put more time, energy, and effort (from kindergarten to college graduation) into the education of students more likely to become social workers, police officers, and teachers, and less into those likely to work on Wall Street. Another would be to influence the students in whom large investments have already been made so they are (somewhat) more likely to become social workers, police officers, and teachers, and less likely to work on Wall Street. The conjecture I make here is just that, at present, with regard to the public good in its educational investment strategies the American education system does less well than it could.

A second way that the undergraduate mission of colleges and universities contributes to the public good is through the development of citizens' democratic competence. Some argue that in ideal conditions higher education would play *no* role in citizen formation. Because everyone, not just those who are fortunate enough to attend college, should become fully competent citizens, civic education would be taken care of in the compulsory education sector (Martin, 2021). But our conditions are nonideal. They are characterized by high (and unjust) levels of material inequality, with graduates being, on average, more likely to be beneficiaries of those inequalities than nongraduates. Given that, graduates have particularly urgent reasons to be able to discern, and to be inclined to give considerable weight to, the interests of nongraduates. To make things more difficult, in many democracies neither the political culture nor the infrastructure that mediates political debate and discourse supports careful and responsible scrutiny of factual claims or of normative reasoning. However, college, especially as structured in the US though also in some other countries, has affordances that support the development of citizens who are skilled at and inclined to deliberate responsibly even within institutions that tilt against deliberative responsibility.[5] Students typically encounter more people who are more unlike them in a variety of ways (for example race, class, religion, ethnicity and political outlook) at college than in high school and in their familial networks. In the US, the system of general education requirements (and, for a large number of nonprofessional degrees, additional liberal arts requirements) ensures that all students in baccalaureate degrees can be required to take courses concerning politically and ethically inflected issues. High-quality

[5] For readers unfamiliar with the US system: typically, in a four-year degree, no more than two-thirds of one's courses comprise one's major area of specialization, and at least one-fourth of one's courses fulfill general education breadth requirements that have nothing to do with one's specialization. One interesting possible upshot of the first part of the argument of this chapter is that higher education systems in other countries have reasons to emulate the US in this respect.

instruction in such courses oriented toward learning how to explore and articulate reasons and to hear and internalize the reasons of others on matters of moral of political importance about which disagreement is inevitable contributes to better citizenship and, thus, the public good.

Why is it so important for higher education to contribute to the public good (understood in the ways I have suggested, or any other way). One obvious answer is that the public *pays*: in the US government spending per full-time equivalent (FTE) student/year on higher education is more than $16,000, which is considerably more than spending per student FTE/year in K-12 education, for example. Another is simply that they are well placed to contribute, especially, as I argued in the previous paragraph, to the development of democratic competence. Of course, actually using breadth requirements to further democratic citizenship might require different pedagogical skills than simply teaching in one's discipline. Most faculty develop skills in teaching their discipline. Instructors who are trying to introduce students to a field, or prepare them for future study in that field, or are focused on specific content delivery have different aims and rely upon different teaching skills than instructors who are trying to emphasize the value of broad exploration of knowledge and liberal arts skill development. A teacher may be able to turn students into expert Spanish speakers, biologists, historians, and philosophers without ever getting them to reflect self-critically on their value commitments, and without getting them to discuss difficult controversial issues to which democratic citizens must contribute with people who disagree with them in a manner that produces fruitful and respectful deliberation. I've argued that even teaching in the disciplines is suboptimal: given that many teachers do not even self-consciously have the learning goals associated with democratic citizenship in mind, it would not be surprising if teaching with respect to democratic skills were even more suboptimal.

Gina Schouten alerts us to a further reason for higher education to contribute to the public good, which has particular force for the more selective and elite parts of the sector. Higher education puts those who do not participate in it, who are already less advantaged than those who do, at a competitive disadvantage:

> The degrees college students receive, the social capital they develop, and the enhanced skills those degrees and networks signal are *positional* goods, or goods whose value depends on the holder's *position* within the overall distribution of the good in the population. A good might be positional, for example, because its value is partly a function of how well it equips its holder to compete for subsequent goods, like jobs or further degrees. My educational credential will be less valuable as a means of securing a job insofar as others' credentials are better than mine; that's true even though my credential *itself* stays exactly the same. Because jobs are in scarce supply, one person's leg up is another person's leg down. The dark side of positional goods, then, is the positional costs they impose on those who lack them. As students in selective institutions of higher education become better skilled and credentialed, those who don't attend such institutions compare less favorably in competitions for scarce jobs . . . Partly by virtue of their very

> educational mission, then, selective colleges and universities impose positional costs on those members of a cohort who do not attend them. Those bearing these costs disproportionally comprise the most unfairly badly off individuals in the cohort, because social class background heavily influences outcomes in primary and secondary education, which in turn influences prospects for successfully securing admission to and persisting in higher education. Selective colleges and universities then confer still greater advantage upon attendees, including not just intrinsically valuable educational experiences but also those skills, networks, and credentials that are instrumentally valuable for securing jobs. In short, selective colleges and universities disproportionally educate already advantaged students and then confer still greater advantage upon them, *to the competitive detriment* of those left out. (Schouten, 2022; see also Brighouse & Swift, 2016, pp. 471–97)

Contribution to the public good (understood in any sensible way, but especially understood in a way that gives special weight to the disadvantaged and induces more privileged students to learn the skills and dispositions needed to give due weight to the interests of others in decisionmaking) mitigates this harm to those who do not attend.

27.5 Taking Teaching and Mentoring Seriously

Suppose you wanted to improve the quality of instruction and mentoring in higher education. How would you go about doing so?

It depends who you are. If you were an administrator, and had enough resources and enough political room for maneuver, you would institute reforms that would create a high-quality professional learning infrastructure and reconfigure the incentive structure so that instructors would use it. You might: require PhD programs to institute teacher training; train a cadre of instructional coaches and require coaching for all first and second year instructors (whether graduate students, faculty, or staff); fund, and create incentives for, the development of high-quality measures of learning. You might require departments to train faculty in protocols for peer observation and require their use in tenure and promotion and salary decisions; and reduce reliance on adjuncts. At research institutions, you might create a track for career teachers who are not only well-compensated, but have full governance and participation rights. A 2017 American Academy for the Arts and Sciences report points to examples of colleges establishing tracks for "teaching professors" whose duties and professional development do not involve disciplinary research, but whose professional status is similar to that of the more traditional tenure track (American Academy of Arts and Sciences, 2017). Generally, you would make teaching, and the quality of teaching, a more central part of the cultural and material fabric of the institution.[6]

[6] For a more detailed discussion of possible reforms see Brighouse (2022a).

Suppose you are a tenured professor. If the above reforms have been executed, then you can, in good conscience, follow the incentives. But imagine, instead, that your institution has not been reformed. Then taking teaching and mentoring seriously is more difficult, and more costly. It is more costly exactly because in doing so you will be ignoring the incentives, thus risking that promotions and raises will be delayed and, if you are at a research institution, risking that your standing in the research community will be (somewhat) diminished. With respect to teaching: you have not just to read the literature about pedagogy in your field but learn how to discern the good literature from the bad. You probably need to devote several hours a semester to observing peers who teach well which, in turn, requires finding out who they are. You have to learn, and practice, new techniques, facing up to the reality of implementation dips (you may experience your teaching getting worse before it gets better because you haven't yet mastered the new techniques). Importantly, for relevant courses and disciplines, when you teach students who will not specialize in your discipline, you have to learn how to orient your teaching toward the knowledge, skills, attitudes, and dispositions associated with competent democratic citizenship. You need to learn how to cajole your students, who are accustomed to watching a teacher do all the hard intellectual work in a classroom, to do that work themselves. In order to do this you probably need to get to know your students, and not just the highly motivated high-achieving students who are proactive in building relationships but, more urgently, the more reserved and recalcitrant, less motivated, students. You need to find peers, or students, who are willing to observe you when you teach and give you frank feedback.

You also need to learn about mentoring, and learn how to be purposeful about building relationships with students. How do you make yourself sufficiently open that students are comfortable approaching you – especially those students who are least comfortable approaching faculty? You need to learn how to access the numerous resources on your campus that are available to support students but which students don't know about, or do know about but don't know what they're for, and you need to learn how to induce students to access them. You need to learn where the mental health resources are on your campus, and how extensive (and how limited) they are. If you are going to help students think about their career trajectories, you need at least to learn something about what careers that students majoring in your subjects do after graduating, and, again, where the career advising resources are on your campus and how extensive (and how limited) they are. If you have learned how to make yourself available to students, your office hours will likely be busier, and will probably overrun, so you need to set them at times of the day and week when students are liable to come, and when you can afford an overrun.

All this involves, at minimum, real time costs. The compensation is the fulfillment that comes from a job well done. But professors whose salaries are governed by strict union contracts will not get paid more for doing these things. And professors at the many institutions (which include, but are by no means limited to, R1s) for which research is the main determinant of pay-raises risk losing salary over time, because much of the time spent in the ways I have described above could otherwise have been spent doing research.

27.6 Why Individual Tenured Professors Are Required to Take Teaching and Mentoring *Seriously*

I've claimed that tenured professors are morally required to spend more time, energy, and effort on improving their teaching and mentoring than the incentive structure supports. Perhaps *considerably* more. And that they are obliged to suffer whatever professional consequences flow from that, even if none of their colleagues do any more than the incentives support. Why? My answer proceeds in two stages. The first, in this section, explains why they have *some* obligation. The second, in Section 27.7, argues that the extent of that obligation is considerable.

When something bad happens, which agent or agents, if any, have obligations to correct it? When it is easy to identify the perpetrator of the harm, and it is feasible for that person to correct it or to make them correct it, that perpetrator has the obligation. But in some cases, it is difficult to identify a specific perpetrator, or impossible for the perpetrator to make restitution or mitigation, or they refuse to and it is impossible to force them to. In those cases, we want to know which nonperpetrating agents, if any, should bear the costs of, and any risks associated with, restitution or mitigation.

The bad in question is suboptimal teaching and mentoring in undergraduate programs, and the consequent harms to students and the public good. Take a tenured professor in a university which has not implemented the kinds of reform mooted in Section 27.2, and whose colleagues have not committed to taking teaching and mentoring seriously in the ways described in Section 27.5. Why should he, at cost to himself, feel obliged to bear the costs of mitigating the resulting harms by taking teaching and mentoring seriously in those ways?

He meets three conditions, each of which separately supports him taking on that obligation, and which, I think, jointly provide conclusive support.

First, he is *relatively privileged*. Professors tend not to feel privileged, but they earn considerably more than the median wage; have jobs that are remarkably stimulating, meaningful, and enjoyable; and, if tenured, have a kind of job security that is unmatched in almost any other profession. Tenured professors at more selective institutions also typically enjoy a remarkable level of control over what they do and over their own workflow (Lawford Smith, 2016; Dunham & Lawford Smith, 2017).

Second, he is *implicated* in the risks students take, and a specific harm to the public good that higher education generates. Let's start with the risks: he derives his livelihood from, and enjoys the benefits described in the previous paragraph thanks to, his employer inducing students to take those risks. If he teaches on a residential campus, the business model depends on students living almost exclusively among others of a similar age, and taking the risks attendant on that choice. Whatever kind of campus he works on, it induces students to take on the risks associated with debt and failure at that campus. And, especially if he works on a selective campus, he is implicated in the positional harm to those who do not attend college that this chapter has discussed (Brighouse & Swift, 2016; Schouten, 2022). Whatever his awareness of the situation, and whatever his attitude toward the institution, in taking his living from it he implicates himself in these risks and harms (Butt, 2007, 2014; Goodin & Barry, 2014).

Third, he is *well placed* to do the work of mitigation. With respect to student learning this is obvious: he has considerable control over what happens in his classroom. He can engage students who might not otherwise be engaged; induce them to take on the intellectual work of the classroom; forge them into a learning community; radiate a sense of excitement and possibility. In a highly individualized system of teaching, in which little control is exerted externally over the instructor, he is better placed than anyone to ensure that valuable learning happens in his classroom, if he has the requisite skills and the will to exercise them. It might not be so obvious that he is well positioned to mitigate the costs and risks that students face through mentoring. After all, most campuses have considerable cadres of student-facing professionals: financial aid specialists, academic deans, mental health counsellors, career advising services and academic advisors. These professional roles are essential. So what is there left for professors to do?

On residential campuses in which students live and study largely with people their own age, and are mostly some distance from their families, they see very few responsible older adults on the kind of iterated basis that enables them to deepen mutual acquaintance. Mainly, those few are their instructors. Their interactions with student service professionals tend to be focused on immediate problems, and the purpose is to get a satisfactory resolution. The professional sees the student once or twice, and knows them only through focus on that problem. But the professor sees his students regularly, and can get to know them intellectually, in interactions that are divorced from any particular problem the student might need help with. In the best circumstances, something that Paul Weithman calls "academic friendship" can emerge (Weithman, 2016). But even in other circumstances, if the teacher can make him or herself available enough, and can be purposeful in their interaction with particular students, they will be the first stop when a problem emerges. Sometimes, if the problem is small and readily solved, they might be the last stop. In other cases, though, they are often the facilitator of interaction with the appropriate student-facing professionals, whose roles are often opaque to students in need. If I may indulge in an anecdote, here's what a graduating senior told me in 2017: "College was great for me, and nothing went badly wrong. But I always knew that if anything did go badly wrong I would come to you and you would give and find me the support that I needed. And I knew I could send my friends to you too." (She had, in fact, sent a friend to me.)

27.7 Why Individual Professors Have a Duty to Change Even in the Absence of Reform

Most tenure-line professors in selective universities currently have both teaching and research duties, have strong incentives to take their research much more seriously than their teaching and mentoring, and lack a well-constructed infrastructure to support improvement in their teaching and mentoring. This section is devoted to arguing that the extent to which individual professors should change their behavior, regardless of whether reforms are introduced to change incentives and regardless of whether they expect their colleagues to comply with the obligations they share, is considerable. They should change their behavior, devoting time energy and attention to improving their pedagogy and to individually and purposefully mentoring students even when it involves taking risks and bearing costs, and even though doing so will be more difficult (as well as less well rewarded) than if appropriate incentives and infrastructure were in place.

How might someone deny the claim I am making? One might hold the view that an agent who is implicated in, or a beneficiary of, an institutional injustice or harm that they have not caused has an obligation to respond to and to obey the rules, and to support effort to correct the injustice or eliminate the bad at the institutional level (as does everybody else). But the agent has no special obligation to go *beyond that* by divesting themselves of any part of the benefit, or making personal contributions to ameliorating the injustice or harm. Let's call this the position *No-contribution*.[7]

Anyone who holds no-contribution, however persuasive they find the analysis and argument I have made so far, will be unpersuaded that they, or any other professor, should change their behavior, absent reform. But the position seems false. Consider Peter and Sam. Peter has a large fortune, whereas Sam is close to destitute. Peter's fortune was inherited from his father. But the reason Sam is close to destitute is that his father left him nothing; and the reason for this was that his father had nothing to leave, it having been stolen by Peter's father. The statute of limitations on theft has long since expired. Peter did not commit any wrong. But it seems implausible to say that he owes Sam *nothing at all*.

At the other end of the spectrum of demandingness in conditions of mass noncompliance with the demands that bear on all of us collectively is what one might call *maximal contribution*. This is the position Peter Singer takes about our individual obligations to the global poor in his famous paper "Famine, Affluence, and Morality." The maximal contributor takes no time for himself. In our context, he relentlessly improves his pedagogical skills, and spends every possible hour mentoring or supporting students, taking up the slack left by his recalcitrant colleagues, and entirely forgoing the pay-raises, promotions, and status associated with research productivity (Singer, 1972).

Few people endorse maximal contribution. But it is far from the only alternative to no-contribution, and my recommendations do not depend on its truth.[8] The conceptual space between no-contribution and maximal contribution is very large, and my position that individual professors are obliged to act differently, and to refrain from merely responding to institutional incentives, only

[7] If *no-contribution* were true then the objector would be right to reject the idea that professors have an obligation to do anything other than follow the existing institutional incentives, even if my analysis of what elite higher education does is right, and even if I am right that professors are implicated in, and beneficiaries of, injustice. But someone could hold *no-contribution* and still think that leaders of elite institutions have obligations to change the incentives to which professors are permitted to respond.

[8] In fact, they may be incompatible with it: if it is true, I suspect that the right thing for most professors to do, unless they are past their late middle age, would be to abandon academic life and do something entirely different.

depends on rejecting *no-sacrifice* and positions very close to it on the spectrum. Consider, for example, the view, advanced by Liam Murphy, which I'll call *fair share contribution*, that in nonideal conditions where others will not comply with the demands of justice, one is required to contribute exactly as much as one would have to contribute if everyone were doing their fair share (Murphy, 2000). In fact, I believe this view must understate what is required of us under nonideal conditions – it is too lenient – but suppose that it is true. It's difficult to calculate "fair share" when it comes to teaching and learning, but with respect to mentoring it is easier. Divide the number of undergraduate students on your campus by the number of instructional faculty, and ask whether that represents the number of students on your campus who would feel that it was easy to call on you for reliable source in a time of crisis, minor or major. If it is that number or above then you are doing your fair share; if not then you are not. Professors would be required to reorient *some*, though *not all*, of their (considerable) discretionary time, energy, and attention in the ways I have suggested.

Why is Murphy's view too lenient? Imagine that you are alone and see two children drowning, both of whom you could easily save with very little cost or risk to yourself. In those circumstances you are morally required to save both. Now imagine a new situation that differs only in that an additional adult is present, who could easily save either child, but whom you know will not lift a finger. In this case your fair share would be saving one child. But, given the noncompliance of the other adult, and that you would be obliged to save both if the other adult were absent, it seems implausible that in the second situation all that you are required to do is save *one* child. Here's the mentoring analogue. Suppose the ratio of faculty to students is 1:17. Then fair share is 17. But suppose 34 needed mentoring and nobody else was around to do it. Then you'd be obliged to mentor 34. Now imagine that the ratio is 1:17, but you know without doubt that a colleague will mentor none, and no-one else will pick up the slack. Then it seems that you are obliged to pick up that slack.

Whatever our obligations are, they should not be sensitive to the addition of morally indolent other people to a situation in the way that Murphy's view makes them.

As long as no-contribution is false, the call for professors to alter their behavior even in the absence of changed incentives and in the absence of others similarly situated doing so has *some* force. The further the truth is from no-contribution, the more force the call has.

As I've said, the obligation to do at least and probably more than one's fair share of taking teaching and learning and mentoring seriously bears risks and costs. That said, the costs and risks attached to doing our duties in nonideal conditions are not *given*. Agents can reduce both. Changed incentives and training help. One way that firefighters, for example, reduce risk is through training so that they are better able to meet the challenges associated with their professional duties. Of course, administrators, departments, and individual senior professors can all reduce the risks to junior professors of becoming better teachers, and of mentoring and supporting students more effectively, by helping to train them, so that less of their time and energy is absorbed by trial and error as they learn how to teach. Higher-quality preparation of teachers while students are in graduate school would also lower the costs and risks to those students of engaging in higher-quality instruction once they are professors.

But, even absent changed incentives and support, the net costs tenured professors experience from investing in becoming better instructors can also be reduced both by adapting their interests and changing their identities, so that they enjoy successful instruction and identify more as instructors. Among the rewards professors get from research is confidence in the satisfaction of a job well done; they are able to enjoy this because the culture of the research enterprise has, ever since Boyle, been one in which members of the community publicly scrutinize and judge one another's performances. The culture of instruction in research universities (and, for that matter, in K-12 schools) in the US, by contrast, is one of secrecy, isolation, and nonjudgment, so that even when one is successful one lacks reason to be confident that one has *been* successful. Inviting colleagues to observe one's teaching; requesting to observe theirs; expanding one's reference group to include other faculty who are invested in continuous improvement in their teaching; consuming the research about instruction in one's discipline and, possibly, contributing to that research, are all ways of entering a culture around instruction that resembles the culture of research and making available to one the reward of some degree of confidence that one is doing a valuable job well. As long as *some* of one's colleagues are doing their part, opportunities are available to participate in such a culture in a small way. But even in the absence of fellow-travelers one can change one's own reward structure somewhat. One of the intrinsic rewards of teaching is seeing the development of individual students. This is quite difficult to experience in a 15-week semester, especially with large classes. But in large research departments, tenured professors at least tend to have a fair amount of say in what classes they teach. Choosing (when possible) to teach first-year students, choosing to teach sequential classes (Fall/Spring), and recruiting from one class to the next, all allow one to see the same students repeatedly, thus gaining the reward (with luck, and good mentoring and instruction) of seeing them grow.

27.8 Concluding Comments

I have argued that professors have duties to improve their teaching and mentoring, that these duties are grounded their benefiting from and implicated in an institution that exposes students to specific risks and imposes certain costs on the disadvantaged, and that these duties hold for individual professors even if the incentive structure does not change and even if their colleagues refrain from doing what duty requires. I conclude by considering some objections.

Somebody might object that not every professor has the capacity to become a good instructor or to develop the expertise needed to mentor students effectively. It wouldn't be surprising if this were true, given that professors are hired almost without regard to their potential at these activities. If I am saying something is obligatory that is, in fact, and contrary to my belief, not possible, then it is not obligatory after all: because "ought implies can," nobody has a duty to do more than they *can* do.[9] Of course, different agents have different potentials and limits. One person might be able to become a superb instructor; another might be able to become a superb mentor; one professor might be able to open themselves up in a way that induces students with mental illnesses to seek help, and become adept at convincing them to go to counseling services and see psychiatrists. Another might be able to help aspiring elementary teachers to become more reflective about their practice; a mediocre teacher of calculus might only be able, even with considerable effort and support, to become a little better than mediocre. My assumption is only that most professors could improve somewhat at these aspects of their job. The task of the moral agent is to figure out what their own space is for moral action, do at least whatever they are morally required to do within it, and attempt, where possible, to expand the space available to them. In doing this, we should beware of our tendency to underestimate our space for moral action, when our own interests might be put at risk by the course morality recommends.

A second objection, which can only be advanced by someone at an elite *research* institution, is that my conclusion undervalues research, which is the central part of the job of a professor at a research institution.

Some staff researchers, many of whose salaries are paid through "soft money," and many of whom are well paid but lack the protections of tenure, do not have any instructional duties, and are not regularly in contact with undergraduates. My call is not directed at them. And professors do not have a duty to violate the terms of their contracts: if doing research is part of one's contractual obligations one should continue to do research, and attempt to do it well. But, typically, even in research institutions, research is held to be coequal with teaching, for tenure-line professors. To the extent that research serves teaching there is no conflict. But the idea that research and teaching are always synergetic seems unlikely; when conflicts arise, professors get to make largely unmonitored choices about which to take more seriously; my call is to make the choice in favor of teaching more often than at present.

A third objection is that people who are implicated in some harm should extricate themselves from that situation, so that they are no longer implicated, rather than continuing to enjoy the benefits associated with their position and compensating by changing the way they approach it. Professors, in other words, should not change their behavior qua professor; they should resign.

Even if something like maximal contribution is correct, there is no duty to divest oneself of the benefits of being implicated in the risks to students and harms to the public good when that would do no good for anyone: think, for example, of resigning and taking a job as a house cleaner. *Nevertheless,* if

[9] Conversely, if more is possible than I believe, then *more* might be obligatory than I think.

something like maximal contribution is correct, it does seem quite plausible that someone's obligations might extend beyond changing behavior within a job to giving it up if they can, thereby, contribute more to the public good. Then it may well be that professors should resign, and seek more lucrative employment that enables them to donate very considerable sums to charities that serve the disadvantaged. Perhaps, if they can become good enough instructors, they should find employment at nonelite institutions (probably at considerably lower salaries). I assume, though, that few of my readers will actually be motivated to take such a dramatic step. The discussion in Section 27.6 was addressed, then, to readers who, either because they are convinced that *nothing like* the *maximal self-sacrifice* view is correct, or because they are weak-willed, will remain in their positions, but are, nevertheless, willing to change their behavior within those positions.

Finally, some readers might suspect me of political complacency. Haven't I implicitly assumed that the prevailing injustices, such as large inequalities of income and wealth and inequalities of educational opportunity are unchanged, and urged beneficiaries of injustice to be dispensed charity?

This objection seems to me to be animated by a quite understandable revulsion against nonideal theorizing of the kind this paper exemplifies. My question is *not* what the world should be like, or what we should do to change it, but *how we should change our behavior within it given that it is not, and will not in the near future be, the way it should be.* I am interested in what *beneficiaries* of that social structure are obliged to do, given the unjust social structure which I, and you, the (typically, relatively advantaged) reader, will inhabit for the foreseeable future. Readers who anticipate large-scale social change in the short- term future will see this as a merely academic exercise, because they believe that the conditions in which those duties hold are very temporary. I think they are wrong about that. Professors can choose simply to enjoy the benefits their institutions confer on them, or to be agents in ameliorating and mitigating some of its bad effects. In doing the latter, though, one is not dispensing charity; one is simply fulfilling the obligations that, even if they are underspecified by one's contract, accompany one's job.[10]

References

American Academy of Arts & Sciences. (2017). *The future of undergraduate education.* Available at: https://www.amacad.org/publication/future-undergraduate-education.

American College Health Association (ACHA). (2016). *National College Health Assessment II: Spring 2016 Reference Group Executive Summary.* Hanover, MD:

[10] Thanks are due to the numerous audiences that have heard or read, and commented on, versions of this chapter including, especially, several undergraduate classes at UW-Madison. I'm especially grateful also for helpful comments to Tony Laden, Jen Morton, Michael McPherson, Kyla Ebels-Duggan, Christopher Martin, Diana Hess, Emma Prendergast, Andree-Anne Cormier, Luke Gangler, Grace Gecewicz and, of course, to Gina Schouten and David O'Brien. Also, thank you to Madelyn Aaronson for editorial and research assistance.

American College Health Association. Available at: https://www.acha.org/documents/ncha/NCHA-II%20SPRING%202016%20US%20REFERENCE%20GROUP%20EXECUTIVE%20SUMMARY.pdf.

Baum, S. (2016). *Student debt: Rhetoric and realities of higher education financing*. London: Palgrave Macmillan.

Bok, D. (2008). *Our underachieving colleges*. Princeton, NJ: Princeton University Press.

Brighouse, H. (2022a). Taking teaching and learning seriously. Really seriously. In S. Cahn, ed., *Academic ethics today: Problems, policies, and prospects for university life*. Lanham, MD: Rowman & Littlefield, pp. 261–72.

Brighouse, H. (2022b). Deliberative responsibility and civic education in universities and colleges in the US. In J. Culp, J. Drerup, I. de Groot, A. Schinkel & D. Yacek, eds., *Liberal democratic education: A paradigm in crisis*. Paderborn: Brill | Mentis, pp. 1–23.

Brighouse, H., & Swift, A. (2016). Equality, priority, and positional goods. *Ethics*, 116(3), 471–97.

Butt, D. (2007). On benefiting from injustice. *Canadian Journal of Philosophy*, 37(1), 129–52.

Butt, D. (2014). A doctrine quite new and altogether untenable: Defending the beneficiary pays principle. *Journal of Applied Philosophy*, 31(4), 336–48.

Dunham, J., & Lawford-Smith, H. (2017). Offsetting race privilege. *Journal of Ethics and Social Philosophy*, 11(2), 1–22.

Goodin, R., & Barry, C. (2014). Benefiting from the wrongdoing of others. *Journal of Applied Philosophy*, 31(4), 363–76.

Johnson, W.B. (2016). *On being a mentor: A guide for higher education faculty*. New York: Routledge.

Lawford Smith, H. (2016). Offsetting class privilege. *Journal of Practical Ethics*, 4(1), 23–51.

Martin, C (2021). *The right to higher education: A political theory*. Oxford: Oxford University Press.

Murphy, L. (2000). *Moral demands in nonideal theory*. Oxford: Oxford University Press.

Rawls, J. (1971). *A theory of justice*. Cambridge MA: Harvard University Press.

Schouten, G. (2022). The case for egalitarian consciousness raising in higher education. *Philosophical Studies*. https://doi.org/10.1007/s11098-022-01808-3.

Singer, P. (1972). Famine, affluence, and morality. *Philosophy and Public Affairs*, 1(3), 229–43.

Weithman, P. (2016). Academic friendship. In H. Brighouse & M. McPherson, eds., *The aims of higher education: Problems of morality and justice*. Chicago IL: University of Chicago Press, pp. 52–73.

28

Racism, Moral Transformation, and Democratic Education

Ilya Zrudlo

28.1 Introduction

It is a basic premise of this chapter that prejudices of all kinds, including racism, are inimical to a democratic society and that democratic education should therefore enable students to overcome them. Beyond simply recognizing the fact that racism is bad and becoming aware of the myriad ways in which it manifests itself, a democratic education should, among other aims, empower students to be able to contribute to a process of change, at least in their own local contexts, in which racism is steadily reduced if not eliminated. Being able to contribute to such a process implies, among other things, that a student is endowed with the capacities required to help *others* overcome racial prejudice. In other words, they need the capacities that would enable them to take practical steps that successfully result in others around them – their families, peers, neighbors, etc. – setting aside racist beliefs, attitudes, and behaviors. But what are these capacities? And how can they be fostered in students?

This chapter offers a modest contribution to the work of answering these critical questions for democratic education. Not only are these questions vital, but they are also quite complex, and demand several complementary approaches and methods from a variety of disciplines. One promising approach, I will argue, is to examine closely actual instances in which young people were able to successfully assist one or more members of their community to overcome racist beliefs, attitudes, and behaviors. A close analysis of such cases, which focuses on the capacities demonstrated by the students involved, would allow us to get a better sense of what some of the requisite capacities are. We may also observe clues as to how these capacities might be deliberately fostered in students. The bulk of my chapter involves a philosophical analysis of one such case in the recent past, constituting what I will call a "moral microhistory." It is the case of the transformation of Derek Black, a former white nationalist.

I first outline my approach, with reference to what Kwame Anthony Appiah (2014) has called a "natural experiment" (p. 22) in moral philosophy. I then briefly summarize the story of the transformation of Derek Black, which has been eloquently captured by the award-winning journalist Eli Saslow (2016, 2018). My philosophical analysis follows, in which I highlight certain details of the story that offer insight into the nature of the capacities the students who interacted with Derek appeared to possess. Two major sets of capacities emerge: capacities relevant to friendship and capacities related to the promotion of truth and justice.

Appiah (2014) explains the "natural experiment" approach by drawing an analogy with certain kinds of research in the sciences that mine historical evidence since the nature of their work does not permit them to carry out laboratory experiments. For example, economists might wonder about the effect of immigration on economic growth. They cannot, of course, carry out society-wide experiments, asking two similar regions of a country to adopt different immigration policies and then measure the results. However, they can examine historical data in order to see if there are any correlations. Examining the historical data constitutes a kind of natural experiment, that is, an experiment that occurred naturally, and whose results one can see in the records to which we have access. Appiah (2014) encourages philosophers to consider taking a similar approach, but in this case focusing on "the moral history of our species" (p. 22). He took this approach in *The Honor Code: How Moral Revolutions Happen* (2010), which examined certain changes in moral norms over several decades. Appiah looked at, for example, changes in norms about the previously widespread practice of dueling.

In this chapter, I focus on the moral transformation of one US college student, Derek Black, and the role of others in this transformation, over a period of a few years in the recent past. This "moral microhistory," as it were, was captured by the journalist Eli Saslow in 2016 in a piece for *The Washington Post*. The article documented the gradual transformation of Derek Black, who eventually cut himself off from the white nationalism with which he had grown up and which he had helped propagate. Saslow (2018) subsequently published a book titled *Rising Out of Hatred: The Awakening of a Former White Nationalist*, which expands on the same story. Derek Black is the son of Don Black and the godson of David Duke – important names in the white nationalist movement. A crucial factor in Derek's transformation was his interactions with several students in college who deliberately befriended him in part to assist him to set aside his views. The process of this transformation – captured in interviews conducted by Saslow as well as a plethora of documentary evidence he gathered from his interviewees, such as emails, student forum posts, text messages, etc. – constitutes the data for my "natural experiment" in moral philosophy.

This approach offers several benefits, beyond addressing the questions related to democratic education that I have posed. First, it offers a fresh perspective on the analysis of racism in contemporary philosophy. Many philosophers have turned their attention to the issue of racism, analyzing, for instance, the different ways in which racism operates (e.g., Liao & Huebner, 2020), what should be done about "race talk" given issues with the very concept of race (e.g., Glasgow, 2008; Wodak, 2021), and the kind of injustice(s) involved in certain racist acts (e.g., Mogensen, 2017). However, very little philosophical work has been carried out on actual instances of the reduction or elimination of racism, such as Derek Black's story. While we are getting increasingly sophisticated accounts of racism itself, there is far less clarity about how it can be overcome, or, better, how it *has* been overcome in particular instances and what we can learn from such cases.

A second upshot of my approach is that it brings back into view a central aim of philosophy: to examine how we ought to live. While it may be an accurate description of some or even most (contemporary) professional ethics to say that it has little influence on our ability to become better people (e.g., Schwitzgebel, 2014), this is, in my opinion, a rather deplorable situation. I would rather echo Pierre Hadot (1995) and argue that philosophy – especially moral philosophy and philosophy of education – ought to help us live better lives. This can be easily lost from view in contemporary professional philosophy. My focus on a real case of moral improvement brings back into view the idea of living better. This is in part because some of the characters in Derek's story take exemplary moral actions and reflecting upon them is thus morally edifying in and of itself (Zagzebski, 2017).

28.2 Summary of the Case Study

Derek Black's father, Don Black, was formerly part of the Ku Klux Klan. Don Black established what is probably the most infamous white nationalist website in history: Stormfront. A number of active members of the forum have gone on to commit hate crimes, including killings (Saslow, 2018). Don groomed his son Derek as a future white nationalist. Saslow (2016) explains that Derek was taught as a child that, "America was a place for white Europeans and that everyone else would eventually have to leave. He was told to be suspicious of other races, of the US government, of tap water and of pop culture." He often accompanied his father on trips to white nationalist meetings. Derek founded the children's version of Stormfront when he was 10 years old and was already speaking at white nationalist political events as a teenager. Around this age, he was actively working to promote the idea of a white genocide and the need to take back the country. He was seen by other white nationalists, including his father, as the heir to the movement, its future mainstream face.

At 21, Derek transferred to New College in Florida, a small liberal arts school, to study history. The school was about three hours away from home, so, for the first time, Derek lived apart from his parents. Early on, he realized that he would be ostracized on campus if he mentioned anything about white nationalism, so he decided not to say anything about this aspect of his life. He made friends with a few other dorm students, including a Peruvian immigrant and an Orthodox Jew. Derek quite liked his new friends and Saslow (2016) explains that "he went from keeping his convictions quiet to actively disguising them," pretending, for example, on one occasion that he had never heard of the website Stormfront. At the same time, however, he continued to secretly promote white nationalist propaganda through the radio program he hosted with his father. Multiple times a week, in the mornings, he would call in to the program and talk about how nonwhite immigration was destroying America.

An older student, who "considered it part of his responsibility to call out others when their behavior demanded it" (Saslow, 2018, ch. 3), eventually found out who Derek was and publicized this information on a student message board. The news spread like wildfire. Derek was immediately ostracized and began receiving threats. On the student message board, for example, one person wrote: "I just want this guy to die a painful death along with his entire family. Is that too much to ask?" (Saslow, 2016). On campus, people would swear at him, throw things at him, and avoid his presence. One student, out of fear of Derek, obtained a permit to carry a concealed weapon and purchased a gun. Some tried to pressure the administration to get him expelled and planned and carried out intimidation and exclusion tactics. They wrote to other students: "Ignore Derek. Heckle him. Make him feel uncomfortable" (Saslow, 2018, ch. 3). Derek did not engage with any of these comments or provocations. He had been used to receiving hate mail and tried to ignore these in a similar way. It appears that he used the experience "as motivation to plan a conference for white nationalists in East Tennessee" (Saslow, 2016). The treatment he received effectively pushed him deeper into white nationalism. However, the messages from some of his (former) friends (including a girl he had developed feelings for prior to the news breaking out about his affiliation with white nationalism) hurt him more than he thought they would. He moved out of the dorms, opting to live alone near school.

A small minority of students felt that ostracizing Derek would not accomplish anything, and that they had a chance to be real activists if they managed to change his mind. One of these students was Derek's (former) friend, Matthew, who was an Orthodox Jew. When Derek's identity was revealed, Matthew started following his activities: his previous posts on Stormfront, his radio show, etc. It became clear to Matthew that anti-Semitism was integral to Derek's white nationalism. Derek himself had posted on Stormfront that "Jews are NOT white"; that "Jews worm their way into power over our society"; and that "They must go" (Saslow, 2016). After some deep reflection, Matthew decided finally to invite Derek to his weekly Shabbat dinner that he held at his campus apartment. Saslow (2016) explains that "Matthew decided his best chance to affect Derek's thinking was not to ignore him or confront him, but simply to include him." For the first dinner, Matthew instructed everyone else who attended to treat Derek like anyone else, and not to bring up white nationalism or the student forum. Derek was quiet and polite at the first dinner he attended, and he ended up coming back again and again. Gradually, Derek rekindled some friendships and found new ones through the Shabbat dinners, including with Matthew's roommate, Allison.

In the months that followed, some of his Shabbat dinner friends, especially Allison, began asking him to clarify his racial beliefs: did he really believe that white people were superior? No, he explained, he just thought each race was better off living on its own. Should immigrants be deported by force? He backtracked: well, not now, perhaps gradual self-deportation would be the way; no one should be forced to leave America (Saslow, 2016). Gradually, over the course of his time in college, his views softened. He slowly stopped posting on Stormfront. He also appeared less and less on the radio show with his dad, giving him various made-up excuses. Allison sent him links to scientific studies, gradually dismantling the conspiracies and falsehoods he had been taught as a child. He was also studying history and became fascinated with the Islamic world. He realized that it had been far ahead of medieval Europe, which he had initially assumed was the cradle of a superior "white" civilization. He also came to understand that the modern concept of race was itself a relatively recent invention. All of this combined to draw him further and further away from the beliefs with which he had grown up.

Shortly after graduation, Derek wrote a public statement disavowing white nationalism and cutting ties with the movement. He was practically disowned by his family as a result. After college, he moved across the country to pursue graduate studies. Saslow offers many more details regarding this fascinating story, to which I have not done justice here, but this summary should offer sufficient background to begin examining specific details of the case, which I will fill out through additional references to Saslow's investigations.

28.3 Capacities Demonstrated by Derek's Friends

What enabled Derek's friends to contribute so decisively to his transformation? Why did they choose to take the kinds of actions they ended up taking, whereas other students avoided Derek, or harassed him? Derek's friends acted very much against the grain of the wider campus ethos, in some cases incurring some of the same ire Derek was attracting. What convictions, attitudes, virtues, and skills did they possess that allowed them to act as they did? I want to highlight two sets of capacities that seem particularly central: capacities relevant to friendship, and capacities related to the promotion of truth and justice.

28.3.1 Capacities Relevant to Friendship

After his repudiation of white nationalism, Derek wrote to a reporter about the path that led him to do so, emphasizing the role his friends played in fostering his transformation:

> [A] critical juncture was when I'd realize that a friend was considered an outsider by the philosophy I supported. It's a huge contradiction to share your summer plans with someone whom you completely respect, only to then realize that your ideology doesn't consider them a full member of society. I couldn't resolve that. (Saslow, 2018, ch. 11)

I will return to the "contradiction" Derek highlights here, but I want to first focus on the process from the point of view of his friends, since it is *their* capacity for friendship that concerns me here.

Saslow's narrative makes it clear that the effort to befriend Derek was at least initially strategic. This was especially the case for Matthew, who wanted to try this approach because he felt that shaming or ostracizing Derek would be useless:

> "There is no better way to make sure Derek keeps these abhorrent views than if we all exclude him," Matthew said. But nonjudgmental inclusion – Matthew believed that tactic had potential, and the more he researched Derek, the more convinced he became. . . . [I]nstead of trying to build a case, Matthew began working to build a relationship in which Derek might be able to learn what the enemy was actually like. "The goal was really just to make Jews more human for him," Matthew said. (ch. 4)

Talking about "tactics" and "goals" may strike some readers as fundamentally incompatible with friendship. How could the friendship be genuine, one might ask, if Matthew had an agenda (regardless of whether Derek was aware of it)?

There are at least three ideas that might motivate reticence to call Matthew's approach here "friendship": (i) that true friendship is about accepting your friends for who they are, not wanting to change them; (ii) that if you want to morally improve your friend, this implies that you feel morally superior to them, and therefore this cannot be a true friendship; and (iii) that it is incompatible with friendship to treat the relationship as a means to some other end. There are grains of truth in these assertions, but they are ultimately untenable, and in fact constitute obstacles to developing the kind of capacity Matthew demonstrated. I will address each in turn.

One assumption embedded in objection (i) is a rather superficial version of the ideal of authenticity: that each person should strive to dig deep within themselves, discover their true selves, and then learn to express this self. Your true friends, from this perspective, are those who encourage you to undertake this journey of self-discovery and unhesitatingly embrace and accept whatever person eventually emerges from within – which is truly "who you are." Wanting to change a friend becomes viewed as an outside imposition, if not a betrayal of the friendship. Much ink has been spilled tracing the Romantic roots of this individualistic and solipsistic notion of authenticity, eviscerating it completely, and retrieving a more serviceable notion of being true to oneself (e.g., Bialystok, 2014; Larmore, 2010; Taylor, 1991; Williams, 2002). Nietzsche offers an alternative version of the ideal of authenticity, arguing that "your true nature lies, not buried deep within you but immeasurably high above you, or at least above that which you usually take yourself to be" (quoted in Jonas & Yacek, 2019, p. 103). From this perspective, a true friend would be one who helps you see your true nature, which is not hidden deep within (which would be inaccessible to outsiders), but rather lies "immeasurably high above you." Someone who accepts you exactly as you are may even hold back your progress, encouraging the development of complacency.

If Matthew had held the idea that friendship was merely about "accepting" your friends, he might not have even reached out in the first place. Juan, the

Peruvian immigrant Derek had met early on in his first semester, similarly held a more dynamic conception of friendship. Saslow (2018) writes:

> Juan had read through some of Derek's Stormfront posts over the summer – "all this bizarre and horrifying stuff about brown people," he remembered – but ultimately Juan trusted his own instincts more than what he read on the internet. If Derek truly despised brown people, why had he spent dozens of hours cultivating a friendship with a Peruvian immigrant? Juan decided to believe that Derek was already in the inevitable process of changing his views. "Glad you are indeed coming back," Juan wrote to Derek. "[New College] can learn a lot from you, and you can learn a lot from it as well." (ch. 3)

Objection (ii), the charge of moral superiority, contains a valid point: that feeling proud of being morally superior to one's friends (even if it is true) is inimical to friendship (and is, moreover, ethically dangerous in and of itself). However, to want to morally improve one's friend is not contrary to friendship. In fact, as Kristjánsson (2020) has argued, along Aristotelian lines, there is a case to be made for the fundamental moral educational nature of friendship: that the central purpose of friendship is the mutual moral improvement of friends. In most cases, friends will naturally be unequal with respect to their development of certain virtues, and therefore can learn from one another to become, for example, more courageous or humble. The uneasiness some may feel about this kind of talk stems from a radical moral egalitarianism that is (rightly) wary of self-righteousness – but this position is ultimately untenable. First, while moral progress cannot and should not be measured in any literal sense, people quite clearly differ in their moral attainments. Second, denying this fact can easily cause one to slide into resentment when one runs into its reality (Jonas & Yacek, 2019). Paradoxically, by shunning those who seek to morally improve others (including oneself) and projecting onto them self-serving attitudes they do not necessarily possess, one can become self-righteous as a result.

That Matthew wanted to help Derek improve morally, then, is not a reason to doubt the genuine nature of the friendship that was established. Thinking like this would have, in fact, hampered Matthew's ability to sincerely build a friendship with Derek.

Finally, objection (iii), about treating the friendship as a means, likewise contains a grain of truth. It is certainly the case that if Matthew thought of or treated the relationship with Derek strictly in an instrumental way, it would not really qualify as a true friendship. However, we can add the nuance (adapted from Kant himself) that a friendship could in a sense be a "means" as long as it is not *solely* conceived in this way. Schwarzenbach (1996), in a paper on civic friendship, argues that these kinds of friendships help bring about a just society. In a footnote accompanying this statement she explains:

> Here we must recognize a class of actions that are both ends in themselves and also constituents in (not "a means to") some wider end. Consider each individual step of a dance; each step is not a mere means to the total dance,

> but each is performed for its own sake and for the sake of the dance as a whole. I believe a similar relationship holds between friendship and justice; for Aristotle friendly civic relationships are valuable for their own sake, and they are necessary constituents of justice. (Schwarzenbach, 1996, p. 107)

We might similarly say that initiating a friendship with Derek was seen as both an end in itself and a means to establishing a more just community (or a constitutive part of a just community, to use Schwarzenbach's preferred terms). In Matthew's case, the relationship was more of a means at first, but then became an end as well:

> It had begun for Matthew as a strictly tactical relationship – to change Derek, who in turn could change the thinking of other white nationalists about Jews and minorities – but now a friendship was growing in its place. They met some nights to play pool at the student union. Matthew bought a cake and threw Derek his birthday party . . . And so after a while Matthew decided he knew Derek well enough to stop scorekeeping their relationship. He gave up on monitoring Derek's morning radio shows to see if his language was somehow softening. He stopped waiting for some kind of public apology or a grand renunciation. (Saslow, 2018, ch. 4)

Even early on, however, Matthew was not overly attached to the results of his relationship-building strategy:

> Midway through the school year, one classmate wrote to Matthew and suggested abandoning outreach to Derek – calling it "a good idea that clearly didn't work." But Matthew was resolute. "The basic principle is that it's our job to push the rock, not necessarily to move the rock," he replied. "That's the only part we can control. Just give it time. We don't know where it will go, but I think he's already started softening." (Saslow, 2018, ch. 4)

The analogy Matthew uses here – "that it's our job to push the rock, not necessarily to move the rock" – expresses succinctly his attitude toward the friendship. He is committed to the friendship even if it will not, in the end, change Derek. This is what saves him from the charge of instrumentalizing the relationship. But the fact that he is pushing the rock, and sees it as his duty, does not invalidate the friendship. Interestingly, this case may constitute an important kind of exception to Kristjánsson's (2020) claim that "people will hardly ever offer the educational *raison d'être* as the explicit motivation for initiating or engaging in friendship" (p. 137).

Thus, our first conclusion is that the kind of capacity for friendship that is required is one that can accommodate an aspirational vision of authenticity and a moral educational aim, while also avoiding a sense of moral superiority and being detached from results. This was the kind of understanding of friendship and associated concepts that was required of Derek's friends.

Having clarified some initial points about the understanding of friendship itself, we can consider some of the capacities Derek's friends required in order to initiate the friendship. Some friendships are not deliberate at all and simply emerge spontaneously, requiring no effort or capacity to initiate per se. In other situations, however, we may go somewhat out of our way to befriend someone. For example, we may strive to develop a friendship with someone who appears to be new on campus or who seems to have few friends. It may also happen that we purposefully make friends with someone who might feel out of place in a particular setting due to a different cultural background or language. We could say that purposefully reaching out and initiating a relationship requires more capacity than simply "falling in" with a group of friends somewhat spontaneously. Initiating a friendship with Derek fell in the former category, and thus required this ability to reach out beyond one's natural associations.

There were at least two further reasons that made it particularly difficult to initiate a friendship with Derek. The first was of course the basic knowledge that had spread about his white nationalist affiliation. His online activity was also open to scrutiny. Imagine being in Matthew's shoes, reading what Derek had written about Jews on Stormfront, and inviting him over regardless. As cited earlier in this section, Juan likewise had read horrible things on Stormfront about "brown people", but reached out to Derek nonetheless.

The second reason it was particularly difficult to initiate a friendship with Derek was the setting of New College campus life, which had been stirred up by the news that one of their students was affiliated with white nationalism. Several of Derek's friends suffered as a result of being associated with him – becoming collateral damage in the ongoing campaign to exclude Derek. Another Jewish student who was involved in the Shabbat dinners, Moshe, reports that "People associated me with Derek or saw me getting in and out of his car, and that made me hugely unpopular" (Saslow, 2018, ch. 7). Around this time, a "student wellness survey suggested "expelling Derek Black and Moshe Ash" as a way to improve the New College community" (Saslow, 2018, ch. 7). Allison lost several of her friends because of her closeness with Derek: some unfriended her on Facebook after they saw her hanging out with him. Allison herself took the greatest risk of all Derek's friends by accepting his invitation to attend a Stormfront conference. She used the visit to gather more information on white nationalism so she could later debate with Derek more effectively.

Becoming friends with Derek therefore took great courage. It also required a certain ability to resist social conformism, which on their campus bent toward excluding Derek. What allowed these friends – Juan, Matthew, Moshe, and Allison especially – to build up this courage and to resist the social pressures on campus? In other words, what motivated and strengthened their efforts to build a friendship with Derek, even in the face of powerful obstacles?

First, as is clear from some of the excerpts I have cited, Derek's friends were motivated by their sense of justice. They felt that they had a chance to be "real activists" by befriending Derek and helping him change his views. I will return in Section 28.3.2 to the importance of their sense of justice, but it should be noted that the capacity to establish a friendship in this case was itself connected to their sense of justice.

A second source of motivation here, I want to suggest, is what Simone Weil called the "power of attention." It is obvious from Saslow's account that those who reached out to Derek *saw* him differently than others did. One way to describe this is that they paid close *attention* to him in the specific sense that Weil uses this term. Attention, Weil ([1947] 1999) explains, is a kind of power: "In the intellectual order, the virtue of humility is nothing less than the power of attention" (p. 128). "Attention consists of suspending our thought, leaving it detached, empty, and ready to be penetrated by the object" (Weil, 1951, p. 111). It is applicable to intellectual pursuits, but also to our relationships with others; in fact, according to Weil (1951), "the love of our neighbor ... is made of [attention]" (p. 114). Again referring to attention as a kind of power, or capacity, Weil (1951) emphasizes the difficulty of directing it to those who suffer: "The capacity to give one's attention to a sufferer is a very rare and difficult thing; it is almost a miracle; it *is* a miracle" (p. 114).

Iris Murdoch ([1970] 2014) famously picked up on Weil's idea of attention in her own work, where she writes that "the characteristic and proper mark of the active moral agent" is "a just and loving gaze directed upon an individual reality" (p. 33). "Human beings are obscure to each other," remarks Murdoch, "in certain respects which are particularly relevant to morality, unless they are mutual objects of attention or have common objects of attention" (p. 32). There are certain veils that obscure our vision of one another and of the moral situations in which we find ourselves, chief among them our "fat relentless ego" (p. 51). "Attention is the effort to counteract such states of illusion" (p. 36), and this is one reason Weil associates it with humility.

Most of Derek's friends appear to have exercised the power of attention in the way described by Weil and Murdoch. While they were all conscious of Derek's association with white nationalism – many of them spent a good amount of time researching his ideology on Stormfront – they somehow managed to look beyond this fact (as Weil might put it, they detached themselves from this thought) and focused their attention on something else. As Murdoch would put it, they focused their attention on Derek's individual reality. What did they see there?

In Kristen Renwick Monroe's (1996) classic study of altruism, she argues that altruism stems from a perception of a common humanity. It seems to me that this is part of what Matthew and the others were able to see in Derek by paying attention: *someone like them, another human being – their common humanity*. Monroe argues that this perception was what empowered individuals who harbored Jews at great personal risk in Nazi Germany. By paying close attention, Matthew and the others were able to *see* commonalities between themselves and Derek, to see a potential friend, which then helped them reach out to befriend him. All those who ostracized Derek, however, saw him merely as *other*: they could not see any common ground between them. Saslow (2018) reports:

> When some of Matthew's other friends privately denigrated Derek's character, calling him a racist and an oppressor, Matthew insisted on treating Derek with respect, even compassion. "In some ways, he just has way bigger versions of the same hang-ups we all have," Matthew told a friend once. He believed it was human nature to separate into groups, to

> define oneself against the other . . . it was natural for people to define themselves partly by what they were not. Everyone had prejudices, Matthew thought, even if Derek's were much more extreme and pronounced. (Saslow, 2018, ch. 4)

Another way of describing Matthew's disposition here is by appealing to the notion of "responsiveness," which has been discussed in recent literature on democracy and education (e.g., Warnick et al., 2018). Responsiveness is thought to be a key democratic virtue, but there are debates as to whether it is warranted when we face someone with morally suspect beliefs. In this case, Matthew was not responsive in the sense that he changed his beliefs or opinions about social reality (this is only one possible "mode" of responsiveness, as Warnick et al. (2018) put it); rather, he was responsive in that he changed *his view of Derek* (or, more precisely, retained an unpopular view in the face of social pressure), thus creating conditions for a friendship to thrive.

Saslow (2016) reports that Matthew remembers thinking to himself: "well, maybe he's [Derek] never spent time with a Jewish person before." This is not a naïve thought. Rather, it is the result of a just and loving gaze, a humble and responsive form of attention, that managed to see a potential friend where everyone else had only seen an enemy. And we know who was right in the end.

Both Weil and Murdoch connect the idea of attention to love – a third source of motivation that I want to highlight in its own right. Modern moral philosophy is notoriously squeamish about love, as Murdoch and others, such as Charles Taylor (1989), have pointed out. Moral philosophers operating from within a broadly Kantian framework, for example, might describe Derek's friend's actions as "supererogatory": they were praiseworthy but not morally obligatory (Urmson, 1958), that is, no one would have been blameworthy for *not* reaching out to Derek.[1] While this point seems true, the use of "obligatory" here might obscure the nature of what Derek's friends did and the relationship between their actions and the aims of social justice.

There is a modern tendency at play here which tends to reduce justice to the individual performance of duty. From within this framework, justice is achieved when everyone does what they ought to do, nothing more and nothing less. Demanding more from someone would be unfair and doing less would be morally blameworthy. Societies should put in place rules to make sure no one is unduly burdened and to punish those who fail in their duties. Supererogatory

[1] Warnick et al. (2018) make a similar point in their discussion of Daryl Davis – an African American musician who went out of his way to befriend members of the Ku Klux Klan, several of whom left the group as a result. They offer the caveat that "we are not saying that all people, particularly African-Americans, have a moral duty to seek out responsive interactions with hate groups, as Davis did. What he did seems to be 'supererogatory' . . . There is also something to the idea that the moral obligation to be responsive belongs much more to White America and to the hate groups themselves, after years of being unresponsive to racial minorities. There are, finally, understandable worries that a responsive posture, and with it some degree of humanization, will be taken as legitimation or normalization of morally repugnant positions. While not holding Davis up as an example for others to follow, however, we do believe that his engagement powerfully illustrates the possibility of responsiveness in *extreme* cases. More precisely, he illustrates both that responsiveness is possible in these extreme cases and that it can yield productive civic achievements. This suggests that responsiveness is also possible and beneficial in less extreme cases" (p. 38).

acts – again, viewed from within this framework – are just a nice bonus as it were, and have nothing to do with justice per se. It is certainly the case that we cannot and should not blame people for simply not acting in a morally heroic fashion. Nevertheless, I think there is a sense in which such actions – imbued with an extra measure of love that goes beyond what is socially expected – *are* necessary, at least in a collective sense, especially if we have the aims of social justice at heart. We live, after all, in what one might call, a little tongue in cheek, the "circumstances of injustice," and it is far from clear that we can improve on these circumstances without a consistent dose of so-called supererogatory actions.

We can turn to Weil (1987) once more for some relevant insights that can help us here:

> It is not easy to fight for justice. It is not enough to discern which is the side of least injustice and, having joined it, to take up arms and expose oneself to the arms of the enemy. No doubt this is beautiful, more than words can say. But on the other side men do exactly the same. What we need in addition is for the spirit of justice to dwell within us. The spirit of justice is nothing other than the supreme and perfect flower of the madness of love. The madness of love turns compassion into a far more powerful motive for any kind of action . . . than splendour, glory or even honour . . . The madness of love imbues a part of the heart deeper than indignation and courage, the place from which indignation and courage draw their strength, with tender compassion for the enemy . . . if the order of the universe is a wise order, there must sometimes be moments when, from the point of view of earthly reason, only the madness of love is reasonable. Such moments can only be those when, as today, mankind has become mad from want of love. (pp. 9–10)

Surely, it was a bit "mad" for Matthew to invite the publicly antisemitic Derek to a Shabbat dinner. Or for Allison to attend a conference for white nationalists. Logically, there was no reason for these individuals to risk themselves: viewed from the perspective of "earthly reason," it was complete madness. And yet, these friends were moved by "tender compassion for the enemy" to try to establish and nurture a relationship with Derek. While these actions may not have been morally obligatory in the technical sense (no one would deserve blame for not carrying them out), it may be that today, when "mankind has become mad from want of love," they are in another sense absolutely necessary.

Paul Ricoeur (1995) puts Weil's point a little more analytically by arguing that love and justice exist in a kind of dialectical relationship: they need one another. Briefly, Ricoeur's point is that the norms of justice can be (and have been) interpreted in very narrow terms, as a kind of self-interested utilitarian calculation. He argues that in order to protect justice from this interpretation, it needs to be complemented by love, which is governed by "the economy of the gift" (p. 33) and "develops a logic of superabundance" (pp. 33–34). It is this logic of superabundance, associated with love, that protects justice from degenerating into utilitarian scorekeeping. Derek's friends' capacity for friendship was motivated by the logic of superabundance associated with love, which strengthens one's ability to promote justice.

Finally, I want to briefly consider the *effect* of the friendships on Derek. Friendship, as can be evidently gleaned from Saslow's narrative, is a powerful means for transformation. Derek cites his friendships as one of the main factors in his eventual repudiation of white nationalism. We can therefore think of friendship as a kind of *power* – but one unlike political or economic power. Hannah Arendt (1958) offers some insight into the kind of power friendship might be:

> Power is actualized only where word and deed have not parted company, where words are not empty and deeds not brutal, where words are not used to veil intentions but to disclose realities, and deeds are not used to violate and destroy but to establish relations and create new realities. (p. 200)[2]

The initial threats Derek had received on the student message board consisted of truly empty words and the threat of brutal deeds. These words were *powerless* to change him, pushing him instead deeper into white nationalism. Those who reached out to Derek, by contrast, used their words and deeds to "establish relations", what eventually became their close friendships with him. And these friendships created a new reality: namely, a transformed Derek.

I want to suggest that these friendships represented for Derek what Douglas Yacek (2019) has called "civic epiphanies": "moments in which we recognize the humanity of those we had previously considered our political enemies" (p. 424). These moments "are central to cultivating a politically beneficial form of open-mindedness" (p. 424). These friendships opened Derek's heart and mind to persuasion, to the moral pull of truth and justice, to which I now turn.

28.3.2 Capacities Related to the Promotion of Truth and Justice

Juan, Matthew, and Allison helped Derek transform not *only* by befriending him. They had specific conversations with him and presented him with facts and arguments, ideas to which he was receptive because of their friendships. Beyond the capacities related to establishing a friendship with Derek, then, were a set of capacities related to the promotion of truth and justice.

Saslow (2018) explains that it was easy for Derek to shrug off the criticisms of "the enemy" – say, people sending him hate mail online – but when the people disagreeing with him were his own friends with whom he had mutual respect, it was much more difficult to ignore. This is what Derek himself wrote following his disavowal of white nationalism:

> "People who disagreed with me were critical in this process," he wrote. "Especially those who were my friends regardless, but who let me know when we talked about it that they thought my beliefs were wrong and

[2] Thank you to Sona Farid-Arbab (2016) for bringing this passage to my attention. See her book (ch.2) for a novel approach to the concept of power in education, which references Arendt among others.

> took the time to provide evidence and civil arguments. I didn't always agree with their ideas, but I listened to them and they listened to me." (Saslow, 2018, ch. 11)

How, then, did Derek's friends disagree with him? How did they let him know that they thought his beliefs were wrong? How did they "provide evidence and civil arguments"? More importantly, what convictions and attitudes enabled them to do so? Allison's example shines in this respect, so, in this section, I will focus on the role she played.[3]

Once she had developed a more trusting relationship with Derek, Allison began to gradually have an increasing number of conversations with him about white nationalism, debating its foundations and pointing out to him its negative influence:

> Allison looked online for arguments against white nationalism and checked out books from the library on the history of racism in the United States. She read several IQ studies so she could pinpoint the scientific flaws in Derek's conclusions. She watched documentaries about the Klan and read through hundreds of messages on Stormfront. (Saslow, 2018, ch. 6)

Especially after attending the white nationalist conference, Allison worked even harder to bring the truth to Derek's attention:

> Every few days, Allison worked to inject white nationalism into their conversations. But Derek dreaded interpersonal conflict, and at first he preferred to talk about his ideology with Allison mostly online, where even a heated argument could feel somehow remote and dispassionate ... Allison began to send him studies from her own online research and also from the scientific journals in her Stigma and Prejudice syllabus, and she targeted her evidence at the basic pillars of Derek's beliefs. (Saslow, 2018, ch. 8)

Ironically, Derek's passion for history had been fueled in part by the way in which white nationalists mythologize the Middle Ages. However, as he began to better understand this period of history, he realized that much of what was said about it on Stormfront was false. He also became fascinated with Islamic history, and how the sciences and arts had flourished in Baghdad where Jews, Christians, and Muslims lived together. These realizations cut against the grain of white nationalism's assumptions.

Returning to part of one of Arendt's (1958) quotes, she says that "Power is actualized ... where words are not used to veil intentions but to disclose realities" (p. 200). The idea of using words to "disclose realities" is particularly helpful. Certain aspects of reality had become entirely obscure to Derek, growing up, as he did, in a white nationalist echo chamber. This ideology had drawn several veils in front of his eyes that prevented him from seeing things as they actually were, whether it was about IQ scores or the history of the Middle Ages. Allison's words

[3] It is worth noting that, in Allison's case, her relationship with Derek eventually took a closer turn, and they began dating at some point during their time together at New College (Saslow, 2018).

disclosed realities that had been obscured for Derek. She took the time to seek out the truth and to patiently bring all these realities to Derek's attention.[4]

Two interrelated convictions seem to have motivated and shaped Allison's efforts here. While it may seem obvious, it is worth noting that she was clearly convinced that there *was* a truth of the matter (about racism, etc.) to be ascertained. She was also convinced that this truth, if presented in the context of a loving friendship, had the power to change Derek's mind. We might say that Allison operated according to a kind of epistemic realism, where there was a real distinction to be made between thinking moved by reasons and thinking clouded by prejudice. Obscuring this distinction, which some strands of postmodern thought appear to do (Fricker, 2007, pp. 2–3), may weaken the ability and commitment of an individual to search out the truth and to promote it in meaningful conversations with others.

If one does not have a strong notion of truth, or confidence in its ability to move another human being, one may fall back on coercion. Derek's friends were convinced that, in the context of the friendships they were nurturing with him, their best weapons against Derek's ideology were truth and justice. On one occasion, Allison responded to one of the many attacks on Derek on the student forum by writing that:

> Attacking a person, especially a person who is not fighting back and has never fought back, is not productive to anybody. What is productive is engaging in meaningful dialogue about how to change these oppressive structures here and elsewhere. Participate in diversity talks, be upset and give a damn, but in a positive way, not in a hostile way. Attacking him [Derek] as a mass gang is not the way to change his views (so throwing things at him in the library, etc., which is what happened the semester after he came back, is not acceptable human behavior either). Talk about it, shed apathy, get involved, but do it constructively. (Saslow, 2018, ch. 8)

In addition to her strong commitment to the truth, Allison was convinced that justice was on her side. And once their friendship was strong enough, she continuously pointed this out to him. Not only, then, did she point out that he was factually wrong in many respects; she also insisted that his views were themselves the cause of injustice and suffering:

> White nationalism wasn't just some academic thought experiment. It was a caustic, harmful ideology that was causing real damage to people's lives, so Allison began to send Derek links about that, too . . . For years Derek had been hearing about the abstract evils of racism, which he had always dismissed as empty rhetoric from his enemies on the liberal left. But he didn't consider Allison an enemy, so now he spent hours on his computer reading through raw data, doing his own research, and debating the

[4] I should add that, of course, Derek himself played a crucial role in all of this. Although I have been focusing throughout, for the purposes of this chapter, on the attitudes and abilities of Derek's friends, we should not lose sight of Derek's own agency in this process of moral transformation. In the final analysis, Derek was able to transform because he was able to demonstrate a degree of responsiveness (Warnick et al., 2018), in the context of trusting friendships.

> evidence with Allison. She wrote to him, saying that even if his intellectual theories about the future of a multicultural America were correct – which they weren't – that still wouldn't justify the damage his racism was inflicting. "It's not just that you're wrong," she told him. "It's that you're actually hurting people." (Saslow, 2018, ch. 8)

When other students attacked Derek, whether online or in person, Allison would express compassion for him (and even occasionally chastise his attackers, as we have seen), but she would also help him understand *why* he was being harassed, connecting this to the injustices he was perpetuating. She wrote to him the following:

> For them, what you believe in are not simply "intellectual ideas." They are abhorrent and dangerous. And to them, it's not just that you believe it – it's that there's a radio show with your name on it. It's that your name is stickied on Stormfront threads. It's that you publicly believe these things. And in that, you're distanced from them. You're not a classmate. You're a public figure. Your vulnerabilities and emotions don't necessarily matter to them. It's not like you haven't done anything that reinforces and spreads the WN [White Nationalist] ideology – you have. To them, you are not a victim – and in general you aren't because, to be frank, you absolutely have done all of those things. They hurt you, yes. Because in their view your public beliefs oppress and hurt others, and yeah, I agree with them. I don't think there are nice ways to say that. (Saslow, 2018, ch. 9)

What were the effects of all these conversations on Derek? First, Allison was able to gradually help Derek tap into *his* sense of justice, which in turn helped him better see the truth. There is a close connection between justice and truth. Miranda Fricker (2007) highlights this connection in her work on epistemic injustice. She insists that a certain kind of fair-mindedness is necessary in order to prevent prejudice from barring our access to truth and knowledge. She thus adds to Bernard Williams' (2002) two virtues of truth (sincerity and accuracy) a third: what she calls the virtue of testimonial justice (Fricker, 2007, pp. 116–18). We could say that Derek was in the grip of the corresponding vice – testimonial injustice – which prevented him from taking seriously any argument against white nationalism that came from outside of his narrow group. Allison's conversations helped bring this vice to his attention and encouraged him to adopt the more fair-minded attitude associated with the virtue of testimonial justice. These conversations also enhanced Derek's responsiveness.

Second, it seems these conversations created a kind of benign cognitive dissonance in Derek, one which may have helped foster the kind of civic epiphany I mentioned at the end of Section 28.3.1 (Yacek, 2019). Saslow (2018) writes:

> [N]ow Derek's brain was also crowded with new ideas, backed by data and dozens of studies, which suggested white nationalism was both dangerous and flawed. If he returned to the radio show, he knew Allison and his other New College friends would be listening and parsing every word. Suddenly he cared about both audiences. How could he possibly appease both? (Saslow, 2018, ch. 8)

Derek told Allison that "My brain now has two ways of thinking, a white nationalist way and a new way ... It's like living in two different realms" (Saslow, 2018, ch. 9). Saslow (2018) continues:

> White nationalism remained embedded in all of his childhood memories, his sense of self, and almost every important relationship he'd had during the first twenty-one years of his life. "It's my community, so I reflexively hear criticism of WN sort of like some people hear your momma's so fat jokes," he wrote to Allison. But if his loyalty was holding his identity in place, his brain was increasingly leading him in a new direction. At nights ... he lay in bed and questioned his assumptions about the world, which included rethinking so much of what he had once believed about the history of Europe. (ch. 9)

This process of reflection, encouraged by his close friends, culminated in his public disavowal of white nationalism, a clear victory for social justice.

28.4 Conclusion

The analysis in this chapter suggests that there are at least two sets of capacities that are particularly important for democratic education to develop in students who are to be empowered to overcome racism in their communities: capacities relevant to friendship and to the promotion of truth and justice.

Students need to be assisted to conceive of friendship as compatible with (if not constituted by) a moral educational aim; at the same time, they need to avoid a sense of moral superiority in the process and be detached from results. To initiate the kinds of friendships we considered, students need to develop the power of attention, focused on the common humanity they share with others; they need to learn to look at the "other" with a just and loving gaze. They also need to be moved by the "madness" of love and its logic of superabundance. With regard to promoting truth and justice, students need a strong conviction in the existence of truth and in its ability to convince others without the need to resort to coercion; the ability to patiently bring relevant truths to the attention of one's friend; and the conviction that justice is on their side and that others will have a sense of justice that can be awakened once they are assisted to see the injustices in which they are involved.

The transformation of Derek Black is, however, only one case, and no case is perfect or universally applicable. This chapter constitutes therefore a modest contribution to a much larger project. Further research is required in order to identify additional capacities that may be required – perhaps by identifying other natural experiments[5] – and, more importantly, to learn about educational

[5] Another moral transformation that has been the object of analysis is that of Christian Picciolini (2015), a former neo-Nazi who now dedicates much of his time to helping others who are caught up in similar ideologies. See Yacek (2021) for a brief discussion of this case (pp. 47–49).

content and methods that can deliberately foster the development of these capacities in students at various levels.

One educational program that appears promising in this regard is the Multi Racial Unity Living Experience (MRULE) at Michigan State University (https://mosaic.msu.edu/mruleICA-program/index.html). The program categorically rejects any us/them divisions and promotes instead the oneness of the human family as a guiding principle. Practically, it involves students from diverse backgrounds in discussion groups and social action projects in order to build relationships and community across difference. The focus on building relationships may assist in developing the capacities I have described that are relevant to friendship, and their discussion groups appear to promote the practice of fair-minded examination of the truth and issues of social justice. Research on this program (Gazel, 2007; Muthuswamy et al., 2006) and other similar ones might be fruitful in generating further insights into the kind of democratic education that can help people overcome racism in their communities.

It is important to acknowledge before closing that democratic education of the kind I have described here is not all that needs to be done to eradicate prejudice and racism in a society. There are structural changes in laws and politics that also need to take place. There is arguably a link between democratic education and the latter changes, but this is not the argument I have advanced here. Suffice it to say that an educational process that fosters the capacities I have been exploring is an important and perhaps essential complement to other strategies.

Imagine if we had thousands upon thousands of students like Juan, Matthew, and Allison, who were able to help facilitate the transformation of some of their peers away from dangerous ideologies. In a world that is, to quote Weil's words again, "mad for want of love," we need more students like these, who can act as true champions of justice, especially when it seems "mad" to do so.

References

Appiah, K. A. (2010). *The honor code: How moral revolutions happen*. New York, NY: W. W. Norton.

Appiah, K. A. (2014). Experimental philosophy. In C. Luetge, H. Rusch & M. Uhl, eds., *Experimental ethics: Towards an empirical moral philosophy*. London: Palgrave Macmillan, pp. 7–25.

Arendt, H. (1958). *The human condition*. 2nd ed. Chicago, IL: University of Chicago Press.

Bialystok, L. (2014). Authenticity and the limits of philosophy. *Dialogue*, 53(2), 271–98.

Farid-Arbab, S. (2016). *Moral empowerment: In quest of a pedagogy*. Wilmette, IL: Baha'i Publishing Trust.

Fricker, M. (2007). *Epistemic injustice: Power and the ethics of knowing*. Oxford: Oxford University Press.

Gazel, J. (2007). Walking the talk: Multiracial discourses, realities, and pedagogy. *American Behavioral Scientist*, 51(4), 532–50.

Glasgow, J. (2008). On the methodology of the race debate: Conceptual analysis and racial discourse. *Philosophy and Phenomenological Research*, 76(2), 333–58. https://doi.org/10.1111/j.1933-1592.2007.00135.x.

Hadot, P. (1995). *Philosophy as a way of life*. Hoboken, NJ: Blackwell.

Jonas, M., & Yacek, D. W. (2019). *Nietzsche's philosophy of education: Rethinking ethics, equality and the good life in a democratic age*. London: Routledge.

Kristjánsson, K. (2020). Learning from friends and terminating friendships: Retrieveing friendship as a moral educational concept. *Educational Theory*, 70(2), 129–49.

Larmore, C. (2010). *The practices of the self*. Chicago, IL: Chicago University Press.

Liao, S., & Huebner, B. (2020). Oppressive things. *Philosophy and Phenomenological Research*, 103(1), 92–113. https://doi.org/10.1111/phpr.12701.

Mogensen, A. (2017). Racial profiling and cumulative injustice. *Philosophy and Phenomenological Research*, 98(2), 452–77. https://doi.org/10.1111/phpr.12451.

Monroe, K. R. (1996). *The heart of altruism: Perceptions of a common humanity*. Princeton, NJ: Princeton University Press.

Murdoch, I. (2014). *The sovereignty of good*. London: Routledge (original work published in 1970).

Muthuswamy, N., Levine, T. R., & Gazel, J. (2006). Interaction-based diversity initiative outcomes: An evaluation of an initiative aimed at bridging the racial divide on a college campus. *Communication Education*, 55(1), 105–21.

Picciolini, C. (2015). *Romantic violence: Memoirs of an American skinhead*. Chicago, IL: Goldmill Group.

Ricoeur, P. (1995). Love and justice. Trans. by D. Pellauer, *Philosophy & Social Criticism*, 21(5/6), 23–39.

Saslow, E. (2016, October 15). The white flight of Derek Black. *The Washington Post*. Available at: https://www.washingtonpost.com/national/the-white-flight-of-derek-black/2016/10/15/ed5f906a-8f3b-11e6-a6a3-d50061aa9fae_story.html.

Saslow, E. (2018). *Rising out of hatred: The awakening of a former white nationalist* [eBook ed.]. New York, NY: Doubleday.

Schwarzenbach, S. A. (1996). On civic friendship. *Ethics*, 107(1), 97–128.

Schwitzgebel, E. (2014). The moral behavior of ethicists and the role of the philosopher. In C. Luetge, H. Rusch & M. Uhl, eds., *Experimental ethics: Towards an empirical moral philosophy*. London: Palgrave Macmillan, pp. 59–64.

Taylor, C. (1989). *Sources of the self: The making of the modern identity*. Cambridge, MA: Harvard University Press.

Taylor, C. (1991). *The ethics of authenticity*. Cambridge, MA: Harvard University Press.

Urmson, J. (1958). Saints and heroes. In A. Melden, ed., *Essays in moral philosophy*. Washington, DC: University of Washington Press, pp. 198-216.

Warnick, B., Yacek, D., & Robinson, S. (2018). Learning to be moved: The modes of democratic responsiveness. *Philosophical Inquiry in Education*, 25(1), 31–46.

Weil, S. (1951). *Waiting for God*. Trans. by E. Craufurd, New York: Harper & Row.

Weil, S. (1987). Are we struggling for justice? Trans. by M. Barbaras. *Philosophical Investigations*, 10(1), 1–10.

Weil, S. (1999). *Gravity and grace*. Trans. by E. Crawford & M. von der Ruhr, London: Routledge (original work published in 1947).

Williams, B. (2002). *Truth and truthfulness: An essay in genealogy*. Hoboken, NJ: Princeton University Press.

Wodak, D. (2021). Of witches and white folks. *Philosophy and Phenomenological Research*, 104(3), 587–605. https://doi.org/10.1111/phpr.12799.

Yacek, D. W. (2019). Should anger be encouraged in the classroom? Political education, closed-mindedness, and civic epiphany. *Educational Theory*, 69(4), 421–37.

Yacek, D. W. (2021). *The transformative classroom: Philosophical foundations and practical applications*. New York, NY: Routledge.

Zagzebski, L. T. (2017). *Exemplarist moral theory*. Oxford: Oxford University Press.

29

Postcolonial Perspectives on Democratic Education

Penny Enslin and Kai Horsthemke

29.1 Introduction

29.1.1 Democracy, Education, and the Postcolonial Challenge

With democratic institutions and practices now widely regarded as under threat (Levitzky & Ziblatt, 2019; Runciman, 2018), education for democracy is, more than ever, an urgent necessity across the globe. Taken together, the concepts "democratic" and "education" – both regarded as valuable social goods in this volume – imply education that prepares citizens to participate in a democratic society through the acquisition of knowledge and values that foster free and equal participation. They entail, too, that education itself is characterized by democratic principles and governed by values and structures that are democratic – and that educational opportunities should be democratic, thus accessible to all. Gutmann captures this interrelationship between democracy and education by describing democratic education as "a political as well as an educational ideal" (Gutmann, 1987, p. 3).

From a postcolonial perspective, this observation is likely to be seen as both self-evident and yet problematic. This is because colonialism and persisting coloniality have created conditions in which opportunities in former colonies for both education and democracy were historically opposed by the imperial powers who colonized large swathes of the globe and such opportunities are currently undermined by globalized conditions that continue to favor the political and economic interests of those former colonial powers. Considered in a postcolonial time, "democracy" is a key concept in Western political theory, but one with a colonial past requiring critical scrutiny. A postcolonial perspective demands a critical revisiting of key political concepts, including a cluster of concepts related to democracy – such as sovereignty, justice, rights, inclusion and citizenship. Education, furthermore, was an instrument of colonialism; colonial masters were inclined to be both parsimonious in its provision and to use its perceived lack as a reason to deny that colonial populations could be capable of self-rule. Thus, both concepts – democracy and education – and their attendant practices are woven into the history of colonialism.

Viewed in anticolonial terms, interpretations of democracy and of education have been heavily influenced by their association with Western modernity and so they require reconstruction within an alternative understanding and ethos. Hence, addressing the past destruction and injustices of colonialism and of ongoing coloniality are currently a major focus of attention in both educational and political theory, as in all academic disciplines. In the discussion that follows, we aim to explore the conceptual, educational, and political challenges involved in articulating a postcolonial perspective on democratic education. In doing so we defend an account of democratic education that retrieves and defends a qualified *universalist, liberal* stance – although we are fully aware that both these concepts tend to be regarded with suspicion by postcolonial, and especially by decolonial, critics.

We develop our argument in the following sections. In Section 29.2, we outline how colonial rule both provoked and rejected demands for self-determination, while rendering democracy difficult to establish in newly independent states after formal decolonization. We defend a conception of postcolonial democracy in which democracy is understood as a universal aspiration, a critical practice with a deliberative range that accommodates particular, local contexts. In Section 29.3, we describe colonial education before considering a currently influential yet problematic approach to decolonial education. While some sense might be made of the notions of postcolonial knowledge and epistemology, we argue that, at its most extreme, the decolonialist position is epistemologically unviable. Finally, in the concluding fourth section of the chapter we outline a perspective on postcolonial democratic education as a form of liberal education, universal in some shared features, that needs to resist the universal presence of neoliberal capitalism as a recent form of coloniality that is universally inimical to both education and democracy.

29.1.2 Postcolonial Thought: Concepts and Controversies

Before proceeding further, because postcolonial debates are marked by vigorous contestation of some complex terms, we will clarify our use of a selection of concepts that are key to our exploration of democratic education in a postcolonial context. Postcolonial thought is a broad and diverse project that sets out to analyze and to counter the effects of colonization of much of the globe by modern European states, from the sixteenth century onward. At its height in the nineteenth century and the first half of the twentieth century, modern colonization dominated large parts of Africa, Asia, the Caribbean, Australasia, Oceania, North America, and the Middle East. This colonial era was characterized by appropriation of natural resources, annexation, and dispossession of indigenous people's land, military and administrative control by the imperial power, impoverishment, occasional genocide and famine, as well as slavery, exploitation of labor, and the enforcement of trade on terms that favored the metropolitan power over its colonized subjects. A key feature of colonization was dismissal of local traditions and culture and the imposition of a racist social order.

An important distinction in the scholarship and activism that set out to address the legacy of the colonial era is that between colonialism and imperialism. Although they are sometimes used interchangeably, our discussion of these two overlapping concepts relies on Said's account: "'imperialism' means the practice, the theory, and the attitudes of a dominating center ruling a distant territory; 'colonialism', which is almost always a consequence of imperialism, is the implanting of settlements on a distant territory" (Said, 1993, p. 8). For our purposes the term "imperialism" refers to the creation of modern empires by European powers during the modern colonial era. Most prominently, Britain's extensive empire stretched at its height across significant portions of the globe, notably in the Indian subcontinent and across the continent of Africa which was carved into spheres of influence by European powers in the scramble for Africa in the late nineteenth century.

Even the very term "postcolonial" is acknowledged to be problematic, because the "post-" prefix can be taken to suggest, misleadingly, that colonialism ended with the achievement of political sovereignty by newly independent states. Thus, we emphasize that our use of this expression does not imply any such clear break. Instead, it refers both to the study of colonialism in all its aspects and to a critical understanding of persistent coloniality. Coloniality prevails in varying forms across most countries, including the former imperial powers with their own now diverse populations as a result of migration from their former colonies as well as from regions destabilized by colonialism's consequences. The postcolonial condition is not static, as in time new forms of domination evolve alongside old ones; hence, the use of the term neocolonialism, a tendency toward new and shifting forms of domination – social, economic, and political. Neocolonial forces comprise the emergence of new imperial powers such as the United States, post-Soviet Russia, and China, as well as globalization, the hegemony of neoliberal capitalism, and the role of powerful multinationals.

Our critical stance is anticolonial, and while this position supports decolonization in general, we will express skepticism about some articulations of decoloniality and particularly about certain applications of decolonial theory to education. Kohn (2010, p. 209) suggests that while "post-colonial theory is associated with the issues of *hybridity*, *diaspora*, representation, narrative, and knowledge/power, theories of decolonization are concerned with revolution, economic inequality, violence and political identity." Yet because of variations within both sets of intersecting theories, the relationship between postcolonialism and decolonization is not always clear-cut, and they may sometimes intersect.

Across the range of theories that comprise the postcolonial and the decolonial, a further point of divergence is the extent to which analysts take as their starting point and major emphasis either the cultural or the material aspects of imperialism and colonialism. Said's *Orientalism* (1978) and *Culture and Imperialism* (1993) have been hugely influential in establishing postcolonial studies in Western universities, with a strong emphasis on literary and cultural studies. This emphasis has, however, been criticized in Marxist approaches to the study of colonialism (for example Lazarus, 2011), which have taken issue with a tendency to view imperialism and colonialism as cultural categories, as against analyzing them as part of the history of capitalism, which imposed on colonized people commodity production within a market system in which all were drawn into capitalist class relations – for the material benefit of the colonizing powers.

A related area of dispute is present in the decolonial literature, in which decolonizers' interest in cultural difference is focused on knowledge – and hence education – as a European or Western imposition on the colonized, although some decolonizers would also treat capitalism as an accompanying European imposition. While not necessarily representative of all expressions of decolonial thinking, Mignolo's significant decolonial challenge calls for "epistemic disobedience," to counter the "epistemic privileges" of Western knowledge and to affirm "the epistemic rights of the racially devalued" (2009, p. 4). This categorical break with the West requires not only epistemological but also – notably for our purposes in this chapter – political delinking as "necessary steps for imagining and building democratic, just, non-imperial/colonial societies" (2009, p. 1). This emphatic rupture with political theories of the West, for Mignolo, includes delinking with the vocabularies of liberalism and Marxism as products of the Enlightenment. Furthermore, as he sees postcolonial thinking as having originated mainly in England and the United States, Mignolo maintains that "it is easier for European intellectuals to endorse postcolonialism … than decolonial thinking" (2011, p. 280).

Mignolo's categorical skepticism toward European political thought, knowledge, and experience allies his decolonial stance with a strongly held opposition to universalism, an opinion central to decolonial thought and indeed orthodoxically prominent in much postcolonial thought, as well as in poststructuralism and some feminist theories. Yet Gopal (2020), for example, takes issue with claims, like Mignolo's, of radical difference between the epistemologies, ethics, economy, and politics of the subjects of colonization and of their colonizers. Gopal's study of anticolonial resistance questions the antiuniversalist stance and presents compelling evidence that opposition to empire in both the colonies and within Britain drew on and reshaped Enlightenment concepts such as freedom and equality (Gopal, 2020).

In political and moral philosophy as well as in education, the antiuniversalist tendency has been widely accepted, particularly by postmodernist and postcolonial thinkers, in vehemently opposing the idea that there are some context-independent values, understandings, and norms. The antiuniversalist position insists instead on cultural relativism – as against a form of universalism that acknowledges and respects particularity, as we aim to do here in articulating our account of democracy and of democratic education. It is understandable that the unjust history and enduring harms of colonialism should encourage repudiation, rejection, and distancing from concepts and ideas that were routinely invoked to justify imperialism and colonialism. The histories of both democracy and education reveal examples of particularistic practices that have expressed a false universalism, sometimes in the form of what Gopal (2020) calls "pretended universality," whose expression aimed to justify colonialist assumptions and practices. However, our exploration of democratic education, starting in the Section 29.2 with democracy in colonial and postcolonial times, shares a refusal to discard universalism as irretrievably tainted by colonialism.

29.2 Democracy and Colonialism

29.2.1 Colonial Rule and the Paradoxes of Liberal Democracy

Repressive colonial rule over native inhabitants of colonies during the age of empire contrasted markedly with the emergence of mass democracy within the metropolitan European states that took place in the nineteenth and twentieth centuries[1]. The gradual establishment of some key features of liberal democracy, such as the widening of political participation and representation, and acceptance of the principle that governments have obligations to meet the needs of citizens who have a right to a say in the affairs of their communities, was confined to the metropole[2]. Imperial rule was, instead, directed at the subjugation of colonial subjects, whose subjection was paid for by their exploitation, while local elites were coopted to service colonial rule (Pitts, 2010).

Stovall (2013) observes a paradoxical contrast between the deeply antidemocratic system of imperial rule in British and French colonies, on the one hand, and the growth of democracy at home. The democracy that grew in the metropole was denied to the masses in the colonies, race and class intersecting and facilitating an alliance of imperialism and liberal democracy. This racial difference was evident, too, in the granting of self-rule to Britain's "dominion" settler colonies, Canada, Australia, New Zealand, and in South Africa, which took place well before the era of decolonization following World War II.

Commentators frequently remark on how liberalism was imbricated in both empire and in Western liberal democratic culture. For some postcolonial theorists and in decolonial thought in particular, liberal democracy was heavily complicit in colonialism. Until independence drew near in the period of formal decolonization after World War II, colonial rulers' opposition to democratic participation for colonized populations was sometimes supported by liberal theorists. Pitts (2010) interprets the relationship between the spread of European empires and liberal thought as one of coincidence and deep intersection. But Parekh (1994) insists on a closer complicity, attributing to liberalism in Britain the role of an ideology that set out to legitimize colonialism, notoriously represented in John Stuart Mill's defense of individual liberty alongside his illiberal dismissal of Eastern societies. Furthermore, Mill both defended the British Empire and argued that Indian subjects lacked the education they would need in order to be able to rule themselves. Chakrabarty's critique of Western

[1] We note that colonial practices varied among the different colonial powers and that processes of decolonization also took different forms in different colonial contexts. See Stovall (2013), for example, on differences between French and British colonialism.

[2] Exclusion based on gender, race, and class has persisted long after these democratic principles achieved widespread acceptance.

political thought is another that rightly rebukes Mill for his defense of empire, and the grounds he offered for it: "According to Mill, Indians or Africans were *not yet* civilized enough to rule themselves. Some historical time of development and civilization (colonial rule and education, to be precise) had to elapse before they could be considered prepared for such a task" (Chakrabarty, 2000, p. 8).

Mill insisted that education had to precede the franchise, a not unfamiliar objection to the extension of the franchise in Europe, but with a racial twist in the colonial context. As Chakrabarty (2000) observes, this stance was of course rejected in nationalist demands for independence. Stovall's (2013) analysis of the paradoxes of empire notes the declared imperial aim of "uplifting" colonial subjects. Yet, "Just as in Britain and France liberal democracy required the creation of an educated populace integrated into the acceptance of a liberal world view, so too in their colonies must the natives be 'civilized' to make democracy possible – at least some day" (Stovall, 2013, p. 7). While compulsory primary education aimed at developing basic literacy and a sense of membership of a "national community" was mandated at home in Britain and France, such educational opportunities were not extended to colonial subjects.

But does the complicity of influential figures like Mill with empire render liberalism incompatible with anticolonial thought? Pitts correctly emphasizes the range of liberalism as "a complex ideology whose exemplars share family resemblances rather than any strict doctrine" (2010, p. 218). Hence Sartori's (2006) observation that liberal theory itself also developed a complex critique of the East India Company and of imperialism. Furthermore, although there is much skepticism within postcolonial thought about liberal ideas – and even more so from a decolonial perspective – it is highly significant that theorists from outside of European and American thought also "adopted and adapted liberal language and categories for reformist or avowedly anti-imperial ends" (Pitts, 2010, p. 218).

On this process of adaptation Gopal (2020, p. 14) persuasively makes the case that processes of decolonial struggle reflected liberal democratic concepts that were drawn from Western theoretical traditions and also, crucially, contributed to their further development[3]. This process of refinement and conceptual enhancement Gopal describes in terms of "pedagogical reciprocity," in which those in the metropole learned from colonial insurgents: "Even as colonial narratives of universal freedom were challenged and queried, the project of something like universal freedom was reconstituted and reframed, rather than discarded" (2020, p. 17).

In his influential argument for "provincializing" Europe, Chakrabarty argues that concepts drawn from European political thought, while associated with a "universal vision" that was denied the colonized while also preached at them, are "both indispensable and inadequate" (Chakrabarty, 2000, p. 6) in non-Western contexts. Provincializing Europe is not a matter of rejecting concepts

[3] Among the examples of "reverse tutelage" explored by Gopal (2020, ch. 8) are the ways in which Caribbean authors like C. L. R. James influenced the opinions of British radicals and liberals on freedom and rights by bringing themes of labor, capitalism, and race to the fore in anticolonial discourse.

like citizenship, human rights, the state, equality before the law, civil society, a public sphere, social justice, popular sovereignty, and democracy (Chakrabarty, 2000, p. 4). Colonial subjects resisting their own subjection invoked liberal concepts of equality and freedom despite the fact that colonialist expressions of those concepts failed to invoke them in universalist terms. Yet to criticize imperialism and colonial rule for failing to live up to such principles is to imply that they ought to be universally applied. Arguments against the oppression, exploitation, and exclusion of indigenous populations from the extension of democracy that was taking place in the metropole are already – and rightly – universalist arguments (see also Culp, 2019, pp. 15, 164, 166–68).

Universalist stances can take varying forms (see also Drerup, 2019, pp. 32–34, 42). At its most objectionable, imperialist universalism selectively picked out ideas from Enlightenment and European thought and cast them in terms convenient to justifying domination of the colonized, while endorsing a selection of colonialists' own particular traditions, practices, and assumptions. These were declared to epitomize an unquestionable standard while dismissing, usually ignorantly, local variants among the colonized as deviant. Yet this one possibly "universalist" stance does not exhaust the range of ways in which universalism can be expressed, and it is what Keane (2018) describes as an "abusive universal." Gopal (2020) argues for an expansive, critical universalism as central to anticolonialism. In proceeding to discuss postcolonial democracy and education, we adopt this perspective on universalism, supporting a postcolonial, democratic universalism while resisting a tendency in decolonial critiques of universalism to retreat in the face of colonialist universalism into a radical particularity, a "will-to-difference" (Gandhi, 1998). It is perhaps unsurprising that coloniality would provoke assertions of far-reaching divergence emphasizing radically contrasting cultural, political, moral, and epistemological differences between the West and the rest. But such radical particularism frequently rests, too, on identifying selective features of a tradition of thought or one of its authors, discarding its broader critical usefulness to the anticolonial project. Discussions of universalism tend to be an all-or-nothing affair; either difference is recognized and respected or the alternative is an oppressive universalism. Locating our understanding of universalism between these two extremes, we maintain that aspiring to a commonly shared universalism in general terms in applying key political concepts can be pursued while at the same time recognizing and valuing the local and the particular. This we will do in relation to democracy and then subsequently in endorsing a postcolonial, liberal democratic education – neither of which we expect to be identically expressed or enacted through like practices in all contexts.

29.2.2 From Colonial Rule to Postcolonial Democracy

Although development of democratic governance was resisted by the colonial powers, resistance on the part of indigenous populations and their twentieth-century independence movements frequently called for political autonomy and the establishment of democratic institutions, although not of course necessarily modeled on those in the West[4]. Such movements and acts of resistance were suppressed, often brutally. How colonies had been governed by imperial powers profoundly affected their futures after formal political decolonization, commonly rendering difficult the successful establishment of viable states with democratic systems.

Political authority during the colonial era focused on control, wielded with the assistance of a combination of displacement and cooption of local traditional authorities and facilitated by categorizing and dividing populations into ethnic groups, tribes, and castes. Structures and practices that were regarded as unconducive to imperial dominance were undermined and destroyed (LiPuma & Koelble, 2009). As Robinson observes of decolonization in Africa, "many colonial institutions were reserved at independence, including the marriage of state institutions and customary rule, with deleterious effects" (2019, p. 1). The states created by imperial powers were granted independence with arbitrarily constructed colonial borders that disregarded ethnic affiliations and differences, partitioning some ethnic groups into different states while forcing others together. Moreover, relations between state and society cast during colonial rule encouraged citizens to distrust the postcolonial state (Robinson, 2019). This was unsurprising, as criticism of colonial authorities had been defined as treasonous and was punished. In effect, many features of indigenous inhabitants' adverse experience of government lingered after the departure of colonial officials, as did the domination, patronage, fragmentation, and inequality fostered by colonial rule.

Colonialism and its political aftermath made it difficult to establish an effective postcolonial state apparatus, yet newly independent states usually adopted democratic constitutions. Given the democratic deficits of colonial rule and the struggles of colonized populations to free themselves from it, the three virtues identified by Sen in defending democracy as a universal value are pertinent to the postcolony:

> [F]irst, the *intrinsic* importance of political participation and freedom in human life; second, the *instrumental* importance of political incentives in keeping governments responsible and accountable; and third, the *constructive* role of democracy in the formation of values and in the understanding of needs, rights, and duties. (Sen, 1999, p. 11)

Each of Sen's three virtues of democracy was denied by colonial rule, and together they begin to address colonialism's democratic deficit. The third of these is particularly relevant to our argument, as Sen observes further that by practicing democracy citizens are given opportunities to learn from each other, to collectively shape and choose their priorities and values. Rights to discuss, critique, and disagree have a central role in formulating and making those choices. For Sen, they also contribute to supporting his argument that democracy is a universal value "that people anywhere may have reason to see as

[4] For example, Keane (2009) contrasts M. K. Gandhi's dedication to Indian self-government, social equality, and universal adult suffrage with a skepticism toward the Westminster model of representative democracy.

valuable" (1999, p. 12). Sen strenuously resists the idea that democracy is either unique to the West or inimical to, say, '"Asian values." However, authoritarian tendencies that assert the incompatibility of democracy with national or local values and practices may be found, of course, within Western and non-Western political traditions.

This stance is developed further by Beetham (2009), who adds popular control and political equality as core democratic principles. Beetham also advances further reasons for regarding democracy as a universal value, by arguing that defense of these core democratic principles "cannot stop at the borders of a country or group of countries, since the considerations from epistemology and a shared human nature underpinning that justification carry universal applicability" (2009, p. 281). Such a position is likely to invite decolonial objections that it fails to recognize diversity between different contexts and their political and social traditions, but Beetham insists that it is both consistent with diversity and avoids licensing unilateral intervention as pretexts for promoting democracy and "regime change." The potential for abuse of power is universal, and there are universal threats to democracy, in all contexts, from authoritarianism, nativist nationalism, paternalism, corruption, fake news, and populism. Resisting all these threats requires universal democratic vigilance, and a role for a suitable form of democratic education to counter these forces, with emphasis on critical thinking as a universal goal.

How democracies recognize diversity has been, in recent attention by many writers, a central focus to deliberation, which we see as a practice in which citizens debate their values and political choices, but whose procedures and styles of communication can and do vary across places and cultures (Young, 1996). In making this observation we share the view that deliberation is a universal, critical political practice that "manifests a universal human competence to reason collectively" (Sass & Dryzek, 2014, p. 4). The close complementarity between democracy and education here points ahead to the argument we will present in Section 29.4 about the characteristics of a postcolonial democratic education. But before that, we consider the characteristics of colonial education and one possible approach to postcolonial education, reflecting on tensions between the universal and the particular in relation to both.

29.3 Colonialism and Decoloniality in Education and Knowledge

29.3.1 From Colonial to Postcolonial Education

While its provision and practices varied across colonies, depending on which imperial power was present, the function of colonial schooling was to serve the colonizing power (Altbach & Kelly, 1978; Carnoy, 1974). The conceptions of knowledge, language medium, curriculum, and ethos were European, while indigenous traditions of upbringing and learning were dismissed as inferior. As Carnoy observed of both colonial education and, crucially, of mass schooling in the metropole too, "far from acting as a liberator, Western formal education came to most countries as part of imperial domination. It was consistent with the goals of imperialism: the economic and political control of the people of one country by the dominant class in another" (1974, p. 3). Alongside the avowed civilizing mission of colonial rule, missionary activities in Africa during the modern colonial era, for example, did not only set out to convert Africans to Christianity.[5] A further aim was the enforcement of a different form of social and economic organization (Carnoy, 1974), providing labor suited to the changing demands of capital.

Colonial dismissal of indigenous traditions and education was hardly an expression of liberal values. Nor was colonial education an example of liberal education. Colonial curricula and educational practices, for both indigenous and settler populations as subjects of the empire, certainly did not reflect the application of liberal thought and, like mass education in Britain, did not remotely match the type of conception of liberal education that was to emerge in the late twentieth century in its Anglo-American expressions. It was also not an expression of any type of liberal universalism. Its witlessness and uncritical qualities are most tellingly reflected in Macaulay's much cited and notorious "Minute on Indian Education" of 1835 (extract in Ashcroft et al., 1995, pp. 428–30), which has rightly drawn the ire of postcolonialist critics. Leela Gandhi comments on how Macaulay's defense of English medium education in India is "a paradigmatic instance of canon formation," assuming works of English literature to be superior to indigenous works because "a single shelf of a good European library was worth the whole native literature of India and Arabia" (Gandhi, 1998, p. 144; see also Culp, 2019, p. 165). For the purposes of the present argument, Macaulay's ill-informed dismissal of Indian literature is a dubious example of universalism; at best it is an expression of imperialist universalism, or simply an ignorant expression of imperialist particularism. If there is an injustice to Macaulay's othering of Asian languages and literature, it is a failure of universalism as a principled openness to difference and to the intrinsic value and extrinsic usefulness of all literatures and the knowledge and art they offer – universally – to those who are willing to be open to their merits. Yet Macaulay's example represents a justification for colonial education that prompts a radical critical distancing from the forms of education it appears to represent and to sanction.

A key feature of all education is the dissemination, sharing, facilitation, development, and production of knowledge. Colonial education was concerned, among many other things, with establishing strict hierarchies along cultural, ethnic, and racial divides, and with upholding the status quo of the privileged, by conceptualizing knowledge as originating with the colonial elites who bestowed it as a "gift" on the "ignorant"colonized majorities, which usually came at a substantial cost to the recipients (Quintero & Garbe, 2013). A significant, vociferous constituency within postcolonial theory has responded to this educational and epistemological imbalance by emphasizing democratization and decolonization processes within educational knowledge (Adebisi,

[5] Ethiopian Christianity long predated the era of European colonialism in Africa. See Barnes (2018) on the history of Christian evangelization in Africa and its educational legacy.

2016; Clemens, 2020; Piedrahita Rodríguez, 2020). Other popular notions include epistemological diversity (Clemens, 2020; Santos, 2014; Santos et al., 2008), the value of indigenous knowledge/s (Adebisi, 2016), and alternative ways of knowing and epistemologies (Adebisi, 2016; Santos, 2014). In addition, certain key concepts have been introduced: "epistemicide" (Bennett, 2017, pp. 153, 154; Brunner, 2020; Lebakeng, 2004; Masaka, 2018; Ndlovu-Gatsheni, 2018; Ramose, 2004; Santos, 2014), "epistemic violence" (Brunner 2016, 2020; Clemens, 2020, p. 17; Garbe, 2013; Spivak, 1988), "epistemic liberation" (Lebakeng, 2004; Masaka, 2018; Ndlovu-Gatsheni, 2018), and – as we saw in Section 29.1.2 – "epistemic disobedience."[6]

29.3.2 Democratic Education, Decolonial Knowledge, and Epistemology

Democratization and decolonization concern recognition, reclamation, legitimization or validation, and protection of previously marginalized, subjugated, and exploited ways of being, ways of doing, and ways of knowing – and thus have an ontological, an ethical, as well as an epistemological dimension. In this section, we focus on the last of these, as a possible starting point for conceptualizing postcolonial, democratic education. What does decolonization of knowledge and epistemology involve? A similar question might be posed regarding democratization of (postcolonial) "knowledge/s" and "epistemology" or "epistemologies," in the commonly preferred plural form. Insofar as colonialism and colonization have involved nonrecognition or misrecognition, subjugation, and exploitation of the prior practical and theoretical knowledge of the colonized, a primary endeavor of decolonial democratic education has been to reclaim, validate, and protect this knowledge from further oppression and exploitation. This is usually coupled with an emphasis on the value and diversity of indigenous, local, or alternative knowledge (systems) and epistemologies. The struggle of formerly marginalized and colonized people for a dignified and sustainable way of life, for personal and communal space, and for self-determination is a foremost political-ethical and educational concern and deserving of unconditional support. Political and cultural diversity have a bearing not only on the 'measurement of democracy' (Koelble & LiPuma, 2008) but also on education (moral and political education, education for global citizenship, etc.). However, can the same be said, as it often is, about "epistemological diversity"? Do the notions of indigenous, local, or alternative knowledge and of diverse epistemologies make sense at all? Is epistemic rationality relevantly like political rationality? Our worry remains that in the process of decolonization and democratization epistemological issues are confused or conflated with questions of social justice. This is especially glaring with Mignolo's notion of epistemic disobedience, the analogy being with "civil disobedience."

[6] "Epistemic disobedience," for Mignolo (2009, 2011), involves "epistemic de-linking," that is, extrication from the Western notions of rationality and modernity, ideals of humanity, and promises of economic growth and financial prosperity: in short, from coloniality's foundations of the concepts and accumulation of knowledge.

Everything arguably depends on the respective understandings of knowledge and epistemology employed within decolonial and postcolonial discourses. Once the philosophically and educationally relevant distinction is made between practical or skill-type knowledge (knowledge-how) and theoretical or propositional knowledge (knowledge-that) – the latter comprising belief, adequate justification, and truth at the very least as necessary conditions – much of the initial attraction and plausibility of ideas like "indigenous knowledge" (in the theoretical sense of "knowledge-that") is likely to wane, unless one is able to make sense of something like "indigenous truth," let alone "indigenous truth*s*." Similarly, the pertinent philosophical understanding of "epistemology" is a normative one: it is concerned with what ought or ought not to be called "knowledge." Epistemology is a domain or division within philosophy that investigates the nature, origin, and conditions of knowledge. It further means "theory of knowledge," that is, theory of the nature, origins, and conditions of knowledge. Thus, any knowledge claim that does not meet the required conditions outlined here is merely that: a knowledge *claim*. Furthermore, "diverse epistemologies" meaningfully refer to foundationalist and nonfoundationalist epistemologies, but not to so-called (multi)cultural, indigenous, or gendered epistemologies.[7] The best way to make sense of such diversity is to acknowledge that particular historical, geographic, and sociocultural experiences of people give rise to particular priorities that shape their epistemic theory and practice. If what has been established here is cogent, it follows that democratization and so-called decolonization of knowledge/epistemology and diverse epistemologies refer neither to a multitude of truths nor to an anything-goes conception of justification, but rather to different experiences connected to particular social locations, or to different social or interpersonal pathways to knowledge. In this sense, reference to "epistemolog*ies*" – like reference to "plural systems of knowledges" (Santos et al., 2008, p. xxxix) or to indigenous, local, or subaltern ways of knowing – is not only unhelpful but also misleading.

Epistemicide has been defined as "the murder of knowledge" (Santos, 2014, p. 92) or "destruction of all alternative knowledges" that involves "the destruction of all social practices and the disqualification of the social agents that operate according to such knowledges" (2014, p. 153). Among the authors we have come across who have employed this notion are Ramose (2004[8]) and Lebakeng (2004).[9] Closely related is the idea of "epistemic violence," which was first introduced by Spivak (1988) and has recently been elaborated by Brunner (2016, 2020). It refers to the kind of violent harm suffered by a person in her capacity as a knower, either because she has not been given the requisite resources to make epistemic sense of her situation or because she is not given

[7] Foundationalist and nonfoundationalist epistemologies coexist because philosophers still disagree about them, even though they agree that only one position can be correct. This is not the case with appeals to "multicultural epistemologies" – which (as their defenders contend) are all equally respectable and valid.

[8] "The history of epistemicide in South Africa raises fundamental questions of justice such as the question of epistemological equality of all the existing paradigms of the peoples of South Africa" (Ramose, 2004, p. 156).

[9] Lebakeng (2004, p. 109) refers to epistemicide as "a destruction of African knowledge systems."

sufficient credibility or has her knowledge claims rejected simply because of who she is, that is, because of her race, ethnicity, sex, or gender.

Epistemicide and epistemic violence are notions that have achieved widespread articulation and, unfortunately, also less-than-critical endorsement. There is a tendency to apply the ideas in question in a rather undifferentiated manner to all kinds of beliefs and worldviews – irrespective of whether they amount to knowledge, let alone emanate from a theory of knowledge. Does rejection of views that underlie rainmaking and ancestor agency amount to the "murder of knowledge systems"? Is the failure to allow flat-earth and geocentric worldviews in geography classrooms a matter of epistemic violence? What about the refusal to teach creationism in biology? Or the unwillingness to allow the counsel of active drug dealers and pimps in career guidance sessions? Do indigenous African women have epistemologies?[10] In what way, if any, can one make sense of the ideas of "alternative knowledges," "fundamentally different epistemologies" (Clemens, 2020, p. 19), and "parity of epistemologies" (Masaka, 2018, p. 294)? The implications of an essentially symmetrical understanding of diverse knowledge systems and epistemologies are deeply troubling, over and above the problem of epistemic relativism. If the alleged epistemological parity can be employed by the historically disempowered against the judgments and interpretational sovereignty of the powerful, then it can also be used to immunize the rulers against criticism of the disempowered. Moreover, regarding epistemic violence and epistemicide, surely there is a difference between rejecting someone's view on the mere grounds that she is black and/or a woman (such a credibility denial would be ethically reprehensible, epistemologically problematic, and indeed irrational[11]), and rejecting the views held or expressed by someone, who happens to be black and/or a woman, on the grounds of faulty or fallacious reasoning (that is, in cases not of *knowledge* but at most of mere knowledge *claims*).

Carefully examined, alternative knowledges (ways of knowing; epistemologies) do not exist, just as there are no alternative facts or alternative truth(s). There is only knowledge and nonknowledge. An alternative to knowledge would be ignorance. Alternative "knowledge" is therefore to be seen as synonymous with nonknowledge/ignorance. If something is knowledge, then it is not alternative. Once this is clear, then a great deal of discussion about epistemicide, epistemic violence, epistemic liberation, and epistemic disobedience has been rendered redundant.

What are the implications of decolonization and decolonized knowledge for education? What does decolonized education consist in, according to theorists like Mignolo, Garbe, Brunner, Clemens and others? Piedrahita Rodríguez (2020, pp. 48, 63) states that "a process of epistemological decolonization, based on the

[10] In a 2010, roundtable during the annual meeting of the Philosophy of Education Society in San Francisco, Claudia Ruitenberg posed the question, "How should the field of educational research respond to claims about indigenous African women's epistemologies?" (Code et al., 2012, p. 137)

[11] What appears to be ignored by colonizers and decolonial theorists alike is the very irrationality of suppressing or rejecting knowledge. If something amounts to knowledge, then it is rationally untenable not to recognize and prize it as such.

principles of Buen Vivir, is necessary, not only for political education, but also for the education system in general, in the search for new forms of education, based on the respect for all forms of life, respect for others and towards nature." Again, the question might be raised as to what this (otherwise perfectly plausible) requirement has to do with *epistemology*. According to Clemens (2020, p. 20), "educational science must focus on multiplicity and social aspects of knowledge," which – somewhat less plausibly – she takes to mean that evidence and truth must be deuniversalized. At this juncture, it might be noted that a prized terrain of decolonial theory, the sociology (and/or social/cultural anthropology) of knowledge, is more accurately called the sociology (and/or social/ cultural anthropology) of *belief*. At its most extreme, that is, in its radical particularism and with its relativist leanings, the decolonialist position is epistemologically incongruous. By contrast, there is an eminently plausible postcolonialist position that takes experiential knowledge and people's epistemic priorities seriously, without thereby advocating a blanket antiuniversalism or throwing out the critical universalist baby with the colonialist bathwater (see also Drerup, 2019, pp. 43–47). Given, for example, many indigenous peoples' experiences of colonization, physical as well as mental slavery, and wide-ranging epistemic violence, it stands to reason that they would have as priorities matters of epistemic transformation and redress. The promise of a critical universalism has in part to do with locality and context-specific relations – but not in terms of any exclusionist, hands-off approach. Rather, it appears to be plausible that the particular historical, geographic, and sociocultural experiences of the formerly colonized and oppressed give rise to particular priorities that shape their epistemic theory and practice. These experiences and priorities also yield conceptual and epistemological tools that are likely to enrich not only our understanding of colonialism, but also education and educational research as a whole (Horsthemke, 2020, p. 4).

29.4 Conclusion: Postcolonial Democracy Education

Must democracy education in a postcolonial time necessarily rest on a decolonizing approach that resists "Western knowledge" and education on the grounds that both are irredeemably tainted by colonialism and its universalizing tendencies? As suggested in our discussion of possibilities for postcolonial democracy and of decolonizing approaches to addressing the legacy of colonialism in knowledge and hence in education, there is an alternative, hybrid middle ground between the two polarities of Western hegemony on the one hand and repudiation of the West and replacing it with a retrieval of the indigenous on the other. Our concluding stance on postcolonial democratic education, which declines to accept either of these polarized possible choices, comprises two key recommendations.

Firstly, arguing from our critique of the political and educational features of colonialism and its enduring harms, we can identify the outlines of a democratic education that has some universal features but is open to enacting them with local variations to match relevant differences in local, national, and regional contexts and their democratically determined priorities. What future citizens need to learn would include central characteristics of democracy as based on the intrinsic value of political freedom, equality, and participation, with strategies for enacting those values and collective priorities fleshed out collaboratively as common goals, by contrast with rule under previous colonial regimes. Universally necessary to democratic education, too, is learning about potential threats to democracy, which all polities face. Such threats include the potential emergence of authoritarian politicians, populist parties, threats to a free press and an independent judiciary, as well as possible local antidemocratic tendencies peculiar to a context and its history.

If democratic education is to be postcolonial, then clearly in every educational context explicit attention should be given to the history and effects of colonialism, attending to both its universal features and to its local features and significance. At appropriate stages in formal education, as well as in open and deliberative public education, citizens need to learn not only about colonialism and how it has affected their own and other societies, but also about debates and controversies in interpreting the history of colonialism.[12] For example, British students need to know about the British Empire, its effects on people in former colonies, and its role in creating the society in which they themselves live, including the diverse traditions, experiences, histories, and literatures of its people. In all contexts, systematic attention is needed to curricula and to the spaces, rituals, and symbols in educational institutions and in public places, including their commemorative statues, through procedures that are in themselves open and democratically deliberative. It is likely that democratic education along these lines would closely resemble some distinctive features of a liberal education: acquiring a capacity for critical thinking, a broad and noninstrumental education that fosters both moral autonomy and attends to the rights and welfare of others. While the principle of noninstrumentality marks out a liberal education as pursued for its own sake as a feature of the good life, this does not preclude extrinsic benefits of education, primarily as a preparation for productive work and employment that benefits individuals and their communities.[13]

This last feature takes us to a second and urgent feature of a postcolonial democratic education, universally understood. There are significant and pressing problems in the current state of globalized neocoloniality that are common across the globe, and a universal threat to democracy and education of citizens in all countries, whether former colonies or previous imperial powers. These derive from the current dominant form of neoliberal capitalism into which

[12] This could include comparison of contrasting analyses of the impact and significance of colonialism, for example Ferguson's *Empire: How Britain Made the Modern World* (2012) and Tharoor's *Inglorious Empire: What Britain Did to India* (2018).

[13] See for example Nussbaum's (2010) defense of liberal education, in which the arts, literature, and humanities support the cultivation of critical thinking and imaginative empathy for others, aimed at democratic, global citizenship while also emphasizing education for employment. In relation to our argument in this chapter, a notable feature of Nussbaum's stance is that it is not a peculiarly "Western" one, as her liberalism embraces, for example, the ideas of the Indian philosopher Tagore.

almost all states have been pulled. This has fostered an unequal global economy in which former colonies remain disadvantaged, compared with the ongoing capacity of the previous imperial powers and new neocolonial forces to shape the global order to their own advantage. Much unaccountable power is wielded by multinational companies. The global political and educational order is profoundly undemocratic. In education, neoliberalism has cast pupils and students as customers, consumers of education for whom learning is an investment in the self and in which they are a means to the ends of the economy. Schools and universities have been colonized by neoliberal imperatives, with curricula increasingly tailored to programs that promote employability and profit above all else (Nussbaum, 2010). These tendencies include managerialist control and competitive league tables that favor educational institutions in rich countries. They are present as much in former colonies as they are in the West and are a universal, shared threat to democracy and to education.

References

Adebisi, F. I. (2016). Decolonizing education in Africa: Implementing the right to education by re-appropriating culture and indigeneity. *Northern Ireland Legal Quarterly*, 67(4), 433–51.

Altbach, P., & Kelly, G. (1978) *Education and colonialism*. London & New York: Longman.

Ashcroft, B., Griffiths G., & Tiffin, H. (Eds.) (1995). *The post-colonial studies reader*. London: Routledge.

Barnes, A. (2018). Christian evangelization and its legacy. In M. Shanguhyia & T. Falola, eds., *The Palgrave handbook of African colonial and postcolonial history*. New York: Palgrave, pp. 239–80.

Beetham, D. (2009). Democracy: Universality and diversity. *Ethics & Global Politics*, 2(4), 284–96.

Bennett, K. (2017). Epistemicide! The tale of a predatory discourse. In S. Cunico & J. Munday, eds., *Translation and Ideology, The Translator*, Special Issue 13(2), 151–69.

Brunner, C. (2016). Gewalt weiter denken in der Kolonialität des Wissens. In A. Ziai, ed., *Postkoloniale Politikwissenschaft. Theoretische und empirische Zugänge*. Bielefeld: Transcript-Verlag, Edition Politik, pp. 91–108.

Brunner, C. (2020). *Epistemische Gewalt*. Bielefeld: Transcript-Verlag.

Carnoy, M. (1974). *Education as cultural imperialism*. New York: Longman.

Chakrabarty, D. (2000). *Provincializing Europe*. Princeton, NJ: Princeton University Press.

Clemens, I. (2020). Decolonizing knowledge: Starting points, consequences and challenges. *Foro de Educación*, 18(1), 11–25. https://doi.org/dx.doi.org/10.14516/fde.733

Code, L., Phillips, D. C., Ruitenberg, C. W., Siegel, H., & Stone, L. (2012). Epistemological diversity: A roundtable. In C. W. Ruitenberg & D. C. Phillips, eds., *Education, culture and epistemological diversity: Mapping a contested terrain*. Dordrecht: Springer, pp. 121–43.

Culp, J. (2019). *Democratic education in a globalized world. A normative theory*. London: Routledge.

Drerup, J. (2019). Global justice, global citizenship education, and the postcolonial critique. *Global Justice: Theory Practice Rhetoric*, 12(1), 27–54. Available at: https://www.theglobaljusticenetwork.org/index.php/gjn/article/download/230/172.

Ferguson, N. (2012). *Empire: How Britain made the modern world*. London: Penguin.

Gandhi, L. (1998). *Postcolonial theory: A critical introduction*. New York: Columbia University Press.

Garbe, S. (2013). Deskolonisierung des Wissens: Zur Kritik der epistemischen Gewalt in der Kultur- und Sozialanthropologie. *Austrian Studies in Social Anthropology*, 1, 1–17. Available at: https://www.univie.ac.at/alumni.ksa/wp-content/uploads/text-documents/ASSA/ASSA-Journal-2013-01-DeskolonisierungDesWissens.pdf.

Gopal, P. (2020). *Insurgent empire: Anticolonial resistance and British dissent*. London: Verso.

Gutmann, A. (1987). *Democratic education*. Princeton, NJ: Princeton University Press.

Horsthemke, K. (2020). The provincialization of epistemology: Knowledge and education in the age of the postcolony. *On_education*, 3(7), 1–5.

Keane, J. (2009). *The life and death of democracy*. New York: W.W. Norton.

Keane, J. (2018). Is democracy a universal ideal? In J. Keane, *Power and humility: The future of monitory democracy*. Cambridge: Cambridge University Press, pp. 439–70.

Koelble, T., & LiPuma, E. (2008). Democratizing democracy: A postcolonial critique of conventional approaches to the measurement of democracy. *Democratization*, 15(1), 1–28.

Kohn, M. (2010). Post-colonial theory. In D. Bell, ed., *Ethics and world politics*. Oxford: Oxford University Press, pp. 200–18.

Lazarus, N. (2011). What postcolonial theory doesn't say. *Race & Class*, 53(1), 3–27.

Lebakeng, T. (2004). Towards a relevant higher education epistemology. In S. Seepe, ed., *Towards an African identity of higher education*. Pretoria: Vista University and Skotaville Media, pp. 109–19.

Levitzky, S., & Ziblatt, D. (2019). *How democracies die: What history reveals about our future*. New York: Penguin Random House.

LiPuma, E., & Koelble, T. (2009). Deliberative democracy and the politics of traditional leadership in South Africa: A case of despotic domination or democratic deliberation? *Journal of Contemporary African Studies*, 27(2), 201–23.

Masaka, D. (2018). The prospects of ending epistemicide in Africa: Some thoughts. *Journal of Black Studies*, 49(3), 284–301.

Mignolo, W. (2009). Epistemic disobedience, independent thought and decolonial freedom. *Theory, Culture & Society*, 26(7-8), 1–23.

Mignolo, W. (2011). Geopolitics of sensing and knowing: On (de)coloniality, border thinking and epistemic disobedience. *Postcolonial Studies*, 14(3), 273–83.

Ndlovu-Gatsheni, S. (2018). *Epistemic freedom in Africa: Deprovincialization and decolonization*. London & New York: Routledge.

Nussbaum, M. (2010). *Not for profit. Why democracy needs the humanities*. Princeton, NJ: Princeton University Press.

Parekh, B. (1994). Decolonizing liberalism. In A. Shtromas, ed., *The end of "Isms"? Reflections on the fate of ideological politics after communism's collapse*. Oxford: Blackwell, pp. 85–103.

Piedrahita Rodríguez, J. A. (2020). La descolonización epistemológica y la educación política en Colombia: Hacia una perspectiva ciudadana del Buen Vivir. *Foro de Educación*, 18(1), 47–65. https://doi.org/dx.doi.org/10.14516/fde.720

Pitts, J. (2010). Political theory of empire and imperialism. *Annual Review of Political Science*, 13, 211–35.

Quintero, P., & Garbe, S. (Eds.) (2013). *Kolonialität der Macht. De/Koloniale Konflikte zwischen Theorie und Praxis*. Münster: Unrast.

Ramose, M. B. (2004). In search of an African philosophy of education. *South African Journal of Higher Education*, 18(3), 138–60.

Robinson, A. L. (2019). Colonial rule and its political legacies in Africa. In N. Cheeseman, ed., *Oxford encyclopedia of African politics*, Oxford: Oxford University Press. https://doi.org/doi.org/10.1093/acrefore/9780190228637.013.1346

Runciman, D. (2018). *How democracy ends*. London: Profile Books.

Said, E. (1978). *Orientalism*. New York: Vintage.

Said, E. (1993). *Culture and imperialism*. London: Vintage.

Santos, B. D. (2014). *Epistemologies of the South: Justice against epistemicide*. London & New York: Routledge.

Santos, B. D., Nunes, J. A., & Meneses, M. P. (2008). Introduction: Opening up the canon of knowledge and recognition of difference. In B. D. Santos, ed., *Another knowledge is possible: Beyond Northern epistemologies*. London & New York: Verso, pp. xvix–lxii.

Sartori, A. (2006). The British Empire and its liberal mission. *The Journal of Modern History*, 78(3), 623–42.

Sass, J., & Dryzek, J. (2014). Deliberative cultures. *Political Theory*, 42 (1), 3–25.

Sen, A. (1999). Democracy as a universal value. *Journal of Democracy*, 10(3), 3–16.

Spivak, G. C. (1988). Can the subaltern speak? In C. Nelson & L. Grossberg, eds., *Marxism and the interpretation of culture*. Urbana-Champaign: University of Illinois Press, pp. 271–313.

Stovall, T. (2013). Empires of democracy. In G. Huggan, ed., *The Oxford handbook of postcolonial studies*. Oxford: Oxford University Press. https://doi.org/0.1093/oxfordhb/9780199588251.013.0010

Tharoor, S. (2018). *Inglorious empire: What the British did to India*. London: Penguin Random House.

Young, I. M. (1996). Communication and the other: Beyond deliberative democracy. In S. Benhabib, ed., *Democracy and difference: Contesting the boundaries of the political*. Princeton, NJ: Princeton University Press, pp. 120–35.

30

Populist Challenges to Democratic Education

Jürgen Oelkers

30.1 The Concept of Liberal Democracy and Education

In its elaborated form, what today is called "liberal democracy" appeared at the cusp of the eighteenth and nineteenth centuries. One of its originators was Jeremy Bentham. He indicated that freedom of the press and speech is essential for this form of democracy and cannot be subject to any censorship by the state or church (Bentham, 1821).[1]

Freedom of the press is synonymous with the "liberty of writing" (Bentham, 1821, p. 15), which also applies to the spoken word, that is to say, the freedom of expression in public meetings.[2] The two belong together. There are three prerequisites or "instruments of conjunction" for this, namely "instruction, excitation, and faculty of correspondence" (Bentham, 1821, p. 24).

Regardless of Bentham's philosophy, this entails two basic norms that must be fulfilled. The first is that an exchange of political arguments between various groups must take place. Available for this are various freely accessible locations and media where opinions can be formed without being limited to any particular elite. The other basic norm is education. Arguments must be elaborated, and the exchange thereof requires tolerance.

Every developed democracy must rely on citizens capable of criticism and articulation. Only in this way can democracy as a form of life continue and assert itself. Democratic coexistence requires social exchange and, hence, a minimum level of willingness to listen to each other and reach an agreement. This applies even between opponents (Inazu, 2016), who can develop tolerance only in joint discussion and not in abstract terms.

As long as speech is free, no one is always right, and everything can be exposed to criticism in public political discussion. The overriding validity of political views is determined by fair and equal elections with the participation of

[1] Bentham addressed his four essays to the citizens of Spain. The essays were meant to support Spanish liberals following the abolition of the inquisition on March 9, 1820, but Bentham was not concerned with exporting the English system of government, which was clearly not considered a representative democracy. Only in the language of lawyers, "that is, in liar's language, the government *is* a government representative of the people" (Bentham, 1821, p. 33).

[2] The call for freedom of speech is older than the call for freedom of the press (Moreau & Holtz, 2005).

responsible citizens. There is no automatic right to determine political policy, only a contest between opinions that never converge and therefore their advocates must provide convincing arguments in elections and to secure votes. Ideally, this occurs freely, without influence and with the aid of personal education.

With his proposal for a radical reform of the English parliament[3], Bentham called for a balancing-out of interests and the elimination of "sinister interests." He who claims to be a "friend of the people" conceals his true interests, which can never be anything other than particular and parochial. The issue is resolved when one considers interests and associates them with various parties or milieus (Bentham, 1817, pp. CCC–CCCII).

A prerequisite for reform is an education sufficient for representative elections, enabling the elected to conduct business mentally and morally, in other words, with integrity, intellectual competency, power of judgment and the skill of active participation in public discussion (Bentham, 1817, pp. 1–4). The same applies to voters in all classes; and, for the lower classes, this should mean an increase of comfort and social recognition (Bentham, 1817, p. 41).[4]

Only in this way can the political responsibility of the electorate be fulfilled. It should permit sovereign decisions formed via the programs and practice of politics. In liberal democracies, this creates the risk for those in government that they will not be elected again, a risk that is treated in discussion but cannot be eliminated. Political systems become authoritarian when an attempt is made to exploit this in order to keep a party or leader in power.

The association between democracy and general education took shape during the eighteenth century, when education began to be addressed to the people, who could therefore no longer be considered the "rabble" (Israel, 2013). Previously, courting the people's voice had often been dismissed as wishful thinking or religious fanaticism, and the idea was met with social disgust or rigid marginalization without any discursive analysis. In other words, public opinion was devoid of the citizens' arguments.

Hence, the education of citizens became central to the pedagogical program of the Enlightenment. Citizens should communicate and influence public opinion, which should not erupt spontaneously in the streets but should be based on arguments raised before the high court of reason. This, at any rate, is how Immanuel Kant and Jürgen Habermas viewed the political public under the Enlightenment. The public is composed of citizens – men and women – and not subjects.

Liberal democracy does not allow a political party or movement to represent the entire people, whatever the convictions of their followers. Representative democracies are developed in such a way that the relevant political groups in a

[3] Written in 1809 in the form of a catechism.

[4] Bentham (1817, pp. 5–9) called for annual elections by secret ballot, equal electoral districts, the right to vote by everyone who pays a certain amount of taxes, and the disqualification of members of parliament who obtain a seat (placement) without an election.

society can win parliamentary seats in an election, and in doing so, must strive for a majority.

On the other hand, a parliamentary democracy inevitably produces problems, indicating how far politics is removed from everyday life and thus having the ability to harm faith in democracy. Thomas Carlyle (1855, p. 127), referring to debates in the English parliament, spoke of a "national palaver" that serves only imaginary purposes and is therefore useless.

From a race-conscious perspective,[5] the form of argumentation[6] frequently used in Germany after 1848 often overlooks the democratic rules of parliamentary discourse. In the latter, arguments and methods count, and every new election can change them. Underlying arguments can be drawn in later, and therefore the person who has won a majority need not necessarily be in the right. Any experience can be contested, but ultimately experience is democracy's corrector and requires general education.

Certain conditions need to be fulfilled for this ideal to be achieved, however. Education systems are liberal when they recognize the maturity of future citizens, foster freedom of speech, gear themselves to modern sciences, guarantee a pluralism of outlook, are religiously neutral, and dispense with any dogmatic claims.

According to this view, education is to be arranged in the schools. It is oriented toward a democratic society and, therefore, to communication between different groups, not toward a particularly powerful group that serves only its own interests and does everything it can to control public education for its own purposes. When this occurs, the meaning of general education in a modern sense, a common value that can serve no parochial interests without being discredited, is deliberately ignored.

"Public" education in this paradigm means educational opportunities that are freely accessible, that is, free of charge, avoid mandatory curricula, apply no admission barriers, are conducted professionally and are guaranteed by binding school legislation. Curricula generally remain stable over a longer period. This usually also applies to private schools and thus serves as a contract for generations. Parents trust that their children will receive educational opportunities just as good or better than the ones they themselves had. The educational offering is recognized on a political level, receives public judgment, and is exposed to criticism.

30.2 Populism

"Populism" is a modern term that has been used in political debates for about 60 years, but is based on much older contexts that refer to the power of the "vox populi" (the voice of the people) (Boas, 2020). This is regularly associated with

[5] The antidemocrat Carlyle applied "palaver" to African tribes in his history of the French Revolution.

[6] The Frankfurt parliament (1848–49) was described as a "talking shop" (*Schwatzbude*) by both left-wing and right-wing critics.

political protests and social movements, usually with the courage of a crowd or the loudness of a marketplace meeting.

Today, the term "vox populi" is used to warn of the danger of populist rhetoric to liberal democracy (Van der Geest et al., 2020). However, the expression was also used in ancient times, where the voice of the people was considered uncontrollable, and "people" (populus) was often synonymous with "rabble." This meaning has not disappeared. It remains, for example, as an expression of fear of spontaneous unrest, such as "mob rule."

However, political opinions usually do not emerge spontaneously and do not descend solely from interests and associated thematic junctures. Opinions are frequently an expression of deep-seated convictions, combined with incorrigible world outlooks that are articulated in public. In this sense "populist" opinions in politics can be seen as immune to, authoritarian, and outside of a plural universe of discourse (Müller, 2016, p.1).

These views often take the form of manifestos formulated for certain target groups, and often involve a clash of cultures. One of their characteristics is a radical simplification of complex conflict issues, whereby they take sides with the issue at hand and seek no compromises. The accompanying binary rhetoric has been part of political theology ever since the pamphlets handed out during the Reformation, and today is often described as "populism."

Such manifestos are often associated with provocations and the language of "failure," also involving suspicions of hypocrisy, betraying their theological origins. Today, politicians are said to be hypocrites when they claim to speak the truth and act for the common good, but are suspected of lying and of merely lining their own pockets. However, this accusation always applies only to the other side.

This suspicion has historical substance; it refers to the masking of actual power (Runciman, 2018) and is applied particularly easily when it is associated with an elite and pursues biased generalizations. It is never one's own failure that is projected at political leaders: they were voted into office and can therefore always be voted out.

But what does "populism" generally mean? In 1954, the American sociologist Edward Shils (1954) gave it a broad and negative interpretation. Previously, "populist" had been used for various purposes, including to describe a political party.[7] Shils understood "populism" as the opposite of civil, orderly, and moderate behavior in everyday politics.

In this contect, Shils referred to "conspiracy theories," a term that arose in the Cold War and which Richard Hofstadter (1964) described as the focus of a "paranoid" style that should not be taken to mean mental pathology. The starting point was fear of communist infiltration, a fear whipped up by politicians and stylized by the media. Since the 1950s, conspiracy theories have been exploited and altered many times, regardless of the context in which they emerged (Thalmann, 2019).

[7] The "Populist Party" or "People's Party" (1892–1909). The party represented the interests and demands of the rural population during the industrialization of the southern and western United States (Brexel, 2004).

For Shils, populist behavior is led by a suspicion of politics and lawful procedures and by faith in one's moral superiority: "suspicion of privacy and the withdrawal of common culture" (Shils, 1956, p. 133). This culture derives from heterogeneous elements, which must grow together, and is based on convictions. Hence it is fragile and subject to disruption (Shils, 1982, p. 236).

In other words, it can easily be split when its common communicative features grow thin and brittle in elections and political decisions, when people start to believe in a conspiracy, or when there is general mistrust in the government. This thesis is supported by the findings of recent research (e.g., Keefer et al., 2021).

As a strategy for political battles, the term "populism" is used in a dual manner. On the one hand, it describes the disrespected other side of a political constellation. "Populists" are always those who have to be marginalized because they dramatically simplify complex problems or because their target groups are loud. On the other hand, the suppressed voice of the people should help express itself without employing the language of the elites or heeding the duty of differentiation any longer.

In media contexts, the point is actually to cement convictions with suggestive messages on one's own channels if possible. There are calls for a fight against the established forces, often connected with missions on the political level. On a public level, a radical simplification of all problems and solutions, tailored according to the enemy-against-enemy pattern, is needed. In this sense, "populism" often means an erasure of differences in complex issues and undermining the rules governing discourse.

However, if "populism" were simply the same as impermissible simplification, many politicians would have to be described as "populists." Differentiation is a requirement of analysis, but not of political publicity, which is designed to influence opinions by suggestive means. Political elections often take the form of the most radical simplification, in other words, a choice between only one "either" and only one "or."

Political movements are often public expressions of protest, and in that sense, are indispensable for democracy. Legitimate protests are aimed at clearly identifiable circumstances, such as the economic collapse of entire regions of the United States, China's increasing influence on legislation in Hong Kong, or Turkey's responsibility for the wave of migration to Europe in 2015. If someone fails to get the attention of the relevant authorities, they will try to draw attention to their problems in another way.

Therefore, in a certain sense, Shils' definition is too narrow and biased.[8] In certain situations, spontaneous "uncivil" conduct is required, and the only question is how far it can go without doing permanent damage to democracy and the rule of law. Often, an uprising is supposed to be for the benefit of, and in the name of, democracy. The subsequent processes determine this benefit.

[8] For other definitions, see Anselmi (2018) or the German collection of Möller (2022).

The rhetoric of political movements always includes references to the "people" to disguise these movements' own parochial interests. For this purpose, they employ an ideological superstructure that sometimes pursues a Manichean world outlook via which rage and hatred can be permanently articulated. Democracy is not a philosophical seminar but a struggle for power that nevertheless follows the rules. But when democracy takes to the streets in certain situations, that does not mean that it can win there.

Political parties can develop identities, not only when they address emergencies but especially when they overcome hostilities and prejudice. Then comes the threat of a homogeneous merger, eliminating the purpose of a balance between them. Voters who are emotionally involved and can only act politically based on prejudice, driven by a mistaken understanding, will not attain a positive result (Mason, 2018, p. 141).

On this view, the border of democracy is clearly defined. He who gains power does not hold on to it for life, whatever the popular references to the people suggest. The framework of democracy is the constitution and the rule of law. The storming of the US Capitol on January 6, 2021 was an attempted coup because it deliberately ignored and attempted to destroy this framework, led by the populist lie of election fraud (Bender, 2021).

When undemocratic movements come into power, even by democratic means, they will try to translate as much of their radical policies as possible into politics. They will almost always do so "in the name of the people." The actual beneficiaries of the newly acquired power remain hidden. They are certain milieus and groups, but never "the" people.

In this way, a hubris is expressed whereby no particular opinion is articulated. Instead, the opinion of those in power is used to express the truth. Only the followers of a group or milieu benefit from it. However, these followers can easily believe previously unmentioned facts if the leadership can convince them that they are true. Those who argue against these facts are treated not as opponents but as traitors.

That is how Donald Trump conducts his permanent election struggle. A charismatic, ruthlessly self-staging Trump has influenced his followers in such a way that with every fresh attack on his enemies, he becomes more and more of a "genius" in their eyes (Rucker & Leonning, 2021). They believe he obeys the voice of the people, unlike the elites. This belief is popular and credible to many groups of voters, who are impervious to any objections, even if obvious lies are disclosed.

They then simply say that the media are corrupt and spread "fake news." Conversely, the liberal media, at least in the United States, are focusing more strongly on their own target groups because they fear losses; they assume the expectations of their audiences and share their principles ("Woke-Media": Ungar-Sargon, 2021).

The strategies of charismatic populism are particularly successful where citizens no longer participate in political processes or go to the elections but adopt fundamental positions that exclude compromises. The political opponent is the enemy. Therefore, all topics have a binary load – "for us and against them." Any election can thus turn into a battle that determines defeat or survival.

On the other hand, there is an unease that is frequently attributed to faulty liberalism which is no longer willing or capable of implementing binding standards and which opens the doors to hedonistic individualism (Deneen, 2018). Liberalism is said to be destroying culture and leading to the release of the "disembedded individual" (Deneen, 2018, p. 87), corresponding to the destruction of the local cultures and traditions on which democracy rests (Deneen, 2018, p. 88).[9]

However, democratic social forms are not the same as thick communities that can drift toward political hostility, as the history of petty-bourgeois fascism has shown. The conviction of a released individual who has lost all cultural connections (Deneen, 2018, p. 66) is just as much distortion as homogeneous communities or collective identities in the political theory of the right-wing (Benoist, 2019).

For John Stuart Mill, liberal democracy is not a cradle of weak norms but a form of government to protect freedom. However, in this way, it is linked to forms of life and education, especially efforts to produce culture. Social forms of life are diverse and are not limited in size. They become "democratic" through rules, convictions, and communication inside and outside, but not for historical eternity. On the other hand, education never has any uniform effects, not even when collectively organized by the state.

However, that does not mean that education guarantees political justification. One must distinguish between the acquisition of education and its use; political participation often consists only in consent or abstention. One either follows a party or abstains from voting. Both are at the cost of one's own judgment, which often takes shape in, and depends on, networks.

Empirically, it can be shown that conservative voters in the United States are more susceptible to conspiracy theories than liberals. The more extreme the views of the conservatives, the stronger this trend (Van der Linden et al., 2020). Opinions are confirmed internally, in isolation from those who are considered enemies. QAnon is one of the most striking examples of this modern phenomenon of conspiracy within democracy.

This populist trend becomes stronger in situations where sustainable arguments and judgment results no longer play a primary role or have any role and where political behavior is merely controlled. In such a situation, the addressees are "users" and not citizens. "Users" do not simply use but pass judgment while wanting others to reach decisions for them. They do not alter the platform on which they move.

30.3 New Media and the Public

The mechanism of brief provocation is known from product advertising and has also been used in election campaigns for a long time. What is new are the ways

[9] "Democracy requires extensive social forms that liberalism aims to deconstruct, particularly shared social practices and commitments that arise from thick communities, not a random collection of unconnected selves entering and exiting an election booth" (Deneen, 2018, p. S. XV).

and means in which social media is used for political campaigns. Political campaigns can address their users directly and communicate with them discreetly. Ronald Reagan was not able to tweet his messages like "make America great again"[10] and had to rely on the distributive effects of the traditional media.

In campaigns today, differentiation between target groups plays a key role, as do figures on voters' behavior, the use of resources, and the presentation of topics in the media. It is not responsible citizens that are the addressees of campaigns, but their psychograms, which set out their conduct, preferences, political options, and information about their origin, where they live, and education.

This strategy has come a long way in a short time, as evidenced by American election campaigns from Barack Obama's first candidacy in 2008 through to the Trump campaign of 2016 (Kreiss, 2016). Political messages can now be adapted to personality profiles, and the political spectrum can then decide where it is worth campaigning and where it is not (Hersh, 2015). There are then two groups of voters, those who are being wooed and those who are not interesting.

For some time now, the increased democratization via the internet has been discussed, as every user can now express themself in public in the virtual networks, and every voice can be raised (Kosinski, 2019) something not possible in the real-world public sphere , which had clear conditions and depended on representation, thus restricting participation. In addition, no one could act anonymously – each player had a name, and their support was linked to their visibility.

The effects of the change are far-reaching. Most public opinion is no longer structured in the manner foreseen by liberalism, that is, a literate society able to compare the arguments of various options and reach a considered opinion. Also, there is not one but several public opinions, from which anyone can choose. Meanwhile, even Jürgen Habermas (2021) who normally favored the reasoning of one public sphere peaks of a "renewed" structural change to the political scene.

Opinions are still being increasingly formulated, but they appear during direct exchanges in the high-speed media, making it difficult to bring a topic to any conclusion and to accept or reject an argument. "Speed" means that more and more time is spent on the web, and waiting is considered exhausting. At the same time, fake news from unidentified sources is accumulating.

In a dimension devoid of rules about criticism, no one can completely shield themselves from obvious nonsense and worse things like racism and religious hatred, whether closeted or explicit. As a user, one is not obliged to listen and can easily switch to other media to find others who think the way one does oneself. This game has no end but can only be continued at its own levels of tension.

In this way, convictions cement themselves and allow no access to any objection. No real dialogue takes place. Anyone who contradicts an opinion can be

[10] Slogan in the 1980 presidential campaign.

eliminated with a single mouse-click, which is something that is theoretically unthinkable for any public political dimension. Public opinion is not a homogeneous echoing space but a forum that brings together various topics from various parties. They can fight each other and heap polemics on each other, but they must not see any enemies eliminated.

Beneath this threshold, too, the following applies: the tasks of social coexistence cannot be fulfilled with isolated communities that have nothing to say to each other but expect rapid authoritarian solutions. The democratic social form rules this out and asserts itself via processes of serious understanding. However, these seem to be changing rapidly, a situation which will have educational consequences, not least because the center of power is shifting.

Without argumentative controls on public opinion, the freedom of the individual increases, but so does the power of groups who control themselves using self-assertion. In a vicious circle of assertion, no authority controls the level of discussion because anything that conforms to expectations is welcome. The "better argument" then asserts itself and requires no discussion. However, that is the basic condition for any civic public space.

A distinction must be made between citizens and consumers, as "citizens do not think and act as consumers" (Sunstein, 2017, p. 167). Therefore, public education cannot refer to consumers but only to future citizens, whether education is offered privately or by the state (Sunstein, 2017, p. 166–67). The reason is straightforward: "Acting together as citizens, people can solve problems that prove intractable for consumers" (Sunstein, 2017, pp. 168).

Consumers act for themselves and not for the common good. Consumption can both benefit and harm coexistence. In this sense, consumer behavior is also political but does not indicate citizens' political conduct or education.

Citizens must be able to circumvent political populism, in other words, identify conspiracy theories, mistrust simple and superficial solutions, repel attacks on democratic institutions, and keep an eye on the common good. On the other hand, if politics develops into an uncontrolled, permanent, and continuous drama, there is a danger that people will refuse to learn, and feelings of resentment will reign.

In his book *The Internet of Us*, the American philosopher Michael Patrick Lynch (2016) referred to another danger. From him comes the expression "Google-knowing": in other words, digital knowledge that is searched for and collected. This knowledge has certain qualities, it is "fast, easy and productive" (Lynch, 2016, p. 179), but only as a store of knowledge.

It cannot take the place of efforts at comprehension. "Google-knowing" is not creative (Lynch, 2016, p. 180) and not even a respected authority can be added to it in a reliably selective manner as teachers have assumed for a long time. Google is a search engine but, at the same time, a new kind of labyrinth. People do not find most of the things they search for, and what they find is often based on the Google error that comprehension can be taught directly (Lynch, 2016, p. 181).

"Public opinion" is always a figure of speech with respect to which one can distinguish between impermissible and permissible forms of expression.

Citizens who speak up and express their opinions use their language and react to any semantic deviations or breaches. This occurs in unexpected circumstances and with a new type of power of opinion in the new media. The results, even those unintended, are taken into account.

The new forms of media have in common that they can be used instantly and individually. Their teaching channels are straightforward and largely free of any conditions, requiring practically no qualifications. Neither do they pursue any aims except influencing and binding user behavior. Their contents can be renewed at one's discretion and are free of knowledge hierarchies or barriers such as social origins or lack of previous knowledge. In this respect, the PISA test is no longer a norm.

A fragmented communications market in a heterogeneous democracy creates high risks for citizens and coexistence, not just because of deliberate processes of false information or "cybercascades" (Sunstein, 2017, p. 135). "To the extent that the process entrenches existing views, spreads falsehood, promotes extremism, and makes people less able to work cooperatively on shared problems, there are dangers for the society as a whole" (Sunstein, 2017).

Education is meant to counteract this or at least clarify it to the extent that people will understand "cybercascades" for what they really are, strategies against the democratic social form and against citizens' power of judgment. However, this must be understood against the background of the populist challenges that also confront the concept of a liberal educational system.

30.4 Populist Challenges to Educational Systems

Schools cannot act independently of the political framework in which they are contained and by which they are framed and financed. Today, many of the world's educational systems are politically authoritarian and pursue objectives that are not connected with the requirements of liberal society. Communist China and the Arab countries, Iran, Russia, and the post-Soviet republics, to say nothing of North Korea, are equally affected. In countries like these, the state is not concerned about any balance of interests but acts solely to exercise and propagate political power.

The basis is a strict state ideology headed by a leader. This ideology employs populist means of communication that turn Shils' negative definition into a deliberately positive one. Instead of distance, it calls for conformity, and instead of division, it calls for cultural uniformity, backed by attacks on foreign conspiracies and consistent separation of what is domestic from what is foreign. The rhetoric formulae and explanations follow the pattern of the political authoritarianism of the interwar period of the twentieth century (Oelkers, 2020).

An example of autocratic reconstruction of society is China's system of social credits to control behavior, which is nothing other than a wide-scale attempt at education designed to rid society of subversion, the only weapon people under a dictatorship have. It is not restructured education, but public opinion, which

Erving Goffman (1971) described as a self-controlled *public order* of interaction that escapes state intervention.

For Goffman, the individual moves inside a public space created by this movement. He is concerned about relationships, contacts, and rituals, including conciliation, in volatile public networks, and not acquiring points in an educational program that rewards good behavior and punishes deviations. Unlike earlier attempts at social control, nothing should be lost, and anyone can be affected by losing trust.[11]

China is ruled by a totalitarian regime that is subject to no democratic control and appears immune to any objections. Inside the country, educated Chinese people well versed in internet communications refer to Western "right-wing populism" and exploit this viewpoint to criticize Western hegemony and construct an ethnoracial identity for their own country (Zhang, 2019).

The authoritarian Chinese educational system is preparing this successfully. Unlike South Korea and Japan, at least in a programmatic sense, the Chinese system has never approached the Western model of education and upbringing. Therefore, it has never accepted pluralism.

The confinement and "reeducaion" of ethnic minorities in camps is well documented and shows how strongly political pressure on opinion causes ideological distortions.[12] Political public opinion has no role to play. In December 2021, the government announced that China is a "democracy that works."[13]

In a democratic society, one can talk of pedagogical "populism," when educational systems take shape with the aid of topics and explanations loaded with emotion and promise alternative solutions that are often based solely on the expressed dissatisfaction of an opposition group. Alternative solutions act as a release from the evil that the other group regards as liberty.

The secular structure of state schools, the theory of evolution in biology lessons, the role and structure of sex education, the treatment of religious minorities, and the picture of history propagated by the school are all included in this. The stronger the unshakable beliefs clash against each other in these zones, the more difficult it is to conduct dialogue, as shown recently by the "school-board wars" in the United States.[14]

Various strategies alter or amend the educational system when the ruling public loses influence and populist trends are evident. They are "populist" in various respects, but especially from the point of view of Shils whereby subjective convictions assume the nature of unshakable truths, parochial identities set the tone, or individual dissatisfaction guides the decisions reached by institutions.

[11] Nevertheless, a dictatorship of tight surveillance, smartly controlled and stored (Strittmatter, 2018), has not appeared yet. The system is still locally fragmented and is based on nontechnical data collection, such as reports and investigations (Drinhausen & Brussee, 2021).

[12] The Chinese gulags are described as "vocational education" (Haitiwaji & Morgat, 2021).

[13] State Council Information Office (2021). For the international political spectrum, China is supposed to represent a new model of democracy.

[14] *The New York Times*, November 16 and 17, 2021.

One of the strategies is geared to the national curriculum and has left and right variants. This means continuous attempts to remove the theory of evolution from biology lessons or at least to relativize it considerably. However, one is also concerned with the new version of history instruction, language policy, the canon of school literature, or sex education, which pose a provocation to the self-conception of, for instance, national conservative or evangelical groups. Not just because of this do they seek close contact with autocrats.

However, it is not just the right-hand side of the political spectrum involved here. Language policy takes center stage wherever there are calls for a symbolic recognition of minorities. At the same time, revisions of history are meant to revise those parts of the social and cultural past, in other words, established historiography, that are stigmatized as "racist."

Moreover, all these tendencies are academically important and should impact the curriculum. However, public discussion is often beset with populist anger that opposes any differentiation. Such anger also applies to gender issues insofar as they are linked to strong beliefs and rigorous morality. The public seeks and exploits this, but at the same time, invalidates a basic principle, the principle of mutual recognition. The public arena then becomes a battlefield.

The COVID-19 pandemic that began in 2020 was accompanied by serious school disputes between the opponents and supporters of compulsory vaccination. They allowed no compromises and sometimes even set families against each other. COVID also fueled conspiracy theories and showed how quickly reason and considered judgment could disappear. A crisis like this also provides an educational experience and can lend force to paranoid trends in the public system of beliefs (Suthaharan et al., 2021; similar findings appear in the Basel study by Kuhn et al., 2021).

A second, increasingly widespread pedagogical strategy calls for instruction in schools and universities to be a "safe space" and aims to prevent mental harm using "trigger warnings." The concept of a pedagogical safe space goes back to Jean-Jacques Rousseau's *Emile* (1762) and is based on the premise that children require protection for their own good. Rousseau had in mind the dangers posed by society, especially in comparison with others.

What Rousseau intended for children can have fatal consequences for adults if the safe space contradicts the freedom of learning and opens the door to a new kind of censorship that casts everything into doubt and supports things that eventually could be harmful. Instead of relying on the free judgments of those who are learning, defense and resistance are conditioned as friendly protection against excessive challenges.

The raison d'être behind this strategy is frequently the populist demarcation of the psychological trauma theory and the protection of an identity that tolerates no overload and which anyone can adopt for themself. Epistemic authorities remain anonymous, and instead of encouraging critical thinking (cf. the articles in Bernecker et al., 2021), they hinder it because the safe space, with constant fresh warnings, can become a permanent phenomenon.

However, even the safe space for children is a problem if it merely involves consumerism in which learning is nothing but "fun" and can interconnect only with similar values. This affects schools and their curriculum. They are compelled to shield themselves from the consumer world but are often unable to draw the boundary. This applies, for instance, to popular learning strategies that avoid efforts that offer no immediate reward.

To this extent, the populist challenge also affects schools themselves. This applies all the more when every controversial topic can be developed into a challenge for schools. At the same time, the value of public schooling is cast into doubt. The danger is that civic responsibility for schools disappears, and schools cannot serve democracy without this trust in it (Stitzlein, 2017).

A third strategy is retrograde and recognizes various features advocated by right-wing and evangelical authors, which also appear in parallel movements and frequently refer to a homogeneous population that survived the past but is now under threat and is meant to be salvaged through education. These features include a return to unquestionable authority at school and at home, strictness and discipline as educational values, a dismantling of democratization, a devaluation of dialogue and discussion, and even the duty of upbringing based on creed or race. It is a mistake to assume that all this lies in the past (Giudici, 2021; Peters & Besley, 2020; especially on the effects of the internet, Watson & Barnes, 2021).

Pedagogical concepts like this always repeat themselves in public debates and merely wait for a suitable discussion forum. Framed in this way, populism comes out into the open as soon as the right opportunity arises. What is decisive is who is believed in the public space based on what arguments or evidence and how minorities emerge. Moreover, whenever there is mention of "populism," the level of education makes no difference on its own (Brühwiler & Goktepe, 2021).

It is also becoming clear today that the Western concept of a liberal education formed after the end of the Cold War has never had global respect and has even been debated inside democracies. One need only consider the market orientation and steady indebtedness of university studies in the United States. State funding of public education has always been strongly opposed and schools' freedom strongly supported. Even in that country, authoritarian concepts of upbringing have never disappeared. They have merely been absent in educational literature on the subject of upbringing.

The restoration of religious undertones to the educational system represents a further populist trend that is spreading massively. This has not yet affected Protestant Central Europe but has certainly affected Catholic countries like Hungary and Poland and orthodox Russia, Islamic Turkey, and Hindu India. These countries have secular public education that is being increasingly repressed, to the applause of various parental groups (Oelkers, 2018).

The arguments employed there join church and state, are nationalist in tone, and reject any liberal theology. Also, there is frequent reference to national opposition, such as the historical fight of Orthodox churches to the spread of Catholicism in Russia and the salvaging of Catholic identity against the backdrop of the Reformation in Poland. Therefore, the nation is a pedagogical point of reference even when the diverse histories are unsustainable but can be told in schools as tales.

The development of educational systems possesses its own kind of logic because various elements appear everywhere and cannot be dismantled. No system lacks strongly funded subjects like mathematics. Information science is part of the general curriculum everywhere. No one has to go without sport in schools, and countries like China invest in top research that the ruling party can only in parts, like the early COVID-19 cases in Wuhan, influence.

However, that does not mean that political interference in these countries weakens or far-reaching autonomy takes shape in education. In his *Esprit des loix* (1748), Montesquieu said that the form of government creates the laws that govern education, not vice versa. According to this logic, democratic upbringing can only exist in a democracy.

However, in reality, increasing cases do not fit into any firm category. They assume a hybrid shape. Countries like Russia are formally a democracy but are assuming increasingly authoritarian features reminiscent of a monarchy and either do not require a liberal public opinion or deliberately neutralize it. Social education then becomes gradually authoritarian because criticism can be widely ignored.

In these systems there is no longer any criticism of schools, at least no public criticism, which is a feature of Western discourse and has always been a challenge or a bone of contention. Criticism of schools is seldom moderate or restrained, but often radical and suggestive regarding the solving of problems and solutions, and always arouses discussions. Schools in an authoritarian system of education do not need this.

This must not be identified with trends to develop the system. Digitalization is the driving force everywhere, whose effects cannot be entirely judged yet. However, it has already altered the lives of children and young people so much that there is an often irresistible pressure on schools and curricula to offer serious and structured subjects. However, in the altered learning environments, this culture must be protected, further developed, and defended against populist trends coming from left and right.

30.5 Perspectives: Education for Democracy

In her literary report on the development of Anglo-Saxon theoretical discourse on democracy and education between 2006 and 2017, the Spanish pedagogue Edda Sant distinguished between three main political concepts of democratic upbringing: education for democracy; education within democracy; and education through democracy (Sant, 2019, pp. 481–83).

The first concept involves traditional upbringing, is suitably established using standards, and is based on state-organized "mass schooling policies" as practiced in almost every liberal democracy. The philosophical principles usually conform to John Dewey's *Democracy and Education* ([1916] 1985). The second concept does not emerge from a democratic society but from free choices, which are supposed to represent a democracy. Education is appropriately understood as individual and competitive. The third concept assumes that democracy and education cannot be separated, the educational policy must be based on citizen participation, and the school itself is a place of democracy. This, too, owes its origins to Dewey and his concept of the school as an "embryonic society."

The first principle, "education for democracy," is preferred with regard to practice in most of the articles examined by Sant, "and has been very successful influencing educational practices worldwide" (Sant, 2019, p. 683). The neoliberal approach is considered elitist and thus unsuitable for the education of all children in a democracy. In contrast, the deliberative and inclusive features of the third principle are integrated into the first one as far as possible.

However, this thesis does not apply worldwide when considering the authoritarian education trends in China and Russia. It also requires expansion. If democracy is to be understood as a form of ruled coexistence, including self-government and popular sovereignty, a government cannot simply prescribe the education of the people in a way that suits it. Education must also shape the ability to object. Only an authoritarian state can raise discipline and conformity to the status of a cult.

Democratic schools are based on transparent rules and call for adaptability on the part of the system – in other words, a transformation that does not alter the basic principles. In addition, various learning channels must be accepted, and deviations from goals must be understood in positive terms. Lastly, one must remember that knowledge acquisition is an independent process.

What makes future education different from schooling in the eighteenth and twentieth centuries is that the state has lost its monopoly over education. Obligatory schooling is no longer synonymous with far-reaching control over the entire teaching environment, but it is not devalued because mass education for democracy cannot exist without a compulsory school attendance.

Therefore, schools will continue to pursue the objectives of public education and must also keep the development of democracy in their sights. In this regard, they are not neutral, but they have no freedom to influence the political opinions that must be propagated. Therefore, apart from a subject curriculum, public schools should stand out with a culture of debate that is bound to the freedom of speech and open exchange. In other words, they should not advocate dogmas or promote only individual sensitivities.

The basic principle of educational organization is that a school career cannot be repeated. General education may offer many opportunities brought by life experience, but schooling has quite specific curricula. One condition is that their progress is irreversible. One can break off schooling but never restart it from the beginning.

Liberal democracy requires both the ability to learn and also formal education in the sense of comprehension skills that cannot be simply attained on the go. This applies all the more when everything that happens can be turned into a political topic. Cognitive arrangements and the creation of educational horizons are necessary, and these cannot be lifted from the internet.

The school has always been a concentration point of knowledge that has never let itself be completely undermined in the entire history of schooling, but has acquired recognized authority in the form of an educational canon or curriculum. A central criterion of school tuition is to improve the existing teaching horizon, raise professional standards, and continuously develop the interests of the individual.

For a long time, society had no alternative but to grow accustomed to education. Since the Reformation, education has been an institution secured by obligatory schooling, determining its own offer, and controlling the media effectively. A transfer of education to the interactive media, which respond to demand, would alter the situation thoroughly and irreversibly.

Only interaction and exchange between various groups, in other words across borders, is a democratic social form. John Dewey ([1916] 1985) observed this correctly, even if he might have underestimated the forms of government in a democracy and the political struggle for power. For him, nefariousness was not a subject. On the other hand, when parties or groups only fight each other, the common good that constitutes a social form is eroded.

Attempts to accept populist rhetoric as left-wing articulation by democratic movements (Laclau, 2005),[15] that refer to Dewey's version of coexistence (Mårdh & Tryggvason, 2017) are not very convincing, all the less so because they do not take into account the consequences of media control over education processes or do not want to recognize them as a danger.

Dewey's theory assumes that every experience "educates," but not every experience contributes to mental and social growth. The objective is to encourage thinking that is tested in experience before it can qualify as thinking. One learns only by reflecting upon experience. That is not the same as the "voice of the people."

References

Anselmi, M. (2018). *Populism. An introduction*. Trans. by Laura Fano Morrisey. London/New York: Routledge.

Bender, M. C. (2021). *"Frankly, we did win this election": The inside story how Trump lost*. New York/Boston: Twelve Books, Grand Central Publishing.

Benoist, A. de (2019). *Contre le libéralisme: La société n'est pas un marché*. Paris: Payot.

Bentham, J. (1817). *Plan of parliamentary reform, in the form of a catechism, with reasons for each article, with an introduction, renewing the necessity of radical, and the inadequacy of moderate, reform*. London: R. Hunter.

Bentham, J. (1821). *On the liberty of the press and public discussion*. London: William Hone.

Bernecker, S., Flowerree, A. K., & Grundmann, T. (Eds.) (2021). *The epistemology of fake news*. Oxford: Oxford University Press.

Boas, G. (2020). *Vox populi: Essays in the history of an idea*. Baltimore, MD: Johns Hopkins University Press.

[15] For social movements, the following should apply: Populism is "a performative act endowed with a rationality of its own" (Laclau, 2005, p. 18).

Brexel, B. (2004). *The populist party. A voice for the farmers in an industrial society*. New York: Rosen.

Brühwiler, C. F., & Goktepe, K. (2021). Populism with a Ph.D.: Education levels and populist leaders. *Journal of Political Power*, 14(3), 449–71. https://doi.org/10.1080/2158379X.2021.1904366.

Carlyle, T. (1855). *Latter-day pamphlets*. Boston/New York: Philipps, Sampson, and Company; J.C. Derby.

Deneen, P. J. (2018): *Why liberalism failed. With a new preface*. New Haven, CT: Yale University Press.

Dewey, J. (1916/1985). *The middle works 1899–1924, vol. 9: Democracy and education 1916*. Ed. by J. A. Boydston; introduced by S. Hook. Carbondale/Edwardsville, IL: Southern Illinois University Press.

Drinhausen, K., & Brussee, V. (2021, March 3): China's social credit system in 2021. From fragmentation toward integration. *Merics China Monitor*. Available at: https://ccn.unistra.fr/websites/ccn/documentation/Cybersecurite/MERICS_ChinaMonitor_67_Social_Credit_System_final_1.pdf (accessed: December 27, 2021).

Giudici, A. (2021). Seeds of authoritarian opposition: Far-right education politics in post war Europe. *European Educational Research Journal*, 20(2), 121–42.

Goffman, E. (1971). *Relations in public. Microstudies of the public order*. Harmondsworth/Middlesex: Penguin Books.

Habermas, J. (2021). Überlegungen und Hypothesen zu einem erneuten Strukturwandel der politischen Öffentlichkeit. In M. Seeliger & S. Sevignani, eds., *Ein neuer Strukturwandel der Öffentlichkeit?* (Leviathan Sonderband 37), Baden-Baden: Nomos, pp. 470–500.

Haitiwaji, G., & Morgat, R. (2021). *Rescapée du goulag Chinois*. Paris: Editions des Equateurs.

Hersh, E. D. (2015). *Hacking the electorate. How campaigns perceive voters*. Cambridge: Cambridge University Press.

Hofstadter, R. (1964, November). The paranoid style in American politics. *Harper's Magazine*, 77–86.

Inazu, J. D. (2016). *Confident pluralism. Surviving and thriving through deep difference*. Chicago, IL: The University of Chicago Press.

Israel, J. (2013). *Democratic enlightenment. Philosophy, revolution, and human rights*. Oxford: Oxford University Press.

Keefer, P., Scartascini, C., & Vlaicu, R. (2021). Trust, populism, and the quality of government. In A. Bågenholm, M. Bauhr, M. Grimes & B. Rothstein, eds., *The Oxford handbook of quality of government*. Oxford: Oxford University Press, pp. 249–67.

Kosinsky, M. (2019, November 21). In *Neue Zürcher Zeitung*, 41.

Kreiss, D. (2016). *Prototype politics. Technology-intensive campaigning and the data of democracy*. Oxford: Oxford University Press.

Kuhn, S. A. K., Lieb, R., Freeman, D., Andreou, C., & Zander-Schellenberg, T., (2021). Coronavirus conspiracy beliefs in the German-speaking general population: Endorsement rates and links to reasoning biases and paranoia. *Psychological Medicine*. DOI: 10.1017/S0033291721001124.

Laclau, E. (2005). *On populist reason*. London/New York: Verso.

Lynch, M. P. (2016). *The internet of us: Knowing more and understanding less in the age of big data*. New York: Liveright.

Mårdh, A., & Tryggvason, Á. (2017). Democratic education and the mode of populism. *Studies in Philosophy and Education*, 36, 601–13.

Mason, L. (2018). *Uncivil agreement. How politics became our identity*. Chicago, IL: The University of Chicago Press.

Möller, K. (Ed.) (2022). *Populismus. Ein Reader*. Berlin: Suhrkamp Verlag.

Moreau, I., & Holtz, G. (Eds.) (2005). *"Parler librement". La liberté de parole au tournant de XVIe auf XVIIe siècle*. Lyon: ENS Editions.

Müller, J.-W. (2016). *What is populism?* Philadelphia, PA: University of Pennsylvania Press.

Oelkers, J. (2018). Autoritarismus und liberale öffentliche Bildung. *Zeitschrift für Pädagogik*, 64(6), 728–48.

Oelkers, J. (2020). Authoritarianism ande in the interwar period. *Paedagogica Historica*, 56, 572–86.

Peters, M. A., & Besley, T. (2020). *The far-right education and violence*. London: Routledge.

Rucker, P., & Leonnig, C. (2021). *A very stable genius. Donald J. Trump's testing of America*. London: Bloomsbury.

Runciman, D. (2018). *Political hypocrisy. The mask of power. From Hobbes to Orwell and beyond*. Rev. ed. with a new afterword by the author, Princeton, NJ: Princeton University Press.

Sant, E. (2019). Democratic education: A theoretical review (2006–2017). *Review of Educational Research*, 89(5), 655–96.

Shils, E. (1954). Populism and the rules of law. In S. Buchanan et al., eds., *University of Chicago Law School conference on jurisprudence and politics*, pp. 99–107.

Shils, E. (1956). *The tournament of secrecy: The background and consequences of American politics*. Glencoe, IL: The Free Press.

Shils, E. (1982). *The constitution of society. With a new introduction by the author*. Chicago, IL: The University of Chicago Press.

State Council Information Office (2021). *China: Democracy that works*. white paper. The State Council Information Office of the People's Republic of China. Available at: www.news.cn/english/2021-12/04/c_1310351231.htm (accessed: December 28, 2021).

Stitzlein, S. M. (2017). *American public education and the responsibility of its citizens. Supporting democracy in the age of accountability*. Oxford: Oxford University Press.

Strittmatter, K. (2018). *Die Neuerfindung der Diktatur. Wie China den digitalen Überwachungsstatt aufbaut und uns damit herausfordert*. 2nd ed., Munich: Piper Verlag.

Sunstein, C. R. (2017). *#republic. Divided democracy in the age of social media*. Princeton, NJ: Princeton University Press.

Suthaharan, P., Reed, E. J., Leptourgos, P., et al. (2021). Paranoia and belief updating during the Covid-19 crisis. *Human Nature Behavior*, 5, 1190–202.

Thalmann, K. (2019). *The stigmatization of conspiracy theory since the 1950's. "A plot to make us look foolish"*. London: Routledge.

Ungar-Sargon, B. (2021). *Bad news: How woke media is undermining democracy*. New York: Encounter Books.

Van der Geest, I., Jansen, H., & Van Klink, B. (Eds.) (2020). *Vox populi: Populism as a rhetorical and democratic challenge*. Cheltenham: Edward Elgar.

Van der Linden, S., Panagopoulos, C., Azevedo, F., & Jost, J. T. (2020). The paranoid style in American politics revisited: An ideological asymmetry in conspirational thinking. *Political Psychology*, 42(1), 32–51.

Watson, S., & Barnes, N. (2021). Online educational populism and New Right 2.0 in Australia and England. *Globalisation, Societies and Education*, 20(22), 208–20. DOI: 10.1080/14767744.2021.1882292 (accessed: December 25, 2021).

Zhang, C. (2019). Right-wing populist discourse on Chinese social media: Identity, otherness, and global imaginaries. *Les Cahiers des Cevipol*, 3, 2–31.

31

Religion and Democratic Education

Brett Bertucio

31.1 Introduction

More than a decade ago, political theorist Mark Lilla commented on the curious and precarious state of contemporary politics: "The way we live now in the West politically is an experiment. Historically considered, most civilizations, in most times and places, have founded their understanding of law and basic political legitimacy on some kind of divine revelation or sanction. In the large sweep of history, the modern West is an extraordinary exception" (Lilla & Myers, 2007). Modern liberal democracy is indeed an exception to the historical norm. The language of "experiment" is often used to indicate both its novelty and its fragility. George Washington (1790) termed the new American nation a "grand experiment," as did translators of Alexis de Toqueville's *Democracy in America* (1835, p. 15). The term has been increasingly used in times of global conflict, particularly during the First and Second World Wars and the end of the Cold War (Michel et al., 2011).[1] In 1989, Francis Fukuyama famously declared the experiment successful. But Fukuyama and his critics now admit the triumph of liberal democracy was either tenuous or illusory (Fukuyama, 1989, 2010; Hughes, 2012; Menand, 2018). Liberalism's enduring weakness seems to be that Enlightenment principles of universalism and rational neutrality lie in tension with diverse preliberal commitments to transcendent, extranational ideals.[2] In a word, modern liberal democracies struggle with the question of religion.

Perhaps no other question so complicates democratic education. Almost by definition, liberal democracies allow for a multiplicity of religious communities among their citizens. Yet the very fact of religious pluralism makes forming a unified citizenry difficult. Navigating minefields involved therein is a major task of democratic education, and theorists advocate a multiplicity of approaches to the problem. To be sure, this description of the issue paints religious commitment in a negative light, as if religion inevitably hampers, or at least

[1] For use of the analysis technology employed here, see Google Ngram Viewer: https://books.google.com/ngrams.

[2] In seriousness, one might say "extraterrestrial" ideals. This is to say, these ideals have as their object things not of this earth. For an analysis of the reemergence of preliberal dynamics in modern democracies, see Reno (2019).

complicates, democracy. It is therefore worth noting that many political theorists view liberal democracy as insufficient unto itself, requiring religious values as a source of morality and public order (Gruenwald, 2009; Kraynak, 2001).

Religion is variously considered a boon, a danger, irrelevant, or an area of civic competence for democratic education. This chapter considers a variety of questions and positions lying at the intersection of religion and democratic formation: Is religion helpful or necessary to democracy? Is religion harmful? Should religious ideas lie outside the sphere of democratic life? Or are they inextricable from democratic coexistence? The answers to each have substantial implications for democratic education. These questions will be considered from both historical and theoretical perspectives, with particular emphasis on the American experience with which the author is most familiar. History, law, and policy in other Western democracies will add a comparative perspective and help highlight universal issues. The chapter concludes with a reconsideration of the modern democratic state along religious lines, questioning the supposed dichotomy between religion and liberal democracy. If modern liberal democracies should properly be considered religious phenomena, then liberal democratic education's purported neutrality toward traditional religion actually obscures a direct rivalry.

31.2 Is Religion Helpful or Even Necessary for Democratic Citizenship?

In his 1796 farewell address, George Washington famously insisted on the necessity of religion for democratic government. "Of all the dispositions and habits, which lead to political prosperity, Religion and Morality are indispensable supports," he held. "And let us with caution indulge the supposition," he continued, "that morality can be maintained without religion. Whatever may be conceded to the influence of refined education on minds of peculiar structure, reason and experience both forbid us to expect that national morality can prevail in exclusion of religious principle" (Washington, 1811, p. 30). His sentiment – that mere secular education was insufficient for civic formation – was reflected in the earliest American federal action involving schooling. The Northwest Ordinance, enacted in 1787 to govern the creation of new states between the Ohio and Mississippi rivers, decreed, "Religion, morality, and knowledge, being necessary to good government and the happiness of mankind, schools and the means of education shall forever be encouraged" (US Congress, 1934). The phrase reflected more sentimental ideal than substantive law, but it indicated that the leaders of the new republic felt that mass education should inculcate religion, and that only a religious citizenry could sustain the nation. When mass schooling did materialize in the early nineteenth century, its aims were explicitly religious. In many places, tax-supported common schools were originally denominational charity schools which continued their mission to bring Protestant belief and morality to indigent children (Kaestle, 1972).

Indeed, explicitly religious aims seem to have been inseparable from state-sponsored education at its origins in many Western democracies. The first

English proposal for universal schooling, Arthur Roebuck's failed 1833 Bill for National Education in the Commons, acknowledged religious tensions in the nation but insisted that schools teach "piety, and a profound respect for the divinity."[3] A successful contemporaneous Dutch law, while likewise acknowledging divisions between Protestant and Catholic citizens, insisted that the new national schools "imprint on [students'] hearts the knowledge and feeling of everything which they owe to the supreme being" (Glenn, 2011, p. 62).

In some democratic nations, this emphasis remains. The Greek constitution, for example, explicitly connects religious and civic education: "Instruction constitutes a fundamental mission of the state. Its purpose is the moral, cultural, professional and physical education of the Hellenes as well as the development of their national and religious consciousness and their formation into free and responsible citizens" (Constitution of Greece, Art. 16.2, cited in Willaime, 2007, p. 58). The Italian Concordat of 1984 acknowledges the Catholic heritage of the nation, and "continues to ensure within the school system the instruction in the Catholic religion in non-university public schools of all levels and types" (Willaime, 2007). Several German Länder (federated states) include religious formation in the official aims of state schools.[4] Until 2008, state schools in Quebec offered explicitly Protestant or Catholic religious formation (Bindewald et al., 2017).

Several Western democracies appeal to religious education as a source of general morality and civic formation. The most notable is perhaps the British Religious Education (RE) system. It is remarkable that the major pieces of British education legislation (the Education Acts of 1870, 1902, and 1944) include conscious clauses for religious dissenters but little in the way of positive descriptions of religious education (Jackson, 2000). It seems religious education in line with the doctrines of the Church of England was such an accepted aspect of state education that legislation need not have mentioned it. During the 1970s, increasing religious pluralism in the UK precipitated a series of changes in RE. Instead of merely teaching Anglican doctrine, teachers combined religious literacy instruction, moral education, and personal exploration of religious traditions (Parker & Freathy, 2012). Current law requires both collective worship in state schools and that RE be nonindoctrinating (Jackson, 2000, p. 127). Unsurprisingly, the nature of RE has been hotly contested. The latest movement – to present students with both the doctrines of various world religions and nonreligious worldviews as possible lifeways – has become an occasion for controversy (Wightwick, 2020; UK Parliament, 2019). Regardless, the continued existence of RE indicates the prevailing intuition of British politicians that – as one member of the House of Lords put it – "we consider religious faith and precept as the spiritual life-blood of the nation and all its citizens" (Jackson, 2000, p. 139).

[3] Commons Sitting of July 30, 1833, Series 3 Volume 20, 139–74.

[4] I use the term "state schools" not as an antgovernment pejorative, but simply to indicate schools in diverse nations which are funded and operated by governments, acknowledging that terms used for these schools vary among democratic nations. It is worth noting that the term "public school" as used in the American context has a rather contentious history involving religious animus (Reese, 2007).

In 2008, due to similar demographic pressures, the province of Quebec instituted a similar program. Under the Ethics and Religious Culture (ERC) curriculum, students are exposed to the beliefs of major world religions and secular worldviews. They are taught respect and tolerance for differing traditions, yet assisted to commit to a certain tradition "after due consideration" (Hoverd et al., 2015). While the framework wherein a young person explores a menu of life options and then selects one independently from family or community seems exceedingly liberal, a similar intuition remains: part of citizenship education is assistance in committing to a comprehensive worldview. Finally, there is good empirical evidence in the American context that religious, particularly Catholic schools, produce more civic-minded students than their public counterparts (Bryk et al., 1993; Glenn, 2016). This may be due to changing notions of patriotism in public schools and the traditionalist impulse of religious schools, but the sorts of prosocial morality inculcated in British RE programs seems to be at play in American religious schools.

These changes to traditional religious education reflect the historical challenge presented by religious pluralism to any explicitly religious civic formation. George Washington may have decreed religion essential to the maintenance of the republic, but he also told his audience, "With slight shades of difference, you have the same religion, manners, habits, and political principles" (Washington, 1811, p. 30). Empirically, the claim was simply false. Religious dissenters from New England Puritanism were critical to founding Rhode Island and Pennsylvania.[5] The early republic included a large proportion of Catholics, who would soon be viewed as a threat to national unity (Franchot, 1994; Pagliarini, 1999). Early American common schools were at least implicitly Protestant institutions, and disagreements over Bible translations led to violence in the mid-nineteenth century.[6] Common school reformers had attempted to define a nondenominational, unified "school theology," but the impossibility of the task resulted in the creation of a parallel public and private school systems. In the Netherlands, a contemporaneous effort toward a consensus school religion resulted in the *schoolstrijd* (school struggle), whose resolution was a system of state funding for a variety of religious schools (Glenn, 2002). In brief, while religion may be a help or even a necessary part of civic formation, the fact of religious pluralism means that state-sponsored schools will struggle to articulate a type of religious formation acceptable to all citizens.

31.3 What of Religious Schools?

If it is the case that religion is helpful for democracy, and the challenges of pluralism make a common religious education in state-sponsored schools

[5] Both states were founded by dissenters with novel notions of religious freedom. See Seiple (2012) and Adams and Emmerich (1990).

[6] The worst of the "Bible Wars" came in Philadelphia in 1844, where nativist riots resulted in at least fourteen deaths and the burning of a Catholic Church. See Lannie and Diethor (1968).

difficult, it may be the case that a degree of state support for religious schools would have democratic benefits. Empirical literature over the last quarter-century gives evidence of the civic benefits of religious belief and religious membership. Religious involvement is linked to increased volunteering (Campbell & Yonish, 2003; Lam, 2002; Park & Smith, 2000; Ruiter & De Graaf, 2006), voting (Putnam & Campbell, 2010), and charitable giving (Regnerus et al., 1998; Wilhelm et al., 2007). Personal religious commitment is associated with engagement in community projects and willingness to help strangers (Bennett & Einolf, 2017; Loveland et al., 2005). Even when controlling for the social effects that come with group membership, religious citizens are more civically engaged according to certain measures (Smidt, 1999).

We might then ask whether the democratic state might better form citizens by financially supporting religious schools. Historically, state funding of religious schools has been a response to diverse communities' demands for a comprehensive education which welcomes their particular religious tradition. For example, the Canadian provinces of Alberta, Ontario, Quebec, and Saskatchewan fund Catholic schools, due to historical concerns of a large Catholic population. In recent decades, a degree of financial support has been extended to other religious schools, mirroring the diversification of religious education in public schools. The majority of Irish children attend schools operated by religious communities but funded by the government, again due to its historical Catholic and Protestant history (Russo & Raniere, 2017). Most Western democracies provide some financial support for religious schools, with varying degrees of government oversight, and often for similar reasons (Glenn, 2005; see generally Glenn, 2011). While the policy is perhaps best described as liberal democratic accommodation of religious citizens, some have suggested that the civic effects of religious schools may justify government support of these schools (Black, 2013; Berner, 2017; Brinig & Garnett, 2009; Campbell, 2008; Giersch, 2014). Baldwin Wong (2021) has gone so far as to suggest that this arrangement might be made under a Rawlsian framework, in which religious schools would provide comprehensive reasons to strengthen students' commitments to political principles.

31.4 Is Religion Harmful to Democracy and Democratic Education?

Considering the challenge religious pluralism poses to a unified citizenry, several Dutch researchers concluded, "Religion is a source of mischief, but also of values" (De Groof et al., 2010). Many political and educational theorists reach a similar conclusion and even assert that religious values cause considerable "mischief" to a nation. Critics of religious influence in education typically express concerns regarding rationality and student autonomy. Both values seem essential to democratic citizenship, and so any mark of religion on education becomes problematic.

Michael Hand has emerged as the principal critic of religious schooling on "rationality" grounds. He conceives of religious belief as by definition nonrational and of education as primarily concerned with rationality. Hand argues that religious education teaches religious propositions, which cannot be known to be true. If schools successfully inculcate these beliefs in students, then they are indoctrinatory, which is antithetical to both rationality and democratic formation (Hand, 2003). In considering discussion of controversial issues in the classroom, Hand indicates that religious reasons, particularly regarding human identity and sexuality, are both arational and harmful, and should be excluded from the classroom (Hand, 2008). Hand's critics contend that his conception of rationality is truncated and therefore flawed, and that as religious propositions indeed make truth claims, they can be the object of reason and thus education. The charge of indoctrination also makes certain empirical assumptions about how religious education is conducted and denies student agency (Groothuis, 2004; Short, 2003).

Nel Noddings has also expressed concerns about rationality in the role of religion in education, albeit with different conclusions. According to Noddings, teachers across subject areas should educate their students for "intelligent belief or unbelief" (Noddings, 1993). She encourages American public school educators within a variety of disciplines to take up the existential and religious questions that naturally occur in their content areas and to help students evaluate beliefs according to either rational or psychological criteria. Her conception of rationality seems to mirror the tenets of political liberalism with interesting consequences. For example, as monotheism tends toward exclusivism, it must be rationally rejected (Noddings, 1993). Elsewhere, Noddings argues that students should be discouraged from belief in hell because of its potential to induce fear (Noddings, 2005). In effect, Noddings' evaluation pits a certain conception of political liberalism against the doctrines of traditional Western religions. When the latter conflict with the former, they are deemed harmful and dangerous to civic formation.

Robert Kunzman criticizes this view as the imposition of an epistemic criterion totally alien to the religious traditions in question. Ironically, Noddings' criterion of liberal tolerance may lead to intolerance in the classroom. He suggests that because religious pluralism remains a challenge to democratic life, part of democratic education must be preparation for religious and ethical disagreement. Kunzman suggests that students should be encouraged to openly share and explore religious beliefs, but not to critically evaluate them, as Noddings would have it, nor to promote acceptance of a belief, as in the case of religious education in the United Kingdom or Quebec (Kunzman, 2005a, 2005b).

However, some theorists worry that certain religious traditions, often evangelical Protestantism, might be diametrically opposed to the sorts of dispositions ideal for liberal democracy. Benjamin Bindewald, Suzanne Rosenblith, and Jennifer James describe incidents where evangelical students display "theological certainty" – they present religious truth claims which are not open to revision (Bindewald & Rosenblith, 2015; James, 2010). This is a problem under certain versions of democratic education which value consensus-building and compromise among students and citizens. All three authors share a concern that these students' concerns not be dismissed, for fear of exodus from the public school system, yet their approaches are very different. James urges teachers to psychologically analyze student religiosity. She argues that theological certainty is in fact a sign of "immature" belief and that encouraging students to adhere to their belief systems will increase trust and eventually lead to openness and the possibility that students will revise their views (James, 2010, p. 632). Bindewald and Rosenblith appeal to Hand's understanding of rationality to guide teachers. They advocate terminating any discussion on epistemically "closed" issues – that is, on issues in which the tenets of liberalism declare only one position may be ethical or reasonable.

Others express concern that religious formation may inhibit autonomy, often considered a critical disposition for democratic life. Emphasis on autonomy may be traced at least back to Rousseau's *Emile*, in which the title character receives protection from undue influence in order to become a citizen worthy of a liberal republic (Rousseau, 2010; see also Callan, 1988, p. 3). Contemporary theorists often describe the freedom to choose one's religion as a fundamental liberty. Explicitly religious education would not only deprive one of that right via undue influence but might create citizens who appeal to authority in democratic debate rather than the dictates of reason or conscience (Callan, 1988). Eamonn Callan goes so far as to label religious upbringing morally impermissible (Callan, 1985).[7] In general, religious groups are suspected of limiting the sort of exploration or critical thinking proper to a free mind (Kerr, 2006). Interestingly, liberal educational theorists often advocate the sort of exploratory religious education featured in the United Kingdom in order to expose students to differing traditions and to critically evaluate their own (Jawoniyi, 2015; Warnick, 2012; Wilson & Ryg, 2015). We might consider this a type of bounded autonomy-encouraging education.

Paula McAvoy's study of insular religious communities advocates for government policies which help exiting members access public education (McAvoy, 2012). Still others contend that young people can be raised in a particular religious community and develop autonomy (Burtt, 2003). Anders Schinkel has argued that subjecting students to the kind of education wherein they critically question their own religious traditions is in fact autonomy-reducing (Schinkel, 2010). A similar critique emerges in the literature on Rawlsian norms of public reasoning in democratic education.

31.5 Should Religious Reasoning Appear in the Democratic Classroom?

During the late-1980s' and 1990s' "explosion of interest" in citizenship,[8] political and educational theorists such as Amy Gutmann (1987), Stephen Macedo (2003), and Eamonn Callan (1997) drew on the work of John Rawls to elucidate

[7] Matthew Clayton (2014) has extended this proscription to any comprehensive philosophical doctrine.

[8] The description belongs to Kymlicka and Norman (1994).

normative principles for deliberation within democratic education. Rawls' *Political Liberalism* (1993), itself a revision and continuation of ideas first proposed in *A Theory of Justice* (1971), served as the foundation for these theories. Faced with the challenge of pluralism, the liberal paradigm seeks to establish a common "public sphere" governed by deliberative norms. Two aspects of these norms are crucial for the Rawlsian citizenship education literature that followed. The first, "public reasoning," demands that in the public sphere, citizens only use reasons which can be understood and accepted by all others. Public reasoning aims to solve only political problems, expresses a political community's commitments to individual rights, and contains only "presently accepted general beliefs and forms of reasoning found in common sense, and the methods and conclusions of science when these are not controversial" (Rawls, 1993, p. 224). Under the norm of public reasoning, citizens should not voice their approval or disapproval of policies by citing religious reason or those that are somehow not immediately accessible to all citizens.

The second key aspect is what Rawls terms the "burdens of judgment." The concept refers to the difficulties of judgment which lead to a plurality of views. The complexity of evidence, necessity of intuitive judgments, and different normative considerations or emphases lead people to disagree regarding both the nature of the good and practical solutions to political problems. A citizen must *accept* the burdens of judgment – that is, she must assent that judgment is difficult and can differ among reasonable people – in order to treat others as equals in democratic deliberation. Rawls takes care to emphasize that to accept the *reasonableness* (and not correctness) of opposing beliefs should not present a threat to comprehensive doctrines: "Above all, [the burdens of judgment] does not argue that we should be hesitant and uncertain, much less skeptical, about our own beliefs" (Rawls, 1993, p. 63).

Yet Gutmann's vision of "democratic" education calls for schools, through the pedagogical expertise of teachers, to temper private family preferences with liberal modes of public reasoning. Macedo follows a similar, albeit even more skeptical, path. He insists that "the success of our civic project relies upon a transformative project that includes the remaking of moral and religious communities" (Macedo, 2003, p. x). He calls for a "non-neutral," "tough-minded" liberalism, a "liberalism with a spine" (Macedo, 2003, p. 5). Interestingly, Macedo does not explicitly advocate for comprehensive liberalism. Rather, he contends that political liberalism is important in order to gain the trust of citizens and transform particular religious and ethical communities through voluntary participation in public schools. In Macedo's view, a "transformative" citizenship education is necessary for the survival of an ordered society. Some comprehensive communities (he names preconciliar Catholicism and fundamentalist Protestantism specifically) espouse illiberal values. A merely "political" liberalism which employs persuasion rather than state intervention will work to convince skeptical citizens of the value of public reasoning. Macedo's ultimate hope is that particular religious and ethical communities themselves promote the spirit of liberalism. In the context of citizenship education, students would be enculturated into the modes of public reasoning and learn to justify their political views, and ultimately their conceptions of the good life, by appeals to universally accessible reasons.

Callan's work takes Gutmann and Macedo's vision a bit further. Like Macedo, he emphasizes the need for a "shared public morality" or a common "constellation of habits, abilities, and attributes" for the survival of the liberal democratic state (Callan, 1997, pp. 2–3). Of course, this means that education is the primary bulwark of democracy, and the state possesses a compelling interest in schooling. Unlike other liberal theorists (and like many multicultural citizenship educators), Callan believes political liberalism to be somewhat of a myth. The demands of liberal modes of public reasoning require that "private" comprehensive doctrines undergo change. First, Callan argues that Rawls' stipulation of "reasonable" pluralism paints liberal theory as the arbiter of permissible comprehensive doctrines. Further, Callan reinterprets Rawls' burdens of judgment to imply the impossibility of holding a liberal public epistemology and a nonliberal comprehensive doctrine. In his view, because reciprocal respect requires that I imaginatively enter the "reasonable" views with which I disagree, the "burdens" necessarily cause me to doubt my own views. Psychologically, Rawls' distinction between public and private realms is untenable. Shifting epistemologies when transitioning between "spheres" "would require a spectacular feat of self-deception that cannot be squared with personal integrity" (Callan, 1997, p. 31).

Because education is concerned with the formation of a unitary person, Callan claims that citizenship education in a liberal democracy must inculcate comprehensive liberalism. Under this model, students would be guided to become "autonomous" thinkers. They would learn to reject claims to tradition or authority and evaluate views on the basis of contemporary articulations of individual rights. While this might be detrimental to some cultural or religious groups, Callan sees these consequences as necessary for the preservation of the democratic order (Callan, 1997, p. 37).

Unsurprisingly, Rawlsian theory and Rawlsian models of civic education have drawn sharp criticism from those who feel religious commitment is a positive force in democratic life. Paul Weithman (2002) argues that the Rawlsian conception of reason is truncated, precluding many forms of reasoned action that are indeed religious. Jeffrey Stout (2004) has famously argued that the norms of public reasoning effectively disenfranchise many citizens. According to Craig Calhoun (2011), those who hold themselves to the standards of public reason as an ideological matter necessarily impoverish their ability to think across difference: "Secularists propose a limit on religion in the public square, which they take to be a basis for equal inclusion, but at the same time insulate themselves from understanding religious discourse, practicing an ironic exclusion" (p. 78). Others have simply observed that the bounds Rawls draws on reason are themselves part of a particular, comprehensive worldview, and thus the demand to conform to public reason itself fails to be accessible to all citizens (Friedman, 2000; Horton, 2003; March, 2015; McConnell, 2007).[9]

[9] Rawls himself would attempt to soften his position in consideration of this critique (see Rawls, 1997).

Among educational theorists, Hanan Alexander is perhaps the most prominent critic of the Rawlsian view. For Alexander, as for Stout, deeming religious reasons irrelevant to democratic life not only disenfranchises students, but fails to take their prior commitments seriously. If schooling is to form democratic citizens, it must take into account their whole personhood. Educators cannot dismiss those things that a citizen values more highly than national membership and expect that schooling be truly formative. It will be either ineffectual or disforming. Alexander argues that the truncation of reason inherent in Rawlsian public reasoning actually has wider negative effects on education, even beyond its democratic aims. The search for a consensus language amidst plural conceptions of the good will often results in the use of quantitative measurement as the sole determinant of educational quality. Ironically, this attempt at neutrality imposes a particular and peculiar vision of the world on children (Alexander, 2015). Indeed, some see Rawlsian democratic education as itself a form of illiberal religion (Neiman, 2002).

31.6 Are Religion and Religious Diversity Inextricable from Democratic Life?

As the change in British RE demonstrates, educators over the last half-century have increasingly acknowledged the fact of religious diversity in democratic nations and sought to prepare young people for life in a pluralistic society. Religious *literacy* education, as distinct from religious education, seeks to inform students about the variety of world religions, but has no component of evaluation or personal commitment. This approach takes a more academic tone and aims to form young citizens who will respect religious difference in the workplace and political life.

In the American context, the movement for religious literacy education is comparatively recent, due in part to the particularities of constitutional law. Again, at its origins, the American common school system was explicitly religious, and sought to transmit pan-Protestant belief and morality (Kaestle, 1983). During the mid-twentieth century, increasing acknowledgment of religious diversity led first to a more ecumenical approach to prayer in public schools, then rather quickly to a Supreme Court ruling that struck down any devotional reading or prayer. In *Abington v. Schempp* (1963), Justice Tom Clark wrote that the Establishment Clause of the First Amendment forbade devotional Bible reading in public schools but did not preclude academic study of religion. Although he counseled educators that awareness of various religious traditions was part of a complete education, many schools were reticent to include study of religious beliefs in the wake of the decision.[10]

A movement toward religious literacy education has gained momentum in the last two decades, prompted by a realization of the relevance of religion to

[10] *Abington School District v. Schempp*, 374 U.S. 203 (1963). On the reticence of American public schools to broach religious topics following *Schempp*, see Nord & Haynes (1998, pp. 23–24).

political life. As American law would generally forbid the sorts of commitment-encouraging education found in other nations, religious literacy curriculum is entirely academic, perhaps with an added component of personal encounter with religious leaders in the community.

Two distinct approaches have emerged, which have substantial consequences for democratic education. Diane Moore's cultural studies approach holds that history, literature, art, and other subjects are opaque without knowledge of religion. She advocates an interdisciplinary curriculum according to the academic norms of the religious studies field. Here, religion is a cultural phenomenon accessible through economic, sociological, and even psychological method. For Moore, the doctrinal elements of religious traditions are less relevant and even noncognizable, as Rawlsian theorists might have it. Her approach asks students to affirm that religions are internally diverse, embedded in culture, and change over time (Moore, 2007, 2015). This understanding has recently been adopted by the leading American professional organization involved in civic education (Marcus et al., 2017).

Unfortunately, practitioners of religions who claim a timeless element to their traditions might take issue with these claims. While democratic education under Moore's framework certainly admits the political salience of religion, students may receive the impression that religious reasoning in the public sphere is arbitrary, or at least has no direct relation to truth claims. This sort of democratic education may risk the alienating and disenfranchising effects of public reasoning norms.

Stephen Prothero offers an alternative approach to religious literacy education which foregrounds doctrinal claims. He depicts the liberal-Protestant attempts toward nonsectarianism and unity in American schooling as partly responsible for the loss of theological depth among American religious communities. Ironically, by imposing an external framework on religious convictions and thus marking their internal logics as nonrational, political liberalism may have contributed to the rise of anti-intellectual trends in American evangelicalism. Prothero's solution calls for students to encounter the theological claims and self-understanding of major religious traditions. Religious literacy which explores doctrinal claims serves as a preparation for public life, given the empirical reality of civic discourse. In Prothero's words, "American political life is, as a factual matter, awash in religious arguments, religious reasons, and religious motivations. What good can it possibly serve for citizens, religious or otherwise, to be ignorant of all this" (Prothero, 2007, p. 173). Empirical work with religious literacy curriculum following this model has shown increases in students' religious tolerance, religious literacy, and support for the rights of religious minorities (Lester, 2013).

31.7 An Alternative Perspective

Liberal political theory tends to depict religion as somehow prior to or at least outside the democratic state. A central problem of public life is therefore how to balance the diverse and often competing religious values of citizens with the need for democratic consensus. This chapter has thus far taken this framing as normative. But recent scholarship in history, legal theory, philosophy, and theology has offered a different view. Instead of an overarching sphere or structure which adjudicates the consequences of religious difference, it may be that the liberal democratic state is itself a religious entity, one which competes with traditional religions for citizens' loyalty.

Brad Gregory's (2012) analysis of the consequences of the Reformation has shown that modern liberal democracies are only possible because of a religious revolution. The religious rivalries which emerged in sixteenth-century Europe, as well as an emerging Protestant conception of autonomous belief, created the conditions under which politics is separable from substantive notions of the good. By jettisoning a once-universal Aristotelian metaphysics, Western societies were left to navigate the political consequences of competing ethical and ontological visions. Prior to the fifteenth-century emergence of univocal metaphysics, Western societies lacked the modern division of life into strict "secular" and "religious" categories (Jones, 2017). Both Gregory and Charles Taylor have recently argued that the modern conception of "religion" as a bounded, discrete life choice separate from politics is only possible in a post-Reformation world (Gregory, 2012; Taylor, 2007).

Nature, of course, abhors a vacuum. In contemporary democracies, a veritable faith in the power of politics or in a particular political structure has arguably replaced traditional religious faith. Despite its ostensible commitment to rationalism, liberal democracy affirms certain anthropological doctrines regarding the reformation of the human condition as articles of faith. In the absence of traditional religion, the attempt to satisfy the human need for justice via politics takes on a religious quality (Deneen, 2005). While more muted than the explicitly religious trappings of the French Revolution, contemporary democracies have their own liturgies, and increasingly their own dogmas (Vermeule, 2017; see also Legutko, 2018). The pageantry of parliamentary procedure, the emotional exaltation of political rallies, and the repetition of pious phrases all mark contemporary liberal regimes. Louis Boyer's (2022) description of this dynamic is instructive:

> When man loses the faith that animated his rituals and his sacrifices, he comes to regret this loss. If he does not miss the substance of the religion, he at least misses the emotion and the feeling of exaltation that were associated with it. He then seeks, either by reviving the past or by instituting new techniques with a psychological basis inspired by the ancient rites, to recover something of that psychological atmosphere which surrounded them, without however giving credence to the original beliefs that had been connected with them. (p. 96)

We think of these rituals and beliefs only as "secular" because of the particular structure of modern political theory. As the modern state takes each individual citizen as its primary subject, it is by design rivalrous with other institutions. It competes for loyalty, and ideally takes precedence over other collective institutions, including religious communities (Cavanaugh, 2011). If this is indeed the case, and we can think of the liberal democratic state as itself a religious body, the dichotomy or tension between democratic education and religion would be a false one. In this view, all education would be religious. The only question that would remain is what sort of religion a society embraces through its schools.

We might say that the particular religions endorsed by various contemporary liberal democracies are species of Rousseauean civil religion. Rousseau intuited the need for all societies, particularly republics, to have some semblance of unifying religion. His "civil religion" required all citizens to assent to articles of faith, including the "sanctity of the social contract and the laws," or risk banishment or execution (Rousseau, 1923, p. 123). Today, the religions imbedded in liberal democracies have their own dogmas, particularly regarding issues of social cohesion and sexual morality. Their liturgies descend from the French Revolutionary festivals and are bound by what Legutko terms "linguistic-political rituals" (2018, p. 126). Carried out in political discourse, emotive rallies, and electoral speeches, these new festivals establish an official language through which to identify those outside the political community. Inevitably, this curiously religious tendency of modern liberal democracy betrays the mythological character of what Rawls would consider merely *political* liberalism. For those interested in classical or integral political theory, this is a natural and expected outcome. Human persons desire truth in all aspects of their lives. By organizing political life around consensus or procedural coherence and thus placing politics at one remove from substantive questions about the good, liberal democracies frustrate the human desire for truth (Vermeule, 2021). These regimes begin to embody a sort of truncated religion constructed from the principles of an increasingly arcane official language.

If this is indeed the case, then what passes for democratic education in many modern democracies is in fact a species of religious education. It can therefore be directly compared to more traditional forms of religious education. We might then ask whether contemporary democratic education succeeds in the aims we most often associate with religious formation: Does it lead young people to the truth about themselves and reality? Does it point toward an authentic salvation from the problems of the human condition? Can it engender true and lasting happiness?[11] If critics of liberal democracy are right, and contemporary democratic faith is in truth a deformed religion, then democratic education as currently conceived would produce malformed young people. Again, the remaining task for democratic formation would be to discover what sort of religious education – however conceived – might produce well-formed young people.

[11] The quintessentially liberal critique would, of course, point to the multiplicity of visions of happiness, truth, and salvation amid a democratic republic as evidence that this line of argument is circular. That is, in advocating for a democratic education that is evaluated via its relation to truth, I am simply arguing for the universal adoption of a particular definition with which others will inevitably disagree. On the contrary, I contend that the fact of disagreement and the embeddedness of conceptions of truth in historical traditions does not preclude the knowability of a universal truth, happiness, or salvation. See McIntyre (1988).

References

Adams, A. M., & Emmerich, C. J. (1990). William Penn and the American heritage of religious liberty. *Journal of Law and Religion*, 8(1–2), 57–70.

Alexander, H. (2015). *Reimagining liberal education: Affiliation and inquiry in democratic schooling*. London: Bloomsbury.

Bennett, M. R., & Einolf, C. J. (2017). Religion, altruism, and helping strangers: A multilevel analysis of 126 countries. *Journal for the Scientific Study of Religion*, 56(2), 323–41.

Berner, A. R. (2017). *Pluralism and American public education: No one way to school*. New York: Palgrave Macmillan.

Bindewald, B., & Rosenblith, S. (2015). Addressing orthodox challenges in the pluralist classroom. *Educational Studies*, 51(6), 497–509.

Bindewald, B. J., Sanatullova-Allison, E., & Hsiao, Y.-L. (2017). Religion and public education in pluralist, democratic societies: Some lessons from the United States and Canada. *Religion & Education*, 44(2), 180–202.

Black, D. W. (2013). Charter schools, vouchers, and the public good. *Wake Forest Law Review*, 47(1), 101–43.

Boyer, L. (2022). *Rite and man: The sense of the sacred and Christian liturgy*. Trans. by M. J. Costelloe, Providence, RI: Cluny Press.

Brinig, M. F., & Garnett, N. S. (2009). Catholic schools, urban neighborhoods, and education reform. *Notre Dame Law Review*, 85(3), 887–954.

Bryk, A. S., Lee, V. E., & Holland, P. B. (1993). *Catholic schools and the common good*. Cambridge, MA: Harvard University Press.

Burtt, S. (2003). Comprehensive educations and the liberal understanding of autonomy. In K. McDonough & W. Feinberg, eds., *Citizenship and education in liberal-democratic societies: Teaching for cosmopolitan values and collective identities*. Oxford: Oxford University Press, pp. 179–207.

Calhoun, C. (2011). Secularism, citizenship, and the public square. In C. Calhoun, M. Juergensmeyer & J. Van Antwerpen, eds., *Rethinking secularism*. Oxford: Oxford University press, pp. 75–91.

Callan, E. (1985). McLaughlin on parental rights. *Journal of Philosophy of Education*, 19(1), 111–18.

Callan, E. (1988). *Autonomy and schooling*. Montreal: McGill-Queen's University Press.

Callan, E. (1997). *Creating citizens: Political education and liberal democracy*. Oxford: Clarendon Press.

Campbell, D. E. (2008). The civic side of school choice: An empirical analysis of civic education in public and private schools. *BYU Law Review*, 2008(2), 487–523.

Campbell, D. E., & Yonish, S. J. (2003). Religion and volunteering in America. In C. Smidt, ed., *Religion as social capital: Producing the common good*. Waco, TX: Baylor University Press, pp. 87–106.

Cavanaugh, W. (2011). *Migrations of the holy: God, state, and the political meaning of the church*. Grand Rapids, MI: William B. Eerdmans.

Clayton, M. (2014). Anti-perfectionist childrearing. In A. Baggattini & C. Macleod, eds., *The nature of children's well-being: Theory and practice*. London: Springer, pp. 123–40.

De Groof, J., van de Donk, W., Lauwers, G., de Goede, P., & Tim Verhappen, T. (2010). *Reflections on religion & education in the Netherlands and Flanders*. Paper presented at Religion, Beliefs, Philosophical Convictions and Education conference, Bruges, Belgium, December 7–9.

de Tocqueville, A. (1835). *Democracy in America*. Trans. by H. Reeve, London: Saunders and Otley.

Deneen, P. (2005). *Democratic faith*. Princeton, NJ: Princeton University Press.

Franchot, J. (1994). *Roads to Rome: The antebellum Protestant encounter with Catholicism*. Berkeley, CA: University of California Press.

Friedman, M. (2000). John Rawls and the political coercion of unreasonable people. In V. Davion & C. Wolf, eds., *The idea of a political liberalism: Essays on Rawls*. Lanham, MD: Rowman and Littlefield, pp. 16–33.

Fukuyama, F. (1989). The end of history? *The National Interest*, 16, 3–18.

Fukuyama, F. (2010). The "end of history" 20 years later. *New Perspectives Quarterly*, 27(1), 7–10.

Giersch, J. (2014). Vouchers for religious schools and the development of democratic values. *The Educational Forum*, 78(2), 142–49.

Glenn, C. L. (2002). *The myth of the common school*. Oakland, CA: Institute for Contemporary Studies.

Glenn, C. L. (2005). What the United States can learn from other countries. In D. Salisbury & J. Tooley, eds., *What America can learn from school choice in other countries*. Washington, DC: Cato Institute, pp. 79–88.

Glenn, C. L. (2011). *Contrasting models of state and school: A comparative historical study of parental choice and state control*. London: Bloomsbury.

Glenn, C. L. (2016). Educating citizens: Who is doing that in the United States? *Italian Journal of Sociology of Education*, 8(1), 56–86.

Gregory, B. (2012). *The unintended reformation: How a religious revolution secularized society*. Cambridge, MA: Belknap Press.

Groothuis, D. (2004). On not abolishing faith schools: A response to Michael Hand and Harvey Siegel. *Theory and Research in Education*, 2(2), 177–88.

Gruenwald, O. (2009). Culture, religion and politics: Why liberal democracy needs God. *Journal of Interdisciplinary Studies*, 21(1), 1–24.

Gutmann, A. (1987). *Democratic education*. Princeton, NJ: Princeton University Press.

Hand, M. (2003). A philosophical objection to faith schools. *Theory and Research in Education*, 1(1), 89–99.

Hand, M. (2008). What should we teach as controversial? A defense of the epistemic criterion. *Educational Theory*, 58(2), 213–28.

Horton, J. (2003). Rawls, public reason and the limits of liberal justification. *Contemporary Political Theory*, 2(1), 5–23.

Hoverd, W., LeBrun, E., & Van Arragon, L. (2015). Religion and education in the provinces of Quebec and Ontario. *Religion and Diversity Project*. Available at: religion_and_education_in_the_provinces_of_quebec_and_ontario_report.pdf (religionanddiversity.ca).

Hughes, C. (2012). *Liberal democracy as the end of history: Fukuyama and postmodern challenges*. London: Routledge.

Jackson, R. (2000). Law, politics and religious education in England and Wales: Some history, some stories and some observations. In M. Leicester, C. Modgil, and S. Modgil, eds., *Spiritual and religious education*. London: Palmer, pp. 126–48.

James, J. (2010). "Democracy is the Devil's snare": Theological certainty and democratic teacher education. *Theory and Research in Social Education*, 38(4), 618–39.

Jawoniyi, O. (2015). Religious education, critical thinking, rational autonomy, and the child's right to an open future. *Religion & Education*, 42(1), 34–53.

Jones, A. W. (2017). *Before church and state: A study of social order in the sacramental kingdom of St. Louis IX*. Steubenville, OH: Emmaus Academic.

Kaestle, C. F. (1972). Common schools before the "common school revival": New York schooling in the 1790s. *History of Education Quarterly*, 12(4), 465–500.

Kaestle, C. F. (1983). *Pillars of the republic: Common schools and American society, 1780–1860*. New York: Hill & Wang.

Kerr, D. (2006). Teaching autonomy: The obligations of liberal education in plural societies. *Studies in Philosophy and Education*, 25(6), 425–56.

Kraynak, R. P. (2001). *Christian faith and modern democracy: God and politics in the fallen world*. Notre Dame, IN: University of Notre Dame Press.

Kunzman, R. (2005a). Educating for more (and less) than intelligent belief or unbelief: A critique of Noddings's vision of religion in public schools. In K. Howe, ed., *Philosophy of education*. Urbana, IL: Philosophy of Education Society, pp. 72–80.

Kunzman, R. (2005b). *Grappling with the good: Talking about religion and morality in public schools*. Albany, NY: SUNY Press.

Kymlicka W., & Norman, W. (1994). Return of the citizen: A survey of recent work on citizenship theory. *Ethics*, 104(2), 352–81.

Lam, P.-Y. (2002). As the flocks gather: How religion affects voluntary association participation. *Journal for the Scientific Study of Religion*, 41(3), 405–22.

Lannie, V. P., & Diethorn, B. C. (1968). For the honor and glory of God: The Philadelphia Bible Riots of 1844. *History of Education Quarterly*, 8(1), 44–106.

Legutko, R. (2018). *The demon in democracy: Totalitarian temptations in free societies*. New York, Books.

Lester, E. E. (2013). *Teaching about religions: A democratic approach for public schools*. Ann Arbor, MI: University of Michigan Press.

Lilla, M., & Myers, J. J. (2007). The stillborn God: Religion, politics, and the modern West. *Carnegie Council*. Available at: https://media-1.carnegiecouncil.org/import/studio/The_Stillborn_God.pdf.

Loveland, M. T., Sikkink, D., Myers, D. J., & Radcliff, B. (2005). Private prayer and civic involvement. *Journal for the Scientific Study of Religion*, 44(1) 1–14.

Macedo, S. (2003). *Diversity and distrust: Civic education in a multicultural democracy*. Cambridge, MA: Harvard University Press.

March, A. F. (2015). Rethinking the public use of religious reason. In T. Bailey & V. Gentile, eds., *Rawls and religion*. New York: Columbia University Press, pp. 97–132.

Marcus, B. P., Blitzer, J., Brady, Seth et al. (2017). Religious studies companion document. In *College, Career & Civic Life (C3) Framework for Social Studies State*

Standards. Silver Spring, MD: National Council for the Social Studies, pp. 92–97.

McAvoy, P. (2012). "There are no housewives on Star Trek": A reexamination of exit rights for the children of insular fundamentalist parents. *Educational Theory*, 62(5), 535–52.

McConnell, M. W. (2007). Secular reason and the misguided attempt to exclude religious argument from democratic deliberation. *Journal of Law, Philosophy and Culture*, 1(1), 159–74.

McIntyre, A. (1988). *Whose justice? Which rationality?* Notre Dame, IN: University of Notre Dame Press.

Menand, L. (2018, September 3). Francis Fukuyama postpones the end of history. *The New Yorker*. Available at: https://www.newyorker.com/magazine/2018/09/03/francis-fukuyama-postpones-the-end-of-history.

Michel, J.-P., Shen, Y. K., Aiden, A. P. et al. (2011). Quantitative analysis of culture using millions of digitized books. *Science*, 331(6014), 176–82.

Moore, D. L. (2007). *Overcoming religious illiteracy: A cultural studies approach to the study of religion in secondary education*. New York: Palgrave Macmillan.

Moore, D. L. (2015). Diminishing religious literacy: Methodological assumptions and analytical frameworks for promoting the public understanding of religion. In A. Dinham & M. Francis, eds., *Religious literacy in policy and practice*. Chicago, IL: Policy Press, pp. 27–38.

Neiman, A. (2002). The very (bad) idea of public reason. *Philosophy of Education Archive*, 135–37.

Noddings, N. (1993). *Educating for intelligent belief or unbelief*. New York: Teachers College Press.

Noddings, N. (2005). Beyond belief? In K. Howe, ed., *Philosophy of education*. Urbana, IL: Philosophy of Education Society, pp. 81–83.

Nord, W. A., & Haynes, C. C. (1998). *Taking religion seriously across the curriculum*. Alexandria, VA: Association for Supervison and Curriculum Development.

Pagliarini, M. A. (1999). The pure American woman and the wicked Catholic priest: An analysis of anti-Catholic literature in antebellum America. *Religion and American Culture*, 9(1), 97–128.

Park, J. Z., & Smith, C. (2000). "To whom much has been given…": Religious capital and community voluntarism among churchgoing Protestants. *Journal for the Scientific Study of Religion*, 39(3) 272–86.

Parker, S. G., & Freathy, R. J. K. (2012). Ethnic diversity, Christian hegemony and the emergence of multi-faith religious education in the 1970s. *History of Education*, 41(3), 381–404.

Prothero, S. (2007). *Religious literacy: What every American needs to know – And doesn't*. New York: HarperLuxe.

Putnam, R. D., & Campbell, D. E. (2010). *American grace: How religion divides and unites us*. New York: Simon & Schuster.

Rawls, J. (1971). *A theory of justice*. Cambridge, MA: Belknap Press.

Rawls, J. (1993). *Political liberalism*. New York: Columbia University Press.

Rawls, J. (1997). The idea of public reason revisited. *The University of Chicago Law Review*, 64(3), 765–807.

Reese, W.J. (2007). Changing conceptions of "public" and "private" in American educational history. In W. Reese, ed., *History, education, and the schools*. New York: Palgrave Macmillan, pp. 95–112.

Regnerus, M. D., Smith, C., & Sikkink, D. (1998). Who gives to the poor? The influence of religious tradition and political location on the personal generosity of Americans toward the poor. *Journal for the Scientific Study of Religion*, 37(3), 481–93.

Reno, R. R. (2019). *Return of the strong gods: Nationalism, populism, and the future of the West*. New York: Simon and Schuster.

Rousseau, J.-J. (1923). *The social contract and discourses*. Trans. by G. D. H. Cole, London: J. M. Dent and Sons.

Rousseau, J.-J. (2010). *Emile, or on education*. Trans. by C. Kelly & A. Bloom, Hanover, NH: Dartmouth College Press.

Ruiter, S., & De Graaf, N. D. (2006). National context, religiosity and volunteering: Results from 53 countries. *American Sociological Review*, 71(2), 191–210.

Russo C., & Raniere, N. (2017). School choice: An overview of selected international perspectives. In R. A. Fox & N. K. Buchanan, eds., *The Wiley handbook of school choice*. Hoboken, NJ: John Wiley & Sons, pp. 46–56.

Schinkel, A. (2010). Compulsory autonomy-promoting education. *Educational Theory*, 60(1), 97–116.

Seiple, C. (2012). The essence of exceptionalism: Roger Williams and the birth of religious freedom in America. *The Review of Faith & International Affairs*, 10(2), 13–9.

Short, G. (2003). Faith schools and indoctrination: A response to Michael Hand. *Theory and Research in Education*, 1(3), 331–41.

Smidt, C. (1999). Religion and civic engagement: A comparative analysis. *The Annals of the American Academy of Political and Social Science*, 565(1) 176–92.

Stout, J. (2004). *Democracy and tradition*. Princeton, NJ: Princeton University Press.

Taylor, C. (2007). *A secular age*. Cambridge, MA: Belknap Press.

U.K. Parliament. (2019, February 8). *Questions and Answers UIN #218805*. Available at: https://questions-statements.parliament.uk/written-questions/detail/2019-02-08/218805.

U.S. Congress. (1934) *United States Code: Ordinance of: The Northwest Territorial Government 1934*. Available at the Library of Congress: https://www.loc.gov/item/uscode1934-001000009/.

Vermeule, A. (2017). Liturgy of liberalism. *First Things*, 269. Available at: https://www.firstthings.com/article/2017/01/liturgy-of-liberalism.

Vermeule, A. (2021). According to truth. In P.E. Waldstein & P.A. Kwasniewski, eds. *Integralism and the common good: Selected essays from The Josias*. Brooklyn, NY: Angelico Press, pp. 310–15.

Warnick, B. R. (2012). Rethinking education for autonomy in pluralistic societies. *Educational Theory*, 64(4), 411–26.

Washington, G. (1790). Letter to Catharine Sawbridge Macaulay Graham. *National Archives*. Available at: https://founders.archives.gov/documents/Washington/05-04-02-0363.

Washington, G. (1811). *Washington's farewell address to the people of the United States*. Hudson, NY: William E. Norman.

Weithman, P. J. (2002). *Religion and the obligations of citizenship*. Cambridge: Cambridge University Press.

Wightwick, A. (2020, June 23). Catholic schools call for changes to RE in Wales to be scrapped. *Wales Online*. Available at: https://www.walesonline.co.uk/news/education/catholic-schools-religious-education-wales-18470657.

Wilhelm, M. O., Rooney, P. M., & Tempel, E. R. (2007). Changes in religious giving reflect changes in involvement: Age and cohort effects in religious giving, secular giving, and attendance. *Journal for the Scientific Study of Religion*, 46(2), 217–32.

Willaime, J.-P. (2007). Different models for religion and education in Europe. In R. Jackson, S. Miedema, W. Weisse, & J. F. Willaime, eds., *Religion and education in Europe: Developments, contexts and debates*. New York/Münster: Waxmann, pp. 57–66.

Wilson T. S., & Ryg, M. A. (2015). Becoming autonomous: Nonideal theory and educational autonomy. *Educational Theory*, 65(2), 127–50.

Wong, B. (2021). Let God and Rawls be friends: On the cooperation between the political liberal government and religious schools in civic education. *Journal of Applied Philosophy*, 38(5), 774–89.

32

The Epistocratic Challenge to Democratic Education

Ben Kotzee

32.1 Introduction

In a handbook of democratic education, one is likely to encounter mostly optimistic assessments of the value of democratic education. However, as the chapters in this section show, democratic education has to deal with a formidable range of challenges. Among the most fundamental of these challenges must be the fact that normative political theory is not universally convinced about the value of the very thing that democratic education is designed to promote – democracy. While defenses of democracy are a staple in normative political theory (see, for instance Hardin, 1999; Goodin, 2003; Gutmann & Thompson, 2004; Landemore, 2013), a countercurrent called "epistocracy" questions the fundamental value of the universal franchise. It holds that political decision-making cannot be entrusted to ordinary citizens, because these ordinary citizens lack the political knowledge and motivation to make wise political choices. It holds that it would be better for society if political decisions were made by only that subsection of the population who have sufficient political knowledge. Indeed, it holds that democracy itself constitutes a form of jeopardy: by sharing political decision-making power too widely, democracy exposes the population to risky political decision-making by an ignorant and capricious electorate.

The debate between democracy and epistocracy goes back to ancient philosophy. Yet, in contemporary culture it has made a striking comeback: during the period 2016 to date, commentators on both sides of the Atlantic have bemoaned, for instance, the election of Donald Trump as the 45th president of the United States and the UK's departure from the European Union following the Brexit referendum. Many political commentators in the period decry democratic decisions like these as "populist" and there is a burgeoning literature on the perils of populism (Roth, 2017; Galston, 2018). While some see populism as a manifestation of national democracy in action (Eatwell & Goodwin, 2018), others see it as demonstrating the credulousness of voters (Milliband, 2020). In this context, the question can legitimately be asked as to exactly how much of the big political decisions we can entrust to the voters and how prepared they truly are to make those decisions.

The critique of populism brings into relief two questions: Should one entrust political decisions to a wide base if that base gets its decisions *wrong*? This is the democratic question. Moreover, should political education focus on broadening the base of political participation through democratic education if broadening that base of participation might simply lead to poor decision-making in future? This is the educational question. In this chapter, I take up these two questions, with a focus on the second.

32.2 The Argument for Epistocracy

> "Thousands of years ago, Plato worried that a democratic electorate would be too dumb, irrational, and ignorant to govern well." (Brennan, 2016, p. 14)

The most famous argument against democracy is the one offered by Plato. In the *Republic*, Plato compares state craft to other crafts (like building, medicine, or navigation). He observes that, when we want to move passengers or cargo by ship, we put a skilled captain in charge of the ship – the passengers are rightly not consulted regarding the ship's lading, husbandry, navigation, etc. When it comes to the ship of state, Plato thinks the same should hold: skilled, knowledgeable, and experienced leaders ("guardians") should be placed in charge of the ship of state, not ordinary people. Indeed, the *Republic* was mostly written as a consideration of the training or education that the guardians (or philosopher kings and queens) should receive.

Another famous proponent of epistocracy was John Stuart Mill (1861). Mill disagreed with Plato that the broad population had no business being involved with politics; indeed, he thought it would be practically important, as well as educative for them, if ordinary people did take part in democracy. However, Mill was also skeptical regarding the extent to which ordinary people are, in fact, able to take part in democratic politics. He was acutely aware that different sections of society enjoy different levels of education; he held that it would be dangerous to entrust the less-educated section of society with too much political power, which they may not be qualified to exercise responsibly. For this reason, Mill proposed a scheme according to which citizens with a more advanced education would be given more votes than ordinary citizens; this is today called "plural voting" or "scholocracy" (Estlund, 2003, p. 54). In a plural voting system, every citizen would receive at least one vote, but the well-educated would receive additional votes.[1]

Mill provided two main justifcations for epistocracy. One motivation was largely practical. In Victorian England the franchise was expanding in the wake of the Reform Acts (1833 and 1867), but many of those newly granted the vote were illiterate. Mill proposed that the risks in expanding the vote to illiterate people could be mitigated by giving more compensatory votes to highly

[1] Mill's scheme is colorfully brought to life in Nevil Shute's novel *In the Wet*. Something like it is also mentioned in Mark Twain's "The Curious Republic of Gondour."

educated people. However, Mill was also motivated by an issue of rationality and, indeed, fairness: decisions should be made based on good reasons and those with merit and intelligence (from *whatever* class they were born into) should be the ones to make those decisions. Indeed, the idea that plural votes should be awarded to *educated* people, from, for instance, the urban clerical class, rather than to potentially less well-educated members of the landed classes, was arguably progressive for his time.

The leading contemporary advocate of epistocracy is Jason Brennan.[2] In his book *Against Democracy,* Brennan holds that our current liberal and democratic political culture regards democracy as definitional of the good life (2016, p. 3); in the book he problematizes this unquestioning assumption of the superiority of democracy. Brennan (2016) makes three broad arguments against democracy:

1. Democracy is not, instrumentally, a very efficient way to govern.
2. Democratic political participation is not, in fact very good for people – it tends to corrupt rather than enlighten and improve them.
3. Epistocracy would be a better way to govern.

In Brennan (2022), he repeats his position, but adds a fourth argument:

4. People have a right to be protected against poor decisions made by incompetent people.[3]

Brennan starts with the empirical claim that the majority of the population do not have the ability or inclination truly to play a productive part in democratic politics. He classifies citizens into three groups that he colorfully calls hobbits, hooligans, and vulcans.

> *Hobbits* are mostly apathetic and ignorant about politics. They lack strong, fixed opinions about most political issues. Often they have no opinions at all. They have little . . . social scientific knowledge; they are ignorant not just of current events but also of the social scientific theories and data needed to . . . understand these events.
>
> *Hooligans* are the rabid sports fans of politics. They have strong and largely fixed worldviews. . . . Hooligans consume political information, although in a biased way. . . . They may have some trust in the social sciences, but cherry-pick data and tend only to learn about research that supports their own views.
>
> *Vulcans* think scientifically and rationally about politics. Their opinions are strongly grounded in social science and philosophy. . . . They are interested in politics, but at the same time dispassionate, in part because they actively try to avoid being biased and irrational. (Brennan, 2016, pp. 4–5)

[2] Others who share Brennan's skepticism about democracy or who support elements of the epistocratic approach include Caplan (2007), Somin (2016), Jeffrey (2018), and Landa and Pevnick (2020). Bell (2016) makes the striking claim that China is a "political meritocracy" – a form of epistocracy.

[3] Brennan is first and foremost a libertarian, and not an epistocrat. He holds that it is only if we leave unchanged the current scope of government power and do not adopt a radically decentralized libertarian government that epistocracy looks like a better alternative (2022, p. 40)

Table 32.1 *Brennan's classification of degree of political interest and knowledge in the population.*

	Informed about politics	Not informed about politics
Interested in politics	Vulcans	Hooligans
Not interested in politics	(Not named by Brennan)	Hobbits

Brennan holds that "[m]ost Americans are either hobbits or hooligans, or fall somewhere in the spectrum in between" (2016, p. 5). He does not offer demographic evidence regarding the distribution of hobbits, hooligans, and vulcans in the population[4]; indeed, this will be an important point later in the chapter. However, purely conceptually, dividing the electorate into groups according to whether they are (i) informed about politics or (ii) interested in politics yields the possible distribution of knowledge and political motivation among the electorate, shown in Table 32.1

Brennan's claim is that a combination of being informed about politics and interested in politics are both important qualifications needed to take part in democracy. Those who are uninformed are likely to make poor decisions. And those who are uninterested are unlikely to spend the time and energy needed to take part effectively. From this, it follows that ideally speaking only vulcans (and not hobbits or hooligans) should take part in politics.

However, Brennan's argument goes deeper than skepticism about the political abilities and tastes of the electorate. He attacks the most common normative arguments made for democracy and for widespread political participation.

> *Instrumental arguments:* democracy is good because it leads to just, efficient, or stable decisions.
> *Aretaic arguments*: democracy is good because it educates, enlightens, and ennobles citizens.
> *Intrinsic arguments:* democracy is good in itself. (Brennan, 2016, p. 7)

His argument against the aretaic value of democracy is largely empirical. Based on some of the more skeptical studies of deliberative democracy in action Brennan notes that, when people are placed in real deliberative settings they tend to:

1. be fairly uninterested in and uninspired by political participation (most people do not truly enjoy taking part in politics)
2. reason in biased ways (exhibiting systematic my-side bias, confirmation bias, disconfirmation bias, etc.)

[4] Based on American National Election Study data, Somin (2016, p. 33) calculates that 25 percent of the population are "know-nothings" when it comes to politics; Bennett (1988, p. 483) puts the number at 29 percent.

3. rapidly sort themselves into political groups (for instance Republican and Democrat) and adopt political positions based on group allegiance rather than deliberative discussion. (Brennan, 2016, pp. 54–73)

Brennan also does not think that democracy has intrinsic value. Attacking philosophers like Christiano, Brennan holds that democracy does not encode equality into political decision-making in any distinctive way. Christiano (1996, 2008) holds that democracy is valuable because it expresses equality through majority voting. If an individual, or a minority, appoints themselves in power over a majority, that individual or minority in effect declares that they are superior to that majority; however, when an individual or a minority accepts the power of majority vote, that individual or minority signals that they regard other voters as their equals. Brennan (2016, p. 120–22) holds that that does not follow. Firstly, equality can be encoded in political systems through principles of human rights – democratic voting is not the only way to encode equality in politics. Furthermore, in other, nonpolitical areas of life, we do not interpret deference to expert knowledge as signaling inequality. When a person visits a doctor for medical advice or when they pay a plumber to fix their hot water, they do not signal that they are not the plumber or doctor's "equal"; rather, they simply follow expert advice. Brennan holds that political decision-making is no different: were the electorate to accept rule by the best-qualified politicians, they would no more signal that they are "inferior" than when they, say, follow an airline pilot's instructions to stay in their seat with their buckles fastened. Next to Christiano, Brennan (2016, chs. 1 and 5) also criticizes intrinsic arguments for the value of democracy offered by figures like Habermas, Estlund, and Rawls.

Because democracy does not have aretaic or intrinsic value, Brennan holds that democracy is at best instrumentally valuable: the value of democracy is determined solely by whether or not it can be shown to lead to the best decision-making. He holds, however, that democracy is not clearly the best decision-making system. He attacks three widely accepted demonstrations of the effectiveness of democratic decision-making: the miracle of aggregation, the Condorcet jury theorem, and the Hong-Page theorem (2016, pp. 177–82). Moreover, he advances considerable empirical evidence regarding exactly how poorly informed the average voter is (2016, pp. 23–53). In particular, he highlights work by Althaus (2003) and Caplan (2007) that shows that patterns of voter ignorance are systematic: uninformed voters do not have random mistaken beliefs that might cancel one another out, but tend to subscribe to the same mistaken beliefs that reinforce one another. For instance, Brennan holds that most American voters are uninformed about the largely positive economic consequences of inward migration into the United States. Those mistaken beliefs translate into systematically different policy preferences: poorly informed voters prefer different policies – for instance, tougher immigration restrictions – than they would have if they had been better informed regarding the facts (2016, p. 192). Brennan holds that this shows that voter ignorance matters and that it leads to poor decision-making in democracies. Because voters are so poorly informed, they tend to make the same (predictable) mistakes again and again (2016, pp. 188–94). Brennan concludes that if that section of the population who were informed regarding the relevant issues were in charge of setting policy, it would lead to systematically better decision-making.

32.3 The Empirical Evidence

Brennan outlines a range of conceptual problems for democracy and puts forward counterarguments against the most common arguments made in favor of democracy. However, in many places the argument against democracy hinges on empirical claims regarding ordinary voters' lack of knowledge about and interest in politics. In political psychology today, there is a substantial and widely discussed body of evidence that backs up Brennan's complaint against the electorate. For instance, in book-length studies, authors like Delli Carpini and Keeter (1996), Althaus (2003), Caplan (2007), Somin (2016), and Achen and Bartels (2016) concur that voters have generally lamentable levels of political knowledge, that they have little motivation to acquire better knowledge, that they suffer from systematic biases in their political decision-making, and that, fundamentally, voters' choices are not democratic in the sense of being the expression of true individual conviction: rather, voting choice in itself is fundamentally group-based and exhibits systematic my-side bias.

32.3.1 Low Levels of Political Knowledge

The empirical literature on the political ignorance of the electorate today is largely founded on survey research conducted on political knowledge in the United States in the 1940s, 1950s, and 1960s. A leading early work in the study of political knowledge was Campbell, Converse, Miller, and Stoke's book *The American Voter* (Campbell et al., 1960). Using data from the University of Michigan's Survey Research Center (that later provided the basis for the American National Election Studies) Campbell et al. showed that voters are often ignorant of basic facts about US elections, such as which party has a majority in the House of Representatives or what policies the two parties support on major political issues. They found that party identification was a more important predictor of voting behavior than ideology, meaning that voters make decisions based largely on partisanship rather than on issues or policy. Expanding on *The American Voter*, Converse used data from the American National Elections Studies to show (like Campbell et al.) that most voters are not consistently left-wing or consistently right-wing in their policy positions: while voters identify strongly with political parties, their policy preferences do not correlate well either with their preferred party's position or, even, with their own policy preferences in other areas. Moreover, voters' policy preferences are not consistent over time, showing great variability even when measured as little as two years apart. Converse found that most voters do not understand or use political or policy terminology in justifying their voting behavior; rather, they reason in terms of loyalty to parties or being attracted to particular candidates. Arguably, the political ignorance of (American) voters is laid bare most starkly in Delli Carpini and Keeter's (1996) book *What Americans Know about Politics and Why It Matters*: about a quarter of voters cannot name the Vice President, about half cannot name the British Prime Minister, and about three quarters cannot name one candidate for the House of Representatives and their party. Admittedly, a number of studies question exactly how much factual political knowledge voters need in order to make good political decisions and a number of authors hold that low-information voters can use information shortcuts to derive sufficient political knowledge from higher-information voters, such as peers, journalists or political representatives (Popkin, 1991; Sniderman et al., 1991; Page & Shapiro, 1992). However, Campbell et al.'s negative conclusions about voters' levels of factual political knowledge are borne out in studies using more recent data (Lewis-Beck et al., 2008).

Importantly for our purposes in this chapter, the increase in general education levels over time seems not to have made a difference: despite the fact that secondary school and university graduation rates rapidly increased after the Second World War, Delli Carpini and Keeter report little real increase in levels of political knowledge in the period (1996, p. 17).

32.3.2 Low Levels of Interest and Motivation to Engage in Democratic Deliberation

Achen and Bartels hold that, next to being very poorly informed, most voters also have little interest in politics or are poorly motivated to invest the cognitive effort required to gather enough information to take part in politics effectively. Achen and Bartels point to studies that show that ordinary people generally have very little desire to take part in political debate and actually quite dislike political disagreement when they encounter it (Achen and Bartels, 2016, p. 301). Indeed, in an empirical study of deliberative democracy in practice, Mutz shows that exposure to political deliberation with those who hold different political views actually decreases people's motivation to take part in politics; although political debate with people who hold different perspectives does increase tolerance of others views, it seems that fundamentally, people do not enjoy political deliberation with others (Mutz, 2006, p. 10).

Far from being surprising, a strong current suggests that it is *rational* for voters not to care much or know much about politics. The reason is that each individual vote in a democracy makes very little difference. Very few voters will ever be in a position to break a tie in an important election; for the most part, the same outcome will arise whichever way one particular voter votes. Indeed, Caplan (2007) holds that because every voter realizes that their vote is only one of millions of votes, it is *rational* for voters not to put cognitive energy into improving their knowledge of politics. He dubs this "rational ignorance" about politics.

32.3.3 Voter Bias

Studies of political knowledge and decision-making confirm that voters suffer from all of the same cognitive biases that psychologists and behavioral economists have identified over the last five decades of bias research (Wilke & Mata, 2012; Blanco, 2017). This is well illustrated by paying attention to the role that framing effects play in determining voter behavior. For instance, Achen and Bartels report that over 60 percent of voters in the US in the 1980s agreed that the government spends too little on "assistance to the poor," but only a little over 20 percent thought the government spends too little on "welfare" (Achen and Bartels, 2016, p. 30).

Rather than decide, rationally, what party to support at the polls, Achen and Bartels present evidence that voters' choices are often influenced by their feelings regarding the state of the economy, whether or not the government of the day is responsible for those economic conditions or not. Misattribution errors by voters led to governments during good times being rewarded and governments during bad times being punished (2016, pp. 111–13). They report a series of historical and contemporary examples: for instance, how the electoral success of the state governments of US oil states goes up and down with the oil price (2016, p. 114). They even explore whether President Wilson's election results in New Jersey were damaged by a spate of shark attacks in 1916 (2016, pp. 120–28).

Today, robust evidence exists regarding the cognitive biases affecting people's political behavior, including confirmation and disconfirmation bias (Kahan et al., 2017), availability bias (Cohen, 2019), and affective contagion (Erisen et al., 2014).

32.3.4 Group-Based Voting Behavior

We have seen that voters are largely ignorant about public affairs and fairly innocent of ideological thinking. What, then, drives people's political choices? Achen and Bartels hold that the most important factor is not ideology, but party affiliation. People see themselves as loyal to a political party; they support the things that the party is for and oppose things that the other party is for. This point about group behavior connects to the point about voters' political ignorance and their own ideological innocence: voters do not support their parties because of the party's ideology, they support their party's policy platforms because they identify with the party (Achen & Bartels, 2016, p. 264).

The "rational choice" picture of democracy holds that voters have a left–right ideology and vote for the party that proposes policies that reflects the voter's preference. However, according to Achen and Bartels, voters

> do not rethink their fundamental political commitments with every election cycle. Insofar as they do consider new issues or circumstances, they often do so not in order to challenge and revise their fundamental commitments, but in order to bolster those commitments by constructing preferences or beliefs consistent with them. (2016, p. 294)

For Achen and Bartels this means that the ideal that voters make rational democratic choices is largely a myth; instead, they merely rationalize, after the fact, positions that correspond with their identity-based party-preference.

In a time that many commentators and academics remark on the polarization that has crept into democratic politics Achen and Bartels's remark rings true:

> Once inside the conceptual framework, the voter finds herself inhabiting a relatively coherent universe. Her preferred candidates, her political opinions, and even her view of the facts will all tend to go together nicely. The arguments of the "other side", if they get any attention at all, will seem obviously dismissible. The fact that none of the opinions propping up her party loyalty are really hers will be quite invisible to her. It will feel like she's thinking. (2016, p. 268)[5]

32.4 Epistocratic Alternatives

If philosophers like Brennan are right that democracy is not an automatically superior form of government, and if political psychologists like Achen and Bartels are right that most democratic voters are ignorant and irrational, what alternative form of government would perform better? We have already encountered Plato's proposal to appoint a group of philosopher kings as absolute rulers and Mill's proposal to give weighted votes to the well-educated. In contemporary political theory, authors like Caplan (2007) and Somin (2016) hold that the answer to voter ignorance lies in limiting the scope of democratic government to make the fewest decisions possible. If only very few decisions were made democratically, the risk that the electorate would make the wrong decision would be reduced.

Caplan proposes that many decisions that are currently made democratically should, instead, be made in the markets – the market should take up the slack. For Caplan, the main problem with democratic decision-making is that voters are rationally irrational: it is rational for voters *not* to invest much cognitive effort in democratic decisions because they know how low a chance they have of affecting the outcome. However, every market transaction that a person participates in is one that they can affect and is one that has direct consequences for them; Caplan holds that it is therefore rational for economic actors to invest much cognitive effort into their market behavior leading to better overall decisions. In addition to expanding the market, Caplan (2007, p. 197) also floats the same epistocratic alternatives as Brennan: an educational requirement for voting rights or a weighting system to provide more votes to the well-educated – especially those well-educated in Caplan's own discipline of economics.

While Caplan advocates the market as an alternative to democratic decision-making, Somin (2016) advocates smaller, more limited government in the round. However, Somin suggests two interesting mechanisms to aid the

[5] This fact that voters largely adopt political positions based on group loyalty is exacerbated by the fact that the policy positions of groups are often set by highly motivated minority groups. As Achen and Bartels write: "Most government decisions [are] decisively influenced by the power and intensity of rival groups . . ." moreover, ". . . intense minorities . . . get their way when the majority is apathetic, uninterested, or unorganized" (2016, p. 218).

efficiency of small government. The first is ease of immigration: if it were possible for voters to vote with their feet and live in the polity that they thought most efficient, immigration would serve as a signal to polities regarding voters' preferences (2016, pp. 119–54). Moreover, Somin advocates robust judicial review in the small state: if democratic decisions were always thoroughly tested in the courts, he holds poor democratic decisions can be vetoed or amended (2016, pp. 155–69). In effect, Somin proposes that the judiciary might serve as an epistocratic check on the electorate.

In analytical political theory today, however, Brennan's proposal for epistocracy is developed in most detail. In addition, it is Brennan's system that gives the most central role to *education* as a tool to select and prepare epistocrats and, thereby, to bolster the epistocratic system. As an alternative to democracy, Brennan outlines a number of possible epistocratic systems that might be more efficient (in the instrumental sense) than democratic systems.

1. *Restricted suffrage*: a system that restricts voting rights to those citizens who demonstrate a basic level of political knowledge in (in effect) a voter qualification test (2016, pp. 211–13). Such a test, Brennan holds, could be modeled on the political knowledge section of the American National Election Survey, be based on current citizenship tests for prospective immigrants (common in many countries), or could simply consist of logic and mathematics puzzles or tests in economics, political science or geography.
2. *Plural voting*: a system modeled on Mill's proposal that each voter would be granted one vote by default, and could earn additional votes for gaining academic qualifications. Brennan does not specify exactly which qualifications would count, but he mentions the possibility of granting specific numbers of votes for finishing high school, for gaining an undergraduate degree, and for gaining a graduate degree (2016, p. 213).
3. *Enfranchisement lottery (with voter education)*: a system in which potential voters are chosen at random and are then compelled to take part in an intensive "competence building process designed to optimize their knowledge about the alternatives on the ballot" (2016, pp. 214–15).
4. *Universal suffrage with epistocratic veto:* a system with universal democratic voting as there is today, but with the addition of an epistocratic council with the power to veto or thwart bad democratic decision-making (2016, pp. 215–18).
5. Government by simulated oracle: a system that uses social scientific surveys to (i) discover the true wishes of the population and (ii) discover the most effective policy programs to bring these about (2016, pp. 220–22).

On the face of it, all of these possible systems should interest democratic or, at least, political educators: 1 and 2 clearly rely on forms of *educational testing*; 2, 3, and (to an extent 4) rely on forms of *political education*; and 5 in effect makes social and political scientists (the readers of this handbook) into *epistocrats*.

Brennan's proposals have attracted some support from authors like Jeffrey (2018) and Landa and Pevnick (2020).

Jeffrey (2018) defends what she calls limited epistocracy. By "limited epistocracy," she means organized bodies of experts or what she calls "specialized institutions." For Jeffrey, a specialized institution is one that

1. houses expertise that constitutes optimal, non-common knowledge about a subject matter,
2. is not primarily political,
3. has epistemic standing to be believed on a particular subject matter of practical importance, and
4. "issues practical verdicts, judgments, and policies that can bind citizens to a certain course of action backed by coercive power" (Jeffrey, 2018, p. 416).

As examples of specialized institutions, Jeffrey cites the World Trade Organization or World Health Organization. Neither of these bodies is elected; they also house expertise that is well outside the ordinary voter's capacity. Their legitimacy is also not democratic or even national – they are international bodies. However, both of these bodies have considerable power to make verdicts, judgments, and policies that bind citizens from many countries around the world. While Jeffrey does not offer specific proposals for how more specialized institutions can be formed or their influence extended, she holds that the de facto power of these institutions is to the good, both epistemically and politically.

Landa and Pevnick (2020) concede that opinion is stacked against epistocracy, but hold that well-functioning representative democracies can result in epistocratic rule, even if they were not designed as epistocracies from the start. Landa and Pevnick hold that, even though ordinary voters in a representative democracy may be ignorant, voters vote for representatives and these representatives' political motivation and knowledge differ fundamentally from that of the voters. Firstly, there exists a strong motivation for representatives to gain accurate political knowledge. Unlike ordinary voters, representatives do not have a small chance of affecting political outcomes – they have a large chance of affecting them. Knowing that they are pivotal to political decisions, representatives have, in Caplan's terms, a rational motivation to gain better and more accurate political knowledge that they can use in affecting decisions in the direction that they would like them to go. Secondly, Landa and Pevnick hold that representatives realize that their chances of reelection are tied to the opinion of voters: this means that representatives have incentives to inform themselves regarding the issues and to make responsible decisions (aiding their reelection chances). While voters in a well-functioning representative democracy may be ignorant and irrational, Landa and Pevnick hold that their *representatives* are incentivized to be informed, rational, and engaged. In effect, Landa and Pevnick hold that representative democracy results in delivering epistocracy with elected representatives as the epistocrats.[6]

[6] Landa and Pevnick also hold that their version of epistocracy "is not – in contrast to commonly discussed epistocratic arrangements – vulnerable to the disagreement or demographic objections. It is not vulnerable to the disagreement objection because the mechanisms at stake do not require that citizens agree that there is a particular subset of citizens who are most capable" (Landa & Pevnick, 2020, p. 6).

32.5 Objections to Epistocracy

Epistocracy is an old idea and different objections have been formulated against it. However, contemporary dicussions focus on the following four objections.

32.5.1 The Demographic Objection

At its most basic, an epistocratic system of government would give more political power to more knowledgeable citizens, or, in the formulation that Brennan takes over from Mill, better *educated* citizens. However, one of the most basic facts about the distribution of knowledge and/or education in society is that it corresponds to predictable unequal socioeconomic patterns. Surveys of the distribution of education in the United States and the United Kingdom, for instance, finds that university degrees (a qualification that Brennan himself considers as a possible voting qualification) are distributed unequally by income, race, gender, school attended, etc. (Crawford et al., 2016; Clotfelter, 2017).

If a university degree, for instance, were the voting qualification, that would change the demography of the electorate: the electorate would contain far more members of the higher than the lower socioeconomic classes. Estlund (2003) holds that this immediately raises a problem of bias for epistocracy. It is natural for voters to vote in their own self-interest, or, at the very least, to vote from a conception of the importance of particular political problems and the desirability of political solutions to solve those problems. Even if epistocratic voters are not *overtly* biased, it is reasonable to expect that they will perceive political problems from the standpoint of their own social position and propose political solutions that make sense from the position of that social position. As Estlund puts it, we might end up with a situation in which "the educated portion of the populace ... disproportionately have epistemically damaging features that countervail the admitted epistemic benefits of education" (Estlund, 2003, p. 62) Others who make a version of the demographic objection are Arlen and Rossi (2022).

32.5.2 The Disagreement Objection

The second objection commonly voiced against epistocracy is the "disagreement" objection. According to the disagreement objection, there is likely to be widespread and serious disagreement about who the most knowledgeable voters *are*. Mill and Brennan consider a university degree as a proxy for being a knower; however, it is unlikely that everyone will agree. Many people hold that a university degree does not, in fact, signal much knowledge at all; indeed, Arum and Roksa (2011) point out how little graduates typically learn at university. Should one therefore hold that an advanced degree, like a master's degree or doctorate is required? Readers of this handbook will all be familiar with PhDs who should not be trusted with any level of political or practical influence. Next to what level of education would be sufficient for voting, one could also ask what field that education should be in: politics and economics as Brennan holds? And what of people who do not have university degrees but have much political knowledge through self-study or experience? The same questions are likely to be asked by anyone considering an epistocratic system and it is highly unlikely that we will all agree about the *criteria* for being included as a member of the epistocratic electorate.

However, next to a general skepticism about the possibility of accurately identifying a competent epistocratic electorate, there are also principled points to make about the legitimacy of any epistocratic system. Talisse (2022) makes the reasonable observation that those liable to be cut out of the electorate by a move to epistocracy – the hobbits and hooligans who would be disenfranchised – are very unlikely to *accept* the move to epistocracy. Because most of the current electorate are hobbits or hooligans, a move to epistocracy would almost certainly be met with widespread, popular resistance. Ironically, this would be so even if the conceptual or philosophical case for epistocracy were established beyond doubt. For, even if one could formulate an epistocratic proposal that gains universal acceptance among the more knowledgeable or educated voters (that is among the vulcans), it is exactly Brennan's contention that most voters are hooligans and hooligans *are not persuaded by the strength of the argument.* If Brennan is right that hooligans (i) outnumber vulcans and (ii) do not make political decisions rationally, then epistocracy is guaranteed *never* to gain popular acceptance.[7]

Indeed, Estlund (2008) holds that this is a problem in principle for epistocracy. He holds that epistocracy cannot be publicly justified in Rawlsian manner, that is, in a way that will gain the assent of all reasonable people. He holds that no purported criterion for being included in the electorate – for instance, holding a certain level qualification or passing a certain voter qualification test – can be justified to the public in such a way that the whole reasonable public would accept it. There will always be reasonable objections that one can make to, for instance, the exact qualification chosen as a voter qualification and there will always be reasonable questions that can be raised to the exact content of the voter qualification test.

32.5.3 The Practicality Objection

A third objection often made against epistocracy is that it is an untried and impractical solution to democracy's problems. Next to conceptual or philosophical proposals, such as those offered by Plato, Mill, and, latterly, Brennan, there simply is no roadmap to epistocracy on the table. Moreover, a number of authors hold that, inasmuch as the epistocratic solution has been worked out by someone like Brennan, the purported solution does not solve the problems of political ignorance, bias, and irrationality.

Somin (2022) holds that current epistocratic proposals are impractical and unworkable in the real world. Like Talisse, he observes that epistocracy would have to be implemented by a real-world government. Such a government would have to formulate voting tests and set up the qualifications checking systems

[7] It seems to follow that there is no democratic route to the adoption of an epistocratic system . . . any epistocracy will have to be established by force. Brennan does not make clear what route to epistocracy he favors, be it via the ballot box, via a revolution, or via a coup.

that are necessary to regulate enfranchisement. Continuing a theme from Estlund's critique of epistocracy, Somin holds that it is likely that whichever political party is in government will use the process to advantage their own supporters (2022, p. 33). Moreover, Somin holds that even if the process works and a real-world government manages to install an epistocratic electorate, there is no guarantee that that epistocratic electorate would be less biased and tribal than the current electorate (even though, it must be acknowledged, they might be less downright ignorant). We have seen already in this chapter that it is a fact of political psychology that *everyone* suffers from the predictable biases like my-side bias and confirmation bias. We have also seen that well-educated people may be good at rationalizing their own position but are equally blind to the position of others. This means that vulcans may be no better suited to rule us than the current democratic electorate. In sum, Somin: writes that "ironically, the main flaw of epistocracy may be that we don't have the knowledge to make it work" (2022, p. 33).

32.5.4 The Epistemic Objection

The practicality and disagreement objections shade over into a last objection: the epistemic objection. Authors like Landemore (2020) and Lafont (2020) hold that the phenomenon of the wisdom of the crowds undermines Brennan's arguments. Voters are not merely individual knowers, but interact with one another and form epistemic groups; such groups they hold, can conceivable possess much more extensive, accurate and useful political knowledge than the group's individual members. One may call this an "optimistic" epistemic argument in that it emphasizes that epistemic groups may possess more political knowledge than Brennan credits. Authors like Gunn (2019) and Reiss (2019), on the other hand, offer a more "pessimistic" epistemic argument. Gunn points out that Brennan has a very high opinion of the social sciences, principally economics. After all, it is on the basis that ordinary people lack knowledge of politics and economics that Brennan concludes they are not fit to take part in decision-making (Brennan, 2016, pp. 28–30). However Gunn holds that the "social sciences do not provide the kind of reliable knowledge of the world offered by the natural sciences" (2019, p. 29); for Gunn the kind of political and economic knowledge that Brennan thinks epistocrats will gain by studying political science and economics is a chimera. Reiss (2019) makes the same point. He holds that political judgments regarding what kinds of social, economic, or political policies to pursue are not the same as technical judgments (for instance, how to build a bridge or fly an aeroplane). In technical matters, the goals are very clear and are external to the technical skills needed to achieve that goal. However, he holds that the opposite is the case in politics. In politics, there are always many different goals that one could pursue, and much of the conflict in politics is about what goal to pursue – not about the objectively best means to attain those goals. For Reiss and Gunn, politics involves making value judgments, and social science cannot specify exhaustively how to do that. It may well be that ordinary voters do not have sufficient political knowledge to solve these questions, but, epistemically speaking, they hold that the social sciences that Brennan and Caplan so admire do not have the answers either.

32.5.5 Brennan's Response

Brennan (2016, 2022) responds in depth to these objections; while it is not possible to rehearse all the responses here, his answers to two of the objections are particularly revealing in the context of this chapter.

Brennan concedes, in line with the disagreement objection, that the population at large will most likely not agree on who, exactly, should make up the epistocratic electorate; as he concedes "people disagree about both who knows more than others and who the experts are" (2016, p. 223). Moreover, he concedes, in line with the practicality objection, that any real-world implementation of epistocracy is liable to manipulation; he writes:

> In the real world, I'd expect there to be a political battle to control what goes on any voter qualification exam. Just as congresspeople now gerrymander districts to help ensure they'll win, they might try to control the exam for their own benefit. (2016, p. 223)

Brennan is very aware voter tests can be abused.[8] However, he thinks that this is not an inherent problem, and that the remedy does not lie in democracy, but rather in designing any epistocratic system that is fair, including, presumably voter qualification tests that cannot be "gamed".[9] Brennan also admits that the demographic objection is serious. He writes: "Political knowledge is not evenly dispersed among all demographic groups ..." People who are already advantaged also have higher levels of political knowledge. This means that "people who belong to these already advantaged groups are likely to acquire more power than people who belong to certain disadvantaged groups. An epistocracy is thus likely to have unfair policies that serve the interests of the advantaged rather than those of the disadvantaged" (2016 , p. 226).

Brennan offers a very interesting answer to this problem. He holds that, as long as the pool of voters in our future epistocracy is large enough voters will not vote selfishly, but "sociotropically." He leans on evidence by Feddersen, Gailmard and Sandroni (2009) to the effect that, voters are aware that their individual vote cannot make much of a difference and, hence, that it is pointless to vote selfishly. By analogy, he holds, an epistocratic electorate, as long as it is large enough, will also realize that it is pointless to vote selfishly and, for this reason, one need not worry unduly about the demographic objection. As Brennan is at pains to hold, individual votes in mass democracies count for very little as issues are rarely decided based on one swing vote. Following Caplan

[8] Historically, the most notorious manipulation of voter qualification tests was the manipulation of literacy tests to disenfranchise black voters in the American South during the Jim Crow era. Brennan deplores that particular injustice (2016, p. 223).

[9] Educational psychologists will counter that it is very hard to design a test that cannot be coached for or otherwise abused. The history of the Scholastic Aptitude Test (SAT) is salutary.

(2007), Brennan regularly stresses that voter ignorance is rational: there is little point to inform oneself of the issues of one's own vote is unlikely to be decisive. Interestingly, Brennan holds that the same applies for *selfish* voting: there is little point to vote selfishly if one's individual vote counts so little. He writes:

> Since individual votes count for so little, selfish voting doesn't survive cost–benefit analysis. Voters instead vote symbolically, to express their commitment to various ideals and show they belong to their political tribe . . . So long as the voting pool in an epistocracy is sufficiently large (in absolute, not percentage terms), large enough to ensure that voters have a low chance of being decisive, voters will vote for what they believe to be in the common good, not for what they believe is in their self-interest. (Brennan, 2022, p. 45)

The answer to the demographic objection, for Brennan, is *to ensure that the group of epistocratic voters is large enough* (even if this group is not strictly demographically representative).

However, next to the hope that a large body of epistocratic voters will vote in sociotropic fashion, Brennan also advances another solution to the demographic problem. Brennan concedes the demographic point that, if a country like the US instituted a voter qualification exam along the lines that he suggests, it is likely that more white, upper-class, employed males would pass it, compared to disadvantaged sections of the community. While he concedes the point, he does not hold that the solution is to give everyone an equal vote:

> My view is that rather than insist everyone vote, we should *fix* those underlying injustices. Let's treat the disease, not the symptoms. As we saw . . . low- and high-information voters have systematically different policy preferences, including preferences for how to deal with these underlying injustices. In the United States, excluding the bottom 80 percent of white voters from voting might be just what poor blacks need. (Brennan, 2016 , p. 228)

Brennan's response is brief, but next to suggesting that voter qualification tests should be fair, he seems to hold that the solution to the demographic problem is to ensure that disadvantaged sections of society overcome their educational and social disadvantages and become capable of passing the voter qualification test. If disadvantaged groups began passing the voter qualification test in greater numbers, this would eventually correct the demographic problem. He adds (in the last sentence from the quotation above) that this process of assisting disadvantaged people to become capable of passing the voting test might, in fact, be helped if it were carried through by an epistocratic government (for instance, one in which some currently advantaged voters – e.g., the "bottom 80 percent of white voters" – did not vote).

32.6 The Challenge

We have outlined both philosophical arguments against democracy and empirical results that raise serious questions about the actual functioning of democratic decision-making in practice. Based on this bleak résumé, a skeptical democratic educator might formulate two challenges for democratic education:

1. *The conceptual challenge*: Perhaps ordinary people should not govern and universal voting should be abandoned. Concomitantly, broad-based democratic education should cease and should be rethought along narrower epistocratic lines.
2. *The empirical challenge*: If most adults are too ignorant, biased, and tribal to be effective voters, it is reasonable to expect that children are equally or more ignorant, biased, and tribal. Against these odds, democratic education may be ineffectual or downright impossible.

32.6.1 The Conceptual Challenge

Let us start with the conceptual challenge. In an epistocratic system in which only a minority of the population (the vulcans) take part in elections, there will be no need to prepare the whole population for democratic participation. In such a system "democratic education," in the sense of "educating children about and for democracy" will clearly be superfluous. While contemporary advocates of epistocracy (like Brennan or Caplan) do not make specific proposals, one can speculate regarding the form that political education in an epistocracy might take.

In what one might call "Platonic" epistocratic political education, one can expect to see narrow-based or "elite" political education for vulcan children (or those assessed to be on track to become vulcans one day) regarding how to play their proper role as epistocrats in society as adults. However, one might also see broader-based political education directed at hobbit and hooligan children (or those on track for hobbit or hooligan status) designed to induce them to accept and support rule by the vulcans, lest the epistocratic system suffers from the legitimacy problems that Estlund and Talisse outline. Indeed, one might speculate that the major role of broader-based political education in an epistocratic system might be to turn hooligan children into hobbit adults. After all, as Brennan makes clear, many of the problems of contemporary democracy (such as tribalism) can be pinned on hooliganism; while hobbits are ignorant, they are (at least) passive in their acceptance of the political status quo. It would therefore make sense for broader-based political education to educate hooligan children to be more hobbit-like as adults. "Platonic" epistocratic political education would surely shake the principles of democratic education to their core. Democratic education means education about democracy, but, in addition, it also means a form of education that is broad-based, inclusive, and equal. A form of political education that has elite and nonelite tracks and is designed to keep the rulers and the ruled in their own lane will be thoroughly *anti*democratic.

Granted, the Platonic model is not the only possible epistocratic model of political education. An epistocratic educational system might give up on democratic education as we currently know it, but might, by the same token, concentrate very heavily on teaching those academic disciplines and topics that epistocrats admire. For instance, it is clear that Caplan believes that study of economics holds the key to greater awareness and understanding of social and political realities. Brennan agrees regarding economics, but also includes the broader social sciences (one assumes that he means the hard or positivistic social sciences, like political science, political psychology, and statistics). An epistocratic educational system might simply choose to give as many students as possible a good grounding in the hard social sciences: the ones who take to this education best will thereupon become vulcans whereas the others might even learn to become slightly less hooligan- or hobbit-like.

Alternatively, it is possible that the epistocratic system might simply give up on providing civic education to children. Brennan himself suggests that testing for epistocratic traits might be easier than educating for them. As he writes: "I worry . . . that breeding competent voters is significantly harder and more likely to fail than *selecting* for them (Brennan, 2016, p. 215). It is possible, therefore, that epistocratic political education may give up on the effort made to educate epistocrats, and would focus its energies instead on a massive testing effort to select the most knowledgeable people to serve as epistocrats (paying no attention to what serendipity it is that turned them into such political sages). In such a system, the focus would shift from political education to political testing.

32.6.2 The Empirical Challenge

The empirical challenge is that, if adult voters are in the main too ignorant, biased, and tribal to be effective voters, then children must be at least as ignorant, biased, and tribal, if not more so. If the literature in political psychology illustrates that adults' ignorance, bias, and tribalism are irredeemable, this will mean that democratic education is pointless; it will never work, because children are destined for life as ignorant, biased tribalists come what may. Even worse, it is possible that, as it is currently set up, democratic education is no different from the deliberative democracy experiments that Mutz (2006) investigated. If even the best attempts at fostering democratic deliberation inevitably degenerate into tribal standoffs between different political camps, it is possible that civic education will only ever increase rather than decrease tribalism. Splits between left and right may simply be inevitable or, where a teacher does manage to unify children around a political standpoint, it might just be because she has succeeded in indoctrinating them into subscribing to her particular brand of biased politics. Genuine, open, deliberative democratic classrooms might simply be a pipedream.

In order to settle the empirical question, one must turn to the literature on the effectiveness of citizenship education – a literature that is almost as old as the political psychology literature about voter knowledge. Unfortunately, the results from that literature are mixed. In a landmark study, Langton and Jennings (1968) reached the same negative conclusions regarding the effectiveness of civic education as Converse (1964) reached about voters' political knowledge. Langton and Jennings interviewed 1,600 American high school students who had taken civic education courses in topics like American Government or Comparative Politics. Langton and Jennings found that civic education does not improve political knowledge, political interest, political efficacy, or tolerance. By contrast, Niemi and Junn (1998) (using data from the Civics Assessment of the US National Assessment of Educational Progress) found that civics classes in the US do increase political knowledge, albeit by roughly one letter grade.

By the 2000s the literature had grown. Manning and Edwards, for instance, report on a number of studies that find that young people have little knowledge of or interest in politics (2014, p. 22). They conducted a systematic literature review study to review the evidence for the effectiveness of civic education programs in reducing this "civic deficit" and found only nine interventional studies on the effectiveness of civic education that meet basic quality criteria like reporting an objective outcome that can be compared against a control group or baseline. Manning and Edwards are critical of the quality of these studies, holding that all nine suffer from "serious methodological weaknesses" (2014, p. 38). Overall, they hold that there is little evidence for "civic education having a discernible or direct effect on voting" (2014, p. 22).

A further review study was carried out by Donvaband and Hoskins (2021). The randomized controlled trial (RCT) is the gold standard of educational effectiveness studies and Donvaband and Hoskins found a more encouraging 25 trials that have been conducted on various civic educational interventions. However, they point out that 25 is still a small number and that the geographic spread is limited: 17 of the studies are from the US or UK. Donvaband and Hoskins do not draw overall conclusions regarding how well civic education's effectiveness is proven through these 25 trials, but their conclusions are somewhat more optimistic than Manning and Edwards: of the studies they reviewed, 15 report positive results, 6 mixed results, and 4 negative results. Despite the preponderance of positive results emerging from the 25 trials, it must be noted that Donvaband and Hoskins did not carry out a true systematic review of RCTs (or "Cochrane review") culminating in the synthesis of data on effect sizes. The results of the 25 studies are reported thematically and are not synthesized statistically (2021, pp. 7–12); moreover, the methodological strengths of the underlying studies are not investigated and compared (2021, pp. 12–14).

On the whole we can conclude that there is a rapidly developing body of evidence on the extent to which civic education in childhood can contribute to solving the problem of political ignorance and disengagement in adulthood. However, it is fair to say that at present there is not enough high-quality research to make one confident that civic education is up to the task of solving the problem of voter ignorance, bias, and tribalism.

32.7 Conclusion: Meeting the Epistocratic Challenge

In the face of the depressing evidence regarding voter ignorance and in the face of mixed evidence regarding the effectiveness of civic education, the more optimistic democratic educator is likely to hold that this exactly proves the need for more high-quality civic education and for more high-class research on its effectiveness. Surely the answer to voter ignorance, bias, and partisanship can *only* lie in educating potential voters more effectively; as Giesinger puts it: "The democratic response to the alleged incompetence of citizens is democratic (political, civic) education" (2022, p. 7). If the evidence does not yet conclusively show that democratic education can move the dial on the democratic deficit, and it is so theoretically obvious that democratic education should in principle move it, this might demonstrate that we do not have enough democratic education programs of sufficient quality *and* that we have not yet collected the right evidence to demonstrate their effectiveness. However, as Giesinger shows, such an answer would beg the question in favor of democratic education by doubling down on what might simply be a fruitless intervention. Giesinger holds that democratic educators need to face up to the fact that education might *not* be the remedy for the democratic deficit. Firstly, it seems descriptively obvious that current educational systems in the democratic world do not produce competent citizens; despite continually rising levels of educational participation around the world, levels of political knowledge seem to be stuck. Secondly, it is possible that political ignorance, apathy, and biased thinking are such irredeemable features of human psychology that they cannot be eradicated (Giesinger, 2022, pp. 7–9).

Giesinger suggests that we should, rather, pay attention to the role that education plays within the epistocratic framework (2022, p. 14). While he does not write directly about democratic education, educational concerns – and discussions of things like what subjects are useful to study at university and/or what topics are important to master within those subjects – feature prominently in Brennan's work. Throughout, Brennan's ambivalence toward the value of education is striking. On the one hand, he seems to hold that ordinary political life provides most people with a bad political education. He writes: "Most common forms of political engagement not only fail to educate or ennoble us but also tend to stultify and corrupt us" (2016, p. 2). This clearly shows that Brennan has an educational concern – he is in favor of education and is against corruption – but complains that our current system corrupts rather than educates. Moroever, it is clear that the political knowledge that Brennan most admires is the knowledge taught in advanced degrees in economics and political science and, at many points, he comes close to suggesting that the height of political education is a graduate degree in economics. If this is so, why not advocate that the whole population (or as many people as are able) be provided with a high-quality, free-at-the-point-of-delivery, graduate-level, education in economics? Would increasing the population of economics graduates to the maximum not lead to the best, most epistocratic, decision-making?

Indeed, as we have seen, Brennan holds that the epistocratic electorate cannot be too small. If the sociotropic effects that he counts on are to be realized, the future epistocratic electorate needs to be large enough that it does not vote selfishly, but votes for the common good. Moreover, he concedes (Brennan, 2016, p. 228, quoted in Section 32.5.5) that the demographic objection does have *some* bite and that it is desirable to ensure that, over time, the epistocratic electorate becomes more diverse by solving what is the root problem – not the poor distribution of votes, but the poor distribution of *knowledge* among the electorate. It therefore appears that Brennan does envisage something like political education to enable a larger and more diverse group of people to be able to pass the voter qualification test. This would not be possible if the general population's political ignorance, bias, and tribalism were utterly beyond improvement, leading one to believe that Brennan holds political edification is still *possible* (at least for a section of the population that he does not specify).

It turns out that, not only does epistocracy pose a problem for democratic education, democratic education also poses a problem for epistocracy. For epistocracy to be complete, it must provide a detailed epistocratic political education program. However, Brennan simply does not answer the question of whether a graduate degree in economics (or political science, or the hard social sciences in general) *would* make a person fit to be part of the epistocracy. Moreover, he does not adduce any evidence that advanced degrees in these subjects do increase political knowledge or decrease political bias or tribalism. Moreover, he does not deal with the vexed question of whether there is a direct causal link between studying these subjects and positive political outcomes or merely a selection effect at work. Crucially, he does not say why it is in principle impossible to provide the entire electorate with a graduate education in economics, which would bring broad-based democracy back through the epistocratic educational door. The only reason why, in principle, only a section of the population should rule, is if there were some magic kernel of knowledge hidden in a graduate education in economics or the "hard social sciences" more broadly, and if only a small number of people were intellectually capable of grasping that kernel of knowledge. Suffice it to say, Brennan does not provide any detailed argument in this regard.

Talisse holds that the real problem is that we do not yet know enough about the nature and extent of political ignorance to design a political system that effectively counters political ignorance. He writes:

> We know that, given the kind of power it collectively wields, the citizenry falls far short of any reasonable threshold of epistemic responsibility. But we don't know whether public ignorance is a problem of objectively unjustified belief, subjectively unjustified beliefs, dysfunctional belief forming processes, flawed processes of belief-revision, or (as is likely) varied combinations of them all. Alas, it would be difficult to design a large-scale research program that could detect the relevant epistemological nuance, so it is not at all clear what democratic theorists ought to offer as a remedy. (2022, p. 21)

Exactly the same holds regarding civic education in the broad: we simply do not know enough about whether civic education is effective enough in countering political ignorance, bias, and tribalism to rescue democracy from the epistocratic challenge. On the other hand, current epistocratic political thought does not have any detailed educational proposal to match the one collectively being put forward by the authors in this handbook.[10] Whereas the battle between

[10] Save a foundational work by Plato and a few passages in Mill.

epistocracy and democracy has hitherto been fought in normative political theory and in political psychology, this chapter maps out the terrain of what will become the educational front of that battle.

References

Achen, C., & Bartels, L. (2016). *Democracy for realists: Why elections do not produce responsive governments*. Princeton, NJ: Princeton University Press.

Althaus, S. (2003). *Collective preferences in democratic politics*. Cambridge: Cambridge University Press.

Arlen, G., & Rossi, E. (2022). Is this what democracy looks like? (Never mind epistocracy). *Inquiry*, 65(1), 1–14.

Arum, R., & Roksa, J. (2011). *Academically adrift: Limited learning on college campuses*. Chicago, IL: University of Chicago Press.

Bell, Daniel. (2016). *The China model: Political meritocracy and the limits of democracy*. Princeton, NJ: Princeton University Press.

Bennett, S. (1988). "Know-nothings" revisited: The meaning of political ignorance today. *Social Science Quarterly*, 69(2), 476–90.

Blanco, F. (2017). Cognitive bias. In J. Vonk & T. Shackelford, eds., *Encyclopedia of animal cognition and behavior*. Basel: Springer. doi: 10.1007/978-3-319-47829-6_1244-1.

Brennan, J. (2016). *Against democracy*. Princeton, NJ: Princeton University Press.

Brennan, J. (2022). Giving epistocracy a fair hearing. *Inquiry*, 65(1), 35–49.

Campbell, A., Converse, P., Miller, W. & Stokes, D. (1960) *The American voter*. Chicago, IL: University of Chicago Press.

Caplan, B. (2007). *The myth of the rational voter: Why democracies choose bad policies*. Princeton, NJ: Princeton University Press.

Christiano, T. (1996). *The rule of the many: Fundamental issues in democratic theory*. London: Routledge.

Christiano, T. (2008). *The constitution of equality: Democractic authority and its limits*. Oxford: Oxford University Press.

Clotfelter, C. (2017). *Unequal colleges in the age of disparity*. Cambridge, MA: Belknap Press.

Cohen, M. (2019). The availability heuristic, political leaders, and decision making. In *Oxford research encyclopedia of politics*. Oxford: Oxford University Press. doi: 10.1093/acrefore/9780190228637.013.1028.

Converse, P. (1964) The nature of belief systems in mass publics. In D. Apter, ed., *Ideology and discontent*. New York: Free Press of Glencoe.

Crawford, C., Gregg, P., Macmillan, L., Vignoles, A., & Wyness, G. (2016). Higher education, career opportunities and intergenerational inequality. *Oxford Review of Economic Policy*, 32(4), 553–75.

Delli Carpini, M., & Keeter, S. (1996). *What Americans know about politics and why it matters*. New Haven, CT: Yale University Press.

Donvaband, S., & Hoskins, B. (2021). Citizenship education for political engagement: A systematic review of controlled trials. *Social Sciences*, 10(5), 1–19.

Eatwell, R., & Goodwin, M. (2018). *National populism: The revolt against liberal democracy*. London: Pelican.

Erisen, C., Lodge, M., & Taber, C. (2014). Affective contagion in effortful political thinking. *Political Psychology*, 35(2), 187–206.

Estlund, D. (2003). Why not epistocracy. In N. Reshotko, ed., *Desire, identity, and existence: Essays in honor of T.M. Penner*. New York: Academic Printing and Publishing, pp. 53–70.

Estlund, D. (2008). *Democratic authority: A philosophical framework*. Princeton, NJ: Princeton University Press.

Feddersen, T., Gailmard, S., & Sandroni, A. (2009). A bias toward unselfishness in large elections: Theory and experimental evidence. *American Political Science Review*, 103, 175–92.

Galston, W. (2018). *Anti-pluralism: The populist threat to liberal democracy*. New Haven, CT: Yale University Press.

Giesinger, J. (2022). Education as the remedy: the justification of democracy and the epistocratic challenge. In J. Culp, J. Drerup, I. de Groot, A. Schinkel, & D. Yacek, eds., *Liberal democratic education: A paradigm in crisis*. Paderborn: Brill, pp. 67–82.

Goodin, R. (2003). *Reflective democracy*. Oxford: Oxford University Press.

Gunn, P. (2019). Against epistocracy. *Critical Review*, 31(1), 26–82.

Gutmann, A., & Thompson, D. (2004). *Why deliberative democracy?* Princeton, NJ: Princeton University Press.

Hardin, R. (1999). *Liberalism, constitutionalism and democracy*. Oxford: Oxford University Press.

Jeffrey, A. (2018). Limited epistocracy and political inclusion. *Episteme*, 15(4), 412–32.

Kahan, D., Peters, E., Cantrell Dawson, E., & Slovic, P. (2017). Motivated numeracy and enlightened self-government. *Behavioural Public Policy*, 1(1), 54–86.

Lafont, C. (2020) *Democracy without shortcuts: A participatory conception of deliberative democracy*. Oxford: Oxford University Press.

Landa, D., & Pevnick, R. (2020). Representative democracy as defensible epistocracy. *American Political Science Review*, 114(1), 1–13.

Landemore, H. (2013). *Democratic reason: Politics, collective intelligence, and the rule of the many*. Princeton, NJ: Princeton University Press.

Landemore, H. (2020). *Open democracy: Reinventing popular rule for the twenty-first century*. Princeton, NJ: Princeton University Press.

Langton, K., & Jennings, M. K. (1968). Political socialization and the high school civics curriculum in the United States. *American Political Science Review*, 62(3), 852–67.

Lewis-Beck, M., Jacoby, W., Norpoth, H., and Weissberg, H. (2008). *The American voter revisited*. Ann Arbor, MI: University of Michigan Press.

Manning, N., & Edwards, K. (2014). Does civic education for young people increase political participation: A systematic review. *Educational Review*, 66(1), 22–45.

Mill, J. S. (1861). *Considerations on representative government*. London: Parker, Son, and Bourn.

Milliband, D. (2020). Brexit, populism, and the future of British democracy. *Horizons: Journal of International Relations and Sustainable Development*, 15, 150–65.

Mutz, D. (2006). *Hearing the other side: Deliberative versus participatory democracy*. Cambridge: Cambridge University Press.

Niemi, R., & Junn, G. (1998). *Civic education: What makes students learn*. New Haven, CT: Yale University Press.

Page, I. & Shapiro, R. (1992). The rational public and democracy. In G. Marcus & R. Hanson, eds., *Reconsidering the democratic public*. University Park, PA: Penn State University Press.

Popkin, S. (1991). *The reasoning voter: Communication and persuasion in presidential campaigns*. Chicago, IL: University of Chicago Press.

Reiss, J. (2019). Expertise, agreement, and the nature of social scientific facts or: Against epistocracy. *Social Epistemology*, 33(2), 183–92.

Roth, K. (2017). The dangerous rise of populism: Global attacks on human rights values. *Journal of International Affairs*, 70, 79–84.

Sniderman, P., Brody, R., & Tetlock, P. (1991). *Reasoning and choice: Explorations in political psychology*. Cambridge: Cambridge University Press.

Somin, I. (2016). *Democracy and political ignorance: Why smaller government is better*. Stanford, CA: Stanford University Press.

Somin, I. (2022). The promise and peril of epistocracy. *Inquiry*, 65(1), 27–34.

Talisse, R. (2022). The trouble with hooligans. *Inquiry*, 65(1), 15–26.

Wilke, A., & Mata, R. (2012). Cognitive bias. In: V. Ramachandran, ed., *Encyclopedia of human behaviour*. London/Burlington, MA: Elsevier/Academic Press, pp. 531–35.

33

Climate Change and Democratic Education

Anders Schinkel

33.1 Introduction

After a number of "school strikes for climate" by Dutch pupils, prime minister Mark Rutte tweeted (@Youth4ClimateNL) that he and minister of Economic Affairs and Climate Eric Wiebes are always open for a conversation – "After school, of course 😉" (NOS, 2019a). Rutte is leader of the VVD, a right-wing liberal party that has been the largest political party (in terms of numbers of seats in parliament) since 2010, the year in which Rutte first became prime minister. He is the longest serving prime minister in Dutch parliamentary history, currently leading his fourth government coalition. The VVD is notoriously conservative, to put it mildly, when it comes to climate policies and environmental policies in general, a fact highlighted in 2015 when Urgenda, an environmental organization founded at the initiative of an environmental activist and a professor in sustainability transition management, won a court case against the state. The court ruled that the state had not done enough to protect its citizens' human rights in the face of climate change, and set emission level reduction targets for the state. The government fought the decision all the way to the supreme court – and lost (Kaminski, 2019). School strikes for climate took off across the world – in the Netherlands at the very same time that the Dutch state appealed against the court decision. Despite this, Rutte stated he found the climate protest "fantastic," while also claiming that his government's climate ambitions were already very high compared to those of other European countries. "Guys, what more do you want?" he said, "You can't possibly ask for more" (NOS, 2019b).

This example is illustrative of democratic countries' failure – so far – to take responsibility for climate change; for their part in causing it, and for implementing the urgently needed mitigation and adaptation measures. It also highlights that climate change as a political and moral problem is interwoven with questions about education, and about democratic education in particular. At first glance it may look like a glorious example of democracy in action that the prime minister of the Netherlands not only takes the time to respond to a school student protest – these are not even voting citizens, after all – but actually invites them over to have a discussion about the issue. On reflection, however, the picture looks quite a bit darker. The supposedly witty "after school, of course" comment tells us a lot about Rutte's (and his government's) views about what young people's priorities ought to be when it comes to spending time in school versus speaking up for better climate policies in order to safeguard a future for themselves and others. Underlying this is a narrow view of what activities count as educational, and what students are in school for. There is also a paternalistic, if not insulting, aspect to the comment – a failure to take these young people seriously as concerned democratic citizens. And this in turn points to one of the main challenges faced by democracies: how to take the interests and rights of those who cannot (yet) vote and of those yet to be born into account. The ecological crises of the Anthropocene – of which climate change is but one, though hugely important, element – reveal and create unprecedented intergenerational tensions that challenge the legitimacy of current forms of democracy. Finally, Rutte's claim that his government was already doing everything one could reasonably ask highlights a structural problem in the relation between current adults and younger generations, between the educators and those to be educated, namely the problem of hypocrisy. In Rutte's case there is the obvious inconsistency between what adults say and what they actually do. But the deeper problem concerns the believability of adults in general as educators, in light of their continued collective failure to mount an adequate response to climate change and other aspects of the ecological crisis the world currently faces (see Schinkel, 2022).

Climate change poses a complex challenge to all forms of governance, but some difficulties are specific to democracies or particularly pronounced in democracies. My purpose in this chapter is to analyze the implications of those difficulties for practices of democratic education. Taken separately, both climate change and democratic education already involve problems of such complexity that the conjunction of the two gives us a topic with so many aspects and layers that the current chapter can never claim to be comprehensive. Even less does it make sense to approach the topic as a "problem" for which we might find "a solution" – a theory of or approach to democratic education that will enable democracies to (finally) "deal with" climate change, or provide the answer to problems of democratic legitimacy (on this point see also Machin, 2013 and Laird, 2017). When it comes to climate change the language of problems (whether '"wicked" or not) is too suggestive of control; on hearing the word "problem" the second word that comes to mind is "solution" or "management." But on the spatiotemporal scale at which the interlocking crises of the Anthropocene emerged (climate change, ecosystem destruction, species extinction, environmental pollution, and so on) we are certainly causal agents, but not in control – that is to say, there is no "we," no collective agent, at the steering wheel of history. It makes more sense, therefore, to look at climate change as a reality – a geophysical, material, economic, moral, and political reality – that requires a *response* in terms of how we live our lives, and the economic, moral, and political direction we decide to take both individually and at various collective levels. A response is not a solution, and taking a new direction does not simply undo the damage of the previous course; but this, and only this, is possible.[1]

I will begin, in Section 33.2, by saying a few words about the understanding of democratic education I rely on in this chapter. We can then move to the substantive issues. In Section 33.3, I set out the main reasons why climate change is such a difficult problem (the term is not entirely avoidable, but keep in mind it should not be taken literally) for democracies, as well as what specific advantages democracies might have for responding to it. This sets the stage for Section 33.4, in which I offer my perspective on what particular challenges, tasks, and opportunities follow for democratic education. In the concluding section, I briefly summarize my findings and raise some questions that I believe merit further consideration.

33.2 The Concept of Democratic Education

The term "democratic education" may refer to (i) education *for* democracy, that is, education that aims to support the functioning of a democracy by enabling young people to participate in it in constructive ways, fostering democratic dispositions, and so on; (ii) democratically organized forms of education (e.g., with participation by parents and/or pupils and students, dialogic teaching models, etc.); and (iii) an education system and/or curriculum shaped according to democratically determined educational policies. In short, the concept of democratic education refers to a particular *general* answer to one or more of three questions about education: What should be the aims and content of education? What form should education take? And who should decide about the form and content of education? The answers one gives to these questions are likely to be interdependent in various ways. In what ways exactly depends in part on one's views on other matters; for instance, if one believes that being able to tell the difference between reliable information and disinformation is vital to the functioning and the survival of democracies, one may wish to limit the extent to which the content of education is settled by popular vote. There are also logical connections between the questions: for instance, the second question implies an answer to the question "Who decides?" but on the practical rather than the policy level; and "democratic education" as a way to organize educational practice may well also be someone's first and best answer to the question how to educate *for* democracy.

[1] This is not to say that there are not also aspects of climate change and its causes that can be identified as more specific problems that may be amenable to solutions in the form of mitigation or adaptation. But the point is that climate change as a (physical-political) whole exceeds this level, and also cannot be seen as a sum of isolated problems. The notion of a problem assumes a stable background against which the problem lights up and in the context of which it needs to be dealt with. But climate change involves everything: it concerns precisely the background – how we as human beings live on this planet – and an adequate response (one that does justice to its moral, political, and practical implications) will require this background to change. A roughly similar point is made by Fiorino (2018, p. 36): "Climate change will always be with us. Given its complexity, irreversibility, and its roots in economic structures and processes, it cannot be seen as a problem that will be 'solved' over the next several decades, or even within a century. It presents a long-term, permanent challenge to governance."

With regard to the first sense of "democratic education," this chapter follows the use of this term explained in the editors' introduction to this volume, meaning that democratic education is understood as a general concept of education for a democratic way of life and a democratic moral character. It is an ideal that can be more or less realized in practice. "Practice" does not necessarily mean civic education classes, nor even formal schooling as a whole; practices of democratic education also occur outside the school. The school strikes for climate are again a case in point; these are not just happenings with potential educational *effects*, but can also be seen as a form of political self-education by young people. The second point made by the editors of this volume is that democratic education is to be distinguished from political education (understood here as education about the political system and preparation for political participation) in that it is equally closely connected to moral education. Democratic education entails the cultivation of a particular attitude toward fellow human beings, namely one of recognition of human beings' fundamental moral equality.

For my purposes in this chapter, it is important to emphasize two points about this concept of democratic education: Firstly, it is an *ideal*, and therefore something that *may* happen in places where people intend it to happen, but equally well may not happen. What actually happens, for instance, in formal educational contexts intended as education for democracy, may be a far cry from the moral-political ideal just described. It may be a place where young people disengage from, rather than come to engage with, political issues. It may in practice limit itself entirely to democratic socialization, and lack a critical-reflective and responsibilizing component (see Biesta, 2011). A related point is that people may become "democratically educated" (or, of course, the opposite) by life, by what they experience and what happens to them, without any educational intention on anyone's part. This lies beyond the scope of "democratic education" as I use the term here, but it is no less important. And secondly, the concept of democratic education can be fleshed out in many ways, leading to as many conceptualizations (see Sant, 2019, for a discussion of eight different discourses of democratic education, which she dubs elitist, liberal, neoliberal, deliberative, multicultural, participatory, critical, and agonistic). In this chapter, I do not offer an argument for one particular conceptualization of democratic education, or for a particular educational approach. Instead, I am interested in how, in the face of climate change, educational practices can come to approximate more closely to the general ideal of democratic education, and how educational practices that do so may contribute to an adequate and just response to the reality of climate change and its effects on human and nonhuman life.

I take the ideal of *democracy* to comprise two fundamental components, one being the moral component, the other being the idea of self-rule, that is, that government acquires additional legitimacy – beyond that based on its effectiveness in dealing with the basic problems of social existence – when those who are governed are ultimately responsible for the rules by which they are governed. The other term in democratic education is no less important; "education," too, is not just a term that denotes schooling and other actual practices in which some people are trying to teach things to other people; it is also a normative concept, an ideal that stipulates what we *hope* happens in such practices. In the fullest sense of the word, education happens when through knowledge and understanding a *perspective* is gained on the subject, meaning that the educated has gained a *personal, informed awareness* of some aspect of the world that they were not informed about and/or not truly aware of before. The world has been opened up a bit more, and the educated are able to notice more, and understand more – while also being more aware of what they do not understand. Education "is inversely related to the extent to which we merely take things for granted" (Schinkel, 2021, p. 107). It is not just a cognitive matter; the very sense of having a perspective, the heightened awareness of this "thing" in the world, has a dimension of feeling to it, apart from any additional emotional and evaluative charge – it is the feeling of noticing, of finding something remarkable (worth noticing) in a mild sense at least, the feeling of interest or importance.[2] There is also an element of responsibility there: the educated person responds to, and feels in touch with, the world – not just a textbook – and has at the same time acquired responsibility for her knowledge and understanding; her answer to the question "How do you know?" no longer just refers to the textbook or some authority, but to her own perception and understanding of the world.

Returning to the three questions about education mentioned earlier in this section, if we look at these through the lense of climate change, we may ask: (i) Does the reality of climate change call for (more) education for democracy, and if so, what should the aims and content of such education be? (ii) Would democratically organized education further liberal democracies' ability and/or their citizens' ability to respond to climate change, more than other forms of education? (iii) Who should decide about education (policy) in the face of climate change? In order to aspire to completeness, an answer to the question as to the implications of climate change for democratic education would have to answer these three questions not just in terms of the concept of democratic education but also in terms of specific conceptualizations. My ambitions are more modest; my focus will be on the first question, on the ways in which the fundamental components of the democratic educational ideal may best be realized in the face of the challenges posed to democracy by climate change, and on how realizing this ideal may help democracies plot a new course in response to those challenges.

33.3 Climate Change as a Challenge for Democracies

Climate change is obviously a difficult problem for any government. One reason for this is its complexity: climate systems, and the impact on them of human actions, are highly complex, involving large numbers of variables and nonlinear

[2] This understanding of "education" leans on Peters (1970) and Whitehead (1962).

causality (feedback loops), and demanding simultaneous consideration of multiple spatial and temporal scales. A related reason is that there are many uncertainties in our understanding of climate change, and thus in predictions about what will happen given various scenarios. Other reasons are the abstractness of climate change – people cannot literally "touch, feel, or smell climate change" (Fiorino, 2018, p. 25) and for a long time there were no noticeable effects at all; the human tendency to discount the future and focus on the present and other ingrained aspects of human psychology; the fact that an adequate response to climate change requires global cooperation, meaning cooperation between very different types of regime, and between governments representing (in some respects) different and conflicting interests; and the fact that any analysis of the problem and of what would count as a good response will depend in part on ideas of the good life, about which no consensus exists.

However, observing that even established democracies have so far failed to mount anything even close to an adequate response to climate change, some commentators have begun to wonder whether democracy as a type of government is actually *capable* of doing so.[3] Perhaps, in light of the urgency of the issue, a more autocratic or authoritarian form of governance is required. It might be that democracies suffer from structural failings – at least when faced with climate change – that will forever prevent them from responding adequately and in time.

I will now briefly discuss the main arguments for why climate change is particularly challenging for democracies; my main guide here will be Di Paola and Jamieson (2018). Drawing on Fiorino (2018) and Lindvall (2021), I will then offer some reasons to think that democracies actually hold particular advantages over autocratic and authoritarian forms of governance when it comes to dealing with such complex, long-term issues as climate change, and subsequently summarize the empirical evidence for the comparative effectiveness of democracies' responses to climate change.

33.3.1 Why Climate Change Is Particularly Challenging for Democracies

Di Paola and Jamieson (2018) discuss essentially the same vulnerabilities of democracies as Fiorino (2018; see p. 45 for a summary overview) and Lindvall (2021, ch. 4), but what makes Di Paola and Jamieson's discussion particularly valuable is that they do so in light of a dual challenge to legitimacy. When democratic governments fail to respond adequately to climate change, their legitimacy can be challenged on grounds of public utility. But when they do come up with effective policies, their legitimacy is likely to become challenged on expressed preference grounds (i.e., on the grounds that their policies are not sufficiently grounded in the consent of the majority of their citizenship). The reason is that effective policies "require democracies to make robust

[3] Lindvall (2021, p. 11) refers (indirectly, through news items) to James Hansen, climate modeller with NASA, and environmental thinker and scientist James Lovelock. Fiorino (2018, p. 1, pp. 37ff.) mentions Lovelock as well, but also 'older' critics like William Ophuls and Robert Heilbroner, and more recent critics Shearman and Smith (2007).

commitments to multilateral cooperation, long-term planning, significant deviations from the status quo, and increased reliance on expert knowledge," while "citizens' expressed preferences may be quite distant from this network of commitments and activities, since the benefits of successfully managing a problem like climate change would mostly accrue not to these citizens, but to spatiotemporally distant people . . . and genetically distant (non-human) nature" (Di Paola & Jamieson 2018, p. 403). This is a dilemma: avoiding one challenge makes democracies vulnerable to the other; somehow, democracies have to find a course between the Scylla of ineffective policy and the Charybdis of relaxing the core democratic principle of popular sovereignty (p. 402). Thus, Di Paola and Jamieson's analysis links two senses in which climate change is challenging for democracies: it is difficult to get an adequate response off the ground, but it is also difficult for a democratic government – and possibly even a democratic *system* of governance – to *survive* climate change. As the consequences of climate change (including climate disasters, problems with the food and water supply, migration of climate refugees, and economic decline) progress, the pressures on governments will mount as citizens' dissatisfaction grows. People may come to have less faith in the democratic process and become more easily persuaded by authoritarian forms of populism (Lindvall, 2021, p. 17).

Di Paola and Jamieson discuss the vulnerabilities of democracies under five headings: weak multilateralism, short-termism, veto players, the contested role of experts, and self-referring decision-making. I will explain each of these in turn.

Weak multilateralism refers to democracies' failure to cooperate sufficiently on a global level. One aspect of the problem (not specific to democracies) is that an effective response to climate change requires international cooperation, but as the need for cooperation increases, so does its cost (the price of obtaining it from every country). A problem specific to democracies is that they are *locally* accountable, and thus wish to preserve strong ties to their local electorate. "Democratic states that attempt to rise to the challenge [of multilateralism] are likely to face challenges on expressed preference grounds. Those that do not may face legitimacy challenges on public utility grounds" (Di Paola & Jamieson, 2018, p. 407).

Short-termism is arguably an ingrained human tendency, but it is one that democracies may be particularly vulnerable to. There can sometimes be legitimate reasons to discount the future and pass the buck to future generations. In the case of climate change, however, short-termism is arguably both "irrational and morally wrong" (p. 408). There are two reasons why, in theory, democracies might be more vulnerable than authoritarian regimes to short-termism. One is that democratic regimes "inherit . . . citizens' bias in favor of the present" and reflect citizens' unawareness and ignorance of long-term processes, risks, etc. p. 408). Filtering these biases and ignorance leads to legitimacy challenges on expressed preference grounds (a problem of *intra*generational legitimacy), but not doing so may lead to legitimacy challenges on grounds of public utility (a problem of *inter*generational legitimacy). The second reason lies in the scheduling of elections and other participatory events. Democracy requires relatively frequent elections, meaning that politicians will constantly be concerned about their own reelection; so the problem of short-termism is "structurally connected to the very fact of popular sovereignty – at least as long as the majority of people discount the future" (p. 410).[4]

Veto players are agents "who can prevent a departure from the status quo" (p. 410). In a democracy, they play a stabilizing role; they may "protect minority interests, prevent destabilizing change, and preserve important values and policies through periods in which they are unpopular" (p. 410). Clearly, they can also become an obstacle to necessary change. With their reliance on checks and balances liberal democracies seem particularly vulnerable to this problem. The "antimajoritarian service" veto players offer "is particularly precious to liberal democracies" (p. 412). But this also means that even an overwhelming majority in favor of strong climate policies can be rendered powerless. In the face of climate change, the temptation may therefore arise to reduce the number of veto players and remove certain checks and balances. However, since veto players "reflect and configure real power structures and promote the interests of real people" (p. 412), doing so can raise legitimacy challenges on both expressed preference and public utility grounds.

Contested role of experts: because in a democracy expertise does not automatically come with political authority, relations "between experts and ordinary citizens are always potentially fraught in a democracy" (p. 414). In the case of climate change scientists' message is particularly unwelcome, because it tells people that the very way in which they live their daily lives is problematic. This is a breeding ground for resentment, a sentiment readily exploited by powerful interests that promote denialism. The existence of free social media, as a matter of principle important to democracy, can work against it here, since the speed and directness of communication favor branding and marketing over expert knowledge and careful argumentation. This characteristic of communication through social media also promotes polarization, since it allows for networked and fragmented communication, meaning that there is no common story to debate, and no agreed-upon facts (p. 416). Di Paola and Jamieson speak of a "nihilistic turn in public epistemology [that] threatens the legitimacy of democracy" (p. 417).

Self-referring decision-making relates to the fact that central to modern democratic theory is the "agency presupposition," which says that "the political community is constituted by agents who initiate and conduct political action, and who themselves, and their interests and welfare, are what matter politically" (p. 419). In the current, deeply interconnected world there is not even a semblance of identity between subject and object of political action anymore; (decisions by) agents in one locality impact agents in other localities, and agents exert unprecedented power over nonagents – animate and inanimate nature, as well as "those living on the periphery of both space and time" (pp. 419–20). There

[4] Lindvall (2021) adds the important observation that "[t]he process of assessing and holding governments accountable is . . . distorted when it comes to climate-related issues. The generation mostly affected by global warming did not elect the politicians who are currently delaying the response, nor will they be able to hold them answerable for their failure" (p. 41).

thus exists an enormous asymmetry of power. Giving more power to nonagents, however, will expose democracies to intragenerational legitimacy challenges on grounds of both expressed preference and public utility. So the dilemma is this: the agency presupposition is fundamental to democracies, and it is threatened by the response climate change calls for; but respecting the presupposition means committing a serious moral wrong.

There are two further features that may make it difficult for democracies to respond to climate change that are not fully covered by the above: democracies, and in particular liberal democracies, guarantee *individual rights and freedoms*, but protecting these may prevent them from, for instance, reducing consumption and other carbon-intensive practices (Fiorino, 2018, p. 52). Secondly, typical of current democracies is that there is *no shared view of the common good* (p. 52). Some will define this primarily in terms of individual (negative) freedoms, others in terms of equal conditions for human flourishing, and yet others will draw nonhumans into the "common." This, too, may hinder a committed response to climate change.

33.3.2 Advantages of Democracies in Responding to Climate Change

At least in theory, democracies also seem to have certain advantages over authoritarian regimes when it comes to their ability to respond to climate change. These can be summarized under four headings: accountability, free flow of information, civil participation, and support for innovation (Fiorino, 2018, pp. 44ff.; Lindvall, 2021, p. 29).

Accountability: Governments in a democracy are accountable to the people, and people can hold them accountable, through elections, but also through referenda, public protest, and even litigation (as in the Urgenda case). This gives democratic governments a strong reason to take people's interests and concerns seriously. It also means that the quality of governance is likely to be better in (full) democracies than in other types of regime, because the level of corruption is likely to be inversely related to the degree of accountability.[5]

Free flow of information: Democracies allow people to access and spread information freely (within limits determined by constitutional or human rights). With regard to climate change, this means that scientific information can be accessed, shared, and debated publicly, without censorship. People can find information about climate change and other environmental issues, and use this to evaluate government policies. Another type of information should also be accessible to citizens; the more democratic a government is, the more transparent it will be about itself and its own decision processes. This, too, supports accountability.

[5] The Economist Intelligence Unit's Democracy Index distinguishes "full" democracies, that meet all basic criteria for being a democracy (elections, political freedom, civil liberty, political participation, effective governance, strong political culture), from "flawed" democracies, that fall short on political participation and culture, "hybrid regimes," which combine democratic and authoritarian features and are deficient on some core criteria of democracy, and "authoritarian" regimes, that "lack even the basic features of democracy" (Fiorino, 2018, p. 18).

Civil participation: This is an important feature of democracies, which guarantee people's freedom to organize themselves politically, form associations, develop political initiatives or solutions to technical, organizational, and other types of problem. Thus, citizens in a democracy are a powerful "resource" and partner for governments seeking ways to respond to climate change, to decarbonize, to transition to renewable energy, etc. Civil participation also enhances support for, and the legitimacy of, policies developed in cooperative ways.

Support for innovation: As Lindvall (2021) observes, "[d]emocracies . . . provide the best conditions for an open and regulated market economy, enabling business enterprises to present innovations and solutions for change and act as a force in the transition process" (p. 29). More generally, due to the previously mentioned advantages, democracies are likely to have a higher learning capacity than other regime types, and therefore have a higher capacity for technological and policy innovation (Fiorino, 2018, p. 48). This is an advantage when faced with issues, like climate change, that demand a fundamental rethinking of many aspects of the way our society is organized.

33.3.3 What Does the Empirical Evidence Say?

Having listed the main theoretical advantages and disadvantages of democracies in the face of (the need to respond to) climate change, it is important to take a look at what the empirical evidence says about how well democracies do compared to nondemocracies. Have democracies so far responded with better or worse mitigation and adaptation policies? Can differences between countries, in terms of how well they perform from a sustainability perspective, be explained, if only in part, by how democratic they are?

Looking at historical emissions of greenhouse gases, it is clear that today's established democracies are responsible for the lion's share of emissions, and thus for the phenomenon of anthropogenic climate change. Lindvall cites figures showing that "the three democratic giants – the EU, Japan and the USA – are accountable for about two-thirds of all historic carbon emissions" (Lindvall 2021, p. 27).[6] It would be rash to conclude that democracy leads to higher emissions, however. As Lindvall observes, "most modern democracies evolved from industrialized nations in Europe and North America, and in the process of their modernization, these countries had a massive impact on the environment" and "[g]rowing prosperity also enabled democracy to take root" (2021, p 26). Industrialization led to high emissions *and* lay at the root, indirectly, of democratization – though obviously it did not *cause* democratization, and some of the largest industrialized nations in the world (Russia, China) have never been well-functioning democracies. With regard to historical emissions, it is also worth noting that nondemocratic regimes did not perform any better (the Soviet Union and China are again cases in point).

[6] Lindvall's source was the website of the Center for Global Development (2022; year updated to my own date of access).

Presently, "people living in democracies are high emitters" (Lindvall, 2021, p. 28), but nondemocracies do not perform much better. In the top 20 of countries in per capita emissions we find both nondemocracies and democracies. What unites some of the worst emitters is a highly influential fossil fuel industry; this explains that the top 20 (i.e., the list of the 20 highest emitters) includes countries like Saudi Arabia, Kazakhstan, Qatar, and the United Arab Emirates, as well as the United States, Australia, and Canada, among others.

What about climate *policies?* Emissions may still be high in democracies, but it may be that they have begun to pursue better policies than authoritarian regimes. Both Lindvall and Fiorino argue that democracy has a positive influence on climate policies. They both refer to the Climate Change Performance Index, which compares countries' climate policies. Lindvall (2021, p. 30) notes that "[a]mong the 13 highest-scoring countries, 7 are classified as full democracies by The Economist Intelligence Unit's Democracy Index," and "[n]ot a single authoritarian country can be found among the high- and medium-scoring countries." Lindvall (2021, p. 45) also cites evidence to suggest that democracies do not actually suffer more from short-termism than nondemocracies; in fact, the opposite may be true. In sum: the more democratic countries are, the greater their commitment to strong climate policies tends to be.

Still, more ambitious policies do not necessarily translate to better actual performance.[7] And the mere fact that current authoritarian regimes do not do better, and perhaps do worse, than democracies is also not very informative about what an *ecological* authoritarian regime might accomplish – none of the existing authoritarian regimes were set up with ecological purposes in view, after all. So the question is, "What explains that some regimes do better than others?" and the distinction democratic vs. nondemocratic is too crude to do so. Some studies suggest that the *level* of democratization matters (Lindvall, 2021, p. 29), others that democracy stock ("the accumulation and development of democratic institutions over time" [Fiorino, 2018, p. 57]) matters. The common denominator here is the *quality* of democratic institutions: how democratic they actually are (how transparent, accountable, etc.), how robust, and how effective (see Fiorino, 2018, pp. 60–61).[8] This is strongly related to state capacity, defined by Lindvall (2021, p. 46) as the capacity of governing institutions to formulate policies, respond to public concerns, implement, organize, regulate, finance, oversee, assess, and evaluate policies – in other words, to exercise effective control over the whole process of policy formulation, implementation, and evaluation, to carry through. That capacity is inversely related to the level of corruption and the level of policy capture by nondemocratic powerful agents, and for that reason closely related to the quality of democracy. The importance of state capacity explains why even strongly democratic countries with a strong

[7] Fiorino (2018, p. 60) cites a study – Bättig and Bernauer (2009) – that showed that democracies, despite making stronger commitments, did not actually perform better.

[8] Historical continuity also matters: "A history of democracy raises expectations about continuity and stability," and this influences the behavior of both politicians, whose time horizon grows, and industry, for which delay of compliance becomes a less attractive strategy (Fiorino, 2018, p. 58).

fossil fuel industry and lobby perform very poorly from an environmental point of view; the presence of such a powerful interest increases corruption and policy capture, and thus cripples the state with regard to climate change. Clearly, the presence of such a powerful interest also negatively affects the quality of democratic governance, both by influencing government decision-making and by manipulating voters (through the support of climate skepticism and denialism).[9]

Fiorino further notes that "[a]mong the most consistent findings in the research is that consensus-based democracies with an ability to integrate goals across policy domains exhibit better environmental and climate performance" (2018, p. 72). He identifies consensus-based democracies with neocorporatist systems, which he opposes to pluralist systems. Where the former are better positioned to get different parties to cooperate and thus to harmonize, for instance, environmental and economic goals, Fiorino argues, the latter tend to show more adversarial and fragmented policy-making. It is difficult to know what to make of this claim and the evidence he cites in support of it. One problem is that neocorporatist systems seem to be by definition vulnerable to policy capture (intimate connections between politics and business are typical of such systems). Another is that how one evaluates the performance evidence depends on what one's criteria are, and how demanding one's standard is, for good climate policy. Fiorino says that "consensus-based, integrating democracies have an advantage in identifying and acting on positive-sum relationships among energy, economic, ecological, and health goals" (2018, p. 73), but more radical environmentalists are likely to be suspicious of policies that, for instance, aim to combine sustainability with economic growth. In general, the less people think we need to do to respond adequately to climate change, the more faith they are likely to have in the capacities of existing democratic systems to rise to the challenge. Conversely, those who believe that an adequate response to climate change requires a complete overhaul of our economic system and way of life are likely to be more pessimistic on this point, and may see the need for either more authoritarian forms of governance, or more radical democratic forms.

33.3.4 The Challenge for Democracies: Conclusion

In sum, there are both theoretical reasons and empirical evidence to suggest that democracies are, in principle, better equipped than other regime types to respond adequately to the challenges posed by climate change; but unambiguous evidence of better performance (as opposed to more ambitious commitments on paper) by democracies is as yet scarce. All authors discussed in this

[9] Lindvall notes that "[t]he policy capture of the fossil fuel industry is particularly evident in the USA" and that "public opinion on climate in the USA was clearly affected" (2021, p. 51). These processes have been well documented; see, for instance, Klein (2015). Perhaps less known is that the same things have been and are going on in many other countries. In the Netherlands, for instance, politics is strongly interwoven with the fossil fuel industry; the Ministry of Foreign Affairs seconded personnel with Shell and vice versa, and the list of influential politicians who worked for Shell before entering politics or moved from politics to Shell is impressive (De Bruijn et al., 2013; Zuidervaart, 2021).

section agree that part of the way forward is to remedy the democratic deficits in existing democracies, that international cooperation needs to be increased, and that the interests of political non-agents (future generations, non-human nature) need to be taken into account more (Fiorino, 2018, pp. 116–7; Di Paola & Jamieson, 2018, pp. 422–3; Lindvall, 2021, pp. 55–9), but only Di Paola and Jamieson observe the tensions involved in these combined suggestions: if governments need to bind themselves more to multilateral agreements and commitments to the well-being of future generations, this will loosen their ties to their present electorate, meaning "perhaps paradoxically, that the democracies of the Anthropocene will have to be more democratic in some respects and less democratic in others" (Di Paola & Jamieson, 2018, p. 423).

33.4 Climate Change as a Challenge for Democratic Education

Among the weaknesses of democracies (with regard to responding to climate change) one stands out as having an obvious connection with education: the problem of voter ignorance, voter manipulation through disinformation, and the contested role of scientific expertise. At first glance it might therefore seem that what is needed, first and foremost, is more and better climate education (as indeed suggested by Lindvall, 2021, p. 57). If all young people acquire the knowledge necessary for a basic understanding of anthropogenic climate change, its causes and consequences, would that not remedy the problem of disinformation and contested expertise? And would it not also make the next generation much more willing to support strong climate policies? The answer is surely "no." Although better knowledge and understanding of climate change will undoubtedly help, it would be naïve to think that this is enough, or even that this is the most important contribution education can make. One flaw in this suggestion is that it neglects the fact that children receive the most influential part of their education, at least when it comes to what they will regard as normal and acceptable ways of living, outside the school – that is, at home and through their day-to-day experience of living in a particular kind of society. Knowledge of the causes and consequences of climate change alone will not be enough to overcome ingrained habits and cherished ways of life. Furthermore, offering scientifically grounded knowledge in schools has never been enough to prevent the most outlandish views from taking hold over the minds of people. The Flat Earth Society (or International Flat Earth Research Society) still exists, after all. (And part of what feeds these theories is the correct observation that some previously "scientific" views are now considered outlandish and in some cases morally repugnant.) A second flaw in the suggestion that what we need most is climate education is that it ignores the moral and especially the political dimension of the issue. Knowing "the facts" does not settle the question of what we ought to do, or who ought to do what. Should rich countries compensate for historical emissions? Should "developing" countries be discouraged from further economic development? Should we introduce reproductive policies to stop population growth? How much should be left to individuals' moral responsibility (for instance, as consumers) and where should governments step in? These are the issues to be decided, so we need moral and political education at least as much as we need climate education.

Since democratic forms of governance still offer our best hope in the face of climate change, we have reason to invest strongly in democratic education. Most of the necessary changes arguably cannot be brought about by education – institutional changes may be needed, for instance, to make sure that democracies are not paralyzed by powerful interests, or held captive by the short-term interests of present electorates (lowering the voting age might be part of that; see, for instance, Sharp, 2021, and for a philosophical argument that supports this, see Merry & Schinkel, 2016) – but democratic education can play its part. The question is: How can democratic education help remedy current democratic deficits, and how can it help overcome the inertia that has characterized democratic countries' response to the fact of climate change?

33.4.1 The Value of Radical Democratic Education

Most of the weaknesses of democracies are closely tied up with the fact that government policy is inevitably strongly geared towards protecting current, short-term interests and meeting the current preferences of the present electorate. For the majority of that electorate, policies with drastic implications for how people live (how they transport themselves, how much and what they can consume) are still too extreme or radical. This means that it is unlikely that a wide consensus will be reached on strong climate policies in the near future (and later than that may be too late). Amanda Machin (2013), indeed, argues that it is an illusion to think a consensus can ever be reached. Whereas dominant theoretical approaches to democracy assume the need for a common understanding of the problem of climate change and a consensus on how to respond, Machin (inspired by Mouffe; see, for instance, Mouffe, 2000, 2005) argues for "radical democracy," for the view that it is not consensus but disagreement that drives political action; rather than seek agreement we must agree to disagree. Consensus-seeking approaches in effect silence all perspectives other than the dominant one(s). Radical democracy celebrates diversity and disagreement, and thereby "revitalizes politics and foments engagement with the issues and the political discussion itself" (Machin, 2013, p. 124). In this vein, one may ask whether democratic education should take the form of *radical* democratic education if it is to help overcome the current inertia. Though not specifically in relation to climate change, Biesta (2011) argues for an agonistic conception of democratic education, exactly because there is fundamental disagreement about what it means to be a good citizen, and because only an agonistic approach allows us to question the presuppositions of the existing order. Instead of a socialization conception of civic education, which would assume a consensus about what it means to be a good democratic citizen, Biesta proposes a subjectification conception, in which learning "is not about the acquisition of knowledge, skills, competencies or dispositions but has to do with an 'exposure' to and engagement with the experiment of democracy" (Biesta, 2011, p. 152).

The agonistic approach can be considered an important correction and supplement to liberal democratic and deliberative approaches. It has descriptive value because the dominant approaches downplay, if not ignore, an important aspect of (democratic) political reality, namely the ineradicability of conflict and disagreement, and underlying that not only the divergence between the interests of different individuals and groups, but also people's emotion-laden perceptions and evaluations – the agonistic approach offers a corrective to overly rationalistic conceptions of the political. It also has prescriptive value, because in times of political disengagement, particularly in the face of the unprecedented crises of the Anthropocene, emphasizing the agonistic dimension of political reality can repoliticize what have come to appear as technical or managerial problems, and thus promote political engagement (for instance, of the kind shown by Greta Thunberg and the movement she inspired). This links up with all of the theoretical advantages of democracies: acknowledging diversity and repoliticizing the issues at stake increases the types of "information" to which citizens are exposed, boosts political participation, supports the emergence of innovative initiatives, and increases (the demand for) accountability.

However, Machin exaggerates her point, because there is no inherent contradiction between acknowledging diversity and disagreement on the one hand, and striving for consensus (or the broadest possible support) on the other hand. In fact, disagreement is implicit in the notion of seeking consensus. Furthermore, it is important to distinguish between seeking consensus for a *decision* and desiring consensus on all points of discussion. The value of the former is that it enhances the legitimacy of the decision taken. Now, Machin argues that "[f]or a democratic decision to be legitimate, there does not need to be substantive agreement on that decision; rather, there is agreement on the importance of democracy" (Machin, 2013, p. 102). This is true, of course, but, firstly, there will still need to be a majority (of representatives) in favor of the decision, otherwise it will be rejected. So it is not necessary to reach a full consensus, only to attain majority support. But that is exactly what already happens, so this is hardly a novel view. Secondly, climate change requires concerted action, and it is unclear how the celebration of disagreement would produce this; policies are only likely to be effective if they enjoy fairly broad popular and corporate support or at least their silent agreement. And one of the problems democracies face is exactly that the kinds of policies that are arguably necessary currently still lack broad support.[10]

But there is a more fundamental problem with Machin's view, which is that she ignores the fact that amidst all the disagreement and the plethora of views on climate change and how to respond to it, there are better and worse views, more and less plausible ones. Some views are better supported by the best available evidence on the causes and consequences of climate change than others; and some views are morally much more defensible than others.

[10] And Machin acknowledges this implicitly: "There appears to be no real grasp by populations that climate change demands urgent attention" (2013, p. 106).

Celebrating disagreement *without* holding on to epistemic and moral standards and notions of intellectual and moral virtue leads to epistemological and moral nihilism and from there either to power play or to political apathy. That said, "plausibility" is not a single scale from implausible to eminently plausible; Machin (2013, p. 115) is surely right to emphasize that there are different plausible perspectives possible on what our attitude toward "the environment ought to be, none of which can claim to be the correct one.

33.4.2 Responsibilizing Democratic Education

The *ideal* of democratic education is that of a practice – or rather an event – in which those who are educated come to a personal, informed awareness of the nature of political reality and, in light of that, a personal and informed understanding and assessment of the value of popular sovereignty and the recognition of human beings' fundamental equality. The nature of political reality is ineradicably but not exclusively conflictual; societies are as much forms of order that manage and repress conflict as forms of collective organization and cooperation. As Leiviskä and Pyy (2021) write in their critical discussion of agonistic models of citizenship education: "Citizenship education should be equally concerned about creating possibilities for justified political resistance as it is about fostering capabilities to take part in collective endeavours" (p. 586). The value of democratic education, thus understood, in light of the challenge of climate change, lies first and foremost in its potential to *responsibilize* students.[11] Democratic education needs to convey that politics *matters*, because it concerns *affairs* that matter. And climate change in fact offers a unique opportunity to do so. No one can honestly say that climate change does not concern them (in at least one sense of the term "concern"). Thus, the enormity and urgency of the issue may themselves help to call forth the response that the issue calls for. Heightened political engagement, civil participation, political initiative, and critical engagement with "information" all begin with responsibilization, with serious personal engagement with (the political dimension of) the world. It is worth noting that Mouffe – and with her, Machin – also stresses the importance of responsibility, which Mouffe (2000, p. 105) connects (in Derridean fashion) with the "undecidability" inherent in any decision (which, after all, literally means a cut-off point: the discussion is cut off, and/or other possibilities of action are cut off). If a certain conclusion followed *inevitably* from an argument, it would not be a decision. Consensus-seeking, too, can be a way to avoid having to take responsibility: it is something one can hide behind (Machin, 2013, p. 107).

There is an important role for *wonder* in education that aims at responsibilization (Schinkel, 2021, ch. 5). Wonder, as Maxime Greene wrote, entails a "shock of awareness" (Greene, 1978, p. 185, cited in Hadzigeorgiou, 2012, p. 999).

[11] Note that I do not use this term in the sense in which it is used in the governmentality literature, where it means that individuals are made (to feel) responsible for tasks that where previously the responsibility of another, usually a state agency (a use closely connected with neoliberalism; see Wakefield & Fleming, 2009, pp. 277–8).

In wonder we see the world as in some way strange or puzzling but at the same time remarkable, as important, worthy of our attention for its own sake. This goes as much for the natural world – in which case wonder may nourish an urge to protect it (Moore, 2005; Washington, 2018) – as for the human world and its political dimension. Wonder highlights that the world eludes our understanding, and this is part of what arrests our gaze. It is a type of experience that is particularly significant if we wish to foster both a personal seriousness and responsibility about the views people come to hold and the intellectual humility to recognize that one cannot claim finality for those views and must therefore recognize not only the existence but also the value of disagreement and diversity of perspectives.

Biesta's subjectification conception of democratic education, which is quite similar to the view I propose here, is inspired not just by agonistic theorists (Mouffe, Rancière), but also by the work of John Dewey. Biesta therefore emphasizes the importance of learning from engagement with and exposure to the experiment of democracy; it is through such engagement that political subjectivity arises – or *may* arise, for this cannot be guaranteed (Biesta, 2011, p. 152). The general truth behind this is that experiences educate. As Paul Kingsnorth (2017) wrote: "Experiences change you. Nothing else changes you" (p. 16). Acknowledging this on the one hand throws into doubt the relative importance of schooling – or, more broadly, of deliberate attempts at education – because everyone who grows up and spends her life in a consumer capitalist society or some other type of (post)industrialized society undergoes an inescapable miseducation about what is normal and acceptable. Democratic education, therefore, ought to begin and take place as much in the transformation of society (its economic basis, power structures, etc.) as in schools. On the other hand, it provides an argument for practices of democratic education that aim to evoke *experiences*, not in a sensationalist sense, but in the sense of moments in which reality breaks through the abstractions students try to absorb every day. This may be the realization that the future looks bleak – though it remains unpredictable, and those who are in school now can still play their part in determining it – but equally the reality of disagreement, of experiencing that others truly do not and cannot see the world the way you do. The task for democratic education in this respect is to make sure that this does not turn young people away from politics, nor make them come to look down upon others.

Finally, one of the main themes of responsibilizing democratic education, in the face of climate change, should be the meaning of democracy and democratic legitimacy itself. If, as we can currently observe, current systems of democratic governance fail to mount an adequate response to climate change, we need fresh perspectives on democracy and new experiments in democracy. We also need to rethink the meaning and comparative importance of the two main grounds of democratic legitimacy (public utility and expressed preference). Do young people, who are not allowed to vote, perceive current climate policies as legitimate? And is it justified to discount those preferences that cannot (or not yet) be expressed through the vote?

33.5 Conclusion

Climate change presents an unprecedented challenge to all forms of governance, but some difficulties are specific to democracies or especially pronounced in democracies. Democracies are bound to "local" electorates, both in space and time, and therefore suffer from short-termism and are deficient in their capacity to cooperate internationally. They suffer also from problems of disinformation and voter manipulation, and their capacity to respond adequately to climate change is undermined by features that are fundamental to them (the role of veto players and the agency presupposition). Still, due to the accountability of governments, the (relatively) free flow of information, the role of civil participation, and the conditions democracies offer for political and technological innovation, democracies also have pronounced advantages over nondemocracies when it comes to responding to climate change. The available empirical evidence, though tentative, supports the idea that democracy is still our best hope. This analysis has a number of implications for democratic education, understood as an ideal of education in which those educated come to a personal, informed awareness of the nature of political reality and a personal and informed understanding and assessment of the value of the two main components of the ideal of democracy: popular sovereignty and the recognition of human beings' fundamental equality. Firstly, we have reason to invest in democratic education – not just climate education. Secondly, radical (or agonistic) democratic education can be considered an important corrective and supplement to other approaches. Thirdly, the primary value of democratic education, in the face of climate change, lies in responsibilizing students – fostering serious personal engagement with the issue.

What can we expect, in practice, of attempts at democratic education? Ideally, democratic education would lead to "responsible" democratic citizens, aware of what is at stake, willing to cooperate despite disagreement, and with the courage to take a stand for their views even if they are unpopular. Biesta (2011, p. 152) writes that democratic politics as a process of subjectification is "driven by a desire for the particular mode of human togetherness . . . to which the name 'democracy' has been given" – a desire that cannot be taught (since it does not operate at the level of cognition) but only be fueled. But at this point it is important to take our eyes off the ideal for a moment. How far removed is it from today's democratic reality? How many people can truly be said to have "a desire for the particular mode of togetherness [we call] democracy"? In line with the acknowledgment that climate change is not a problem we can solve but a present and future reality that calls for a response in terms of the path we take, individually and collectively, it seems best to see the ideal of democratic education, in the hands of dedicated teachers, as a lure or an irritation – something that may cause something to stir in the minds of students.

Can we expect governments to support and promote democratic education, if this is conceived of as a potentially *subversive* practice, rather than a merely socializing one? (Or is truly democratic socialization necessarily potentially subversive?) If not, the question is how such a practice could become widespread. Another important question is how we can begin to take seriously the (mis)educative effects of fundamental features of (post)industrialized and/or consumer capitalist societies; that is, how democratic education can come to be seen as a public responsibility, rather than one of schools and parents alone. For this is what it would take for governments to truly put education at the center (Jamieson, 2020).

References

Bättig, M. B., & Bernauer, T. (2009). National institutions and global public goods: Are democracies more cooperative in climate change policy? *International Organization*, 63, 281–308.

Biesta, G. (2011). The ignorant citizen: Mouffe, Rancière, and the subject of democratic education. *Studies in Philosophy and Education*, 30, 141–53.

Center for Global Development (2022). *Developed countries are responsible for 79 percent of historical carbon emissions*. Available at: https://www.cgdev.org/media/who-caused-climate-change-historically.

De Bruijn, W., Van Huijkelom, T., & Metze, M. (2013, October 23). Het ministerie van Shell-zaken: De innige samenwerking van Shell en de Nederlandse overheid. *De Groene Amsterdammer*, 43. Available at: https://www.groene.nl/artikel/het-ministerie-van-shell-zaken.

Di Paola, M., & Jamieson, D. (2018). Climate change and the challenges to democracy. *University of Miami Law Review*, 72(2), 369–424.

Fiorino, D. J. (2018). *Can democracy handle climate change?* Cambridge: Polity Press.

Greene, M. (1978). *Landscapes of learning*. New York: Teachers College Press.

Hadzigeorgiou, Y. (2012). Fostering a sense of wonder in the science classroom. *Research in Science and Education*, 42, 985–1005.

Jamieson, D. (2020, June 18). Can democracies beat climate change? *Politico*. Available at: https://www.politico.eu/article/can-democracies-beat-climate-change.

Kaminski, I. (2019, December 20). Dutch supreme court upholds landmark ruling demanding climate action. *The Guardian*. Available at: https://www.theguardian.com/world/2019/dec/20/dutch-supreme-court-upholds-landmark-ruling-demanding-climate-action.

Kingsnorth, P. (2017). *Confessions of a recovering environmentalist*. London: Faber & Faber.

Klein, N. (2015). *This changes everything*. London: Penguin Books.

Laird, S. (2017). Learning to live in the Anthropocene: Our children and ourselves. *Studies in Philosophy and Education*, 36(3), 265–82.

Leiviskä, A., & Pyy, I. (2021). The unproductiveness of political conflict in education: A Nussbaumian alternative to agonistic citizenship education. *Journal of Philosophy of Education*, 55(4–5), 577–88.

Lindvall, D. (2021). Democracy and the challenge of climate change. Discussion Paper 3/2021. Strömsborg: International IDEA. Available at: https://www.idea.int/publications/catalogue/democracy-and-challenge-climate-change.

Machin, A. (2013). *Negotiating cimate change: Radical democracy and the illusion of consensus*. London: Zed Books.

Merry, M. S., & Schinkel, A. (2016). Voting rights for older children and civic education. *Public Affairs Quarterly*, 30(3), 197–213.

Moore, K. D. (2005). The truth of the barnacles: Rachel Carson and the moral significance of wonder. *Environmental Ethics*, 27(3), 265–77.

Mouffe, C. (2000). *The democratic paradox*. London/New York: Verso.

Mouffe, C. (2005). *On the political*. London/New York: Routledge.

NOS (2019a, February 8). Rutte nodigt klimaatspijbelaars uit voor gesprek. *NOS Nieuws*. Available at: https://nos.nl/artikel/2271061-rutte-nodigt-klimaatspijbelaars-uit-voor-gesprek.

NOS (2019b, February 7). Rutte tegen jongeren: 'We doen al veel aan klimaat, vraag niet meer'. *NOS Nieuws*. Available at: https://nos.nl/artikel/2270913-rutte-tegen-jongeren-we-doen-al-veel-aan-klimaat-vraag-niet-meer.

Peters, R. (1970). *Ethics & education*. London: George Allen & Unwin.

Sant, E. (2019). Democratic education: A theoretical review. *Review of Educational Research*, 89(5), 655–96.

Schinkel, A. (2021). *Wonder and education: On the educational importance of contemplative wonder*. London: Bloomsbury.

Schinkel, A. (2022). Education in the Anthropocene: A sober assessment. In J. Drerup, F. Felder, V. Magyar-Haas & G. Schweiger, eds., *Creating green citizens: Bildung, Demokratie, und der Klimawandel*. Berlin: Springer, pp. 73–96.

Sharp, M. (2021, December 2). Climate crisis fuels push to drop voting age to 16. *National Observer*. Available at: https://www.nationalobserver.com/2021/12/02/news/climate-crisis-fuels-push-drop-voting-age-16.

Shearman, D. J. C., & Smith, J. W. (2007). *The climate challenge and the failure of democracy*. Westport, CT: Praeger.

Wakefield, A., & Fleming, J. (2009). Responsibilization. In A. Wakefield & J. Fleming, eds., *The Sage dictionary of policing*. Thousand Oaks, CA: Sage, pp. 277–8.

Washington, H. (2018). *A sense of wonder towards nature: Healing the world through belonging*. London: Routledge.

Whitehead, A. N. (1962). *The aims of education and other essays*. London: Ernest Benn.

Zuidervaart, B. (2021, November 15). De lijntjes tussen Shell en het Binnenhof zijn kort. *Trouw*.

34

The COVID-19 Pandemic and Democratic Education

Johannes Giesinger

34.1 Introduction

Since early 2020, the COVID-19 pandemic has impacted people's lives around the world both directly and indirectly. It has directly affected those who became sick from the virus or who died, and it has had an indirect impact on virtually everybody through the measures taken to combat the virus's spread. In the sphere of education, the closure of schools – in conjunction with the instigation of remote teaching – was the most drastic measure. It changed students' as well as their parents' lives overnight, and redefined the work of teachers. At the same time, there was, or still is, widespread controversy on both the pandemic and the political response to it – from lockdowns and mask mandates to vaccination – that also affects the realm of democratic education. The question is how teachers and schools should handle this kind of disagreement, and what can *legitimately* be taught regarding the coronavirus.

According to a common – though not uncontroversial – view in political philosophy, questions of *legitimacy* can be distinguished from questions of (distributive) *justice* (Rawls, 1993; Peter, 2009; Pettit, 2012). While the latter refer to what is owed to people, the former are concerned with the justification of the use of political power. The question is: Which measures can legitimately be pursued by the state in the face of deep-rooted political and ethical disagreement in society? It needs to be asked, in this context, how political decision-making processes must be set up in order to lead to decisions that can legitimately be enforced. Democracy provides a specific scheme of legitimacy – its basic idea is that those subjected to political decisions must in some way or other be involved in the decision-making process. In what follows, I rely on a *deliberative* understanding of democracy according to which democratic decision-making is not reducible to voting, but should be embedded in a culture of public deliberation, where individuals engage in the practice of giving and asking for reasons (Habermas, 1992; Gutmann & Thompson, 2004). According to the deliberative conception, democratic legitimacy hinges on people's participation in the public exchange of reasons.

The COVID-19 crisis has raised issues of political legitimacy, for some of the political measures adopted to combat the virus were not acknowledged as legitimate by some parts of the populace. In addition, the crisis has raised problems of (educational) justice that are related to the issue of democratic education. The concept of democratic education might be understood in various ways; for instance, it might refer to educational practice itself and to the relationship between teacher and learner, or to the aims pursued in educational practice. In the latter case, democratic education is an education *for democracy* – the focus lies on fostering the capacity for democratic participation. Within the deliberative model, this amounts to the initiation of students into practices of public deliberation.

It has mostly been assumed that the closure of schools has exacerbated social inequalities in education, and that this might also affect the realization of democratic aims. Should we conclude, then, that it was unjust to shut down the schools? Maybe the more important question is what we can learn, from the COVID-19 experience, for the ongoing debate on issues of justice and legitimacy in the field of education. I address justice-related problems in Section 34.2, before turning to questions of legitimacy in Section 34.3.

34.2 Educational Justice, Democratic Education, and the COVID-19 Pandemic

In 2020, the schools were shut down in many countries around the world, but it is important to note that different countries handled the situation very differently. Sweden, for instance, never fully closed all its schools, while in Switzerland schools were closed only for a few months in spring 2020. In countries such as Germany or the United Kingdom, by contrast, schools were shut down again in late 2020, and did not fully open until the spring (United Kingdom) or the summer (Germany) of 2021 (UNESCO, 2022). In the United States, many public schools were closed for long periods, while private schools returned to in-person schooling as soon as possible. James Dwyer (2022) notes that "a substantial portion of parents and other people, at least in the US, were profoundly disappointed in the performance of public school systems in time of crisis" (p. 36).

Whether the COVID crisis will exacerbate educational inequalities in the long term is an empirical question that must be answered by looking at the varying circumstances in different countries.[1] Whatever future studies will show, it is easy to explain why the closure of schools might lead to growing social inequalities within the education system.

The shift to remote teaching during the pandemic highlighted inequalities in the technical conditions in different families. While some students were technically well equipped, others had to share a device with their parents or siblings,

[1] Recent studies include Engzell et al. (2021), Hammerstein et al. (2021).

and had to overcome a range of technical obstacles simply in order to participate in class activities online. Also, there are differences in the digital skills of students or their parents, that is, their ability to use the available equipment effectively for learning.

A further problem could have arisen out of precarious spatial conditions in the family home: some students have a room of their own where they can work in a quiet atmosphere, while others lack any kind of privacy at home.

In addition, students had to deal with very different social conditions in the family. Some were fully supported in their school-related work by their parents or other family members, while others struggled with conflicts within the family, had to care for siblings or grandparents, or were neglected or abused by those who should have cared for them. Well-educated parents – many of them working in home-offices during the pandemic – were especially well prepared to help their children with their schoolwork, and to motivate or discipline them if necessary.

These explanations refer to the living conditions of the family. Apart from that, the quality of schooling that children have access to is also an important factor: while some schools – due to having a well-functioning digital infrastructure and a motivated staff – could offer high-quality remote teaching, others had problems in adjusting to the new situation. So, many children from disadvantaged backgrounds were not only facing difficulties in their home environment, but were also less supported by their schools and teachers than students from socially privileged families.

All these factors might *explain* growing social inequalities in education. In order to evaluate whether this amounts to an injustice, we have to take normative considerations into account. Let us take a brief look at the debate on principles of educational justice, in relation to the problem of democratic education. The most common idea in this field is that educational inequalities due to social background are unjust. This idea is expressed in the "meritocratic" conception of educational justice, as formulated by Harry Brighouse and Adam Swift (2008), which is influenced by John Rawls' principle of fair equality of opportunity (Rawls, 1971). According to the meritocratic conception, Brighouse and Swift write, "[a]n individual's prospects for educational achievement may be a function of that individual's talent and effort, but it should not be influenced by her social class background" (Brighouse & Swift, 2008, p. 447). This principle states, then, that inequalities caused by differences of "talent" or "effort" are morally acceptable, while social inequalities should be fully neutralized. Even if we consider this as too demanding, we might well agree that exacerbating existing social inequalities is unjust. A further question is how considerations of educational justice are related to the problem of democratic education.

It is often assumed that the meritocratic idea is an important feature of the liberal-democratic model of society where all persons should have fair access to attractive social positions, regardless of the social position of their parents. Still, the meritocratic idea is not directly tied to democratic educational aims, or a democratic political structure. It seems possible, for instance, to allocate positions of political power in accordance with merit without establishing a democratic system of equal suffrage. While the meritocratic principle is neutral with regard to substantive educational considerations, other conceptions of educational justice are oriented toward specific aims. Amy Gutmann – in her seminal *Democratic Education* (1987, p. 136) – has proposed a threshold conception of educational justice, according to which everyone should be educated in a way that prepares him or her for democratic participation. This defines the substantive aims of education, and also the threshold level that should be reached by everyone. It is also assumed, then, that educational inequalities above this level are acceptable. Elizabeth Anderson (1999, see also Anderson, 2007) works with a broad understanding of democratic equality that is not limited to specifically political competencies, but refers to the notion of "a community in which people stand in relations of equality to others" (Anderson, 1999, p. 289). In order to function as a democratic equal, Anderson says, a person needs capabilities in three different spheres – they have to be able to function "as a human being, as a participant in a system of cooperative production, and as a citizen of a democratic state" (p. 317). This sets requirements regarding material resources and individual rights, but it can also be used to define a basic level of education that enables persons to give shape to their personal lives, to access the labor market, and to take part in political processes. The politically relevant capacities entail – as both Gutmann and Anderson will agree – the ability to participate in public deliberation.

The COVID-19 crisis, then, might not only exacerbate social inequalities in education, but also exclude some persons from the democratic community, possibly in the long term. To the extent that this is the case, school closures can be described as an injustice. However, considerations of social and educational justice need to be weighed against other justice-oriented concerns, such as the demand to save lives. With regard to possible pandemics in the future, we can say that there is a pro tanto reason to keep schools open – or not to shut them down for long periods of time – but that this reason might be overridden by stronger reasons in a particular situation. For instance, if there were a highly lethal virus that affected primarily children and adolescents, it would probably be morally required to close schools despite its negative educational effects.

Taking the stance that school closures are pro tanto unjust highlights a feature of education that has mostly been overlooked in past debates on educational justice and democratic education: namely, the spatial and temporal structure of schooling with its specific social characteristics. The school systems of many countries have previously been criticized as unjust, but giving up on in-person schooling seems to worsen the situation, at least for some groups of students. We should not idealize traditional forms of schooling, but rather think more closely about how in-person schooling might be improved by making changes to the spatial setup of schools and classrooms, the temporal structures of teaching and learning, and its social organization.

Moreover, we should think about which functions educational institutions have – and which they should have – in a democratic society (Drerup, 2022, p. 81; Dwyer, 2022, p. 39). The breakdown of in-person schooling has revealed that schools, as they are set up in our liberal democracies, are not merely institutions for teaching and learning, but perform other social functions as well. What these functions are also depends on specific contexts: in the United States, for instance, providing food to children seems to be an important function of public schools – consequently, school closures led to a shortage of food in many families (Dwyer, 2022, p. 39; Levinson, 2020). Another function of schools lies in detecting child neglect and abuse. In addition, schools typically provide different forms of counseling, and organize various kinds of social activities (Dwyer, 2022, p. 39). It is a matter for further debate whether all of these – and more – functions should be provided by educational institutions. It seems clear, though, that schools in a democracy should not be narrowly focused on promoting deliberative capacities, but should do so in a social environment that supports students' flourishing overall.

For many, the experience of the COVID-19 pandemic has emphasized the importance of educational institutions in a democracy. In this regard, it should be noted that those factors that have likely exacerbated educational inequalities during the pandemic are also at work in common forms of schooling – the technical, spatial, and social aspects mentioned at the beginning of this section become relevant in situations where students have to do school-related work at home, especially the classical homework. This is work typically done in the social and spatial context of the family, on one's own and potentially with the support of parents. The insight that parents from different social backgrounds differ in their ability to help their children is not new. One reaction is the demand to abolish homework altogether and to extend the time that students spend in the school environment. This strategy aims at reducing the influence of parents on the learning process of students. The COVID-19 crisis has – by contrast – strengthened the educational role of parents, turning some of them into assistant teachers. Instead of weakening their role, it would of course also be possible to improve all potential parents' ability to support their children educationally. This would require an overall reduction of social and educational inequalities: once all parents have at least a decent education, and live under decent material conditions, the effects of family background will be reduced, even in the case of a further pandemic. Another proposal – made by Anca Gheaus (2022) – is to ensure that children do not fully depend on their parents (or a single parent), but have access to multiple adults in parent-like roles – even outside of institutional contexts. While the COVID-19 crisis has made child-rearing more private, communal practices of caring for children might not only improve their wellbeing overall, but also help mitigate the social and educational disadvantages of some children.

The COVID-19 situation, then, gives rise to broad considerations regarding the social and institutional organization of democratic education. If we want to promote democratic educational justice, it does not suffice to go back to the status quo ante, but we have to explore new ways in supporting students to function as equals in the democratic community. As I would like to suggest – in Section 34.3 – this is also relevant for democratic legitimacy, to the extent that legitimacy depends on people's ability to participate in public deliberation (Giesinger, 2022).

34.3 Political Legitimacy, Democratic Education, and the COVID-19 Pandemic

The COVID-19 pandemic has highlighted issues of political legitimacy that also affect educational problems. It is common to ask which kinds of education are legitimate, given ongoing disagreement on basic questions. For instance, it has long been contested whether – or in which way – scientific theories (such as evolution theory) should be taught in public schools, given that some religious groups consider these theories incompatible with their own beliefs. In the pandemic, the scientific view of the virus and its effects as well as the scientific justification of measures to combat the virus have been rejected by some. This raises the question, as I have said, of how teachers should handle these kinds of disagreement.

As I would like to point out, there is a second way to discuss the problem of legitimacy in relation to democratic education: education might be considered as being among the conditions of legitimacy itself (or at least, as instrumental to these conditions), meaning that a lack of democratic education undermines democratic legitimacy. Here, then, the basic question is how education needs to be set up to ensure the legitimacy of the democracy. The main idea pursued in this section is that taking this second perspective provides an answer to the first question. Before I turn to educational issues, I have to say more about the concept of legitimacy and the challenges to legitimacy that arose during the pandemic.

In a democracy, decision-making processes, in order to lead to legitimate results, must in some way or other be rooted in democratic practices and procedures. According to an influential strand in political philosophy – that refers both to Jürgen Habermas (1992) and John Rawls (1993) – a key element of democratic legitimacy is that political decisions can be justified to those subjected to them – Fabienne Peter calls this the "justificationist view of legitimacy" (Peter, 2021, p. 396). This view often goes along with a deliberative model of democracy, according to which the democratic process crucially consists of a free exchange of reasons. Democratic deliberation is then considered as constitutive for political legitimacy, as Peter explains: "If the aim of political decision-making is a justified political decision, it becomes clear why political deliberation is an essential feature of politically legitimate decision-making. In political deliberation, possible decisions and their pro tanto justifications are critically examined. If all goes well, then political deliberation supports legitimate political decisions, i.e. decisions that are overall justified" (Peter, 2021, p. 396).

For one, the deliberative practice of reason-giving influences whether citizens *in fact* accept political decisions: political stability depends on whether citizens consider the decision-making process as legitimate. In the COVID-19 pandemic, some people refused to acknowledge the legitimacy of the measures taken by governments. The question of whether decisions are acknowledged as legitimate can be distinguished from the question of whether they *should* be seen as justified. The fact that the COVID-19 measures were rejected by some does not mean that they were unjustified.[2]

The focus on deliberation raises the question of what conditions must be satisfied to ensure an appropriate form of collective reasoning: Peter (2021) distinguishes "participation" norms from the "epistemic" norms of a "well-ordered deliberation" (p. 396). The former norms regulate who should be allowed to take part in political deliberation. In a democracy, the basic idea is that everyone should have an equal say in the political process. Epistemic norms determine what can be "validly asserted in political deliberation" (p. 396). Here, the idea is that discursive assertions should satisfy certain epistemic conditions, for example, that they should be true or justified, or at least not obviously untenable.

In the COVID-19 crisis, some opponents of official policies may have felt marginalized in the political process as their assertions were often not treated as valid contributions to the discourse – by political leaders, by experts, or by major media outlets. However, these critics were never excluded from public debate, as they could always freely express their views, and even protest in the streets. One reason why their views were to some extent sidelined in the political discourse was that they were seen as epistemically problematic – as unjustified or simply false. To cite one extreme example, Donald Trump – then president of the United States – suggested, in a White House press briefing, that one could inject bleach into oneself to fight the virus.

While it can be rationally debated whether mask mandates, lockdowns, or school closures are justified in a pandemic, many opponents of such measures relied on untenable empirical views or defended unfounded conspiracy theories. It should be noted that liberal theory typically assumes that individuals are entitled to hold epistemically problematic views and lead their personal lives in accordance with them. For Rawls (1993, p. 58), for instance, so-called comprehensive doctrines – ethical and religious views – must satisfy only minimal epistemic standards to count as "reasonable," that is, as acceptable within the political-liberal framework.[3] Martha Nussbaum even states that the reasonableness of comprehensive doctrines should only depend on its ethical qualities, that is, on whether it is compatible with a basic notion of equal respect: "So long as people are reasonable in the ethical sense, why should the political conception denigrate them because they believe in astrology, or crystals, or the Trinity?" (Nussbaum, 2011, p. 28). It might be added that people are also entitled to their own medical views – for instance, they might rely on homeopathy and oppose vaccination. These kinds of views are then to be considered as "reasonably" contested.

[2] It should also be noted that defenders of deliberative models of democracy will acknowledge that political legitimacy does not solely rest on public deliberation, but in addition depends on practical mechanisms, such as voting, in cases where a consensus cannot be reached.

[3] In particular, a comprehensive doctrine, to count as reasonable, must be "more or less consistent and coherent" (Rawls, 1993, p. 59).

As the pandemic has made clear, however, medical views held in private can become publicly relevant, to the extent that they are related to collective decision-making.[4] It is one thing if the belief in a conspiracy theory regarding vaccines impacts people's personal decision-making, another if it leads them to spread unfounded views in the course of public deliberation on pandemic measures. In order to collectively address those issues that affect us all – such as issues of public health – we need to be able to refer to a shared reality, or at least to shared epistemic norms that allow us to settle disagreement. Public deliberation runs into problems if some parts of the populace refuse to accept those norms, and cannot be reached by evidence and arguments. These problems are of course, not completely new. The debate on climate change, for instance, has similar characteristics. Some people deny that global warming is caused by human behavior, or that it is happening at all. As Anderson notes, empirical disagreement in current political debates is often "politically motivated," in that it is rooted in specific political identities (Anderson, 2020, p. 7). Anderson adds that these debates typically take place "against a deeper background of shared values" (p.7). Those who deny anthropogenic climate change, for instance, might agree that it is morally required to prevent human suffering if this is possible. So, they claim that global warming is not real, or that it cannot be prevented. In the case of the COVID-19 pandemic, it was often claimed that COVID-19 is "just like the flu." Playing down the gravity of the disease in this way suggests a deeper agreement that people should be protected from serious diseases.

Let us now consider the role of democratic education in this context. My basic idea is that some form of education is necessary to establish and sustain a culture of public deliberation – which is constitutive for democratic legitimacy. In this sense, then, education is of instrumental value for democratic legitimacy (Peter, 2021, p. 404). As suggested, a well-ordered deliberation is regulated by participation and epistemic norms. With regards to both these norms, democratic education is relevant: it prepares students for participation in the democratic process and enables them to make valid contributions. It might be added that classroom discussions themselves amount to a form of quasi-public deliberation and are in this sense not merely instrumental for the development of deliberative competencies, but form part of a diverse set of practices in which reasons on politically relevant issues are exchanged. In classroom discussions, students should learn to follow the epistemic norms of deliberations. As mentioned, these norms – however they are spelled out in detail – are set up to ensure that contributions are epistemically valid, or at least not fully beside the point. Education, then, should promote students' capacity for good reasoning.

Here, we might refer to well-known programs of "critical thinking.". Nicholas Burbules argues, in this context, that "the traditional model of teaching and promoting critical thinking – fostering the skills and dispositions of being a critical thinker, advocating for and trying to model critical thinking in our own

[4] It should be noted that political liberals such as Rawls or Nussbaum would not deny that political deliberation depends on the acceptance of certain epistemic norms. Nussbaum writes that participation in the political life requires "a respect for argument and the public exchange of reasons" (Nussbaum, 2011, p. 37).

speech and behaviour – is no longer enough" (Burbules, 2022, p. 9). He goes on to say that we should think about "a different kind of intervention – one that is sensitive to the psychological, emotional, and tribal dynamics that have combined to create a culture actively hostile to critical thinking" (p. 9).

It seems clear that however this new kind of intervention is set up, the basic epistemic standards of deliberative democracy cannot be abandoned. The aim must be, then, to work against the distortions – or the "epistemic pathologies" – of political discourse. These pathologies might be characterized in various ways, but I would like to point out three aspects: epistemic distrust, epistemic irresponsibility, and the lack of open-mindedness:

1. *Epistemic distrust*: The COVID-19 crisis is characterized by a deep and generalized distrust of some people regarding official information on the pandemic, especially information coming from medical experts. Those people often consider themselves as the "true critical thinkers" (Burbules, 2022, p. 9) who have deeper insights in the goings-on in the world. Education itself – learning from others – requires some degree of epistemic trust. If trust is lacking in students, then, the endeavor of democratic education is set up for failure from the outset. Teachers who advocate for epistemic standards might be specially distrusted by those students who are opposed to the "mainstream view" on COVID-19 and other issues. A look into recent psychotherapeutic research gives a hint as to how teachers might react in such situations to build up trust. As Peter Fonagy and Elizabeth Allison (2014; see also Duschinsky & Collver, 2019, and Duschinsky & Foster, 2021) write, epistemic trust might be established and maintained by a kind of intervention they characterize as "mentalizing." This means that psychotherapists or teachers show understanding and recognition of others' mental states – their thoughts and feelings. The idea is that this does not only foster epistemic trust, but at the same time enables the other to mentalize their own thoughts and feelings better, that is, to become aware of them, to understand them and reflect on them. This might help them get access to underlying emotional states – such as fear, shame, or anger – that influence how they process information. So, instead of addressing students with epistemically untenable views exclusively on the cognitive level – in trying to refute their assertions referring to evidence and arguments – teachers should also pay attention to building up relationships of trust. It might well be that students' ability for epistemic trust – that is developed in the family as well as in school – also shows itself in the political domain, in the assessment of experts' views. It is also clear, however, that students should not only be taught to trust, but be equipped with the ability to critically assess what they hear from experts, from teachers, or their parents. Epistemic trust must be complemented with a healthy dose of epistemic vigilance in all spheres of life.
2. *Epistemic irresponsibility*: To be epistemically responsible, as the term is used here, means to stand ready to justify one's assertions. An epistemically irresponsible person, by contrast, utters all kinds of false, misleading, or nonsensical views without ever responding seriously to the demand for reasons.

Social media platforms such as Twitter and Facebook have played a role in establishing a culture of epistemic irresponsibility as anyone can circulate arbitrary information on these platforms, without being held to account. Those who spread disinformation online might be banned from social media platforms, but they usually do not have to take epistemic responsibility as they cannot be forced to engage in serious deliberation on their claims. The classroom situation is different: here, teachers and learners stand face to face – at least if schooling takes place in-person – and it is much more difficult to escape accountability. Initiating students into epistemic practices does not only mean that they are supported in developing epistemic skills, but also that they should learn to take epistemic responsibility. If epistemically problematic views are put forward in the classroom deliberation, teachers should address them by demanding reasons. This should not be done, however, in a way that pushes students into the corner and exposes them in front of the class. Rather, the demand for justification should be motivated by genuine interest in and for students' views and emotional states.

3. *Lack of open-mindedness*: Giving up long-held beliefs is never easy, but in a "healthy" epistemic environment, persons should be open to new evidence that does not affirm what they already believe. Recent political and technological developments seem to have created an epistemic atmosphere in which many people outright reject arguments that run contrary to their values or empirical beliefs. We might refer, in this context, to the phenomenon of "group polarization" and to the "cognitive biases" at work in our processing of information, in particular the so-called confirmation bias that leads us to select new information on the basis of our belief system. In a group – and especially on social media – people's views are mutually confirmed by the members of the group, leading to stronger and more extreme views (Anderson, 2021, p. 13). In this regard, there is also talk of epistemic bubbles or echo chambers (Nguyen, 2020). The aim of education should be, then, to cultivate an attitude of open-mindedness, or at least to prevent students from being extremely biased with regard to new information. This presupposes that (1) the teacher themself is trusted, and (2) that students take epistemic responsibility. It requires that, on the one hand, various and possibly also problematic epistemic perspectives can be brought into the classroom discourse, and on the other hand, that students accept the basic norms of epistemic practices which allow us to deal with disagreement.

Working against the epistemic pathologies of deliberation is a key element of a democratic education set up to ensure political legitimacy. In this sense, then, a failure of education does not only constitute an injustice (see Section 34.2), but also poses a threat to legitimacy. Now, if a certain form of education is necessary for democratic legitimacy, it cannot be illegitimate to promote this kind of education. Advocating for basic epistemic norms in school might not be uncontroversial, but it is legitimized by a specific understanding of legitimacy. It is clear that this conception of democratic legitimacy is itself not immune from critique. However, even if the deliberative account of legitimacy is rejected, it might be acknowledged that collective decision-making depends on a shared sense of the epistemic norms guiding the decision-making process.

At the same time, the concern for upholding legitimacy puts clear-cut constraints on what can be legitimately taught in schools: students should not be influenced in partisan or ideological ways but be enabled to form their own political views on controversial issues. If it would be legitimate to transmit partisan views in school, it would be possible to manipulate the democratic process through education, bringing young people to accept a particular political perspective over which there is reasonable disagreement.[5]

Against this background, it should be discussed, for instance, whether teachers are allowed or even obligated, in the context of a pandemic, to advocate for certain controversial courses of action, for example, to recommend being vaccinated. On the one hand, this recommendation corresponded to official state policy, in many countries. It could be argued, then, that teachers in public schools should act in line with official recommendations, and in this sense function as agents of the state. After all, these recommendations came from legitimately elected governments. It should also be noted that teachers themselves had to enforce certain rules – such as mask mandates – in the classroom amid diverging views on these matters.

On the other hand, however, democratic governments mostly represent a majority view of society, and are not committed to promote only policies that are generally accepted, or generally acceptable. Typically, they are to some extent in line with partisan views over which there can be reasonable disagreement. In the United States, some Republican state governments were themselves opposed to common measures to fight the virus and refused to allow schools to require masks or vaccinations for their students (Burbules, 2022, p. 9). From a philosophical perspective, it seems problematic to commit teachers to promoting official government positions. Regardless of who is in power in a particular country or state, teachers should be committed to basic epistemic norms and discuss ongoing policy issues on this basis. So, while it might not be the teachers' job to motivate students to get the vaccine, even if the government recommends or mandates it, teachers should debunk false and misleading claims about the vaccine, including widespread conspiracy theories in this field. They might hold students who advocate for untenable views to account, asking them for reasons. Assuming that there are some basic epistemic norms that will be acknowledged by any open-minded person, teachers should defend these norms, trying to address the epistemic pathologies of public deliberation.

[5] It is understood, here, that it is legitimate for teachers to advocate for basic political principles over which reasonable agreement can be expected. It can be noted that some normative commitments (such as the commitment to political equality) form part of the conditions of legitimacy.

34.4 Conclusion

What then does the COVID-19 experience teach us for the future of democratic education? Democratic education depends on a robust form of institutionalized schooling that ensures everyone has access to an education that enables them to function as a democratic equal and overcome social disadvantages. To the extent that the pandemic has exacerbated educational inequalities due to social background, this has made it difficult for already disadvantaged students to develop the capacities necessary for democratic participation. At the same time, it should be emphasized that education systems in most Western countries fell short of basic requirements of justice, even before the pandemic.

However, ensuring a decent education for everyone is not only a matter of justice, but is also instrumental with regard to the conditions of legitimacy. As has been pointed out, public deliberation is a core feature of democratic legitimacy. Young people should thus be enabled to participate in deliberations and make epistemically valid contributions. The pandemic has brought out deep-rooted disagreement in empirical matters, and this has raised urgent questions concerning the epistemic norms of public discourse. In democratic education there is no alternative to taking a reasons-based approach: addressing disagreement in this way is legitimate because democratic legitimacy itself depends on a commitment to evidence and argument. It might be claimed, then, that programs of critical thinking should be strengthened. However, the purely cognitive approach typically taken by these programs does not seem to be sufficient to overcome the epistemic pathologies that currently pervade the public discourse. More thought should be given to other forms of educational intervention that address students on both the cognitive and the emotional level, in order to encourage them to remain open to the demands of reason.

References

Anderson, E. (1999). What is the point of equality? *Ethics*, 109(2), 287–337.

Anderson, E. (2007). Fair opportunity in education: A democratic equality Perspective. *Ethics*, 117(4), 595–622.

Anderson, E. (2020). The epistemology of justice. *The Southern Journal of Philosophy*, 58(1), 6–29.

Anderson, E. (2021). Epistemic bubbles and authoritarian politics. In E. Edenberg & M. Hannon, eds., *Political epistemology*. Oxford: Oxford University Press, pp. 11–29.

Brighouse, H., & Swift, A. (2008). Putting educational equality in its place. *Education Finance and Policy*, 3(4), 444–66.

Burbules, N. (2022). Promoting critical thinking in anti-critical thinking times: Lessons from COVID Discourse. *Philosophical Inquiry in Education*, 19(1), 5–10.

Drerup, J. (2022). *Kinder, Corona und die Folgen. Eine kritische Bestandsaufnahme.* Frankfurt/New York: Campus.

Duschinsky, R., & Collver, J. (2019). "Trust comes from a sense of feeling one's self understood by another mind": An interview with Peter Fonagy. *Psychoanalytic Psychology*, 36(3), 224–27.

Duschinksy, R., & Foster, S. (2021). *Mentalizing and epistemic trust: The work of Peter Fonagy and colleagues at the Anna Freud Centre*. Oxford: Oxford University Press.

Dwyer, J. G. (2022). Homeschooling by choice and homeschooling by force. *Philosophical Inquiry in Education*, 29(1), 36–41.

Engzell, P., Frey, A., & Verhagen, M. (2021). Learning loss due to school closures during the Covid-19 pandemic. *Proceedings of the National Academy of Sciences*, 118(17), 1–7. doi: 10.1073/pnas.2022376118.

Fonagy, P., & Allison E. (2014): The role of mentalizing and epistemic trust in the therapeutic relationship. *Psychotherapy*, 51(3), 372–80.

Gheaus, A. (2022). Childhood after COVID: Children's interests in a flourishing childhood and a more communal childrearing. *Philosophical Inquiry in Education*, 29(1), 65–71.

Giesinger, J. (2022). Education as the remedy: The justification of democracy and the epistocratic challgenge. In J. Culp, J. Drerup, I. de Groot, A. Schinkel & D. Yacek, eds., *Liberal democratic education: A paradigm in crisis*. Münster: Brill/Mentis, pp. 67–81.

Gutmann, A. (1987). *Democratic education*. Princeton, NJ: Princeton University Press.

Gutmann, A., & Thompson, D. (2004). *Why deliberative democracy?* Princeton, NJ: Princeton University Press.

Habermas, J. (1992). *Faktizität und Geltung. Beiträge zur Diskurstheorie des Rechts und des demokratischen Rechtsstaats*. Frankfurt am Main: Suhrkamp.

Hammerstein, S., König, C., Dreisörner, T., & Frey, A. (2021). Effects of school-related school closures on student achievement – a systematic review. *Frontiers in Psychology*, 12, 746289. doi: 10.3389/fpsyg.2021.746289.

Levinson, M. (2020). *Education ethics during a pandemic*. Available at: https://ethics.harvard.edu/files/center-for-ethics/files/17educationalethics2.pdf (accessed: May 25, 2022).

Nguyen, C. T. (2020). Echo chambers and epistemic bubbles. *Episteme*, 17(2), 141–61.

Nussbaum, M. (2011). Perfectionist liberalism and political liberalism. *Philosophy and Public Affairs*, 39(1), 3–45.

Peter, F. (2009). *Democratic legitimacy*. New York: Routledge.

Peter, F. (2021). Epistemic norms of political deliberation. In M. Hannon & J. de Ridder, eds., *Routledge handbook of political epistemology*. New York: Routledge, pp. 395–406.

Pettit, P. (2012). Legitimacy and justice in republican perspective. *Current Legal Problems*, 65, 59–82.

Rawls, J. (1971). *A theory of justice*. Cambridge, MA: Harvard University Press.

Rawls, J. (1993). *Political liberalism*. New York: Columbia University Press.

UNESCO (2022): *COVID-19 education response*. Available at: https://covid19.uis.unesco.org/global-monitoring-school-closures-covid19/country-dashboard.

35

Teacher Neutrality, Pedagogical Impartiality, and Democratic Education

Bruce Maxwell

35.1 Introduction

Having students learn about, discuss, and deliberate over contested social issues has long been a mainstay of democratic education because it is thought to provide opportunities to develop civic skills and virtues associated with citizenship in a liberal democratic society: articulating a point of view, attentiveness to others' ideas, perspective-taking, argumentation, respect for the facts, and so on. For teachers, however, the choice to engage their students with controversial political issues comes with its share of professional risks and pedagogical challenges. One of the reasons teachers frequently cite to explain why they prefer not to raise politically sensitive matters in class is that their pedagogical decision-making is under constant scrutiny. Many teachers fear that if they are perceived as inviting criticism of views that are cherished by certain students and their families, school administrators, or other members of the school community, they could face disciplinary action at work (Camicia, 2008; Journell, 2012; Swalwell & Schweber, 2016; Westheimer, 2015; Zimmerman & Roberston, 2017). The jurisprudence on teacher free speech confirms the legitimacy of this worry. The legal record shows that disagreements between teachers and their employers about what teachers have the right to say or teach about in class can almost always be traced back to a teacher's choice to use material considered to be objectionable on ethical, religious, or political grounds (Maxwell et al., 2018).

A common strategy that teachers use to mitigate the professional risks associated with teaching about sensitive issues is to adopt a stance of impartiality when teaching or talking about them in class and to avoid revealing their personal viewpoints to students. Particularly in light of the common belief that students' opinions are easily influenced by those of their teachers, by being impartial, teachers send the message that they understand that students are there to learn about the issues and develop their thinking skills rather than to absorb the viewpoints of their teachers.

For teachers, then, one of the things that makes impartiality so attractive is that it provides shelter against the charge that they are using their position of authority to promote a particular standpoint while at the same time cohering pedagogically with the standard justification for teaching and learning about controversial political issues in schools in democratic societies.

Indeed, the prima facie benefits of dealing with politically sensitive issues impartially – for students educationally, for teachers professionally, and for school–home relations – appear to be so many and so obvious that handling controversial issues in the classroom impartially is widely considered to be a basic professional expectation in teaching. A duty of impartiality features commonly in codes of ethical conduct for teachers (Maxwell & Schwimmer, 2016). In addition, research on teachers' perceptions of unprofessional behavior has revealed that using their position of authority to promote personal views, in particular those with a religious basis, is not only one of the most common forms of unethical behavior; it is considered one of the most serious as well (Barrett et al., 2012)

Despite being such a widely recognized professional obligation in teaching, the duty of impartiality is contested among both educational scholars and educators themselves. Three main objections to it recur in the educational literature on teacher impartiality. One is that teacher impartiality is not *ethically* desirable. Teachers have a duty to raise students' consciences about hidden and not-so-hidden forms of social injustice, call them out when they see them, and encourage their students to do the same (see, for example, Agostinone-Wilson, 2005; Ayers et al., 1998). From this perspective, the duty of neutrality is a myth that at best supports the status quo and, at worst, oppression (Moglen, 1996). A second objection to the duty of neutrality in teaching is that it is not *pedagogically* desirable. This idea pushes back against the common view among teachers that teaching students "how to think" requires teachers to avoid ever disclosing their personal views in class. Educationalists from Warnock (1975) to Kelly (1986) and Noddings (1993) have argued against this standard view by pointing out the educational advantages of teacher disclosure. A committed teacher who speaks openly about their personal views while remaining balanced and objective, they claim, makes a better model of democratic citizenship and appropriate civic behavior. The third and most radical objection to the idea that teachers have a professional duty to remain impartial when dealing with controversial issues in class is that teacher impartiality is not even *possible* (see for example Apple, 2004; Appelbaum, 2009; Reboul, 1977). Proponents of this view point out that every aspect of instruction, from the topics teachers choose to teach to the microchoices teachers make while planning and conducting a lesson, are inevitably value laden. If teachers cannot but be biased, they are fooling both themselves and their students by pretending otherwise. By the same token, the professional expectation of impartiality that teachers are generally held to by parents, society and the teaching profession is unreasonable.

This chapter defends the duty of impartiality as a professional expectation that society and the teaching profession can reasonably expect of educators against these objections. Essentially, it will argue that they are each based on different misconceptions about impartial teaching and teacher neutrality: about the definition of "controversial issue," about the pedagogical value for teachers and students of being flexible about neutrality, and about what constitutes a reasonable standard of impartiality. The chapter is structured as follows. It begins by revisiting Kelly's classic typology of the teacher's role in dealing with controversial issues in class. Next, by way of a critique of the ethical objection to teacher impartiality, the chapter raises the definitional question of how to conceptualize "controversial issues" in the context of civic and democratic education. After rehearsing and pointing out the key limitations of the main criteria that have been introduced in the academic literature on teaching and learning about controversial issues – namely, the epistemic, behavioral, and political criteria – the chapter puts forward what I argue is a more workable praxiological, or practice-centered, conceptualization. The chapter then proceeds to describe and challenge three received ideas about pedagogical impartiality and teacher neutrality in the context of teaching and learning about controversial issues: that teacher disclosure is indoctrination, that students can always tell what a teacher thinks about an issue, and that pedagogical impartiality and teacher neutrality are impossible ideals because education is an inherently partisan endeavor.

35.2 Neutrality and Impartiality in Teaching

Kelly's typology, used by multiple scholars over decades as a conceptual frame for research and theorizing on teacher impartiality (see, for example, Hess & McAvoy, 2014; Journell, 2016; Morris, 2011), is so compelling because it describes and labels the four main professional stances that educators are commonly drawn to in relation to teaching and learning about controversial issues.

The first is *exclusive neutrality*. Teachers who adhere to the perspective of exclusive neutrality simply avoid teaching about controversial subjects. Two factors inform this choice in Kelly's (1986) reading: either the teacher believes that it is the responsibility of parents and private communities, not schools, to help young people navigate complex evaluative issues or they believe that it is not possible for them as teachers to guarantee a fair and impartial hearing for all sides in a debate.

The second perspective in Kelly's (1986) typology is *exclusive partiality*. Teachers who adopt this perspective on teaching about controversial issues willingly introduce controversial subject matter in their teaching and openly promote a particular evaluative standpoint – normally, the one they personally favor – on the issue under discussion. When teachers adopt this perspective, they speak openly about their personal beliefs in front of their students, make no effort to avoid a one-sided presentation of the topic, and tend to discourage or dismiss dissenting views as illegitimate.

When teachers adopt *neutral impartiality*, the third category in Kelly's (1986) typology, they also embrace the discussion of controversial issues. Contrary to exclusive partiality, however, with neutral impartiality, teachers deliberately hold back from divulging their personal views to their students. When teachers adopt this role, they focus on dealing with the different sides of the issue in a fair and balanced way and on facilitating students' acquisition of critical reflection skills. The teacher endeavors to present a balanced view of the issues by searching out and seriously considering multiple perspectives, by encouraging the class to become as fully and accurately informed about the issues at stake as possible, by carefully weighing the arguments and evidence for and against, and so on. From this perspective, revealing the teacher's own view is a potential distraction from these endeavors. As Kelly (1986) notes, a teacher's choice to adopt neutral impartiality is often based on an awareness that, because they are in a position of authority over students, their own views risk unduly interfering with the process of students thinking through the issues themselves and arriving at considered opinions of their own.

The fourth category in Kelly's (1986) typology, *committed impartiality*, is identical to neutral impartiality except in one crucial respect. With committed impartiality, teachers deliberately disclose to students their own personal evaluative perspectives on the controversial topic at hand. For Kelly (1986), the pedagogical interest of adopting committed impartiality is that it models the skills in democratic dialogue and rational deliberation that teachers want their students to develop. The posture illustrates by example that one can have strongly held personal convictions about an ethically or politically charged question, yet still give the matter a fair hearing.

As mentioned, Kelly's typology has proven to be so useful in scholarship on teaching and learning about controversial issues because it accurately picks out and labels the full set of pedagogical stances that educators tend to gravitate towards when faced with the pedagogical challenges and professional risks associated with controversial issues in class. A less often recognized strength of Kelly's typology, however, is that it also provides a conceptual tool to get a handle on an important but frequently neglected distinction. Deftly avoiding getting bogged down in semantics about the sense precise meaning of "neutrality" and "impartiality" in teaching (for etymological discussions of these distinctions see, for example, Gravel & Lefebvre, 2012; Heybach, 2014), Kelly quietly introduces stipulative definitions of "neutrality" and "impartiality" in the context of teaching and learning about controversial issues. In his terms, "neutrality" refers to the act of *teacher positioning* with regard to a controversial issue. "Impartiality," by contrast, refers to the *pedagogical approach* the teacher adopts in dealing with controversial issues. According to Kelly's definitions then, a "neutral" teacher is one who abstains from divulging their personal viewpoints to students while a "committed" teacher is one who makes their personal viewpoints known to students. An "impartial" teacher, on the other hand, is one who seeks to teach about a controversial topic in a way that is fair, balanced, and unbiased whereas a "partial" teacher makes no such attempt. Partial teachers seek to promote a particular viewpoint on the topic under discussion as if it were the only one correct perspective.

Kelly's distinction between "impartial" versus "partial" teaching lines up neatly with a distinction that Michael Hand (2007, 2008; Hand & Levinson, 2012) employs in his more recent work on controversial issues in teaching. This is the distinction between "directive" and "nondirective" teaching. In Hand's (2007) language, to teach directively means "to provide pupils with substantive guidance, to teach moral questions with a view to promoting

Table 35.1 *Glossary of terms related to teaching about controversial issues*

Teacher positioning	**Neutrality:** The teacher does not disclose their own viewpoint on a controversial issue to students **Committedness:** The teacher discloses their own viewpoint on a controversial issue to students
Pedagogical approach	**Impartiality:** Teaching about a controversial issue in way that avoids favoring or promoting a particular viewpoint *(synonym for "nondirective teaching")* **Partiality:** Teaching about a controversial issue in a way that favors or promotes a particular viewpoint *(synonym for "directive teaching")*
Conceptions of the teacher's role	**Exclusive neutrality:** The teacher avoids discussing controversial issues with students *(abstention from teaching about controversial issues)* **Committed partiality:** The teacher discloses their own viewpoint on a controversial issue and teaches about it in a way that favors or promotes their own viewpoint *(synonym for "exclusive partiality")* **Neutral impartiality:** The teacher does not disclose their own viewpoint on a controversial issue and teaches about it in a way avoids favoring or promoting their own viewpoint *(most teachers' preferred stance)* **Committed impartiality:** The teacher discloses their own viewpoint on a controversial issue and teaches about it in a way that avoids favoring or promoting their own viewpoint *(advocated by Journell, Kelly, and Warnock)* **Neutral partiality:** The teacher does not disclose their own viewpoint on a controversial issue and teaches about it in a way that favors or promotes their own viewpoint *(conceptually possible but deceptive and difficult to achieve)*

particular answers to those questions" (p. 69). A teacher who teaches directively is a partial teacher in Kelly's terms. To teach nondirectively means to "make a deliberate attempt not to steer pupils towards particular answers but rather to be as even-handed as possible in the presentation of conflicting views" (p. 69). A teacher who engages in nondirective teaching, then, is impartial.

What is useful about these distinctions is that they highlight how teacher disclosure is not only conceptually distinct from the pedagogical approach the teacher adopts in teaching about a controversial issue. Neutrality and impartiality are also distinguishable in practice. Following Kelly's lead, but tidying up the terminology somewhat, these mix and match options yield four conceptions of the teacher's role in teaching about controversial issues: committed partiality (Kelly's "exclusive partiality"), neutral impartiality, committed impartiality, and neutral partiality. The latter conception of the teacher's role, which refers to a situation in which a teacher does not disclose their own viewpoint about a controversial issue but nevertheless teaches about it a in way that favors or promotes their own viewpoint, does not feature in Kelly's typology. This is likely due to the fact that, because it is deceptive and difficult to achieve in practice, it is rarely encountered in teaching. Table 35.1 provides a synthesis of the terminology related to teaching about controversial issues discussed in this section.

35.3 Defining "Controversial Issues"

As mentioned, some educators and scholars object to the professional expectation that teachers adopt a pedagogical stance of impartiality when dealing with controversial issues on ethical grounds (see for example Agostinone-Wilson, 2005; Appelbaum, 2009; Apple, 2004; Heybach, 2014). Their concern is that, when it comes to issues like systemic racism, gender discrimination, trans- and homophobia, and the history of slavery, adopting an impartial pedagogical stance goes squarely against teachers' mandate to endorse public values like social justice, political equality, and human dignity and rights, and to inculcate a commitment to these values among their students. In the case of unambiguous gross violations of the basic values of the liberal democratic political order, the teacher has an obligation to speak out against them. Remaining neutral on such matters, or teaching about them impartially by seeking "balance" and giving various perspective on them "equal time," is simply not acceptable. From this perspective, teachers need to see that adhering to the duty of impartiality can tacitly serve a discriminatory and illiberal political agenda. Far from embracing impartiality, the call then is for teachers to "confront the cult of neutrality" in teaching, in Agostinone-Wilson's (2005) words.

As legitimate as these concerns are, there is something amiss about this argument against teacher impartiality. The gist of the argument seems to be as follows. Teachers need to be skeptical about the duty of impartiality because some issues that some people *consider* to be controversial – for example, whether gay people or racialized minorities deserve fair and equal treatment – are in fact not controversial, at least when analyzed in terms of their consistency with basic liberal democratic values that teachers are justified in promoting. If this interpretation is accurate, then the argument is not against teacher impartiality per se but only against teacher impartiality *in relation to these specific noncontroversial issues*. For surely there are some genuinely controversial political stances even when all parties accept the same basic liberal democratic values framework. The trouble with the argument, in other words, is that, even if we accept that teachers should teach committedly or directively about certain specific issues, it does not follow that adopting an impartial stance in teaching is never justified. Unless of course the claim is that the liberal democratic framework yields a decisive answer to each and every issue. This, however, seems obviously implausible as it amounts to denying that, in the final analysis, there is even such thing as a genuinely controversial issue for those who adhere to liberal democratic values. Indeed, the very raison d'□tre of the supreme courts of constitutional democracies like the United States and Canada is to examine just such difficult questions from a legal standpoint as they are brought before the court.

This apparent confusion in the social justice education objection to teacher impartiality seems to call for greater definitional clarity. So what is this thing called a controversial issue? Michael Hand (2008) in his critical analysis of the literature provides what is perhaps the most comprehensive review of the main criteria that have emerged in recent scholarship to delineate the notion of "controversial issue" in teaching. Following the lead of other educationalists, Hand takes as a starting point that some issues warrant teacher impartiality – or indirective teaching to use Hand's term – and some issues warrant teacher partiality – or directive teaching as he calls it. The conceptual task is then to identify the criterion that most convincingly allow us to separate out those issues in relation to which issues teachers should teach about impartially from those requiring a partial pedagogical approach.

The first criterion Hand considers is the epistemic criterion. Associated with Dearden's classic 1981 essay "Controversial Issues and the Curriculum," the epistemic criterion states that issues in relation to which there is only one view that passes the test of reasonability should be taught partially. In Dearden's hands, a "reasonable view" is essentially one that is based on convincing arguments and sound evidence. Dearden deploys a linguistic argument in support of the epistemic criterion and as a means of rejecting the notion that an issue is controversial merely because people do, in fact, disagree about it. Children and other nonexperts can be found engaging in heated debates about questions to which there is a known, available, and undisputed answer. The spelling of certain words, the authors of particular books, and the explanations of well-understood natural phenomena are some of the examples Dearden gives to illustrate. In Dearden's sense, then, to say that a question is "uncontroversial" is to say that no two reasonable and fully informed individuals would disagree about it. Insofar as, say, bullying or racial discrimination are, in this sense, uncontroversially bad or wrong or that human-induced climate change is a real phenomenon, these are issues that should be taught about partially according to the epistemic criterion.

The second criterion is the behavioral criterion. Elaborated in Peter Gardner's (1984) critique of the epistemic criterion, Gardner argues essentially that whether a particular standpoint is controversial has nothing to do with the degree to which it is supported by reason and sound evidence. After all, some people do in fact consider viewpoints that would seem to satisfy the epistemic criterion – for example, that the theory of evolution is an accurate account of the origin of species – to be controversial. At the same time, Gardner points out, there are issues that people do not disagree about or simply have no opinion on that are the subject of reasonable disagreement: why the Roman Empire fell, for instance, or the precise reasons behind the great stock market crash of 1929. At this point, both are dead issues at least for nonspecialists. Yet according to the epistemic criterion, it would be *inaccurate* to describe the theory of evolution as controversial and *necessary* to describe the fall of the Roman Empire as "controversial." Clearly, both descriptions fly in face of how the word "controversial" is used in ordinary language. On these grounds, Gardner rejects the epistemic criterion of controversial issues in favor of the behavioral criterion. The behavioral criterion stipulates that an issue is "controversial," and hence requiring an impartial approach in teaching, if as a matter of fact people genuinely disagree about it.

The third criterion of controversial issues that Hand discusses is the political criterion. Mirroring the social justice education argument, the political criterion states that teachers are not only justified in adopting a partial stance when teaching about issues in relation to which a particular position is compatible with the basic rights and liberties underlying liberal democratic societies. As agents of the state, they are positively required to do so. As Hand articulates it, proponents of this view hold that since the liberal democratic state is entitled to use its coercive power to uphold the public values that are constitutive of the liberal democratic political order, so too do public school teachers have a professional obligation to promote views on matters of public concern that are entailed by public values. The political criterion can, for example, be deployed as a basis for arguing that sexual practices that some consider deviant – homosexuality, for example – should not be treated as a controversial issue (Hand, 2007). According to the political criterion, a clear position on strictly private matters relating to sexual behavior is entailed by basic individual rights and freedoms; as long as it is consensual, the decision to engage in homosexual interaction is a purely private affair.

I argued above that, when used as grounds for objecting to teachers' duty of impartiality, the political criterion falls short. Hand (2008) recognizes as well that, clearly, not all issues that are controversial in fact (i.e., according to the behavioral criterion) are controversial according to the political criteria. Hand's reservations about the political criterion are different. He argues against the political criterion because it seems to require teachers to adopt a decidedly *uneducational* approach to teaching and learning about controversial issues. In dealing with contested issues with their students, Hand suggests, the teacher's goal should not be to enforce public values as such but rather to teach in a way that helps students come to rationally endorse those values. Teachers do this best, he says, when they help students develop the ability to reason about contested issues and come to conclusions of their own based on reasons, facts, and arguments, even if doing so means taking seriously – provisionally and for educational purposes – views that may not be rationally defensible from the point of view of shared public values.

35.4 Limitations of the Epistemic, Behavioral, and Political Criteria

For different reasons, then, the epistemic, behavioral, and political criteria all have trouble adequately distinguishing those issues that teachers should teach about impartially from those that they should teach about partially.

Both the epistemic and behavioral criteria, as we saw, are consistent with at least one way "controversial" is used in ordinary language. As the respective arguments of Dearden and Gardner make clear, however, "controversial" is used in two discrete and, indeed, contradictory senses. "Controversial" means both "disagreed about by experts" (the epistemic criterion) *and* "disagreed about by laypeople" (the behavioral criterion). The linguistic arguments, then, only take us so far. I would add here that both the epistemic and behavioral criteria gloss over an important distinction between controversies about observable matters of fact and controversies over value-laden issues. At least as the phrase is used by educators in the context of civic education or education for critical reflection, "controversial issue" implies that a person's views on the issue relate in some way to their evaluative perspective – their personal values – and thus cannot be readily settled on the basis of facts and evidence alone. Teachers are not normally tempted to engage their students in balanced discussions of such matters as the various possible spellings of the capital city of the Indian state of Maharashtra, who is the true author of Macbeth, or why it rains. Nor do they feel in any way compelled to adopt a neutral stance in relation to such issues, keeping their personal opinions to themselves. From an educator's perspective, what makes a controversial issue controversial in the relevant sense is that it is, for whatever reason, *normatively delicate for the people discussing it.*

For its part, the political criterion has the advantage of assuming that "controversial issues" have, by definition, a strong normative dimension, but it too faces obstacles as a standard to help educators distinguish between issues that should be taught impartially and those that should be taught partially. First, as suggested, the political criterion seems to underestimate the difficulty involved in moving from consensus over a set of *public values* to consensus over which *substantive viewpoints* follow from those values. Some normative standpoints like whether homosexuality should be tolerated, whether slavery is wrong, and whether women and men deserve equal pay for equal work follow uncontroversially from the basic liberal democratic values framework. However, a great many substantive positions are genuinely controversial in this regard.

Following Bialystok (2014), one promising strategy to get around this limitation of the political criterion is to suggest that teachers are justified in teaching partially about normative viewpoints which "have legislative backing," that is, those that are consistent with the laws and constitutionally recognized rights and freedoms of the state. As attractive as this approach may seem on first glance, however, it risks sending a message to students about law that is particularly problematic in the context of democratic education: that the law is fixed and immutable and that the justice of current law is not a legitimate subject of debate (Tanchuk et al., 2021).

A second limitation of the political criterion was pointed out by Hand (2008). If the educational purpose of teaching and learning about controversial issues is to help students develop a capacity for independent thought and judgment about complex social issues, then shutting down debate about issues that students themselves (or their family members and others around them) consider to be contested seems to run counter to this aim.

Third and finally, it takes only a moment's reflection to realize that the political criterion presupposes a highly selective reading of the political values of the liberal democratic political order. To be sure, social justice, political equality, and personal autonomy are core public values but so are tolerance, dialogue, and a commitment to negotiation and discussion as a way of resolving public disputes. Promoting these values in the classroom means, it would seem, creating space for dissenting views, hearing people out, and encouraging calm and respectful dialogue between students who hold possibly incommensurable views. The political criterion, in other words, seems to arbitrarily prioritize some public values while deprioritizing others.

35.5 A Praxiological Conception of Controversial Issues

These considerations point, I think, toward the need for a praxiological, or practice-centered, conception of "controversial issues" in which the meaning assigned to the term is directly linked to the context of a particular educational practice – in this case the practice of teaching about controversial issues as a form of civic education. The epistemological, behavioral, and political criteria all run into conceptual trouble, it seems, because they approach the definitional task back to front. They begin by attempting to define "controversial" in the abstract and then proceed to apply it to the domain of practice rather than taking as a starting point educators' experience dealing with controversial issues with students in schools.

Such a praxiological conception of "controversial issue" has three main features. First, it is *phenomenological*. This means understanding controversial issues as issues that are experienced as controversial in the teacher's work environment. Defining "controversial issue" this way breaks the impasse generated by the linguistic arguments in favor of the epistemic versus behavioral criteria. By defining "controversial issue" in local terms, it doesn't matter whether a particular topic or view is considered controversial by either experts or laypeople. Being considered controversial by students and parents is sufficient to call an issue "controversial" because that is what matters from an educator's standpoint.

This phenomenological definition implies a second feature of the praxiological conception of "controversial issues," namely, that controversial issues are *floating*. This means that what is experienced as controversial varies from community to community, school to school, and perhaps even from class to class. Indeed, from the teacher's perspective, the fact that what counts as controversial varies depends on where one teaches is a normal and expected aspect of teaching about controversial issues. In one area, for example, the theory of evolution may be delicate, with some parents demanding that the school present "alternative theories" (for a discussion of this issue, see Goldston & Kyzer, 2009). In another area, such complaints are unthinkable. In a particular school, a large number of students are skeptical about the scientific evidence about climate change while in another school, the students are demanding permission to miss school to attend climate protests (for a discussion of this issue, see Clarke et al., 2022). The reasons for these differences are rarely a mystery. They are the direct result of demographic facts about the student body and the communities that students grow up in, and in this way, facts that teaches have no choice but to work with.

One may object that teachers have an obligation to teach partially about matters that are the subject of consensus among members of the scientific community. To add to the familiar examples of global warming and evolution, other examples are that vaccines don't cause autism or that the COVID-19 virus was not created by big pharma.

A direct response to this objection lies, in fact, in the third feature of the praxiological conception of controversial issues: *teleological*. The idea here is that the justification for whether a teacher should adopt a stance of impartiality in relation to a particular issue is inseparable from the teacher's pedagogical intention in a particular didactic context. For example, take a science teacher who has to teach about vaccines in a biology class. In this context, the scientifically debunked claim that vaccines cause autism might be an excellent starting point to present the specific biochemical mechanisms behind vaccination that undermine the vaccine–autism link theoretically. Presenting the triangulating epidemiological research on the connection between vaccination rates and rates of autism would show that it is not credible empirically either. However, if a teacher – perhaps even the same science teacher with the same class on the same day – shifts their pedagogical intention from teaching about biology to teaching to help students develop skills in critical reflection then the teacher would, if one accepts the teleological feature of "controversial issues," be justified in adopting an impartial stance. From the point of view of this pedagogical aim, failing to move into an impartial teaching mode centered on dialogue and debate, sifting through the arguments, and allowing students to voice dissenting views would deny an important educational opportunity to precisely those students who stand to benefit from the opportunity most.

The same teleological considerations provide an answer to the objection based on the political criterion, discussed at length already in this chapter, that certain topics like bullying, racism, and tolerance of homosexuality should always be taught about partially. Commenting on research by Oulton and colleagues (2004), Hand (2008) reacts with some bewilderment to the finding that teachers routinely name "racism" and "bullying" when asked to list the controversial issues they teach about and that only a small minority of teachers say that they would try to influence students' views on these issues. When considered from the point of view of the teacher and their likely pedagogical intention, these results are a small wonder. If the teacher's students themselves view racism, bullying, or homosexuality as contested issues, refusing to meet them on their own terms and let the ideas and arguments, rather than the teacher's view, lead the discussion would be to deny an opportunity that students might never otherwise ever have, an opportunity to think about the issues in a respectful discursive environment that is open to a diversity of opinions. As Hand (2008) points out himself, creating such an environment is essential to an educational, as opposed to uneducational, approach to teaching and learning about public values.

35.6 Teacher Neutrality as a Pedagogical Tool

It was observed in the introduction of this chapter that there is a long and venerable strand of argument in the academic literature that neutrality in teaching is not pedagogically desirable – or at least that there are good educational reasons for teachers to give preference to a committed standpoint over a neutral standpoint when teaching about controversial issues. Some of the most influential work on the topic of teacher neutrality by Warnock (1975), Kelly

(1986), and Noddings (1993) advance this view, positioning themselves against what they perceive to be the default position among educators. To teachers who believe that their job of teaching students "how to think" rather than "what to think" requires them to abstain from disclosing their personal viewpoints, these authors point to the educational value of teaching about controversial issues commitedly. When teachers intentionally disclose their views while maintaining a pedagogical stance of impartiality, they argue, they offer themselves as a model of intellectual responsibility, demonstrating to their students through their actions that it is possible to have an opinion about a contested issue and yet still engage in a balanced and critical examination of the evidence for and against. Furthermore, committed impartiality exemplifies how working through controversial questions is not just about reasoning and knowing the facts but also learning to recognize and manage one's own emotional responses to the issues at stake. It shows that a person can have strong feelings about an issue and still be open minded about the possibility that they may be wrong. In addition, from the point of view of citizenship education, committed impartiality is better at simulating in the classroom the real conditions of public discussion and dialogue; normally, people do not dissimulate their views when they discuss contested issues. Finally, and especially when discussing a topic that nearly everyone feels strongly about, a teacher's insistence on adhering to a neutral standpoint risks sending students the message that the discussion is, in Warnock's (1975) words, mere "play acting." In these circumstances, teacher impartiality risks being perceived as disrespectful to the topic and to the others present in the room and, for these reasons, potentially an impediment to a forthright and meaningful exchange of ideas. Journell (2016) summarizes the apparently overwhelming educational argument in favor of committed impartiality this way:

> With a committed impartiality approach, teachers can model appropriate ways in which to articulate and defend one's political opinions in a pluralistic society. For students who agree with their teachers' opinions, seeing their teacher model tolerant political discourse will demonstrate the value of showing deference to the beliefs of those who hold opposing views. For students who disagree with their teachers' beliefs, a committed impartiality approach allows students to articulate their own opinions in a safe environment and provides experience working with authority figures who hold political beliefs that are different from their own. (p. 105)

As compelling as this argument in favor of committed impartiality is, it has two limitations that are both linked to the deeper problem of not taking into account sufficiently the teacher's perspective on the professional risks and pedagogical challenges associated with teaching about controversial issues.

One limitation of recommending that teachers systematically prioritize committed impartiality is that it overlooks the fact that teachers' well-documented preference for neutral impartiality is driven as much by pragmatic reasons, as

Journell's (2011c) own research has shown as educational reasons (see also Hess, 2004). Committed impartiality exposes teachers to considerably greater professional risk. They know that parents and school leaders are highly sensitive to teacher disclosure in class. They know as well that if their position on a public issue runs counter to the cherished personal beliefs of parents or students, or if it has the potential to tarnish the school's public image, they risk facing accusations of "indoctrination" or "abuse of authority." Teachers also know that it is very difficult to predict which statements will attract negative attention and which statements will be met with indifference in the school community. In this context, it is entirely reasonable for a teacher to adhere to a stance of neutral impartiality when dealing with controversial issues.

The other reason why caution is required in categorically endorsing committed impartiality as *the* right or best approach to teaching about controversial issues is that it underestimates how useful it can be for teachers to be flexible and adaptive about disclosure. Indeed, one of the most significant outcomes of Diana Hess's longstanding research program on teaching about controversial political issues is the way it so convincingly documents how and why teachers tend to pivot between neutral impartiality and committed impartiality as a means of managing the complex social dynamics that such content occasions (Hess & McAvoy, 2014). Teachers tend to gravitate toward neutral impartiality for the pragmatic and educational reasons already mentioned. Yet teachers sometimes decide to step out of the role of neutral mediator out of concern for student comfort and wellbeing. This can happen when a small minority of pupils find themselves defending a particular side of an issue. When this occurs, these pupils can face strong intellectual and social pressure to either concede to the majority or fall silent. And if the topic is sensitive enough, there is a danger that the social dynamic created in class by the teacher will spill over into nonteaching situations – after school or during breaks – over which the teacher has little or no control. To protect such pupils from being ostracized, and to keep the debate moving forward, one option open to a teacher is to strategically exercise their authority by taking the side of the students who hold the minority view.

In sum, the teacher's perspective on the issue of disclosure and positioning, valuably highlighted in Hess and McAvoy's (2014) work, helps us see that neutrality may be best understood as a pedagogical tool. In addition to offering shelter from the professional risks involved in discussing controversial issues with students, teachers sometimes feel that keeping the focus on the issues and away from their personal opinions is the best way to promote students' engaged and critical thinking. At other times, however, all but the most ardent proponents of neutral impartiality would concede that always withholding one's personal view does not best serve their students' interests. The lesson to draw from the practice-centered portrait of teacher neutrality Hess paints is that the right approach to disclosure is an adaptive one according to which the decision to disclose or withhold is determined by the intricacies of particular pedagogical circumstances. It should not be decided in advance.

35.7 Three False Assumptions about Neutrality and Impartiality in Teaching

As significant as the teacher perspective undoubtedly is for grounding academic discussions of teacher neutrality and impartiality, teachers' understanding of these issues is by no means infallible. This section discusses three rather disparate and seemingly incorrect assumptions about teacher neutrality and impartiality that crop up repeatedly in the academic literature and that many teachers appear to adhere to as well. It is important to correct these false assumptions because, as we will see, each of them can lead to errors of professional judgment in relation to teaching and learning about controversial issues.

35.7.1 Committed Teaching Is Indoctrination

One of these false assumptions is that not adopting a neutral stance in teaching about controversial issues is tantamount to indoctrinating students. This concern has emerged in the empirical research on teacher disclosure as one of the reasons teachers most commonly cite for why a stance of neutrality with respect to controversial issues is pedagogically preferable (see Hess 2004, Hess & McAvoy, 2014, Parker, 2010).

Educators in liberal democratic societies are of course right to be wary of indoctrination. Still "indoctrination" refers to a particular kind of instructional intervention and it is far from clear that committed impartiality fits the description. For an instructional act to count as indoctrination it must, it seems, meet three criteria. It has to (i) be concerned with imparting beliefs that have political or sectarian content, (ii) employ nonrational instructional methods, and (iii) involve deliberateness. To indoctrinate someone, in other words, means not just to tilt a person toward certain partisan or sectarian beliefs. As commentators on indoctrination in education have long pointed out, "indoctrination" implies *intentionally* imbuing a person with certain partisan or sectarian beliefs using noneducational methods (Kazepides, 1983; Peters, 1965; Reboul, 1977).

If we accept this characterization of normally indoctrination, then the mere disclosure of personal views to students is not indoctrination as such. Adopting a committed stance on a controversial issue is not indoctrination unless the teacher does so *in order to* irrationally or uneducationally influence their students to accept the teacher's viewpoint. This, of course, is not the case insofar at the teacher adopts an impartial pedagogical approach to the subject matter. By contrast, committed partiality, typically advocated by proponents of the social justice education argument against teacher neutrality as we saw, does fit the description of "indoctrination" when the persuasive tactics teachers deploy to direct students' opinion toward a particular standpoint tip toward uneducational through the use of coercion, belittling, manipulation, intimidation, etc.

Running disclosure together conceptually with indoctrination is more than a mere semantic error. As Hess (2004) observes, anxiety over indoctrination can lead teachers to avoid dealing with controversial issues altogether. For others, it means rigidly adhering to neutral impartiality. When either of these things happens, the false assumption that teaching about controversial issues from a committed standpoint amounts to indoctrination has significant negative educational implications. When it leads teachers to adopt neutral exclusivity, it is responsible for denying students opportunities to practice skills essential to democratic participation. When it leads teachers to categorically eschew committed impartiality, it deprives students of the benefits of teacher disclosure and positive discursive role modelling, and prevents teachers from using disclosure as pedagogical tool to help manage the complex interpersonal dynamics inherent to teaching and learning about controversial issues.

35.7.2 Students Always Know Their Teacher's Views

Another mistaken assumption that can potentially turn teachers toward exclusive neutrality is the belief that, no matter how hard they try to be impartial, subtle cues in how they speak about controversial issues or in the way they select and treat content will reveal their viewpoint to their students. The claim, in other words, is that teacher neutrality, though attractive in theory, is not psychologically possible in practice. Especially when coupled with the received idea just discussed – namely, that disclosure implies indoctrination – the inference from this claim that teachers should avoid dealing with controversial issues altogether is a natural one for teachers to make. If students always know their teachers views anyway, what is the point in pretending to teach impartially and feigning neutrality? Faced with this perception, the choice then is between committed partiality, which, as we know, most teachers consider professionally risky and pedagogically questionable, and exclusive neutrality (avoidance of controversial issues), the latter being the safer and thus more attractive option.

The question of whether teacher neutrality is psychologically possible has been explored by several researchers but perhaps the most sophisticated and enlightening work on this topic are Wayne Journell's studies on teacher neutrality and impartiality in the context of US presidential election campaigns (see Journell, 2011a, 2011b, 2011c, 2012, 2016; Payne & Journell, 2019). With regard to the question of whether students can usually discern their teacher's political leanings, the key finding from Journell's research is that students are rather less astute than many educators seem to think.

Journell's work is premised on a distinction between what I will label "objective impartiality" and "apparent impartiality." Objective impartiality refers to the teacher's capacity to teach about an issue in an unbiased way from the point of view of an outside observer. Apparent impartiality refers to the teacher's capacity to teach about an issue in an unbiased way from the point of view of the teacher's students.

The main conclusions of the research on objective and apparent impartiality are the following. With regard to objective impartiality, Journell found in his class observations of teachers who adopt a standpoint of neutral impartiality – that is, teachers who don't disclose their views and strive in good faith to teach about the issues in a fair and balanced way – that they regularly make value judgments about the issues and place more emphasis on educational resources and considerations that are consistent with their personal views (Journell, 2011a, 2011b, 2011c). Consistent with this observation, research by Goldston and Kyzer (2009) found that teachers who self-identify as impartial pedagogically prioritize aspects of the curriculum that cohere with their personal beliefs and deemphasize aspects that do not. Similarly, Niemi and Niemi (2007) found that teachers are frequently unaware that partisan statements they make in class are, in fact, clearly partisan.

Based on these findings, one might think that students can pick up on these kinds of cues and readily infer the teacher's viewpoint from them. Not so. In fact, with regard to apparent impartiality, Journell (2011a) found that students are surprisingly unperceptive about the objective indicators that would normally betray a teacher's political bias to an outside observer. When asked, students often guess wrongly about their teacher's view and when they do guess correctly it is often based on considerations that relate to the teacher's social location – considerations like the teacher's ethnicity or perceived social class – rather than what teacher says in class or how the teacher handles the material.

As Journell (2016) points out, this research raises the question of whether, in light of these dynamics, it might be preferable from an educational perspective for teachers to be forthright with their students about their political commitment as doing so may make students more attentive to forms of teacher bias such as the lack of balance of the information presented in class. Be that as it may, Journell's findings on apparent objectivity in teaching do provide grounds for skepticism toward the widespread belief among educators that students can generally read *what* their teacher thinks about an issue from *how* they teach about it.

35.7.3 Impartial Teaching Is Not Possible

A classic and powerful objection to the demand that teachers remain impartial when dealing with controversial issues is that education is inherently and inevitably partisan (iterations of this idea are discussed in Agostinone-Wilson, 2005; Appelbaum, 2009; Apple, 2004; Heybach, 2014; Kelly & Brandes, 2001; Moglen, 1996; Norman, 1975; Reboul, 1977). Commentators have long observed that instruction and the curriculum convey and promote normatively laden standpoints, often in hidden ways. The very choice of topics to discuss – an international conflict versus the environment or biotechnology versus social inequalities, for example – already says something about the relative importance of these issues for the teacher. The particular words teachers use to frame discussions carry normative weight and teachers' choices about which arguments and positions to focus on, and which to set aside, send messages to students about whose perspectives matter. Furthermore, and as we saw in the summary of Journell's research, such value-laden pedagogical choices are rarely intentional. Very often, neither the teacher nor their students are consciously aware of the forms of bias at play in a teaching situation. Indeed, one might add that even the professional expectation that educators teach about controversial issues in an impartial way is backgrounded by a normatively tinged ideal of individualism and democratic citizenship, one that values independent mindedness, the ability to think for oneself and question authority, caring about and staying informed about public issues, and playing an active role in public life.

It is to be expected, then, that the effect of these hidden biases can be to normalize or even legitimize forms of unjust dominance and, in this way, support forms of oppression. Even the filters through which one perceives fair and nonideological teaching can be tainted with prejudice. A case in point is the entirely plausible anecdote related by Appelbaum (2009) of a teacher who, in teaching about the colonization of the western United States by Europeans, sought balance by including a unit on Indigenous perspectives. Much to the teacher's surprise, the unit was met by student accusations that the teacher was attempting to impose their own political views on the class.

In pedagogical terms, what follows from the claim that teacher impartiality is, at best, an unattainable ideal and, at worst, an insidious apology for the unjust status quo? For many commentators, the answer is that teachers should abandon neutral impartiality in favor of committed partiality. They should refuse to play the role of impartial spectator, speak truth to power, call out social injustice when they see it, open students' eyes to oppression, and challenge students who express illiberal views in class.

This move from the myth of teacher impartiality to the call to take on education for social justice, however, overlooks the crucial matter of how *teachers themselves* are likely to react to the realization that impartial teaching is something of a myth. We know that most teachers are concerned about unduly influencing their students for educational reasons and that they are anxious about the potential negative fallout for themselves as professionals if they openly promote a contested view in class (Camica, 2008; Hess, 2004; Hess & McAvoy, 2014; Swalwell & Schweber, 2016). Against this background, a completely understandable response to the realization that unbiased teaching is impossible is a sense of paralysis about teaching about controversial issues that, once again, would make neutral exclusivity (i.e., avoiding teaching about controversial issues altogether) – with all the undesirable educational implications for students that that entails – seem like a very attractive option for teachers indeed.

Whatever one's opinion may be about how educators should adapt their practice to the fact that impartial teaching is, strictly speaking, not a realistic pedagogical goal, one thing seems certain. Parents, society, and the teaching profession will continue to expect teachers to strive to teach about controversial issues in fair and balanced way and avoid promoting their own partisan beliefs in class. When we know that educating is inherently normative but continue to impose on teachers a duty of impartiality, is there any way for educators to navigate between the Scylla of neutral exclusivity and the Charybdis of committed partiality?

One promising place to look for an answer to this question, it seems, is in the judicial standard of "evenhandedness" that has emerged in the jurisprudence on teacher free speech in the classroom (see Maxwell et al., 2018). In litigation between a teacher and their employer over alleged breaches of the duty of impartiality or the right to state personal viewpoints about controversial issues in class, the courts frequently return to the tributary professional obligation for teachers to use the authority they exercise over students in a reasonable and responsible way. Linked to the public interest of maintaining public trust in teachers and the school system, and providing protection for students as a captive audience, the judicial standard is that teachers must not be seen as using their position of authority to promote their own personal views on contested or sensitive issues. In the hands of the courts, respecting the standard of evenhandedness does not necessarily require teachers to abstain from expressing their personal views in class or even feigning strict pedagogical impartiality. All it requires is for teachers to make good-faith attempts to seek balance in the treatment of controversial issues and to avoid teaching with the intent of purposefully imposing their perspective about sensitive or controversial topics on their students. There is no simple recipe for avoiding a perception of abuse of authority in this sense, but doing so would seem to imply, among other things, encouraging students to consider several competing viewpoints, treating students who adhere to views one disagrees with respectful, and generally conducting oneself in a way in class that models honest intellectual inquiry. Courts do not expect teachers to be impartial in the sense of being perfectly objective or even shedding their personal beliefs at the classroom door. Given the deeply and inherently normative nature of education – which judges, incidentally, routinely recognize in such cases – doing so would be unreasonable because the standard is unattainably high. To paraphrase Justice Abella of the Supreme Court of Canada, what society can reasonably expect of teachers is that they adhere to a conception of impartial teaching that has been used by good teachers for centuries: to do their best to let the facts and arguments guide the discussion and not the personal views of the teacher (Loyola High School v. Quebec (Attorney General), 2009, para. 78).

35.8 Conclusion

Scholars and educators committed to providing young people with a civic education adapted to citizenship in liberal democratic society are naturally drawn to the idea of teaching and learning about controversial issues. Dialogue and debate about contested public questions not only simulates the deliberative processes characteristic of democracy as a way of life. When teachers succeed in creating conditions of deliberation that are inclusive, informed, respectful, and reason-based, they also model an ideal of democratic discussion that most students are, unfortunately, unlikely to encounter other than at school. Owing to the fact that the questions and topics that are best suited to developing the skills and virtues of democratic citizenship are often emotionally charged, coupled with an awareness that students are vulnerable to teacher influence, society and the teaching profession expect teachers to handle controversial issues in class in an impartial way. However, scholars and teachers alike express concerns about how realistic the duty of impartiality in teaching is and question whether it is even educationally or professionally desirable. Far from being of mere academic interest, these concerns can have a concrete impact on teachers' decision-making about whether and how to address controversial issues with their students in class, driving them either toward committed partiality – which stands in tension with professional norms and exposes teachers to considerable professional risk – or neutral exclusivity – thus depriving their students of important civic educational opportunities. This chapter has tried to defend the duty of impartiality as a legitimate professional expectation by showing that a number of key reservations voiced about pedagogical impartiality and teacher neutrality are not well founded. As we saw, the idea that pedagogical impartiality necessarily serves the status quo appears to be based on a fuzzy distinction between what should and what should not be considered a controversial issue. The view that teachers need to choose between neutrality, or never disclosing their personal views to students, and committedness, or always doing so, is a false dichotomy that obscures the educational value of using teacher disclosure as a flexible pedagogical tool. For its part, the notion that impartiality is not pedagogically possible because of the inherently normative nature of education excludes teacher impartiality essentially by decree. What teaching needs, the chapter suggested, is a reasonable standard of impartiality that is attainable for teachers despite the unavoidably value-laden nature of teaching. As we saw, just such a standard can be found in the legal criterion of evenhandedness that expects teachers to exercise their position of authority responsibly, to prioritize following the questions where they lead over their personal opinions, and to strive in good faith to give a fair hearing to multiple viewpoints on the issue at hand.

References

Agostinone-Wilson, F. (2005). Fair and balanced to death: Confronting the cult of neutrality in the teacher education classroom. *Journal for Critical Education Policy Studies*, 3(1), 1–17.

Appelbaum, B. (2009). Is teaching for social justice a "liberal bias"? *Teachers College Record*, 111(2), 376–408.

Apple, M. (2004). *Ideology and curriculum*. London: Routledge.

Ayers, W., Hunt, J. A., & Quinn, T. (1998). *Teaching for social justice. A democracy and education reader*. New York: New Press.

Barrett, D. E., Casey, J. E., Visser, R. D., & Headley, K. N. (2012). How do teachers make judgments about ethical and unethical behaviors? Toward the development of a code of conduct for teachers. *Teaching and Teacher Education*, 28(6), 890–98.

Bialystok, L. (2014). Politics without "brainwashing": A philosophical defence of social justice education. *Curriculum Inquiry*, 44(3), 413–40.

Camicia, S. P. (2008). Deciding what is a controversial issue: A case study of social studies curriculum controversy. *Theory & Research in Social Education*, 36(4), 298–316.

Clarke, P. T., Anderson, M., & Yoh, A. (2022). "Hey Mom, I missed school today to save the planet!": Mandatory attendance and student activism – A Canadian perspective. *International Journal of Educational Reform*, 31(1), 3–24.

Dearden, R. F. (1981). Controversial issues and the curriculum. *Journal of Curriculum Studies*, 13(1), 37–44.

Gardner, P. (1984). Another look at controversial issues and the curriculum. *Journal of Curriculum Studies*, 16(4), 379–85.

Goldston, M. J. D., & Kyzer, P. (2009). Teaching evolution: Narratives with a view from three southern biology teachers in the USA. *Journal of Research in Science Teaching: The Official Journal of the National Association for Research in Science Teaching*, 46(7), 762–90.

Gravel, S., & Lefebvre, S. (2012). Impartialité et neutralité autour du programme québécois éthique et culture religieuse. *Le programme d'éthique et culture religieuse: l'exigeante conciliation entre le soi, l'autre et le nous*, 191–213.

Hand, M. (2007). Should we teach homosexuality as a controversial issue? *Theory and Research in Education*, 5(1), 69–86.

Hand, M. (2008). What should we teach as controversial? A defense of the epistemic criterion. *Educational Theory*, 58(2), 213–28.

Hand, M., & Levinson, R. (2012). Discussing controversial issues in the classroom. *Educational Philosophy and Theory*, 44(6), 614–29.

Hess, D. E. (2004). Controversies about controversial issues in democratic education. *PS: Political Science & Politics*, 37(2), 257–61.

Hess, D. E. (2009). *Controversy in the classroom: The democratic power of discussion*. New York: Routledge.

Hess, D. E., & McAvoy, P. (2014). *The political classroom: Evidence and ethics in democratic education*. London: Routledge.

Heybach, J. A. (2014). Troubling neutrality: Toward a philosophy of teacher ambiguity. *Philosophical Studies in Education*, 45, 43–54.

Journell, W. (2011a). Teachers' controversial issue decisions related to race, gender, and religion during the 2008 Presidential Election. *Theory & Research in Social Education*, 39, 348–92.

Journell, W. (2011b). Teaching politics in secondary education: Analyzing instructional methods from the 2008 Presidential Election. *The Social Studies*, 102(6), 231–41.

Journell, W. (2011c). The disclosure dilemma in action: A qualitative look at the effect of teacher disclosure on classroom instruction. *Journal of Social Studies Research*, 35(2), 217–44.

Journell, W. (2012). Ideological homogeneity, school leadership, and political intolerance in secondary education: A study of three high schools during the 2008 Presidential Election. *Journal of School Leadership*, 22, 569–99.

Journell, W. (2016). Teacher political disclosure as parrhēsia. *Teachers College Record*, 118(5), 1–36.

Kazepides, T. (1983) Socialization, initiation and indoctrination. In D. H. Kerr, ed., *Philosophy of education 1982: Proceedings of the 38th annual meeting of the philosophy of education society*. Normal, IL: Philosophy of Education Society, Illinois State University, pp. 309–18.

Kelly, T. E. (1986). Discussing controversial issues: Four perspectives on the teacher's role. *Theory & Research in Social Education*, 14(2), 113–38.

Kelly, D. M., & Brandes, G. M. (2001). Shifting out of "neutral": Beginning teachers' struggles with teaching for social justice. *Canadian Journal of Education/Revue canadienne de l'education*, 437–54.

Loyola High School v. Quebec (Attorney General), 2009 SCC 12. Available at: https://scc-csc.lexum.com/scc-csc/scc-csc/en/item/14703/index.do.

Maxwell, B., & Schwimmer, M. (2016). Seeking the elusive ethical base of teacher professionalism in Canadian codes of ethics. *Teaching and Teacher Education*, 59, 468–80.

Maxwell, B., McDonough, K., & Waddington, D. I. (2018). Broaching the subject: Developing law-based principles for teacher free speech in the classroom. *Teaching and Teacher Education*, 70, 196–203.

Moglen, H. (1996). Unveiling the myth of neutrality: Advocacy in the feminist classroom. In P. Meyer Spacks, ed., *Advocacy in the classroom: Problems and possibilities*. London: Palgrave Macmillan, pp. 204–12.

Morris, R. W. (2011). Cultivating reflection and understanding: Foundations and orientations of Québec's Ethics and Religious Culture Program. *Religion & Education*, 38(3), 188–211.

Niemi, N. S., & Niemi, R. G. (2007). Partisanship, participation, and political trust as taught (or not) in high school history and government classes. *Theory & Research in Social Education*, 35(1), 32–61.

Noddings, N. (1993). *Educating for intelligent belief or unbelief.* New York: Teachers College Press.

Norman, R. (1975). The neutral teacher? In S. C. Brown, ed., *Philosophers discuss education*. London: Palgrave Macmillan, pp. 172–87.

Oulton, C., Day, V., Dillon, J., & Grace, M. (2004). Controversial issues – teachers' attitudes and practices in the context of citizenship education. *Oxford review of education*, 30(4), 489–507.

Parker, W. (2010). Listening to strangers: Classroom discussion in democratic education. *Teachers College Record*, 112(11), 2815–32.

Payne, K. A., & Journell, W. (2019). "We have those kinds of conversations here. . .": Addressing contentious politics with elementary students. *Teaching and Teacher Education*, 79, 73–82.

Peters, R. S. (1965). Education as initiation. In R. D. Archambault, ed., *Philosophical analysis and education*. London: Routledge and Kegan Paul, pp. 87–110.

Reboul, O. (1977). *L'endoctrinement. Presses de l'Université de France.*

Swalwell, K., & Schweber, S. (2016). Teaching through turmoil: Social studies teachers and local controversial current events. *Theory & Research in Social Education*, 44(3), 283–315.

Tanchuk, N., Rocha, T., & Krus, M. (2021). Is comprehensive liberal social justice education brainwashing? *Philosophy of Education*, 77(2). doi: 10.47925/77.2.044.

Warnock, M. (1975). The neutral teacher. In S. C. Brown, ed., *Philosophers discuss education*. London: Palgrave Macmillan, pp. 159–71.

Westheimer, J. (2015). *What kind of citizen? Educating our children for the common good*. New York: Teachers College Press.

Zimmerman, J, & Robertson, E. (2017). *The case for contention: Teaching controversial issues in American schools*. Chicago, IL: University of Chicago Press.

Index

Printed in the United States
by Baker & Taylor Publisher Services